Praise for
Deterring and Detecting Money Laundering and Terrorist Financing
by
Ehi Eric Esoimeme

"It is with great pleasure I am writing to endorse Ehi Eric Esoimeme's book because it has so much to offer to financial institutions and practitioners as it sets complex matters in a structured, case based and holistic manner.

As someone who has worked in Russia on anti-corruption matters for over twenty years now and as a former bank board member and anti-corruption expert at the Russian Chamber of Commerce, I cannot help but underscore the importance of this book to take a hard-long look at the issue of money-laundering being executed on a global scale these days. I see one critical component in this book which attempts to adopt the case study methodology to highlight a dangerous trend of money laundering overlapping with terrorist financing especially at a time when global banking in pursuit of gains becomes less vigilant and discriminatory.

This month, a well-known Russian banker, Alexander Lebedev, released in Russia a book called "The Hunt for a Banker" which talks at length and in great detail about corruption and money-laundering in Russian banking and its connectivity to the global banking. His book does not aim to highlight or analyze existing money laundering schemes but it tells the story of its size, scope and reach.

Hence the value of Mr. Esoimeme's book for financial institutions and professionals in many jurisdictions is so much higher because it offers a framework and terms of reference when dealing with such a colossal problem.

Russia does not have a good record when it comes to money laundering. It would be enough to mention the Organized Crime and Corruption Reporting Project ongoing investigation that covers several jurisdictions with regard to Russian banks' scheme.

Plus, the issue of politically exposed persons in countries with systemic corruption and their use of financial institutions still remains a palpable challenge given their ties with organized and ethnic crime groups who may be related to terrorist activities' financing.

Russia is a member of the Financial Action Task Force and two Financial Action Task Force-style regional bodies, the Committee of Experts on the Evaluation of Anti–Money Laundering Measures (MONEYVAL) and the Eurasian group on combating money laundering and financing of terrorism (EAG).

The International Narcotics Control Strategy Report (INCSR) (an annual report by the Department of State to Congress prepared in accordance with the Foreign Assistance Act) categorised Russia as a Country/Jurisdiction of Primary Concern in respect of Money Laundering and Financial Crimes; even though Russia is deemed largely compliant for 13 of the FATF 40 recommendations.

Global regulators and enforcers are talking to each other but the sheer vastness of the challenge does not provide an easy solution as one-size-fits-all. So, this book is a great chance to help change all that."

—Anatoly Yakorev, director, Center for Business Ethics & Compliance (Moscow, Russian Federation)

"Ehi Eric Esoimeme has provided a valuable consolidated source of information assisting an efficient comparison between the different approaches to anti-money laundering and counter terrorism financing measures in Nigeria, the United States of America and the United Kingdom. Nigeria is often perceived and evaluated as a higher risk nation, but as a valued global trading partner with extensive oil reserves it is essential that business is conducted within this enhanced risk profile. By providing a single source of reference, Ehi's texts should provide an invaluable reference aid to business development departments, trade finance teams as well as those in the regulatory world who concentrate on the specific and very technical details of fighting financial crime."

—Patricia Robertson, chartered FCSI, CDipAF, director, senior compliance and management consultant, Westport Global Ltd (United Kingdom); specialist FCA compliance consultant

"Ehi Eric Esoimeme reaches his target audience in a well-documented analysis and comparison of anti-money laundering laws across Nigeria, United States and the United Kingdom. He seeks to provide a clear understanding of their anti-money laundering and counter-terrorist financing (AML/CTF) obligations and money laundering (ML) and terrorist financing (TF) risks and achieves this.

Ehi Eric Esoimeme makes no qualms about the intention of the book and the text lives up to the title. Esoimeme keeps the text focused on the legislation as it relates to the three nations and offers comparisons that include case studies to draw out our understanding. Esoimeme's passion for the topic of anti-money laundering is clear as he takes the reader through a detailed analysis across an encompassing range of anti-money laundering topics. Topics such as human trafficking rarely receive the appropriate focus in many parts of the world and Esoimeme does well to bring topics such as this to the fore.

Ehi Eric Esoimeme set out to compare the anti-money laundering laws of the three nations and offers an in-depth review of the contrasts. Readers seeking a better understanding of anti-money laundering legislation are offered a concise outline with much to learn for those seeking to further their understanding.

"Deterring and Detecting Money Laundering and Terrorist Financing" is aimed at financial institutions and designated non-financial businesses and its professionals, under-graduates and post-graduate researchers. It is a must read for anti-money laundering professionals and students looking for a strong foundation in which to build their knowledge."

—Daniel Rogers, managing director, AML360.com (Asia Pacific, United Kingdom, Middle East, and North America)

"This book has provided a thorough comparison and discussion of the money laundering laws in Nigeria, the United States and the United Kingdom. It has made several recommendations about which approach is best and what reforms are necessary.

The need for this book is most viable for the financial industry, given Ehi's ability to pass excellent commentary on the substantive English law (where he studied law initially) and therefore

his knowledge and familiarity of the statutory construct of English criminal law, in both procedural, rule-based legislation (such as the Money Laundering Regulations 2017) and the definitional statutes (such as the Fraud Act 2006)."
—Uju Ogubunka, PhD, FCIB, president, Bank Customers Association of Nigeria (BCAN) and former registrar/chief executive, the Chartered Institute of Bankers of Nigeria (CIBN)

"I like the discussion on charities and aggressive de-risking within financial institutions.

The case study in this book is really appreciated; my preferred one is the transaction laundering (new methods of money laundering) which shows the new trends on ML scenarios.

Key points are having a good Know Your Customer policy (onboarding and refresh initiatives) and an effective fine-tuned transaction activity monitoring tool and Suspicious Activity Reporting system.

I really liked the chapter on modern slavery. I learnt a lot, and this is more complete than what we could have found in other specialized reviews such as the Association of Certified Anti–Money Laundering Specialists (ACAMS) Today paper I read recently on that matter."
—Mustapha Bouzizoua, compliance officer (financial crimes), HSBC private banking (France)

"I liked the case study on third party payment processors and the case study of employment risk. It was simple, straight to the point and showed the low values potentially involved.

I found the chapter on modern slavery really useful. This is a very topical subject at this moment, particularly in the United Kingdom."
—Andrew Fleming, ICA AML Dip, Global AML risk framework manager at HSBC Global Banking and Markets (London, United Kingdom)

"Ehi Esoimeme engages with issues that many either oversimplify or avoid altogether. He admirably met the challenge of reconciling legal, jurisdictional and operational issues akin to money laundering. Of course, full or actual reconciliation is not always possible. Creating an understanding of the complexity of language to help "finders of fact" register this as a genuine vocational and workable anti–money laundering commodity and professional resource was but one crucial challenge ably achieved. One cannot reduce issues of law and acquisitive financial crime to a state of simplicity that does not exist.

Equally, money laundering, being such an amorphous entity as a crime, is arguably de facto immeasurable in a full and real sense. Many texts address specific points of reference and requisite money laundering criminality, but here we see a splendidly holistic approach to presenting answers to the questions it poses.

Writing a widely acceptable book on the massive issue of money laundering and the fragmented state of the law across key jurisdictions—as in Nigeria, the United Kingdom and the United States of America—needs order and method, as well as a flexible and running thread to connect cohesion and meaning to it all. This book provides this.

The comparatives and overlaps are well presented and neatly contextualized to keep them proportionate. The highest quality grasp of legal theory resonates throughout. A dynamic and synergy in the linking chapters engages the reader in the style I have come to know from Ehi Esoimeme. Current challenges are clear, and future remedies and workable answers and methods and policies are explained or hinted at. The book encourages conceptual thought as well as finite and robust guidance for learning.

In essence, what we have in this superb text is clarity and not mere description of the challenges and issues it addresses.

Therefore you, as either a fellow professional or an infrequent but interested observer of money laundering, knowing what money laundering is, how it has advanced more than ever with new ways, what it causes and how we attempt to govern this massive spectre of crime legally and operationally, cannot help but benefit from this book—whatever your vocation or whatever part you have in combating it."

—Ian Ross, compliance, financial crime specialist and trainer, Intersol Global (UK)

DETERRING AND DETECTING MONEY LAUNDERING AND TERRORIST FINANCING

A COMPARATIVE ANALYSIS OF ANTI–MONEY LAUNDERING AND COUNTERTERRORISM FINANCING STRATEGIES

Second Edition

Ehi Eric Esoimeme
DSC Publications Ltd.

ISBN-13: 9789782787798
ISBN-10: 9782787795
Published by DSC Publications Ltd.
203 Ikorodu Road, Obanikoro
Lagos, Nigeria

Printed and bound in the United States of America
Charleston, SC

To God Almighty for his sufficient grace and mercies throughout my life and for giving me the inspiration, strength, and motivation to write this excellent book

ACKNOWLEDGEMENTS

I take this opportunity to express my deep sense of gratitude to Mr. Ian Ross for his encouragement and support and for contributing the foreword to this book.

I wish to express my awed gratitude to the editorial team that assisted me in this project. They showed tremendous zeal in the preparatory stages of this work, which must be duly recognized. I am grateful to Anatoly Yakorev, director, Center for Business Ethics & Compliance (Moscow, Russian Federation); Patricia Robertson, chartered FCSI, CDipAF, director, senior compliance and management consultant, Westport Global Ltd (United Kingdom); Daniel Rogers, managing director, AML360.com (Asia Pacific, United Kingdom, Middle East, and North America); Dr. Uju Ogubunka, FCIB, president, Bank Customers Association of Nigeria (BCAN); Mustapha Bouzizoua, compliance officer (financial crimes), HSBC Private Banking (France); Andrew Fleming, ICA AML Dip, global AML risk framework manager, HSBC Global Banking and Markets (London, United Kingdom); and Melissa Brown Levine, owner/senior editor at Brown Levine Productions (Hampton, Georgia).

I express my sincere appreciation to my mother, Dr. Angela Esoimeme, for her unwavering support, encouragement, and supreme patience. I consider myself particularly fortunate to have her as my mother. She created an environment of homely peace and tranquility while I strove to ensure that this publication was of unequaled excellence.

TABLE OF CONTENTS

FOREWORD TO THE SECOND EDITION

The eagerly awaited second edition to *Deterring and Detecting Money Laundering and Terrorist Financing* has now come to be. It is my honour and privilege to make my modest contribution to it at this juncture.

What is refreshing and authentically different about all publications by Ehi Eric Esoimeme is his 'needs and wants' analysis approach, and, again, we see impactive areas astutely researched and clearly identified for this book. The structure of the *second edition* represents expediency and efficiency, as well as unshakable legality, as a baseline. We also see consistency of approach imbued with innovation. Not many authors achieve this.

Therefore, without question, the content lives up to the title. The subject matter is addressed incisively in key areas. Moreover, the book provides keen perspectives based on sound legal imperatives, but with added lines of practical and compliance-viable guidance to follow.

This world-class publication rightly, in my view, holds a place amongst the best publications and contributions to countering money laundering and terrorist financing. It is an immensely supportive and valuable resource for lawyers, auditors, academics, investigators, compliance teams, etc., bolstering an organisations' resilience to money laundering and terrorist financing.

In short, the book is useful to all involved in the anti-money laundering/counter-terrorist financing cause.

—Ian Ross, compliance, financial crime specialist and trainer, Intersol Global (UK)

Accredited Counter Fraud Specialist

Certified Internal Controls Auditor

International Academy of Investigative Psychology

Preface to the Second Edition

A diverse mix of regulations and standards has been developed to counter money laundering and terrorist financing. Most significant amongst these are the Recommendations of the Financial Action Task Force (FATF), an inter-governmental body established in 1989 at the G7 summit in Paris as a result of the growing concern over money laundering.

Although countries have followed the advice of the FATF by enacting laws that require financial institutions and designated non-financial businesses and professions (DNFBPs) to implement certain measures that can combat money laundering and terrorist financing, the approaches adopted in these different countries are not identical.

Scope of the Book

The first edition to this book compared the approaches adopted in Nigeria, the United States and the United Kingdom in relation to reporting requirements, money laundering offences, politically exposed persons, cash couriers, compliance officers, offences of bribery, plea bargaining, customer due diligence measures, record keeping and level of compliance. This edition adds eight new topics to the existing chapters. They are assessing risks and applying a risk-based approach, terrorist financing offence, private banking, prepaid cards, modern slavery, fraud, tax evasion and confiscation and provisional measures.

Purpose of the Book
The focus of the second edition is on providing accountable institutions with a clear understanding of their anti-money laundering and counter-terrorist financing (AML/CTF) obligations. The comparative approach adopted by this book ensures that readers will achieve the following:

i. remain familiar with the concepts of money laundering and terrorist financing;
ii. become aware of the threat money laundering and terrorist financing poses to bankers or practitioners;
iii. maintain a proportionate and risk-level-based approach to those threats;
iv. adopt the AML/CTF procedures appropriate to that level of risk; and
v. review and maintain those procedures regularly.

Target Audience
The concepts in this book are aimed at financial institutions and DNFBPs, as well as undergraduate and postgraduate researchers.

Content of the Book
The second edition consists of 19 chapters, followed by a number of appendices that set out other generally applicable material. The book incorporates a range of case studies that financial institutions and designated non-financial institutions will, hopefully, find helpful in appreciating the overall context of, and obligations within, the AML/CTF framework.

The book provides guidance on the following:

- money laundering process, regulation of diamond dealers and other DNFBPs, as well as regulation of hawala and other alternative remittance systems, international bodies and national government agencies charged with fighting money laundering and terrorist financing (Chapter 1);
- country-level and reporting entity-level risk assessments, and the measures to prevent the misuse of

non-profit organisations and third-party payment processors (Chapter 2);

- suspicious activity reports, currency transaction reports, further information orders, disclosure orders and information sharing within the financial sector (Chapter 3);
- money laundering offence, penalties and lifetime management of ancillary orders (Chapter 4);
- terrorist financing, jurisdiction, penalties and policies and procedures involved in the seizure/forfeiture of terrorist property (Chapter 5);
- current measures to reduce the money laundering risks associated with politically exposed persons (Chapter 6);
- innovative methods to reduce the money laundering risks associated with private banking accounts (Chapter 7);
- strategic measures that meet the goal of financial inclusion (that is, preserving innovation and the many legitimate uses and societal benefits offered by prepaid cards) without compromising the measures that exist for combating money laundering, terrorist financing and other illicit transactions through the financial system (Chapter 8);
- calculated processes to prevent the smuggling of the proceeds of crime overseas for the purpose of avoiding the reach of law enforcement agencies (Chapter 9);
- complete understanding of the role and responsibilities of the compliance officer (Chapter 10);
- timely procedures for combating predicate offences for money laundering—e.g. modern slavery (Chapter 11), the offence of bribery (Chapter 12), fraud (Chapter 13) and tax evasion (Chapter 14);
- authorized measures for freezing or seizing property laundered or proceeds from instrumentalities used in, or intended for use in, money laundering or predicate offences (Chapter 15 and Chapter 16);
- conscientious assistance that helps firms gain confidence that their customer due diligence obligations have been properly carried out (Chapter 17);
- institutional record keeping maintenance (Chapter 18).

Details of Competing Books Either Published or in Preparation and How This Book Distinguishes Itself from Them

Several books have adopted the comparative approach. Notable amongst them are Nicholas Ryder's *Money Laundering–An Endless Cycle?: A Comparative Analysis of the Anti-Money Laundering Policies in the United States of America, the United Kingdom, Australia and Canada* (Routledge 2013) and Waleed Alhosani's *Anti-Money Laundering: A Comparative and Critical Analysis of the UK and UAE's Financial Intelligence Units* (Palgrave Macmillan 2016).

Although the aforementioned books may have touched on the issue of money laundering, none of them addressed the issue in broad terms as it is done in this book. This book provides guidance on how to combat money laundering/terrorist financing and the predicate offences for money laundering—e.g. fraud, tax evasion and modern slavery. This book also uses a mix of methodologies as opposed to focusing on just one. In addition to the comparative methodology, the book adopts the case study methodology. This methodology was not used in the first edition. The case study methodology helps the reader to understand better and act in compliance with the law in relation to money laundering and terrorist financing.

Ehi Eric Esoimeme Esq., LLM
Deputy Editor in Chief of DSC Publications Ltd.
Member: Association of Certified Anti-Money Laundering Specialists
Email: ehiesoimeme@yahoo.com

Table of Cases

Tables of Legislation

SECONDARY LEGISLATION

CBN (Anti-Money Laundering and Combating the Financing of Terrorism in Banks and Other Financial Institutions in Nigeria) Regulations, 2013

Anti-Money Laundering/Combating the Financing of Terrorism (AML/CFT) Regulations for Designated Non-Financial Businesses and Professions in Nigeria, 2013

TERTIARY LEGISLATION

Nigerian Financial Intelligence Unit: Anti-Money Laundering/ Combating the Financing of Terrorism (AML/CFT) Reporting Guidelines 2012

Central Bank of Nigeria Revised Guidelines on Stored Value/Prepaid Card Issuance and Operations 2012

Central Bank of Nigeria Guidelines for Card Issuance and Usage in Nigeria

SECONDARY LEGISLATION
Codified Bank Secrecy Act Regulations (31 CFR Chapter X)

TERTIARY LEGISLATION
The Joint Money Laundering Steering Group JMLSG, *Prevention of Money Laundering/Combating Terrorist Financing* (2017) revised version, Guidance for the United Kingdom Financial Sector Part I, June 2017 [Amended December 2017]

Joint Money Laundering Steering Group JMLSG, *Prevention of money laundering/combating terrorist financing*, 2017 Revised Version, Guidance for the UK financial sector Part II, June 2017 (Amended December 2017)

Senior Management Arrangements, Systems and Controls (SYSC) 2017

INDIA
TERTIARY LEGISLATION
Policy Guidelines for Issuance and Operation of Prepaid Payment Instruments in India 2016

REPUBLIC OF KOREA
PRIMARY LEGISLATION
Republic of Korea Criminal Act, No 293, Sep 18 1953 as last amended by Act No 10259 April 15 2010

LIST OF ABBREVIATIONS

ACAMS	Association of Certified Anti-Money Laundering Specialists (this is the largest international membership organization dedicated to enhancing the knowledge, skills and expertise of AML/CTF and financial crime detection and prevention professionals)
ACSRT	African Centre for the Study and Research on Terrorism
ACH	Automated Clearing House
AFF	Department of Justice's Assets Forfeiture Fund
AML	Anti-Money Laundering
APG	Asia Pacific Group
ARO	European Asset Recovery Office
ATM	Automated Teller Machine
AUSA	Assistant U.S. Attorney
BCCI	Bank of Credit and Commerce International
BED	Bank Examination Department
BNIs	Bearer Negotiable Instruments
BSA	Bank Secrecy Act
CAC	Corporate Affairs Commission
CAFRA	Civil Asset Forfeiture Reform Act of 2000
CARIN	Camden Asset Recovery Inter-Agency Network

CBN	Central Bank of Nigeria
CBP	Cross Border Protection
CDD	Customer Due Diligence
CEMA	Customs & Excise Management Act
CEO	Chief Executive Officer
CFT	Combating the Financing of Terrorism
CTF	Counter-Terrorist Financing
CFT	Countering the Financing of Terrorism (also used for combating the financing of terrorism)
CFR	Code of Federal Regulations
CFRs	Consumer Fraud Reports
CIP	Customer Identification Program
CPC	Criminal Procedure Code
CTRs	Currency Transaction Reports
DFS	Department of Financial Services
DHL	Dalsey, Hillblom and Lynn (founders of DHL Worldwide Express)
DNFBPs	Designated non-financial businesses and professions
DNFIs	Designated non-financial institutions
DPA	Deferred Prosecution Agreement
DSS	Department of State Services
DVSA	Driving Vehicle Standards Agency
DVD	Digital Versatile Disc
EAG	Eurasian group on combating money laundering and financing of terrorism
ECHR	European Convention on Human Rights
EDD	Enhanced Due Diligence
EFCC	Economic and Financial Crimes Commission
EO	Executive Order
FATF	Financial Action Task Force, an intergovernmental body whose purpose is to develop and promote broad AML/CTF standards, both at national and international levels
FBI	Federal Bureau of Investigation

FCUA	Federal Credit Union Act
FCA	Financial Conduct Authority, the UK regulator of the financial services industry
FCMB	First City Monument Bank
FCPA	Foreign Corrupt Practices Act
FCT	Federal Capital Territory, Abuja
FDIA	Federal Deposit Insurance Act
FDIC	Federal Deposit Insurance Corporation
FFIEC	Federal Financial Institutions Examination Council
FinCEN	Financial Crimes Enforcement Network, a bureau of the U.S. Department of the Treasury. The Director of FinCEN is appointed by the Secretary of the Treasury and reports to the Treasury Under Secretary for Terrorism and Financial Intelligence. FinCEN's mission is to safeguard the financial system from illicit use and combat money laundering and promote national security through the collection, analysis, and dissemination of financial intelligence and strategic use of financial authorities.
FINTECH	Financial Technology
FIU	Financial Intelligence Unit
FROs	Financial Reporting Orders
FSAPs	Financial Sector Assessment Programs
FSAs	Financial Stability Assessments
FSB	Financial Stability Board
FSMA	Financial Services and Markets Act 2000
FTC	Federal Trade Commission
FTOs	Foreign Terrorist Organizations
GIABA	Inter-Governmental Action Group against Money Laundering in West Africa
GTB	Guarantee Trust Bank
HNWI	High net worth individuals
HMRC	Her Majesty's Revenue and Customs

HMT	Her Majesty's Treasury
HIS	U.S. Immigration and Customs Enforcement's Homeland Security Investigations
IAIS	International Association of Insurance Supervisors
IBC	International Business Corporations
ICAEW	Institute of Chartered Accountants in England and Wales
ICPC	Independent Corrupt Practices and Other Related Offences Commission
ID	Identity Document
ILO	International Labour Organisation
IMF	International Monetary Fund
INCSR	International Narcotics Control Strategy Report
IOSCO	International Organization of Securities Commissions
IOTAs	Interest on Trust Accounts
IPOB	Indigenous People of Biafra
IRS	Internal Revenue Service
ISA	Investments and Securities Act
ISD	Insurance & Surveillance Department
JMLSG	Joint Money Laundering Steering Group
KYC	Know Your Customer
LCTR	Large Currency Transaction Report
ML	Money Laundering
MLPA	Money Laundering Prohibition Act
MONEYVAL	Committee of Experts on the Evaluation of Anti-Money Laundering Measures
MSB	Money Services Business
MVTS	Money or Value Transfer Services
NAICOM	National Insurance Commission
NBFCs	Non-Banking Financial Companies
NCA	The National Crime Agency, the UK's financial intelligence unit

NCS	Nigeria Customs Service
NDLEA	National Drug Law Enforcement Agency
NDIC	Nigeria Deposit Insurance Corporation
NFIU	Nigerian Financial Intelligence Unit (this is the Nigerian arm of the global financial intelligence Units (FIUs) domiciled within the EFCC as an autonomous unit and operating in the African Region. The NFIU seeks to comply with international standards on combating Money Laundering and Financing of Terrorism and proliferation)
NGO	Nongovernmental Organization
NIA	National Intelligence Agency (this is a government division tasked with overseeing foreign intelligence and counterintelligence operations and has its headquarters in Abuja)
NSL	National Security Letter
NMLRA	National Money Laundering Risk Assessment
NOMS	National Offender Management Service
NPOs	Non-Profitable Organisations
NPPS	New Payment Products and Services
NPC	National Planning Commission
NTFRA	National Terrorist Financing Risk Assessment
NRA	National Risk Assessment
NRAS	National Risk Assessment Secretariat
NFPT	National Focal Points on Terrorism
NFP	National Focal Point
NCUA	National Credit Union Administration
OCC	Office of the Comptroller of the Currency
OCP	Organised Crime Partnership
OFAC	Office of Foreign Assets Control
PEPs	Politically Exposed Persons
PICs	Private Investment Companies
PIN	Personal Identification Number
PML	Prevention of Money Laundering Rules 2005
PND	Place No Debit

POCA	Proceeds of Crime Act 2002
POS	Point of Sale
PPIs	Pre-paid Payment Instruments
PSPs	Payment services providers
PUPID	Payable upon Proper Identification
PUK	Personal Unblocking Key
RCCs	Remotely Created Cheques
RBA	Risk-Based Approach
RBS	Risk Based Supervision
RRS	Rapid Response Squad
RUSI	Royal United Services Institute
RVs	Recreational Vehicles
SAN	Senior Advocate of Nigeria
SARs	Suspicious Activity Reports
SCPOs	Serious Crime Prevention Orders
SDGTs	Specially Designated Global Terrorists
SEC	Securities and Exchange Commission
SFO	Serious Fraud Office
SCIID	State Criminal Investigation and Intelligence Department, Yaba
SCUML	Special Control Unit on Money Laundering
SIID	Special Insured Institutions Department
SROs	Self-Regulatory Organisations
SSS	The State Security Service (SSS) is also known as Department of State Services (DSS). This body is the main body responsible for intelligence gathering in Nigeria.
STRs	Suspicious Transaction Reports
SYSC	FCA Sourcebook: Senior Management Arrangements, Systems and Controls
TF	Terrorist Financing
TTF	Topical Trust Funds
TFI	Office of Terrorism and Financial Intelligence
TRO	Travel Restriction Order

UDHR	Universal Declaration of Human Rights
UNILAG	University of Lagos
UNODC	United Nations Office on Drugs and Crime
UNSC	United Nations Security Council
UHNWI	Ultra-High Net Worth Individuals
USA PATRIOT Act	Uniting and Strengthening America by Providing Appropriate Tools Required to Intercept and Obstruct Terrorism Act of 2001
USC	U.S. Code
U.S. Treasury	U.S. Department of the Treasury
USMS	U.S. Marshals Service
USAO	United States Attorney's Office
UKFIU	UK Financial Intelligence Unit
VAT	Value Added Tax
Wi-Fi	Wireless Fidelity, meaning you can access or connect to a network using radio waves, without needing to use wires.

CHAPTER 1

INTRODUCTION TO MONEY LAUNDERING AND TERRORIST FINANCING

Money laundering and terrorist financing are financial crimes with potentially devastating social and financial effects. From the profits of the narcotics trafficker to the assets looted from government coffers by dishonest public officials, criminal proceeds have the power to corrupt and ultimately destabilize communities or entire economies. Terrorist networks are able to facilitate their activities if they have financial means and access to the financial system. In both money laundering and terrorist financing, criminals can exploit loopholes and other weaknesses in the legitimate financial system to launder criminal proceeds, finance terrorism, or conduct other illegal activities, and ultimately, hide the actual purpose of their activity.[1]

1.1 What is Money Laundering?

Money laundering is the processing of the proceeds of crime to disguise their illegal origin. Once these proceeds are successfully 'laundered' the criminal is able to enjoy these monies without revealing their original source.[2]

---

1 Federal Financial Institutions Examination Council (2014), 'Bank Secrecy Act/Anti-Money Laundering Examination Manual', Available at: https://www.occ.treas.gov/publications/publications-by-type/other-publications-reports/ffiec-bsa-aml-examination-manual.pdf (accessed 10 January 2017).

2 International Association of Insurance Supervisors (2004), '5 Guidance paper on anti-money laundering and combating the financing of terrorism', Available at: https://www.iaisweb.org/page/supervisory-material/guidance-papers (accessed 5 February 2017).

Money laundering requires an underlying, primary, profit-making crime (such as corruption, drug trafficking, market manipulation, fraud, tax evasion), along with the intent to conceal the proceeds of the crime or to further the criminal enterprise. These activities generate financial flows that involve the diversion of resources away from economically and socially-productive uses—and these diversions can have negative impacts on the financial sector. They also have a corrosive, corrupting effect on society and the economic system as a whole.[3]

Money laundering takes many forms, including:

i.   Trying to turn money raised through criminal activity into 'clean' money (that is, classic money laundering);
ii. Handling the benefit of acquisitive crimes such as theft, fraud and tax evasion;
iii. Handling stolen goods;
iv. Being directly involved with any criminal or terrorist property, or entering into arrangements to facilitate the laundering of criminal or terrorist property; and
v.   Criminals investing the proceeds of their crimes in the whole range of financial products.[4]

1.2 Stages of Money Laundering

Although money laundering is a diverse and often complex process, it basically involves three independent steps that can occur simultaneously;

---

3 International Monetary Fund (2017), 'Anti-Money Laundering/Combating the Financing of Terrorism', Available at: https://www.imf.org/external/np/leg/aml-cft/eng/ (accessed 5 September 2017).

4 The Joint Money Laundering Steering Group JMLSG: Prevention of money laundering/combating terrorist financing 2017 Revised Version: Guidance for the UK financial sector Part I, June 2017 (Amended December 2017), Preface.

1.2.1 Placement

The placement stage is the stage at which funds from illegal activity, or funds intended to support illegal activity, are first introduced into the financial system. The goal is to introduce the unlawful proceeds into the financial system without attracting the attention of financial institutions or law enforcement. This can be done when a customer makes several cash deposits into one account or into different accounts in different banks; none of which will be over ten thousand US dollars. These transactions are designed to circumvent the Bank's obligation to report any cash deposit over ten thousand dollars on a Currency Transaction Report as described in **31 CFR §1010.330.**

1.2.2 Layering

The layering stage involves further disguising and distancing the illicit funds from their illegal source through the use of a series of parties and/or transactions designed to conceal the source of the illicit funds. A person who was successful in the placement stage is likely to move to this stage which appears to be more complex.

Shell companies, typically registered in offshore havens, are a common tool in the layering phase of money laundering. These companies, whose directors often are local attorneys acting as nominees, obscure the beneficial owners through restrictive bank secrecy laws and attorney-client privilege. They are usually incorporated in jurisdictions such as the Cayman Islands or Channel Islands which restrict disclosure of a company's beneficial owner.

The complex case included here provides a "textbook" typology as an example of misuse of corporate vehicles in the layering phase of money laundering.

CASE STUDY ON THE MISUSE OF CORPORATE VEHICLES IN THE LAYERING PHASE OF MONEY LAUNDERING: THE QUEEN OF THE SOUTH CASE

Based on the best-selling book by the same name written by Spanish author Arturo Pérez Reverte, Queen of The South is a serialized crime drama that centers on the Mexican drug business. The telenovela tells the story of Teresa Mendoza, whose life is thrown upside down when her boyfriend, El Guero, is killed by the organized crime gang for which he has been flying planes. She trades his notebook to the head of the gang, Epifanio Vargas (Zurita), in exchange for her help escaping to Spain. There, she gets a job as a waitress in a brothel, and gradually works her way up to running the place's books. She begins a relationship with a smuggler, and learns the ropes of the trade from him, only for tragedy to strike. While trying to out-run the authorities, their boat crashes into rocks, killing him and leading to her being sent to prison.

In jail, Teresa Mendoza links up with Colombian Patricia O'Farrell (Urgel), who knows the location of a huge cocaine stash, hidden by her late boyfriend from the Russian mafia. On their release, the pair work out a risky deal with Oleg Yasikov (Jiménez) to sell it back, giving them the cash to set up in the drug business, with Yasikov's help.[5]

After many years in the drug business, Teresa Mendoza rose up to become the leader of the Mexican drug cartel, and made so much money from the drug business. Teresa Mendoza knew that by using funds from the drug cartel business, she risks drawing the authorities' attention to the underlying criminal activity and exposing herself to criminal prosecution. In order to benefit freely from the proceeds of her crime, she hired the services of a lawyer to help her conceal the illicit origin of these funds by registering companies in offshore tax havens. The idea was to invest large sums of money into these companies, and later wire some of the profits made from these companies back to her bank accounts in Mexico.

To kick start the process of money laundering, Teresa Mendoza physically delivered the monies made from her drug business to her lawyer in Mexico who then deposited the funds into his bank account in Mexico, and later transferred the funds to his bank accounts in panama for the sole purpose of registering shell companies for Teresa Mendoza (this is the Placement Phase of Money Laundering).

5 Pulsamerica (2017), 'MEDIA: Queen of the South vs. La Reina Del Sur', Available at: http://www.pulsamerica.co.uk/2017/07/culture-queen-of-the-south-vs-la-reina-del-sur/ (accessed 28 September 2017).

Teresa Mendoza's lawyer registered these companies with nominee directors, officeholders, and shareholders. There was no way the Bank would have stopped him from transferring the money from Mexico to panama since they thought it was his own money. He also employed the services of individual couriers to transport part of the cash in checked or carry-on baggage or on their persons. Each of the courier men carried amounts below ten thousand US dollars (this is the Layering Phase of Money Laundering).

The funds that were invested in panama were later wired to Teresa Mendoza's bank accounts in Mexico. Teresa Mendoza withdrew the funds and used them to purchase houses and luxury cars (this is the Integration Phase of Money Laundering which will be discussed in more detail in the next section).

1.2.3 Integration

Once the origin of the funds/assets has been obscured, through placement and layering, the criminal can use the funds which now appear legitimate. They may be invested in legitimate business or used to buy property (both residential and commercial) or other investments, set up a trust or even settle litigation, among other activities. Integration is the most difficult stage of money laundering to detect.[6]

This case study below provides a "textbook" typology as an example of the use of real estate agents in the integration phase of money laundering. The scheme established here was intended to launder criminal proceeds through real estate investment.

CASE STUDY ON THE USE OF REAL ESTATE AGENTS IN THE INTEGRATION PHASE OF MONEY LAUNDERING: THE ADEEL MIRZA CASE

---

6 Chartered Institute of Legal Executives (2015), 'Anti-money Laundering Guidance notes', Available at: http://www.cilex.org.uk/pdf/CILEx%20DRAFT%20 AML%20Guidance%20Member%20Consultation%20January%202015.pdf (accessed 5 September 2017).

Adeel Mirza, a 45-year-old financial adviser who pleaded guilty to 10 counts of fraud and deception in 2013, had been ordered to pay four million one hundred eighty thousand seven hundred eighty-eight pounds. The confiscation order must be paid within 12 months, otherwise a 6-year default sentence will be imposed.

Mirza made widespread use of fraudulent documents to assist him in arranging fraudulent mortgages for his clients, who included heroin dealer Riaz Mohammed and a corrupt solicitor. The financial investigation by the National Crime Agency (United Kingdom) uncovered a tangled web of complex multi-million-pound financial transactions involving fraudulent mortgages, bank accounts and properties being held in the names of unsuspecting members of Mirza's family, including one property purchased in the name of a deceased individual. The investigation also identified offshore bank accounts held in Switzerland and Jersey, and an offshore company based in Jersey that owned 15 rental properties. Mirza was sentenced to six years in 2013 and made subject to a Financial Reporting Order.

On the 24th of September, 2015, the confiscation hearing at Southwark Crown Court found that Mirza's benefit from criminal conduct was eight million two hundred ninety-eight thousand four hundred seventy-six pounds, with the realizable amount in assets being four million one hundred eighty thousand seven hundred eighty-eight pounds. The assets include the luxury family home in Wanstead, Bentley Continental and Range Rover motor vehicles, watches and jewelry, 14 other rental properties in London, and cash held in the United Kingdom and offshore bank accounts.[7]

Case Comment

Real estate agents in particular are involved in the vast majority of real estate transactions and therefore can play a key role in detecting

---

7 National Crime Agency (2015), 'financial-adviser-who-arranged-fraudulent-mortgages-for-a-heroin-dealer-ordered-to-pay-back-more-than-4m', Available at: http://www.nationalcrimeagency.gov.uk/news/710-financial-adviser-who-arranged-fraudulent-mortgages-for-a-heroin-dealer-ordered-to-pay-back-more-than-4m (accessed 26 September, 2015).

money laundering and terrorist financing schemes. Because they are in direct contact with buyers and sellers, real estate agents generally know their clients better than the other parties in the transactions. Therefore, they are well placed to detect suspicious activity or identify red flag indicators.

If the real estate agents who were involved in the buying and selling of properties for Mirza, had done their due diligence properly, the above scenario could have been prevented.

The Financial Action Task Force (FATF) Recommendations recognise the importance of customer due diligence, record-keeping and reporting requirements for the real estate sector.

CASE STUDY: MONEY LAUNDERING BEING ACCOMPLISHED WITHOUT THE INTRODUCTION OF MONEY INTO THE FINANCIAL SYSTEM

It is worth noting that the money laundering process does not always have to begin with the deposit of the proceeds of crime in a bank. Criminals may decide to launder their illicit funds through a local car dealership as seen in the Michael Paul Boyter case study below or through trade in diamonds as seen in the Danny Koort and Jeanette Rosen case study below.

Case 1.1: United States Department of Justice v. Michael Paul Boyter and Anthony Reuben Riley

Michael Paul Boyter, 54, and Anthony Reuben Riley, 53, both of Shreveport, were two of the owners and operators of Mike's Auto Sales and A-1 Auto Finance Company. Boyter and Riley shamelessly facilitated drug trafficking by allowing drug dealers to launder their money and obtain vehicles that they otherwise would have been unable to purchase without detection by law enforcement.

According to evidence presented at the guilty pleas, Boyter and Riley engaged in a conspiracy to commit money laundering beginning in 1996 and continuing through November 2010. The defendants' scheme concerned the sale and financing of used and new vehicles to individuals who derived, or represented that they derived, significant income from the distribution of illegal drugs. The defendants knowingly accepted cash from drug dealers, allowed vehicle purchases in the names of nominees, and falsified records of payments received. The defendants also provided false information to multiple local and federal law enforcement agencies, including the Shreveport Police Department and the Harrison County Sheriff's Office, to facilitate the release of vehicles seized from drug dealers.

In 2009 and 2010, the Federal Bureau of Investigation (FBI) conducted multiple "sting" operations using cooperating individuals to purchase vehicles from Mikes Auto Sales. During the undercover operations, Boyter, Riley, and others accepted large cash payments toward the purchase of vehicles, registered the vehicles in the name of nominees, and failed to report cash received in excess of ten thousand dollars as required by federal law. These operations proved that the defendants routinely accepted large amounts of money thought to be drug proceeds and skimmed cash from down payments by manipulating records to show lower sales prices and reduced amounts of down payments.

The defendants were sentenced on February 18, 2014 by U.S. District Judge Elizabeth E. Foote, on charges arising out of a money laundering conspiracy operated from the businesses. Boyter was sentenced to 60 months in prison for wire fraud and tax evasion charges. He was also ordered to pay two hundred ninety thousand three hundred eighty-one dollars restitution and two hundred thousand dollars fine. Riley was sentenced to 15 months in prison for the failure to file Form 8300 charges and was ordered to pay one hundred thousand dollars fine. As part of their plea agreements with the United States, both men also agreed to forfeit property of Mike's Auto Sales and A-1 Auto Finance, and to pay a money judgment of one million three hundred thousand dollars.

Since the sentencing, the properties where the businesses were housed were sold and funds in bank and brokerage accounts were seized.[8]

---

8 United States Department of Justice (2017), 'U.S. Attorney's Office presents more than $1 million in proceeds from money laundering case to law enforcement agencies', Available at: https://www.justice.gov/usao-wdla/pr/us-attorney-s-office-presents-more-1-million-proceeds-money-laundering-case-law (accessed 26 April 2017).

Case 1.2: R v. Danny Koort and Jeanette Rosen (Unreported)

A couple who ran a diamond trading business were convicted of money laundering on the 28th of October 2016 at the Old Bailey after a joint investigation by the National Crime Agency (NCA) and City of London Police.

Danny Koort and Jeanette Rosen are thought to have laundered up to fifty-three million pounds for organised crime groups in under two years, based on diary entries showing their deals from January 2013 to November 2014.

Koort was jailed for 11 years and Rosen 10 years.

Dutch national Koort, 52, and Rosen, 48, both of East Finchley, London, used code names – such as Fiat, Honda, Champagne, Cristal and Caviar – in the diaries to refer to customers.

Notes made on envelopes inside the diaries showed at least twenty million pounds was laundered between April and November 2014.

The couple ran a legitimate diamond dealing business but used it as cover to clean the money.

Rosen, acting on Koort's behalf, took part in a series of street exchanges with couriers to transfer the massive sums of cash.

Accomplice Andrew Russell, 54, of Ongar in Essex, was also convicted of money laundering and jailed for four years.

NCA officers arrested Russell on 25 July 2014 with one hundred and ninety eighty thousand pounds in cash in a holdall in his car.

He had been under surveillance at a meeting at an Essex hotel where he collected a large bag. He then bought a holdall from Argos and filled it with the cash. Later that day officers photographed Russell and Rosen meeting in a street but Russell did not transfer the money to her.

City of London Police arrested Rosen on 28 November 2014 when she was carrying just short of one hundred and seventy thousand pounds in a bag in a central London street.

Police searched her office where they found two hundred thirty-five thousand two hundred and fifteen euro and seventeen thousand one hundred and sixty-five pounds in cash.

The officers also searched her black Mercedes and discovered 10 pay-as-you-go mobile phones – nine with code names written on.

A search of Rosen and Koort's home discovered a piece of paper headed "my big friend" with calculations for sums in sterling and Euros ending with an outstanding amount of sixty thousand one hundred pounds. Investigators also found a bag containing counterfeit notes.

NCA senior investigating officer Tony Luhman said: "Koort and Rosen had enormous sums of money going through their books and were clearly doing a lot of business with many organised crime groups.

"Their conviction removes a money laundering facility on which numerous other criminals have depended, and now makes life harder for crooks looking to clean their dirty cash."[9]

Case Comment

The Financial Action Task Force (FATF) has acknowledged the vulnerability of dealers in diamonds by recommending that such business activity should be subject to anti-money laundering/countering the financing of terrorism (AML/CFT) requirements. All countries in the world have to have laws which put these requirements on diamond dealers.

There are six of the FATF's 40 Recommendations that are of direct relevance for diamond dealers:

- FATF Recommendation 1 – Assessing the risks and applying a risk-based approach (RBA): This would allow national authorities to allocate more resources to the monitoring of a diamond dealing business in case a country identifies the diamond dealing business as posing a high level of risk;
- FATF Recommendation 22 – Requires diamond dealers to implement customer due diligence (CDD) measures. With regard to any transaction in cash equal to or above the

---

9 National Crime Agency (2016), 'Diamond dealers thought to have laundered more than £50m', Available at: http://www.nationalcrimeagency.gov.uk/index.php/news-media/nca-news/944-diamond-dealers-thought-to-have-laundered-more-than-50m (accessed 8 January 2017).

applicable designated threshold of fifteen thousand dollars/ euro, diamond dealers are required to know their customers and to collect enough information to be satisfied that the transaction is legitimate.

Danny Koort and Jeanette Rosen used their expertise and experience in the diamond industry, to aid their clients in avoiding detection by law enforcement agents.

They used code names – such as Fiat, Honda, Champagne, Cristal and Caviar – in the diaries to refer to customers.

Recommendation 10 of the Financial Action Task Force Recommendations prohibits financial institutions from keeping anonymous accounts or accounts in obviously fictitious names.

This Recommendation applies to diamond dealers when they engage in any cash transaction with a customer equal to or above the applicable designated threshold.

Danny Koort and Jeanette Rosen were engaged in cash transactions way above fifteen thousand dollars/euro;

- FATF Recommendation 23 – Requires, in particular, that diamond dealers to send suspicious transaction reports (STRs) to the authorities. Whenever the dealer suspects or has reasonable grounds to suspect that funds are the proceeds of a criminal activity, or are related to terrorist financing he must report this information to the financial intelligence unit (FIU) for further analysis.

Danny Koort and Jeanette failed to report customers they knew to be engaged in various suspicious and high-risk activities. If they had filed their Suspicious Transaction Reports with the National Crime Agency (United Kingdom), they may not have been charged and convicted for money laundering;

- FATF Recommendation 28 – Dealers in diamonds should be regulated and monitored for compliance with the AML/ CFT requirements, namely customer due diligence (CDD), recordkeeping, and reporting. Furthermore, criminals or their associates should be prevented from being accredited, licensed, or being the beneficial owner of a significant or controlling interest in, or holding a management function in a diamond dealing business, e.g. by evaluating persons on the basis of a "fit and proper" test;

- FATF Recommendation 32 – Measures should be in place to detect the cross-border transportation of cash and bearer negotiable instruments. Countries may specify that precious diamonds are to be considered as bearer negotiable instruments, hence persons carrying diamonds would be subject to a declaration or disclosure requirement;

- FATF Recommendation 34 – Guidelines and feedback should be provided to diamond dealers by competent authorities including their supervisors.

In addition to the above, the money laundering process can also begin with the stashing of cash in a wardrobe as detailed in the Daniel Harris case study or keeping cash in chests of drawers as seen in the Shawn Abubakar and Altin Nase case study below.

Case 1.3: R v. Daniel Harris (Unreported)

National Crime Agency officers found the sum of one hundred and twenty thousand pounds in March 2016 when they raided Daniel Harris's home as part of an investigation into a drug smuggling ring.

One hundred and eighteen thousand pounds was hidden in a holdall inside his baby daughter's wardrobe.

In custody he claimed to officers that the cash was for legal fees for a relative who had been arrested in Spain.

He could not explain why he kept the large sum of money in cash in his child's wardrobe and said he did not know whether the money was criminal.

A judge ordered him to forfeit the money on 19 May, 2017 under the Proceeds of Crime Act 2002.

Harris did not argue against the forfeiture.

The raid on his house was part of an investigation into a cocaine delivery service in which cocaine dealers on mopeds posed as trainee-taxi drivers learning the Knowledge.

Ten men were convicted of drug offences following the NCA investigation.

Harris was found guilty of money laundering but not guilty of drug offences.

A judge ruled that cash seized from Daniel Harris, 37, was the proceeds of crime.[10]

Case 1.4: R v. Shwan Abubaker and Altin Nase (Unreported)

Shwan Abubaker (38) from Derby and Altin Nase (41) from London, were arrested by officers from the joint Organised Crime Partnership (OCP) in July 2015.

They were initially stopped in their car for a drugs search. However, when the vehicle was searched, officers found a large black holdall on the back seat which contained approximately two hundred and sixty-nine thousand pounds.

Abubaker was identified as the driver and when he was searched, officers found an additional two thousand pounds cash. Nase was found to be in possession of a key fob which would later lead officers to a flat in East London.

When the flat was searched, investigators found two kilos of cocaine – with a potential street value of over four hundred and forty thousand pounds - in a holdall in the bottom of a wardrobe and an additional three hundred thousand five hundred pounds cash in two separate chests of drawers.

The following day Abubaker was charged with one count of money laundering and Nase two counts of money laundering and possession of Class A drugs with intent to supply.

They were remanded in custody.

---

10 National Crime Agency (2017), 'Almost £120,000 clawed back from money launderer', Available at: http://www.nationalcrimeagency.gov.uk/news/1095-almost-120-000-clawed-back-from-money-launderer (accessed 27 May 2017).

Both Nase and Abubaker pleaded guilty at Blackfriars Crown Court on the 6th of November, 2015 and were sentenced to 9 years and two years 8 months respectively.

Matt McMillan from the Organised Crime Partnership said:

"Both Abubaker and Nase were involved in laundering money all around the UK and their brazen approach – transporting and being in possession of large quantities of cash – showed they thought they were below the radar of law enforcement."

The total amount of money seized as a result of this investigation was six hundred and twenty-six thousand pounds.[11]

Case Comment

It can be inferred from information available on the National Crime Agency (NCA) website that Nase and Abubaker never intended to launder the proceeds of their crime through a bank. They intended to launder the proceeds through designated non-financial businesses and professions like Lawyers, accountants, Real estate agents, Dealers in precious metals and dealers in precious stones and Casinos.

If the police had not stopped them, Nase and Abubaker may have approached a lawyer or an accountant to carry out transactions for them concerning the following activities:

- managing of their money;
- buying and selling of real estate;
- creation, operation or management of legal persons or arrangements, and buying and selling of business entities.

They may have also approached Real estate agents to carry out transactions for them concerning the buying and selling of real estate.

---

11 National Crime Agency (2015), 'drug dealers hide over 300,000 in chest of drawers', Available at: http://www.nationalcrimeagency.gov.uk/news/738-drug-dealers-hide-over-300-000-in-chest-of-drawers (accessed 5 July 2015).

They may have laundered the proceeds by purchasing precious metals and stones in amounts above the designated threshold or they may have laundered the proceeds by betting in casinos.

Nase and Abubaker would be successful in laundering the proceeds of their crime, if a Lawyer, Accountant and Real estate agent fails to apply customer due diligence and record-keeping requirements set out in the Financial Action Task Force Recommendations 10, 11, 12, 15, and 17 when they prepare for and carry out the activities stated above.

1.3 Terrorist Financing

The motivation behind terrorist financing is ideological as opposed to profit-seeking, which is generally the motivation for most crimes associated with money laundering. Terrorism is intended to intimidate a population or to compel a government or an international organization to do or abstain from doing any specific act through the threat of violence. An effective financial infrastructure is critical to terrorist operations.

Terrorist groups develop sources of funding that are relatively mobile to ensure that funds can be used to obtain material and other logistical items needed to commit terrorist acts. Thus, money laundering is often a vital component of terrorist financing.

Terrorists generally finance their activities through both unlawful and legitimate sources. Unlawful activities, such as extortion, kidnapping, and narcotics trafficking, have been found to be a major source of funding. Other observed activities include smuggling, fraud, theft, robbery, identity theft, use of conflict diamonds, and improper use of charitable or relief funds. In the last case, donors may have no knowledge that their donations have been diverted to support terrorist causes.

Other legitimate sources have also been found to provide terrorist organizations with funding; these legitimate funding sources are a key difference between terrorist financiers and traditional criminal organizations. In addition to charitable donations, legitimate sources include foreign government sponsors, business ownership, and personal employment.

Although the motivation differs between traditional money launderers and terrorist financiers, the actual methods used to fund terrorist operations can be the same as or similar to those methods
used by other criminals that launder funds. For example, terrorist
financiers use currency smuggling, structured deposits or withdrawals from bank accounts; purchases of various types of monetary instruments; credit, debit, or prepaid cards; and funds transfers. There
is also evidence that some forms of informal banking (e.g., "hawala")
have played a role in moving terrorist funds. Transactions through
hawalas are difficult to detect given the lack of documentation, their
size, and the nature of the transactions involved. Funding for terrorist attacks does not always require large sums of money, and the
associated transactions may not be complex.[12]

CASE STUDY ON HAWALA AND ALTERNATIVE REMITTANCE SYSTEMS

The word "hawala" comes originally from the Arabic language and
means transfer or remittance. Hawala provides a fast and cost-effective method for worldwide remittance of money or value, particularly
for persons who may be outside the reach of the traditional financial
sector. In some nations hawala is illegal, in others the activity is considered a part of the "gray" economy. It is therefore difficult to accurately measure the total volume of financial activity associated with
the system, however, it is estimated that the figures are in the tens of
billions of dollars, at a minimum. Officials in Pakistan, for example,
estimate that more than seven billion dollars flow into the nation
through hawala channels each year. Other Alternative Remittance or
Informal Value Transfer Systems include "hundi," "fei ch 'ien," "chit
system," "poey kuan" and the black-market peso exchange.

The very features which make hawala attractive to legitimate
customers (mainly expatriates remitting money to relatives in their

---

12 Central Bank of Nigeria (2011), 'ANTI-MONEY LAUNDERING/COMBAT-
ING THE FINANCING OF TERRORISM (AML/CFT) RISK BASED SUPERVI-
SION (RBS) FRAMEWORK', Available at: https://www.cbn.gov.ng/Out/2012/
CCD/CBN%20APPROVED%20FRAMEWORK.pdf (accessed 6 February 2017).

home country) — efficiency, anonymity, and lack of a paper trail—also make the system attractive for the transfer of illicit funds. As noted in a report of the Asia Pacific Group (APG) on Money Laundering, the terrorist events of September 2001 had brought into focus the ease with which alternative remittance and underground banking systems may be utilized to conceal and transfer illicit funds. Not surprisingly, concerns in this area have led many nations to reexamine their regulatory policies and practices in regard to hawala and other alternative remittance systems.[13]

What is Being Done to Address Hawala?

In October 2001 the FATF expanded its mandate to deal with the issue of the funding of terrorist acts and terrorist organisations, and took the important step of creating the Eight (later expanded to Nine) Special Recommendations on Terrorist Financing. The **FATF Recommendations** were revised a second time in 2003 and a third time in 2012, and these, together with the Special Recommendations, have been endorsed by over 180 countries, and are universally recognised as the international standard for anti-money laundering and countering the financing of terrorism (AML/CFT). Recommendation fourteen of the **FATF Recommendations 2012** which was formerly Special Recommendation 6 as at October 2001 deals with alternative remittance and contains four major elements:

- Jurisdictions should require licensing or registration of persons or legal entities providing money or value transfer services, including through informal systems or networks.[14] But a country need not impose a separate licensing or registration system with respect to natural or legal persons already licensed or registered as financial institutions (as defined by the FATF Recommendations) within that country, which,

---

13 U.S. Department of the Treasury (2010), 'Hawala and Alternative Remittance Systems', Available at: https://www.treasury.gov/resource-center/terrorist-illicit-finance/Pages/Hawala-and-Alternatives.aspx (accessed 10 September 2017).

14 FATF Recommendations (2012), Recommendation 14.

under such license or registration, are permitted to perform money or value transfer services, and which are already subject to the full range of applicable obligations under the FATF Recommendations.[15] See Chap. 8 of this Book for a full discussion of the regulatory practices adopted by Nigeria, the United States, the United Kingdom and India regarding licensing and registration of Money or Value Transfer Services providers.

- Any natural or legal person working as an agent should also be licensed or registered by a competent authority, or the money or value transfer services provider, including informal systems or networks should maintain a current list of its agents accessible by competent authorities in the countries in which the money or value transfer services provider and its agents operate.[16]

- Jurisdictions should ensure that money or value transfer services, including informal systems or networks, are subject to effective systems for monitoring and ensuring compliance with the relevant measures called for in the FATF Recommendations. Countries should also take measures to ensure that money or value transfer services providers that use agents include them in their AML/CFT programmes and monitor them for compliance with these programmes. [17]

- Jurisdictions should be able to impose sanctions on money or value transfer services, including informal systems or networks, that fail to obtain a license/register and that fail to comply with relevant FATF Recommendations.[18]

1.4 International Bodies/Organisations

This section of the chapter highlights the different international bodies charged with fighting money laundering and terrorist financing.

---

15 FATF Recommendations (2012), Interpretive Note to Recommendation 14.
16 FATF Recommendations (2012), Recommendation 14.
17 FATF Recommendations (2012), Recommendation 14.
18 FATF Recommendations (2012), Recommendation 14 .

1.4.1 Financial Action Task Force

The Financial Action Task Force (FATF) is an inter-governmental body established in 1989 by the Ministers of its Member jurisdictions. The objectives of the FATF are to set standards and promote effective implementation of legal, regulatory and operational measures for combating money laundering, terrorist financing and other related threats to the integrity of the international financial system. The FATF is therefore a "policy-making body" which works to generate the necessary political will to bring about national legislative and regulatory reforms in these areas.

The FATF has developed a series of Recommendations that are recognised as the international standard for combating of money laundering and the financing of terrorism and proliferation of weapons of mass destruction. They form the basis for a co-ordinated response to these threats to the integrity of the financial system and help ensure a level playing field. First issued in 1990, the FATF Recommendations were revised in 1996, 2001, 2003 and most recently in 2012 to ensure that they remain up to date and relevant, and they are intended to be of universal application.

The FATF monitors the progress of its members in implementing necessary measures, reviews money laundering and terrorist financing techniques and counter-measures, and promotes the adoption and implementation of appropriate measures globally. In collaboration with other international stakeholders, the FATF works to identify national-level vulnerabilities with the aim of protecting the international financial system from misuse.

The FATF's decision making body, the FATF Plenary, meets three times per year.[19]

1.4.2 Basel Committee

The Basel Committee (the committee) is the primary global standard-setter for the prudential regulation of banks and provides a

---

19 Financial Action Task Force (2017), *'Who we are'*, *Available at:* http://www.fatf-gafi.org/pages/aboutus/ (accessed 5 September 2017).

forum for cooperation on banking supervisory matters. Its mandate is to strengthen the regulation, supervision and practices of banks worldwide with the purpose of enhancing financial stability.[20]

The committee has a long-standing commitment to promote the implementation of sound AML/CFT policies and procedures that are critical in protecting the safety and soundness of banks and the integrity of the international financial system.

Following an initial statement in 1988, it has published several documents in support of this commitment. In September 2012, the committee reaffirmed its stance by publishing the revised version of the core principles for effective banking supervision, in which a dedicated principle (BCP 29) deals with the abuse of financial services.[21]

1.4.3 The Wolfsberg Group of International Financial Institutions

The Wolfsberg Group is an association of eleven global banks, which aims to develop financial services industry standards, and related products, for Know Your Customer, Anti-Money Laundering and Counter Terrorist Financing policies.

The Group came together in 2000, at the **Château Wolfsberg** in north-eastern Switzerland, in the company of representatives from Transparency International, including Stanley Morris, and Professor Mark Pieth of the University of Basel, to work on drafting anti-money laundering guidelines for Private Banking. The Wolfsberg Anti-Money Laundering Principles for Private Banking were subsequently published in October 2000, revised in May 2002 and again most recently in June 2012.

The Group then published a Statement on the Financing of Terrorism in January 2002, and also released the Wolfsberg Anti-Money Laundering Principles for Correspondent Banking in November 2002 and the Wolfsberg Statement on Monitoring

---

20 Basel Committee on Banking Supervision (2017), *'Basel Committee Charter'*, *Available at:* http://www.bis.org/bcbs/about.htm (accessed 5 September 2017).
21 Basel Committee on Banking Supervision: *Sound management of risks related to money laundering and financing of terrorism 2014,* Paragraph 2.

Screening and Searching in September 2003. In 2004, the Wolfsberg Group focused on the development of a due diligence model for financial institutions, in co-operation with Banker's Almanac, thereby fulfilling one of the recommendations made in the Correspondent Banking Principles.

During 2005 and early 2006, the Wolfsberg Group of banks actively worked on four separate papers, all of which aim to provide guidance with regard to a number of areas of banking activity where standards had yet to be fully articulated by lawmakers or regulators. It was hoped that these papers would provide general assistance to industry participants and regulatory bodies when shaping their own policies and guidance, as well as making a valuable contribution to the fight against money laundering. The papers were all published in June 2006, and consisted of two sets of guidance: Guidance on a Risk Based Approach for Managing Money Laundering Risks and AML Guidance for Mutual Funds and Other Pooled Investment Vehicles. Also published were frequently asked questions (FAQs) on AML issues in the Context of Investment and Commercial Banking and FAQs on Correspondent Banking, which complement the other sets of FAQs available on the site: on Beneficial Ownership, Politically Exposed Persons and Intermediaries.

In early 2007, the Wolfsberg Group issued its Statement against Corruption, in close association with Transparency International and the Basel Institute on Governance. It describes the role of the Wolfsberg Group and financial institutions more generally in support of international efforts to combat corruption. The Statement against Corruption identifies some of the measures financial institutions may consider in order to prevent corruption in their own operations and protect themselves against the misuse of their operations in relation to corruption. Shortly thereafter, the Wolfsberg Group and The Clearing House Association LLC issued a statement endorsing measures to enhance the transparency of international wire transfers to promote the effectiveness of global anti-money laundering and anti-terrorist financing programmes.

In 2008, the Group decided to refresh its 2003 FAQs on politically exposed persons (PEPs), followed by a reissued Statement on Monitoring, Screening & Searching in 2009. 2009 also saw the publication of the first Trade Finance Principles and Guidance on Credit/Charge Card Issuing and Merchant Acquiring Activities. The Trade Finance Principles were expanded upon in 2011 and the Wolfsberg Group also replaced its 2007 Wolfsberg Statement against Corruption with a revised, expanded and renamed version of the paper: Wolfsberg Anti-Corruption Guidance. This Guidance takes into account a number of recent developments and gives tailored advice to international financial institutions in support of their efforts to develop appropriate Anti-Corruption programmes, to combat and mitigate bribery risks associated with clients or transactions and also to prevent internal bribery.

Most recently, focus has expanded to the emergence of new payment methods and the Group published Guidance on Prepaid & Stored Value Cards, which considers the money laundering risks and mitigants of physical Prepaid and Stored Value Card Issuing and Merchant Acquiring Activities, and supplements the Wolfsberg Group Guidance on Credit/Charge Card Issuing and Merchant Acquiring Activities of 2009.[22]

1.4.4 International Monetary Fund

The International Monetary Fund (IMF) is an organization of 189 countries, working to foster global monetary cooperation, secure financial stability, facilitate international trade, promote high employment and sustainable economic growth, and reduce poverty around the world.[23]

During the past 15 years, the IMF has helped shape domestic and international AML/CFT policies. Staff work has included more than 120 AML/CFT assessments, numerous involvements in Article IV consultations, Financial Sector Assessment Programs (FSAPs), and inputs into the design and implementation of financial

---

22 Wolfsberg Group (2017), *'Global Banks: Global Standards'*, *Available at:* http://www.wolfsberg-principles.com/ (accessed 6 September 2017).

23 International Monetary Fund (2017), *'About the IMF'*, *Available at:* http://www.imf.org/en/About (accessed 10 September 2017).

integrity-related measures in Fund-supported programs, as well as many capacity development activities and research projects. The IMF staff has been particularly active in providing financial integrity advice in the context of surveillance, evaluating countries' compliance with the international AML/CFT standard, and in developing programs to help them address shortcomings. The fund also analyzes global and national AML/CFT regimes and how they interact with issues such as virtual currencies, Islamic finance, costs of and mitigating strategies for corruption, and the withdrawal of correspondent banking relationships.

In line with a growing recognition of the importance of financial integrity issues for the IMF, the AML/CFT program has evolved over the years. In 2004, the Executive Board agreed to make AML/CFT assessments and capacity development a regular part of IMF work. In 2011, the Board discussed a report on the evolution of the AML/CFT program over the previous five years. Directors supported the mandatory coverage of financial integrity issues in specific circumstances and further specified in the 2012 Guidance Note on the inclusion of AML/CFT in surveillance and financial stability assessments (FSAs). Staff is required to discuss AML/CFT issues in the context of Article IV consultations in cases where money laundering, terrorism financing, and related crimes (such as corruption or tax crimes) are serious enough to threaten domestic stability, balance of payments stability, or the effective operation of the international monetary system. In the 2014 review of the Fund's AML/CFT strategy, the Board encouraged staff to continue its efforts to integrate financial integrity issues into its surveillance and in the context of Fund-supported programs, when financial integrity issues are critical to financing assurances or to achieve program objectives. The Board also decided that AML/CFT should continue to be addressed in all FSAPs but on a more flexible basis.

In 2009, the IMF launched a donor-supported trust fund—the first in a series of Topical Trust Funds—to finance capacity development in AML/CFT that complemented the IMF's existing financing accounts. The first phase ended in April 2014. Considering the success of the program and continuing high demand for capacity development in this area, a new five-year phase started in May 2014. Donors (France, Japan, Luxembourg, the Netherlands, Norway, Qatar, Saudi Arabia, Switzerland and the United Kingdom) have pledged more than $25 million to support this new phase. The contribution to the Topical Trust Fund has helped deliver $6.5 million annually in direct technical assistance and training to more than 40 countries.[24]

1.4.5 The World Bank

The World Bank is a vital source of financial and technical assistance to developing countries around the world. It is not a bank in the ordinary sense but a unique partnership to reduce poverty and support development. Established in 1944, the World Bank Group is headquartered in Washington, D.C.[25]

The World Bank and International Monetary Fund developed a unique Reference Guide to Anti-Money Laundering (AML) and Combating the Financing of Terrorism (CFT) in an effort to provide practical steps for countries implementing an AML/CFT regime in accordance with international standards. The Guide, authored by Paul Allan Schott, describes the global problem of money laundering and terrorist financing on the development agenda of individual countries and across regions. It explains the basic elements required to build an effective AML/CFT legal and institutional framework and summarizes the role of the World Bank and the International Monetary Fund in fighting money laundering and terrorist financing.

The primary objective of this joint Bank-Fund project is to ensure that the information contained in the Reference Guide is useful and easily accessible by developing countries that are working to

---

24 International Monetary Fund (2017), *The IMF and the Fight Against Money Laundering and the Financing of Terrorism*', *Available at:* http://www.imf.org/en/About/Factsheets/Sheets/2016/08/01/16/31/Fight-Against-Money-Laundering-the-Financing-of-Terrorism (accessed 10 September 2017).

25 The World Bank (2017), *What we do*', *Available at:* http://www.worldbank.org/en/about/what-we-do (accessed 10 September 2017).

establish and strengthen their policies against money laundering and the financing of terrorism. Additionally, this Guide is intended to contribute to global understanding of the devastating consequences of money laundering and terrorist financing on development growth, and political stability and to expand the international dialogue on crafting practical solutions to implement effective AML/CFT regimes.[26]

1.4.6 The International Organization of Securities Commission

The International Organization of Securities Commissions (IOSCO), established in 1983, is the acknowledged international body that brings together the world's securities regulators and is recognized as the global standard setter for the securities sector. IOSCO develops, implements, and promotes adherence to internationally recognized standards for securities regulation, and is working intensively with the G20 and the Financial Stability Board (FSB) on the global regulatory reform agenda.[27]

IOSCO's membership regulates more than 95% of the world's securities markets. Its members include over 120 securities regulators and 80 other securities markets participants (i.e. stock exchanges, financial regional and international organizations etc.). IOSCO is the only international financial regulatory organization which includes all the major emerging markets jurisdictions within its membership.[28]

IOSCO has adopted the principle that regulators should require securities (including derivatives) market intermediaries to have in

---

26 The World Bank (2016), *'Comprehensive Reference Guide to AML/CFT'*, Available at: http://web.worldbank.org/WBSITE/EXTERNAL/TOPICS/EXTFINAN-CIALSECTOR/EXTAML/0,, contentMDK:20746893~menuPK:2495265~pagePK:210058~piPK:210062~theSitePK:396512,00.html (accessed 10 September 2017).

27 The International Organization of Securities Commissions (2017), 'About IOSCO', Available at: https://www.iosco.org/about/?subsection=about_iosco (accessed 6 September 2017).

28 The International Organization of Securities Commissions (2017), *'Fact Sheet'*, *Available at:* https://www.iosco.org/about/pdf/IOSCO-Fact-Sheet.pdf (accessed 6 September 2017).

place policies and procedures designed to minimize the risk of the use of an intermediary's business as a vehicle for money laundering.[29] IOSCO subsequently endorsed principles to address the application of the client due diligence process in the securities industry (CIBO).[30]

1.4.7 International Association of Insurance Supervisors

The International Association of Insurance Supervisors (IAIS) is a voluntary membership organization of insurance supervisors and regulators from more than 200 jurisdictions in nearly than 140 countries. In addition to its Members, more than 130 Observers representing international institutions, professional associations and insurance and reinsurance companies, as well as consultants and other professionals participate in IAIS activities.[31]

The IAIS has given AML and CFT high priority. In October 2003 the IAIS approved and issued the *Insurance core principles and methodology*, which revised the core principles for the supervision of insurers. Compliance with the Insurance Core Principles is required for a supervisory system to be effective. In accordance with Insurance Core Principle 28, the Recommendations of the FATF applicable to the insurance sector and to insurance supervision must be satisfied to reach this objective.[32]

---

29 The International Organization of Securities Commissions: Objectives and Principles of Securities Regulation 2003, Principle 8.5.

30 The International Organization of Securities Commissions: Principles on Client Identification and Beneficial Ownership for the Securities Industry 2004. See also The International Organization of Securities Commissions: Final Report, Anti Money Laundering Guidance for Collective Investment Schemes 2005, 3.

31 International Association of Insurance Supervisors (2017), 'About the IAIS', *Available at:* https://www.iaisweb.org/page/about-the-iais (accessed 10 September 2017).

32 International Association of Insurance Supervisors: Guidance Paper on Anti-Money Laundering and Combating the Financing of Terrorism October 2004, Paragraph 3.

1.4.8 Transparency International

In 1993, a few individuals decided to take a stance against corruption and created Transparency International. Now present in more than 100 countries, the movement works relentlessly to stir the world's collective conscience and bring about change. Much remains to be done to stop corruption, but much has also been achieved, including:

i.   the creation of international anti-corruption conventions;
ii. the prosecution of corrupt leaders and seizures of their illicitly gained riches;
iii. national elections won and lost on tackling corruption;
iv. companies held accountable for their behaviour both at home and abroad.[33]

1.4.9 Egmont Group

The Egmont Group is a united body of **156 Financial Intelligence Units (FIUs)**. The Egmont Group provides a platform for the secure exchange of expertise and financial intelligence to combat money laundering and terrorist financing (ML/TF). This is especially relevant as FIUs are uniquely positioned to cooperate and support national and international efforts to counter terrorist financing and are the trusted gateway for sharing financial information domestically and internationally in accordance with global Anti Money Laundering and Counter Financing of Terrorism (AML/CFT) standards.

The Egmont Group continues to support the efforts of its international partners and other stakeholders to give effect to the resolutions and statements by the United Nations Security Council, the G20 Finance Ministers, and the Financial Action Task Force (FATF). The Egmont Group is able to add value to the work of member FIUs by improving the understanding of ML/TF risks amongst its stakeholders. The organisation is able to draw upon operational experience to

---

33 Transparency International (2017), 'Overview', Available at: https://www.transparency.org/whoweare/organisation (accessed 10 September 2017).

inform policy considerations; including AML/CFT implementation and AML/CFT reforms. The Egmont Group is the operational arm of the international AML/CFT apparatus.

The Egmont Group recognises sharing of financial intelligence is of paramount importance and has become the cornerstone of the international efforts to counter ML/TF. Financial Intelligence Units (FIUs) around the world are obliged by international AML/CFT standards to exchange information and engage in international cooperation. As an international financial intelligence forum, the Egmont Group both facilitates and prompts this amongst its member FIUs.[34]

1.5 Role of Government Agencies in Implementing AML/CFT Regulations

1.5.1 Nigeria

Certain government agencies play a critical role in implementing anti-money laundering and counter-terrorist financing (AML/CFT) Regulations, developing examination guidance, ensuring compliance with the **Money Laundering Prohibition Act, 2011 (as amended),** and enforcing the **Money Laundering Prohibition Act, 2011 (as amended)** in the country. These agencies include the Central Bank of Nigeria (CBN), Nigeria Deposit Insurance Corporation (NDIC), Economic and Financial Crimes Commission/Nigerian Financial Intelligence Unit (EFCC/NFIU), Federal Ministry of Trade and Investment, Nigeria Custom Service, etc.

There is no financial institution in Nigeria that is currently and temporarily exempted from the requirements of the law and regulation to establish an AML/CFT Program. All government bodies in the country are therefore required to support the fight against money laundering and terrorist financing.

---

34 Egmont Group (2017), 'About', Available at: https://www.egmontgroup.org/en/content/about (accessed 3 October 2017).

1.5.1.1 Central Bank of Nigeria

The law and regulation on AML/CFT authorize the CBN to require financial institutions to establish AML Programs, file certain reports and keep certain records of transactions. The relevant provisions have been extended to cover not only traditional deposit money banks but other financial institutions such as discount houses, micro-finance banks, finance houses, bureau de change, operators of credit card systems, etc. under the regulatory purview of the CBN, including their foreign branches, affiliates and subsidiaries.

The CBN, NFIU, Securities and Exchange Commission (SEC) and the National Insurance Commission (NAICOM) are required to collaborate among themselves to carry out consolidated AML/CFT supervision/examination, carry out oversight and enforcement functions of regulated institutions in order to eliminate any arbitrages. These regulatory agencies are empowered to use their authority to enforce compliance with appropriate banking rules and regulations, including compliance with the **Money Laundering Prohibition Act, 2011 (as amended)**.[35]

1.5.1.2 Nigerian Financial Intelligence Unit

The Nigerian Financial Intelligence Unit (NFIU) was established by **sections 1(2) and 12(2) of the Economic and Financial Crimes Commission (Establishment) Act, 2004.** Apart from being the coordinating entity for the receipt and analysis of financial disclosure of Currency Transaction Reports and Suspicious Transaction Reports in line with Nigeria's anti-money laundering and combating the financing terrorism (AML/CFT) regime, NFIU also disseminates intelligence gathered thus to competent authorities. NFIU draws its responsibilities directly from the 40 Recommendations of the Financial Action Task Force (FATF),

---

35 Central Bank of Nigeria (2011), 'Anti-Money Laundering/Combating the Financing of Terrorism (AML/CFT) Risk Based Supervision (RBS) Framework', Available at: https://www.cbn.gov.ng/Out/2012/CCD/CBN%20APPROVED%20 FRAMEWORK.pdf (accessed 10 January 2017).

the global coordinating body for Anti-Money Laundering and Combating the Financing of Terrorism (AML/CFT) efforts. It also draws its powers from the **EFCC (Establishment) Act of 2004** and the **Money Laundering (Prohibition) Act of 2011 (as amended).** The laws require financial institutions and designated non-financial institutions to submit records of financial transactions to the NFIU.

It is domiciled at EFCC being a law enforcement agency and has three central roles which are receiving, analysis of financial intelligence and dissemination of such intelligence to end-users.

Additionally, NFIU engages in the following:

- Monitoring Compliance with AML/CFT Requirements – to ensure compliance by reporting entities.
- Training and Research – to enhance the knowledge base of stakeholders and aid AML/CFT policy formulation.
- Enhance Public Awareness on AML/CFT Issues – through publicity in the print and electronic media, publication of newsletters etc.
- Advisory Role – the NFIU provides inputs that help to fine-tune extant AML/CFT policies, regulations and laws based on findings from topology studies on money laundering/terrorism financing.

Generally, NFIU expands the frontier regarding the coordination, implementation and awareness on Anti-Money Laundering and Countering Terrorism Financing as well as partnering government, the legislature and international organisations including other FIUs in distillation of financial and non-financial sectors for national and international investments.

The NFIU became a full member of Egmont Group of Financial Intelligence Units in 2007, and the coordinating FIU in West African sub-Region as it helps the Inter-Governmental Action Group against Money Laundering in West Africa (GIABA), in the enforcement of AML/CFT regime. NFIU is broadly segmented into the Legal/Research and Cooperation, Strategic Analysis, Monitoring and

Analysis, ICT and Administration and is headed by a Director who is the chief accounting officer assisted by heads of Units.[36]

On the 5th of July, 2017, the EGMONT Group of Financial Intelligence Units made a decision, by consensus, to suspend the membership status of the NFIU, Nigeria, following repeated failures on the part of the FIU to address concerns regarding the protection of confidential information, specifically related to the status of suspicious transaction report (STR) details and information derived from international exchanges, as well as concerns on the legal basis and clarity of the NFIU's independence from the Economic and Financial Crimes Commission (EFCC). The measure is to remain in force until immediate corrective actions are implemented. The NFIU, Nigeria is now excluded from all Egmont Group events and activities. The Egmont Group expressed its hope that the Nigerian authorities will address these concerns to enable the Egmont Group to lift the suspension as soon as possible.[37]

In its commitment to accelerate the establishment of an autonomous Nigeria Financial Intelligence Unit (NFIU), the Nigerian Senate on the 27th day of July, 2017 passed the Nigerian Financial Intelligence Agency Bill as a central body in Nigeria responsible for receiving, requesting, analysing and disseminating financial intelligence reports and other information to law enforcement agencies.

This followed the consideration of the report of the Committee on Anti-Corruption and Financial Crimes presented to the Senate by its chairman, Sen. Chukwuka Utazi during plenary.

The Bill, which was only read for the first time on Thursday July 20, 2017, passed second reading on Tuesday and was approved by the upper legislative chamber on Thursday, exactly one week after.

---

36 Economic and Financial Crimes Commission (2017), 'Nigeria Financial Intelligence Unit', Available at: https://efccnigeria.org/efcc/nfiu (accessed 22 February 2017).

37 Egmont Group (2017), 'CO-CHAIRS' STATEMENT - 24TH PLENARY OF THE EGMONT GROUP OF FINANCIAL INTELLIGENCE UNITS', Available at: https://egmontgroup.org/en/content/co-chairs%E2%80%99-statement-24th-plenary-egmont-group-financial-intelligence-units (accessed 3 October 2017).

With the passage of the Bill, the risk of Nigeria being expelled from the Egmont Group has been reduced by half as the bill is just waiting for presidential assent to become law.[38]

1.5.1.3 Federal Ministry of Trade and Investment

The Federal Ministry of Trade and Investment is the competent supervisory authority for designated non-financial institutions (DNFIs), which include casinos, real estate agents, dealers in precious stones, and the legal and accounting professions. The DNFIs were not regulated for AML/CFT measures before the enactment of the **Money Laundering Prohibition Act (MLPA), 2011. Sections 3, 4, 5, 7, 9 and 25 of the MLPA, 2011** have, however, expanded the definition of reporting entities to include DNFIs.

Sections 4 and 5 of MLPA, 2011 empower the Ministry to monitor all DNFIs in Nigeria and ensure appropriate compliance with AML/CFT requirements. Under **section 5(6) of the MLPA**, the Ministry can impose sanctions on defaulting DNFIs. The supervisory functions of the Ministry are conducted through the Special Control Unit on Money Laundering (SCUML). **Section 7(2) of the EFCC Act, 2004** empowers the Commission to prosecute any designated non-financial institution for any breach of the MLPA.[39]

1.5.1.4 Special Control Unit Against Money Laundering (SCUML)

The establishment of SCUML in 2005 was as a commitment by Nigeria, through the Federal Government constituted Presidential Inter-Agency Committee, to the Financial Action Task Force (FATF).

---

38 The Vanguard (2017), 'How EGMONT Group suspended Nigeria, accused Magu of sharing confidential information to media', Available at: https://www.vanguardngr.com/2017/07/egmont-group-suspended-nigeria-accused-magu-sharing-confidential-information-media/ (accessed 3 October 2017).

39 Central Bank of Nigeria (2011), 'Anti-Money Laundering/Combating the Financing of Terrorism (AML/CFT) Risk Based Supervision (RBS) Framework', Available at: https://www.cbn.gov.ng/Out/2012/CCD/CBN%20APPROVED%20FRAMEWORK.pdf (accessed 10 January 2017).

The objectives were to remedy identified inadequacies of AML/CFT legislation and institutional framework for implementation in Nigeria.

Nigeria's response, led to the passage of the **Money Laundering (Prohibition) Act 2004, currently the Money Laundering Prohibition Act, 2011 (as amended),** and legally included Designated Non-Financial Institutions (DNFIs) in the anti-money laundering/combatting the financing of terrorism (AML/CFT) regime.

Nigeria being a cash-based economy, vested the supervisory responsibility on the Federal Ministry of Commerce and Industry (now Federal Ministry of Industry, Trade & Investment), which established the Special Control Unit against Money Laundering (SCUML).

The statutory responsibility of SCUML, as expressed in its vision, is 'to be a world-class regulatory unit - one that becomes a benchmark in the supervision, monitoring and regulation of the Designated Non-Financial Institutions (DNFI) as regards compliance to Nigeria's Anti Money Laundering and Combating the Financing of Terrorism AML/CFT regime'.[40]

SCUML currently enforces **the Money Laundering Prohibition Act, 2011 (as amended), Terrorism Prevention Act 2013** and other pieces of legislation relevant to AML/CFT on: Accountants and Accounting firms; Trust and company services Providers; Estate surveyors and valuers; Business outfits dealing in Jewelleries; car dealers; dealers in luxury goods; chartered accountants; audit firms; tax consultants; clearing and settlement companies; Hotels; Casinos; Supermarkets; Dealers in precious stones and metals; Dealers in Real Estate Developers, Estate Agents and Brokers; Hospitality industry; Consultants and consulting companies; Importers and dealers in cars or any other automobiles; Dealers in mechanized farming equipment and machineries; Practitioners of mechanized farming; and Non-governmental organizations and any other business(es) as may be designated from time to time by the Federal Ministry of Trade and Investment.

In SCUML's efforts to serve as a structure for curtailing Money Laundering and Terrorist Financing in the DNFI sector and

---

40 Anti-Money Laundering/Combating the Financing of Terrorism (AML/CFT) Regulations for Designated Non-Financial Businesses and Professions in Nigeria 2013, Regulation 1.3.

sanitizing the sector to create an enabling environment for promotion of commerce and investment, it ensures effective supervision of DNFI's which includes amongst others, registration, inspection on a risk based-approach, ensuring rendition of statutory reports (cash-based transaction reports, currency transaction reports, suspicious transaction reports), training and manpower development.

All efforts are aimed at adding value to investigations by providing data relating to DNFIs, which will facilitate an enabling environment for the promotion of investment in Nigeria. In this effort to sanitize the business environment, it collaborates with key stakeholders such as Self-Regulatory Organisations (SROs), Non-Profitable Organisations (NPOs), National Planning Commission (NPC), Corporate Affairs Commission (CAC) etc.

SCUML works in collaboration with Economic and Financial Crimes Commission "EFCC" (the coordinating agency for Nigeria's AML/CFT regime) and the Nigerian Financial Intelligence Unit "NFIU" (the national repository of financial disclosures of cash-based transaction reports, currency transaction reports and suspicious transaction reports).[41]

1.5.1.5 The National Insurance Commission (NAICOM)

The National Insurance Commission is a statutory agency of the Federal Government of Nigeria established by the law to regulate and supervise the Nigerian Insurance Sector. The Commission derives its regulatory powers from the **National Insurance Commission Act 1997 and the Insurance Act 2003.**

The principal object of the Commission is to ensure the effective administration, supervision, regulation and control of insurance business in Nigeria.

Accordingly, insurance/reinsurance companies, Insurance Brokers, Loss Adjusters and Agents fall within the regulatory purview of the Commission.[42]

---

41 Special Control Unit against Money Laundering (2017), 'About Us', Available at: http://www.scuml.org/scuml/index.php/about-us (accessed 3 January 2017).
42 National Insurance Commission (2014), 'About the National Insurance Com-

1.5.1.6 The Securities And Exchange Commission (SEC)

The Securities and Exchange Commission (SEC), Nigeria is the apex regulatory institution of the Nigerian capital market supervised by the Federal Ministry of Finance.

The Commission has evolved over time having started with the establishment of the Capital Issues Committee in 1962 by the government as an essential arm of the Central Bank of Nigeria. This was purely an ad-hoc, non-statutory committee, which later metamorphosed into SEC in 1979, following a comprehensive review of the Nigerian financial system, with the promulgation of **SEC Decree No. 71 of 1979.** Successive reviews of this earlier enactment led to the introduction of a new legislation, the **Investments and Securities Act (ISA) No 45 of 1999.** The ISA No. 45 of 1999 was repealed with the promulgation of the ISA No. 25 of 2007, which gives the Commission its current power.[43]

This legislation further enlarged the powers of the Nigerian SEC, while saddling it with the dual responsibilities of:

- Regulating the capital market with a view to protecting investors; and
- Developing the capital market in order to enhance its allocative efficiency, and pave the way for a private sector led economy.[44]

The Act also empowers the Commission with a board of nine (9) members including the Chairman, the Director General, three Executive Commissioners, two Non-Executive Commissioners, Representatives of the Federal Ministry of Finance and Central Bank of Nigeria.[45]

---

mission (NAICOM)', Available at: http://naicom.gov.ng/content?id=10 (accessed 6 March 2014).

43 Securities and Exchange Commission (2014), 'About Us', Available at: http://www.sec.gov.ng/about-us.html (accessed 5 March 2014).

44 The Investments and Securities Act, 2007, s. 13.

45 The Investments and Securities Act, 2007, s. 3.

1.5.1.7 The Nigeria Customs Service (NCS)

The **Customs & Excise Management Act (CEMA) Cap 45, Law of the Federation of Nigeria, 2004** vests Legal Authority in the Nigeria Customs Service (NCS) to act on behalf of the Federal Government of Nigeria in all Customs matters. The Nigeria Customs Service is charged with the duty of controlling and managing the administration of the Customs and Excise laws. The NCS collects the revenue of Customs and Excise and accounts for same in such manner as provided for by the relevant legislation.[46]

Section 2 of the Money Laundering Prohibition Act, 2011 (as amended) empowers NCS to report declaration in respect of information on the cross-border transportation of cash or negotiable instrument in excess of ten thousand US dollars or its equivalent by individuals in and out of the country to the CBN and EFCC.

1.5.1.8 The Nigeria Deposit Insurance Corporation (NDIC)

The Nigeria Deposit Insurance Corporation is responsible for insuring all deposit liabilities of licensed banks and other financial institutions operating in Nigeria,[47] providing assistance in the interest of depositors in case of imminent or actual financial difficulties;[48] guaranteeing payments to depositors in case of imminent suspension of payments by insured banks and other financial institutions[49] and assisting the authorities in the formulation and implementation of banking policy.[50]

Bank Supervision in the NDIC is the responsibility of three departments, namely, Bank Examination Department (BED), Insurance & Surveillance Department (ISD) and Special Insured Institutions Department (SIID). As the names imply, on-site examination is carried out by BED and SIID while the ISD is charged

---

46   Customs & Excise Management Act (CEMA) Cap 45, Law of the Federation of Nigeria, 2004, s. 4 (1)

47   Nigeria Deposit Insurance Corporation Act 2006, s. 2 (1) (a)

48   Nigeria Deposit Insurance Corporation Act 2006, s. 2 (1) (b)

49   Nigeria Deposit Insurance Corporation Act 2006, s. 2 (1) (c)

50   Nigeria Deposit Insurance Corporation Act 2006, s. 2 (1) (d)

with the responsibility of maintaining off-site surveillance over all insured banks. Both the On-site and Off-site supervision ensure that the insured institutions remain healthy at all times and/or where there are problems, they would be detected and addressed promptly. In addition, supervision protects the bank depositors, encourages competition among banks and assists in efficient and orderly payment system.[51]

1.5.1.9 The National Focal Point (NFP)

In realization of the African Union's Plan of Action made in 2002 in Algiers, the 53 (fifty-three) member nations of the Union were required to establish a forum to facilitate timely exchange and sharing of ideas and intelligence in combating terrorism within the continent. This led to the establishment of the African Centre for the Study and Research on Terrorism (ACSRT).

Member countries were also mandated to establish national focal points on terrorism (nfpt). in compliance, the nigerian government established the national focal point (nfp) coordinated by the department of state services (dss). the national focal point membership is drawn from several stakeholder government ministries, departments and agencies.

The activities of the national focal point include:

(i) Conducting research and analysis on terrorism-related matters in order to provide prompt and proactive response to terrorist threats;

(ii) Collation, integration and preparation of input provided by intelligence services with a view to advising the relevant authorities on counter terrorism policies;

(iii) Identifying, penetrating and monitoring of extremist/fundamentalist groups and suspected NGOs with a view to intercepting the recruitment process of terrorists;

---

51 Nigeria Deposit Insurance Corporation (2017), 'Supervisory Activities', Available at: http://ndic.gov.ng/supervision/ (accessed 16 January, 2017).

(iv)   Implementation of all policies on counter terrorism and its financing by monitoring the activities of financial institutions;

(v)   Developing and maintenance of a national repository data-base on terrorist groups;

(vi)   Maintaining and updating of data-base on the movement and activities of passengers from risk countries;

(vii) Maintenance of security watch-list on individuals and groups; and

(viii) Maintenance of close watch and regulation of the use of explosives in liaison with relevant government agencies or parastatals.[52]

1.5.2 United States

Certain government agencies play a critical role in implementing the Bank Secrecy Act (BSA) regulations, developing examination guidance, ensuring compliance with the BSA, and enforcing the BSA. These agencies include the U.S. Treasury, FinCEN, and the federal banking agencies (Board of Governors of the Federal Reserve System (Federal Reserve), Federal Deposit Insurance Corporation (FDIC), National Credit Union Administration (NCUA), and Office of the Comptroller of the Currency (OCC).

1.5.2.1 U.S. Treasury

The BSA authorizes the Secretary of the Treasury to require financial institutions to establish AML programs, file certain reports, and keep certain records of transactions. Certain BSA provisions have been extended to cover not only traditional depository institutions, such as banks, savings associations, and credit unions, but also nonbank financial institutions, such as money services businesses, casinos,

---

52 Central Bank of Nigeria (2011), 'Anti-Money Laundering/Combating the Financing of Terrorism (AML/CFT) Risk Based Supervision (RBS) Framework', Available at: https://www.cbn.gov.ng/Out/2012/CCD/CBN%20APPROVED%20 FRAMEWORK.pdf (accessed 10 January 2017).

brokers/dealers in securities, futures commission merchants, mutual funds, insurance companies, and operators of credit card systems.

The United States Department of the Treasury is fully dedicated to combating all aspects of money laundering at home and abroad, through the mission of the Office of Terrorism and Financial Intelligence (TFI). TFI utilizes the Department's many assets - including a diverse range of legal authorities, core financial expertise, operational resources, and expansive relationships with the private sector, interagency and international communities - to identify and attack money laundering vulnerabilities and networks across the domestic and international financial systems.[53]

1.5.2.2 Financial Crimes Enforcement Network (FINCEN)

The Financial Crimes Enforcement Network (FinCEN) is a bureau of the U.S. Department of the Treasury. The Director of FinCEN is appointed by the Secretary of the Treasury and reports to the Treasury Under Secretary for Terrorism and Financial Intelligence. FinCEN's mission is to safeguard the financial system from illicit use and combat money laundering and promote national security through the collection, analysis, and dissemination of financial intelligence and strategic use of financial authorities.

FinCEN carries out its mission by receiving and maintaining financial transactions data; analyzing and disseminating that data for law enforcement purposes; and building global cooperation with counterpart organizations in other countries and with international bodies.

FinCEN exercises regulatory functions primarily under the **Currency and Financial Transactions Reporting Act of 1970, as amended by Title III of the Uniting and Strengthening America by Providing Appropriate Tools Required to Intercept and Obstruct Terrorism, USA PATRIOT Act of 2001 and other legislation, which legislative framework is commonly referred to as the "Bank Secrecy Act" (BSA).** The BSA is the nation's first and most comprehensive Federal anti-money

---

53 U.S. Department of the Treasury (2017), 'Money Laundering', Available at: https://www.treasury.gov/resource-center/terrorist-illicit-finance/Pages/Money-Laundering.aspx (accessed 3 January 2017).

laundering and counter-terrorism financing (AML/CFT) statute. In brief, the BSA authorizes the Secretary of the Treasury to issue regulations requiring banks and other financial institutions to take a number of precautions against financial crime, including the establishment of AML programs and the filing of reports that have been determined to have a high degree of usefulness in criminal, tax, and regulatory investigations and proceedings, and certain intelligence and counter-terrorism matters. The Secretary of the Treasury has delegated to the Director of FinCEN the authority to implement, administer, and enforce compliance with the BSA and associated regulations.

Congress has given FinCEN certain duties and responsibilities for the central collection, analysis, and dissemination of data reported under FinCEN's regulations and other related data in support of government and financial industry partners at the Federal, State, local, and international levels. To fulfill its responsibilities toward the detection and deterrence of financial crime, FinCEN:

- Issues and interprets regulations authorized by statute;
- Supports and enforces compliance with those regulations;
- Supports, coordinates, and analyzes data regarding compliance examination functions delegated to other Federal regulators;
- Manages the collection, processing, storage, dissemination, and protection of data filed under FinCEN's reporting requirements;
- Maintains a government-wide access service to FinCEN's data, and networks users with overlapping interests;
- Supports law enforcement investigations and prosecutions;
- Synthesizes data to recommend internal and external allocation of resources to areas of greatest financial crime risk;
- Shares information and coordinates with foreign financial intelligence unit (FIU) counterparts on AML/CFT efforts; and
- Conducts analysis to support policymakers; law enforcement, regulatory, and intelligence agencies; FIUs; and the financial industry.

FinCEN serves as the FIU for the United States and is one of more than 100 FIUs making up the Egmont Group, an international entity focused on information sharing and cooperation among FIUs. An FIU is a central, national agency responsible for receiving (and, as permitted, requesting), analyzing, and disseminating to the competent authorities' disclosures of financial information:

- concerning suspected proceeds of crime and potential financing of terrorism or
- required by national legislation or regulation in order to combat money laundering and terrorism financing.

As one of the world's leading FIUs, FinCEN exchanges financial information with FIU counterparts around the world in support of U.S. and foreign financial crime investigations.

The basic concept underlying FinCEN's core activities is "follow the money." The primary motive of criminals is financial gain, and they leave financial trails as they try to launder the proceeds of crimes or attempt to spend their ill-gotten profits. FinCEN partners with law enforcement at all levels of government and supports the nation's foreign policy and national security objectives. Law enforcement agencies successfully use similar techniques, including searching information collected by FinCEN from the financial industry, to investigate and hold accountable a broad range of criminals, including perpetrators of fraud, tax evaders, and narcotics traffickers. More recently, the techniques used to follow money trails also have been applied to investigating and disrupting terrorist groups, which often depend on financial and other support networks.[54]

1.5.2.3 Federal Banking Agencies

The federal banking agencies are responsible for the oversight of the various banking entities operating in the United States,

---

54 Financial Crimes Enforcement Network (2017), 'What we do', Available at: https://www.fincen.gov/what-we-do (accessed 10 January 2017).

including foreign branch offices of U.S. banks. The federal banking agencies are charged with chartering (The National Credit Union Administration, NCUA and Office of the Comptroller of the Currency, OCC), insuring (The Federal Deposit Insurance Corporation, FDIC and NCUA), regulating, and supervising banks. **12 USC 1818(s)(2) and 1786(q)** require that the appropriate federal banking agency include a review of the BSA compliance program at each examination of an insured depository institution. The federal banking agencies may use their authority, as granted under **section 8 of the Federal Deposit Insurance Act (FDIA)** or **section 206 of the Federal Credit Union Act (FCUA),** to enforce compliance with appropriate banking rules and regulations, including compliance with the BSA.

The federal banking agencies require each bank under their supervision to establish and maintain a BSA compliance program. In accordance with the **USA PATRIOT Act,** FinCEN's regulations require certain financial institutions to establish an AML compliance program that guards against money laundering and terrorist financing and ensures compliance with the BSA and its implementing regulations. When the USA PATRIOT Act was passed, banks under the supervision of a federal banking agency were already required by law to establish and maintain a BSA compliance program that, among other things, requires the bank to identify and report suspicious activity promptly. For this reason, **31 CFR 1020.210** states that a bank regulated by a federal banking agency is deemed to have satisfied the AML program requirements of the USA PATRIOT Act if the bank develops and maintains a BSA compliance program that complies with the regulation of its federal functional regulator governing such programs. This manual refers to the BSA compliance program requirements for each federal banking agency as the "BSA/AML compliance program."

Banks should take reasonable and prudent steps to combat money laundering and terrorist financing and to minimize their vulnerability to the risk associated with such activities. Some banking organizations have damaged their reputations and have been required to pay civil money penalties for failing to implement adequate controls within their organization resulting in noncompliance with the BSA. In addition, due to the AML assessment required as part of the application process, BSA/AML concerns can have an impact on the bank's strategic plan. For this reason, the federal banking agencies' and FinCEN's commitment to provide guidance that assists banks in complying with the BSA remains a high supervisory priority.

The federal banking agencies work to ensure that the organizations they supervise understand the importance of having an effective BSA/AML compliance program in place. Management must be vigilant in this area, especially as business grows and new products and services are introduced. An evaluation of the bank's BSA/AML compliance program and its compliance with the regulatory requirements of the BSA has been an integral part of the supervision process for years.

As part of a strong BSA/AML compliance program, the federal banking agencies seek to ensure that a bank has policies, procedures, and processes to identify and report suspicious transactions to law enforcement. The agencies' supervisory processes assess whether banks have established the appropriate policies, procedures, and processes based on their BSA/AML risk to identify and report suspicious activity and that they provide sufficient detail in reports to law enforcement agencies to make the reports useful for investigating suspicious transactions that are reported.

On July 19, 2007, the federal banking agencies issued a statement setting forth the agencies' policy for enforcing specific anti-money laundering requirements of the BSA. The purpose of the *Interagency Statement on Enforcement of Bank Secrecy Act/Anti-Money Laundering Requirements* (Interagency Enforcement Statement) is to provide greater consistency among the agencies in enforcement decisions in BSA matters and to offer insight into the considerations that form the basis of those decisions.[55]

---

55 Federal Financial Institutions Examination Council (2014), 'Bank Secrecy Act/Anti-Money Laundering Examination Manual', Available at: https://www. ffiec.gov/bsa_aml_infobase/documents/BSA_AML_Man_2014_v2.pdf (accessed 20 February 2017).

1.5.2.4 Office of Foreign Assets Control (OFAC)

Office of Foreign Assets Control (OFAC) of the US Department of the Treasury administers and enforces economic and trade sanctions based on U.S. foreign policy and national security goals against targeted foreign countries, terrorists, international narcotics traffickers, and those engaged in activities related to the proliferation of weapons of mass destruction. OFAC acts under the President's wartime and national emergency powers, as well as under authority granted by specific legislation, to impose controls on transactions and freeze assets under U.S. jurisdiction. Many of the sanctions are based on United Nations and other international mandates, are multilateral in scope, and involve close cooperation with allied governments.

OFAC requirements are separate and distinct from the BSA, but both OFAC and the BSA share a common national security goal. For this reason, many financial institutions view compliance with OFAC sanctions as related to BSA compliance obligations; supervisory examination for BSA compliance is logically connected to the examination of a financial institution's compliance with OFAC sanctions.[56]

1.5.3 United Kingdom

Certain government agencies play a critical role in implementing Money Laundering Regulations, developing examination guidance, ensuring compliance with the Money Laundering Regulations, and enforcing the Money Laundering Regulations. These agencies include HM Treasury, National Crime Agency, HM Revenue and Customs, the Revenue and Customs Prosecutions Office, Crown Prosecution Service, Financial Conduct Authority and the Joint Money Laundering Steering Group.

---

56 Ibid.

1.5.3.1 HM Treasury

The Treasury is responsible for appointing supervisors and for the **Money Laundering, Terrorist Financing and Transfer of Funds (Information on the Payer) Regulations 2017** (the Regulations) which set out the role of the supervisors and gives them powers to effectively monitor their respective sectors. In order to improve the transparency and accountability of supervision and to encourage good practice, the Treasury has worked with supervisors to produce annual reports, which covers supervisory activities.

The Treasury has 28 appointed AML/CTF supervisors which oversee eight broad sectors and a diverse range of firms which include financial institutions, credit institutions, law firms, accountancy firms, estate agents and casinos. Some have been supervisors for AML/CTF purposes since the Regulations were first implemented in 1993; others were introduced when the Regulations were updated in 2007 and 2017. The supervisors are a highly diverse group including large global professional bodies, smaller professional and representative bodies, and a number of public sector organisations. In each area of supervision, the supervisor's approach needs to be proportionate to the nature and associated risks of the firm being supervised.

All supervisors are expected to attend the AML Supervisors Forum which meets on a quarterly basis, and is chaired by Paul Simkins, Director of Quality Assurance, Professional Standards at the Institute of Chartered Accountants in England and Wales (ICAEW), which is one of the professional body supervisors. Supervisors meet on a regular basis in smaller affinity groups based on the industry sector they supervise to encourage the exchange of sector relevant material.[57]

---

57 HM Treasury (2012-13), 'Anti-money laundering and counter terrorist finance supervision report', Available at: https://www.gov.uk/government/publications/anti-money-laundering-and-counter-terrorist-finance-supervision-reports/anti-money-laundering-and-counter-terrorist-finance-supervision-report-2012-13 (accessed 7 February 2017).

1.5.3.2 National Crime Agency

The UK Financial Intelligence Unit (UKFIU) sits at the heart of the UK's response to money laundering and terrorist financing. As one of over 150 (Egmont Group) FIUs across the world the National Crime Agency receive, analyse and distribute financial intelligence gathered from Suspicious Activity Reports (SARs). These SARs are received predominantly from the private sector following identification of suspicious activity. The information contained within SARs alert law enforcement domestically and internationally to potential money laundering or terrorist financing and is used to build a better understanding of the risks to the UK.[58]

The UKFIU is the single point of contact for UK law enforcement with international Financial Intelligence Units (FIUs). The UKFIU participates on behalf of the UK within the Egmont Group of FIUs, utilising the European FIU system (FIU.NET) on behalf of the UK and processing inbound and outbound requests for criminal asset tracing intelligence through the Camden Asset Recovery Inter-Agency Network (CARIN) and the European Asset Recovery Office (ARO).

The UKFIU assists investigators in tracing and identifying the proceeds of crime and other crime related property which may become subject to subsequent restraint, freezing, seizure or confiscation orders. These would be made by a competent judicial authority in the course of criminal or, as far as possible under the national law of the jurisdiction concerned, civil proceedings. UKFIU International facilitates the sharing of information from overseas jurisdictions relating to the funding of serious organised crime and money laundering.

Any information shared by the UKFIU is strictly controlled and safeguarded ensuring compliance with national provisions on data protection and privacy. As a minimum, exchanged information is protected by the same confidentially provisions that apply to information from domestic sources obtained by the receiving FIU.

---

58 National Crime Agency (2015), 'Suspicious Activity Reports (SARs) Annual Report', Available at: http://www.nationalcrimeagency.gov.uk/publications/677-sars-annual-report-2015/file (accessed 10 February 2017).

The UKFIU International Team receives assistance requests from partners overseas via these networks and searches against databases available to them to collect information on subjects. This information is then assessed for relevance to the request; all relevant information is suitably formatted. The information is then entered into a UKFIU intelligence report for dissemination to the requesting party.

This same process is used when SARs are identified as possessing potential relevance to an overseas jurisdiction; a formatted report is prepared and spontaneously disseminated via the secure networks.[59]

In July 2016 the UKFIU produced a guidance document aimed at providing the correct pathways when concerns are raised in respect of vulnerable persons. The SARs regime is not a route to report a crime and this document signposts the reporter to the most appropriate reporting routes.

The latest SAR glossary codes (dated 16 January 2017) provides clarification on reporting routes. As of July 2016, the UKFIU changed its processes for requesting a defence under the **Proceeds of Crime Act 2002** and the **Terrorism Act 2000**. Please see the two documents below for information:

I. 'Requesting a defence from the NCA under POCA and TACT', Available at: http://www.nationalcrimeagency.gov.uk/publications/713-requesting-a-defence-under-poca-tact/file (accessed 29 December 2017).

II. 'Changes to the 'Consent' Approach; Requesting A Defence Under POCA & TACT from 18th July 2016', Available at: http://www.nationalcrimeagency.gov.uk/publications/712-changes-to-the-consent-approach-requesting-a-defence-under-poca-tact/file (accessed 29 December 2017).

---

59 Ibid.

A SAR is a piece of information that alerts law enforcement of potential money laundering or terrorist financing. This could be large cash purchases or a series of large, out of character deposits.

The UKFIU receives more than 400,000 SARs a year. These are used by a wide variety of law enforcement bodies to help investigate all levels and types of criminal activity; from benefit fraud to international drug smuggling, human trafficking to terrorist financing.

The UKFIU identifies the most sensitive SARs and sends them to the appropriate organisations for investigation. The remainder are made available to UK law enforcement bodies via a secure channel.[60]

1.5.3.3 HM Revenue and Customs

HM Revenue and Customs (HMRC) has a unique dual role in helping to tackle money laundering and terrorist financing:

- As a supervisor under the **Money Laundering, Terrorist Financing and Transfer of Funds (Information on the Payer) Regulations 2017**, HMRC seeks to register all Money Service Businesses (MSBs), subject them to a fit and proper test and seek to maximise their compliance with the Regulations.
- As a law enforcement agency HMRC seeks to take appropriate and effective enforcement action against MSBs that fail to comply with the Regulations, or facilitate money laundering or terrorist financing.

HMRC is also responsible for the supervision of high value dealers, trust or company service providers and accountancy service providers

---

60 National Crime Agency (2016), 'UK Financial Intelligence Unit', Available at: http://www.nationalcrimeagency.gov.uk/about-us/what-we-do/economic-crime/ ukfiu (accessed 8 February 2017).

for compliance with the Money Laundering Regulations, as well as having a much wider law enforcement role.[61]

1.5.3.4 The Revenue and Customs Prosecutions Office

The Revenue and Customs Prosecutions Office prosecutes money laundering, drug trafficking and certain tax offences investigated by HMRC.

1.5.3.5 Crown Prosecution Service

The Crown Prosecution Service prosecutes crime, money laundering and terrorism offences in England and Wales. The Procurator Fiscal and Public Prosecution Service of Northern Ireland play similar roles in Scotland and Northern Ireland respectively.

1.5.3.6 Financial Conduct Authority

The Financial Conduct Authority (FCA) has statutory objectives under the Financial Services and Markets Act 2000 (FSMA) that include protecting and enhancing the integrity of the UK financial system. The integrity of the UK financial system includes it's not being used for a purpose connected with financial crime.[62]

The FCA has supervisory responsibilities under the **Money Laundering, Terrorist Financing and Transfer of Funds (Information on the Payer) Regulations 2017** for authorised firms and businesses such as leasing companies and providers of safe deposit boxes. The FCA also has functions under other legislation such as **schedule 7 to the Counter-Terrorism Act 2008.**

---

61 HM Revenue and Customs (2016), 'The money service business action plan', Available at: http://webarchive.nationalarchives.gov.uk/20090211213308/http://www.hmrc.gov.uk/mlr/money-service-busplan.pdf (accessed 22 February 2017).
62 Financial Services and Markets Act 2000, s. 6

1.5.3.7 The Joint Money Laundering Steering Group (JMLSG)

The Joint Money Laundering Steering Group is made up of the leading UK Trade Associations in the Financial Services Industry. Its aim is to promulgate good practice in countering money laundering and to give practical assistance in interpreting the UK Money Laundering Regulations. This is primarily achieved by the publication of industry Guidance.[63]

---

63 JMLSG (2017), 'Joint Money Laundering Steering Group (JMLSG)', Available at: http://www.jmlsg.org.uk/ (accessed 29 December 2017).

CHAPTER 2

Assessing Risks and Applying a Risk-Based Approach

Risk can be defined as the likelihood of an event and its consequences. In simple terms, risk can be seen as a combination of the chance that something may happen and the degree of damage or loss that may result from such an occurrence. In the context of money laundering/terrorist financing (ML/TF), risk means:

- At the national level: threats and vulnerabilities presented by ML/TF that put at risk the integrity of a Country's financial system and the safety and security of its citizens.
- At the reporting entity level: threats and vulnerabilities that put the reporting entity at risk of being used to facilitate ML/TF.[64]

In the context of ML/TF, a risk-based approach is a process that encompasses the following:

- The risk assessment of your business activities and clients using certain prescribed elements;
- The mitigation of risk through the implementation of controls and measures tailored to the identified risks;

---

64 Financial Transactions and Reporting Analysis Centre of Canada: Guidance on the Risk-Based Approach to Combatting Money laundering and Terrorist Financing 2015, page 4.

- Keeping client identification and, if required, beneficial ownership and business relationship information up to date in accordance with the assessed level of risk; and
- The ongoing monitoring of transactions and business relationships in accordance with the assessed level of risk.[65]

The text of the Financial Action Task Force Recommendations (Recommendation 1) lays out a number of basic principles with regard to risk assessment. First, it calls on countries to "identify, assess and understand" the money laundering/terrorist financing (ML/TF) risks they face, and states that countries should also designate "an authority or mechanism to co-ordinate actions to assess risks". The goal of the standard is to ensure that countries can mitigate their ML/TF risks effectively, and the risk assessment is clearly intended to serve as the basis for application of the risk-based approach, i.e., "to ensure that measures are commensurate with the risks identified." The text of the Recommendation adds that the "[risk-based] approach" (and therefore the risk assessment process on which it is based) should also be "an essential foundation" in allocating anti-money laundering and combating the financing of terrorism (AML/CFT) resources efficiently. Furthermore, the Recommendation indicates that risk assessments carried out by countries should be used for determining higher and lower risks that may then be addressed by applying enhanced measures or allowing simplified measures respectively. The Recommendation concludes by requiring that financial institutions and designated non-financial businesses and professions (DNFBPs) should also be able to identify, assess and take effective action to mitigate ML/TF risks.[66]

---

65 Financial Transactions and Reporting Analysis Centre of Canada: Guidance on the Risk-Based Approach to Combatting Money laundering and Terrorist Financing 2015, page 5.

66 Financial Action Task Force (2013), 'FATF Guidance: National money laundering and Terrorist Financing Risk Assessment', Available at: http://www.fatf-gafi.org/media/fatf/content/images/National_ML_TF_Risk_Assessment.pdf (accessed 13 August 2017).

This chapter is structured to help countries and reporting entities better understand what the risk-based approach is and take inventory of their risks relating to products, services and delivery channels, clients and business relationships, geography and other relevant factors. It will also help in implementing effective mitigation measures and in monitoring the money laundering and terrorist financing risks reporting entities may have or encounter as part of their activities and business relationships.

Section 2.1 focuses on country level risk-assessments while Section 2.2 focuses on the reporting entity level risk-assessments.

2.1 National Risk Assessment

Successful implementation of a risk-based approach to combating money-laundering and terrorist financing depends on a sound understanding of the threats and vulnerabilities. Where a country is seeking to introduce a risk-based approach at a national level, this will be greatly aided if there is a national understanding of the risks facing the country. This understanding can flow from a national risk assessment.[67]

The process of risk assessment can be divided into a series of activities or stages: *identification, analysis,* and *evaluation.* The three stages are briefly described below:

    I.   In general terms, the process of ***identification*** in the context of an ML/TF risk assessment starts by developing an initial list of potential risks or risk factors countries face when combating ML/TF. These will be drawn from known or suspected threats or vulnerabilities. Ideally at this stage, the identification process should attempt to be comprehensive; however, it should also be dynamic in the sense that new or previously undetected risks identified may also be considered at any stage in the process.

---

67 The Financial Action Task Force: Guidance on the Risk-Based Approach to Combating Money Laundering and Terrorist Financing 2007, para. 2.3.

II. *Analysis* lies at the heart of the ML/TF risk assessment process. It involves consideration of the nature, sources, likelihood and consequences of the identified risks or risk factors. Ultimately, the aim of this stage is to gain a holistic understanding of each of the risks – as a combination of threat, vulnerability and consequence in order to work toward assigning some sort of relative value or importance to them. Risk analysis can be undertaken with varying degrees of detail, depending on the type of risk and the purpose of the risk assessment, as well as based on the information, data and resources available.

III. *Evaluation* in the context of the ML/TF risk assessment process involves taking the risks analysed during the previous stage to determine priorities for addressing them, taking into account the purpose established at the beginning of the assessment process. These priorities can contribute to development of a strategy for their mitigation.[68]

A national risk assessment should be tailored to the circumstances of the individual country, both in how it is executed, and its conclusions. Factors that may influence the risk of money laundering and terrorist financing in a country could include the following:

- Political environment;
- Legal environment;
- A country's economic structure;
- Cultural factors, and the nature of civil society;
- Sources, location and concentration of criminal activity;
- Size of the financial services industry;
- Composition of the financial services industry;
- Ownership structure of financial institutions;

---

68 Financial Action Task Force (2013), 'FATF Guidance: National money laundering and Terrorist Financing Risk Assessment', Available at: http://www.fatf-gafi. org/media/fatf/content/images/National_ML_TF_Risk_Assessment.pdf (accessed 13 August 2017).

- Corporate governance arrangements in financial institutions and the wider economy;
- The nature of payment systems and the prevalence of cash-based transactions;
- Geographical spread of financial industry's operations and customers;
- Types of products and services offered by the financial services industry;
- Types of customers serviced by the financial services industry;
- Types of predicate offences;
- Amounts of illicit money generated domestically;
- Amounts of illicit money generated abroad and laundered domestically;
- Main channels or instruments used for laundering or financing terrorism;
- Sectors of the legal economy affected;
- Underground areas in the economy.[69]

2.1.1 Nigeria

Nigeria is yet to conduct its own National Risk Assessment of Money laundering and terrorist financing.

2.1.2 United States

On the 6th of December, 2015, the U.S. Department of the Treasury issued the National Money Laundering Risk Assessment (NMLRA) and the National Terrorist Financing Risk Assessment (NTFRA). The purpose of these assessments is to help the public and private sectors understand the money laundering and terrorist financing methods used in the United States, the risks that these activities pose to the U.S. financial system and national security, and the status of current efforts to combat these methods. In doing so, these

---

69   The Financial Action Task Force: Guidance on the Risk-Based Approach to Combating Money Laundering and Terrorist Financing 2007, para. 2.24.

assessments enable the U.S. Government and financial institutions to more effectively detect and combat illicit finance.

This is the first NTFRA, and the NMLRA builds and expands on a previous Treasury money laundering report issued in 2005. The methodology for these reports is based on guidance set out in 2013 by the Financial Action Task Force (FATF), the international standard-setting body for anti-money laundering and counter-terrorist financing safeguards, of which the United States is a founding member.[70] The 2013 FATF Guidance presents a process for conducting a risk assessment at the national level. This approach uses the following key concepts for National Money Laundering Risk Assessment:

- **Threats**: These are the predicate crimes that are associated with money laundering. In some cases, specific crimes are associated with specific money laundering methods. Understanding the threat environment is essential to understanding the vulnerabilities that create money laundering opportunities, and to understanding the residual risks.
- **Vulnerability**: This is what facilitates or creates the opportunity for money laundering. It may relate to a specific financial sector or product, or a weakness in regulation, supervision, or enforcement, or reflect unique circumstances in which it may be difficult to distinguish legal from illegal activity.
- **Consequence**: Not all money laundering methods have equal consequences. The methods that allow for the most amount of money to be laundered most effectively or most quickly present the greatest potential consequences.
- **Risk**: Risk is a function of threat, vulnerability, and consequence. It represents a summary judgment.

The NMLRA uses all available information to identify as objectively as possible the priority money laundering risks to the United States. The fact-finding and assessment process involved:

---

70 FATF Guidance, National Money Laundering and Terrorist Financing Risk Assessment, February 2013.

- Identifying the nature and volume of predicate financial crime in the United States to determine the source of domestic illicit proceeds;
- Tallying the money laundering methods identified through civil and criminal investigations and criminal prosecutions;
- Assessing the deterrent effect of domestic regulation, supervision, and enforcement on potential money laundering methods; and
- Using the foregoing research and analysis to identify residual money laundering risks in the United States.

The 2013 FATF guidance also prescribes a process for conducting a risk assessment at the national level for Terrorist Financing. This approach uses the following key concepts:

- **Threat:** A threat is a person or group of people, or activity with the potential to cause harm to, for example, the state, society, the economy, etc. In the TF context this includes terrorist groups and their facilitators, as well as radicalized individuals that seek to exploit the United States and U.S financial system to raise and move funds.
- **Vulnerability:** A vulnerability is something that can be exploited to facilitate TF, both in the raising of funds for terrorist networks and the moving of funds to terrorist organizations. It may relate to a specific fundraising method or financial product used to move funds, or a weakness in regulation, supervision, or enforcement, or reflect unique circumstances in which it may be difficult to distinguish legal from illegal activity.
- **Consequence:** Not all TF methods have equal consequences. The methods that allow for the greatest amount of money to be raised or moved most effectively present the greatest potential TF consequences.
- **Risk:** Risk is a function of threat, vulnerability, and consequence.

Throughout the NTFRA, potential TF threats, vulnerabilities and residual risks were identified, analyzed and evaluated in the following manner:

- Using the 2011 *National Strategy for Counterterrorism* and Congressional testimony from senior U.S. government officials, identifying the terrorist groups that the U.S. government has determined pose the most significant threat to the United States and the prime ways that these groups are financed, particularly where the United States and its financial system were involved;
- Cataloging the TF methods disclosed in criminal investigations and prosecutions and violations of Office of Foreign Assets Control (OFAC) sanctions for supporting individuals and entities designated for their support of terrorist groups;
- Analyzing financial institution reporting and cross-referencing with law enforcement counterterrorism (CT) investigations and/or OFAC designations;
- Comparing the above information with intelligence reporting to validate or refute the information;
- Assessing the extent to which domestic laws and regulations, law enforcement investigations and prosecutions, regulatory supervision, and enforcement activity and international outreach and coordination mitigate identified TF threats and vulnerabilities; and
- Using the aforementioned research and analysis to identify residual TF risks facing the United States.

The United States is the world's largest financial system and U.S. financial institutions play a central role in the global economy, processing trillions of dollars of transactions from around the world every day. While this position exposes the United States to increased risks for illicit finance, the U.S. Government has developed a robust regulatory framework, complemented by law enforcement and supervision efforts, which make it more difficult and costly for criminals and terrorists to access and use the U.S. financial system.[71]

The NMLRA finds that the United States has effectively kept pace with innovation, such that, criminals pursuing money laundering opportunities rely on costly and burdensome methods to mask their identities from financial institutions in order to open and maintain accounts. These include, but are not limited to, using cash, other monetary instruments, shell companies, and conducting transactions below customer identification thresholds. The report also finds that the U.S. framework for anti-money laundering and counter terrorist financing effectively narrows many of the most significant vulnerabilities that money launderers seek to exploit through a core set of tools, including targeted financial sanctions, law enforcement investigations and prosecutions and regulatory preventive measures, and by working to enhance international standards.[72]

The NTFRA finds that the U.S. Government has made it substantially more difficult for terrorist organizations to raise and move money through the U.S. financial system since the September 11, 2001 attacks. A notable trend highlighted in the report is a decrease in the use of the U.S banking system for terrorist financing-related transactions, as terrorists are forced into more expensive and less efficient methods to facilitate terrorist financing, such as cash smuggling. Such channels outside of the regulated financial system are riskier than straightforward bank transfers, making them more vulnerable to disruption and exposure. Nonetheless, the wealth and resources of the United States will continue to make it an attractive target for a wide range of terrorist

---

71 U.S. Department of the Treasury (2015), 'Treasury Department Publishes National Money Laundering Risk Assessment and National Terrorist Financing Risk Assessment', Available at: https://www.treasury.gov/press-center/press-releases/Pages/jl0072.aspx (accessed 12 August 2017).

72 U.S. Department of the Treasury (2015), 'National Money Laundering Risk Assessment', Available at: https://www.treasury.gov/resource-center/terrorist-illicit-finance/Documents/National%20Money%20Laundering%20Risk%20Assessment%20%E2%80%93%2006-12-2015.pdf (accessed 11 August 2017).

organizations seeking to fund their activities, and the risk of terrorist financing through the U.S. financial system persists.[73]

The review for these assessments was led by the Treasury Department's Office of Terrorist Financing and Financial Crimes, and developed in close coordination with offices and bureaus in the Treasury Department, the Department of Justice, the Department of Homeland Security, the Department of State, and across the intelligence community and staffs of the Federal functional regulators.[74]

2.1.3 United Kingdom

On the 15th of October, 2015, the UK Government published an assessment of the money laundering and terrorist financing risks faced by the UK. This National Risk Assessment (NRA), which is the first of its kind in the UK, draws on data from UK law enforcement and intelligence agencies, anti-money laundering supervisory agencies, government departments, industry bodies, and private sector firms.[75] The assessment followed the three key stages identified in FATF guidance, of identification, assessment and evaluation.[76]

The NRA warned that the country's banking, accountancy and legal services sectors were at a high risk of exposure to handling corrupt money.

---

73 U.S. Department of the Treasury (2015), 'National Terrorist Financing Risk Assessment', Available at: https://www.treasury.gov/resource-center/terrorist-illicit-finance/Documents/National%20Terrorist%20Financing%20Risk%20Assessment%20%E2%80%93%2006-12-2015.pdf (accessed 11 August 2017).

74 U.S. Department of the Treasury (2015), 'Treasury Department Publishes National Money Laundering Risk Assessment and National Terrorist Financing Risk Assessment', Available at: https://www.treasury.gov/press-center/press-releases/Pages/jl0072.aspx (accessed 12 August 2017).

75 HM Treasury and Home Office (2015), 'UK national risk assessment of money laundering and terrorist financing', Available at: https://www.gov.uk/government/uploads/system/uploads/attachment_data/file/468210/UK_NRA_October_2015_final_web.pdf (accessed 13 August 2017).

76 Financial Action Task Force (2013), 'FATF Guidance: National money laundering and Terrorist Financing Risk Assessment', Available at: http://www.fatf-gafi.org/media/fatf/content/images/National_ML_TF_Risk_Assessment.pdf (accessed 13 August 2017).

"The same factors that make the UK an attractive place for legitimate financial activity – its political stability, advanced professional services sector and widely understood language and legal system – also make it an attractive place through which to launder the proceeds of crime," said the report by the Treasury and Home Office.

The report emphasised how little is known about the true volume of corrupt money moving in and out of the UK, with the financial sector as a whole said to be facing "significant intelligence gaps, in particular in relation to 'high-end' money laundering".

It said: "There are known professional enablers within the legal sector who are facilitating money laundering through the purchase of property with criminal proceeds, and the creation of complex corporate structures and offshore vehicles to conceal the ownership and facilitate the movement of criminal assets.

"Although there are few complicit professional enablers known within the legal sector relative to the size of the sector as a whole, the potential impact they can have on money laundering remains high given their ability to conceal and disguise large sums of criminal money. They also pose a threat to the reputation and integrity of the vast majority in the legal sector who are not complicit in money laundering".

While referring to the true amount of corrupt money moving through the UK as 'an intelligence gap', the report observed: "Some non-governmental organisations estimate that between twenty-three billion pounds and fifty-seven billion pounds is laundered within and through the UK each year. The National Crime Agency assesses that hundreds of billions of dollars are laundered through UK banks and their subsidiaries each year."[77]

---

77 HM Treasury and Home Office (2015), 'UK national risk assessment of money laundering and terrorist financing', Available at: https://www.gov.uk/government/uploads/system/uploads/attachment_data/file/468210/UK_NRA_October_2015_final_web.pdf (accessed 13 August 2017). See also The Guardian (2015), 'UK banks at high risk of exposure to laundered money, says report', Available at: https://www.theguardian.com/money/2015/oct/15/report-uk-banks-high-risk-aiding-money-laundering (accessed 12 August 2017).

The NRA found that while the UK's response to money laundering and terrorist financing risks is well developed, more could be done to strengthen the UK's anti-money laundering (AML) and counter-terrorist financing (CTF) regime, including in the following areas:

- understanding of certain types of money laundering, and particularly in relation to 'high-end' money laundering, where the proceeds are often held in bank accounts, real estate or other investments, rather than cash
- consistency of the UK's supervisory regime, and specifically the understanding and application of a risk-based approach to supervision;
- priority given to combating money laundering by law enforcement agencies and the effectiveness of their response.[78]

2.2 Risk Assessment for Financial Institutions

A reasonably designed risk-based approach provides the means by which a financial institution identifies the criteria to assess potential money laundering and terrorist financing risks. A reasonably implemented risk-based process also provides a framework for identifying the degree of potential money laundering and terrorist financing risks associated with customers and transactions and allows for an institution to focus on those customers and transactions that potentially pose the greatest risk of money laundering (ML) and terrorist financing (TF).

Inherent risk assessment should address the different categories of risk exposure to ML and TF. The Financial Action Task Force requires that inherent risk assessment address the following specific categories of risk:

---

78 HM Treasury and Home Office (2015), 'UK national risk assessment of money laundering and terrorist financing', Available at: https://www.gov.uk/government/uploads/system/uploads/attachment_data/file/468210/UK_NRA_October_2015_final_web.pdf (accessed 13 August 2017).

2.2.1 Client Risk

This is risk associated with types of clients that buy or use the financial institution's products and services. Categories of clients that may indicate a higher risk could include:

- politically exposed persons (PEPs);
- clients conducting their business relationship or transactions in unusual circumstances, such as geographic distance from the financial institution for which there is no reasonable explanation;
- clients whose nature, structure or relationship make it difficult to identify the ultimate beneficial owner(s) of significant or controlling interests, including clients that are corporations with the ability to issue bearer shares;
- cash (and cash equivalent) intensive businesses including:
  - Money services businesses (for example, remittance houses, foreign exchange businesses, money transfer agents, bank note traders, cash couriers or other businesses offering money transfer or movement facilities);
  - Casinos, betting and other gaming-related businesses;
  - Businesses that, while not normally cash-intensive, generate substantial amounts of cash for certain lines of activity; and
- charities and other non-profit organizations that are not monitored or supervised.

> **BOX 2.1: RISK ASSESSMENT FOR POLITICALLY EXPOSED PERSONS**
>
> The amount of corruption and abuse of public funds by some government leaders and public officials over recent years have given great cause for concern internationally. Those people are collectively known as politically exposed persons (PEPs).[79] PEPs are individuals who are or have been

79 Hopton, D. (2009), Money Laundering: A Concise Guide for All Business (2nd Edition Gower) 108

entrusted with prominent public functions and an immediate family member or a known close associate of such a person.[80]

There are special challenges in entering into financial transactions and business relationships with PEPs. Typical customer due diligence (CDD) measures may prove insufficient for PEPs as financial transactions and business relationships with these individuals present a higher money laundering risk and hence require greater scrutiny than "normal" financial transactions and business accounts. To reduce the money laundering risk associated with PEPs, international conventions and national laws require that firms apply a risk-based approach to their compliance programs.[81]

Adopting a risk-based approach implies the adoption of a risk management process for dealing with money laundering and terrorist financing. This process encompasses recognising the existence of the risk(s) at the Customer Due Diligence stage, undertaking an assessment of the risk(s) at the Enhanced Due Diligence stage and developing strategies to manage and mitigate the identified risks at the Enhanced on-going monitoring stage.[82]

Customer Due Diligence

Customer Due Diligence/know your customer is intended to enable a financial institution to form a reasonable belief that it knows the true identity of each customer and, with an appropriate degree of confidence, knows the type of transactions the customer is likely to undertake.[83]

---

80 The Financial Action Task Force (FATF): International Standards on Combating Money Laundering and the financing of terrorism and proliferation, (The FATF Recommendations) 2012, Recommendation 12.

81 Choo, K. K. R. (2008), Politically exposed persons (PEPs): risk and mitigation, 11 (4) JMLC, 371 – 387

82 FATF Guidance on the Risk Based Approach to combating money laundering and terrorist financing, (High Level principles and procedures) 2007, Paragraph 1.8.

83 FATF Guidance on the Risk Based Approach to combating money laundering and terrorist financing, (High Level principles and procedures) 2007, Paragraph 3.10.

Failure of firms taking adequate steps to identify PEPs may lead to corrupt PEPs opening accounts without being detected and in the process avoiding enhanced due diligence and ongoing monitoring. For example, in the late 1980s, a large multinational bank in London opened accounts for Ibrahim and Mohamed Sani Abacha, who represented themselves as commodity and oil dealers. The bank failed to make note of the Father's position at the time as a General in the Army. By the late 1990s, it was discovered that the two brothers had amassed and deposited, either for themselves or on behalf of others, approximately six hundred and sixty million dollars with the London bank. It was later revealed that Sani Abacha brothers and other members of the Abacha circle had allegedly stolen an estimated four billion three hundred million dollars over a number of years.[84]

In situations where the money-laundering risk associated with the business relationship is increased, for example, where the customer is a PEP, banks must carry out enhanced due diligence on the customer.[85]

Enhanced Due Diligence

The Enhanced Due Diligence (EDD) should give firms a greater understanding of the customer and their associated risk than standard due diligence. It should provide more certainty that the customer and/or beneficial owner is who they say they are and that the purposes of the business relationship are legitimate; as well as increasing opportunities to identify and deal with concerns that they are not.[86]

---

84 Otusanya, O.J. (2012), The Role of offshore financial centres in elite money laundering practices: evidence from Nigeria, 15(3) JMLC, 336 – 361.

85 Otusanya, O.J. (2012), The Role of offshore financial centres in elite money laundering practices: evidence from Nigeria, 15(3) JMLC, 336 – 361.

86 Financial Conduct Authority (2015), 'Financial crime: a guide for firms Part 1: A firm's guide to preventing financial crime', Available at: https://www.handbook.fca.org.uk/handbook/document/FC1_FCA_20140612.pdf (accessed 28 December 2017). See also Uniting and Strengthening America by Providing

It is for each firm to decide the steps it takes to determine whether a PEP is seeking to establish a business relationship for legitimate reasons.[87] Firms must take adequate measures to establish the source of wealth and source of funds which are involved in the business relationship in order to allow the firm to satisfy itself that it does not handle the proceeds from corruption or other criminal activity. The measures firms should take to establish the PEP's source of wealth and the source of funds will depend on the degree of risk associated with the business relationship, and where the individual sits on the PEP continuum. Firms should verify the source of wealth and the source of funds on the basis of reliable and independent data, documents or information where the risk associated with the PEP relationship is particularly high.[88] In countries where the declarations ought to be publicly available and are not still available, firms should insist that they see the declaration and if they are not given the declaration they should not open the account.

Once the source of wealth and source of funds are established banks will need to analyse the information for "red flag" for corrupt PEP activity.[89] In all cases if a bank suspects that the funds are proceeds of criminal activity, the bank is required to file a Suspicious Transaction Report with the Financial Intelligence

Appropriate Tools Required to Intercept and Obstruct Terrorism Act 2001, s. 312 (2) (B) I, II which states that the enhanced due diligence policies and procedures enables firms in the United States to ascertain for any such foreign bank, the shares of which are not publicly traded, the identity of each owners of the foreign bank and the nature and extent of the ownership interest of each such owner.

87 The Joint Money Laundering Steering Group JMLSG, *Prevention of Money Laundering/Combating Terrorist Financing* (2017) revised version, Guidance for the United Kingdom Financial Sector Part I, June 2017 (Amended December 2017), Paragraph 5.5.29.

88 The Joint Money Laundering Steering Group JMLSG, *Prevention of Money Laundering/Combating Terrorist Financing* (2017) revised version, Guidance for the United Kingdom Financial Sector Part I, June 2017 (Amended December 2017), Paragraph 5.5.30.

89 Greenberg, T. (2009), 'Stolen Asset Recovery: Politically Exposed Persons, A Policy Paper on Strengthening Preventive Measures', Available at: http://www.u4.no/recommended-reading/stolen-asset-recovery-politically-exposed-persons-a-policy-paper-on-strengthening-preventive-measures/ (accessed 28 December 2017).

Unit.[90] A risk based approach for the reporting of suspicious activity under these circumstances is not applicable.[91] A risk based approach is however appropriate for the purpose of identifying suspicious activity, for example by directing additional resources at those areas a financial institution has identified as higher risk and in this case to customers who are identified as PEPs.[92]

Senior Management Approval

The FATF standard requires banks to obtain senior management approval for establishing a business relationship with PEPs and continuing a business relationship with a customer who is subsequently found to be a PEP or becomes a PEP.[93] The group AML/CTF officer should be involved in the PEP approval process since he is in the best position to say that a person should not be accepted regardless of the size of the account.[94]

Enhanced on Going Monitoring

As due diligence is an ongoing process, a bank is required to take measures to ensure account profiles of politically exposed persons are current and monitoring should be

---

90 Greenberg, T. (2009), 'Stolen Asset Recovery: Politically Exposed Persons, A Policy Paper on Strengthening Preventive Measures', Available at: http://www.u4.no/recommended-reading/stolen-asset-recovery-politically-exposed-persons-a-policy-paper-on-strengthening-preventive-measures/ (accessed 28 December 2017).

91 FATF Guidance on the Risk Based Approach to combating money laundering and terrorist financing, (High Level principles and procedures) 2007, Paragraph 3.16.

92 FATF Guidance on the Risk Based Approach to combating money laundering and terrorist financing, (High Level principles and procedures) 2007, Paragraph 3.17.

93 The Financial Action Task Force (FATF): International Standards on Combating Money Laundering and the financing of terrorism and proliferation, (The FATF Recommendations) 2012, Recommendation 12.

94 Greenberg, T. (2009), 'Stolen Asset Recovery: Politically Exposed Persons, A Policy Paper on Strengthening Preventive Measures', Available at: http://www.u4.no/recommended-reading/stolen-asset-recovery-politically-exposed-persons-a-policy-paper-on-strengthening-preventive-measures/ (accessed 28 December 2017).

risk-based. Banks should consider whether risk profiles should be adjusted or suspicious activity reported when the activity is inconsistent with the profile.

Failure of firms to subject PEPs to heightened monitoring may lead to corrupt PEPs laundering money through the Bank.

The Panama Papers revealed that Former Delta State governor, James Ibori, working through a Swiss asset management firm, Clamorgan S.A. in Geneva, established limited liability companies and foundations in secret offshore tax havens to hide some of the funds he looted from the state's treasury. Mr. Ibori enlisted his immediate family as beneficiaries of the offshore companies and foundations.[95]

From the revelation, it could be argued that James Ibori's personal Bank in Nigeria conducted business without implementing adequate procedures and internal controls, as appropriate and practical, to detect and timely report suspicious activity and large currency transactions. This explains why large amount of funds were moved from the Nigerian Bank to Geneva, undetected.

The following measures should have been put in place by James Ibori's Bank to prevent money laundering:

- The Bank's anti-money laundering risk assessment process should have adequately evaluated and distinguished customers with heightened anti-money laundering risks, including politically exposed persons like James Ibori.
- The Bank's manual cash transaction monitoring for unusual activity should have been commensurate with the size of the Bank, volume of transactions, customer base, or geographic footprint.

95 Ogundipe, S. (2016), '#PanamaPapers uncovers how Ibori the thief organised massive stealing of Delta funds', Available at: http://www.premiumtimesng.com/news/headlines/201265-panamapapers-uncovers-how-ibori-the-thief-organised-massive-stealing-of-delta-funds.html (accessed 5 April 2016).

- The Bank should have employed automated systems to detect and monitor suspicious activity.
- The Large Cash Transaction Report (LCTR) should not have been manually reviewed for potential structuring activity; such review may not capture transactions below ten thousand US dollars, rendering it useless for monitoring for patterns of structuring.

If the accounts of James Ibori were effectively monitored and properly scrutinized, the Bank would have been able to detect that the funds deposited into the account were not commensurate with the legitimate income of the Governor.

BOX 2.2: RISK ASSESSMENT FOR CHARITIES AND NON-PROFIT ORGANIZATIONS

To assess the risk of charities and other non-profit organizations, a financial institution should conduct adequate due diligence on the organization. At a minimum, the bank must obtain the following identifying information from charities and non-governmental organizations before opening the account:

- Name of account;
- Mailing address;
- Contact telephone and fax numbers;
- Some form of official identification number, such as tax identification number;
- Description of the purpose or activities of the account holder as stated in a formal constitution; and
- Copy of documentation confirming the legal existence of the account holder such as register of charities.
- Financial institutions/DNFBPs shall verify the information referred to above, by at least one of the following –
- Obtaining an independent undertaking from a reputable and known firm of lawyers or accountants confirming the documents submitted;

- Obtaining prior bank references; and
- Accessing public and private databases or official sources.

In addition to required Customer Identification Program (CIP) information, due diligence for charities and non-governmental organizations should focus on other aspects of the organization, such as the following:

(i)   Geographic locations served including headquarters and operational areas;
(ii) Organizational structure;
(iii) Donor and volunteer base;
(iv) Funding and disbursement criteria including basic beneficiary information;
(v)   Record keeping requirements;
(vi) Its affiliation with other charity organizations; and
(vii) Internal controls and audits.[96]

For accounts that financial institution management considers to be higher risk, stringent documentation, verification and transaction monitoring procedures should be established. NGO accounts that are at higher risk for ML/TF concerns include those operating or providing services in Syria and Iraq where the Islamic State of Iraq and the Levant (ISIL) have a strong hold, and those conducting unusual or suspicious activities or lacking proper documentation.

There have been reports that International banks, including HSBC, UBS and NatWest, have frozen accounts held by UK-registered charities and international non-governmental organisations delivering aid in areas such as Syria, Gaza and Iraq, over fears that the money could end up financing

---

96 Federal Financial Institutions Examination Council (2014), 'Bank Secrecy Act/Anti-Money Laundering Examination Manual', Available at: https://www.ffiec.gov/bsa_aml_infobase/documents/BSA_AML_Man_2014_v2.pdf (accessed 20 February 2017).

terrorism.[97] This approach which is known as the 'wholesale de-risking approach' is a wrong approach. Rather than Banks applying the wholesale de-risking approach to UK-registered charities, they should apply the risk-based approach by enhancing the measures used to combat terrorist financing through non-governmental organisations. Enhance Due Diligence (EDD) for these accounts should include:

(i)   Evaluating the principals;
(ii)   Obtaining and reviewing the financial statements and audits;
(iii) Verifying the source and use of funds; and
(iv)   Evaluating large contributors or grantors to the non-governmental organizations.

2.2.2 Business Relationship Risk

This is risk associated with the client's stated purpose in dealing with the financial institution. Categories of business relationships that may indicate a higher risk could include:

- intermediary structures, such as holding companies, numbered companies or trusts, that have no apparent business purpose or that make beneficial owners difficult to identify;
- accountants, lawyers or other professionals holding commingled funds accounts where the beneficial ownership of the funds may be difficult to verify;
- use of the financial institution's products or services by clients of clients, for example, clients of correspondent banks and third-party payment processors;
- providing account services to third party payment processors.

---

97 The Guardian (2015), 'Banks block charity donations over terrorism funding fears', Available at: https://www.theguardian.com/society/2015/mar/05/banks-block-charity-donations-over-terrorism-funding-fears (accessed 28 August 2017).

BOX 2.3: RISK ASSESSMENT FOR THIRD PARTY PAYMENT PROCESSORS

The financial institution's systems should be adequate to manage the risks associated with its relationships with third-party payment processors and the management should have the ability to implement its monitoring and reporting systems effectively.

Non-bank or third-party payment processors (processors) are bank or other financial institution customers that provide payment-processing services to merchants and other business entities. Traditionally, processors primarily contract with retailers that have physical locations in order to process the retailers' transactions.[98]

These merchant transactions primarily included credit card payments but also covered automated clearing house (ACH) transactions, Remotely Created Cheques (RCCs), debit and prepaid cards transactions. With the expansion of the internet, retail borders have been eliminated. Processors now provide services to a variety of merchant accounts, including conventional retail and internet-based establishments, prepaid travel, telemarketers and internet gaming enterprises.

Third-party payment processors often use their commercial bank accounts to conduct payment processing for their merchant clients. For example, the processor may deposit into its account RCCs generated on behalf of a merchant client, or act as a third-party sender of ACH transactions. In either case, the financial institution does not have a direct relationship with the merchant. The increased use by processor customers, particularly telemarketers of RCCs also raises the risk of fraudulent payments being processed through the processor's bank account.[99]

---

98 Central Bank of Nigeria (2011), 'ANTI-MONEY LAUNDERING/COMBATING THE FINANCING OF TERRORISM (AML/CFT) RISK BASED SUPERVISION (RBS) FRAMEWORK', Available at: https://www.cbn.gov.ng/Out/2012/CCD/CBN%20APPROVED%20FRAMEWORK.pdf (accessed 6 February 2017).
99 Central Bank of Nigeria (2011), 'ANTI-MONEY LAUNDERING/COMBAT-

Financial institutions offering account services to processors should develop and maintain adequate policies, procedures and processes to address risks related to these relationships. At a minimum, these policies should authenticate the processor's business operations and assess their risk level. A financial institution may assess the risks associated with payment processors by considering the following:

(i) Implementing a policy that requires an initial background check of the processor (using for example, state incorporation departments, internet searches and other investigative processes) and of the processor's underlying merchants on a risk-adjusted basis in order to verify their creditworthiness and general business practices;

(ii) Reviewing the processor's promotional materials, including its Web site to determine the target clientele. A financial institution may develop policies, procedures and processes that restrict the types of entities for which it will allow processing services. These entities may include higher risk entities such as offshore companies, online gambling-related operations, telemarketers and online pay lenders. These restrictions should be clearly communicated to the processor at account opening stage;

(iii) Determining whether the processor re-sells its services to a third party who may be referred to as an agent or provider of independent sales institution opportunities or internet service provider (gateway) arrangements;

(iv) Reviewing the processor's policies, procedures and processes to determine the adequacy of its due diligence standards for new merchants;

ING THE FINANCING OF TERRORISM (AML/CFT) RISK BASED SUPERVISION (RBS) FRAMEWORK', Available at: https://www.cbn.gov.ng/Out/2012/CCD/CBN%20APPROVED%20FRAMEWORK.pdf (accessed 6 February 2017).

(v)   Requiring the processor to identify its major customers by providing information such as the merchant's name, principal business activity and geographic location;

(vi)   Verifying directly or through the processor that the merchant is operating a legitimate business by comparing the merchant's identifying information against public record databases, fraud and financial institution check databases;

(vii)   Reviewing corporate documentation including independent reporting services and, if applicable, documentation on principal owners; and

(viii) Visiting the processor's business operations centre.[100]

Refer to Ehi Eric Esoimeme's book on the Risk-Based Approach to Combating Money Laundering and Terrorist Financing for further information on third-party payment processors. The book is available for sale on Amazon.

CASE STUDY ON TRANSACTION LAUNDERING THROUGH THIRD-PARTY PAYMENT PROCESSORS

A Reuters examination found that a network of dummy online stores offering household goods has been used as a front for internet gambling payments.

The seven sites, operated out of Europe, purport to sell items including fabric, DVD cases, maps, gift wrap, mechanical tape, pin badges and flags. In fact, they are fake outlets, part of a multinational system to disguise payments for the forty billion dollars global online gambling industry, which is illegal in many countries and some U.S. states.

---

100 Federal Financial Institutions Examination Council (2014), 'Bank Secrecy Act/Anti-Money Laundering Examination Manual', Available at: https://www.ffiec.gov/bsa_aml_infobase/documents/BSA_AML_Man_2014_v2.pdf (accessed 20 February 2017).

The findings raise questions about how e-commerce is policed worldwide. They also underline a strategy which fraud specialists say regulators, card issuers and banks have yet to tackle head-on.

That strategy is "transaction laundering" - when one online merchant processes payment card transactions on behalf of another, which can help disguise the true nature of payments.

Credit card companies including Visa and Mastercard require all online purchases to be coded so they can see what type of purchase is being processed and block it if it is illegal in a particular country. The codes are known as Merchant Category Codes. Gambling transactions, for example, are given the code of 7995 and subject to extra scrutiny.

The scheme found by Reuters involved websites which accepted payments for household items from a reporter but did not deliver any products. Instead, staff who answered helpdesk numbers on the sites said the outlets did not sell the product advertised, but that they were used to help process gambling payments, mostly for Americans.

The dummy stores came to Reuters' attention in late 2016, when an anonymous document posted on the internet pointed to three online outlets that advertised products but did not actually deliver any. In December, a reporter placed an order for a yard of burlap cloth on one of the sites, myfabricfactory.com, a website run by a UK company called Sarphone Ltd. The fabric, advertised in U.S. dollars at six dollars and forty-eight cents per yard, has "many uses including lightweight drapes," the website says. Sarphone did not respond to requests for comment.

This order went unmet. After a few weeks an email from My Fabric Factory arrived saying the product was out of stock. The payment was refunded.

When a reporter called the helpline number given on the site, the call was answered by someone who gave her name as Anna Richardson. She said she was employed by Agora Online Services, a payment services provider. Payment services providers (PSPs) verify, process and code card transactions.

Richardson said Agora processes payments for poker and works with "hundreds" of online gambling sites. Asked which references on the reporter's card statement would be for online gambling,

Richardson said, "If you have been using a betting site of any sort ... they are normally processed by us."

It was not possible to verify Richardson's identity. The My Fabric Factory email came from Agora's email address, info@agrsupport. net. Agora, headquartered in Iceland and linked to companies from the UK to Germany, is owned by a Mauritius-based company, DueXX Ltd, according to Orbis, a company database. Andrej Brandt, one of two directors of Agora and listed as the sole point of contact on DueXX's website, declined to comment.

"Thank you very much for your interest but I don't like to share my views and insights," he said via text message after Reuters presented its findings. "I presume you understand."

The other director of Agora, Joerg Henning, could not be reached.

Reuters placed orders for household products on six other websites, all owned by companies in the UK. All the orders went unfilled and payment was refunded without comment. The sites used the same mail server as one of Agora's web addresses, agrsupport.net, according to domain name records.

The site helplines were answered by three individuals who all said they worked for Agora, a company that specialized in processing gambling payments. One was the woman who identified herself as Anna Richardson. Another gave her name as Lucy, and the third, who did not give his name, told the reporter, "Most of the people who gamble and end up having our charges on their accounts are Americans. Gambling is illegal in America." The staff said they were based in Germany.

When Reuters made payments on the seven sites, in each case the reporter's credit details were processed by Deutsche Payment, a payment processor headquartered in Berlin. Its website says it is certified by the PCI Security Standards Council, a global payment card security body. It was included in Visa Europe's May 2017 list of approved agents. Deutsche Payment did not respond to requests for comment.[101]

---

101   Reuters (2017), 'Exclusive: Fake online stores reveal gamblers' shadow banking system', Available at: https://uk.reuters.com/article/us-gambling-usa-dummies-exclusive-idUKKBN19D137 (accessed 27 August 2017).

2.2.3 Product/Service Risk

This is risk associated with the financial institution's products/services that enable clients to move funds. Categories of products and services that may indicate a higher risk could include:

- deposit-taking, especially cash, and insurance products that allow large one-time or regular payments, pre-payments or deposits, to be made and subsequently withdrawn from deposit or deposit-like accounts (for example, side accounts);
- "free look" or "cooling off" periods coupled with premium refunds, for example, in some life insurance products;
- cash values, early cash surrender and loan provisions, and provisions for deposit, accumulation and withdrawal of funds with relative ease and speed, for example, non-registered segregated funds;
- trade finance services where
  - the financial institution is not able to assess whether the values of goods or services being imported or exported are reasonable; or
  - Financial Institutions confirm, advise or make payments under letters of credit for purposes of their clients' buying or selling goods internationally.
- credit accounts in respect of which large credit balances are allowed to be maintained, for example, some credit and corporate card products;
- payable through accounts that permit clients of a foreign correspondent bank to draw drafts (or cheques) on Canadian-based accounts;
- lock boxes for the use of clients of foreign correspondent banks that permit such banks to collect payments due from their clients domiciled in Canada; and
- pouch services and similar international commercial payment services.

A firm should take care with customers whose identity is verified under a variation from the standard and who wish to migrate to other

products in due course. The verification of identity undertaken for a basic bank account may not be sufficient for a customer migrating to a higher risk product. Firms should have processes defining what additional due diligence, including where appropriate further evidence of identification, is required in such circumstances.[102]

For example, a customer may have opened a savings account with the bank and provided basic information to the bank like his legal name, permanent address, telephone number, date and place of birth and occupation. The bank may have verified this information provided by confirming the full name and date of birth from an official document (such as birth certificate, passport, identity card, social security records) and confirming the permanent address (such as utility bill, tax assessment, bank statement, a letter from a public authority). The customer may decide to migrate to a domiciliary/current account by making a formal application to the bank. The bank, on receiving this application, must ask the customer to provide at least two bank references from people who have a current account. The bank must also ask the client to provide information about his source of income and the source of the funds that the particular client expects to use in concluding the single transaction or transactions in the course of the business relationship. This information must be verified by the bank using original or certified true copies of documents that would be provided by the customer. Sources of income or wealth include inheritance, divorce settlement and property sale.

2.2.4 Delivery Channel Risk

A new breed of entrepreneurs is creating financial technology (fintech) which could change the whole game – and many of them are based in the UK. These online companies are using software to offer greater transparency, better rates, and democratise the way the financial sector is run.

---

102 Joint Money Laundering Steering Group JMLSG, *Prevention of money laundering/combating terrorist financing*, 2017 Revised Version, Guidance for the UK financial sector Part II, June 2017 (Amended December 2017), Paragraph 1.17.

Currently leading the pack on money transfer is Transferwise, created by former Skype engineers and backed by Sir Richard Branson, which is making a big name for itself by offering rates banks can't match.[103]

Transferwise allows for non-face-to-face business relationships. This may increase the risk of identity fraud or customers providing inaccurate information potentially to disguise illegal activity if effective measures to address this risk are not employed. Against this backdrop, Transferwise has adopted alternative identification mechanisms, which can provide adequate risk mitigation measures.

If you open a Transferwise Account and use certain of the Services, they will verify some of your information like Name and Address. These may be made directly or through third parties, including checking commercial databases or credit reports. They may ask you for further information, requiring you to provide your date of birth, a taxpayer identification number and other information that will allow them to reasonably identify you. This could include requiring you to take steps to confirm ownership of your email address or financial instruments, ordering a credit report from a credit reporting agency, or verifying your information against third party databases or through other sources. They may also ask to see your driver's license or other identifying documents at any time. TransferWise reserves the right to close, suspend, or limit access to your TransferWise Account and/or the Services in the event they are unable to obtain or verify this information.

A TransferWise Account is subject to withdrawal limits. If your withdrawal request exceeds the current limit, they may decline your request and require you provide additional documents to them so that they could carry out additional checks or impose additional obligations before allowing the money to be withdrawn.[104]

---

103 The Guardian (2015), 'Fintech revolutionaries storm the barricades of traditional banking', Available at: https://www.theguardian.com/small-business-network/2015/apr/24/fintech-traditional-banking-tech-investors (accessed 27 August 2017).

104 TransferWise (2017), 'Electronic Communications Policy', Available at: https://transferwise.com/electronic-communications-policy (accessed 27 August 2017).

2.2.5 Geographic Location Risk

This is risk associated with places in which a financial institution's activities are carried out. Where financial institutions have subsidiaries or branches in such places, this may mitigate or elevate the risk. Categories of countries that indicate a higher risk include countries:

- subject to national sanctions, embargoes or similar measures, such as the *Special Economic Measures Act* or measures prescribed under the USA PATRIOT Act;
- subject to United Nations Security Council (UNSC) sanctions;
- identified by credible sources as providing funding or support for terrorist activities or the proliferation of weapons of mass destruction;
- identified by credible sources as having significant levels of corruption or other criminal activity;
- that are not members of the FATF, and in particular, countries that are subject to monitoring by the FATF or otherwise identified by the FATF as lacking appropriate AML/CFT regulatory requirements; and
- where legislation prohibits or unduly restricts access to client information by the Compliance Officer.

2.2.6 Employee Risk

A financial institution should assess the risks that the employee may pose taking into consideration any appropriate risk variables before making a final determination. Financial institutions will determine the due diligence requirements appropriate to each employee. Financial institutions are required to understand an employee's background, conflicts of interest and their susceptibility to money laundering complicity.

Banks are advised not to use the Employee Profiling methodology, to assess the risk posed by potential employees. Employee profiling, being a one-size-fits-all assessment methodology, may not be the best option. Banks should use a flexible approach that can adapt as risks evolve. Since the approach used to combat money laundering is more like a flexible approach, the methodology used to assess employee risk should also be flexible. Banks should label employees in sensitive positions as high risk, just as how they label customers. Banks would need to apply enhanced scrutiny to such employees. Money Laundering Reporting Officers, for example, should be labeled high-risk. Measures would have to be put in place to mitigate the risk (s) associated with high-risk employees.

CASE STUDY ON EMPLOYEE RISK

A local banker admitted in San Diego federal court on October 15 2015 that he caused Citibank to fail to report suspicious transactions and fail to maintain an effective anti-money laundering compliance program. Raymundo Navarrette, 51, pleaded guilty to bank bribery.

In his plea agreement, Navarrette admitted that he used his position within Citibank, as well as knowledge he gained as a result of his career in finance, to aid his clients in avoiding detection by Citibank's AML compliance program.

Navarrette recruited and failed to report Citibank customers he knew to be engaged in various suspicious and high-risk activities, according to the plea agreement.

Prosecutors said that in exchange for cash, in-kind compensation, and other things of value exceeding one thousand dollars, Navarrette agreed to undermine Citibank's obligations as a domestic financial institution.

Navarrette counseled customers on the specifics of Citibank's AML parameters, to include providing people with internal-use-only Citibank AML guidelines, prosecutors said.

Navarrette also devised schemes in which shell bank accounts in non-threatening business sectors would be established and maintained by his clients for the purpose of engaging in large volumes of cash transactions, without triggering Citibank's AML reporting obligations, according to prosecutors.[105]

---

105 TIMES OF SAN DIEGO (2015), 'Banker Admits to Bribery, Aiding Clients to Launder Money', Available at: https://timesofsandiego.com/business/2015/10/15/banker-admits-to-bribery-aiding-clients-to-launder-money/ (accessed 27 August 2017).

2.2.7 Internal Controls

Certain risk control measures are prescribed by regulatory requirements. These cannot be qualified or bypassed by inherent risk assessments. They include, for example:

- client identification and ascertaining identity (subject to prescribed exemptions);
- determining under prescribed circumstances whether a client is a PEP or is acting on behalf of a third party;
- reporting suspicious transactions and suspicious attempted transactions, large cash transactions and large Electronic Funds Transfer; and
- record keeping.

The information obtained through the Customer Identification Program should allow the bank to determine the customer's risk profile at account opening. Banks should monitor their lower-risk customers through regular suspicious activity monitoring and customer due diligence processes. If there is indication of a potential change in the customer's risk profile (e.g., expected account activity, change in employment or business operations), management should reassess the customer risk rating and follow established bank policies and procedures for maintaining or changing customer risk ratings.[106]

For example, the Customer Identification Program may have determined that a potential customer is a taxi driver whose main source of funds is derived from salary payment from a Bank and that the transactions are commensurate with the funds. The taxi driver may decide to later register as a bureaux de change operator to feed his family. He may not inform his Bank of these new changes. An effective monitoring system should be able to detect a deviation in a customer's activity from anticipated activity identified at account opening like when a taxi driver who usually received the sum of forty thousand naira into his account

---

106 Federal Financial Institutions Examination Council (2014), 'Bank Secrecy Act/Anti-Money Laundering Examination Manual', Available at: https://www.ffiec.gov/bsa_aml_infobase/documents/BSA_AML_Man_2014_v2.pdf (accessed 20 February 2017).

is now receiving five hundred thousand naira. The Bank must re-assess the taxi driver's risk profile by designating him or her as a high-risk customer. The Currency exchanges specifically are an important link in the money laundering chain. Once the money has been exchanged, it is difficult to trace its origin. Banks must therefore enhance the due diligence of the taxi driver by obtaining the following information on him:

- Purpose of the account.
- Source of funds and wealth (e.g., inheritance, divorce settlement, property sale). The Bank should consider whether, in some circumstances, evidence of source of wealth or income should be required (for example, if from an inheritance, see a copy of the will and if it is from property sale, see a copy of the deed of assignment and receipt).
- Banking references.
- Domicile (where the business is organized).
- Proximity of the customer's residence, place of employment, or place of business to the bank.
- Description of the customer's primary trade area and whether international transactions are expected to be routine.
- Description of the business operations, the anticipated volume of currency and total sales, and a list of major customers and suppliers.
- Explanations for changes in account activity.

Financial institutions should take into account the risk of tipping-off when performing the enhanced due diligence (EDD) process on the taxi driver. If the institution reasonably believes that performing the EDD process will tip-off the taxi driver, it may choose not to pursue that process, and should file a Suspicious Transaction Report. Institutions should ensure that their employees are aware of, and sensitive to, these issues when conducting EDD.

CASE STUDY ON RISK ASSESSMENT FOR FINANCIAL INSTITUTIONS

Case 2.1: Financial Crimes Enforcement Network v. Gibraltar Private Bank and Trust Company Number 2016-01

Gibraltar failed to adequately assess the money laundering risks associated with its customers. Risk assessment procedures are a key component of a compliance program because they permit a financial institution to assess its particular risks associated with its business lines, practices, and clientele and to design a program that can reasonably assure and monitor Bank Secrecy Act (BSA) compliance. While Gibraltar undertook several AML risk assessments between February 2008 and October 2014, Gibraltar failed to adequately risk rate its high-risk customers and their respective accounts, leaving the Bank ill-equipped to adequately monitor transactions based on a customer's particular level of risk or the account's purpose and expected activity. Moreover, on some occasions, when Gibraltar detected a deviation in a customer's activity from anticipated activity identified at account opening, it would change the anticipated activity in the account rather than changing customer's risk rating, even when the customer should have been identified as high risk. This practice undermined the purpose of conducting risk ratings and caused Gibraltar to apply insufficient transaction monitoring to accounts it should have identified as high-risk and limited Gibraltar's ability to detect red flags of suspicious activity.

For example, Gibraltar did not adequately risk rate its high net-worth private banking customers, like Scott Rothstein. As a result, the Bank applied insufficient scrutiny to his and related accounts, and missed the following significant red flags:

- Rothstein used his account to conduct millions of dollars of intrabank and interbank funds transfers sent in large, round-dollar amounts. The continued movement of large round-dollar amounts within accounts at the same institution is red flag activity indicative of a Ponzi scheme.
- The account also processed unexplained funds transfer activity and payments and receipts with no links to legitimate services provided. The Bank should have identified that this activity was not expected for the Rothstein accounts and, as unexpected activity, should have investigated it further.

- A significant volume of highly suspicious transactional activity involved multiple Interest on Trust Accounts ("IOTAs") controlled by Rothstein that did not match his customer information file. An IOTA is an account set up by an attorney to hold client funds received for future use, and cannot be used to support ongoing transaction activity. Had Gibraltar applied appropriate scrutiny to Rothstein's accounts, it would have identified as suspicious Rothstein's improper use of IOTAs to support his massive Ponzi scheme.

In addition, in 2011, Gibraltar's customer risk profiles were generally incomplete, stale, and lacking in sufficient analysis and validation. Some account files lacked sufficient supporting documentation to validate the risk profiles of the beneficial owners or authorized signers. Such files also were generally missing descriptions regarding the source of funds, financial capacity, expected activity, and the purpose of the account. By failing to have complete and accurate information, Gibraltar was unable to accurately risk rate such accounts either at account opening or when updating its account risk ratings. Further, when updating its account risk ratings, rather than soliciting updated and more accurate information from customers to conduct a comprehensive assessment, Gibraltar would simply review its account risk ratings based on average account activity that the Bank did not validate with the customer's expected activity.

In 2013, the risk rating methodology of all deposit accounts was also considered deficient. The methodology did not consider the volume of customer activity by transaction type (e.g., cash activity, wire activity, and Automated Clearing House activity). The type of transaction being used by the account is an important factor in identifying an expected volume of customer activity. This is important because such information is necessary to identify baselines with which to compare actual activity for transaction monitoring.

For over three years, Gibraltar did not have up-to-date, accurate, and verified information to enable it to conduct its annual risk assessment. Gibraltar's information was unreliable because, from 2011 through 2014, it failed to complete a full cycle of annual high-risk account reviews. In fact, in 2014, the Bank had conducted only 44 (or 7%) annual high-risk reviews out of 590 high-risk customer information files.

In sum, Gibraltar's transaction and suspicious activity monitoring deficiencies from 2008 through 2013, combined with its overall risk assessment and risk rating deficiencies, demonstrate Gibraltar's continuous failure to maintain an anti-money laundering compliance program that adequately identified the risks posed by its products, services, customers, and its customers' activities.

FinCEN determined that the penalty in this matter will be four million dollars, of which two million five hundred thousand dollars will be concurrent with the penalty imposed by the Office of the Comptroller of the Currency (OCC). Accordingly, this penalty will be satisfied by paying one million five hundred thousand dollars to the United States Department of the Treasury and by paying two million five hundred thousand dollars in satisfaction of, and in accordance with, the penalty imposed by the OCC.[107]

Case 2.2: Financial Crimes Enforcement Network v. Bethex Federal Credit Union Number 2016-06

The Financial Crimes Enforcement Network (FinCEN) determined that grounds exist to assess a civil money penalty against Bethex Federal Credit Union (Bethex or the Credit Union), pursuant to the Bank Secrecy Act (BSA) and regulations issued pursuant to that Act.

From 2011 through 2012, Bethex failed to conduct a risk assessment that incorporated all of its products and services including wire transfers processed for its domestic and international Money Service Business (MSB) accounts. Bethex processed transactions for MSB customers in over 30 countries, including jurisdictions with high money laundering risks such as Mexico, Ghana, Bangladesh, China,

---

107 United States of America Department of the Treasury Financial Crimes Enforcement Network (2016), 'IN THE MATTER OF: Gibraltar Private Bank and Trust Company Coral Gables, Florida', Available at: https://www.fincen.gov/sites/default/files/enforcement_action/Gibraltar_%20Assessment.pdf (accessed 27 April, 2017).

Pakistan, and South Korea. Bethex failed to conduct any risk assessment in 2011 and conducted an inadequate risk assessment in 2012 because it did not assess the risk of its MSB clients. An operational and organizational risk assessment is a vital part of a compliance program, as it permits the financial institution to assess the particular risks posed by its business lines, practices, and clientele and establish appropriate controls to mitigate those risks. Bethex's failure to conduct an adequate risk assessment left Bethex ill-equipped to implement necessary AML controls when its MSB transaction activity nearly quadrupled from one billion three hundred million dollars in 2010, to two billion seven hundred million dollars in 2011, and finally to four billion dollars in 2012.

In view of the above stated facts, FinCEN determined that Bethex willfully violated the program and reporting requirements of the BSA and its implementing regulations, and that grounds exist to assess a civil money penalty for these violations. **31 U.S.C. § 5321** and **31 C.F.R. § 1010.820**. FinCEN determined that the appropriate penalty in this matter is five hundred thousand dollars.[108]

2.3 Discussion

The Inter-Governmental Action Group against Money Laundering in West Africa (**GIABA**) had confirmed in its Seventh Follow up Report on Nigeria that Nigeria has consolidated its efforts in carrying out its AML/CFT national risk assessment in line with the requirement of Financial Action Task Force (FATF) Recommendations. This assessment is targeted at clear understanding of the AML/CFT vulnerabilities and the deployment of resources and attentions to areas that are more vulnerable using the AML/CFT Risk-Based Approach (RBA) Framework. According to GIABA, steps are currently being put in place to reposition and transfer the National Risk Assessment

---

108   United States of America Department of the Treasury Financial Crimes Enforcement Network (2016), 'IN THE MATTER OF: Bethex Federal Credit Union Bronx, New York', Available at: https://www.fincen.gov/sites/default/files/enforcement_action/2016-12-15/Bethex%20Assessment_Final.pdf (accessed 25 April 2017).

Secretariat (NRAS) to the NFIU as is obtainable in other jurisdictions. To this end, the NFIU has applied for funds that will enable it effectively commence and run the NRAS, especially in the areas of capacity building, infrastructure, and sourcing of experts.[109]

Although this could be viewed as a form of positive development, it is necessary to state that the report that confirmed this development was released in May 2015. As at 12 August 2017 Nigeria is still yet to conduct its own National Risk Assessment.

2.4 Conclusion

Nigeria should identify, assess, and understand the money laundering and terrorist financing risks for the country, and should take action, including designating an authority or mechanism to coordinate actions to assess risks, and apply resources, aimed at ensuring the risks are mitigated effectively. Based on that assessment, Nigeria should apply a risk-based approach (RBA) to ensure that measures to prevent or mitigate money laundering and terrorist financing are commensurate with the risks identified. This approach should be an essential foundation to efficient allocation of resources across the anti-money laundering and countering the financing of terrorism (AML/CFT) regime and the implementation of risk-based measures throughout the FATF Recommendations. Where Nigeria identifies higher risks, it should ensure that its AML/CFT regime adequately addresses such risks. Where Nigeria identifies lower risks, it may decide to allow simplified measures for some of the FATF Recommendations under certain conditions.[110]

---

109 The Inter-Governmental Action Group against Money Laundering in West Africa (**GIABA**) (2015), 'Seventh Follow up Report Mutual Evaluation Nigeria May 2015', Available at: http://www.giaba.org/media/f/932_7th%20FUR%20Nigeria%20-%20English.pdf (accessed 7 April 2017).

110 The Financial Action Task Force Recommendations 2012, Recommendation 1.

CHAPTER 3

REPORTING REQUIREMENTS

The Financial Action Task Force (FATF), the independent intergovernmental body that develops and promotes policies to protect the global financial system against money laundering, terrorist financing and financing the proliferation of weapons of mass destruction, advised countries to enact laws that mandate financial institutions and designated nonfinancial businesses and professions (DNFBPs) to file certain reports. These reports are to be filed when a financial institution or DNFBP suspects or has reasonable grounds to suspect that funds are the proceeds of a criminal activity or are related to terrorist financing.[111]

Although countries have followed the advice of the FATF, the reporting requirements in different countries are not the same. For example, Nigeria and the United States require financial institutions to file suspicious transaction reports (STRs) and currency transaction reports (CTRs),[112] while countries like the

---

111 The Financial Action Task Force (FATF): International Standards on Combating Money Laundering and the financing of terrorism and proliferation (The FATF Recommendations) (2012), Recommendation 20, 23.

112 Money Laundering Prohibition Act 2011 (as amended), s. 6, s. 2 and s. 10. See also the Codified Bank Secrecy Act Regulations 2010 (31 CFR, s. 1020.320 (b) (1), s. 1022.320 (b) (1) and s. 1010.311).

United Kingdom require financial institutions to file only a suspicious activity report (SAR).[113]

This chapter, therefore, compares the reporting requirements in Nigeria with those of the United States and the United Kingdom. The aim of such comparison is to determine if Nigeria needs to adopt the approach in these countries or if there is no need for reform.

This chapter briefly highlights the relevant money laundering/terrorist financing laws and regulations in Nigeria, the United States and the United Kingdom. It will then compare the reporting requirements in Nigeria with those of the United States and the United Kingdom under five subheadings: 'What to File', 'Where to File', 'When to File', 'Confidentiality of SARs' and 'Penalties'. The chapter will later analyse issues that arise from the earlier comparison, with the aim of determining if there is need for reform.

3.1 Relevant Money Laundering/Terrorist Financing Laws and Regulations

3.1.1 Nigeria

The laws enacted to combat money laundering and terrorist financing in Nigeria include: the **Money Laundering Prohibition Act 2011 (as amended), Terrorism (Prevention) Act, 2011 (as amended), Economic and Financial Crimes Commission (Establishment) Act, 2004, Central Bank of Nigeria (CBN) (Anti-Money Laundering and Combating the Financing of Terrorism in Banks and other Financial Institutions in Nigeria) Regulations 2013, Anti-Money Laundering/ Combating the Financing of Terrorism (AML/CFT) Regulations for Designated non- Financial Businesses and Professions in Nigeria 2013** and the **Anti-Money Laundering/Combating the Financing of Terrorism (AML/CFT) Reporting Guidelines 2012**.

---

113 The Joint Money Laundering Steering Group JMLSG, *Prevention of Money Laundering/Combating Terrorist Financing* (2017) revised version, Guidance for the United Kingdom Financial Sector Part I, June 2017, Paragraph 6.33. Please note that STR and SAR are the same even if the names are different. For more information, see Ellinger, E.P. (2011) *Modern Banking Law*, 5th edition (Oxford University Press), 97.

3.1.2 United States

The laws enacted to combat money laundering and terrorist financing in the United States include: the **Currency and Foreign Transactions Reporting Act of 1970 (which legislative framework is commonly referred to as the 'Bank Secrecy Act' or 'BSA') as amended, Uniting and Strengthening America by Providing Appropriate Tools Required to Intercept and Obstruct Terrorism (USA PATRIOT ACT) Act of 2001, Title 18 of the United States Code, Codified Bank Secrecy Act (BSA) Regulations (31 CFR)**, the **Bank Secrecy Act/Anti-Money Laundering Examination Manual 2014** and the **Bank Secrecy Act/ Anti-Money Laundering Examination Manual for Money Service Businesses 2008.**

3.1.3 United Kingdom

The laws enacted to combat money laundering and terrorist financing in the United Kingdom include: **Proceeds of Crime Act 2002 (as amended), Criminal Finances Act 2017, Terrorism Act 2000, Anti-Terrorism Crime and Security Act 2001, Money Laundering, Terrorist Financing and Transfer of Funds (Information on the Payer) Regulations 2017, the Financial Conduct Authority Handbook, Senior Management Arrangements, Systems and Controls (SYSC)** and the **Joint Money Laundering Steering Group (JMLSG): Prevention of money laundering/combating terrorist financing, 2017 Revised Version: Guidance for the UK Financial Sector Part I, Part II and Part III.**

3.2 Reporting Requirements

3.2.1 Nigeria

3.2.1.1 What to File

A financial institution or designated non-financial institution is required to report any suspicious transaction relating to money laundering and terrorist financing.[114] A transaction is deemed to be suspicious if it involves a frequency which is unjustifiable or unreasonable[115] or is surrounded by conditions of unusual or unjustified complexity.[116] It is also deemed suspicious if it appears to have no economic justification or lawful objective[117] or in the opinion of the financial institution or designated non-financial institution involves terrorist financing or is inconsistent with the known transaction pattern of the account or business relationship.[118] The report required to be filed is called a Suspicious Transaction Report (STR).[119]

In addition to reporting any suspicious transaction, a financial institution or designated non-financial institution is also required to report a transfer to or from a foreign country of funds or securities by a person or body corporate including a money service business of a sum exceeding ten thousand US dollars or its equivalent.[120] The law also requires a financial institution or designated non-financial institution to report in writing any single transaction, lodgement or transfer of funds in excess of five million naira or its equivalent in the case of an individual or ten million naira or its equivalent in the case of a body corporate.[121] The report required to be filed is called a Currency Transaction Report (CTR).[122]

---

114 Money Laundering Prohibition Act 2011 (as amended), s. 6 (2)

115 Money Laundering Prohibition Act 2011 (as amended), s. 6 (1) (a)

116 Money Laundering Prohibition Act 2011 (as amended), s. 6 (1) (b)

117 Money Laundering Prohibition Act 2011 (as amended), s. 6 (1) (c)

118 Money Laundering Prohibition Act 2011 (as amended), s. 6 (1) (d), See also the CBN (Anti-Money Laundering and Combating the Financing of Terrorism in Banks and Other Financial Institutions in Nigeria) Regulations, 2013, Regulation 31 (1) for the definition of a Suspicious Transaction.

119 Nigerian Financial Intelligence Unit: Anti-Money Laundering/Combating the Financing of Terrorism (AML/CFT) Reporting Guidelines 2012, Paragraph 2.

120 Money Laundering Prohibition Act 2011 (as amended), s. 2 (1)

121 Money Laundering Prohibition Act 2011 (as amended), s. 10 (1)

122 Nigerian Financial Intelligence Unit: Anti-Money Laundering/Combating the Financing of Terrorism (AML/CFT) Reporting Guidelines 2012, Paragraph 2.

3.2.1.2 Where to File

A financial institution or a designated non-financial institution is required to file a STR with the Economic and Financial Crimes Commission (EFCC).[123]

A financial institution or a designated non-financial institution is also required to file a CTR with the Central Bank of Nigeria, Securities and Exchange Commission or the EFCC in writing.[124]

Designated non-financial institutions like Casinos and Real Estate Agents are required to provide the Special Control Unit against Money Laundering with a copy of what they filed with the EFCC.[125]

Upon receiving the STR or CTR from a financial institution or designated non-financial institution, EFCC may order the Bank to halt any transaction on the account. The order is called a 'Place No Debit' (PND) order.

It is only when an ex-parte order has been made by the Court that the Chairman of the EFCC will issue a PND order addressed to the Manager of the Bank as person in control of the account to freeze the account.[126]

A bank who receives a PND order from the EFCC must immediately freeze the suspect's account. There have been cases in the past where bank officials deliberately ignore EFCC order of PND on

---

123 Money Laundering Prohibition Act 2011 (as amended), s. 6 (2) (c)

124 Money Laundering Prohibition Act 2011 (as amended), s. 2 (1), s. (10) (1)

125 Anti-Money Laundering/Combating the Financing of Terrorism (AML/CFT) Regulations for Designated Non-Financial Businesses and Professions in Nigeria 2013, Regulation 6

126 By Section 34(1) of the Economic and Financial Crimes Commission (Establishment) Act, 2004, the Chairman of the Economic and Financial Crimes Commission or any officer authorized by him may, if satisfied that the money in the account of a person is made through the commission of a money laundering offence, apply to the Court exparte for power to issue or instruct a bank examiner or such other appropriate regulatory authority to issue an order as specified in Form B of the Schedule to the EFCC Act, addressed to the manager of the bank or any person in control of the financial institution where the account is or believed by him to be or the head office of the bank or other financial institution to freeze the account. See Dangabar v. F.R.N. (2014) 12 N.W.L.R. (Pt. 1422) 575 at 611 for more on this.

suspects account or inform suspect about the PND to enable them make withdrawals using their ATM cards. The EFCC has stated that it would no longer condone such behaviour.[127]

CASE STUDY: EFCC ORDER OF "PLACE NO DEBIT" ON SUSPECTS ACCOUNT

Former First Lady, Patience Jonathan had filed a two hundred-million-naira fundamental rights enforcement suit against Skye Bank Plc sometime in September, 2016, following the freezing of four bank accounts, which she claims the Economic and Financial Crimes Commission (EFCC) has used to inconvenience and embarrass her.

The four accounts, lodged with Skye Bank Plc, are in the name of four companies which is said to have a balance of thirty-one million four hundred thousand dollars.

The four companies are Pluto Property and Investment Company Limited; Seagate Property Development & Investment Co. Limited; Trans Ocean Property and Investment Company Limited and Development Company Limited and Globus Integrated Service Limited.

In an affidavit filed before the Court and deposed to by one Sammie Somiari, a legal practitioner on behalf of Patience Jonathan, the deponents claim that the EFCC **placed a No Debit Order** on the four accounts in July in the course of probing one Waripamo Dudafa, a former Special Adviser on Domestic Affairs to former President Goodluck Jonathan.

After its investigations, the EFCC went ahead to file an amended 17-count against Dudafa and seven others, including the four companies, with the defendants being accused of conspiring to conceal the monies which the EFCC claimed they ought to have known formed parts of the proceeds of an unlawful act.

---

127 Economic and Financial Crimes Commission (2017), 'Anti-Graft War: EFCC Sensitizes Compliance Officers of Banks', Available at: https://efccnigeria.org/efcc/news/2654-anti-graft-war-efcc-sensitizes-compliance-officers-of-banks (accessed 10 October 2017).

In the affidavit however, Sammie Somiari claims that it was Dudafa who helped Mrs Patience Jonathan to open the four bank accounts which the EFCC froze.

According to him, Dudafa had on March 22, 2010 brought two Skye Bank officers, Demola Bolodeoku and Dipo Oshodi, to meet the former first lady at home to open five accounts.

He, however, claimed that after the five accounts were opened, Mrs Patience Jonathan later discovered that Dudafa opened only one of the accounts in her name while the other four were opened in the names of companies belonging to Dudafa.

Somiari added "that Mrs Jonathan complained about this to Honourable Dudafa, who at her prompting and instance promised to effect the change of the said accounts to the applicant's name; and to effect this change, Honourable Dudafa brought the said bank manager, Mr. Dipo Oshodi, who claimed to have effected the changes. This was about April 2014.

"The bank official, Mr. Dipo Oshodi, as it would appear did not effect or reflect the instruction of the applicant to change the said accounts to her name(s) despite repeated requests.

The deponent also claims that Mrs Patience Jonathan who is said to be away for an urgent medical treatment abroad, is the sole signatory to the accounts as the money belongs to her.

The affidavit also said that the ATM credit cards bearing the said companies' names were brought to Mrs Jonathan by the bank manager who promised to replace them once the cards bearing the changed names were available, but he never did.

"However, since 2010 up until 2014 and thereafter, Mrs Jonathan had been using the cards on the said accounts and operating the said accounts without let or hindrance. Even in May, June and July 2016, the former First Lady traveled overseas for medical treatment and was using the said credit cards abroad up until July 7, 2016 or thereabouts when the cards stopped functioning."

In her fundamental rights action before the court, the wife of the former President is asking the court to compel the EFCC to immediately vacate the "No Debit Order" placed on her accounts.

She also says the action of the EFCC without a court order or prior notice to her is illegal, overbearing and constitutes a breach of her fundamental rights as enshrined in **Section 33, 34, 35 & 36 of the 1999 Constitution**.

She wants the court to order Skye Bank to pay her damages in the sum of two hundred million naira for what she termed a violation of her right to own personal property under **Section 44 of the Constitution**.[128]

3.2.1.3 When to File

A financial institution that suspects or has reason to suspect that funds are the proceeds of a criminal activity or are related to terrorist financing, is required to report its suspicions **immediately and without delay.**[129] The report is expected to be filed not later than within 24 hours.[130]

All suspicious transactions, including attempted transactions are to be reported regardless of the amount involved.[131]

The CTR on the other hand is to be filed within 7 days from the date of the transaction.[132]

3.2.1.4 Confidentiality of STRS/Tipping Off (General Rule)

Financial institutions, their directors, officers and employees (permanent and temporary) are prohibited from disclosing the fact that a report is required to be filed with the competent authorities.[133]

---

128 Channels Television (2016), 'Patience Jonathan Sues EFCC For Placing 'No Debit Order' On $31.4m Account', Available at: https://www.channelstv.com/2016/09/10/patience-jonathan-sues-efcc-for-placing-no-debit-order-on-31-4m-account/ (accessed 10 October 2017).
129 Money Laundering Prohibition Act 2011 (as amended), s. 6 (2)
130 CBN (Anti-Money Laundering and Combating the Financing of Terrorism in Banks and Other Financial Institutions in Nigeria) Regulations, 2013, Regulation 31 (3)
131 CBN (Anti-Money Laundering and Combating the Financing of Terrorism in Banks and Other Financial Institutions in Nigeria) Regulations, 2013, Regulation 32 (7)
132 Money Laundering Prohibition Act 2011 (as amended), s. 2 (1), s. 10 (1)
133 Money Laundering Prohibition Act 2011 (as amended), s. 16 (1) (a)

3.2.1.5 Confidentiality of STRS/Tipping Off (Exception)

There are no exceptions to the general rule.[134]

3.2.1.6 Penalties

A person who discloses the fact that a report is required to be filed is liable on conviction to imprisonment for a term of not less than two years or a fine of not less than ten million naira.[135]

A person who fails to file a STR or CTR would be liable to imprisonment for a term of not less than 3 years or a fine of ten million naira or to both, in the case of an individual and twenty-five million naira in the case of a body corporate.[136]

3.2.2 United States

3.2.2.1 What to File

3.2.2.1.1 Banks

Every bank is required to file a report of any suspicious transaction relevant to a possible violation of law or regulation.[137] A transaction requires reporting if it is conducted or attempted by, at, or through the bank, it involves or aggregates at least five thousand dollars in funds or other assets, and the bank knows, suspects or has reason to suspect that:

  i. The transaction involves funds derived from illegal activities or is intended or conducted in order to hide or disguise funds or assets derived from illegal activities (including,

---

134 Money Laundering Prohibition Act 2011 (as amended), s. 16 (1) which provides for no exception to the General Rule

135 Money Laundering Prohibition Act 2011 (as amended), s. 16 (2) (a)

136 Money Laundering Prohibition Act 2011 (as amended), s. 16 (2) (b)

137 Codified Bank Secrecy Act Regulations (31 CFR, s. 1020.320 (a) (1))

without limitation, the ownership, nature, source, location, or control of such funds or assets) as part of a plan to violate or evade any federal law or regulation or to avoid any transaction reporting requirement under federal law or regulation,

ii. The transaction is designed to evade any requirements of this chapter or of any other regulations promulgated under the Bank Secrecy Act, or

iii. The transaction has no business or apparent lawful purpose or is not the sort in which the particular customer would normally be expected to engage, and the bank knows of no reasonable explanation for the transaction after examining the available facts, including the background and possible purpose of the transaction.[138]

A suspicious transaction shall be reported by completing a Suspicious Activity Report (SAR).[139]

In addition to filing of a SAR, Banks are required to file a report of each deposit, withdrawal, exchange of currency or other payment or transfer, by, through or to such financial institution which involves a transaction in currency of more than ten thousand US dollars. This report is referred to as a Currency Transaction Report.[140]

3.2.2.1.2 Money Service Businesses

Every money service business is required to file a report of any suspicious transaction relevant to a possible violation of law or regulation.[141] A transaction requires reporting if it is conducted or attempted by, at or through a money service business, involves or aggregates funds or other assets of at least two thousand dollars and the money service business knows, suspects or has reason to suspect that the transaction (or a pattern of transactions of which the transaction is a part):

---

138 Codified Bank Secrecy Act Regulations (31 CFR, s. 1020.320 (a) (2))
139 Codified Bank Secrecy Act Regulations (31 CFR, s. 1020.320 (b) (1))
140 Codified Bank Secrecy Act Regulations (31 CFR, s. 1010.311)
141 Codified Bank Secrecy Act Regulations (31 CFR, s. 1022.320 (a) (1))

i.   Involves funds derived from illegal activity or is intended or conducted in order to hide or disguise funds or assets derived from illegal activity (including without limitation, the ownership, nature, source, location, or control of such funds or assets) as part of a plan to violate or evade any federal law or regulation or to avoid any transaction reporting requirement under Federal law or regulation

ii. Is designed, whether through structuring or other means, to evade any requirements of this chapter or of any other regulations promulgated under the Bank Secrecy Act, as amended.

iii. Serves no business or apparent lawful purpose, and the reporting money service business knows of no reasonable explanation for the transaction after examining the available facts, including the background and possible purpose of the transaction.

iv. Involves use of the money service business to facilitate criminal activity.[142]

A suspicious transaction shall be reported by completing a Suspicious Activity Report – MSB ('SAR-MSB')[143]

In addition to filing a SAR, a money service business is also required to file a report of each deposit, withdrawal, exchange of currency or other payment or transfer, by, through or to such financial institution which involves a transaction in currency of more than ten thousand dollars.[144]

CASE STUDY: NEED FOR A MONEY SERVICE BUSINESS TO TERMINATE OR DISCIPLINE AGENTS WHO REPEATEDLY VIOLATE ANTI-MONEY LAUNDERING RULES THROUGH THEIR STRUCTURING ACTIVITY

---

142 Codified Bank Secrecy Act Regulations (31 CFR, s. 1022.320 (a) (2))

143 Codified Bank Secrecy Act Regulations (31 CFR, s. 1022.320 (b) (1))

144 Codified Bank Secrecy Act Regulations (31 CFR, s. 1010.311)

Case 3.1: United States Department of Justice v. Western Union Company 17-015

The Western Union Company, a global money services business headquartered in Englewood, Colorado, had on the 19th day of January 2017 agreed to forfeit five hundred and eighty-six million US dollars and enter into agreements with the Justice Department, the Federal Trade Commission (FTC), and several United States Attorney's Offices, including the Central District of California.

In its agreement with the Justice Department, Western Union admits to criminal violations, including willfully failing to maintain an effective anti-money laundering (AML) program and aiding and abetting wire fraud.

According to admissions contained in a deferred prosecution agreement (DPA) and an accompanying statement of facts filed on the 19th of January, 2017, between 2004 and 2012, Western Union violated **U.S. laws – the Bank Secrecy Act (BSA) and anti-fraud statutes** – by processing hundreds of thousands of transactions for Western Union agents and others involved in an international consumer fraud scheme.

As part of the scheme, fraudsters contacted victims in the United States and falsely posed as family members in need or promised prizes or job opportunities. The fraudsters directed the victims to send money through Western Union to help their relative or claim their prize. Various Western Union agents were complicit in these fraud schemes, often processing the fraud payments for the fraudsters in return for a cut of the fraud proceeds.

Western Union knew of, but failed to take corrective action against, Western Union agents involved in or facilitating fraud-related transactions. Beginning in at least 2004, Western Union recorded customer complaints about fraudulently induced payments in what are known as consumer fraud reports (CFRs). In 2004, Western Union's Corporate Security Department proposed global guidelines for discipline and suspension of Western Union agents that processed a materially elevated number of fraud transactions. In these guidelines, the Corporate Security Department effectively recommended automatically suspending any agent that paid 15 CFRs within 120 days. Had Western Union implemented these proposed guidelines, it would have prevented significant fraud losses to victims and would have resulted in corrective action against more than 2,000 agents worldwide between 2004 and 2012.

Court documents also show Western Union's BSA failures spanned eight years and involved, among other things, the acquisition of a significant agent that Western Union knew prior to the acquisition had an ineffective AML program and had contracted with other agents that were facilitating significant levels of consumer fraud. Despite this knowledge, Western Union moved forward with the acquisition and did not remedy the AML failures or terminate the high-fraud agents.

Similarly, Western Union failed to terminate or discipline agents who repeatedly violated the BSA and Western Union policy through their structuring activity in the Central District of California, the Eastern District of Pennsylvania, New York City and elsewhere. The BSA requires financial institutions, including money services businesses such as Western Union, to file currency transaction reports (CTRs) for transactions in currency greater than ten thousand dollars in a single day. To evade the filing of a CTR and identification requirements, criminals will often structure their currency transactions so that no single transaction exceeds the ten thousand dollars threshold. Financial institutions are required to report suspected structuring where the aggregate number of transactions by or on behalf of any person exceeds more than ten thousand dollars during one business day. Western Union knew that certain of its U.S. Agents were allowing or aiding and abetting structuring by their customers. Rather than taking corrective action to eliminate structuring at and by its agents, Western Union, among other things, allowed agents to continue sending transactions through Western Union's system and paid agents bonuses. Despite repeated compliance reviews identifying suspicious or illegal behavior by its agents, Western Union almost never identified those agents as the subjects of required reports to law enforcement

In the Central District of California, an investigation by the FBI's Los Angeles Field Office, IRS Criminal Investigation and local partners into Western Union's largest West Coast agent found that U.S.

Shen Zhou International in Monterey Park sent more than three hundred and ten million dollars in Western Union transactions to China – approximately 50 percent of which were structured. The owner of Shen Zhou – Zhihe "Frank" Wang, 60, of Monterey Park – pleaded guilty late 2013 to one count of structuring international transactions to evade reporting requirement in Santa Ana federal court. Wang admitted making numerous transmission to China in two thousand five hundred dollars amounts, which is just below the three thousand dollars amount that triggers various BSA reporting and record-keeping requirements for money transmitters, as well as the ten thousand dollars amount that triggers CTR filings. Despite finding repeated violations of Western Union policies, Western Union took no disciplinary action against Shen Zhou beyond one 90-day probation in January 2006 during which Shen Zhou continued to process transactions.

Based on information uncovered in the Shen Zhou investigation, further investigation by the FBI into Western Union and its "China Corridor" agents found widespread structuring violations. Despite the fact that these high-volume agents failed multiple compliance reviews and continued to aid their customers in illegal activity, Western Union took little to no discipline against the agents, continued to allow the agents to process money transfers and actively encouraged the China Corridor agents to expand their businesses. Between 2003 and 2012, the top five China Corridor agents in the United States structured hundreds of millions of dollars in Western Union transactions.

FBI's investigation uncovered hundreds of millions of dollars being sent to China in structured transactions designed to avoid the reporting requirements of the Bank Secrecy Act, and much of the money was sent to China by illegal immigrants to pay their human smugglers," said U.S. Attorney Decker. "In the case being prosecuted by my office, a Western Union agent has pleaded guilty to federal charges of structuring transactions – illegal conduct the company knew about for at least five years. Western Union documents indicate that its employees fought to keep this agent – as well as several other high-volume independent agents in New York City – working for Western Union because of the high volume of their activity. This action today will ensure that Western Union effectively controls its agents and prevents the use of its money transfer system for illegal purposes.

"Los Angeles defendant Wang's company was considered to be among the largest Western Union agents in the United States as over three hundred and ten million dollars was sent to China in a span of five years, half of which was illegally structured and transmitted using false identification," said Deirdre Fike, the Assistant Director in Charge of the FBI's Los Angeles Field Office. "Rather than ensuring their high-volume agents were operating above-board, Western Union rewarded them without regard to the blatant lack of compliance and illegal practices taking place. **This settlement should go a long way in thwarting the proceeds of illicit transactions being sent to China to fund human smuggling or drug trafficking, as well as to interrupt the ease with which scam artists flout U.S. banking regulations in schemes devised to defraud vulnerable Americans.**"

In taking responsibility for their actions, Western Union had agreed to cooperate and forfeit more than five hundred million dollars for their role in circumventing Bank Secrecy Act reporting requirements.

Western Union entered into a DPA in connection with a two-count felony criminal information filed on the 19th day of January 2017 in the Middle District of Pennsylvania that charges Western Union with willfully failing to maintain an effective AML program and aiding and abetting wire fraud. Pursuant to the DPA, Western Union has agreed to forfeit five hundred and eighty-six million dollars and also agreed to enhanced compliance obligations to prevent a repeat of the charged conduct, including creating policies and procedures:

- for corrective action against agents that pose an unacceptable risk of money laundering or have demonstrated systemic, willful or repeated lapses in compliance;
- that ensure that its agents around the world will adhere to U.S. regulatory and AML standards; and
- that ensure that the company will report suspicious or illegal activity by its agents or related to consumer fraud reports.

"As this case shows, wiring money can be the fastest way to send it – directly into the pockets of criminals and scam artists," said Acting Assistant Attorney General David Bitkower of the Justice Department's Criminal Division. "Western Union is now paying the price for placing profits ahead of its own customers. Together with our colleagues, the Criminal Division will both hold to account those who facilitate fraud and abuse of vulnerable populations, and also work to recoup losses and compensate victims."

In a related case, Western Union agreed to settle charges by the FTC in a complaint filed on January 19, 2017, in the U.S. District Court for the Middle District of Pennsylvania, alleging that the company's conduct violated the FTC Act. The complaint charges that for many years, fraudsters around the world have used Western Union's money transfer system even though the company has long been aware of the problem, and that some Western Union agents have been complicit in fraud. The FTC's complaint alleges that Western Union declined to put in place effective anti-fraud policies and procedures and has failed to act promptly against problem agents. Western Union has identified many of the problem agents but has profited from their actions by not promptly suspending and terminating them.

"Western Union owes a responsibility to American consumers to guard against fraud, but instead the company looked the other way, and its system facilitated scammers and rip-offs," said FTC Chairwoman Edith Ramirez. "The agreements we are announcing today will ensure Western Union changes the way it conducts its business and provides more than half billion dollars for refunds to consumers who were harmed by the company's unlawful behavior."

In resolving the FTC charges, Western Union agreed to a monetary judgment of five hundred and eighty-six million dollars and to implement and maintain a comprehensive anti-fraud program with training for its agents and their front-line associates, monitoring to detect and prevent fraud-induced money transfers, due diligence on all new and renewing company agents, and suspension or termination of noncompliant agents.

The FTC order prohibits Western Union from transmitting a money transfer that it knows or reasonably should know is fraud-induced, and requires it to:

- block money transfers sent to any person who is the subject of a fraud report;
- provide clear and conspicuous consumer fraud warnings on its paper and electronic money transfer forms;
- increase the availability of websites and telephone numbers that enable consumers to file fraud complaints; and
- refund a fraudulently induced money transfer if the company failed to comply with its anti-fraud procedures in connection with that transaction.

In addition, consistent with the telemarketing sales rule, Western Union must not process a money transfer that it knows or should know is payment for a telemarketing transaction. The company's compliance with the order will be monitored for three years by an independent compliance auditor.

Since 2001, the Justice Department has charged and convicted 29 owners or employees of Western Union agents for their roles in fraudulent and structured transactions.

The investigation into Western Union was conducted by the FBI's Los Angeles Field Office and its local partners; the United States Postal Inspection Service's Philadelphia Division's Harrisburg, Pennsylvania, Office; Internal Revenue Service (IRS) Criminal Investigation; U.S. Immigration and Customs Enforcement's Homeland Security Investigations (HSI), Philadelphia; the Office of Inspector General for the Board of Governors of the Federal Reserve System and the Consumer Financial Protection Bureau; the United States Department of Treasury, Office of Inspector General; the Broward County (Florida) Sheriff's Office; and the United States Department of Labor.

The case is being prosecuted by Assistant U.S. Attorney Gregory W. Staples of the Santa Ana Branch Office, along with Trial Attorney Margaret A. Moeser of the Criminal Division's Money Laundering and Asset Recovery Section's Bank Integrity Unit and Assistant U.S. Attorneys in the Middle District of Pennsylvania, the Eastern District of Pennsylvania and the Southern District of Florida. Assistant United States Attorney Frank Kortum of the Asset Forfeiture Section, along with asset forfeiture attorneys in the other U.S. Attorney's Offices and the Money Laundering and Asset Recovery Section, provided significant assistance in this matter. The Justice Department appreciates the significant cooperation and assistance provided by the FTC in this matter.[145]

3.2.2.2 Where to File

3.2.2.2.1 Banks

The SAR is to be filed with the Financial Crimes Enforcement Network (FinCEN) in a central location, to be determined by FinCEN, as indicated in the instructions to the SAR.[146]

The CTR is to be filed with the Commissioner of Internal Revenue, unless otherwise specified.[147]

3.2.2.2.2 Money Service Businesses

The SAR-MSB is to be filed in a central location to be determined by FinCEN, as indicated in the instructions to the SAR-MSB.[148]

The CTR is to be filed with the Commissioner of Internal Revenue, unless otherwise specified.[149]

---

145 United States Department of Justice (2017), 'Western Union Admits Anti-Money Laundering and Consumer Fraud Violations, Will Forfeit $586 Million in Settlement with Justice and FTC', Available at: https://www.justice.gov/usao-cdca/pr/western-union-admits-anti-money-laundering-and-consumer-fraud-violations-will-forfeit (accessed 27 April 2017).

146 Codified Bank Secrecy Act Regulations (31 CFR, s. 1020.320 (b) (2))

147 Codified Bank Secrecy Act Regulations (31 CFR, s. 1010.306 (a) (3))

148 Codified Bank Secrecy Act Regulations (31 CFR, s. 1022.320 (b) (2))

149 Codified Bank Secrecy Act Regulations (31 CFR, s. 1010.306 (a) (3))

3.2.2.3 When to File

3.2.2.3.1 Banks

A bank is required to file a SAR no later than 30 calendar days after the date of initial detection by the bank of facts that may constitute a basis for filing a SAR. If no suspect was identified on the date of the detection of the incident requiring the filing, a bank may delay filing a SAR for an additional 30 calendar days to identify a suspect. In no case is reporting to be delayed more than 60 calendar days after the date of initial detection of a reportable transaction. In situations involving violations that require immediate attention, such as, for example, on-going money laundering schemes, the bank shall notify by telephone, an appropriate law enforcement authority in addition to filing timely a SAR.[150]

A CTR is also required to be filed by the bank within 15 days following the day on which the reportable transaction occurred.[151]

3.2.2.3.2 Money Service Businesses

A money service business is required to file each SAR-MSB no later than 30 calendar days after the date of the initial detection by the money service business of facts that may constitute a basis for filing a SAR-MSB.[152]

A CTR is also required to be filed by the money service business within 15 days following the day on which the reportable transaction occurred.[153]

3.2.2.4 Confidentiality of Sars/Tipping Off (General Rule)

---

150 Codified Bank Secrecy Act Regulations (31 CFR, s. 1020.320 (b) (3))

151 Codified Bank Secrecy Act Regulations (31 CFR, s. 1010.306 (a) (1))

152 Codified Bank Secrecy Act Regulations (31 CFR, s. 1022.320 (b) (3))

153 Codified Bank Secrecy Act Regulations (31 CFR, s. 1010.306 (a) (1))

3.2.2.4.1 Banks and Money Service Businesses

No bank/money service business and no director, officer, employee, or agent of any bank/money service business is to disclose a SAR or any information that would reveal the existence of a SAR. Any bank, and any director, officer, employee, or agent of any bank/money service business that is subpoenaed or otherwise requested to disclose a SAR or any information that would reveal the existence of a SAR, shall decline to produce the SAR or such information. The bank/money service business is also to notify FinCEN of any such request and the response thereto.[154]

3.2.2.5 Confidentiality of SARS/Tipping Off (Exceptions)

3.2.2.5.1 Banks and Money Service Businesses

The disclosure by a bank/money service business, or any director, officer, employee, or agent of a bank/money service business of:

i.   A SAR, or any information that would reveal the existence of a SAR, to FinCEN or any Federal, State, or Local Law enforcement agency, or any Federal regulatory authority that examines the bank/money service business for compliance with the Bank Secrecy Act, or any State regulatory authority administering a State law that requires the bank/money service business to comply with the Bank Secrecy Act or otherwise authorizes the State authority to ensure that the bank/money service business complies with the Bank Secrecy Act; or[155]

ii. The underlying facts, transactions and documents upon which a SAR is based, including but not limited to, disclosures to another financial institution, or any director, officer,

---

154 Codified Bank Secrecy Act Regulations (31 CFR, s. 1020.320 (e) (1), s. 1022.320 (d) (1))

155 Codified Bank Secrecy Act Regulations (31 CFR, s. 1020.320 (e) (1) (A) (1), s. 1022.320 (d) (1) (A) (1))

employee, or agent of a financial institution, for the preparation of a Joint SAR; or[156]

iii. The sharing by a bank/money service business, or any director, officer, employee, or agent of the bank/money service
business, of a SAR, or any information that would reveal the
existence of a SAR, within the bank's/money service business's corporate organizational structure for purposes consistent with Title II of the Bank Secrecy Act as determined by
regulation or in guidance is not prohibited.[157]

3.2.2.6 Penalties

3.2.2.6.1 Civil Penalty

i. For any wilful violation, committed on or before October 12,
1984, of any reporting requirement for financial institutions,
the Secretary may assess upon any domestic financial institution, and upon any partner, director, officer, or employee
thereof who wilfully participates in the violation, a civil penalty not to exceed one thousand dollars.[158]

ii. For any wilful violation committed after October 12, 1984 and
before October 28, 1986, of any reporting requirement for financial institutions, the Secretary may assess upon any domestic financial institution, and upon any partner, director, officer,
or employee thereof who wilfully participates in the violation, a
civil penalty not to exceed ten thousand dollars.[159]

iii. For any wilful violation committed after October 27, 1986, of
any reporting requirement for financial institutions under
this part (except §103.24, §103.25 or §103.32), the Secretary

---

156 Codified Bank Secrecy Act Regulations (31 CFR, s. 1020.320 (e) (1) (A) (2),
s. 1022.320 (d) (1) (A) (2))

157 Codified Bank Secrecy Act Regulations (31 CFR, s. 1020.320 (e) (1) (B), s.
1022.320 (d) (1) (B))

158 Codified Bank Secrecy Act Regulations (31 CFR, s. 1010.820 (a))

159 Codified Bank Secrecy Act Regulations (31 CFR, s. 1010.820 (b))

may assess upon any domestic financial institution, and upon any partner, director, officer, or employee thereof who wilfully participates in the violation, a civil penalty not to exceed the greater of the amount (not to exceed $100,000) involved in the transaction or twenty-five thousand dollars.[160]

3.2.2.6.2 Criminal Penalty

Any person who violates any provision, may, upon conviction thereof, be fined not more than two hundred and fifty thousand dollars or be imprisoned not more than 5 years, or both.[161]

3.2.3 United Kingdom

3.2.3.1 What to File

A firm's nominated officer must report any transaction or activity that, after his evaluation, he knows or suspects, or has reasonable grounds to know or suspect, may be linked to money laundering or terrorist financing, or to attempted money laundering or terrorist financing.[162] Such report is called a Suspicious Activity Report.[163]

Having knowledge means actually knowing something to be true. In a criminal court, it must be proved that the individual in fact knew that a person was engaged in money laundering. That said, knowledge can be inferred from the surrounding circumstances; so,

160   Codified Bank Secrecy Act Regulations (31 CFR, s. 1010.820 (f))
161   Codified Bank Secrecy Act Regulations (31 CFR, s. 1010.840 (b))
162   Proceeds of Crime Act 2002 (as amended), s. 331; the Joint Money Laundering Steering Group JMLSG, *Prevention of money laundering/combating terrorist financing*, 2017 Revised Version, Guidance for the UK financial sector Part I June 2017 (Amended December 2017), Paragraph 6.33.
163   Joint Money Laundering Steering Group JMLSG, *Prevention of money laundering/combating terrorist financing*, 2017 Revised Version, Guidance for the UK financial sector Part I June 2017 (Amended December 2017), Chapter 6, See also Lilley, P. (2006), *Dirty Dealing: The Untold Truth About Global Money Laundering, International Crime and Terrorism*, Kogan Page Limited, United Kingdom.

for example, a failure to ask obvious questions may be relied upon by a jury to imply knowledge. The knowledge must, however, have come to the firm (or to the member of staff) in the course of business, or (in the case of a nominated officer) as a consequence of a disclosure under **Section 330 of the Proceeds of Crime Act (POCA) or Section 21A of the Terrorism Act.** Information that comes to the firm or staff member in other circumstances does not come within the scope of the regulated sector obligation to make a report. This does not preclude a report being made should staff choose to do so, or are obligated to do so by other parts of these Acts.[164]

Suspicion is more subjective and falls short of proof based on firm evidence. Suspicion has been defined by the courts as being beyond mere speculation and based on some foundation, for example:

"A degree of satisfaction and not necessarily amounting to belief but at least extending beyond speculation as to whether an event has occurred or not"; and

"Although the creation of suspicion requires a lesser factual basis than the creation of a belief, it must nonetheless be built upon some foundation."[165]

A transaction which appears unusual is not necessarily suspicious. Even customers with a stable and predictable transactions profile will have periodic transactions that are unusual for them. Many customers will, for perfectly good reasons, have an erratic pattern of transactions or account activity. So, the unusual is, in the first instance, only a basis for further enquiry, which may in turn require judgement as to whether it is suspicious. A transaction or activity may not

---

164 Joint Money Laundering Steering Group JMLSG, *Prevention of money laundering/combating terrorist financing*, 2017 Revised Version, Guidance for the UK financial sector Part I June 2017 (Amended December 2017), para. 6.10

165 Joint Money Laundering Steering Group JMLSG, *Prevention of money laundering/combating terrorist financing*, 2017 Revised Version, Guidance for the UK financial sector Part I, Paragraph 6.11

be suspicious at the time, but if suspicions are raised later, an obligation to report then arises.[166]

A member of staff, including the nominated officer, who considers a transaction or activity to be suspicious, would not necessarily be expected either to know or to establish the exact nature of any underlying criminal offence, or that the particular funds or property were definitely those arising from a crime or terrorist financing.[167]

Transactions, or proposed transactions, such as '419' scams, are attempted advance fee frauds, and not money laundering; they are therefore not reportable under POCA or the Terrorism Act, unless the fraud is successful, and the firm is aware of resulting criminal property.[168]

The objective test of suspicion would likely be met when there are demonstrated to be facts or circumstances, known to the member of staff, from which a reasonable person engaged in a business subject to the Money Laundering Regulations would have inferred knowledge, or formed the suspicion, that another person was engaged in money laundering or terrorist financing.[169]

To defend themselves against a charge that they failed to meet the objective test of suspicion, staff within financial sector firms would need to be able to demonstrate that they took reasonable steps in the particular circumstances, in the context of a risk-based approach, to know the customer and the rationale for the transaction, activity or instruction. It is important to bear in mind that, in

---

166 Joint Money Laundering Steering Group JMLSG, *Prevention of money laundering/combating terrorist financing*, 2017 Revised Version, Guidance for the UK financial sector Part I, Paragraph 6.12

167 Joint Money Laundering Steering Group JMLSG, *Prevention of money laundering/combating terrorist financing*, 2017 Revised Version, Guidance for the UK financial sector Part I, Paragraph 6.13

168 Joint Money Laundering Steering Group JMLSG, *Prevention of money laundering/combating terrorist financing*, 2017 Revised Version, Guidance for the UK financial sector Part I, Paragraph 6.14

169 Joint Money Laundering Steering Group JMLSG, *Prevention of money laundering/combating terrorist financing*, 2017 Revised Version, Guidance for the UK financial sector Part I, Paragraph 6.15

practice, members of a jury may decide, with the benefit of hindsight, whether the objective test has been met.[170]

Depending on the circumstances, a firm being served with a court order in relation to a customer may give rise to reasonable grounds for suspicion in relation to that customer. In such an event, firms should review the information it holds about that customer across the firm, in order to determine whether or not such grounds exist.[171]

3.2.3.2 Where to File
To avoid committing a failure to report offence, nominated officers must make their disclosures to the National Crime Agency (NCA). The national reception point for disclosure of suspicions, and for seeking consent to continue to proceed with the transaction or activity, is the UK Financial Intelligence Unit (FIU) within the NCA.[172]

3.2.3.3 When to File
Such reports must be made as soon as is reasonably practicable after the information comes to the nominated officer.[173]

The SARs consent regime has the practical effect of preventing an activity from going ahead for an initial notice period of 7 days,[174] and where appropriate, for a period of 31 days known as the 'moratorium

---

170 Joint Money Laundering Steering Group JMLSG, *Prevention of money laundering/combating terrorist financing*, 2017 Revised Version, Guidance for the UK financial sector Part I, Paragraph 6.16

171 Joint Money Laundering Steering Group JMLSG, *Prevention of money laundering/combating terrorist financing*, 2017 Revised Version, Guidance for the UK financial sector Part I, Paragraph 6.17

172 Joint Money Laundering Steering Group JMLSG, *Prevention of money laundering/combating terrorist financing*, 2017 Revised Version, Guidance for the UK financial sector Part I, Paragraph 6.40

173 Joint Money Laundering Steering Group JMLSG, *Prevention of money laundering/combating terrorist financing*, 2017 Revised Version, Guidance for the UK financial sector Part I June 2017 (Amended December 2017), Paragraph 6.33

174 Proceeds of Crime Act 2002 (as amended), s. 335 (5), s. 336 (7)

period'.[175] The moratorium period allows law enforcement agencies to gather evidence to determine whether further action, such as restraint of the funds, should take place.

There are times when law enforcement agents may not have sufficient time to gather evidence related to particularly complex activities, which are linked to overseas grand corruption or other serious crime. The provisions in the **United Kingdom Criminal Finances Act 2017** provide for the extension of the moratorium period by a court, for up to 31 days. This can be repeated up to 186 days (approximately 6 months), from the end of the initial 31-day moratorium period. The process will have judicial oversight and the interested party will be notified that an application has been made to extend the moratorium period.[176]

3.2.3.4 Confidentiality of SARS/Tipping Off (General Rule)

A person is not to disclose a SAR if such disclosure is likely to prejudice any investigation that might be conducted following the disclosure and the information on which the disclosure is based came to the person in the course of a business in the regulated sector.[177]

3.2.3.5 Confidentiality of SARS/Tipping Off (Exception)

i.   An employee, officer or partner of an undertaking does not commit an offence if the disclosure is to an employee, officer or partner of the same undertaking.[178]

ii. A person does not commit an offence in respect of a disclosure by a credit institution or a financial institution if—

   a.   The disclosure is to a credit institution or a financial institution,

---

175 Proceeds of Crime Act 2002 (as amended), s. 335 (6), s. 336 (8)
176 Criminal Finances Act 2017, s. 10
177 Proceeds of Crime Act 2002 (as amended), s. 333A (1)
178 Proceeds of Crime Act 2002 (as amended), s. 333B (1)

    b. The institution to whom the disclosure is made is situated in an EEA State or in a country or territory imposing equivalent money laundering requirements, and

    c. Both the institution making the disclosure and the institution to which it is made belong to the same group.[179]

iii. A professional legal adviser or a relevant professional adviser does not commit an offence under section 333A if—

(a) The disclosure is to professional legal adviser or a relevant professional adviser,

(b) both the person making the disclosure and the person to whom it is made carry on business in an EEA State or in a country or territory imposing equivalent money laundering requirements, and

(c) Those persons perform their professional activities within different undertakings that share common ownership, management or control.[180]

3.2.3.6 Penalties

3.2.3.6.1 Tipping Off

A person guilty of the offence of tipping off is liable on summary conviction to imprisonment for a term not exceeding 3 months or to a fine not exceeding level 5 on the standard scale or to both[181] and on conviction on indictment, to imprisonment for a term not exceeding two years, or to a fine, or to both.[182]

---

179 Proceeds of Crime Act 2002 (as amended), s. 333B (2)

180 Proceeds of Crime Act 2002 (as amended), s. 333B (4), See also Proceeds of Crime Act 2002 (as amended), s. 333C and D for more exceptions.

181 Proceeds of Crime Act 2002 (as amended), s. 333A (4) (a)

182 Proceeds of Crime Act 2002 (as amended), s. 333A (4) (b)

3.2.3.6.2 Failure to File a Sar

A person guilty of not filing a SAR is liable on summary conviction for a term not exceeding 6 months or to a fine not exceeding the statutory maximum or to both,[183] and on conviction on indictment, to imprisonment for a term not exceeding five years or to a fine or to both.[184]

CASE STUDY ON FAILURE TO FILE TIMELY AND COMPLETE SUSPICIOUS ACTIVITY REPORTS

Case 3.2: Financial Crimes Enforcement Network v. Great Eastern Bank of Florida No. 2002-02

During the relevant time period, Great Eastern failed to file Suspicious Activity Reports (SARs) on transactions for at least six customers that it "knew, suspected, or had reason to suspect" were reportable as suspicious under the Bank Secrecy Act (BSA). For example, Great Eastern failed to file a SAR on a customer that engaged in suspicious wire transfer activity in one Great Eastern account. The account received over nine hundred thousand dollars in 29 wire transfers from a foreign company, most of which was wired out the following day to the customer's account at another bank. The activity could not be supported by the normal operations of the customer's business. Indeed, this same customer engaged in nearly identical activity in another account at Great Eastern, and Great Eastern did file a SAR on the customer's activity in the other account, thus demonstrating that it did in fact recognize such behavior as suspicious.

In addition, Great Eastern failed to file a timely SAR for a customer that had millions of dollars of incoming and outgoing wires transfers, many from the same source.

Great Eastern only analyzed the transaction after it was specifically required to do so by the Federal Deposit Insurance Corporation (FDIC) in 1999, and only then determined that there was no

---

183 Proceeds of Crime Act 2002 (as amended), s. 334 (2) (a)
184 Proceeds of Crime Act 2002 (as amended), s. 334 (2) (b)

apparent business reason for the large amounts of wire transfer activity for this customer and filed a SAR. The information available to Great Eastern when it finally filed the SAR two years after the fact was the same information available to it at the time of the transaction. Great Eastern should have detected this transaction and have filed a SAR before being required to do so by the FDIC, two years after the transaction occurred.

1. Failure to File Complete SARs

For at least 14 other customer transactions, Great Eastern filed SARs, but in these SARs the Bank failed to include required information about the suspicious activity that it had in its files at the time it filed the SAR. For example, during the relevant time period, as noted above Great Eastern filed a SAR on a customer identifying wire transfers totaling over nine hundred thousand dollars that were wired out of the account almost immediately, but did not file a SAR on identical transactions engaged in by the same customer in another Great Eastern account. As an alternative to filing a second SAR, Great Eastern could have included this activity in the SAR that was filed, but it failed to do so, thus understating the scope of the suspicious activity by one-half.

During the relevant time period, Great Eastern filed a SAR which merely stated that a customer made a seventy-one thousand two hundred and fifty dollars deposit to an account that had minimal activity prior to that time. The report did not adequately describe the alleged suspicious activity and, therefore, the SAR failed to include important required information that was readily available to Great Eastern – that is, why it was filing the SAR. The SAR failed to report that six of the checks in the deposit were sequentially numbered checks from a single account in even thousand-dollar amounts. Furthermore, the SAR failed to report that the traveler's check portion of the deposit was comprised of 236 checks from 10 banks. The SAR failed to report that wire transfers shortly after the deposit transferred the majority of the funds out of the account. This failure to indicate on the form why the Bank thought the transaction was suspicious undermines the utility of the SAR in alerting law enforcement to transactions that deserve investigation.

Similarly, Great Eastern filed a SAR that simply reported a fifty thousand dollars deposit of money orders. The SAR did not describe the monetary instruments by denomination, issuer, or place of origin as explicitly required by the instructions to the SAR form. The SAR did not state that there was little activity in the account but for the deposit and did not indicate that the customer withdrew the funds soon after the deposit. Again, the SAR did not provide law enforcement with important information about the transaction and why it believed the transaction was suspicious based on information that was readily available to the bank.

In addition, Great Eastern failed to maintain sufficient documentation to support the filing of numerous SARs. With respect to SARs filed on 14 customers, the files contained only a portion of the necessary documentation required by the SAR regulations. In some cases, documents included in the file as supporting documentation were not legible. Supporting documentation is an important means of preserving evidence and enabling law enforcement to follow up on a SAR. Therefore, Great Eastern failed to file SARs that were timely and complete in accordance with **31 U.S.C. §5318(g)** and **31 CFR §1010.320.**[185]

Case 3.3: Financial Crimes Enforcement Network v. Korea Exchange Bank No. 2003-04

FinCEN determined that between March 1998 and May 2001, the Broadway Branch of the Korea Exchange Bank failed to file approximately thirty-nine (39) suspicious activity reports ("SARs") involving nearly thirty-two million dollars in suspicious transactions, in a timely manner in violation of **31 U.S.C. §5318(g)** and **31 CFR §1010.320.**

---

185   United States of America Department of the Treasury Financial Crimes Enforcement Network (2002), 'IN THE MATTER OF GREAT EASTERN BANK OF FLORIDA MIAMI FLORIDA', Available at: https://www.fincen.gov/sites/default/files/enforcement_action/geassessfinal.pdf (accessed 2 April 2017).

A bank must report any transaction involving or aggregating to at least five thousand dollars that it "knows, suspects, or has reason to suspect" (i) involves funds derived from illegal activities or is conducted to disguise funds derived from illegal activities, (ii) is designed to evade the reporting or recordkeeping requirements of the BSA (e.g., structuring transactions to avoid currency transaction reporting) or (iii) "has no business or apparent lawful purpose or is not the sort in which the particular customer would normally be expected to engage, and the bank knows of no reasonable explanation for the transaction after examining the available facts, including the background and possible purpose of the transaction." **31 USC §5318(g)** and **31 CFR §1010.320**.

As an FDIC-supervised bank, the Broadway Branch was on notice of the SAR requirements and the need to have policies and procedures in place to ensure these requirements are met. Section 326.8(b) of the FDIC's regulations requires a bank to develop and administer a program to assure compliance with the BSA. According to the FDIC, at a minimum, the bank's system of internal controls must be designed to "identify reportable transactions at a point where all of the information necessary to properly complete the required reporting forms can be obtained." See, FDIC Manual of Exam Policies, Financial Recordkeeping and Reporting Regulations, Section 9.4. The system must also "ensure that all required reports are completed accurately."

Information in the reports of examination of the Broadway Branch by the FDIC shows that the Branch knew, suspected or had reason to suspect that certain transactions were "suspicious" within the meaning of the BSA but failed to file SARs for these transactions. In its March 31, 1999 examination report, the FDIC specifically cited the Branch for the failure to establish or implement an adequate system of internal controls for the identification, investigation, documentation, and reporting of suspicious transactions. The FDIC also found inadequate BSA and SAR compliance in the October 18, 1999 and March 31, 2001 examinations of the Branch.

To comply with the SAR rule, a financial institution must be able to determine whether transactions are in fact reportable. Therefore, a financial institution is required to have in place systems to identify the kinds of transactions that may be a high risk for money laundering or that exhibit indicia of suspicious activity, taking into account the type of products and services it offers and the nature of its customers. Otherwise, a financial institution cannot assure that it is in fact reporting suspicious transactions as required by the BSA. In this case, the record shows that during the relevant time period, the Broadway Branch had information about its customers and their transactions that caused it to "know, suspect, or have reason to suspect" that many transactions were reportable suspicious transactions, yet the Branch failed to report these transactions because its procedures to identify, analyze, document, or report suspicious activity were not properly implemented. As a result, the Broadway Branch violated the SAR requirements of **31 U.S.C. §5318(g)** and **31 CFR §1010.320**.

1. Frequent Large Cash Deposits

The Broadway Branch's review of cash deposits in large amounts was inadequate for the identification of suspicious patterns of activity. As a result, the Branch failed to timely file SARs regarding suspicious transactions by at least five (5) customers in violation of **31 U.S.C. §5318(g)** and **31 CFR §1010.320.**

For example, in a span of two months thirty-seven cash deposits in excess of ten thousand dollars, totaling almost one million two hundred thousand dollars, were made to the account of a company that imported wigs for wholesale sales. Despite the unusual cash deposit activity on the customer's account that lacked any apparent legal or business purpose, the Branch failed to detect and report the suspicious pattern of transactions. The FDIC noted in its March 31, 1999 report of examination that, because the customer had such an exceptionally high volume of cash deposits over the past year, the FDIC was unable to review more than two months of activity in the account. In June 1999, the Branch filed a SAR in response to the FDIC's citation of the Branch in its examination findings for SAR filing violations.

2. Frequent Large Cash Deposits Followed by Wire Transfers

The Broadway Branch failed to implement adequate procedures to detect suspicious patterns of activity involving numerous cash deposits in large amounts followed by outgoing wire transfers. As a result, the Branch failed to timely file at least eleven (11) SARs for suspicious transactions by at least five (5) customers in violation of **31 U.S.C. §5318(g)** and **31 CFR §1010.320**.

For example, one customer, an individual who imported wigs and purported to be a business partner of the company discussed above, made numerous cash deposits in amounts over ten thousand dollars to his accounts at the Bank that aggregated to over thirteen million dollars from 1986 through 1999 and to his account at the Branch that aggregated to over three million eight hundred thousand dollars from May 1998 through February 1999. The Branch did not know or make an attempt to verify the business relationship between the two businesses or to determine the actual origin of these funds. Most of the currency placed in the account that the individual opened at the Branch in May 1998 was wired out shortly after its deposit. Withdrawals on this account included over seventy (70) wire transfers, through foreign banks, to a number of beneficiaries primarily located in Korea and Japan. The Branch did not attempt to determine the actual business of the majority of the beneficiaries of these transfers and all of the requests for transfer were submitted by facsimile from the company rather than the individual customer. In June 1999, the Branch filed a SAR on these transactions in response to the FDIC's examination findings.

3. Wire Transfers Structured to Avoid Recordkeeping Requirements

The Broadway Branch's review of its inward and outward wire remittance was inadequate for the identification of suspicious patterns of activity designed to evade the regulations promulgated under the BSA. As a result, FinCEN determined that the Branch failed to file SARs for suspicious transactions by at least four (4) non-customers and two (2) customers in violation of **31 U.S.C. §5318(g)** and **31 CFR §1010.320**.

For example, in one instance, the FDIC noted sixty-five (65) wire transfers, all but two of which were between two thousand nine hundred and fifty dollars and two thousand nine hundred and eighty dollars, from the same group of non-bank customers to the same group of beneficiaries. These transactions, all of which were conducted in cash, appear to have been structured to circumvent the recordkeeping requirements for funds transfers of three thousand dollars or more appearing in **31 CFR §1010.410(e)**. In its March 31, 2001 report of examination, the FDIC concluded that the Branch should have filed SARs regarding these transactions, given the volume, frequency, and commonality of the customers involved.

4. Cash Deposits Structured to Avoid CTR Reporting Requirements

While the Broadway Branch identified successive cash deposits of just under ten thousand dollars by certain customers as potentially suspicious activity that warranted investigation, the Branch did not undertake the due diligence necessary to make an informed decision or meaningful analysis of whether the activity was actually suspicious and whether a SAR should be filed. The Branch's process for documenting client profiles and investigating suspicious activity was inadequate. As a result, the Branch failed to timely file SARs for suspicious transactions by at least three (3) customers in violation of **31 U.S.C. §5318(g)** and **31 CFR §1010.320**.

For example, the Branch identified the high volume of cash transaction activity within the business checking account of one customer as potentially suspicious and included the activity on the Branch Suspicious Activity Investigation Log for investigation. For a period of 15 months, the customer made one hundred fifty-five (155) cash deposits to the account, aggregating seven hundred and sixty-six dollars. Of these transactions, twenty-nine were in amounts ranging from eight thousand dollars to ten thousand dollars, including five at exactly ten thousand dollars. None of the deposits was over the CTR threshold of ten thousand dollars. These transactions appeared to have been structured to circumvent the Branch's obligation to report any cash deposit over ten thousand dollars on a CTR as described in **31 CFR §1010.330**.

The Branch did not file a SAR regarding these transactions because the U.S. Compliance Officer concluded that the cash activity appeared normal and that there was no indication of suspicious activity. During its March 31, 2001 examination of the Branch, the FDIC noted that the Branch could not produce any analysis or documentation to support the U.S. Compliance Officer's assertion that the cash activity appeared normal. If an investigation and analysis was performed by the Branch, it was not documented. The FDIC concluded that the Branch should have filed SARs regarding these transactions.[186]

CASE STUDY ON FAILURE TO FILE TIMELY CURRENCY TRANSACTION REPORTS

Case 3.4: Financial Crimes Enforcement Network v. Sovereign Bank No. 2002-01

FinCEN determined that from June 1998, through May 2001, Sovereign failed to file timely approximately 2000 Currency Transaction Report ("CTR") forms for currency transactions in amounts greater than ten thousand dollars as required by **31 CFR §1010.330**, promulgated under **§5313 of the Bank Secrecy Act**.

FinCEN had determined that Sovereign's failures to file CTRs were willful. Over a two-year period, Sovereign had experienced a number of extraordinary events, including several mergers and acquisitions and systems conversions. These events strained Sovereign's compliance systems, leading to the failure to file CTRs primarily for new cash management customers in Pennsylvania and New Jersey that had been acquired through the mergers and acquisitions. While Sovereign BSA compliance personnel or its internal auditors ultimately identified each

186 United States of America Department of the Treasury Financial Crimes Enforcement Network (2003), 'IN THE MATTER OF KOREA EXCHANGE BANK NEW YORK', Available at: https://www.fincen.gov/sites/default/files/enforcement_action/koreaexchangeassessment.pdf (accessed 3 May 2017).

of these problems, the recurring nature of the problems should have alerted Sovereign and particularly the group responsible for arranging cash pickups and deliveries for these new customers ("Group"), to the need to more fully evaluate its BSA compliance procedures and systems completely and thoroughly at an earlier time.

In particular, Sovereign relied on third party vendors without adequate internal controls to assure BSA compliance. First, for a year after it acquired the cash management business, Sovereign believed that its outside vendors, several armored car services that picked up and delivered cash to and from the Bank's customers, prepared and filed the necessary CTRs for the pick-ups and deliveries for these customers.

However, Sovereign did not have sufficient internal controls in place to verify this belief and did not monitor or test the vendors' performance of this function. In fact, the vendors did not prepare or file the CTRs for these customers. As a result, from June 1998 though March 1999, Sovereign failed to file about 1155 CTRs.

Second, when Sovereign discovered that neither the outside vendors nor the Bank's branches had filed the required CTRs, the Group assumed responsibility for preparing and filing CTRs. The Group obtained a list from the vendors of the customers taking advantage of the cash pick-up and delivery service but did not verify that the list was complete. Because some of these customers were not on the vendors' lists, Sovereign failed to file timely an additional approximately 241 CTRs for a five-month period between March and August 1999 for reportable cash transactions by customers missing from the list.

Lastly, from July 1999 through May 2001, the Group relied on a third-party currency handling service to prepare reports of the currency orders by the Bank's customers who received cash from or delivered cash to these third-party vendors. The Group would identify reportable transactions from the information in the vendor's reports and prepare and file the necessary CTRs. The BSA Compliance Department, in turn, would compare the CTRs prepared by the Group to the same vendor's report. Beginning in July 1999, however, the report provided by the vendor did not list all the transactions.

The Bank did not test the accuracy of the vendor's reports against the Bank's own records of such currency transactions by these customers and did not monitor or test the accuracy of the resulting CTRs. Because of undetected inaccuracies in the vendor's reports, Sovereign failed to file over about 578 additional CTRs between July 1999 and May 2001.

FinCEN had determined that Sovereign failed to implement sufficient internal controls and testing to ensure that it filed accurate and timely CTRs, even after it was on notice that there were significant deficiencies in its BSA compliance. Therefore, FinCEN had concluded that Sovereign's failures to file CTRs constitute willful violations of the BSA.[187]

3.3 Discussion

The previous section compared the reporting requirements in Nigeria with those of the United States and the United Kingdom. This section analyses the issues that arose from the comparison, with the aim of determining if there is need for reform.

3.3.1 What to File

As stated earlier, Nigerian and US money laundering laws require financial institutions to file currency transaction reports (CTRs) and suspicious transaction reports (STRs), while the United Kingdom's law requires that financial institutions file only suspicious activity reports (SARs). Is it necessary for Nigerian and US money laundering laws to mandate financial institutions to file CTRs since they are not required by the United Kingdom?

The question can be answered by looking briefly into the history behind the **US Bank Secrecy Act**. In 1970, Congress passed the **Currency and Foreign Transactions Reporting Act**, commonly known as the **Bank Secrecy Act**, which established requirements for record keeping and reporting by private individuals, banks and other financial institutions. The Bank Secrecy Act was designed to help identify the source, volume

---

187   United States of America Department of the Treasury Financial Crimes Enforcement Network (2002), 'IN THE MATTER OF SOVERIGN BANK', Available at: https://www.fincen.gov/sites/default/files/enforcement_action/sovereign-bank.pdf (accessed 28 April, 2017).

and movement of currency and other monetary instruments transported or transmitted into or out of the United States or deposited in financial institutions. The statute requires individuals, banks and other financial institutions to file currency reports with the US Department of the Treasury, properly identify persons conducting transactions and maintain a paper trail by keeping appropriate records of financial transactions. These records enable law enforcement and regulatory agencies to pursue investigations of criminal tax and regulatory violations, if warranted, and provide evidence that is useful in prosecuting money laundering and other financial crimes.

In April 1996, a suspicious activity report (SAR) was developed to be used by all banking organizations in the United States. A banking organization is required to file a SAR whenever it detects a known or suspected criminal violation of federal law, a suspicious transaction related to money laundering activity or a violation of the **Bank Secrecy Act.**[188]

Legislators did not remove the CTR requirement, even though the SAR seeks to achieve the same objective, which is identifying the source, volume and movement of currency and preventing money laundering.

The international law the United States based its 1996 development on required financial institutions to file both a CTR and a STR.[189] This international law has been updated several times, with the most recent version requiring only an STR to be filed.[190]

Since the CTR requirement seeks to achieve a similar objective as the SAR requirement, it's no surprise that the UK money laundering law does not include the CTR requirement. This strengthens the argument that it may not be necessary for a financial institution to be required by law to file a CTR.

---

188 Federal Financial Institutions Examination Council (2014), 'Bank Secrecy Act/Anti-Money Laundering Examination Manual', Available at: https://www.occ.treas.gov/publications/publications-by-type/other-publications-reports/ffiec-bsa-aml-examination-manual.pdf (accessed 10 January 2017).

189 The Forty Recommendations of the Financial Action Task Force on Money Laundering (1990), Recommendations 16, 24; The Financial Action Task Force on Money Laundering, The Forty Recommendations (1996), Recommendations 15, 23.

190 The Financial Action Task Force (FATF): International Standards on Combating Money Laundering and the financing of terrorism and proliferation, (The FATF Recommendations) 2012, Recommendation 20.

3.3.2 When a Transaction Requires Reporting

As stated earlier, the Nigerian and United Kingdom money laundering laws require all suspicious transactions, including attempted transactions, to be reported, regardless of the amount involved. This position is different from that of the **US Bank Secrecy Act**, which sets a particular threshold for reporting. This section of the chapter seeks to determine which of these requirements is preferable.

A threshold requirement appears to allow businesses to flourish because bank customers who engage in transactions below five thousand dollars will not have their transactions stalled by ongoing investigations. However, the threshold mechanism can be circumvented with techniques like smurfing.[191]

Therefore, the 'no threshold rule' is preferable.

3.3.3 Confidentiality of Sars

The **Nigerian Money Laundering Prohibition Act 2011 (MLPA 2011) (as amended)** provides no exceptions to the general rule of tipping off, which is contrary to the positions of the United Kingdom and the United States. This section of the chapter seeks to determine if the tipping-off provision in **MLPA 2011** needs to be amended to include detailed exceptions.

The tipping-off provision, as currently drafted, could cause serious problems for financial institutions and designated nonfinancial institutions. First, it is not clear if a disclosure by a financial institution to law enforcement agents is permitted. Second, it is not clear if a disclosure by a financial institution to another financial institution is permitted. Third, it is not clear if a disclosure by a professional legal adviser to another professional legal adviser is permitted. All these disclosures are stated in both the UK and US laws as clear exceptions to the general rule of tipping off.

---

191   Smurfing is the act of breaking down a transaction into smaller transactions to avoid regulatory requirements or an investigation by the authorities. For more on Smurfing, see Farlex (2017), 'the Free Dictionary', Available at: http://financial-dictionary.thefreedictionary.com/Smurfing (accessed 6 September 2017).

In view of the above arguments, the tipping-off provision in **MLPA 2011** needs to be amended to contain detailed exceptions like those of the United Kingdom and the United States.

3.3.4 Further Information Orders

The **United Kingdom's Criminal Finances Act 2017** allows the National Crime Agency or police to obtain further information from a financial institution pursuant to an Order of Court where the Suspicious Activity Report (SAR) does not contain all the necessary information to enable effective investigations or intelligence development. The intention is to increase the quality of SARs, and to enable improved intelligence analysis for the better identification of risks and threats.[192]

A further information order is an order requiring the respondent to provide—

(a) the information specified or described in the application for the order, or
(b) such other information as the court or sheriff making the order thinks appropriate, so far as the information is in the possession, or under the control, of the respondent.[193]

A further information order must specify—

(a) how the information required under the order is to be provided, and
(b) the date by which it is to be provided.[194]

---

192 Criminal Finances Act 2017, s. 12, s. 37

193 Proceeds of Crime Act 2002 (as amended), s. 339ZH (3); Terrorism Act 2000 (as amended), s. 22B (3)

194 Proceeds of Crime Act 2002 (as amended), s. 339ZH (7); Terrorism Act 2000 (as amended), s. 22B (7)

If a person fails to comply with a further information order made by a magistrates' court, the magistrates' court may order the person to pay an amount not exceeding £5,000.[195]

Although the USA PATRIOT Act made no mention of any procedure that would require FinCEN to approach a Court of Law to obtain a Further Information Order, the USA PATRIOT Act does allow FinCEN to request for additional information from a financial institution without an Order of Court to that effect.

According to **Section 314(a) of the USA PATRIOT Act (31 CFR 1010.520),** FinCEN may solicit, on its own behalf and on behalf of appropriate components of the Department of the Treasury, whether a financial institution or a group of financial institutions maintains or has maintained accounts for, or has engaged in transactions with, any specified individual, entity, or organization. Before an information request under this section is made to a financial institution, FinCEN or the appropriate Treasury component shall certify in writing in the same manner as a requesting law enforcement agency that each individual, entity or organization about which FinCEN or the appropriate Treasury component is seeking information is engaged in, or is reasonably suspected based on credible evidence of engaging in, terrorist activity or money laundering. The certification also must include enough specific identifiers, such as date of birth, address, and social security number, that would permit a financial institution to differentiate between common or similar names, and identify one person at FinCEN or the appropriate Treasury component who can be contacted with any questions relating to its request.

Section 314(a) of the USA PATRIOT Act does not provide for any penalty in an event where a financial institution fails to respond to a FinCEN request.

However, FinCEN being the regulatory authority for financial institutions, still has the power to fine a financial institution for violating **Section 314(a) of the USA PATRIOT Act.**

---

195   Proceeds of Crime Act 2002 (as amended), s. 339ZH (8); Terrorism Act 2000 (as amended), s. 22B (8)

Although Nigeria's Money Laundering/Terrorist Financing Laws and Regulations failed to provide for further information orders just like the USA PATRIOT Act, it did provide for alternative measures.

Under the **Economic and Financial Crimes Commission (Establishment) Act, 2004**, the Chairman of the Economic and Financial Crimes Commission, or any officer authorized by him has the power to seek and receive information from any person, authority, corporation or company without let or hindrance in respect of offences it is empowered to enforce under the **Economic and Financial Crimes Commission (Establishment) Act, 2004**.[196]

A person who willfully obstructs the Economic and Financial Crimes Commission or any authorized officer of the Commission in exercise of this power; or fails to comply with any lawful enquiry or requirements made by any authorized officer in accordance with **Section 38 (1) of the Economic and Financial Crimes Commission (Establishment) Act, 2004**, commits an offence under this Act and is liable on conviction to imprisonment for a term not exceeding five years or to a fine of twenty thousand naira or to both such imprisonment and fine.[197]

3.3.4.1 Conditions for the Making of Further Information Order in the United Kingdom

A magistrates' court or (in Scotland) the sheriff may, on an application made by a law enforcement officer, make a further information order if satisfied that either condition 1 or condition 2 is met.[198]

Condition 1 for the making of a further information order is met if—

(a) the information required to be given under the order would relate to a matter arising from a disclosure made under Part 1 of the **Criminal Finances Act 2017** and **section 21A of the Terrorism Act 2000**,

---

196 Economic and Financial Crimes Commission (Establishment) Act, 2004, s. 38 (1)

197 Economic and Financial Crimes Commission (Establishment) Act, 2004, s. 38 (2)

198 Proceeds of Crime Act 2002 (as amended), s. 339ZH (1); Terrorism Act 2000 (as amended), s. 22B (1)

(b) the respondent is the person who made the disclosure or is otherwise carrying on a business in the regulated sector,

(c) the information would assist in investigating whether a person is involved in the commission of a terrorist financing offence or a money laundering offence or in determining whether an investigation of that kind should be started, and

(d) it is reasonable in all the circumstances for the information to be provided.[199]

Condition 2 for the making of a further information order is met if—

(a) the information required to be given under the order would relate to a matter arising from a disclosure made under a corresponding disclosure requirement,

(b) an external request has been made to the National Crime Agency for the provision of information in connection with that disclosure,

(c) the respondent is carrying on a business in the regulated sector,

(d) the information is likely to be of substantial value to the authority that made the external request in determining any matter in connection with the disclosure, and

(e) it is reasonable in all the circumstances for the information to be provided.[200]

The application must—

(a) specify or describe the information sought under the order, and

(b) specify the person from whom the information is sought ("the respondent").[201]

---

199 Proceeds of Crime Act 2002 (as amended), s. 339ZH (4); Terrorism Act 2000 (as amended), s. 22B (4)

200 Proceeds of Crime Act 2002 (as amended), s. 339ZH (5); Terrorism Act 2000 (as amended), s. 22B (5)

201 Proceeds of Crime Act 2002 (as amended), s. 339ZH (2); Terrorism Act 2000 (as amended), s. 22B (2)

The above stated provisions are not seen present in the Nigerian and the United States Anti-Money Laundering and Counter-Terrorist Financing Laws.

3.3.5 Disclosure Orders

The **United Kingdom's Criminal Financing Act** amended the **Proceeds of Crime Act 2002** and the **Terrorism Act 2000** to provide for disclosure orders, an effective and flexible means of obtaining information in a money laundering and terrorist financing investigation.

A disclosure order can require any person considered to have information relevant to an investigation to answer questions, provide information or to produce documents.

A disclosure order would allow an investigator to have access to important information and documentation that might be difficult to obtain under other investigative orders or would otherwise require multiple applications to court.[202]

Under existing legislation in Nigeria, law enforcement agencies cannot use disclosure orders for money laundering investigations.

Although the United States Bank Secrecy Act Regulations made no mention of any procedure that would require FinCEN to approach a Court of Law to obtain a Disclosure Order, Section 314 (a) of the USA PATRIOT Act does allow for information sharing between government agencies and financial institutions.

In the United States, a law enforcement agency investigating terrorist activity or money laundering may request that FinCEN solicit, on the investigating agency's behalf, certain information from a financial institution or a group of financial institutions. When submitting such a request to FinCEN, the law enforcement agency shall provide FinCEN with a written certification, in such form and manner as FinCEN may prescribe. At a minimum, such certification must: State that each individual, entity, or organization about which the law enforcement agency is seeking information is engaged in, or is reasonably suspected based on credible evidence of engaging in, terrorist activity or money

---

202   Criminal Finances Act 2017, s. 7, s. 35

laundering; include enough specific identifiers, such as date of birth, address, and social security number, that would permit a financial institution to differentiate between common or similar names; and identify one person at the agency who can be contacted with any questions relating to its request. Upon receiving the requisite certification from the requesting law enforcement agency, FinCEN may require any financial institution to search its records to determine whether the financial institution maintains or has maintained accounts for, or has engaged in transactions with, any specified individual, entity, or organization.

In addition to the above, law enforcement agencies may issue out grand jury subpoenas, and National Security Letters.

National Security Letters (NSLs) are written investigative demands that may be issued by the local Federal Bureau of Investigation (FBI) and other federal governmental authorities in counterintelligence and counterterrorism investigations to obtain the following:

- Telephone and electronic communications records from telephone companies and Internet service providers.
- Information from credit bureaus.
- Financial records from financial institutions.

Banks that receive NSLs must take appropriate measures to ensure the confidentiality of the letters and should have procedures in place for processing and maintaining the confidentiality of NSLs.

In Nigeria, the Chairman of the Economic and Financial Crimes Commission, or any officer authorized by him may by a Freezing Order issued under Section 34 (1) of the Economic and Financial Crimes Commission (Establishment) Act, 2004, or by any subsequent order, direct a bank or other financial institution to supply any information and produce books and documents relating to the account and to stop all outward payments, operations or transactions (including any bill of exchange) in respect of the account of the arrested person. The Economic and Financial Crimes Commission (Establishment) Act, 2004 made no mention of Disclosure Orders.[203]

---

203 Economic and Financial Crimes Commission (Establishment) Act, 2004, s. 34 (2)

The Chairman of the Economic and Financial Crimes Commission, or any officer authorized by him may also seek and receive information from any person, authority, corporation or company without let or hindrance in respect of offences it is empowered to enforce under the Economic and Financial Crimes Commission (Establishment) Act, 2004.[204]

3.3.5.1 Money Laundering Investigation

Before the enactment of the United Kingdom **Criminal Finances Act**, disclosure orders were used for confiscation, civil recovery and exploitation proceeds investigations, but they could not be used in money laundering investigations.

The United Kingdom **Criminal Finances Act** amended the **Proceeds of Crime Act 2002** to allow for disclosure orders to be used for money laundering investigations.[205] This is not the case for Nigeria.

Investigators face increasingly complex investigations. Disclosure orders will give law enforcement agencies an effective, efficient and flexible means of obtaining information in an investigation, particularly in the early stages.

3.3.5.2 Terrorist Financing Investigation

The United Kingdom **Criminal Finances Act** allows for disclosure orders to be used for terrorist financing investigations. This is not the case for Nigeria and the United States.

SCHEDULE 5A of the United Kingdom's Terrorism Act 2000 (as amended) laid down the procedure for obtaining a disclosure order:

(1) A judge may, on the application of an appropriate officer, make a disclosure order if satisfied that each of the requirements for the making of the order is fulfilled.

---

204 Economic and Financial Crimes Commission (Establishment) Act, 2004, s. 38 (1)
205   Criminal Finances Act 2017, s. 7

(2) The application must state that a person or property speci-fied in the application is subject to a terrorist financing in-vestigation and the order is sought for the purposes of the investigation.

(3) A disclosure order is an order authorising an appropriate of-ficer to give to any person the officer considers has relevant information notice in writing requiring the person to do any or all of the following with respect to any matter relevant to the terrorist financing investigation concerned—

  (a) answer questions, either at a time specified in the notice or at once, at a place so specified;

  (b) provide information specified in the notice, by a time and in a manner so specified;

  (c) produce documents, or documents of a description, specified in the notice, either at or by a time so specified or at once, and in a manner so specified.

(4) Relevant information is information (whether or not con-tained in a document) which the appropriate officer con-cerned considers to be relevant to the investigation.

(5) A person is not bound to comply with a requirement imposed by a notice given under a disclosure order unless evidence of authority to give the notice is produced.

(6) An appropriate officer may not make an application under this paragraph unless the officer is a senior police officer or is authorised to do so by a senior police officer.

Requirements for making of disclosure order

These are the requirements for the making of a disclosure order.

(1) There must be reasonable grounds for suspecting that a per-son has committed an offence under any of sections 15 to 18 or that the property specified in the application is terrorist property.

(2) There must be reasonable grounds for believing that in-formation which may be provided in compliance with a

requirement imposed under the order is likely to be of substantial value (whether or not by itself) to the terrorist financing investigation concerned.

(3) There must be reasonable grounds for believing that it is in the public interest for the information to be provided, having regard to the benefit likely to accrue to the investigation if the information is obtained.

Offences

(1) A person commits an offence if without reasonable excuse the person fails to comply with a requirement imposed under a disclosure order.

(2) A person guilty of an offence under sub-paragraph (1) is liable—

(a) on summary conviction in England and Wales, to imprisonment for a term not exceeding 51 weeks, or to a fine, or to both;

(b) on summary conviction in Northern Ireland, to imprisonment for a term not exceeding 6 months, or to a fine not exceeding level 5 on the standard scale, or to both.

(3) A person commits an offence if, in purported compliance with a requirement imposed under a disclosure order, the person—

(a) makes a statement which the person knows to be false or misleading in a material particular, or

(b) recklessly makes a statement which is false or misleading in a material particular.

(4) A person guilty of an offence under sub-paragraph (3) is liable—

(a) on conviction on indictment, to imprisonment for a term not exceeding 2 years, or to a fine, or to both;

(b) on summary conviction in England and Wales, to imprisonment for a term not exceeding 12 months, or to a fine, or to both;

(c) on summary conviction in Northern Ireland, to imprisonment for a term not exceeding 6 months, or to a fine
not exceeding the statutory maximum, or to both.

(5) In relation to an offence committed before the coming into
force of **section 281(5) of the Criminal Justice Act 2003** (alteration of penalties for certain summary offences), the reference in subparagraph (2)(a) to 51 weeks is to be read as a
reference to 6 months.

(6) In relation to an offence committed before the coming into
force of **section 282 of the Criminal Justice Act 2003** (increase in maximum sentence on summary conviction of offence triable either way), the reference in sub-paragraph (4)
(b) to 12 months is to be read as a reference to 6 months.

3.3.6 Information Sharing

The UK's Criminal Financing Act allows the regulated sector (e.g.
banks, lawyers, accountants) to share information between themselves, on a voluntary basis, where they have a suspicion of money
laundering and terrorist financing.[206]

Nigeria on the other hand does not permit the regulated sector
to share information between themselves, where they have a suspicion of money laundering and terrorist financing.

The United States allows for voluntary information sharing between financial institutions but does not allow for sharing between
financial institutions and designated non-financial institutions like
lawyers and accountants.[207]

Information sharing can assist governments and their agencies
in the fight against terrorism and money laundering. They can prevent terrorist organizations from accessing their financial services,
assist governments in their efforts to detect suspected terrorist financing and promptly respond to governmental enquiries.

---

206 Criminal Finances Act 2017, s. 11, s. 36. See also the Proceeds of Crime Act
2002 (as amended), s. 339ZB and the Terrorism Act 2000 (as amended), s. 21CA
207 Section 314(b) of the USA PATRIOT Act (31 CFR 1010.540)

3.3.6.1 Conditions for Voluntary Disclosures Within the UK Regulated Sector

3.3.6.1.1 Money Laundering

A person (A) may disclose information to one or more other persons if conditions 1 to 4 are met.[208]

Condition 1 is that—
(a) A is carrying on a business in the regulated sector as a credit institution, financial institution, professional legal adviser and a relevant professional adviser,
(b) the information on which the disclosure is based came to A in the course of carrying on that business, and
(c) the person to whom the information is to be disclosed (or each of them, where the disclosure is to more than one person) is also carrying on a business in the regulated sector as a credit institution, financial institution, professional legal adviser and a relevant professional adviser (whether or not of the same kind as A).[209]

Condition 2 is that—

(a) an NCA authorised officer has requested A to make the disclosure, or
(b) the person to whom the information is to be disclosed (or at least one of them, where the disclosure is to more than one person) has requested A to do so.[210]

Condition 3 is that, before A makes the disclosure, the required notification has been made to an NCA authorised officer (see section 339ZC (3) to (5)).[211]

---

208 Proceeds of Crime Act 2002 (as amended), s. 339ZB (1)
209 Proceeds of Crime Act 2002 (as amended), s. 339ZB (2)
210 Proceeds of Crime Act 2002 (as amended), s. 339ZB (3)
211 Proceeds of Crime Act 2002 (as amended), s. 339ZB (4)

Condition 4 is that A is satisfied that the disclosure of the information will or may assist in determining any matter in connection with a suspicion that a person is engaged in money laundering.[212]

A person may disclose information to A for the purposes of making a disclosure request if, and to the extent that, the person has reason to believe that A has in A's possession information that will or may assist in determining any matter in connection with a suspicion that a person is engaged in money laundering.[213]

A disclosure request must—

(a) state that it is made in connection with a suspicion that a person is engaged in money laundering,
(b) identify the person (if known),
(c) describe the information that is sought from A, and
(d) specify the person or persons to whom it is requested that the information is disclosed.[214]

Where the disclosure request is made by a person mentioned in section 339ZB(3)(b), the request must also—

(a) set out the grounds for the suspicion that a person is engaged in money laundering, or
(b) provide such other information as the person making the request thinks appropriate for the purposes of enabling A to determine whether the information requested ought to be disclosed under section 339ZB (1).[215]

3.3.6.1.2 Terrorist Financing

A person (A) may disclose information to one or more other persons if—

---

212 Proceeds of Crime Act 2002 (as amended), s. 339ZB (5)
213 Proceeds of Crime Act 2002 (as amended), s. 339ZB (6)
214 Proceeds of Crime Act 2002 (as amended), s. 339ZC (1)
215 Proceeds of Crime Act 2002 (as amended), s. 339ZC (2)

(a) conditions 1 to 4 are met, and

(b) where applicable, condition 5 is also met.[216]

Condition 1 is that—

(a) A is carrying on a business in the regulated sector as a credit institution, financial institution, professional legal adviser and a relevant professional adviser,

(b) the information on which the disclosure is based came to A in the course of carrying on that business, and

(c) the person to whom the information is to be disclosed (or each of them, where the disclosure is to more than one person) is also carrying on a business in the regulated sector as a credit institution, financial institution, professional legal adviser and a relevant professional adviser (whether or not of the same kind as A).[217]

Condition 2 is that—

(a) a constable has requested A to make the disclosure, or

(b) the person to whom the information is to be disclosed (or at least one of them, where the disclosure is to more than one person) has requested A to do so.[218]

Condition 3 is that, before A makes the disclosure, the required notification has been made to a constable (see section 21CB (5) to (7)).[219]

Condition 4 is that A is satisfied that the disclosure of the information will or may assist in determining any matter in connection with—

(a) a suspicion that a person is involved in the commission of a terrorist financing offence, or

---

216 Terrorism Act 2000 (as amended), s. 21CA (1)
217 Terrorism Act 2000 (as amended), s. 21CA (2)
218 Terrorism Act 2000 (as amended), s. 21CA (3)
219 Terrorism Act 2000 (as amended), s. 21CA (4)

(b) the identification of terrorist property or of its movement or use.[220]

Condition 5 is that, before making the disclosure request, the person making the request (or at least one of them, where the request is made by more than one person) has notified a constable that the request is to be made.[221]

Condition 5 does not apply where the disclosure request concerned is made by a constable.[222]

A person may disclose information to A for the purposes of making a disclosure request if, and to the extent that, the person has reason to believe that A has in A's possession information that will or may assist in determining any matter of the kind mentioned in paragraph (a) or (b) of subsection (5).[223]

A disclosure request must—

(a) state that it is made in connection with—
    (i) a suspicion that a person is involved in the commission of a terrorist financing offence, or
    (ii) the identification of terrorist property or of its movement or use,
(b) identify the person or property (so far as known),
(c) describe the information that is sought from A, and
(d) specify the person or persons to whom it is requested that the information is disclosed.[224]

3.4 Conclusion

This chapter compared the reporting requirements in Nigeria with those of the United States and the United Kingdom. It has also

220 Terrorism Act 2000 (as amended), s. 21CA (5)
221 Terrorism Act 2000 (as amended), s. 21CA (6)
222 Terrorism Act 2000 (as amended), s. 21CA (7)
223 Terrorism Act 2000 (as amended), s. 21CA (8)
224 Terrorism Act 2000 (as amended), s. 21CB (1)

analysed issues that arose from the comparison to determine the need for reform. This section focuses on those areas that need reform.

Based on the arguments in Section 3.3 of this chapter, the following reforms to the Nigeria and United States Money Laundering/ Terrorist Financing laws and regulations are recommended:

I. **Sections two and ten of MLPA 2011** should be deleted, and section six should remain intact. In other words, firms should be required to file only STRs and should no longer be required to file CTRs.

II. **Section 16 (1) (a) of MLPA 2011** and **Regulation 31 (6) of CBN (Anti–Money Laundering and Combating the Financing of Terrorism in Banks and other Financial Institutions in Nigeria) Regulations 2013** should be amended to include exceptions to the general rule of tipping off, as stated in the **US Codified Bank Secrecy Act Regulations 2010**.[225] Alternatively, the exceptions could be added to **Section 333B, 333D (1) and (2) and 333D (3) of the United Kingdom's Proceeds of Crime Act 2002 (as amended)**.

III. The **Economic and Financial Crimes Commission (Establishment) Act, 2004** should be amended to enable the Economic and Financial Crimes Commission obtain further information from SARs reporters to allow them conduct effective and informed analysis, and to build a stronger intelligence picture on money laundering and terrorist financing. The failure of a country to take active measures to ensure that further information orders becomes a routine part of all law enforcement inquiries related to crime with financial gain may negatively impact on financial investigation as a report by Europol just revealed that money laundering goes mostly uninvestigated, despite banks alerting police to record numbers of suspicious transactions. The report revealed that European banks flagged almost one million transactions

---

225 Codified Bank Secrecy Act Regulations (2010), s 1020.320 (e) (1) (A) (1), s 1022.320 (d) (1) (A) (1), s 1020.320 (e) (1) (A) (2), s 1022.320 (d) (1) (A) (2), s 1020.320 (e) (1) (B), s 1022.320 (d) (1) (B).

suspected of laundering money in 2014, the latest year for which data is available. But only one in 10 of these was investigated and the reason may be due to low quality SARs. Europol is now urging banks to improve the data they provide to help law enforcement authorities to follow up. In Italy alone, Europol found the sums of money involved in such transactions amounted to 164 billion euros ($195 billion) in 2014 - roughly one tenth of the country's economy. However, Europol estimates the amount confiscated as a result of any police investigation was barely 1 percent of criminal proceeds in the European Union. Two-thirds of transactions suspected of laundering money in Europe come from Britain and the Netherlands, according to the report, although this is due in part to the size of the financial centers in London and Amsterdam. In its analysis, the European Union police agency found that there were more than 350,000 suspicious cases in 2014 reported to the United Kingdom police authorities - roughly two thirds higher than in 2006. Dutch authorities were alerted to 277,000 suspect transactions in that year.[226]

IV. The **USA PATRIOT Act** and the **Economic and Financial Crimes Commission (Establishment) Act, 2004** should be amended to include Disclosure Orders. A disclosure order would allow an investigator to have access to important information and documentation that might be difficult to obtain under other investigative orders or would otherwise require multiple applications to court.

V. The **Nigerian Money Laundering Prohibition Act 2011 (as amended)** should be modified to permit firms in the regulated sector to share information between themselves, to allow them to work together to build a clearer picture of how money launderers and terrorist financiers operate, and use that to inform the financial intelligence unit and to protect themselves.

---

226 Reuters (2017), 'Europol urges action after record number of money laundering tip-offs', Available at: http://www.reuters.com/article/us-finance-moneylaundering/europol-urges-action-after-record-number-of-money-laundering-tip-offs-idUSKCN1BG2JB (accessed 2 October 2017).

CHAPTER 4

MONEY LAUNDERING OFFENCE

The Financial Action Task Force (FATF) has advised countries to do the following: (i) criminalize money laundering; (ii) apply the crime of money laundering to all serious offences, with a view to including the widest range of predicate offences; (iii) extend predicate offences for money laundering to conduct that occurred in another country when it would have constituted a predicate offence had it occurred domestically and (iv) apply effective, proportionate and dissuasive criminal sanctions to natural persons convicted of money laundering.[227]

While countries followed the advice of the FATF by criminalizing money laundering and have implemented all the above recommendations, the approaches taken by these countries are different.

This chapter compares the approaches taken by Nigeria with those of the United States and the United Kingdom under four subheadings: 'The Crime of Money Laundering', 'Predicate Offences for Money Laundering (Domestic Crimes)', 'Predicate Offences for Money Laundering (Foreign Crimes)' and 'Penalties'. This chapter will also analyse issues that arise from the comparison to determine if there is need for reform.

---

227 The Financial Action Task Force (FATF): International Standards on Combating Money Laundering and the Financing of Terrorism and Proliferation, (The FATF Recommendations) 2012, Interpretive Note to Recommendation 3

4.1 The Crime of Money Laundering

The FATF has advised countries to criminalise money launder-ing on the basis of the **United Nations Convention against Illicit Traffic in Narcotic Drugs and Psychotropic Substances 1988 (the Vienna Convention)** and the **United Nations Convention against Transnational Organized Crime, 2000 (the Palermo Convention).**[228]

The Vienna Convention requires each party to adopt such mea-sures as may be necessary to establish as criminal offences under its domestic law, when committed intentionally:

i.   The conversion or transfer of property, knowing that such property is derived from any offence or offences established in accordance with **subparagraph (a) of paragraph 1 (Article 3)**, or from an act of participation in such offence or offenc-es, for the purpose of concealing or disguising the illicit ori-gin of the property or of assisting any person who is involved in the commission of such an offence or offences to evade the legal consequences of his actions;[229]

ii. The concealment or disguise of the true nature, source, loca-tion, disposition, movement, rights with respect to, or owner-ship of property, knowing that such property is derived from an offence or offences established in accordance with **sub-paragraph (a) of paragraph 1 (Article 3)** or from an act of participation in such an offence or offences;[230]

iii. The acquisition, possession or use of property, knowing, at the time of receipt, that such property was derived from an offence or offences established in accordance with or from an act of participation in such offence or offences;[231]

---

228 Ibid.

229 United Nations Convention Against Illicit Traffic in Narcotic Drugs and Psy-chotropic Substances, 1988, Article 3 (1) (b) (i)

230 United Nations Convention Against Illicit Traffic in Narcotic Drugs and Psy-chotropic Substances, 1988, Article 3 (1) (b) (ii)

231 United Nations Convention Against Illicit Traffic in Narcotic Drugs and Psy-chotropic Substances, 1988, Article 3 (1) (c) (i)

iv. The possession of equipment or materials or substances listed in Table I and Table II, knowing that they are being or are
to be used in or for the illicit cultivation, production or[232]

v. Publicly inciting or inducing others, by any means, to commit any of the offences established in accordance with this
article or to use narcotic drugs or psychotropic substances
illicitly;[233]

vi. Participation in, association or conspiracy to commit, attempts to commit and aiding, abetting, facilitating and counselling the commission of any of the offences established in
accordance with this article.[234]

Subparagraph (a) of paragraph 1 (Article 3) of the Vienna Convention
lists the following offences:

i. The production, manufacture, extraction; preparation, offering, offering for sale, distribution, sale, delivery on any
terms whatsoever, brokerage, dispatch, dispatch in transit,
transport, importation or exportation of any narcotic drug
or any psychotropic substance contrary to the provisions of
the 1961 Convention, the 1961 Convention as amended or
the 1971 Convention;

ii. The cultivation of opium poppy, coca bush or cannabis plant
for the purpose of the production of narcotic drugs contrary to the provisions of the 1961 Convention and the 1961
Convention as amended;

iii. The possession or purchase of any narcotic drug or psychotropic substance for the purpose of any of the activities enumerated in (i) above;

---

232 United Nations Convention Against Illicit Traffic in Narcotic Drugs and Psychotropic Substances, 1988, Article 3 (1) (c) (ii)

233 United Nations Convention Against Illicit Traffic in Narcotic Drugs and Psychotropic Substances, 1988, Article 3 (1) (c) (iii)

234 United Nations Convention Against Illicit Traffic in Narcotic Drugs and Psychotropic Substances, 1988, Article 3 (1) (c) (iv)

iv. The manufacture, transport or distribution of equipment, materials or of substances listed in Table I and Table II, knowing that they are to be used in or for the illicit cultivation, production or manufacture of narcotic drugs or psychotropic substances.

The Palermo Convention requires each State Party to adopt, in accordance with fundamental principles of its domestic law, such legislative and other measures as may be necessary to establish as criminal offences, when committed intentionally:

i. The conversion or transfer of property, knowing that such property is the proceeds of crime, for the purpose of concealing or disguising the illicit origin of the property or of helping any person who is involved in the commission of the predicate offence to evade the legal consequences of his or her action;[235]
ii. The concealment or disguise of the true nature, source, location, disposition, movement or ownership of or rights with respect to property, knowing that such property is the proceeds of crime;[236]

Subject to the basic concepts of its legal system:

iii. The acquisition, possession or use of property, knowing, at the time of receipt, that such property is the proceeds of crime;[237]
iv. Participation in, association with or conspiracy to commit, attempts to commit and aiding, abetting, facilitating and counselling the commission of any of the offences established in accordance with this article.[238]

---

235 United Nations Convention Against Transnational Organized Crime and the Protocol There to 2004, Article 6 (1) (a) (i)

236 United Nations Convention Against Transnational Organized Crime and the Protocol There to 2004, Article 6 (1) (a) (ii)

237 United Nations Convention Against Transnational Organized Crime and the Protocol There to 2004, Article 6 (1) (b) (i)

238 United Nations Convention Against Transnational Organized Crime and the Protocol There to 2004, Article 6 (1) (b) (ii)

Although countries have followed the advice of the FATF by criminalising money laundering on the basis of the Vienna Convention
and the Palermo Convention, the approaches in these countries are
different.

This section compares the approaches in Nigeria with those of
the United States and the United Kingdom.

4.1.1 Nigeria
The Nigerian Money Laundering Prohibition Act 2011 (as amended)
makes it a money laundering offence for any person or body corporate in or outside Nigeria, to directly or indirectly:

 i. Conceal or disguise the origin of;[239]
 ii. Convert or transfer;[240]
 iii. Remove from the jurisdiction; or[241]
 iv. Acquire, use, retain or take possession or control of;[242]

Any fund or property, knowingly or reasonably ought to have known
that such fund or property is, or forms part of the proceeds of an
unlawful act.[243]

A person also commits the offence of money laundering if he
or she:

 i. Conspires with, aids, abets or counsels any other person to
    commit the offence of money laundering;[244]
 ii. Attempts to commit or is an accessory to an act or offence of
    money laundering; or[245]

---

239 Money Laundering Prohibition Act 2011 (as amended), s. 15 (2) (a)
240 Money Laundering Prohibition Act 2011 (as amended), s. 15 (2) (b)
241 Money Laundering Prohibition Act 2011 (as amended), s. 15 (2) (c)
242 Money Laundering Prohibition Act 2011 (as amended), s. 15 (2) (d)
243 Money Laundering Prohibition Act 2011 (as amended), s. 15 (2)
244 Money Laundering Prohibition Act 2011 (as amended), s. 18 (a)
245 Money Laundering Prohibition Act 2011 (as amended), s. 18(b)

iii. Incites, procures or induces any other person by any means whatsoever to commit the offence of money laundering.[246]

4.1.2 United States

The U.S. Bank Secrecy Act (Statute) (1970) (as amended) is to the effect that:

(a)

(1) Whoever, knowing that the property involved in a financial transaction represents the proceeds of some form of unlawful activity, conducts or attempts to conduct such a financial transaction which in fact involves the proceeds of specified unlawful activity[247]—

(A)

i. With the intent to promote the carrying on of specified unlawful activity; or[248]

ii. With intent to engage in conduct constituting a violation of section 7201 or 7206 of the Internal Revenue Code of 1986; or[249]

(B) Knowing that the transaction is designed in whole or in part—

i. To conceal or disguise the nature, the location, the source, the ownership, or the control of the proceeds of specified unlawful activity; or[250]

ii. To avoid a transaction reporting requirement under State or Federal law,[251]

Shall be guilty of the offence of money laundering

---

246 Money Laundering Prohibition Act 2011 (as amended), s. 18 (c)
247 Bank Secrecy Act (Statute) 18 U.S. Code s. 1956 (a) (1)
248 Bank Secrecy Act (Statute) 18 U.S. Code s. 1956 (a) (1) (A) (i)
249 Bank Secrecy Act (Statute) 18 U.S. Code s. 1956 (a) (1) (A) (ii)
250 Bank Secrecy Act (Statute) 18 U.S. Code s. 1956 (a) (1) (B) (i)
251 Bank Secrecy Act (Statute) 18 U.S. Code s. 1956 (a) (1) (B) (ii)

A financial transaction shall be considered to be one involving the proceeds of specified unlawful activity if it is part of a set of parallel or dependent transactions, any one of which involves the proceeds of specified unlawful activity, and all of which are part of a single plan or arrangement.[252]

(2) Also, whoever transports, transmits or transfers, or attempts to transport, transmit, or transfer a monetary instrument or funds from a place in the United States to or through a place outside the United States or to a place in the United States from or through a place outside the United States.[253]—

(A) With the intent to promote the carrying on of specified unlawful activity; or[254]

(B) Knowing that the monetary instrument or funds involved in the transportation, transmission, or transfer represent the proceeds of some form of unlawful activity and knowing that such transportation, transmission, or transfer is designed in whole or in part[255]—

(i) To conceal or disguise the nature, the location, the source, the ownership, or the control of the proceeds of specified unlawful activity; or[256]

(ii) To avoid a transaction reporting requirement under State or Federal law,[257]

Shall be guilty of the offence of money laundering

(3) Whoever, with the intent—

i. To promote the carrying on of specified unlawful activity;[258]

---

252 Bank Secrecy Act (Statute) 18 U.S. Code s. 1956 (a) (1) (B)
253 Bank Secrecy Act (Statute) 18 U.S. Code s. 1956 (a) (2)
254 Bank Secrecy Act (Statute) 18 U.S. Code s. 1956 (a) (2) (A)
255 Bank Secrecy Act (Statute) 18 U.S. Code s. 1956 (a) (2) (B)
256 Bank Secrecy Act (Statute) 18 U.S. Code s. 1956 (a) (2) (B) (i)
257 Bank Secrecy Act (Statute) 18 U.S. Code s. 1956 (a) (2) (B) (ii)
258 Bank Secrecy Act (Statute) 18 U.S. Code s. 1956 (a) (3) (A)

    ii. To conceal or disguise the nature, location, source, ownership, or control of property believed to be the proceeds of specified unlawful activity; or[259]

    iii. To avoid a transaction reporting requirement under State or Federal law,[260]

Conducts or attempts to conduct a financial transaction involving property represented to be the proceeds of specified unlawful activity, or property used to conduct or facilitate specified unlawful activity, shall be guilty of the offence of money laundering.

The term "represented" means any representation made by a law enforcement officer or by another person at the direction of, or with the approval of, a Federal official authorized to investigate or prosecute violations of this section.[261]

Title 18, United States Code, Section 1956(h) is to the effect that Any person who conspires to commit any offence defined in that section or section 1957 shall be subject to the same penalties as those prescribed for the offence the commission of which was the object of the conspiracy.

CASE STUDY ON CONSPIRACY TO COMMIT MONEY LAUNDERING

Case 4.1: United States Department of Justice v. Marlen Manukyan

Marlen Manukyan, 41, of Brooklyn, New York, pled guilty to one count of conspiracy to commit money laundering, in violation of Title 18, United States Code, Section 1956(h). As part of his plea agreement, Manukyan agreed to restitution in the amount of one hundred twenty-four thousand nine dollars.

According to court documents, from August to November 2013, Manukyan opened bank accounts using counterfeit driver's licenses that he knew would be used to conduct financial transactions involving

---

259 Bank Secrecy Act (Statute) 18 U.S. Code s. 1956 (a) (3) (B)
260 Bank Secrecy Act (Statute) 18 U.S. Code s. 1956 (a) (3) (C)
261 Bank Secrecy Act (Statute), 18 U.S. Code s. 1956 (a) (3)

funds derived from unlawful activities. Specifically, from August 1, 2013 to August 9, 2013, Manukyan opened multiple bank accounts using the identities of two individuals without their permission using counterfeit Pennsylvania Driver's Licenses. These accounts received money from two illicit sources for the next several months.

First, Manukyan's co-conspirators filed fraudulent tax returns with the Internal Revenue Service (IRS) using the stolen identities of various individual taxpayers without the taxpayers' knowledge or consent. The fraudulent tax refunds (minus fees) were sent to several of the bank accounts that were set-up by the defendant. Co-conspirators then withdrew the money through cash withdrawals or debit card transactions. In total, Manukyan's co-conspirators filed approximately 71 fraudulent tax returns with the IRS.

Second, Manukyan's co-conspirators engaged in a scheme to defraud individuals who were seeking to buy used recreational vehicles (RVs) on the internet. To perpetrate this scheme, the defendant's co-conspirators used fake names and advertised on internet websites that they had used RVs for sale. Interested purchasers were told to send their money by wire transfer to a bank account in the name of a shell company that Manukyan opened using a counterfeit driver's license. Specifically, a retired couple was defrauded into believing that they had reached an agreement to purchase a used RV. The individuals sent thirty-nine thousand nine hundred sixty dollars by wire transfer to complete the purchase, but the couple never received the RV and the co-conspirators ceased communicating with the victims once they received the money. The defendant and his co-conspirators caused the bank to send thirty-nine thousand dollars by international wire transfer from the shell company's bank account to a bank account in the name of another individual in Moscow, Russia.

Manukyan was scheduled to be sentenced on March 16, 2017, before United States District Judge Darrin P. Gayles. At sentencing, the defendant faces up to twenty years in prison.[262]

---

262 United States Department of Justice (2017), 'New York Resident Pleads Guilty in South Florida to Money Laundering Conspiracy Involving Stolen Identity Tax Fraud and Recreational Vehicles Fraud Schemes', Available at: https://www.justice.gov/usao-sdfl/pr/new-york-resident-pleads-guilty-south-florida-money-laundering-conspiracy-involving (accessed 27 April 2017).

4.1.3 United Kingdom

The UK Proceeds of Crime Act 2002 (as amended) makes it a money laundering offence[263] for a person to:

i. Conceal criminal property;[264]
ii. Disguise criminal property;[265]
iii. Convert criminal property;[266]
iv. Transfer criminal property;[267]
v. Remove criminal property from England and Wales or from Scotland or from Northern Ireland.[268]
vi. **Enter into or become concerned in an arrangement which he knows or suspects facilitates (by whatever means) the acquisition, retention, use or control of criminal property by or on behalf of another person.[269]**
vii. Acquire criminal property;[270]
viii. Use criminal property;[271]
ix. Have possession of criminal property.[272]
x. Attempt, conspire or incite another to commit the above offences[273]
xi. Aid, abet, counsel or procure the commission of the above offences[274]

The act of 'Entering into or becoming concerned in an arrangement which a person knows or suspects facilitates (by whatever means) the acquisition, retention, use or control of criminal property by or

---

263 Proceeds of Crime Act 2002 (as amended), s. 340 (11) (a)
264 Proceeds of Crime Act 2002 (as amended), s. 327 (1) (a)
265 Proceeds of Crime Act 2002 (as amended), s. 327 (1) (b)
266 Proceeds of Crime Act 2002 (as amended), s. 327 (1) (c)
267 Proceeds of Crime Act 2002 (as amended), s. 327 (1) (d)
268 Proceeds of Crime Act 2002 (as amended), s. 327 (1) (e)
269 Proceeds of Crime Act 2002 (as amended), s. 328 (1)
270 Proceeds of Crime Act 2002 (as amended), s. 329 (1) (a)
271 Proceeds of Crime Act 2002 (as amended), s. 329 (1) (b)
272 Proceeds of Crime Act 2002 (as amended), s. 329 (1) (c)
273 Proceeds of Crime Act 2002 (as amended), s. 340 (11) (b)
274 Proceeds of Crime Act 2002 (as amended), s. 340 (11) (c)

on behalf of another person' is not a money laundering offence in Nigeria and United States but it is a money laundering offence in the United Kingdom as stated above.

Arrangement is not defined in Part 7 of the Proceeds of Crime Act (POCA). The arrangement must exist and have practical effects relating to the acquisition, retention, use or control of property.

An agreement to make an arrangement will not always be an arrangement. The test is whether the arrangement does in fact, in the present and not the future, have the effect of facilitating the acquisition, retention, use or control of criminal property by or on behalf of another person.

Bowman v Fels [2005] EWCA Civ 226 held that s. 328 does not cover or affect the ordinary conduct of litigation by legal professionals, including any step taken in litigation from the issue of proceedings and the securing of injunctive relief or a freezing order up to its final disposal by judgment.

Dividing assets in accordance with the judgment, including the handling of the assets which are criminal property, is not an arrangement. Further, settlements, negotiations, out of court settlements, alternative dispute resolution and tribunal representation are not arrangements. However, the property will generally still remain criminal property and you may need to consider referring your client for specialist advice regarding possible offences they may commit once they come into possession of the property after completion of the settlement.[275]

The recovery of property by a victim of an acquisitive offence will not be committing an offence under either **s.328 or s.329 of POCA**.[276]

---

275 The Law Society (2013), 'Chapter 5 - Money laundering offences', Available at: https://www.lawsociety.org.uk/support-services/advice/practice-notes/aml/money-laundering-offences/ (accessed 18 August 2017).

276 The Law Society (2013), 'Chapter 5 - Money laundering offences', Available at: https://www.lawsociety.org.uk/support-services/advice/practice-notes/aml/money-laundering-offences/ (accessed 18 August 2017).

4.2 Predicate Offences for Money Laundering (Domestic Crimes)

The FATF has advised countries to apply the crime of money laundering to all serious offences, with a view to including the widest range of predicate offences.

According to the FATF, Predicate offences may be described by reference to all offences; or to a threshold linked either to a category of serious offences, or to the penalty of imprisonment applicable to the predicate offence (threshold approach); or to a list of predicate offences; or a combination of these approaches.[277]

This section compares the approaches in Nigeria with those of the United States and the United Kingdom.

4.2.1 Nigeria

The Nigerian Money Laundering Prohibition Act 2011 (as amended) applies the crime of money laundering to a list of predicate offences and also to any other criminal act specified in the Nigerian Money Laundering Law or any other law in Nigeria.[278]

The predicate offences listed in the Nigerian Money Laundering Law includes: participation in an organized criminal group, racketeering, terrorism, terrorist financing, trafficking in persons, smuggling of migrants, sexual exploitation, sexual exploitation of children, illicit trafficking in narcotic drugs and psychotropic substances, illicit arms trafficking, illicit trafficking in stolen goods, corruption, bribery, fraud, currency, counterfeiting, counterfeiting and piracy of products, environmental crimes, murder, grievous bodily injury, kidnapping, hostage taking, robbery or theft, smuggling (including in relation to customs and excise duties and taxes), extortion, forgery, piracy, insider trading and market manipulation.[279]

---

277 The Financial Action Task Force (FATF): International Standards on Combating Money Laundering and the Financing of Terrorism and Proliferation, (The FATF Recommendations) 2012, Interpretive Note to Recommendation 3

278 Money Laundering Prohibition Act 2011 (as amended), s. 15 (6)

279 Money Laundering Prohibition Act 2011 (as amended), s. 15 (6)

4.2.2 United States

The U.S. Bank Secrecy Act (Statute) applies the crime of money laundering to a list of predicate offences.[280]

The predicate offences listed in the **U.S. Bank Secrecy Act (Statute)** include: an offence under section 32 (relating to the destruction of aircraft), section 37 (relating to violence at international airports), section 115 (relating to influencing, impeding, or retaliating against a Federal official by threatening or injuring a family member), section 152 (relating to concealment of assets; false oaths and claims; bribery), section 175c (relating to the variola virus), section 215 (relating to commissions or gifts for procuring loans), section 351 (relating to congressional or Cabinet officer assassination), any of sections 500 through 503 (relating to certain counterfeiting offences), section 513 (relating to securities of States and private entities), section 541 (relating to goods falsely classified), section 542 (relating to entry of goods by means of false statements), section 545 (relating to smuggling goods into the United States.), section 549 (relating to removing goods from Customs custody), section 554 (relating to smuggling goods from the United States.), section 555 (relating to border tunnels), section 641 (relating to public money, property, or records), section 656 (relating to theft, embezzlement, or misapplication by bank officer or employee), section 657 (relating to lending, credit, and insurance institutions), section 658 (relating to property mortgaged or pledged to farm credit agencies), section 666 (relating to theft or bribery concerning programs receiving Federal funds), section 793, 794, or 798 (relating to espionage), section 831 (relating to prohibited transactions involving nuclear materials), section 844 (f) or (i) (relating to destruction by explosives or fire of Government property or property affecting interstate or foreign commerce), section 875 (relating to interstate communications), section 922 (l) (relating to the unlawful importation of firearms), section 924 (n) (relating to firearms trafficking), section 956 (relating to conspiracy to kill,

---

280 Bank Secrecy Act (Statute) 18 U.S. Code s. 1956 (c) (7) (A), (C), (D), (E) and (F)

kidnap, maim, or injure certain property in a foreign country), section 1005 (relating to fraudulent bank entries), 1006 [2] (relating to fraudulent Federal credit institution entries), 1007 [2] (relating to Federal Deposit Insurance transactions), 1014 [2] (relating to fraudulent loan or credit applications), section 1030 (relating to computer fraud and abuse), 1032 [2] (relating to concealment of assets from conservator, receiver, or liquidating agent of financial institution), section 1111 (relating to murder), section 1114 (relating to murder of United States law enforcement officials), section 1116 (relating to murder of foreign officials, official guests, or internationally protected persons), section 1201 (relating to kidnaping), section 1203 (relating to hostage taking), section 1361 (relating to wilful injury of Government property), section 1363 (relating to destruction of property within the special maritime and territorial jurisdiction), section 1708 (theft from the mail), section 1751 (relating to Presidential assassination), section 2113 or 2114 (relating to bank and postal robbery and theft), section 2252A (relating to child pornography) where the child pornography contains a visual depiction of an actual minor engaging in sexually explicit conduct, section 2260 (production of certain child pornography for importation into the United States), section 2280 (relating to violence against maritime navigation), section 2281 (relating to violence against maritime fixed platforms), section 2319 (relating to copyright infringement), section 2320 (relating to trafficking in counterfeit goods and services), section 2332 (relating to terrorist acts abroad against U.S. nationals), section 2332a (relating to use of weapons of mass destruction), section 2332b (relating to international terrorist acts transcending national boundaries), section 2332g (relating to missile systems designed to destroy aircraft), section 2332h (relating to radiological dispersal devices), section 2339A or 2339B (relating to providing material support to terrorists), section 2339C (relating to financing of terrorism), or section 2339D (relating to receiving military-type training from a foreign terrorist organization) of this title, section 46502 of title 49, U.S. Code, a felony violation of the Chemical Diversion and Trafficking Act of 1988 (relating to precursor and essential chemicals), section

590 of the Tariff Act of 1930 (19 U.S.C. 1590) (relating to aviation smuggling), section 422 of the Controlled Substances Act (relating to transportation of drug paraphernalia), section 38 (c) (relating to criminal violations) of the Arms Export Control Act, section 11 (relating to violations) of the Export Administration Act of 1979, section 206 (relating to penalties) of the International Emergency Economic Powers Act, section 16 (relating to offences and punishment) of the Trading with the Enemy Act, any felony violation of section 15 of the Food and Nutrition Act of 2008 (relating to supplemental nutrition assistance program benefits fraud) involving a quantity of benefits having a value of not less than five thousand dollars, any violation of section 543(a)(1) of the Housing Act of 1949 (relating to equity skimming), any felony violation of the Foreign Agents Registration Act of 1938, any felony violation of the Foreign Corrupt Practices Act, or section 92 of the Atomic Energy Act of 1954 (42 U.S.C. 2122) (relating to prohibitions governing atomic weapons), environmental crimes,[281] a felony violation of the Federal Water Pollution Control Act (33 U.S.C. 1251 et seq.), the Ocean Dumping Act (33 U.S.C. 1401 et seq.), the Act to Prevent Pollution from Ships (33 U.S.C. 1901 et seq.), the Safe Drinking Water Act (42 U.S.C. 300f et seq.), or the Resources Conservation and Recovery Act (42 U.S.C. 6901 et seq.); or[282] any act or activity constituting an offence involving a Federal health care offence.[283]

Predicate offences also include any act or activity constituting an offence listed in section 1961 (1) of title 18 except an act which is indictable under subchapter II of chapter 53 of title 31;[284] and also any act or acts constituting a continuing criminal enterprise, as that term is defined in section 408 of the Controlled Substances Act (21 U.S.C. 848);[285]

---

281 Bank Secrecy Act (Statute) 18 U.S. Code s. 1956 (c) (7) (D)

282 Bank Secrecy Act (Statute) 18 U.S. Code s. 1956 (c)(7) (E)

283 Bank Secrecy Act (Statute) 18 U.S. Code s. 1956 (c)(7) (F)

284 Bank Secrecy Act (Statute) 18 U.S. Code s. 1956 (c)(7) (A)

285 Bank Secrecy Act (Statute) 18 U.S. Code s. 1956 (c)(7) (C)

4.2.3 United Kingdom

The UK Proceeds of Crime Act 2002 (as amended) applies the crime of money laundering to all predicate offences.[286]

4.3 Predicate Offences for Money Laundering (Foreign Crimes)

The FATF has advised countries to extend predicate offences for money laundering to conduct that occurred in another country, which constitutes an offence in that country, and which would have constituted a predicate offence had it occurred domestically (double criminality test).

According to the FATF, countries could also provide that the only prerequisite is that the conduct would have constituted a predicate offence, had it occurred domestically (single criminality test).[287]

This section compares the approaches in Nigeria with those of the United States and the United Kingdom.

4.3.1 Nigeria

The Nigerian Money Laundering Prohibition Act 2011 (as amended) remains silent with regards to the application of the above tests.

The reason for such silence could be as a result of the fact that the **Nigerian Criminal Code Act 2004** applies the single criminality test to offences partially committed in Nigeria.[288]

It could therefore be inferred from the above facts that the same test may be applied to 'predicate offences for money laundering' occurring outside Nigeria.

---

286 Proceeds of Crime Act 2002 (as amended), s 340 (2) (a), See also The Joint Money Laundering Steering Group JMLSG, *Prevention of money laundering/combating terrorist financing* 2017 Revised Version, Guidance for the UK financial sector Part I, June 2017 (Amended December 2017), Appendix II, Paragraph 1.

287 The Financial Action Task Force (FATF): International Standards on Combating Money Laundering and the Financing of Terrorism and Proliferation, (The FATF Recommendations) 2012, Interpretive Note to Recommendation 3

288 Criminal Code Act 2004, s. 12, See also Nwadialo, F. (S.A.N) (1987), *The Criminal Procedure of the Southern States of Nigeria* (2nd Edition MIJ Professional Publishers Limited), 14 – 15.

4.3.2 United States

The United States extends predicate offences for money laundering to conduct that would have constituted a predicate offence, had it occurred domestically (single criminality test).

This test is therefore limited to a list of predicate offences and the value of funds involved in a transaction. The predicate offences include:

i. the manufacture, importation, sale, or distribution of a controlled substance (as such term is defined for the purposes of the Controlled Substances Act);[289]

ii. murder, kidnapping, robbery, extortion, destruction of property by means of explosive or fire, or a crime of violence (as defined in section 16);[290]

iii. fraud, or any scheme or attempt to defraud, by or against a foreign bank (as defined in paragraph 7 of section 1(b) of the International Banking Act of 1978));[291]

iv. bribery of a public official, or the misappropriation, theft, or embezzlement of public funds by or for the benefit of a public official;[292]

v. smuggling or export control violations involving—
   a. an item controlled on the United States Munitions List established under section 38 of the Arms Export Control Act (22 U.S.C. 2778); or
   b. an item controlled under regulations under the Export Administration Regulations (15 C.F.R. Parts 730–774);[293]

vi. an offence with respect to which the US would be obligated by a multilateral treaty, either to extradite the alleged offender or to submit the case for prosecution, if the offender were found within the territory of the United States; or[294]

---

289 Bank Secrecy Act (Statute) 18 U.S. Code s. 1956 (c) (7) (B) (i)
290 Bank Secrecy Act (Statute) 18 U.S. Code s. 1956 (c) (7) (B) (ii)
291 Bank Secrecy Act (Statute) 18 U.S. Code s. 1956 (c) (7)(B) (iii)
292 Bank Secrecy Act (Statute) 18 U.S. Code s. 1956 (c) (7) (B)(iv)
293 Bank Secrecy Act (Statute) 18 U.S. Code s. 1956 (c) (7) (B) (v)
294 Bank Secrecy Act (Statute) 18 U.S. Code s. 1956 (c) (7) (B) (vi)

vii. trafficking in persons, selling or buying of children, sexual exploitation of children, or transporting, recruiting or harbouring a person, including a child, for commercial sex acts;[295]

The value involved in a transaction or series of related transactions includes funds or monetary instruments of a value exceeding ten thousand dollars.[296]

4.3.3 United Kingdom

The United Kingdom applies both the single criminality test and the double criminality test to conducts occurring abroad. The single criminality test is limited to predicate offences punishable for more than one year while the double criminality test is limited to predicate offences punishable for less than a year.[297]

4.4 Penalties

The FATF has advised countries to apply effective, proportionate and dissuasive criminal sanctions to natural persons convicted of money laundering.

The FATF has also advised countries to apply criminal liability and sanctions to legal persons and where that is not possible (due to fundamental principles of domestic law), civil or administrative liability and sanctions should apply.[298]

This section compares the approaches in Nigeria with those of the United States and the United Kingdom.

---

295 Bank Secrecy Act (Statute) 18 U.S. Code s. 1956 (c)(7) (B) (vii)

296 Bank Secrecy Act (Statute) 18 U.S. Code s. 1956 (f)(2)

297 Proceeds of Crime Act 2002, s. 340 (2) (b), See also Serious Organised Crime and Police Act 2005, s 102 (1-7), The Proceeds of Crime Act 2002 (Money Laundering: Exceptions to Overseas Conduct Defence) Order 2006, Article 2

298 The Financial Action Task Force (FATF): International Standards on Combating Money Laundering and the Financing of Terrorism and Proliferation, (The FATF Recommendations) 2012, Interpretive Note to Recommendation 3

4.4.1 Nigeria

A person who commits the offence of money laundering is liable on conviction to a term not less than 7 years but not more than 14 years imprisonment.[299]

A body corporate who commits the offence of money laundering is liable on conviction to a fine of not less than 100% of the funds and properties acquired as a result of the offence committed; and withdrawal of licence.[300]

In addition to the penalty prescribed above, the Court may order a person convicted of an offence of fraud and money laundering to make restitution to the victim of the false pretence or fraud by directing that person-

(a) where the property involved is money, to pay to the victim an amount equivalent to the loss sustained by the victim;

in any other case -

(i) to return the property to the victim or to a person designated by him; or
(ii) to pay an amount equal to the value of the property, where the return of the property is impossible or impracticable.
(2) An order of restitution may be enforced by the victim or by the prosecutor on behalf of the victim in the same manner as a judgment in a civil action.[301]

CASE STUDY: RESTITUTION ORDERS WHERE A PERSON IS CHARGED WITH BOTH FRAUD AND MONEY LAUNDERING

A 22 years old internet fraudster, Bike John Niye was sentenced to one and half years imprisonment by a Lagos State High Court sitting

---

299 Money Laundering Prohibition Act 2011 (as amended), s. 15 (3)
300 Money Laundering Prohibition Act 2011 (as amended), s. 15 (4)
301 Advance Fee Fraud and other Fraud Related Offences Act 2006, s. 11

in Ikeja, for defrauding one Laura Wallmam of Indiana, United States of America the sum of fifty-three thousand five hundred dollars. Justice A Akinlade slammed the prison term on Niye having found him guilty of the four-count charge bordering on obtaining money by false pretense and attempt to obtain money by false pretense, preferred against him by the Economic and Financial Crimes Commission, EFCC.

Reports showed that Niye presented himself to Wallmam as businessman who operates a 'moving' company and needed money to get some of his goods out of storage. He met Wallmam in a dating site and has been in a relationship with her using a fictitious name, Toby Encore.

His journey to prison began on May 27th, 2010 when officials of the National Drug Law Enforcement Agency, NDLEA and DHL Courier Services intercepted a suspicious parcel containing a Teddy Bear and a Blackberry handset sent from the USA to the convict by Wallmam. The parcel was examined and it was discovered that it contained the sum of forty thousand dollars, a Blackberry handset, and a white lady's photograph concealed in the Teddy Bear. The parcel was to be delivered to an address in Alapere, a suburb of Lagos with the name Tobi Encore and a Nigerian phone number also belonging to the same recipient. With the phone number, the convicted fraudster was traced and upon finding him, he was handed over to the EFCC for further investigations.

Upon investigation, Operatives of the Commission discovered that the name Tony Encore was used by the fraudster to deceive the American in order to defraud her. It was found out that his real name is Bike John Niye. The operatives also discovered that it was Niye who instructed the victim to conceal all the items in a Teddy Bear.

Investigations also revealed that Niye has been receiving various sums of money from the victim via Western Union totaling about twenty-five thousand dollars before the parcel which finally landed him in jail. To enable him collect the sent funds via Western Union, findings revealed that Niye obtained a Driver's license with a forged identity bearing the name Nathan Omarkeh. He usually destroys the identity card after collecting money sent to him.

In addition to the one and half year jail term, Niye is to refund the sum of forty-eight thousand five hundred dollars as restitution to the victim.[302]

4.4.2 United States

A person who commits the offence of money laundering shall be sentenced to a fine of not more than five hundred thousand dollars or twice the value of the property involved in the transaction, whichever is greater, or imprisonment for not more than twenty years, or both.[303]

In addition to the sentence that may be imposed under the **Bank Secrecy Act (Statute)**, the Court may also impose other orders, known as ancillary orders e.g. supervised release and restitution orders.

Under **18 U.S. Code § 3583 subsection (a)**, the Court is required to impose a term of supervised release to follow imprisonment when supervised release is required by statute or, except as provided in subsection (c), when a sentence of imprisonment of more than one year is imposed. The court may depart from the United States Sentencing Commission Guidelines Manual 2016 and not impose a term of supervised release if supervised release is not required by statute and the court determines, after considering the factors set forth in section 3553(a)(1), (a)(2)(B), (a)(2)(C), (a)(2)(D), (a)(4), (a)(5), (a)(6), and (a)(7), that supervised release is not necessary.

In determining whether to impose a term of supervised release, the court is required by statute to consider, among other factors:

(i) the nature and circumstances of the offence and the history and characteristics of the defendant;

---

302 Uwujaren, W. (2012), 'Court Jails Fraudster Over $53,500 Romance Scam', Available at: https://efccnigeria.org/efcc/news/84-court-jails-fraudster-over-53-500-romance-scam (accessed 30 August 2017).

303 Bank Secrecy Act (Statute) 18 U.S. Code s. 1956 (a) (1) (2) (3)

(ii) the need to afford adequate deterrence to criminal conduct, to protect the public from further crimes of the defendant, and to provide the defendant with needed educational or vocational training, medical care, or other correctional treatment in the most effective manner;

(iii) the need to avoid unwarranted sentence disparities among defendants with similar records who have been found guilty of similar conduct; and

(iv) the need to provide restitution to any victims of the offence.[304]

The court shall order, as an explicit condition of supervised release, that the defendant not commit another Federal, State, or local crime during the term of supervision.[305]

CASE STUDY: SUPERVISED RELEASE AND RESTITUTION ORDERS

Allen Weintraub, 48, of Boynton Beach, was sentenced on April 24, 2014 by U.S. District Judge Donald Graham to 111 months in prison, three years of supervised release, and was ordered to forfeit one hundred forty thousand two hundred eighty dollars and forty-seven cents and to pay the same amount in restitution to two victims of a scheme to sell Facebook shares.

In February 2014, Weintraub pled guilty to two counts of mail fraud. According to an agreed factual proffer, in February 2012, Weintraub, using an alias, steered potential investors seeking to purchase pre-IPO stock of Facebook to the website of Private Stock Transfer Inc. by posting a response on www.quora.com. In that post, Weintraub claimed that he had purchased Facebook stock from Private Stock Transfer Inc. When victims went to the website and sought information on purchasing Facebook stock, Weintraub responded representing that Private

---

304 See the United States Sentencing Commission (2016), ' Guidelines Manual 2016 ', Available at: https://www.ussc.gov/sites/default/files/pdf/guidelines-manual/2016/GLMFull.pdf (accessed 20 August 2017); See also 18 U.S.C. § 3583(c)

305 18 U.S.C. § 3583(d)

Stock Transfer Inc. had thousands of Facebook shares available for purchase. He directed that various forms be completed which represented that victims were purchasing shares described as "Facebook Inc. by and through PST Investment III, Inc. Class A shares on a one for one conversion basis." PST Investment III Inc. was another company associated with Weintraub. After the victims sent payment to Weintraub's bank accounts, Weintraub issued and mailed stock certificates for PST Investment III shares that would convert to Facebook shares on a one-for-one basis once Facebook went public. In reality, neither Weintraub nor Private Stock Transfer Inc. had any Facebook shares. The two victims were defrauded a total of four hundred and fourteen thousand dollars.

This case was prosecuted by Assistant U.S. Attorney Lois Foster-Steers.[306]

4.4.3 United Kingdom

A person who commits the offence of money laundering is liable on summary conviction, to imprisonment for a term not exceeding six months or to a fine not exceeding the statutory maximum or to both,[307] or on conviction on indictment, to imprisonment for a term not exceeding 14 years or to a fine or to both.[308]

In addition to the sentence that may be imposed under the **Proceeds of Crime Act 2002 (as amended),** the judge or magistrate may also impose other orders, known as ancillary orders. Some ancillary orders are aimed at redressing the harm caused by an offender, such as compensation orders. Others aim to prevent future re-offending or repeat victimisation, including criminal behaviour orders and exclusion orders.

It is up to the judge or magistrate to decide whether an ancillary order is appropriate or necessary, taking into account the circumstances of the offence and the offender. In many cases the

---

306 Federal Bureau of Investigation (2014), 'Facebook Fraudster Sentenced', Available at: https://www.fbi.gov/contact-us/field-offices/miami/news/press-releases/facebook-fraudster-sentenced (accessed 6 September 2017).

307 Proceeds of Crime Act 2002, s. 334 (1) (a)

308 Proceeds of Crime Act 2002, s. 334 (1) (b)

prosecution will invite the court to make relevant orders. There are a number of different ancillary orders available including:

- criminal behaviour orders;
- compensation orders;
- confiscation orders (Crown Court only);
- deprivation orders;
- disqualification from driving;
- drink banning orders;
- disqualification from being a company director;
- financial reporting order;
- football banning orders;
- forfeiture orders;
- parenting orders;
- restitution orders;
- restraining orders;
- serious crime prevention order (Crown Court only); and
- sexual harm prevention orders.[309]

4.5 Discussion

The previous section compared the approaches in Nigeria with those of the United States and the United Kingdom. This section will analyse issues that arose from the comparison to determine if there is need for reform.

4.5.1 Predicate Offences for Money Laundering (Domestic Crimes)

As stated earlier, the **Nigerian Money Laundering Prohibition Act 2011 (as amended)** applies the crime of money laundering to a list of predicate offences and also to any other criminal act specified in the money laundering law or any other law in Nigeria.

---

309 The Sentencing Council for England and Wales (2017), 'Ancillary Orders', Available at: https://www.sentencingcouncil.org.uk/about-sentencing/types-of-sentence/ancillary-orders/ (accessed 20 August 2017).

The United States, on the other hand, applies the crime of money laundering to a list of predicate offences, while the United Kingdom applies it to all predicate offences.

The US approach could be regarded as a good law to the extent that it applies the crime of money laundering to the most serious offences. However, the US approach violates Article 7 of the Universal Declaration of Human Rights (UDHR), which prohibits laws that discriminate against human beings.[310]

The discrimination is on the basis that people who commit less serious crimes are allowed to launder the proceeds generated from such crimes, while people who commit serious crimes or crimes not listed in the Bank Secrecy Act are not allowed to launder proceeds generated from such crimes.

The United Kingdom's approach, on the other hand, does not discriminate against persons, as it applies the crime of money laundering to all predicate offences.

Nigeria's approach is similar to that of the United Kingdom. The only difference is that it applies the crime of money laundering to a list of predicate offences. This is the case even when the same law also applies the crime of money laundering to all predicate offences.

In view of the above arguments, there is no need for Nigeria to apply the crime of money laundering to a list of predicate offences, since it is already applied to all offences.

4.5.2 Predicate Offences for Money Laundering (Foreign Crimes)

The **Nigerian Criminal Code Act 2004** applies the single criminality test to foreign crimes partially committed in Nigeria.

The United States, on the other hand, applies the single criminality test to serious crimes that are committed outside the United States. This test is, therefore, limited to the value of funds involved in a transaction.

---

310 The Universal Declaration of Human Rights (1948), Article 7; Odibei, F.F. (2011), *Cases and Materials on Human Rights Law,* 1st edition (Pearl Publishers), 196–197.

The United Kingdom applies the single criminality test to serious crimes that are committed outside the United Kingdom. This test is not limited to any value of funds as it is in the United States.

The Nigerian approach appears to be in line with **Article 2 (2) of the Vienna Convention**, which mandates countries to carry out their obligations in a manner consistent with the principles of sovereign equality and territorial integrity of countries and that of nonintervention in the domestic affairs of other countries.

The US and UK approaches appear to be inconsistent with these principles. They both establish their jurisdictions over offences committed abroad, provided that the offence is a serious offence.

This approach is also inconsistent with **Article 2 (3) of the Vienna Convention**, which mandates that countries should not exercise jurisdiction and performance of functions in the territory of another country that are exclusively reserved for the authorities of that other country by its domestic law.

In view of the above arguments, the Nigerian approach is a good approach.

The United States and United Kingdom are advised to adopt the Nigerian approach by applying the single criminality test to foreign crimes partially committed within their jurisdictions.

4.5.3 Lifetime Management of Ancillary Orders

The Lifetime Management Team within the National Crime Agency (NCA), United Kingdom, has responsibility for managing a number of high-priority and significant serious and organised criminals. These criminals have been convicted of serious offences, and law enforcement have secured additional restrictions on them at court to prevent them from re-offending. Key powers used include:

I. **Serious Crime Prevention Orders**
    Serious Crime Prevention Orders (SCPOs) are civil orders to prevent or deter serious crime. Breach of an SCPO is a criminal offence punishable by up to five years imprisonment and an unlimited fine. The restrictions that an SCPO can include

are wide-ranging. As long as they are shown to be proportionate, justified and necessary to the circumstances of the case, they can include restrictions on communications devices, conducting specific types of business, bank accounts, associating with criminal associates, and geographic restrictions. The order lasts for up to five years.

II. **Travel Restriction Orders**

A Travel Restriction Order (TRO) can be imposed on any offender convicted of a drug trafficking offence and sentenced to four years or more in prison, regardless of nationality. The aim of the order is to reduce re-offending through restricting the movements of convicted drug traffickers. UK passport holders (including those with dual nationality) may be required to surrender their passports to the court. The TRO comes into effect upon the offender's release from prison and its minimum length is two years. The penalty for breach of a TRO is up to five years' imprisonment and/or a fine.

III. **Financial Reporting Orders**

Financial Reporting Orders (FROs) may be made by a court, on the application of a prosecutor, following a conviction for certain offences. They require a convicted criminal to report their financial details at regular intervals. This can be for a period of up to 20 years for those sentenced to life, or a maximum of 15 years for other sentences.

IV. **Licence Conditions**

The National Offender Management Service (NOMS) monitors the behaviour of offenders released from prison on parole licence through the use of standard and bespoke licence conditions. The Lifetime Management Team works closely with NOMS to develop licence conditions imposed on offenders of interest to the NCA. The imposition of licence conditions can deter and frustrate offenders from committing further offences. If the offender breaks one or more of the conditions, such as by travelling abroad, they can be sent back to prison. The Lifetime Management Team and NOMS work together to ensure offenders comply with those conditions.

The Lifetime Management Team uses a wide range of investigative and intelligence techniques to monitor individuals' compliance with these restrictions. In particular, the Lifetime Management Team works closely with partners to exchange information on these individuals to identify and reduce their opportunities for returning to criminal activity.[311]

It is worth noting that the Nigerian Money Laundering Laws/ Regulations do not provide for the above mentioned Ancillary orders. Once a criminal has served his or her time the criminal will no longer be subject to restrictions that could prevent him or her from re-offending. This is contrary to the U.S. and U.K. approach.

4.6 Conclusion

This chapter compared the approaches in Nigeria with those of the United States and United Kingdom on the basis of the 'criminalization of money laundering' and other related subtopics. It has also analysed issues that arose from the comparison to determine if there is need for reform. This section focuses on those areas that need reform.

Based on the arguments canvassed in Section 4.5, the following reforms to the **Nigerian Money Laundering Prohibition Act 2011 (as amended)** are recommended:

I.   The crime of money laundering should not be applied to a list of predicate offences since it is already applied to all offences.

II. The **Nigerian Money Laundering Prohibition Act 2011 (as amended)** should be amended to include the single criminality test, even if it is already included in the Nigerian Criminal Code Act.

---

311 National Crime Agency (2017), 'Lifetime Management', Available at: http:// www.nationalcrimeagency.gov.uk/about-us/what-we-do/lifetime-management (accessed 18 August 2017).

III. The **Economic and Financial Crimes Commission (Establish-ment) Act, 2004** should be amended to include ancillary orders. **Ancillary orders are designed to frustrate criminality, both in and out of prison. They can restrict the number of mobile phones or computers that offenders can access, limit the amount of cash they can carry, require them to surrender passports and provide financial information at regular intervals.** The United Kingdom National Crime Agency rigorously enforces these orders and takes action if people breach the terms. Many career criminals regard prison as an interruption which rarely marks the end of their involvement in organised crime. This is why the NCA has a policy of Lifetime Management. Once a criminal is on the NCA's radar they will stay on it. These orders can include a wide variety of restrictions, all designed to limit the ability for criminals to engage in illegal activity.[312]

---

312 National Crime Agency (2017), 'Updated list of active ancillary orders published', Available at: http://www.nationalcrimeagency.gov.uk/index.php/news-media/nca-news/1145-updated-list-of-active-ancillary-orders-published-2 (accessed 18 August 2017).

CHAPTER 5

TERRORIST FINANCING OFFENCE

The Financial Action Task Force (FATF) has advised Countries to criminalise terrorist financing on the basis of the Terrorist Financing Convention, and should criminalise not only the financing of terrorist acts but also the financing of terrorist organisations and individual terrorists even in the absence of a link to a specific terrorist act or acts.[313]

This Recommendation was developed with the objective of ensuring that countries have the legal capacity to prosecute and apply criminal sanctions to persons that finance terrorism. Given the close connection between international terrorism and, inter alia, money laundering, another objective of the Recommendation is to emphasise this link by obligating countries to include terrorist financing offences as predicate offences for money laundering.[314]

According to the FATF, the terrorist financing offence should have the following characteristics:

i. Terrorist financing offences should extend to any person who wilfully provides or collects funds by any means, directly or indirectly, with the unlawful intention that they should be used, or in the knowledge that they are to be used, in full or in part: (a) to carry out a terrorist act(s); (b) by a terrorist organisation; or (c) by an individual terrorist.

---

313 The FATF Recommendations 2012, Recommendation 5
314 The FATF Recommendations 2012, Interpretive Note to Recommendation 5

ii. Criminalising terrorist financing solely on the basis of aiding and abetting, attempt, or conspiracy is not sufficient to comply with this Recommendation.

iii. Terrorist financing offences should extend to any funds, whether from a legitimate or illegitimate source.

iv. Terrorist financing offences should not require that the funds: (a) were actually used to carry out or attempt a terrorist act(s); or (b) be linked to a specific terrorist act(s).

v. Countries should ensure that the intent and knowledge required to prove the offence of terrorist financing may be inferred from objective factual circumstances.

vi. Effective, proportionate and dissuasive criminal sanctions should apply to natural persons convicted of terrorist financing.

vii. Criminal liability and sanctions, and, where that is not possible (due to fundamental principles of domestic law), civil or administrative liability and sanctions, should apply to legal persons. This should not preclude parallel criminal, civil or administrative proceedings with respect to legal persons in countries in which more than one forms of liability is available. Such measures should be without prejudice to the criminal liability of natural persons. All sanctions should be effective, proportionate and dissuasive.

viii. It should also be an offence to attempt to commit the offence of terrorist financing.

ix. It should also be an offence to engage in any of the following types of conduct:

(a) Participating as an accomplice in an offence, as set forth in paragraphs 2 or 9 of this Interpretive Note;

(b) Organising or directing others to commit an offence, as set forth in paragraphs 2 or 9 of this Interpretive Note;

(c) Contributing to the commission of one or more offence(s), as set forth in paragraphs 2 or 9 of this Interpretive Note, by a group of persons acting with a common purpose.[315]

---

315 The FATF Recommendations 2012, Interpretive Note to Recommendation 5

While countries have followed the advice of the FATF by criminalizing terrorist financing and have implemented all the above recommendations, the approaches taken by these countries are different.

This chapter compares the approaches taken by Nigeria with those of the United States and the United Kingdom under four subheadings: 'Offences', 'Jurisdiction', 'Penalties' and 'Freezing, Seizure and Forfeiture of Funds'. This chapter will also analyse issues that arise from the comparison to determine if there is need for reform.

5.1 Offences

Article 4 (a) of the International Convention for the Suppression of the Financing of Terrorism requires each State Party to adopt such measures as may be necessary to establish as criminal offences under its domestic law the offences set forth in article 2.

Article 2 of the International Convention for the Suppression of the Financing of Terrorism criminalises the financing of terrorism as it states that:

1. Any person commits an offence within the meaning of the Convention if that person by any means, directly or indirectly, unlawfully and wilfully, provides or collects funds with the intention that they should be used or in the knowledge that they are to be used, in full or in part, in order to carry out:
   (a) An act which constitutes an offence within the scope of and as defined in the Convention for the Suppression of Unlawful Seizure of Aircraft, done at The Hague on 16 December 1970; Convention for the Suppression of Unlawful Acts against the Safety of Civil Aviation, done at Montreal on 23 September 1971; Convention on the Prevention and Punishment of Crimes against Internationally Protected Persons, including Diplomatic Agents, adopted by the General Assembly of the United Nations on 14 December 1973; International Convention against the Taking of Hostages, adopted by the General Assembly of the United Nations on 17 December 1979; Convention on the Physical Protection of Nuclear Material, adopted at Vienna on 3 March 1980; Protocol for

the Suppression of Unlawful Acts of Violence at Airports Serving International Civil Aviation, supplementary to the Convention for the Suppression of Unlawful Acts against the Safety of Civil Aviation, done at Montreal on 24 February 1988; Convention for the Suppression of Unlawful Acts against the Safety of Maritime Navigation, done at Rome on 10 March 1988; Protocol for the Suppression of Unlawful Acts against the Safety of Fixed Platforms located on the Continental Shelf, done at Rome on 10 March 1988 and International Convention for the Suppression of Terrorist Bombings, adopted by the General Assembly of the United Nations on 15 December 1997 or

(b) Any other act intended to cause death or serious bodily injury to a civilian, or to any other person not taking an active part in the hostilities in a situation of armed conflict, when the purpose of such act, by its nature or context, is to intimidate a population, or to compel a government or an international organization to do or to abstain from doing any act.

3. **For an act to constitute an offence set forth in paragraph 1, it shall not be necessary that the funds were actually used to carry out an offence referred to in paragraph 1, subparagraphs (a) or (b).**

4. Any person also commits an offence if that person attempts to commit an offence as set forth in paragraph 1 of this article.

5. Any person also commits an offence if that person:
    (a) Participates as an accomplice in an offence as set forth in paragraph 1 or 4 of this article;
    (b) Organizes or directs others to commit an offence as set forth in paragraph 1 or 4 of this article;
    (c) Contributes to the commission of one or more offences as set forth in paragraphs 1 or 4 of this article by a group of persons acting with a common purpose. Such contribution shall be intentional and shall either:
        (i) Be made with the aim of furthering the criminal activity or criminal purpose of the group, where such

activity or purpose involves the commission of an offence as set forth in paragraph 1 of this article; or

(ii) Be made in the knowledge of the intention of the group to commit an offence as set forth in paragraph 1 of this article.

5.1.1 Nigeria
Section 13 of the Terrorism (Prevention) Act, 2011 (as amended), makes the financing of terrorism a criminal offence as it states that:

13 (1) *"Any person or body corporate, who, in or outside Nigeria -*

  (a) solicits, acquires, provides, collects, receives, possesses or makes available funds, property or other services by any means, whether legitimate or otherwise, to -

   (i) terrorist organisation, or

   (ii) individual terrorist, directly or indirectly, willingly with the unlawful intention or knowledge or having reasonable grounds to believe that such funds or property will be used in full or in part in order to commit or facilitate an offence under this Act or in breach of the provisions of this Act,

  (b) attempts to do any of the acts specified in paragraph (a) of this subsection, and

  (c) possesses funds with the unlawful intention that it be used or knowing that it will be used, directly or indirectly, in whole or in part, for the purpose of committing or facilitating the commission of a terrorist act by terrorists or terrorist groups, commits an offence under this Act."[316]

13 (2) *"Any person who knowingly enters into or becomes involved, participates as an accomplice, organizes or directs others in an arrangement -*

  (a) which facilitates the acquisition, retention or control by or on behalf of another person of terrorist fund by concealment, removal out of jurisdiction, transfer to a nominee or in any other way, or

---

316 Terrorism (Prevention) Act, 2011 (as amended), s. 13 (1)

> (b) as a result of which funds or other property is to be made
> available for the purpose of terrorism or for the benefit of -
> > (i)   terrorist individual,
> > (ii) terrorist organization, or
> > (iii) proscribed organization,
> > > commits an offence under this Act. "[317]

13 (3) "For an act to constitute an offence under this section, it is not necessary that the funds or property were actually used to commit any offence of terrorism."[318]

> 13 (4) "An offence under this section shall apply, regardless of whether
> the person alleged to have committed the offence is in the same
> country or a different country from the one in which -
> > (a) the terrorist, terrorist group or proscribed organisation is located; or
> > (b) the terrorist act occurred or is planned to occur."[319]

Section 15 of the Economic and Financial Crimes Commission (Establishment) Act, 2004, also makes the financing of terrorism a criminal offence as it states that:

> 15(1) "A person who willfully provides or collects by any means directly
> or indirectly, any money from any other person with intent that the
> money shall be used or is in the knowledge that the money shall be
> used for any act of terrorism, commits an offence under this Act
> and is liable on conviction to imprisonment for life."

> 15 (2) "Any person who commits or attempts to commit a terrorist act
> or participates in or facilitates the commission of a terrorist act,
> commits an offence under this Act and is liable on conviction to
> imprisonment for life."

> 15 (3) "Any person who, makes funds, financial assets or economic re-
> sources or financial or other related services available for use of
> any other person to commit or attempt to commit, facilitate or

---

317 Terrorism (Prevention) Act, 2011 (as amended), s. 13 (2)

318 Terrorism (Prevention) Act, 2011 (as amended), s. 13 (3)

319 Terrorism (Prevention) Act, 2011 (as amended), s. 13 (4)

participate in the commission of a terrorist act is liable on conviction to imprisonment for life."

Section 46 of the Economic and Financial Crimes Commission (Establishment) Act, 2004 defines terrorism as:

(a) "*any act which is a violation of the Criminal Code or the Penal Code and which may endanger the life, physical integrity or freedom of, or cause serious injury or death to, any person, any number or group of persons or causes or may cause damage to public or property, natural resources, environmental or cultural heritage and is calculated or intended to -*
  (i) *intimidate, put in fear, force, coerce or induce any government, body, institution, the general public or any segment thereof, to do or abstain from doing any act or to adopt or abandon a particular standpoint, or to act according to certain principles; or*
  (ii) *Disrupt any public service, the delivery of any essential service to the public or to create a public emergency; or*
  (iii) *Create general insurrection in a state...*"
(b) "*any promotion, sponsorship of, contribution to, command, aid, incitement, encouragement, attempt, threat, conspiracy, organization or procurement of any person, with the intent to commit any act referred to in paragraph (a) (i), (ii) and (iii).*"

The above provisions appear to be in line with Article 2 of the International Convention for the Suppression of the Financing of Terrorism and Recommendation 5 of the FATF Recommendations as they do not require that the funds meant to finance terrorism were actually used to carry out or attempt a terrorist act(s); or be linked to a specific terrorist act(s).

5.1.2 United States
Section 2339C of Title 18 of the United States Code prohibits the financing of terrorism.

In general, whoever, in a circumstance described in subsection (b) of the 18 U.S. Code § 2339C, by any means, directly or indirectly, unlawfully and willfully provides or collects funds with the intention that such funds be used, or with the knowledge that such funds are to be used, in full or in part, in order to carry out—

(A) an act which constitutes an offence within the scope of a treaty specified in subsection (e) (7), as implemented by the United States, or

(B) any other act intended to cause death or serious bodily injury to a civilian, or to any other person not taking an active part in the hostilities in a situation of armed conflict, when the purpose of such act, by its nature or context, is to intimidate a population, or to compel a government or an international organization to do or to abstain from doing any act, shall be punished accordingly.[320]

The term "treaty" means—

(A) the Convention for the Suppression of Unlawful Seizure of Aircraft, done at The Hague on December 16, 1970;

(B) the Convention for the Suppression of Unlawful Acts against the Safety of Civil Aviation, done at Montreal on September 23, 1971;

(C) the Convention on the Prevention and Punishment of Crimes against Internationally Protected Persons, including Diplomatic Agents, adopted by the General Assembly of the United Nations on December 14, 1973;

(D) the International Convention against the Taking of Hostages, adopted by the General Assembly of the United Nations on December 17, 1979;

(E) the Convention on the Physical Protection of Nuclear Material, adopted at Vienna on March 3, 1980;

(F) the Protocol for the Suppression of Unlawful Acts of Violence at Airports Serving International Civil Aviation,

---

320 18 U.S. Code § 2339C (a) (1)

supplementary to the Convention for the Suppression of Unlawful Acts against the Safety of Civil Aviation, done at Montreal on February 24, 1988;

(G) the Convention for the Suppression of Unlawful Acts against the Safety of Maritime Navigation, done at Rome on March 10, 1988;

(H) the Protocol for the Suppression of Unlawful Acts against the Safety of Fixed Platforms located on the Continental Shelf, done at Rome on March 10, 1988; or

(I) the International Convention for the Suppression of Terrorist Bombings, adopted by the General Assembly of the United Nations on December 15, 1997.[321]

Attempts and Conspiracies

Whoever attempts or conspires to commit an offence under **18 U.S. Code § 2339C (a) (1)** shall be punished accordingly.[322]

Relationship to Predicate Act

For an act to constitute an offence set forth in this subsection, it shall not be necessary that the funds were actually used to carry out a predicate act.[323]

Concealment

—Whoever—

(1)

(A) is in the United States; or

(B) is outside the United States and is a national of the United States or a legal entity organized under the laws

---

321 18 U.S. Code § 2339C (e) (7)

322 18 U.S. Code § 2339C (a) (2)

323 18 U.S. Code § 2339C (a) (3)

of the United States (including any of its States, districts, commonwealths, territories, or possessions); and

(2) knowingly conceals or disguises the nature, location, source, ownership, or control of any material support or resources, or any funds or proceeds of such funds—

(A) knowing or intending that the support or resources are to be provided, or knowing that the support or resources were provided, in violation of section 2339B of this title; or

(B) knowing or intending that any such funds are to be provided or collected, or knowing that the funds were provided or collected, in violation of subsection (a), shall be punished accordingly.[324]

The above provisions appear to be in line with Article 2 of the International Convention for the Suppression of the Financing of Terrorism and Recommendation 5 of the FATF Recommendations as it does not require that the funds meant to finance terrorism were actually used to carry out or attempt a terrorist act(s); or be linked to a specific terrorist act(s).

5.1.3 United Kingdom

Part 3 of the Terrorism Act 2000 criminalises terrorist financing and makes it an offence to: use, possess, or raise funds for the purposes of terrorism, or enter into arrangements to provide funds or property for that purpose.

Use and Possession

(1) A person commits an offence if he uses money or other property for the purposes of terrorism.

(2) A person commits an offence if he—

(a) possesses money or other property, and

---

324 18 U.S. Code § 2339C (c) (1) (2)

(b) intends that it should be used, or has reasonable cause to suspect that it may be used, for the purposes of terrorism.[325]

Fund Raising

(1) A person commits an offence if he—
    (a) invites another to provide money or other property, and
    (b) intends that it should be used, or has reasonable cause to suspect that it may be used, for the purposes of terrorism.

(2) A person commits an offence if he—
    (a) receives money or other property, and
    (b) intends that it should be used, or has reasonable cause to suspect that it may be used, for the purposes of terrorism.

(3) A person commits an offence if he—
    (a) provides money or other property, and
    (b) knows or has reasonable cause to suspect that it will or may be used for the purposes of terrorism.

(4) In this section a reference to the provision of money or other property is a reference to its being given, lent or otherwise made available, whether or not for consideration.[326]

Since 2001, 62 persons have been charged under terrorism legislation (TACT 2000) with terrorist fundraising offences.

Funding Arrangements

A person commits an offence if—

    (a) he enters into or becomes concerned in an arrangement as a result of which money or other property is made available or is to be made available to another, and

---

325   United Kingdom Terrorism Act 2000, s. 16
326   United Kingdom Terrorism Act 2000, s. 15

(b) he knows or has reasonable cause to suspect that it will or may be used for the purposes of terrorism.[327]

Money Laundering

A person commits an offence if he enters into or becomes concerned in an arrangement which facilitates the retention or control by or on behalf of another person of terrorist property—

(a) by concealment,
(b) by removal from the jurisdiction,
(c) by transfer to nominees, or
(d) in any other way.

It is a defence for a person charged with an offence under subsection (1) to prove that he did not know and had no reasonable cause to suspect that the arrangement related to terrorist property.[328]

The above provisions appear to be in line with **Article 2 of the International Convention for the Suppression of the Financing of Terrorism and Recommendation 5 of the FATF Recommendations** as it does not require that the funds meant to finance terrorism were actually used to carry out or attempt a terrorist act(s); or be linked to a specific terrorist act(s).

CASE STUDY ON THE NEXUS BETWEEN TERRORISM AND TERRORISM FINANCING

Before an individual or group of individuals can be guilty of funding terrorism, the group or organization which they support must have been designated as a terrorist organization.

Let me use the case of the **Federal Government of Nigeria v. Indigenous People of Biafra (IPOB)**, to expatiate on this point.

---

327 United Kingdom Terrorism Act 2000, s. 17
328 United Kingdom Terrorism Act 2000, s. 18

On the 20th of September, 2017, the Attorney General of the Federal Republic of Nigeria and Minister of Justice, Mr. Abubakar Malami (SAN), obtained an interim order proscribing IPOB and declaring the secessionist group as a terrorist organization on behalf of the Federal Government. The Order was made pursuant to **Section 2 of the Terrorism (Prevention) Act, 2011 (as amended).**

The order was granted by the acting Chief Judge of the Federal High Court, Justice Abdu Kafarati, in chambers.

The judge held, "That an order, declaring that the activities of the respondent (Indigenous People of Biafra) in any part of Nigeria, especially in the South-East and South-South regions of Nigeria, amount to **acts of terrorism** and illegality, is granted."[329]

An "act of terrorism" means an act which is deliberately done with malice, aforethought and which:

(a) may seriously harm or damage a country or an international organization;

(b) is intended or can reasonably be regarded as having been intended to—

    (i)   unduly compel a government or international organization to perform or abstain from performing any act,

    (ii) seriously intimidate a population,

    (iii) seriously destabilize or destroy the fundamental political, constitutional, economic or social structures of a country or an international organization, or

    (iv) otherwise influence such government or international organization by intimidation or coercion; and

(c) involves or causes, as the case may be—

    (i)   an attack upon a person's life which may cause serious bodily harm or death;

    (ii) kidnapping of a person;

    (iii) destruction to a Government or public facility, a transport system, an infrastructure facility, including an

---

329 The Punch (2017), 'Court proscribes IPOB, FG says group gets funds from France', Available at: http://punchng.com/court-proscribes-ipob-fg-says-group-gets-funds-from-france/ (accessed 25 September 2017).

information system, a fixed platform located on the continental shelf, a public place or private property, likely to endanger human life or result in major economic loss;

(iv) the seizure of an aircraft, ship or other means of public or goods transport and diversion or the use of such means of transportation for any of the purposes in paragraph (b) (iv) of this subsection;

(v) the manufacture, possession, acquisition, transport, supply or use of weapons, explosives or of nuclear, biological or chemical weapons, as well as research into, and development of biological and chemical weapons without lawful authority;

(vi) the release of dangerous substance or causing of fire, explosions or floods, the effect of which is to endanger human life;

(vii) interference with or disruption of the supply of water, power or any other fundamental natural resource, the effect of which is to endanger human life:

(d) an act or omission in or outside Nigeria which constitutes an offence within the scope of a counter terrorism protocols and conventions duly ratified by Nigeria.

Justice Kafarati, who heard the Attorney General of the Federation's motion in chambers, had, in addition to directing the Federal Government to gazette the order, ordered it to publish it in two national dailies.

It is worth noting that the Federal Government has already gazetted the order of the Federal High Court in Abuja, and has commenced moves to notify banks, Nigerian embassies abroad and foreign missions operating in Nigeria from further relating with IPOB.[330]

What the designation of IPOB as a terrorist organization by the Nigerian Court means is that anybody who solicits, acquires, provides,

---

330 The Punch (2017), 'FG gazettes IPOB ban, to write banks, embassies, foreign missions', Available at: http://punchng.com/fg-gazettes-ipob-ban-to-write-banks-embassies-foreign-missions/ (accessed 26 September 2017).

collects, receives, possesses or makes available funds, property or other services by any means, whether legitimate or otherwise, to IPOB on or after the 20th of September, 2017 commits a terrorism financing offence in Nigeria. The conduct would not however amount to a terrorism financing offence in the United States of America since the spokesman for the American Embassy in Nigeria, Russell Brooks, told SUNDAY PUNCH on the 22nd day of September, 2017 that the US government does not view IPOB as a terrorist group.[331]

In the United States, there are two main authorities for terrorism designations of groups and individuals. Groups can be designated as Foreign Terrorist Organizations (FTOs) under the Immigration and Nationality Act. Under Executive Order (EO) 13224 a wider range of entities, including terrorist groups, individuals acting as part of a terrorist organization, and other entities such as financiers and front companies, can be designated as Specially Designated Global Terrorists (SDGTs).

The Department of State is authorized to designate FTOs and SDGTs, while the Department of the Treasury designates only SDGTs. Both departments pursue these designations in cooperation with the Department of Justice. All of the Department of State's designations can be found at: http://www.state.gov/j/ct/list/index.htm. All State FTO and EO designations can also be found at the Office of Foreign Assets Control (OFAC) of the US Department of the Treasury' website.

The Secretary of State designates Foreign Terrorist Organizations in accordance with section **219 of the Immigration and Nationality Act.** The legal criteria for designating a group as a Foreign Terrorist Organization are:

- The organization must be a foreign organization;
- The organization engages in terrorist activity or terrorism, or retains the capability and intent to engage in terrorist activity or terrorism; and

---

331 The Punch (2017), 'We don't see IPOB as terrorist organisation – US', Available at: http://punchng.com/we-dont-see-ipob-as-terrorist-organisation-us/ (accessed 25 September 2017).

- The terrorist activity or terrorism of the organization threatens the security of United States nationals or the national security of the United States.

Under Executive Order 13224, the Secretary of State, in consultation with the Secretary of the Treasury and the Attorney General, may designate foreign individuals or entities that he determines have committed, or pose a significant risk of committing, acts of terrorism that threaten the security of U.S. nationals or the national security, foreign policy, or economy of the U.S.; or, the Secretary of the Treasury, in consultation with the Secretary of State and the Attorney General, may designate individuals or entities that are determined:

- To be owned or controlled by, or act for or on behalf of an individual or entity listed in the Annex to the Order or by or for persons determined to be subject to the Order;
- To assist in, sponsor, or provide financial, material, or technological support for, or financial or other services to or in support of, acts of terrorism or individuals or entities designated in or under the Order; or
- To be otherwise associated with certain individuals or entities designated in or under the Order.

For Foreign Terrorist Organizations, once an organization is identified, we prepare a detailed "administrative record," which is a compilation of information, typically including both classified and open source information, demonstrating that the statutory criteria for designation have been satisfied.

- If the Secretary of State, in consultation with the Attorney General and the Secretary of the Treasury, decides to make the designation, Congress is notified of the Secretary's intent to designate the organization seven days before the designation is published in the Federal Register, as section 219 of the Immigration and Nationality Act requires.
- Upon the expiration of the seven-day waiting period and in the absence of Congressional action to block the designation,

notice of the designation is published in the Federal Register, at which point the designation takes effect.

For Specially Designated Global Terrorists, As with FTO designations, an "administrative record" is prepared for E.O. 13224 designations. Once it is completed and the Secretary of State or the Secretary of the Treasury designates an individual or entity, the Office of Foreign Assets Control (OFAC) of the Department of the Treasury takes appropriate action to block the assets of the individual or entity in the United States or in the possession or control of U.S. persons, including notification of the blocking order to U.S. financial institutions, directing them to block the assets of the designated individual or entity.

- Notice of the designation is also published in the Federal Register. OFAC also adds the individual or entity to its list of Specially Designated Nationals, by identifying such individuals or entities as Specially Designated Global Terrorists (SDGTs), and posts a notice of this addition on the OFAC website.
- Designations remain in effect until the designation is revoked or the Executive Order lapses or is terminated in accordance with U.S. law.

It is unlawful for a person in the United States or subject to the jurisdiction of the United States to knowingly provide "material support or resources" to a designated FTO.[332]

The act of financing IPOB would not also amount to a terrorism financing offence in the United Kingdom since the Press Officer to the UK high commission in Nigeria, Joe Abuku, told the PUNCH Newspaper that the group was not a proscribed organisation under the British law.[333]

---

332 U.S. Department of State (2012), 'Bureau of Counterterrorism and Countering Violent Extremism', Available at: https://www.state.gov/j/ct/rls/other/des/266614.htm (accessed 27 September 2017).

333 The Punch (2017), 'UK seeks clarification about Kanu's status, whereabouts from FG', Available at: http://punchng.com/uk-seeks-clarification-about-kanus-status-whereabouts-from-fg/ (accessed 30 September 2017).

Under the **UK Terrorism Act 2000**, the Home Secretary may proscribe an organisation if she believes it is concerned in terrorism, and it is proportionate to do. For the purposes of the **UK Terrorism Act 2000**, this means that the organisation:

- commits or participates in acts of terrorism;
- prepares for terrorism;
- promotes or encourages terrorism (including the unlawful glorification of terrorism); or
- is otherwise concerned in terrorism.[334]

"Terrorism" as defined in the **UK Terrorism Act 2000**, means the use or threat which: involves serious violence against a person; involves serious damage to property; endangers a person's life (other than that of the person committing the act); creates a serious risk to the health or safety of the public or section of the public; or is designed seriously to interfere with or seriously to disrupt an electronic system. The use or threat of such action must be designed to influence the government or an international governmental organisation or to intimidate the public or a section of the public and be undertaken for the purpose of advancing a political, religious, racial or ideological cause.

What determines whether proscription is proportionate?

If the statutory test is met, the Secretary of State will consider whether to exercise her discretion to proscribe the organisation. In considering whether to exercise this discretion, the Secretary of State will take into account other factors, including:

- the nature and scale of an organisation's activities;
- the specific threat that it poses to the UK;
- the specific threat that it poses to British nationals overseas;
- the extent of the organisation's presence in the UK; and
- the need to support other members of the international community in the global fight against terrorism.[335]

---

334 UK Terrorism Act 2000, s. 3 (5)

335 Home Office (2013), 'Proscribed Terrorist Organisations', Available at: https://www.gov.uk/government/uploads/system/uploads/attachment_data/

CASE STUDY ON INADEQUATE RISK AND COMPLIANCE FUNCTIONS THAT OPEN THE DOOR TO THE FINANCING OF TERRORIST ACTIVITIES

On September 7, 2017, US banking regulators ordered Pakistan's Habib Bank to shutter its New York office after nearly 40 years, for repeatedly failing to heed concerns over possible terrorist financing and money laundering.

Habib, Pakistan's largest private bank, neglected to watch for compliance problems and red flags on transactions that potentially could have promoted terrorism, money laundering or other illicit ends, New York banking officials said.

The state's Department of Financial Services (DFS), which regulates foreign banks, also slapped two hundred and twenty-five million dollars fine on the bank, although that is much smaller than the six hundred and twenty-nine million six hundred thousand dollars penalty initially proposed.

Habib has operated in the United States since 1978, and in 2006 was ordered to tighten its oversight of potentially illegal transactions but failed to comply.

New York regulators said Habib facilitated billions of dollars of transactions with Saudi private bank, Al Rajhi Bank, which reportedly has links to al Qaeda, and failed to do enough to ensure that the funds were not laundered or used for terrorism.

"DFS will not tolerate inadequate risk and compliance functions that open the door to the financing of terrorist activities that pose a grave threat to the people of this State and the financial system as a whole," DFS Superintendent Maria Vullo said in a news release.

"The bank has repeatedly been given more than sufficient opportunity to correct its glaring deficiencies, yet it has failed to do so."

Habib permitted at least 13,000 transactions that were not sufficiently screened to ensure they did not involve sanctioned countries, the agency said.

---

file/612076/20170503_Proscription.pdf (accessed 30 September 2017).

And the bank improperly used a "good guy" list to rubber stamp at least \$250 million in transactions, including those by an identified terrorist and an international arms dealer, regulators said.

In an August letter to the Pakistan Stock Exchange, Habib company secretary Nausheen Ahmad called the proposed fine of six hundred and twenty-nine million six hundred thousand dollars "outrageous" and "capricious" and said the bank had decided to close its New York operations "in an orderly manner."

But DFS said Habib will have to surrender its license after it meets the agency's requirements.[336]

BOX 5.1: DISCLOUSURE OF INFORMATION

Where a person believes or suspects that another person has committed a terrorism financing offence in the UK and bases his belief or suspicion on information which comes to his attention in the course of a trade, profession, business or employment,[337] the person commits an offence if he does not disclose to a constable as soon as is reasonably practicable—

(a) his belief or suspicion, and
(b) the information on which it is based.[338]

It is a defence for a person charged with an offence of non-disclosure to prove that he had a reasonable excuse for not making the disclosure.[339]

A professional legal adviser is not required to make a disclosure of—

---

336 The Times of India (2017), 'US shuts Pakistan's Habib Bank over terror financing concerns', Available at: http://timesofindia.indiatimes.com/business/international-business/us-ousts-pakistani-bank-amid-money-laundering-concerns/articleshow/60420888.cms (accessed 10 September 2017).

337 UK Terrorism Act 2000, s. 19 (1)

338 UK Terrorism Act 2000, s. 19 (2)

339 UK Terrorism Act 2000, s. 19 (3)

(a) information which he obtains in privileged circumstances, or

(b) a belief or suspicion based on information which he
obtains in privileged circumstances.[340]

For the purpose of this section information is obtained by an
adviser in privileged circumstances if it comes to him, otherwise than with a view to furthering a criminal purpose—

(a) from a client or a client's representative, in connection with the provision of legal advice by the adviser
to the client,

(b) from a person seeking legal advice from the adviser,
or from the person's representative, or

(c) from any person, for the purpose of actual or contemplated legal proceedings.[341]

A person guilty of an offence of failing to disclose information relating to a terrorism financing offence shall be liable—

(a) on conviction on indictment, to imprisonment for a
term not exceeding five years, to a fine or to both, or

(b) on summary conviction, to imprisonment for a term
not exceeding six months, or to a fine not exceeding
the statutory maximum or to both.[342]

Under the Nigerian Terrorism Prevention Act 2011 as
amended, where a person has information which he knows
or believes to be of material assistance in-

(a) preventing the commission by any person or an organization of an act of terrorism, or

---

340 UK Terrorism Act 2000, s. 19 (5)

341 UK Terrorism Act 2000, s. 19 (6)

342 UK Terrorism Act 2000, s. 19 (8)

(b) securing the apprehension, prosecution or conviction of another person for an offence under the Terrorism Prevention Act 2011 (as amended) and fails to disclose such information to any law enforcement or security officer as soon as reasonably practicable, commits an offence under the Terrorism Prevention Act and is liable on conviction to imprisonment for a term of not less than ten years.[343]

It is a defence for a person charged with Concealing of information about acts of terrorism to prove that he or she—

(a) did not know and had no reasonable cause to suspect that the disclosure was likely to affect a terrorist investigation; or
(b) has a reasonable excuse for the non-disclosure or interference.[344]

Just like the United Kingdom Terrorism Act 2000, the Nigerian Terrorism Prevention Act 2011 does not require disclosure by a legal practitioner of any information, belief or suspicion based on any information, which he obtained in privileged circumstances.[345]

Information is obtained by a legal practitioner in privileged circumstances where it is disclosed to him by –

(a) his client in connection with the provisions of legal advice, not being a disclosure with a view to furthering a criminal purpose; or

---

343 Nigerian Terrorism (Prevention) Act, 2011 (as amended), s. 8 (1)
344 Nigerian Terrorism (Prevention) Act, 2011 (as amended), s. 8 (2)
345 Nigerian Terrorism (Prevention) Act, 2011 (as amended), s. 8 (3)

> (b) **any person for the purpose of actual or contemplat-
> ed legal proceeding and not with a view to furthering
> a criminal purpose.**[346]

5.2 Jurisdiction

Article 7 of the International Convention for the Suppression of the Financing of Terrorism requires each State Party to take such measures as may be necessary to establish its jurisdiction over the offences set forth in article 2 of the convention when:

(a) The offence is committed in the territory of that State;

(b) The offence is committed on board a vessel flying the flag of that State or an aircraft registered under the laws of that State at the time the offence is committed;

(c) The offence is committed by a national of that State.

2. A State Party may also establish its jurisdiction over any such offence when:

(a) The offence was directed towards or resulted in the carrying out of an offence referred to in article 2, paragraph 1, subparagraph (a) or (b), in the territory of or against a national of that State;

(b) The offence was directed towards or resulted in the carrying out of an offence referred to in article 2, paragraph 1, subparagraph (a) or (b), against a State or government facility of that State abroad, including diplomatic or consular premises of that State;

(c) The offence was directed towards or resulted in an offence referred to in article 2, paragraph 1, subparagraph (a) or (b), committed in an attempt to compel that State to do or abstain from doing any act;

(d) The offence is committed by a stateless person who has his or her habitual residence in the territory of that State;

---

346 Nigerian Terrorism (Prevention) Act, 2011 (as amended), s. 8 (4)

(e) The offence is committed on board an aircraft which is operated by the Government of that State.

4. Each State Party shall likewise take such measures as may be necessary to establish its jurisdiction over the offences set forth in article 2 in cases where the alleged offender is present in its territory and it does not extradite that person to any of the States Parties that have established their jurisdiction in accordance with paragraphs 1 or 2.

5. When more than one State Party claims jurisdiction over the offences set forth in article 2, the relevant States Parties shall strive to coordinate their actions appropriately, in particular concerning the conditions for prosecution and the modalities for mutual legal assistance.

6. Without prejudice to the norms of general international law, this Convention does not exclude the exercise of any criminal jurisdiction established by a State Party in accordance with its domestic law.

5.2.1 Nigeria

The Federal High Court located in any part of Nigeria, regardless of the location where the offence is committed, has jurisdiction to -

(a) try offences under the **Terrorism (Prevention) Act, 2011 (as amended)** or any other related enactment;
(b) hear and determine proceedings arising under the **Terrorism (Prevention) Act, 2011 (as amended)**.

The Federal High Court has jurisdiction to impose any penalty provided for an offence under the **Terrorism (Prevention) Act, 2011 (as amended)**, or any other related law.[347]

The Federal High Court has jurisdiction over terrorist financing offences that take place outside Nigeria when the offence was

---

347 Terrorism (Prevention) Act, 2011 (as amended), s. 32 (2)

commenced in Nigeria and completed outside Nigeria and the victim is -

(i)   a citizen or resident of Nigeria,

(ii) not a citizen of any country but ordinarily resident in Nigeria,

(iii) in transit or has a link with Nigeria,

(iv) dealing with or on behalf of the Government of Nigeria, or a citizen of Nigeria or an entity registered in Nigeria, or

(v)   the alleged offender is in Nigeria and not extradited to any other country for prosecution.[348]

The Nigerian approach appears to be in line with **Article 7 of the International Convention for the Suppression of the Financing of Terrorism,** which requires its parties to cover terrorist financing offences committed fully or partly in their own territories.

5.2.2 United States

There is jurisdiction over terrorist financing offences that take place in the United States in the following circumstances—

(A) a perpetrator was a national of another state or a stateless person;

(B) on board a vessel flying the flag of another state or an aircraft which is registered under the laws of another state at the time the offence is committed;

(C) on board an aircraft which is operated by the government of another state;

(D) a perpetrator is found outside the United States;

(E) was directed toward or resulted in the carrying out of a predicate act against—

(i) a national of another state; or

---

348 Terrorism (Prevention) Act, 2011 (as amended), s. 32 (1)

(ii) another state or a government facility of such state, including its embassy or other diplomatic or consular premises of that state;

(F) was directed toward or resulted in the carrying out of a predicate act committed in an attempt to compel another state or international organization to do or abstain from doing any act; or

(G) was directed toward or resulted in the carrying out of a predicate act—

(i) outside the United States; or

(ii) within the United States, and either the offence or the predicate act was conducted in, or the results thereof affected, interstate or foreign commerce.

There is jurisdiction over terrorist financing offences that take place outside the United States in the following circumstances—

(A) a perpetrator is a national of the United States or is a stateless person whose habitual residence is in the United States;

(B) a perpetrator is found in the United States; or

(C) was directed toward or resulted in the carrying out of a predicate act against—

(i) any property that is owned, leased, or used by the United States or by any department or agency of the United States, including an embassy or other diplomatic or consular premises of the United States;

(ii) any person or property within the United States;

(iii) any national of the United States or the property of such national; or

(iv) any property of any legal entity organized under the laws of the United States, including any of its States, districts, commonwealths, territories, or possessions.

The United States approach to foreign crimes appear to be in line with **Article 7 of the International Convention for the Suppression**

of the Financing of Terrorism, which requires its parties to cover terrorist financing offences committed partly in their own territories.[349]

5.2.3 United Kingdom

Compared to Nigeria and the United States, the United Kingdom's
approach seems to go beyond the scope of **Article 7 of the
International Convention for the Suppression of the Financing of
Terrorism** as it applies the single criminality test to terrorism financing offences that are committed outside the United Kingdom. The
perpetrator need not have any link with the United Kingdom for the
test to apply. This is not a good approach.

Section 63 (1) of the United Kingdom Terrorism Act 2000 is to
the effect that:

If—

(a) a person does anything outside the United Kingdom, and
(b) his action would have constituted the commission of an offence under any of sections 15 to 18 if it had been done in
the United Kingdom, he shall be guilty of the offence. This
is known as a test of "single criminality" for the following
reasons:

I.   The conduct can be committed anywhere and is regarded as "criminal conduct" only by reference to the law of
the UK, and

II. The conduct need not be regarded as criminal in the jurisdiction where it is committed.

5.3 Penalties

**Article 4 (b) of the International Convention for the Suppression of
the Financing of Terrorism** requires each State Party to adopt such
measures as may be necessary to make terrorist financing offences

---

349 18 U.S. Code § 2339C (b)

punishable by appropriate penalties which take into account the grave nature of the offences.

5.3.1 Nigeria

A person guilty of an offence under **Section 13 (1) of the Terrorism (Prevention) Act, 2011 (as amended)** is liable on conviction to imprisonment for a term of not less than ten years and not more than life imprisonment while a person who commits an offence under Section 13 (2) of the Act is liable on conviction to life imprisonment.

Where the offence is committed by a corporate body, it is on conviction liable to a fine of not less than hundred million naira, in addition to -

(a) the prosecution of the principal officers of the corporate body who, on conviction are liable to imprisonment for a term of not less than ten years; or

(b) the winding-up of the corporate body and prohibition from its reconstitution or incorporation under any form or guise.

Notwithstanding subsection (3) of this section, and on application of the Attorney -General, the prison sentence imposed on a person convicted of an offence referred to in that subsection may be reduced in such manner as the court deems fit where that person has, before any proceeding, made possible or facilitated the identification of other accused persons and their sponsors or who, after the commencement of the proceedings, has made possible or facilitated the arrest of such persons.[350]

In any trial for an offence under this Act, the court shall have power, notwithstanding anything to the contrary in any other enactment, adopt all legal measures necessary to avoid unnecessary delays and abuse in the conduct of matters.[351]

---

350 Terrorism (Prevention) Act, 2011 (as amended), s. 32 (4)
351 Terrorism (Prevention) Act, 2011 (as amended), s. 32 (5)

Subject to the provisions of the Constitution of the Federal Republic of Nigeria, an application for stay of proceedings in respect of any criminal matter brought under this Act shall not be entertained until judgment is delivered.[352]

5.3.2 United States

Whoever violates **Section 2339C subsection (a) shall be fined under the 18 U.S. Code**, imprisoned for not more than 20 years, or both while whoever violates subsection (c) shall be fined under the 18 U.S. Code, imprisoned for not more than 10 years, or both.

Whoever knowingly provides material support or resources to a foreign terrorist organization, or attempts or conspires to do so, shall be fined under title 18 or imprisoned not more than 20 years, or both, and, if the death of any person results, shall be imprisoned for any term of years or for life. To violate this paragraph, a person must have knowledge that the organization is a designated terrorist organization (as defined in subsection (g)(6)), that the organization has engaged or engages in terrorist activity (as defined in **section 212(a)(3)(B) of the Immigration and Nationality Act**), or that the organization has engaged or engages in terrorism (as defined in **section 140(d)(2) of the Foreign Relations Authorization Act**, Fiscal Years 1988 and 1989).[353]

In addition to the sentence that may be imposed under **Title 18 U.S. Code**, the Court may also impose other orders, known as ancillary orders e.g. supervised release and restitution orders.

Under **18 U.S. Code § 3583 subsection (a)**, the Court is required to impose a term of supervised release to follow imprisonment when supervised release is required by statute or, except as provided in subsection (c), when a sentence of imprisonment of more than one year is imposed. The court may depart from the United States Sentencing Commission Guidelines Manual 2016 and not impose a term of supervised release if supervised release is not required by statute and the court determines, after considering the factors set

352 Terrorism (Prevention) Act, 2011 (as amended), s. 32 (6)

353 18 U.S. Code § 2339B (a) (1)

forth in section 3553(a)(1), (a)(2)(B), (a)(2)(C), (a)(2)(D), (a)(4), (a)(5), (a)(6), and (a)(7), that supervised release is not necessary.

In determining whether to impose a term of supervised release, the court is required by statute to consider, among other factors:

(i)   the nature and circumstances of the offence and the history and characteristics of the defendant;
(ii)   the need to afford adequate deterrence to criminal conduct, to protect the public from further crimes of the defendant, and to provide the defendant with needed educational or vocational training, medical care, or other correctional treatment in the most effective manner;
(iii) the need to avoid unwarranted sentence disparities among defendants with similar records who have been found guilty of similar conduct; and
(iv)   the need to provide restitution to any victims of the offence.[354]

The court shall order, as an explicit condition of supervised release, that the defendant not commit another Federal, State, or local crime during the term of supervision.[355]

CASE STUDY: SUPERVISED RELEASE AND RESTITUTION ORDERS

Allen Weintraub, 48, of Boynton Beach, was sentenced on April 24, 2014 by U.S. District Judge Donald Graham to 111 months in prison, three years of supervised release, and was ordered to forfeit one hundred forty thousand two hundred eighty dollars and forty-seven cents and to pay the same amount in restitution to two victims of a scheme to sell Facebook shares.

---

354 See the United States Sentencing Commission (2016), ' Guidelines Manual 2016 ', Available at: https://www.ussc.gov/sites/default/files/pdf/guidelines-manual/2016/GLMFull.pdf (accessed 20 August 2017); See also 18 U.S.C. § 3583(c)
355 18 U.S.C. § 3583(d)

In February 2014, Weintraub pled guilty to two counts of mail fraud. According to an agreed factual proffer, in February 2012, Weintraub, using an alias, steered potential investors seeking to purchase pre-IPO stock of Facebook to the website of Private Stock Transfer Inc. by posting a response on www.quora.com. In that post, Weintraub claimed that he had purchased Facebook stock from Private Stock Transfer Inc. When victims went to the website and sought information on purchasing Facebook stock, Weintraub responded representing that Private Stock Transfer Inc. had thousands of Facebook shares available for purchase. He directed that various forms be completed which represented that victims were purchasing shares described as "Facebook Inc. by and through PST Investment III, Inc. Class A shares on a one for one conversion basis." PST Investment III Inc. was another company associated with Weintraub. After the victims sent payment to Weintraub's bank accounts, Weintraub issued and mailed stock certificates for PST Investment III shares that would convert to Facebook shares on a one-for-one basis once Facebook went public. In reality, neither Weintraub nor Private Stock Transfer Inc. had any Facebook shares. The two victims were defrauded a total of four hundred and fourteen thousand dollars.

This case was prosecuted by Assistant U.S. Attorney Lois Foster-Steers.[356]

5.3.2.1 Civil Penalty

In addition to any other criminal, civil, or administrative liability or penalty, any legal entity located within the United States or organized under the laws of the United States, including any of the laws of its States, districts, commonwealths, territories, or possessions, shall be liable to the United States for the sum of at least ten thousand dollars, if a person responsible for the management or control of that legal entity has, in that capacity, committed an offence set forth in subsection (a).[357]

---

356 Federal Bureau of Investigation (2014), 'Facebook Fraudster Sentenced', Available at: https://www.fbi.gov/contact-us/field-offices/miami/news/press-releases/facebook-fraudster-sentenced (accessed 6 September 2017).

357 18 U.S. Code § 2339C (f)

5.3.3 United Kingdom

A person guilty of the offence of 'terrorist financing' shall be liable—

(a) on conviction on indictment, to imprisonment for a term not exceeding 14 years, to a fine or to both, or

(b) on summary conviction, to imprisonment for a term not exceeding six months, to a fine not exceeding the statutory maximum or to both.[358]

In addition to the sentence that may be imposed under the **Terrorism Act 2000**, the judge or magistrate may also impose other orders, known as ancillary orders. Some ancillary orders are aimed at redressing the harm caused by an offender, such as compensation orders. Others aim to prevent future re-offending or repeat victimisation, including criminal behaviour orders and exclusion orders.

It is up to the judge or magistrate to decide whether an ancillary order is appropriate or necessary, taking into account the circumstances of the offence and the offender. In many cases the prosecution will invite the court to make relevant orders. There are a number of different ancillary orders available including:

- criminal behaviour orders;
- compensation orders;
- confiscation orders (Crown Court only);
- deprivation orders;
- disqualification from driving;
- drink banning orders;
- disqualification from being a company director;
- financial reporting order;
- football banning orders;
- forfeiture orders;
- parenting orders;
- restitution orders;
- restraining orders;

---

358 United Kingdom Terrorism Act 2000, s. 22

- serious crime prevention order (Crown Court only); and
- sexual harm prevention orders.[359]

5.4 Freezing, Seizure and Forfeiture of Funds

Article 8 (1) of the International Convention for the Suppression of the Financing of Terrorism requires each State Party to take appropriate measures, in accordance with its domestic legal principles, for the identification, detection and freezing or seizure of any funds used or allocated for the purpose of committing the offences set forth in article 2 as well as the proceeds derived from such offences, for purposes of possible forfeiture.

Article 8 (2) of the International Convention for the Suppression of the Financing of Terrorism requires each State Party to take appropriate measures, in accordance with its domestic legal principles, for the forfeiture of funds used or allocated for the purpose of committing the offences set forth in article 2 and the proceeds derived from such offences.

5.4.1 Nigeria

The **Terrorism (Prevention) Act, 2011 (as amended)** allows for the freezing, seizure and forfeiture of terrorist cash.

5.4.1.1 Freezing Orders

The law enforcement agencies have powers to freeze or maintain custody over terrorist property or fund for the purpose of investigation, prosecution or recovery of any property or fund which the law enforcement and security agencies reasonably believe to have been involved in or used in the perpetration of terrorist activities in Nigeria or outside Nigeria.[360]

---

359 The Sentencing Council for England and Wales (2017), 'Ancillary Orders', Available at: https://www.sentencingcouncil.org.uk/about-sentencing/types-of-sentence/ancillary-orders/ (accessed 20 August 2017).

360 Terrorism (Prevention) Act, 2011 (as amended), s. 1 A (5) (d)

5.4.1.2 Seizure of Cash

The National Security Adviser or the Inspector General of Police with the approval of the President may seize any cash where he has reasonable grounds to suspect that the cash -

(a) is intended to be used for the purposes of terrorism;
(b) belongs to, or is held on trust for, a proscribed organization; or
(c) represents properly obtained through acts of terrorism.[361]

The National Security Adviser or the Inspector General of Police may seize the cash if –

(a) the seizure is incidental to an arrest search; or
(b) The property is liable to forfeiture upon process issued by the court following an application made by the Attorney General, the National Security Adviser or the Inspector General of Police with the approval of the President.[362]

The National Security Adviser or the Inspector General of Police may exercise his powers, whether or not any proceeding has been brought for an offence in connection with the terrorist cash.[363]

The judge in Chambers shall not make an order for seizure of the cash unless he is satisfied that there are reasonable grounds for suspecting that the cash —

(a) is intended to be used for the purposes of terrorism;
(b) consists of resources of a proscribed organization; or
(c) is, or represents, a property obtained through terrorist activities.[364]

Subject to subsection (8) of this section, any order made under subsection (4) of this section shall remain valid for a period of 60 days

---

361 Terrorism (Prevention) Act, 2011 (as amended), s. 12 (1)
362 Terrorism (Prevention) Act, 2011 (as amended), s. 12 (2)
363 Terrorism (Prevention) Act, 2011 (as amended), s. 12 (3)
364 Terrorism (Prevention) Act, 2011 (as amended), s. 12 (4)

by the Judge in Chambers until the production of the cash before the court in the proceedings against any person for an offence with which the cash is connected.[365]

The cash seized shall be deposited in an escrow account by the officer who effected the seizure.[366] The cash with the interest may be released to the owner by order of the Judge in chamber where-

(a) the conditions under subsection (4) of this section are no longer met; or

(b) the proceedings are not brought in connection with the cash seized.[367]

For the purposes of this section, 'cash' means

(a) Coins and notes in any currency;

(b) Postal order;

(c) Travelers' cheques;

(d) Bankers' drafts,

(e) Bearer bonds and bearer shares; or

(f) Such other monetary instruments as the Minister charged with the responsibility for Finance may, by regulations, specify.[368]

5.4.1.3 Forfeiture

Whenever any person is convicted of an offence under the **Terrorism (Prevention) Act, 2011 (as amended)**, the court in passing sentence shall, in addition to any punishment which the court may impose in respect of the offence, order the forfeiture of any -

(a) terrorist fund with accrued interest,

(b) terrorist property,

---

365 Terrorism (Prevention) Act, 2011 (as amended), s. 12 (5)

366 Terrorism (Prevention) Act, 2011 (as amended), s. 12 (6)

367 Terrorism (Prevention) Act, 2011 (as amended), s. 12 (7)

368 Terrorism (Prevention) Act, 2011 (as amended), s. 12 (8)

(c) article, substance, device or material by means of which the offence was committed, or

(d) conveyance used in the commission of the offence, which is reasonably believed to have been used in the commission of the offence or for the purpose of or in connection with the commission of the offence and which may have been seized under this Act or is in the possession or custody or under the control of the convicted person, to the Federal Government of Nigeria.[369]

5.4.2 United States

Section 981 of title 18 of the United States Code allows for the seizure and forfeiture of terrorist cash while Chapter 1 of the Asset Forfeiture Policy Manual (2016) provides guidelines for pre-seizure planning.

5.4.2.1 Seizure and Forfeiture

Any property, real or personal, acquired or maintained by any person with the intent and for the purpose of supporting, planning, conducting, or concealing any Federal crime of terrorism (as defined in section 2332b(g)(5)) against the United States, citizens or residents of the United States, or their property, or which constitutes or is derived from proceeds traceable to a violation, of **section 2339C of title 18** is subject to forfeiture to the United States and may be seized by the Attorney General and, in the case of property involved in a violation investigated by the Secretary of the Treasury or the United States Postal Service, the property may also be seized by the Secretary of the Treasury or the Postal Service, respectively.

Seizures shall be made pursuant to a warrant obtained in the same manner as provided for a search warrant under the **Federal Rules of Criminal Procedure**, except that a seizure may be made without a warrant if—

---

369 Terrorism (Prevention) Act, 2011 (as amended), s. 32 (3)

(A) a complaint for forfeiture has been filed in the United States district court and the court issued an arrest warrant in rem pursuant to the **Supplemental Rules for Certain Admiralty and Maritime Claims**;

(B) there is probable cause to believe that the property is subject to forfeiture and—

    (iii) the seizure is made pursuant to a lawful arrest or search; or

    (iv) another exception to the Fourth Amendment warrant requirement would apply; or

(C) the property was lawfully seized by a State or local law enforcement agency and transferred to a Federal agency.

Notwithstanding the provisions of **rule 41(a) of the Federal Rules of Criminal Procedure**, a seizure warrant may be issued pursuant to **section 981 subsection b of title 18** by a judicial officer in any district in which a forfeiture action against the property may be filed under **section 1355(b) of title 28**, and may be executed in any district in which the property is found, or transmitted to the central authority of any foreign state for service in accordance with any treaty or other international agreement. Any motion for the return of property seized under **section 981 of title 18** shall be filed in the district court in which the seizure warrant was issued or in the district court for the district in which the property was seized.

If any person is arrested or charged in a foreign country in connection with an offence that would give rise to the forfeiture of property in the United States under **section 981 of title 18** or under the Controlled Substances Act, the Attorney General may apply to any Federal judge or magistrate judge in the district in which the property is located for an ex parte order restraining the property subject to forfeiture for not more than 30 days, except that the time may be extended for good cause shown at a hearing conducted in the manner provided in **rule 43(e) of the Federal Rules of Civil Procedure**.

The application for the restraining order shall set forth the nature and circumstances of the foreign charges and the basis for belief that the person arrested or charged has property in the United States that would be subject to forfeiture, and shall contain a statement that the restraining order is needed to preserve the availability of property for such time as is necessary to receive evidence from the foreign country or elsewhere in support of probable cause for the seizure of the property under **section 981 subsection b of title 18**.

Property taken or detained under **section 981 of title 18** shall not be repleviable, but shall be deemed to be in the custody of the Attorney General, the Secretary of the Treasury, or the Postal Service, as the case may be, subject only to the orders and decrees of the court or the official having jurisdiction thereof. Whenever property is seized under **section 981 subsection c of title 18**, the Attorney General, the Secretary of the Treasury, or the Postal Service, as the case may be, may—

(1) place the property under seal;
(2) remove the property to a place designated by him; or
(3) require that the General Services Administration take custody of the property and remove it, if practicable, to an appropriate location for disposition in accordance with law.

For purposes of **section 981 of title 18**, the provisions of the customs laws relating to the seizure, summary and judicial forfeiture, condemnation of property for violation of the customs laws, the disposition of such property or the proceeds from the sale of such property under **section 981 of title 18**, the remission or mitigation of such forfeitures, and the compromise of claims (19 U.S.C. 1602 et seq.), insofar as they are applicable and not inconsistent with the provisions of **section 981 of title 18**, shall apply to seizures and forfeitures incurred, or alleged to have been incurred, under **18 U.S.C. § 981**, except that such duties as are imposed upon the customs officer or any other person with respect to the seizure and forfeiture of property under the customs laws shall be performed with respect to seizures and forfeitures of property under **section 981 of title 18** by such officers, agents, or other persons as may be authorized or designated for that purpose by the Attorney General, the Secretary of the Treasury, or the Postal Service, as the case may be. The Attorney General shall have sole responsibility for disposing of petitions for remission or mitigation with respect to property involved in a judicial forfeiture proceeding.

Notwithstanding any other provision of the law, except **section 3 of the Anti-Drug Abuse Act of 1986**, the Attorney General, the Secretary of the Treasury, or the Postal Service, as the case may be, is authorized to retain property forfeited pursuant to **section 981 of title 18**, or to transfer such property on such terms and conditions as he may determine—

(1) to any other Federal agency;
(2) to any State or local law enforcement agency which partici- pated directly in any of the acts which led to the seizure or forfeiture of the property.

The Attorney General, the Secretary of the Treasury, or the Postal Service, as the case may be, shall ensure the equitable transfer pursu- ant to **section 981 subsection e (2) of title 18** of any forfeited prop- erty to the appropriate State or local law enforcement agency so as to reflect generally the contribution of any such agency participating directly in any of the acts which led to the seizure or forfeiture of such property. A decision by the Attorney General, the Secretary of the Treasury, or the Postal Service pursuant to **section 981 subsec- tion e (2) of title 18** shall not be subject to review. The United States shall not be liable in any action arising out of the use of any property the custody of which was transferred pursuant to **section 981 of title 18** to any non-Federal agency. The Attorney General, the Secretary of the Treasury, or the Postal Service may order the dis-continuance of any forfeiture proceedings under **section 981 of title 18** in favor of the institution of forfeiture proceedings by State or local authori- ties under an appropriate State or local statute. After the filing of a complaint for forfeiture under **section 981 of title 18**, the Attorney General may seek dismissal of the complaint in favor of forfeiture proceedings under State or local law.

Whenever forfeiture proceedings are discontinued by the United States in favor of State or local proceedings, the United States may transfer custody and possession of the seized property to the appropriate State or local official immediately upon the initiation of the proper actions by such officials. Whenever forfeiture proceedings are discontinued by the United States in favour of State or local proceedings, notice shall be sent to all known interested parties advising them of the discontinuance or dismissal. The United States shall not be liable in any action arising out of the seizure, detention, and transfer of seized property to State or local officials. The United States shall not be liable in any action arising out of a transfer under paragraph (3), (4), or (5) of **section 981 subsection e of title 18**.[370]

5.4.2.2 Pre-Seizure Planning

The intent of pre-seizure planning is to ensure the various components of the Department of Justice (Department) work together as a team, assuring that asset forfeiture is used as an efficient and cost-effective law enforcement tool consistent with the public interest. To that end, pre-seizure planning provides the Government with the opportunity to make informed decisions on matters regarding the financial impact of seizing/restraining, forfeiting, and managing assets, and on all matters affecting the Government's ability to efficiently dispose of assets following forfeiture. Specifically, pre-seizure planning consists of anticipating issues and making fully informed decisions concerning what property should be seized or restrained, how and when it should be seized or restrained, and, most important, whether the property should be forfeited at all. Pre-seizure discussions should answer at least the following questions, depending on asset type and circumstance:

(1) *What is being seized, who owns it, and what are the liabilities against it?* Determine the full scope of the seizure to the extent possible. For example, if a house is being seized, are the contents also to be seized? If a business is being seized, are the

---

370 18 U.S.C. § 981. See also Asset Forfeiture and Money Laundering Section (AFMLS) (2016), 'Asset Forfeiture Policy Manual', Available at: https://www.justice.gov/criminal-afmls/file/839521/download (accessed 15 October 2017).

buildings in which it operates, the property upon which it is located, the inventory of the business, and the operating or other bank accounts, accounts receivable, accounts payable, etc., also to be seized? All ownership interests in each asset must be identified to the extent possible as well as existing/potential liabilities involving the asset.

(2) *Should the asset be seized or even targeted for forfeiture?* If the asset has a negative or marginal net equity at the time of seizure, should it be seized and forfeited? Over time, what is the likelihood that the asset will depreciate to a negative or marginal value? What law enforcement benefits are to be realized from seizure and forfeiture? Is a restraining or protective order an adequate alternative to seizure given the circumstances? Can any anticipated losses be avoided or mitigated through careful planning on the part of the participants? Will custody, forfeiture, and/or disposal of the asset impose unduly significant demands on U.S. Marshals Service (USMS) or United States Attorney's Office (USAO) resources and/or require a considerable infusion of funds from the Department of Justice's Assets Forfeiture Fund (AFF)?

(3) *How and when is the asset going to be seized/forfeited?* Determine whether immediate seizure is necessary or if restraint of the asset is sufficient to preserve and protect the Government's interest. The type and content of the seizing instrument and authority for both the investigative agency and the USMS to enter or cross private property must be identified and procured in advance of seizure or restraint to ensure that each agency has the necessary information and legal authority to effectuate its seizure and post-seizure responsibilities.

(4) *What management and disposition problems are anticipated, and how will they be resolved?* Any expected logistical issues involving the maintenance, management, or disposition of the asset should be discussed and resolved as early as possible.

(5) *If negative net equity, management, and disposition problems are identified, what are the alternatives to forfeiture?* That is, is it possible to instead release the property to a lienholder, allow tax

foreclosure and target any proceeds thereof, turn to state or local forfeiture action, etc.?

(6) *Is any negative publicity anticipated?* If publicity or public relations concerns are anticipated, appropriate public affairs personnel should be advised and consulted. Consider preparing a press release announcing the basis and purpose of the seizure, restraint, and forfeiture.

The U.S. Attorney (or in administrative forfeiture cases, the agent in charge of a field office) is responsible for ensuring that proper and timely pre-seizure planning occurs in asset forfeiture cases within each federal judicial district. All pre-seizure planning meetings must include, at a minimum, as applicable, the Assistant U.S. Attorney (AUSA) or investigative agent in charge of the forfeiture matter (and, if applicable, the AUSA in charge of the related criminal matter), investigative agents, and the appropriate USMS representative (which should include a representative from the district where the property is to be seized and/or managed if different from the district where the action is to be filed). A federal regulatory agency representative may also attend in forfeiture cases involving federal regulatory matters, as appropriate.

As a general rule, the lead agency will process all the assets. The lead agency is the agency that initiates the investigation. Another agency may be designated a lead agency if provided for in a task force agreement or memorandum of understanding. Ordinarily, assets must be processed by the lead agency only and shall not be divided among multiple agencies. For instance, a cash seizure of $800,000 may not be divided into two $400,000 seizures to be separately credited to two agencies. Or, a seizure of two vehicles may not be divided into two seizures of one vehicle each to be credited to two different agencies. Although exceptions may be made in extraordinary circumstances to permit individual seizures to be allocated to different agencies, no such allocation may be made without the express consent of the lead prosecuting office.

In asset forfeiture cases involving more than one federal judicial district, the United States Attorney's Office (USAO) instituting the forfeiture action shall have primary responsibility, in coordination with the lead investigative agency, to ensure that all Asset Forfeiture

Program participants are notified and that proper and timely pre-seizure planning occurs in all districts in which assets will be seized.[371]

5.4.2.3 Anti-Terrorist Forfeiture Protection

An owner of property that is confiscated under any provision of law relating to the confiscation of assets of suspected international terrorists, may contest that confiscation by filing a claim in the manner set forth in the **Federal Rules of Civil Procedure (Supplemental Rules for Certain Admiralty and Maritime Claims)**, and asserting as an affirmative defense that—

(1) the property is not subject to confiscation under such provision of law; or
(2) the innocent owner provisions of **section 983 (d) of title 18, United States Code**, apply to the case.

In considering a claim filed under this section, a court may admit evidence that is otherwise inadmissible under the Federal Rules of Evidence, if the court determines that the evidence is reliable, and that compliance with the Federal Rules of Evidence may jeopardize the national security interests of the United States.[372]

5.4.3 United Kingdom

The **Anti-Terrorism Crime and Security Act 2001** allows for the freezing, seizure and forfeiture of terrorist cash.

5.4.3.1 Freezing Orders

The Treasury may make a freezing order if the following two conditions are satisfied:

---

371 Asset Forfeiture and Money Laundering Section (AFMLS) (2016), 'Asset Forfeiture Policy Manual', Available at: https://www.justice.gov/criminal-afmls/file/839521/download (accessed 15 October 2017).

372 18 U.S.C. § 987

The first condition is that the Treasury reasonably believes that—

(a) action to the detriment of the United Kingdom's economy (or part of it) has been or is likely to be taken by a person or persons, or
(b) action constituting a threat to the life or property of one or more nationals of the United Kingdom or residents of the United Kingdom has been or is likely to be taken by a person or persons.

If one person is believed to have taken or to be likely to take the action the second condition is that the person is—

(a) the government of a country or territory outside the United Kingdom, or
(b) a resident of a country or territory outside the United Kingdom.[373]

A freezing order may include provision that a person—

(a) must provide information if required to do so and it is reasonably needed for the purpose of ascertaining whether an offence under the order has been committed;
(b) must produce a document if required to do so and it is reasonably needed for that purpose.

In particular, an order may include—

(a) provision that a requirement to provide information or to produce a document may be made by the Treasury or a person authorised by the Treasury;
(b) provision that information must be provided, and a document must be produced, within a reasonable period specified in the order and at a place specified by the person requiring it;

---

373 Anti-terrorism, Crime and Security Act 2001, s. 4.

(c) provision that the provision of information is not to be taken to breach any restriction on the disclosure of information (however imposed);

(d) provision restricting the use to which information or a document may be put and the circumstances in which it may be disclosed;

(e) provision that a requirement to provide information or produce a document does not apply to privileged information or a privileged document;

(f) provision that information is privileged if the person would be entitled to refuse to provide it on grounds of legal professional privilege in proceedings in the High Court or (in Scotland) on grounds of confidentiality of communications in proceedings in the Court of Session;

(g) provision that a document is privileged if the person would be entitled to refuse to produce it on grounds of legal professional privilege in proceedings in the High Court or (in Scotland) on grounds of confidentiality of communications in proceedings in the Court of Session;

(h) provision that information or a document held with the intention of furthering a criminal purpose is not privileged.[374]

A freezing order may include provision requiring a person to disclose information as mentioned below if the following three conditions are satisfied.

The first condition is that the person required to disclose is specified or falls within a description specified in the order.

The second condition is that the person required to disclose knows or suspects, or has grounds for knowing or suspecting, that a person specified in the freezing order as a person to whom or for whose benefit funds are not to be made available—

(a) is a customer of his or has been a customer of his at any time since the freezing order came into force, or

---

374 Anti-terrorism, Crime and Security Act 2001, Schedule 3, Para. 5

(b) is a person with whom he has dealings in the course of his business or has had such dealings at any time since the freezing order came into force.

The third condition is that the information—

(a) on which the knowledge or suspicion of the person required to disclose is based, or
(b) which gives grounds for his knowledge or suspicion, came to him in the course of a business in the regulated sector.

The freezing order may require the person required to disclose to make a disclosure to the Treasury of that information as soon as is practicable after it comes to him.

The freezing order may include—

(a) provision that **Schedule 3A to the Terrorism Act 2000 (c. 11)** is to have effect for the purpose of determining what is a business in the regulated sector;
(b) provision that the disclosure of information is not to be taken to breach any restriction on the disclosure of information (however imposed);
(c) provision restricting the use to which information may be put and the circumstances in which it may be disclosed by the Treasury;
(d) provision that the requirement to disclose information does not apply to privileged information;
(e) provision that information is privileged if the person would be entitled to refuse to disclose it on grounds of legal professional privilege in proceedings in the High Court or (in Scotland) on grounds of confidentiality of communications in proceedings in the Court of Session;
(f) provision that information held with the intention of furthering a criminal purpose is not privileged.[375]

---

375 Anti-terrorism, Crime and Security Act 2001, Schedule 3, Para. 6

5.4.3.2 Seizure of Cash

An authorized officer (a constable, a customs officer or an immigration officer) may seize any cash if he has reasonable grounds for suspecting that it is terrorist cash. An authorised officer may also seize cash part of which he has reasonable grounds for suspecting to be terrorist cash if it is not reasonably practicable to seize only that part.[376]

For the purposes of **Schedule 1 to the Anti-terrorism, Crime and Security Act 2001 (as amended)**, "Cash" means—

(a) coins and notes in any currency,

(b) postal orders,

(c) cheques of any kind, including travellers' cheques,

(d) bankers' drafts,

(e) bearer bonds and bearer shares,

(f) **gaming vouchers,**

(g) **fixed-value casino tokens,**

(h) **betting receipts,** found at any place in the United Kingdom.[377]

This definition goes beyond the definition provided under the United States and Nigeria counter-terrorism law. Nigeria and the United States definition of cash do not include gaming vouchers, fixed-value casino tokens and betting receipts.

The inclusion of these items in the definition of cash helps to prevent the funding of terrorism through proceeds from online/offline gambling.

5.4.3.2.1 Detention of Seized Cash

While the authorised officer continues to have reasonable grounds for his suspicion, cash seized under Schedule 1 may be detained initially for a period of 48 hours. The period for which the cash or any

---

376 Anti-terrorism, Crime and Security Act 2001, Schedule 1, Para. 2

377 Anti-terrorism, Crime and Security Act 2001, Schedule 1, Para. 1 and the Criminal Finances Act 2017, s. 38

part of it may be detained may be extended by an order made by a magistrates' court or (in Scotland) the sheriff; but the order may not authorise the detention of any of the cash—

(a) beyond the end of the period of three months beginning with the date of the order, and

(b) in the case of any further order under this paragraph, beyond the end of the period of two years beginning with the date of the first order.

A justice of the peace may also exercise the power of a magistrates' court to make the first order under sub-paragraph (2) extending the period. An application to a justice of the peace or the sheriff for an order under sub-paragraph (2) making the first extension of the period—

(a) may be made and heard without notice of the application or hearing having been given to any of the persons affected by the application or to the legal representative of such a person, and

(b) may be heard and determined in private in the absence of persons so affected and of their legal representatives.]

An order under sub-paragraph (2) must provide for notice to be given to persons affected by it.

An application for an order under sub-paragraph (2)—

(a) in relation to England and Wales and Northern Ireland, may be made by the Commissioners of Customs and Excise or an authorised officer,

(b) in relation to Scotland, may be made by a procurator fiscal, and the court, sheriff or justice may make the order if satisfied, in relation to any cash to be further detained, that one of the following conditions is met.

The first condition is that there are reasonable grounds for suspecting that the cash is intended to be used for the purposes of terrorism and that either—

(a) its continued detention is justified while its intended use is further investigated or consideration is given to bringing (in the United Kingdom or elsewhere) proceedings against any person for an offence with which the cash is connected, or

(b) proceedings against any person for an offence with which the cash is connected have been started and have not been concluded.

The second condition is that there are reasonable grounds for suspecting that the cash consists of resources of an organisation which is a proscribed organisation and that either—

(a) its continued detention is justified while investigation is made into whether or not it consists of such resources or consideration is given to bringing (in the United Kingdom or elsewhere) proceedings against any person for an offence with which the cash is connected, or

(b) proceedings against any person for an offence with which the cash is connected have been started and have not been concluded.

The third condition is that there are reasonable grounds for suspecting that the cash is property earmarked as terrorist property and that either—

(a) its continued detention is justified while its derivation is further investigated or consideration is given to bringing (in the United Kingdom or elsewhere) proceedings against any person for an offence with which the cash is connected, or

(b) proceedings against any person for an offence with which the cash is connected have been started and have not been concluded.[378]

5.4.3.2.2 Payment of Detained Cash Into An Account

If cash is detained under this Schedule for more than 48 hours, it is to be held in an interest-bearing account and the interest accruing on it is to be added to it on its forfeiture or release.

In the case of cash seized under paragraph 2(2), the authorised officer must, on paying it into the account, release so much of the cash then held in the account as is not attributable to terrorist cash.

Sub-paragraph (1) does not apply if the cash is required as evidence of an offence or evidence in proceedings under this Schedule.[379]

5.4.3.2.3 Release of Detained Cash

A magistrates' court or (in Scotland) the sheriff may direct the release of the whole or any part of the cash if satisfied, on an application by the person from whom it was seized, that the conditions in paragraph 3 for the detention of cash are no longer met in relation to the cash to be released.

A authorised officer or (in Scotland) a procurator fiscal may, after notifying the magistrates' court, sheriff or justice under whose order cash is being detained, release the whole or any part of it if satisfied that the detention of the cash to be released is no longer justified.

But cash is not to be released—

(a) if an application for its forfeiture under paragraph 6, or for its release under paragraph 9, is made, until any proceedings in pursuance of the application (including any proceedings on appeal) are concluded,

---

378 Anti-terrorism, Crime and Security Act 2001, Schedule 1, Para. 3
379 Anti-terrorism, Crime and Security Act 2001, Schedule 1, Para. 4

(b) if (in the United Kingdom or elsewhere) proceedings are started against any person for an offence with which the cash is connected, until the proceedings are concluded.[380]

5.4.3.3 Seizure of Listed Assets

An authorised officer may seize any item of property if the authorised officer has reasonable grounds for suspecting that it is a listed asset.

A "listed asset" means an item of property that falls within one of the following descriptions of property—

(a) precious metals;
(b) precious stones;
(c) watches;
(d) artistic works;
(e) face-value vouchers;
(f) postage stamps.[381]

The inclusion of certain portable items of property (such as precious metals and jewels) in the definition of cash helps to prevent the funding of terrorism through precious metals and precious stones.

This provision is not seen present in the Nigerian and United States counter-terrorism financing law.

Allowing law enforcement agencies to seize certain portable items of property (such as precious metals and jewels), in addition to cash, helps to prevent the funding of terrorism through precious metals and precious stones.

5.4.3.4 Forfeiture

While cash is detained under this Schedule 1 of the Anti-terrorism, Crime and Security Act 2001 (as amended), an application for the forfeiture of the whole or any part of it may be made—

380 Anti-terrorism, Crime and Security Act 2001, Schedule 1, Para. 5
381 Anti-terrorism, Crime and Security Act 2001 (as amended), Schedule 1, Para. 10A (1) and the Criminal Finances Act 2017, Schedule 3.

(a) to a magistrates' court by the Commissioners of Customs and Excise or an authorised officer,

(b) (in Scotland) to the sheriff by the Scottish Ministers.

The court or sheriff may order the forfeiture of the cash or any part of it if satisfied that the cash or part is terrorist cash.

In the case of property earmarked as terrorist property which belongs to joint tenants one of whom is an excepted joint owner, the order may not apply to so much of it as the court or sheriff thinks is attributable to the excepted joint owner's share.

An excepted joint owner is a joint tenant who obtained the property in circumstances in which it would not (as against him) be earmarked; and references to his share of the earmarked property are to so much of the property as would have been his if the joint tenancy had been severed.[382]

5.4.3.4.1 Appeal Against Forfeiture

Any party to proceedings in which a forfeiture order is made who is aggrieved by the order may appeal—

(a) in relation to England and Wales, to the Crown Court,

(b) in relation to Scotland, to the Court of Session,

(c) in relation to Northern Ireland, to a county court.

An appeal must be made—

(a) within the period of 30 days beginning with the date on which the order is made, or

(b) if sub-paragraph (6) applies, before the end of the period of 30 days beginning with the date on which the order under section **3(3)(b) of the Terrorism Act 2000 (c. 11)** referred to in that sub-paragraph comes into force.

---

382 Anti-terrorism, Crime and Security Act 2001 (as amended), Schedule 1, Para. 10A (1) and the Criminal Finances Act 2017, Schedule 1 Para. 6

The appeal is to be by way of a rehearing. The court hearing the appeal may make any order it thinks appropriate. If the court upholds the appeal, it may order the release of the cash.

Where a successful application for a forfeiture order relies (wholly or partly) on the fact that an organisation is proscribed, this sub-paragraph applies if—

(a) a deproscription appeal under section 5 of the Terrorism Act 2000 is allowed in respect of the organisation,

(b) an order is made under section 3(3)(b) of that Act in respect of the organisation in accordance with an order of the Proscribed Organisations Appeal Commission under section 5(4) of that Act (and, if the order is made in reliance on section 123(5) of that Act, a resolution is passed by each House of Parliament under section 123(5)(b)), and

(c) the forfeited cash was seized under this Schedule on or after the date of the refusal to deproscribe against which the appeal under section 5 of that Act was brought.[383]

5.4.3.4.2 Application of Forfeited Cash

Cash forfeited, and any accrued interest on it—

(a) if forfeited by a magistrates' court in England and Wales or Northern Ireland, is to be paid into the Consolidated Fund,

(b) if forfeited by the sheriff, is to be paid into the Scottish Consolidated Fund.

But it is not to be paid in—

(a) before the end of the period within which an appeal against a forfeiture may be made, or

(b) if a person appeals against a forfeiture order, before the appeal is determined or otherwise disposed of.[384]

---

383 Anti-terrorism, Crime and Security Act 2001 (as amended), Schedule 1, Para. 7

384 Anti-terrorism, Crime and Security Act 2001, Schedule 1, Para. 8

5.4 Discussion

5.4.1 Classification of Crimes in the United Kingdom

In the UK, crimes are classified as summary, indictable and either way offences.[385] Summary offences are the least serious offences, typically what one might view as 'technical monitoring' offences, though also including minor assaults and low value criminal damage. They are tried in the Magistrates' Court. These offences are usually punishable by imprisonment for a maximum term of 6 months and sometimes 12 months.[386]

Indictable offences are the most serious offences. These offences include murder and rape. These offences are tried in the Crown Court by a judge and jury and are usually punishable with a maximum term in excess of 12 months.[387]

Either way offences mean an offence triable either way.[388] It is for the Magistrates' Court to decide whether the offence appears to it more suitable for summary trial or for trial on indictment.[389]

The **United Kingdom Terrorism Act 2000** made the offence of 'terrorist financing' an either way offence. A person guilty of the offence of 'terrorist financing' shall be liable—

---

385 Ormerod, D. (2011), Smith and Hogan's Criminal Law (13th Edition Oxford University Press) 32, see also Allen, M. (2011), Criminal Law (11th Edition Oxford University Press) 14.

386 See Reed, A. and Fitzpatrick, B. (2009), Criminal Law (4th Edition Sweet and Maxwell Limited) 5; For Examples of summary offences see Licensing Act 2003, s. 146; Animal Welfare Act 2006, s. 8; Communications Act 2003, s. 127; Criminal Justice and Public Order Act, 1994, s. 166; Criminal Justice and Public Order Act 1994, s. 167; Communications Act 2003, s. 363.

387 Reed, A. and Fitzpatrick, B (2009), Criminal Law (4th Edition Sweet and Maxwell Limited) 5, See also Monaghan, N. (2012), Criminal Law Directions (2nd Edition Oxford University Press 2012) 6. For examples of Indictable offences see Theft Act 1968, s. 7, s. 8, s. 9 and s. 10.

388 Crime and Disorder Act 1998, s. 51

389 Reed, A. and Fitzpatrick, B. (2009), Criminal Law (4th Edition Sweet and Maxwell Limited) 5. For examples of Either way offences see Bribery Act 2010, s. 11 (1); Copyright, Designs and Patents Act 1988, s. 107 (4); Trade Marks Act 1994, s. 92 (6).

(a) on conviction on indictment, to imprisonment for a term not exceeding 14 years, to a fine or to both, or

(b) on summary conviction, to imprisonment for a term not exceeding six months, to a fine not exceeding the statutory maximum or to both.

The United States and Nigeria on the other hand made the offence of 'terrorist financing' an indictable offence.

Terrorist financing being a very serious offence should not be classified as an either way offence. The approach being adopted by the United States and Nigeria is a more preferable approach.

5.4.2 Lifetime Management of Ancillary Orders

The Lifetime Management Team within the National Crime Agency (NCA), United Kingdom, has responsibility for managing a number of high-priority and significant serious and organised criminals. These criminals have been convicted of serious offences, and law enforcement have secured additional restrictions on them at court to prevent them from re-offending. Key powers used include:

I. **Serious Crime Prevention Orders**

Serious Crime Prevention Orders (SCPOs) are civil orders to prevent or deter serious crime. Breach of an SCPO is a criminal offence punishable by up to five years imprisonment and an unlimited fine. The restrictions that an SCPO can include are wide-ranging. As long as they are shown to be proportionate, justified and necessary to the circumstances of the case, they can include restrictions on communications devices, conducting specific types of business, bank accounts, associating with criminal associates, and geographic restrictions. The order lasts for up to five years.

II. **Travel Restriction Orders**

A Travel Restriction Order (TRO) can be imposed on any offender convicted of a drug trafficking offence and sentenced to four years or more in prison, regardless of nationality. The aim of the order is to reduce re-offending through restricting the movements of convicted drug traffickers. UK passport holders (including those with dual nationality) may be required to surrender their passports to the court. The TRO comes into effect upon the offender's release from prison and its minimum length is two years. The penalty for breach of a TRO is up to five years' imprisonment and/or a fine.

III. **Financial Reporting Orders**

Financial Reporting Orders (FROs) may be made by a court, on the application of a prosecutor, following a conviction for certain offences. They require a convicted criminal to report their financial details at regular intervals. This can be for a period of up to 20 years for those sentenced to life, or a maximum of 15 years for other sentences.

IV. **Licence Conditions**

The National Offender Management Service (NOMS) monitors the behaviour of offenders released from prison on parole licence through the use of standard and bespoke licence conditions. The Lifetime Management Team works closely with NOMS to develop licence conditions imposed on offenders of interest to the NCA. The imposition of licence conditions can deter and frustrate offenders from committing further offences. If the offender breaks one or more of the conditions, such as by travelling abroad, they can be sent back to prison. The Lifetime Management Team and NOMS work together to ensure offenders comply with those conditions.

The Lifetime Management Team uses a wide range of investigative and intelligence techniques to monitor individuals' compliance with these restrictions. In particular, the Lifetime Management Team works closely with partners to exchange information on these individuals to identify and reduce their opportunities for returning to criminal activity.[390]

It is worth noting that the Nigerian Terrorist Financing Laws/ Regulations do not provide for the above mentioned Ancillary

---

390 National Crime Agency (2017), 'Lifetime Management', Available at: http://www.nationalcrimeagency.gov.uk/about-us/what-we-do/lifetime-management (accessed 18 August 2017).

orders. **Once a criminal has served his or her time the criminal will no longer be subject to restrictions that could prevent him or her from re-offending. This is contrary to the U.S. and U.K. approach.**

5.5 Conclusion

In view of the arguments canvassed in this chapter, the following reforms are recommended:

I.   The United Kingdom is advised to adopt the approach of the United States and Nigeria by making the Terrorist Financing Offence only an indictable offence and not an Either Way Offence.

II. The United Kingdom is advised to adopt the Nigerian approach by applying the single criminality test to foreign crimes partially committed within its jurisdiction.

III. The Nigerian Terrorism (Prevention) Act, 2011 (as amended) should be modified to include ancillary orders. **Ancillary orders are designed to frustrate criminality, both in and out of prison. They can restrict the number of mobile phones or computers that offenders can access, limit the amount of cash they can carry, require them to surrender passports and provide financial information at regular intervals.** The United Kingdom National Crime Agency rigorously enforces these orders and takes action if people breach the terms. Many career criminals regard prison as an interruption which rarely marks the end of their involvement in organised crime. This is why the NCA has a policy of Lifetime Management. Once a criminal is on the NCA's radar they will stay on it. These orders can include a wide variety of restrictions, all designed to limit the ability for criminals to engage in illegal activity.[391]

---

391   National Crime Agency (2017), 'Updated list of active ancillary orders published', Available at: http://www.nationalcrimeagency.gov.uk/index.php/news-media/nca-news/1145-updated-list-of-active-ancillary-orders-published-2 (accessed 18 August 2017).

CHAPTER 6

POLITICALLY EXPOSED PERSONS

Individuals who have, or have had, a high political profile and those who hold, or have held, public office can pose a higher money laundering risk, as their positions may make them vulnerable to corruption. These people are collectively known as politically exposed persons (PEPs).[392]

The risk associated with such individuals extends to members of their immediate families and to other known close associates. PEP status itself does not, of course, incriminate individuals or entities. It does, however, put the customer, or the beneficial owner, into a higher-risk category[393] that requires financial institutions to apply additional measures in order to reduce the risk.[394]

A PEP is defined as 'an individual who is or has, at any time in the preceding year, been entrusted with prominent public functions and an immediate family member, or a known close associate, of such a person'.[395]

---

392 The Joint Money Laundering Steering Group JMLSG, *Prevention of money laundering/combating terrorist financing 2017* Revised Version, Guidance for the UK financial sector Part I, June 2017 (Amended December 2017), Paragraph 5.5.13

393 Ibid.

394 The Financial Action Task Force (FATF): International Standards on Combating Money Laundering and the financing of terrorism and proliferation, (The FATF Recommendations) 2012, Recommendation 12

395 Money Laundering Prohibition Act 2011 (as amended), s. 25 (a) (b), See also Section 312 of the US Patriot Act Final Regulation and Notice of Proposed Rule Making 2005. See also the Money Laundering, Terrorist Financing and Transfer of Funds (Information on the Payer) Regulations 2017, Regulation 35 (12); JMLSG, *Prevention of Money Laundering*, Guidance for the United Kingdom Financial Sector Part I, June 2017 (Amended December 2017), Paragraph 5.5.15.

The Financial Action Task Force (FATF) requires that countries apply the PEP definition to only those holding such a position *outside* their jurisdictions.[396]

The United Nations Office on Drugs and Crime (UNODC), on the other hand, requires that countries apply the PEP definition to those holding such positions both inside and outside their jurisdictions.[397]

While some countries have adopted the approach of the FATF, others have adopted that of UNODC. For example, Nigeria and the United Kingdom apply the PEP definition to those holding such positions both inside and outside the country,[398] while the United States applies the PEP definition to those holding such positions outside their respective countries.[399]

The best approach is one that strikes a balance between protecting the financial system against corrupt PEPs and upholding equality before the law.

6.1 Application of the Peps Definition

A PEP is defined as 'an **individual who is or has, at any time in the preceding year, been entrusted with prominent public functions** and **an immediate family member**, or a **known close associate**, of such a person'.[400]

Individuals entrusted with prominent public functions include: heads of state, heads of government, ministers and deputy or assistant ministers; members of parliament or of similar legislative bodies;

---

396 The Financial Action Task Force (FATF): International Standards on Combating Money Laundering and the financing of terrorism and proliferation, (The FATF Recommendations) 2012, Recommendation 12

397 United Nations Convention against Corruption (2004), Article 52 (1)

398 The Nigerian Money Laundering Prohibition Act 2011 (as amended), s 25 (a) (b); the United Kingdom Money Laundering, Terrorist Financing and Transfer of Funds (Information on the Payer) Regulations 2017, Regulation 35 (12) (a).

399 USA Patriot Act of 2001: Uniting and Strengthening America By Providing Appropriate Tools Required To Intercept and Obstruct Terrorism, s. 312 (a) (3) (B)

400 The Financial Action Task Force (FATF): International Standards on Combating Money Laundering and the financing of terrorism and proliferation, (The FATF Recommendations) 2012, Recommendation 12

members of the governing bodies of political parties; members of supreme courts, of constitutional courts or of any judicial body the decisions of which are not subject to further appeal except in exceptional circumstances; members of courts of auditors or of the boards of central banks; ambassadors, charges d'affaires and high-ranking officers in the armed forces; members of the administrative, management or supervisory bodies of State-owned enterprises; directors, deputy directors and members of the board or equivalent function of an international organisation.[401]

"Family member" of a politically exposed person includes: a spouse or civil partner of the PEP; children of the PEP and the spouses or civil partners of the PEP's children; parents of the PEP.[402]

"Known close associate" of a PEP means an individual known to have joint beneficial ownership of a legal entity or a legal arrangement or any other close business relations with a PEP. It also means an individual who has sole beneficial ownership of a legal entity or a legal arrangement which is known to have been set up for the benefit of a PEP.[403]

Financial institutions are required to verify the identity of customers, to take reasonable steps to determine the identity of beneficial owners of funds deposited into high –value accounts and to conduct enhanced scrutiny of accounts sought or maintained by or on behalf of individuals who are, or have been, entrusted with prominent public functions and their family members and close associates. Such enhanced scrutiny shall be reasonably designed to detect suspicious transactions for the purpose of reporting to competent authorities and should not be so construed as to discourage or prohibit financial institutions from doing business with any legitimate customer.[404]

---

401 The United Kingdom Money Laundering, Terrorist Financing and Transfer of Funds (Information on the Payer) Regulations 2017, Regulation 35 (14)

402 The United Kingdom Money Laundering, Terrorist Financing and Transfer of Funds (Information on the Payer) Regulations 2017, Regulation 35 (12) (b)

403 The United Kingdom Money Laundering, Terrorist Financing and Transfer of Funds (Information on the Payer) Regulations 2017, Regulation 35 (12) (c)

404 United Nations Convention Against Corruption 2004, Article 52 (1)

This section will determine the approach that is being adopted by Nigeria, the United States and the United Kingdom with regards to the application of the definition of PEPs.

6.1.1 Nigeria

Nigeria applies the PEP definition to those holding such a position inside and outside the country.[405]

6.1.2 United States

The United States apply the PEP definition to those holding such positions outside the country.[406] The United States refers to PEPs as Senior Foreign Political Figures and limits the application of the definition to Senior Foreign Political Figures who maintain a private banking account with a U.S. financial institution.[407]

6.1.3 United Kingdom

The United Kingdom applies the PEP definition to those holding such a position inside and outside the country.[408]

6.2 Discussion

The previous section compared the approaches adopted in Nigeria, the United States and the United Kingdom with regard to the application of the PEP definition. The best approach is one that strikes

---

405 Money Laundering Prohibition Act 2011 (as amended), s. 25 (a) (b)

406 Uniting and Strengthening America By Providing Appropriate Tools Required To Intercept and Obstruct Terrorism (USA PATRIOT ACT) ACT of 2001, s. 312 (a) (3) (B)

407 Uniting and Strengthening America By Providing Appropriate Tools Required To Intercept and Obstruct Terrorism (USA PATRIOT ACT) ACT of 2001, s. 312 (a) (3) (B), See also Section 312 of the US Patriot Act Final Regulation and Notice of Proposed Rule Making 2005

408 The United Kingdom Money Laundering, Terrorist Financing and Transfer of Funds (Information on the Payer) Regulations 2017, Regulation 35 (12) (a).

a balance between protecting the financial system against corrupt PEPs[409] and upholding equality before the law.[410]

6.2.1 Protecting the Financial System Against Corrupt Peps

As stated earlier, Nigeria and the United Kingdom apply the PEP definition to those holding such positions inside and outside the country, while the United States applies the definition only to those holding such positions outside the country. This section will determine which of the above approaches is more likely to protect the financial system against corrupt PEPs.

The Nigerian and the United Kingdom approaches protects the financial system against individuals who are, or have been, entrusted with prominent public functions both inside and outside the country.

The US approach, on the other hand, protects the financial system against individuals who are or have been entrusted with prominent public functions outside their respective countries.

There appears to be no protection against individuals who are, or who have been, entrusted with prominent public functions within the United States. However, such protection may not be needed since cases of corruption have been rare in the United States.[411]

6.2.2 Upholding Equality Before the Law

This section will determine if the approaches adopted in Nigeria, the United States and United Kingdom directly violate the human rights of PEPs by looking into the conditions that must be cumulatively met in

---

409 Transparency International (2017), 'Corruption Perceptions Index 2016', Available at: https://www.transparency.org/news/feature/corruption_perceptions_index_2016 (accessed 27 December 2017).

410 African Charter on Human and Peoples Rights (1981), Article 2; American Convention on Human Rights (1969), Article 1, 24; European Convention on Human Rights (1950) as amended, Article 14; Rehman, J. (2010), International Human Rights Law, 2nd edition (Pearson Education Limited), 214.

411 Transparency International (2017), 'Corruption Perceptions Index 2016', Available at: https://www.transparency.org/news/feature/corruption_perceptions_index_2016 (accessed 27 December 2017).

order to be considered direct discrimination. These conditions include differential treatment, prohibited grounds without objective and reasonable justification and no reasonable relationship of proportionality.[412]

6.2.2.1 Differential Treatment

One of the conditions that must exist in direct discrimination is that there must be a given difference in treatment, which may concern the exercise of any right set forth by law. [413]

The Nigerian and the UK approaches do not create any difference in treatment concerning the exercise of any right set forth by law. It applies the PEP definition to those holding such positions both inside and outside Nigeria and the UK.

The US approach, on the other hand, does create a difference in treatment concerning the exercise of certain rights set forth by law. The US requires financial institutions to perform enhanced due diligence for individuals who are, or have been, entrusted with prominent public functions in other countries. Such due diligence is not performed on individuals who are, or have been, entrusted with prominent public functions in the United States.

Enhanced due-diligence measures could interfere with the private life of an individual when a financial institution, in trying to establish the source of income and source of wealth of a PEP, gets hold of information that the political figure never wanted anyone to see. The information could relate to that person's legitimate part-time business. This could definitely interfere with the PEP's private life.

The above scenario would not occur if the political figure held such a position in the United States.

---

412 Belgian Linguistic Case (1979 -80) 1 EHRR 252, Para 10; Swedish Engine Driver's Union v. Sweden (1979–80) 1 EHRR, 617, Para 45, 47, 48; National Union of Belgian Police v. Belgium (1979–80) 1 EHRR 578, Para 44, 46; Engel and Others v. The Netherlands (No.1) (1979–80) 1 EHRR 647, Para 72; The Republic of Ireland v. The United Kingdom (1979–80) 2 EHRR 25, Para 226.

413 See Belgian Linguistic Case (1979–80) 1 EHRR 252, Para 10; National Union of Belgian Police v. Belgium (1979–80) 1 EHRR 578, Para 44, 46.

Since the Nigerian and UK approaches do not create any difference in treatment with regard to PEPs, it does not directly discriminate against them. Therefore, there is no need to determine whether or not the Nigerian approach meets the other direct discrimination requirements.

6.2.2.2 Prohibited Grounds

The respective human rights conventions provide that discrimination could be on the grounds of sex, race, colour, national or social origin, property, birth or other status.[414] The US approach does discriminate on the grounds of a person's national origin.

6.2.2.3 Without Objective and Reasonable Justification

The third condition for an action to be considered direct discrimination is that the distinction or difference in treatment would have no objective and reasonable justification. The existence of such a justification must be assessed in relation to the aim and effects of the measure under consideration.[415] This means that we have to look at the aims and objectives in order to determine if the US approach has reasonable justification.

The aim of the application of the PEP definition to foreign individuals holding such positions is to reduce the risk of corrupt PEPs in countries where corruption is at a high level. The United States is not among these.[416]

Therefore, the US approach has objective and reasonable justifications.

---

414 African Charter on Human and Peoples' Rights (1981) Article 2; American Convention on Human Rights, Article 1; European Convention on Human Rights (1950) as amended, Article 14.

415 See Belgian Linguistic Case (1979–80) 1 EHRR 252, Para 10; National Union of Belgian Police v. Belgium (19790–80) 1 EHRR 578, Para 46.

416 Transparency International (2017), 'Corruption Perceptions Index 2016', Available at: https://www.transparency.org/news/feature/corruption_perceptions_index_2016 (accessed 27 December 2017).

6.2.2.4 No Reasonable Relationship of Proportionality

An individual's right to equality is likewise violated when it is clearly established that there is no reasonable relationship of proportionality between the means employed and the aim.[417] In other words, the state must strike a fair balance between the protection of the interests of the community and respect for the rights and freedoms safeguarded by the human rights convention.[418] Hence, if the measure in question creates no impediment to the exercise of the individual rights enshrined in the convention, then it would be a fair balance.[419]

The approach of the United States does interfere with an individual's right to a private life. Therefore, their approach does not strike a fair balance between the protection of the interests of the community and respect for the rights and freedoms safeguarded by the human rights convention.

The US approach directly discriminates against a PEP's right to a private life.

6.3 Conclusion

This chapter compared the approaches in Nigeria, the United States and United Kingdom with regard to the application of the PEP definition. It has analysed issues that arose from the comparison to determine if there is a need for reform.

Based on the outlined arguments, the United States is recommended to extend the application of the PEP definition to individuals who hold prominent public functions within the United States.

This recommended approach would strike a fair balance between the protection of the interests of the community and respect for the rights and freedoms safeguarded by the human rights convention.

---

417 Belgian Linguistic Case (1979–80) 1 EHRR 252, Para 10; National Union of Belgian Police v. Belgium (1979–80) 1 EHRR 578, Para 46.

418 See Belgian Linguistic Case (1979–80) 1 EHRR 252, Para 7.

419 See Belgian Linguistic Case (1979–80) 1 EHRR 252, Para 13.

CHAPTER 7

PRIVATE BANKING

This chapter will focus on one aspect of our banking system—private banking—that may be particularly attractive to criminals who want to launder money. Private banking is probably unfamiliar to most people since, by and large, private banks cater to extremely wealthy clients. Private banks go far beyond providing routine banking services. They market themselves to clients by offering services to meet the special needs of the very wealthy, including providing investment guidance, estate planning, tax assistance, offshore accounts, and, in some cases, complicated schemes designed to ensure the confidentiality of financial transactions.

To open an account in a private bank, prospective clients usually must deposit a substantial sum, often one million dollars or more. In return for this deposit, the private bank assigns a private banker or relationship manager to act as a liaison between the client and the bank, and to facilitate the client's use of a wide range of financial services and products. These products and services often span the globe, enabling a client to make use of a variety of corporate, investment and trust vehicles, estate and tax planning, and other financial services. In essence, private banks seek to provide global wealth management for the wealthy. Private banks typically charge fees based upon the amount of client "assets under management" and the particular products and services used by the client. These fees can exceed one million dollars per client each year.[420]

While many of the products and services offered by private banks are also available through retail banking operations, there are at least two key differences. First, private banks offer an inside advocate—the private banker—whose mission is to help his or her clients make easy use of the bank's products and services. For example, many retail banks provide wire transfer services, but a private banker will routinely arrange complex wire transfers for a client who simply calls in by phone to request them. Retail banks may offer offshore services, but a private banker is an expert in facilitating the creation of offshore trusts and corporations, opening accounts for clients, and arranging transactions on their behalf. Retail banks will allow clients to open multiple accounts, but a private banker will not only create these accounts for a client, but also keep track of the assets in each account and arrange transactions among them.[421]

A second key difference between private banks and retail banks is that a private bank provides its clients with a team of specialists under the coordinated direction of the private banker. These specialists include investment managers, trust officers, estate planners, and other financial experts, all prepared to act in concert. The private banker orchestrates their services with a degree of coordination that is often difficult or impossible to achieve in retail banking.[422]

The Financial Action Task Force requires Countries and financial institutions to identify and assess the money-laundering or terrorist-financing risks that may arise in relation to the development of new business practices, including new delivery mechanisms. In

---

420 The Permanent Subcommittee On Investigations (1999), 'Private Banking and Money Laundering: A Case Study of Opportunities and Vulnerabilities', Available at: https://www.hsgac.senate.gov/subcommittees/investigations/hearings/ private-banking-and-money-laundering-a-case-study-of-opportunities-and-vulnerabilities (accessed 28 December 2017).

421 Ibid.

422 Ibid.

the case of financial institutions, such a risk assessment should take place prior to the launch of new business practices or the use of new or developing technologies. Appropriate measures should be taken to manage and mitigate those risks.[423]

This chapter compares the approach adopted by Nigeria and the United States with that of the United Kingdom to determine if Nigeria and the United States should adopt the approach of the United Kingdom or if there is no need for reform.

The comparison falls under the following subheadings: Definition of Private Banking, Definition of a Private Banking Account and Definition of Private Banking Activities.

7.1 Definition of Private Banking

7.1.1 Nigeria

The Central Bank of Nigeria's Anti-Money Laundering/Combating the Financing of Terrorism (AML/CFT) Risk Based Supervision (RBS) Framework, 2011 defines private banking as providing personalised financial services to wealthy clients.[424] In particular, a financial institution must establish appropriate, specific, and (where necessary) enhanced due diligence (EDD) policies, procedures and controls that are reasonably designed to enable the financial institution to detect and report instances of money laundering through such accounts. Central Bank of Nigeria (CBN) AML/CFT Regulations, 2013 mandate enhanced scrutiny to detect and, if appropriate, report transactions that may involve proceeds of corruption for private banking accounts that are requested or maintained by or on behalf of a senior foreign/local political figure or the individual's immediate family and close associates.[425]

---

423 The FATF Recommendations, Recommendation 15

424 Central Bank of Nigeria's Anti-Money Laundering/Combating the Financing of Terrorism (AML/CFT) Risk Based Supervision (RBS) Framework, 2011, Paragraph 3.12

425 Central Bank of Nigeria (Anti-Money Laundering and Combating the Financing of Terrorism in Banks and Other Financial Institutions in Nigeria) Regulations, 2013, Regulation 16 (b)

7.1.2 United States

Under the **Federal Financial Institutions Examination Council: Bank Secrecy Act/Anti-Money Laundering Examination Manual, 2014**, private banking is defined as providing personalised financial services to wealthy clients.[426] **Section 312 of the USA PATRIOT Act** added **subsection (i) to 31 USC 5318 of the BSA**. This subsection requires each U.S. financial institution that establishes, maintains, administers, or manages a private banking account in the United States for a non-U.S. person to take certain AML measures with respect to these accounts. In particular, a bank must establish appropriate, specific, and, where necessary, EDD policies, procedures, and controls that are reasonably designed to enable the bank to detect and report instances of money laundering through such accounts. In addition, section 312 mandates enhanced scrutiny to detect and, if appropriate, report transactions that may involve proceeds of foreign corruption for private banking accounts that are requested or maintained by or on behalf of a senior foreign political figure or the individual's immediate family and close associates. On January 4, 2006, FinCEN issued a final regulation **(31 CFR 1010.620)** to implement the private banking requirements of **31 USC 5318(i).**

7.1.3 United Kingdom

The United Kingdom uses the term *wealth management* to describe private banking activities, as opposed to Nigeria and the United States, which use the term *private banking*. According to the **Joint Money Laundering Steering Group's Prevention of Money Laundering/Combating Terrorist Financing, 2017 Revised Version: Guidance for the UK Financial Sector Part II: Sectoral Guidance, June 2017 (amended December 2017),** wealth management is the provision of investment services, including advice, discretionary fund management and brokerage to private investors,

---

426 Federal Financial Institutions Examination Council (2014), 'Bank Secrecy Act/Anti-Money Laundering Examination Manual', Available at: https://www.occ. treas.gov/publications/publications-by-type/other-publications-reports/ffiec-bsa-aml-examination-manual.pdf (accessed 10 January 2017).

ranging from the mass affluent to high and ultra-high-net-worth individuals (HNWIs and UHNWIs). Some wealth managers are parts of banks or private banks and may also provide banking services to the same clients. The services are characterised by their bespoke nature, tailored to a client's particular needs and may comprise some or all of the following:

- Execution-only brokerage
- Personalised and detailed advice
- Discretionary portfolio management
- Financial planning
- Bespoke investment solutions
- Investments in markets in a wide range of jurisdictions, including emerging markets, small investment centres, and metropolitan countries
- High-value transactions (for HNWIs and UHNWIs)
- Current account banking (where the wealth manager is part of a private bank)[427]

The definition provided by the United Kingdom for private banking appears to be very detailed. This is so even when the United Kingdom did not use the term *private banking* but, rather, *wealth management.*

7.2 Definition of a Private Banking Account

7.2.1 Nigeria

A private banking account is an account (or any combination of accounts), either a so-called private bank account or maintained at a financial institution, that satisfies all three of the following criteria:

---

427 The Joint Money Laundering Steering Group, *Prevention of money laundering/combating terrorist financing* 2017 Revised Version, Guidance for the UK Financial Sector Part II: Sectoral Guidance June 2017 (Amended December 2017), para. 5.1

(i)   Requires a minimum aggregate deposit of funds or other assets of not less than fifty thousand dollars or its equivalent;

(ii)   Is established on behalf of or for the benefit of one or more Nigerian or non-Nigerian persons who are direct or beneficial owners of the account;

(iii)   Is assigned to, or is administered by, in whole or in part, an officer, employee, or agent of a financial institution acting as a liaison between a financial institution covered by the regulation and the direct or beneficial owner of the account.[428]

If an account satisfies the last two criteria in the definition of a private banking account as described above, but the institution does not require a minimum balance of fifty thousand dollars or its equivalent, then the account does not qualify as a private banking account under this rule. However, the account is subject to the internal controls and risk-based due diligence included in the institution's general AML Compliance program.[429]

With regard to the minimum-deposit requirement, a private banking account is an account (or combination of accounts) that requires a minimum deposit of not less than fifty thousand dollars or its equivalent. A financial institution may offer a wide range of services that are generically termed *private banking*, and even if certain (or any combination, or all) of the financial institution's private banking services do not require a minimum deposit of not less than fifty thousand dollars or its equivalent, these relationships should be subject to a greater level of due diligence under the financial institution's risk-based AML compliance Program.[430]

---

428   Central Bank of Nigeria's Anti-Money Laundering/Combating the Financing of Terrorism (AML/CFT) Risk Based Supervision (RBS) Framework, 2011, Paragraph 5.13

429   Central Bank of Nigeria's Anti-Money Laundering/Combating the Financing of Terrorism (AML/CFT) Risk Based Supervision (RBS) Framework, 2011, Paragraph 3.12

430   Central Bank of Nigeria's Anti-Money Laundering/Combating the Financing of Terrorism (AML/CFT) Risk Based Supervision (RBS) Framework, 2011, Paragraph 5.13

7.2.2 United States

For purposes of **31 CFR 1010.620,** a *private banking account* is an account (or any combination of accounts) maintained at a bank that satisfies all three of the following criteria:

(i) Requires a minimum aggregate deposit of funds or other assets of not less than one million dollars;

(ii) Is established on behalf of or for the benefit of one or more non-U.S. persons who are direct or beneficial owners of the account;

(iii) Is assigned to, or is administered by, in whole or in part, an officer, employee, or agent of a bank acting as a liaison between a financial institution covered by the regulation and the direct or beneficial owner of the account.

With regard to the minimum deposit requirement, a *private banking account* is an account (or combination of accounts) that requires a minimum deposit of not less than one million dollars. A bank may offer a wide range of services that are generically termed *private banking,* and even if certain (or any combination, or all) of the bank's private banking services do not require a minimum deposit of not less than one million dollars, these relationships should be subject to a greater level of due diligence under the bank's risk-based BSA/AML compliance program but are not subject to **31 CFR 1010.620.**

7.2.3 United Kingdom

The **Joint Money Laundering Steering Group's Prevention of Money Laundering/Combating Terrorist Financing 2017 Revised Version: Guidance for the UK Financial Sector Part II: Sectoral Guidance, June 2017 (amended December 2017)** does not specifically define a private banking account.

7.3. Definition Of Private Banking Activities

7.3.1 Nigeria

Under the **Central Bank of Nigeria's Anti-Money Laundering/ Combating the Financing of Terrorism (AML/CFT) Risk Based Supervision (RBS) Framework, 2011**, private banking activities are generally defined as providing personalised services to higher-net-worth customers (e.g., estate planning, financial advice, lending, investment management, bill paying, mail forwarding, and maintenance of a residence). Private banking has become an increasingly important business line for large and diverse banking organizations and a source of enhanced fee income.

Nigerian financial institutions manage private banking relationships for both domestic and international customers. Typically, thresholds of private banking service are based on the amount of assets for management and on the need for specific products or services (e.g., real estate management, closely held company oversight, money management). The fees charged are ordinarily based on asset thresholds and the use of specific products and services.[431]

7.3.2 United States

Under the **Federal Financial Institutions Examination Council: Bank Secrecy Act/Anti-Money Laundering Examination Manual, 2014**, private banking activities are generally defined as providing personalised services to higher-net-worth customers (e.g., estate planning, financial advice, lending, investment management, bill paying, mail forwarding, and maintenance of a residence). Private banking has become an increasingly important business line for large and diverse banking organizations and a source of enhanced fee income.

U.S. banks may manage private banking relationships for both domestic and international customers. Typically, thresholds of private banking service are based on the amount of assets under management and on the need for specific products or services (e.g., real estate management, closely held company oversight, money

---

431 Central Bank of Nigeria's Anti-Money Laundering/Combating the Financing of Terrorism (AML/CFT) Risk Based Supervision (RBS) Framework, 2011, Paragraph 5.33

management). The fees charged are ordinarily based on asset thresholds and the use of specific products and services.

Private banking arrangements are typically structured to have a central point of contact (i.e., relationship manager) that acts as a liaison between the client and the bank and facilitates the client's use of the bank's financial services and products. Typical products and services offered in a private banking relationship include the following:

- Cash management (e.g., checking accounts, overdraft privileges, cash sweeps, and bill-paying services).
- Funds transfers.
- Asset management (e.g., trust, investment advisory, investment management, and custodial and brokerage services).
- The facilitation of shell companies and offshore entities (e.g., private investment companies (PIC), international business corporations (IBC), and trusts).
- Lending services (e.g., mortgage loans, credit cards, personal loans, and letters of credit).
- Financial planning services including tax and estate planning.
- Custody services.
- Other services as requested (e.g., mail services).[432]

Privacy and confidentiality are important elements of private banking relationships. Although customers may choose private banking services simply to manage their assets, they may also seek a confidential, safe, and legal haven for their capital. When acting as a fiduciary, banks have statutory, contractual, and ethical obligations to do the following:

- Ascertain the source(s) of funds deposited into a private banking account and the purpose and expected use of the account

432 Federal Financial Institutions Examination Council (2014), 'Bank Secrecy Act/Anti-Money Laundering Examination Manual', Available at: https://www.occ.treas.gov/publications/publications-by-type/other-publications-reports/ffiec-bsa-aml-examination-manual.pdf (accessed 10 January 2017).

- Review the activity of the account to ensure that it is consistent with the information obtained about the client's source of funds, and with the stated purpose and expected use of the account, and to file a SAR, as appropriate, to report any known or suspected money laundering or suspicious activity conducted to, from, or through a private banking account

7.3.3 United Kingdom
The United Kingdom money laundering laws/regulations do not specifically define private banking activities like Nigeria and the United States do, but they do define private banking. The United Kingdom's definition of "wealth management" or "private banking" is sufficient to cover all private banking activities.

7.4. Conclusion
There is need for the United Kingdom to expressly define the criteria that qualifies a bank account for private banking. This would allow people to know whether or not their bank account qualifies as a private banking account.

CASE STUDY ON PRIVATE BANKING AND MONEY LAUNDERING

Case 7.1: Financial Crimes Enforcement Network v. Riggs Bank. No. 2004-01
FinCEN had determined that Riggs willfully violated the suspicious activity and currency transaction reporting requirements of the **Bank Secrecy Act (BSA)** and its implementing regulations, and that Riggs had willfully violated the anti-money laundering program ("AML program") requirement of the BSA and its implementing regulations.

Extensive and frequent suspicious cash, monetary instrument, and wire activity at Riggs occurred within the accounts held by the government of a foreign country, politically exposed persons of that country, and the companies owned by such persons, where very little monitoring of activity was performed by the bank. Within this relationship, there were a number of transactions that exhibited classic indicators of suspicious activity, or at a minimum lacked any reasonable business or economic purpose, but were never identified and reported. These transactions included:

- aggregate cash withdrawals from the accounts of the government, politically exposed persons, and government employees that totaled tens of millions of dollars over a 2-year period, the majority of which were conducted through payable upon proper identification (PUPID) transactions. PUPID transactions are funds transfers for which there is no specific account to deposit the funds into and the beneficiary of the funds is not a bank customer. For example, an individual may transfer funds to a relative or an individual who does not have an account relationship with the bank that receives the funds transfer. In this case, the beneficiary bank may place the incoming funds into a suspense account and ultimately release the funds when the individual provides proof of identity. In some cases, banks permit noncustomers to initiate PUPID transactions. These transactions are considered extremely high risk and require strong controls;

- dozens of sequentially numbered international drafts drawn from a politically exposed person's account on 3 dates over a 2-month period, totaling millions of dollars, and made payable to the account holder, which were returned to Riggs for crediting back to the account; and

- dozens of sequentially numbered cashier's checks purchased from the same above-listed account on 3 different dates over a period of six months, totaling tens of millions of dollars, and made payable to the account holder, half of which were returned to Riggs for deposit back into the account.

Riggs also failed to identify, monitor, and report suspicious activity related to the accounts of another foreign government, its politically exposed persons, and the companies owned by such persons. This was among Riggs' largest depository relationships; however, the relationship manager for these accounts had little or no supervision. Riggs failed to monitor the activity in these accounts, despite various indicators in early 2003 that should have alerted it to the high-risk nature of the relationship, including publication of a newspaper article alleging official corruption and Riggs' receipt of a subpoena requiring documents regarding the relationship.5 Meanwhile, Riggs failed to implement controls or monitor the ongoing activity.

As a result of these deficiencies, Riggs could not properly identify, evaluate, and report suspicious activity occurring in the relationship, including activity by its employee, the relationship manager. Riggs failed to discover that the relationship manager had signatory authority over two accounts within the relationship, received funds from a government account within the relationship, and failed to file SARs on a timely basis. Examples of the relationship manager's suspicious transactions with respect to this relationship include:

- alteration of a check from the account of a politically exposed person who is the relative of a government official; and
- over one million dollars in wire transfers from accounts owned by the government into the account of a private investment corporation owned by the relationship manager at another U.S. bank.

Riggs also failed to identify, evaluate, and report on suspicious activity occurring in the accounts owned by the government involving transactions by and for the benefit of politically exposed persons, including:

- cash deposits into the account of a private investment corporation owned by a politically exposed person who is a government official, totaling millions of dollars, over a 2-year period; and

- wire transfers, totaling hundreds of thousands of dollars, from a government account to the personal account of another government official who had signature authority over the government account.

FinCEN has determined that by failing (1) to establish and implement an adequate AML program, (2) to file timely, accurate, and complete Suspicious Activity Reports (SARs), and (3) to file accurate and complete Currency Transaction Reports (CTRs) as described in Section III, above, Riggs willfully violated the AML program, SAR, and CTR provisions of the BSA and a civil money penalty is due pursuant to **31 USC §5321** and **31 CFR 1010.820**. In light of the seriousness of the violations, their continuing and ongoing nature, the potential harm they pose to the public, and taking into account the financial resources of Riggs, FinCEN has determined that the appropriate penalty amount in this matter is twenty-five million dollars.[433]

Case 7.2: The Evans Case Study

Chukwudumeme Onwuamadike, a notorious, high-profile kidnap kingpin, popularly called "Evans," was arrested on 10 June 2017 in his mansion on Magodo Estate, Lagos, after a shootout with operatives of the Inspector-General of Police Intelligence Response Team and men of the Lagos State Police Command.

The arrested kingpin's wife, Uchenna Onwuamadike, who is reportedly based in Ghana, has begged Nigerians to have mercy on her husband and family. In an interview, she said, and I quote, "The twenty million naira they said he sent to me through transfer was given to one Hausa man to pay into an account in Ghana to be used in paying our rent and furnish the house in Ghana. I know he banks with Guarantee Trust Bank (GTB) only. Their staff used to visit us in the house."

---

433 United States of America Department of the Treasury Financial Crimes Enforcement Network (2004), 'IN THE MATTER OF: Riggs Bank, N.A.', Available at: https://www.fincen.gov/sites/default/files/enforcement_action/riggsassessment3.pdf (accessed 10 April 2017).

What this means is that Evans utilized GTB's private banking services. Private banking is probably unfamiliar to most Nigerians since, by and large, private banks cater to extremely wealthy clients. Indeed, most of the private banks require their clients to deposit assets in excess of one million dollars. The banks charge their customers a fee for managing those assets and for providing the specialised services of the private banks. Some of those services include traditional banking services such as checking and savings accounts. But private banks go far beyond providing routine banking services. They market themselves to clients by offering services to meet the special needs of the very wealthy, including providing investment guidance, estate planning, tax assistance, offshore accounts, and, in some cases, complicated schemes designed to ensure the confidentiality of financial transactions. Most of the time, private bankers travel as tourists so the authorities will not know that they are visiting clients on business.

Ordinarily, the level of diligence carried out in wealth management/private banking will be higher than that needed for normal retail banking. The relationship manager attached to Evans ought to have done his due diligence properly. The source of Evans's wealth, the nature of his business, and the extent to which his business history presented an increased risk for money laundering and terrorist financing ought to have been considered by his relationship manager. Evans's bank account ought to have been subject to GTB's highest levels of scrutiny, including requirements for senior management approval, prior to opening an account, heightened monitoring, and annual reviews of account developments by the private bank head.

CHAPTER 8

PREPAID CARDS

Prepaid cards are payment cards where money is on deposit with the issuer, but the card account is not linked to a current or savings account. The individual transaction limits, the daily transaction limits, and the maximum amount that can be loaded on the card are specified by the issuer.[434]

Prepaid cards were introduced in the payments market at the end of the 1990's as an alternative to credit cards (which require the card issuer to evaluate the cardholder's minimum level of creditworthiness) and debit cards (which entail the existence of a payment account at a bank or financial institution). Prepaid cards began as a device used to pay for goods and services where the issuer did not need to conduct any analysis on the cardholder's credit standing or bear the cost for opening and managing a payment account.[435]

Today the functionality of prepaid cards varies significantly, as they have evolved from a replacement for store gift certificates and limited-purpose closed-loop applications to, in some cases,

---

434 See the Central Bank of Nigeria Revised Guidelines on Stored Value/Prepaid Card Issuance and Operations 2012 for more on Prepaid Cards.

435 Financial Action Task Force (2013), 'GUIDANCE FOR A RISK BASED-APPROACH: PREPAID CARDS, MOBILE PAYMENTS AND INTERNET-BASED PAYMENT SERVICES', Available at: http://www.fatf-gafi.org/media/fatf/documents/recommendations/Guidance-RBA-NPPS.pdf (accessed 12 January 2017).

embody all the functionalities of a payment instrument tied to a payment account.[436]

Prepaid cards can be issued as smart cards, magnetic stripe cards, Internet accounts, Internet wallets, mobile accounts, mobile wallets, paper vouchers, and any such instrument that can be used to access the prepaid amount.[437]

The prepaid cards that can be issued are classified under three categories: (i) closed-loop prepaid cards, (ii) semi-closed-loop prepaid cards, and (iii) open-loop prepaid cards.

Closed-loop prepaid cards are payment instruments issued to facilitate the purchase of goods and services. These instruments do not permit cash withdrawal or redemption. As these instruments do not facilitate payments and settlement for third-party services, issue and operation of such instruments are not classified as payment systems.[438] Given their low-risk characteristics, closed-loop cards, specifically cards that do not allow reloads or withdrawals, remain outside the scope of this chapter.

Semi-closed-loop prepaid cards are payment instruments that are redeemable at a group of clearly identified merchant locations or establishments, which contract specifically with the issuer to accept the payment instruments. These instruments do not permit cash withdrawal or redemption by the holder.[439]

Open-loop prepaid cards are payment instruments that can be used for the purchase of goods and services at any card-accepting merchant locations (point-of-sale terminals) and also permit cash withdrawal from Automated Teller Machines.[440]

---

436 Financial Action Task Force (2013), 'GUIDANCE FOR A RISK BASED-APPROACH: PREPAID CARDS, MOBILE PAYMENTS AND INTERNET-BASED PAYMENT SERVICES', Available at: http://www.fatf-gafi.org/media/fatf/documents/recommendations/Guidance-RBA-NPPS.pdf (accessed 12 January 2017).

437 Policy Guidelines for Issuance and Operation of Prepaid Payment Instruments in India 2016, para. 2.3

438 Policy Guidelines for Issuance and Operation of Prepaid Payment Instruments in India 2016, para. 2.4

439 Policy Guidelines for Issuance and Operation of Prepaid Payment Instruments in India 2016, para. 2.5.

440 Policy Guidelines for Issuance and Operation of Prepaid Payment Instruments in India 2016, para. 2.6.

The Financial Action Task Force (FATF) has referred to open-loop prepaid cards as New Payment Products and Services (NPPS) that could be misused for money laundering (ML) and terrorist-financing (TF) purposes. This is due to certain characteristics of open-loop prepaid cards, one of which is anonymity. The risk posed by anonymity (not identifying the customer) can occur when the card is purchased, registered, loaded, reloaded, or used by the customer. The level of risk posed by anonymity is relative to the functionality of the card and the existence of anti–money laundering and countering the financing of terrorism (AML/CFT) risk mitigation measures, such as funding or purchasing limits, reload limits, cash access, and whether the card can be used outside the country of issue. Prepaid cards can be funded in various ways with different degrees of customer due diligence (CDD), including through banks/the Internet, at small retail shops, or at automated teller machines.[441]

The FATF has also referred to prepaid cards as payment instruments that could facilitate financial inclusion.[442]

Financial inclusion involves providing access to an adequate range of safe, convenient, and affordable financial services to disadvantaged and other vulnerable groups, including low-income, rural, and undocumented persons, who have been underserved or excluded from the formal financial sector. Financial inclusion also involves making a broader range of financial products and services available to individuals who currently only have access to basic financial products.[443]

James H. Freis Jr., the former director of US Department of the Treasury's Financial Crimes Enforcement Network (FinCEN), stated,

---

441 Financial Action Task Force (2013), 'GUIDANCE FOR A RISK BASED-APPROACH: PREPAID CARDS, MOBILE PAYMENTS AND INTERNET-BASED PAYMENT SERVICES', Available at: http://www.fatf-gafi.org/media/fatf/documents/recommendations/Guidance-RBA-NPPS.pdf (accessed 12 January 2017).

442 Financial Action Task Force (2013), 'FATF GUIDANCE Anti-Money Laundering and Terrorist Financing Measures and Financial Inclusion', Available at: http://www.fatf-gafi.org/media/fatf/documents/reports/AML_CFT_Measures_and_Financial_Inclusion_2013.pdf (accessed 13 January 2017).

443 Ibid.

Prepaid cards have become widely accepted products within the financial system in recent years, and for very good reasons. Not only are these products popular with consumers for convenience and security reasons, there are also benefits for the businesses, employers, governments and banks that issue and market these products. One reason these products are widely used is that prepaid cards are often regarded as a type of validation into the mainstream of the US financial system. Without them, consumers can't shop online or reserve a hotel room. And for the unbanked, one of the only other options is operating on a cash-only basis, which presents its own risks, or purchasing money orders or cashier's checks, which are less flexible and may carry an additional expense.[444]

As stated above, prepaid cards could promote or expand financial inclusion and, at the same time, could be used as a tool to foster money laundering. On this basis, the FATF has advised countries and their financial institutions to design AML/CFT measures that meet the goal of financial inclusion without compromising the measures that exist for the purpose of combating crime.[445] This has been the biggest challenge for several countries, including the United Kingdom and the United States, as has been stated by the former director of FinCEN[446] and the Financial Conduct Authority (FCA).[447]

---

444 Freis, J H. (2010), 'Prepared Remarks of James H Freis, JR, Director FinCEN, Delivered at the Money Transmitter Regulators Association 2010 Annual Meeting and Examiner's School Olympic Village CA', Available at: https://www.fincen.gov/sites/default/files/shared/20100901.pdf (accessed 10 January 2017).

445 Financial Action Task Force (2011), 'FATF GUIDANCE Anti-Money Laundering and Terrorist Financing Measures and Financial Inclusion', Available at: http://www.fatf-gafi.org/media/fatf/content/images/AML%20CFT%20measures%20and%20financial%20inclusion.pdf (accessed 13 January 2017).

446 Freis, J H. (2010), 'Prepared Remarks of James H Freis, JR, Director FinCEN, Delivered at the Money Transmitter Regulators Association 2010 Annual Meeting and Examiner's School Olympic Village CA', Available at: https://www.fincen.gov/sites/default/files/shared/20100901.pdf (accessed 10 January 2017).

447 Financial Conduct Authority (2013), 'Anti-Money Laundering Annual Report 2012/13', Available at: http://www.fca.org.uk/static/documents/anti-money-laundering-report.pdf (accessed 4 December 2016).

The following research question explores how the right balance can be found:

How can countries design AML/CFT measures that meet the goal of financial inclusion (that is, preserving innovation and the many legitimate uses and societal benefits offered by prepaid cards) without compromising the measures that exist for combating money laundering, terrorist financing, and other illicit transactions through the financial system?

The FATF has provided countries with some guidance on how the right balance can be found, but this guidance provides countries with several alternatives, giving them the opportunity to select the best options that they think may best suit them.[448] It is worth noting that some countries have adopted different regulatory approaches, leading to different possible results. This chapter intends to compare the regulatory practices adopted by Nigeria, the United States, the United Kingdom, and India with the aim of determining the best approach among the ones already provided by the FATF. The FATF has not adopted such a comparative approach in any of its documents published. It may sometimes provide some brief information into the regulatory practices adopted by some countries, but it has not tried to compare the approaches adopted by those countries. This is what makes this present research very relevant. The result would add to the already existing literature drawn up by the FATF.

8.1 Licensing/Registration of Providers of Prepaid Cards

The Financial Action Task Force (FATF) has stated that where prepaid cards fall within the definition of money or value transfer services (MVTS) in the glossary to the FATF recommendations, the provider should be licensed or registered, supervised, and subject to anti–money laundering and countering the financing of terrorism

---

448 Financial Action Task Force (2013), 'GUIDANCE FOR A RISK BASED-APPROACH: PREPAID CARDS, MOBILE PAYMENTS AND INTERNET-BASED PAYMENT SERVICES', Available at: http://www.fatf-gafi.org/media/fatf/documents/recommendations/Guidance-RBA-NPPS.pdf (accessed 12 January 2017).

(AML/CFT) measures.[449] These requirements for MVTS have obvious implications for financial inclusion. For example, poor migrant workers often rely on MVTS providers to send remittances home.[450]

Countries have adopted different practices regarding licensing and registration of MVTS providers. This research intends to compare the practices of certain countries, with the aim of finding the best practice; that is, the practice that promotes financial inclusion and also makes the product less attractive for money laundering. It is worth noting that the United Kingdom categorizes prepaid cards as electronic money.[451]

8.1.1 Nigeria

Only deposit-taking banks or financial institutions licensed by the Central Bank of Nigeria (CBN) with clearing capacity are allowed to issue stored value/prepaid cards. Other deposit-taking institutions without clearing capacity can issue in conjunction with those with clearing capacity.[452]

Operators, including mobile/telecommunications operators, wishing to operate money transfer schemes with stored value/prepaid cards shall do so with requisite approval from the CBN and, at all times, in strict conjunction with licensed deposit-taking banks or financial institutions.[453]

---

449 Financial Action Task Force (2013), 'GUIDANCE FOR A RISK BASED-APPROACH: PREPAID CARDS, MOBILE PAYMENTS AND INTERNET-BASED PAYMENT SERVICES', Available at: http://www.fatf-gafi.org/media/fatf/documents/recommendations/Guidance-RBA-NPPS.pdf (accessed 12 January 2017).

450 Financial Action Task Force (2013), 'GUIDANCE FOR A RISK BASED-APPROACH: PREPAID CARDS, MOBILE PAYMENTS AND INTERNET-BASED PAYMENT SERVICES', Available at: http://www.fatf-gafi.org/media/fatf/documents/recommendations/Guidance-RBA-NPPS.pdf (accessed 12 January 2017).

451 See the United Kingdom Electronic Money Regulations 2011, Regulation 2, See also Financial Conduct Authority, 'The FCA's role under the Electronic Money Regulations 2011 Our Approach', Available at: http://www.fca.org.uk/static/documents/emoney-approach.pdf (accessed 10 January 2017).

452 Central Bank of Nigeria Revised Guidelines on Stored Value/Prepaid Card Issuance and Operations 2012, para. 3.1

453 Central Bank of Nigeria Revised Guidelines on Stored Value/Prepaid Card Issuance and Operations 2012, para. 3.9

8.1.2 United States

The US approach is a bit different from the UK's approach. The United States classifies some companies carrying on the business of prepaid cards as money service businesses. Most states in the United States require money service businesses operating within their territory and carrying on the prepaid card business to be licensed with the state banking department.[454] Such money service businesses are also required to be registered with the Financial Crimes Enforcement Network (FinCEN).[455] The "fit and proper test" applies here just like it does in the United Kingdom, but it differs when it comes to registration. The aim of the registration is to collect certain information so as to help FinCEN determine which entity should be responsible for implementing AML/CFT measures. This is different from the UK approach, which allows registration on the basis of the "fit and proper test," but, all the same, they are both similar on the "fit and proper" requirement, although the Financial Conduct Authority (FCA) has more prudential requirements than certain states in the United States.

8.1.3 United Kingdom

The United Kingdom uses the authorisation/registration approach. Authorisation is for certain firms[456] while registrations are for small electronic money institutions.[457] The authorisation approach is similar to the licensing approach adopted by the FATF. Directors of an

---

454 For example, see California's law: Division 1.2 Money Transmission Act, Chapter 3: Licenses: 2030 – 2033, see also Colorado law: Money Transmitter Law, Section 12 – 52 – 108, C.R.S, see also Florida's law: The 2013 Florida Statutes 560.1401, Florida Statutes. See also Atlas, A. (2013), 'Money Transmitter License information for all states', Available at: http://moneytransmitterlicense.blogspot.co.uk/ (accessed 1st of December 2013).

455 See 31 U.S.C 5330, 31 CFR 1022.380 as amended by FinCEN, see also Freis, J H (2011), 'Remarks of James H Freis, JR, Director FinCEN: Money Transmitter Regulators Association 2011 Annual Conference Jacksonville, FL', Available at: https://www.fincen.gov/news/speeches/remarks-james-h-freis-jr-director-financial-crimes-enforcement-network-0 (accessed 5 October 2013).

456 The United Kingdom Electronic Money Regulations 2011, Regulation 5

457 The United Kingdom Electronic Money Regulations 2011, Regulation 12, 13

institution have to be fit and proper persons before the institution can be authorised to carry on the business of prepaid cards.[458]

8.1.4 India

Compared to Nigeria, the United Kingdom, and the United States, India adopts a stricter approach. Only banks that have been permitted to provide mobile banking transactions by the Reserve Bank of India shall be permitted to launch mobile payment instruments (mobile wallets and mobile accounts).[459] Nonbanking financial companies (NBFCs) and other persons would be permitted to issue only semiclosed system payment instruments, including mobile phone-based prepaid payment instruments.[460] Semiclosed system payment instruments are like closed-loop prepaid cards. They are payment instruments redeemable at a group of clearly identified merchant locations/establishments, which contract specifically with the issuer to accept the payment instruments. These instruments do not permit cash withdrawal or redemption by the holder.[461] The "fit and proper test" is not present, but as stated above, nonbanking entities would not be authorised to issue open-loop prepaid cards.

8.2 Thresholds

The use of thresholds is an important consideration with respect to customer due diligence (CDD) and prepaid cards. Thresholds can be used as an effective risk-mitigating tool for open-loop prepaid cards and, therefore, as a measure to allow for the application of simplified CDD. The FATF has stated that the level of threshold will vary between countries, depending on the level of risk posed by

---

458   The United Kingdom Electronic Money Regulations 2011, Regulation 6
459   Policy Guidelines for Issuance and Operation of Prepaid Payment Instruments in India 2016, para. 3.2.
460   Policy Guidelines for Issuance and Operation of Prepaid Payment Instruments in India 2016, para. 3.3.
461   Policy Guidelines for Issuance and Operation of Prepaid Payment Instruments in India 2016, para. 2.5.

prepaid cards in that country, and should be determined based on risk assessment.[462]

The FATF has stated that where prepaid cards are of lower risk and sufficiently low loading or usage limits are applied, countries should still require financial institutions to give sufficient attention to the detection of smurfing and structuring schemes intended to circumvent the thresholds and suspicious activity reports. For example, countries could consider applying thresholds to allow the financial institution to carry out the first three steps of CDD by relying on the customer's statements.[463]

Countries have adopted different levels of practices regarding thresholds. This section intends to compare such practices, with the aim of finding the best practice.

8.2.1 Nigeria

Paragraph 5.2 of the **Central Bank of Nigeria Revised Guidelines on Stored Value/Prepaid Card Issuance and Operations 2012** is to the effect that no prepaid card shall be issued beyond the limits of a stored value card to a person or a corporate organization. Where a customer desires to do transactions beyond the limits prescribed above, full Know Your Customer (KYC) rules would be required.[464]

The maximum amount that can be loaded on the stored value card shall not exceed fifty thousand naira per day.[465]

The maximum balance on the stored value card shall not exceed two hundred and fifty thousand naira at any time.[466]

---

462 Financial Action Task Force (2013), 'GUIDANCE FOR A RISK BASED-APPROACH: PREPAID CARDS, MOBILE PAYMENTS AND INTERNET-BASED PAYMENT SERVICES', Available at: http://www.fatf-gafi.org/media/fatf/documents/recommendations/Guidance-RBA-NPPS.pdf (accessed 12 January 2017).

463 Ibid.

464 Central Bank of Nigeria Revised Guidelines on Stored Value/Prepaid Card Issuance and Operations 2012, para. 5.2

465 Central Bank of Nigeria Revised Guidelines on Stored Value/Prepaid Card Issuance and Operations 2012, para. 4.2

466 Central Bank of Nigeria Revised Guidelines on Stored Value/Prepaid Card Issuance and Operations 2012, para. 4.3

Prepaid cards issued will operate at least within the minimum KYC requirements prescribed by the CBN.[467] However, loadable limits (in naira and foreign currency) and daily balances will be determined by the issuing bank.[468]

8.2.2 United States

Providers of prepaid cards in an arrangement that does not fall within the definition of a prepaid program under **31 CFR 1010 100 (FF) (4) (iii)** will not be required to obtain customer information.[469] For example, prepaid access to funds less than one thousand dollars through a device or vehicle that does not allow international use, transfers between prepaid cards, products within one prepaid card, or loads from nondepository sources, does not require a provider to collect customer identification. This is a little different from the UK approach on the basis of international use.

---

467 The Central Bank of Nigeria requires banks to obtain basic customer information such as passport photograph, name, place and date of birth, gender, address, telephone number, etc. where an account is limited to a maximum single deposit amount of twenty thousand naira and maximum cumulative balance of two hundred thousand naira at any point in time. Evidence of information provided by customer or verification of same is not required. But where the maximum single deposit is fifty thousand naira and the maximum cumulative balance is four hundred thousand-naira, customer information obtained are to be verified against similar information contained in the official data-bases e.g. National Identity Management Commission (NIMC), Independent National Electoral Commission (INEC) Voters Register, Federal Road Safety Commission (FRSC) etc. For more on this, see Central Bank of Nigeria (2013), 'Introduction of Three-Tiered Know Your Customer (KYC) Requirements', Available at: https://www.cbn.gov.ng/out/2013/ccd/3%20tiered%20kyc%20requirements.pdf (accessed 4 February 2017).

468 Central Bank of Nigeria Guidelines for Card Issuance and Usage in Nigeria, para. 6.1

469 Freis, J H (2011), 'Remarks of James H Freis, JR, Director FinCEN: Money Transmitter Regulators Association 2011 Annual Conference Jacksonville, FL', Available at: https://www.fincen.gov/news/speeches/remarks-james-h-freis-jr-director-financial-crimes-enforcement-network-0 (accessed 5 October 2013).

8.2.3 United Kingdom

Regulation 38 of the Money Laundering, Terrorist Financing and Transfer of Funds (Information on the Payer) Regulations 2017 is to the effect that a financial institution or credit institution is not required to apply customer due diligence measures in the circumstances mentioned in regulations 27, 28, 30, and 33 to 37, provided that:

(a) the maximum amount which can be stored electronically is 250 euros, or (if the amount stored can only be used in the United Kingdom), 500 euros;

(b) the payment instrument used in connection with the electronic money ("the relevant payment instrument") is—
(i) not reloadable; or
(ii) is subject to a maximum limit on monthly payment transactions of 250 euros, which can only be used in the United Kingdom;

(c) the relevant payment instrument is used exclusively to purchase goods or services;

(d) anonymous electronic money cannot be used to fund the relevant payment instrument:
(i) if the device cannot be recharged, the maximum amount stored in the device is no more than one hundred and fifty euro; or
(ii) If the device can be recharged, a limit of two thousand five hundred euros is imposed on the total amount transacted in a calendar year, except when an amount of a thousand euro or more is redeemed in the same calendar year by the bearer (within the meaning of Article 3 of the electronic money directive).

The above exceptions do not apply to any transaction that consists of the redemption in cash, or a cash withdrawal, of the monetary value of the electronic money, where the amount redeemed exceeds one hundred euros.[470]

---

470 The Money Laundering, Terrorist Financing and Transfer of Funds (Information on the Payer) Regulations 2017, Regulation 38 (2)

The issuer of the relevant payment instrument must carry out sufficient monitoring of its business relationship with the users of electronic money and of transactions made using the relevant payment instrument to enable it to detect any unusual or suspicious transactions.[471]

8.2.4 India

Compared to Nigeria, the United Kingdom, and the United States, which allow for a complete exemption from CDD so long as the prepaid product meets the threshold requirements, India allows for complete exemption only when semiclosed prepaid payment instruments are issued.

The following types of semiclosed prepaid payment instruments can be issued in carrying out customer due diligence as detailed:

i. Up to Rs.10,000/- by accepting minimum details of the customer, provided the amount outstanding at any point of time does not exceed Rs.10,000/-, and the total value of reloads during any given month also does not exceed Rs.10,000/-. These can be issued only in electronic form.

ii. From Rs.10,001/- to Rs.50,000/- by accepting any "officially valid document," as defined under Rule 2(d) of the Prevention of Money Laundering (PML) Rules 2005, as amended from time to time. Such prepaid payment instruments (PPIs) can be issued only in electronic form and should be nonreloadable in nature.

iii. Up to Rs.1,00,000/- with full KYC and can be reloadable in nature. The balance in the PPI should not exceed Rs.1,00,000/- at any point of time.[472]

---

471 The Money Laundering, Terrorist Financing and Transfer of Funds (Information on the Payer) Regulations 2017, Regulation 38 (3)

472 Policy Guidelines for Issuance and Operation of Prepaid Payment Instruments in India 2016, para. 7.2

Banks can issue open prepaid payment instruments after full KYC in addition to the semiclosed PPIs listed above.[473]

The maximum value of any prepaid payment instruments (where specific limits have not been prescribed, including the amount transferred as per paragraph 10.2) shall not exceed Rs 50,000/-.[474]

CASE STUDY: CIRCUMVENTING THE THRESHOLD MECHANISM THROUGH THE PURCHASE OF MULTIPLE ATM CARDS

The National Drug Law Enforcement Agency (NDLEA) had, on October 17, 2015, arrested a thirty-four-year-old man (name withheld) suspected to be working for an international criminal organisation.

The suspect was in possession of 108 automatic teller machine (ATM) debit cards.

The arrest took place at the Murtala Muhammed International Airport (MMIA) Lagos while the suspect was attempting to board a Qatar Airline flight to China. The debit cards belonged to five commercial banks. The suspect was arrested in connection with alleged money laundering.

The suspect was immediately transferred to the Assets and Financial Investigation Directorate of the Agency for investigation.

First City Monument Bank (FCMB) had the highest number of cards with fifty-eight. Stanbic IBC Bank had twenty-eight cards, Zenith Bank nineteen, Fidelity Bank six, and Diamond Bank two.

"Mrs. Victoria Egbase, the director of assets and financial investigation, said that the agency had established a prima facie case of financial crime against the suspect. She said that the chairman/chief executive of the NDLEA, Ahmadu Giade, had ordered the transfer of the case to the EFCC for further investigation."

---

473 Policy Guidelines for Issuance and Operation of Prepaid Payment Instruments in India 2016, para. 7.3

474 Policy Guidelines for Issuance and Operation of Prepaid Payment Instruments in India 2016, para. 7.1

The agency quoted the suspect as saying in his statement that he was asked to take the cards to China.[475]

8.3 Discussion

As stated earlier, Nigeria, the United States, and the United Kingdom have adopted the risk-based approach for prepaid cards while India has adopted the wholesale derisking approach.

This section determines what the best approach is. The best approach is likely the one that meets the goal of financial inclusion without compromising the measures that exist for combating money laundering, terrorist financing, and other illicit transactions through the financial system.

8.3.1 De-Risking

The FATF has stated that "derisking" should never be an excuse for a bank/country to avoid implementing a risk-based approach in line with the FATF standards. The FATF recommendations only require financial institutions to terminate customer relationships, on a case-by case basis, where the money laundering and terrorist-financing risks cannot be mitigated. This is fully in line with AML/CFT objectives. What is not in line with the FATF standards is the wholesale cutting loose of entire classes of customer, without taking into account, seriously and comprehensively, their level of risk or risk mitigation measures for individual customers within a particular sector.

India has adopted the wholesale derisking approach, as opposed to Nigeria, the United States, and the United Kingdom, which have adopted the risk-based approach.

Although the Indian approach could drastically reduce the money-laundering risks associated with prepaid cards, the approach promotes financial exclusion, as it excludes all non-financial institutions from carrying on the business of prepaid cards.

---

475 The Guardian (2015), 'NDLEA arrests man with 108 ATM cards at MMIA', Available at: http://guardian.ng/news/ndlea-arrests-man-with-108-atm-cards-at-mmia/ (accessed 30 August 2017).

Nigeria, the United States, and the United Kingdom, on the other hand, have adopted approaches that could foster financial inclusion and, at the same time, mitigate the money-laundering risks associated with prepaid cards.

The authorisation approach adopted by Nigeria, the United States, and the United Kingdom ensures that only fit and proper persons are allowed to carry on the business of prepaid cards.

Rather than applying the wholesale derisking approach to non-deposit-taking banks, operators, including mobile/telecommunications operators, wishing to operate money transfer schemes in Nigeria with stored value/prepaid cards can do so with requisite approval from the Central Bank of Nigeria and, at all times, in strict conjunction with licensed deposit-taking banks or financial institutions.

8.3.2 Simplified Due Diligence

As stated earlier, India does not allow for complete exemption from CDD where the product meets the threshold requirements. This is contrary to the approach being adopted by Nigeria, the United States, and the United Kingdom, which allow for complete exemption from CDD where the product meets the threshold requirements.

Measures that ensure that more clients use formal financial services therefore increase the reach and effectiveness of the anti–money laundering/counterterrorist financing (AML/CFT) controls.[476]

India's approach to thresholds would preclude most individuals in the intended target market from accessing basic financial products, as most people typically do not have residential addresses that could be confirmed by reference to formal documentation.

The enforcement of full account opening procedures often excludes some segments of the population from financial services. This keeps them out of the formal economy and indirectly promotes the

---

476 Bester, H., Chamberlain, D., De Koker, L., Hougaard, C., Short, R., Smith, A. and Walker, R. (2008), 'Implementing FATF Standards in Developing Countries and Financial Inclusion: Findings and Guidelines', Available at: http://www.cenfri.org/documents/AML/AML_CFT%20and%20Financial%20Inclusion.pdf (accessed 31 December 2017).

informal sector. This is particularly so among the lower-income earn-ers, poor, and socially disadvantaged segment of the population, the majority of whom live in the rural areas.

8.4 Conclusion

The risk-based approach should be the cornerstone of an effective AML/CFT system and is essential to properly managing risks and facilitating financial inclusion. The FATF expects financial institu-tions to identify, assess, and understand their money-laundering and terrorist-financing risks and take commensurate measures in order to mitigate them. This does not imply a "zero failure" approach.

This chapter concludes that Nigeria, the United States, and the United Kingdom have the best approach to mitigating the money-laundering risks associated with prepaid cards, the reason being that they have adopted the risk-based approach and not the wholesale derisking approach.

CHAPTER 9

CASH COURIERS

The Financial Action Task Force (FATF)—an independent intergovernmental body that develops and promotes policies to protect the global financial system against money laundering, terrorist financing and financing the proliferation of weapons of mass destruction—has advised countries to enact laws that require all persons who physically transport currency or bearer negotiable instruments (BNIs) in excess of fifteen thousand US dollars or Euros to submit a truthful declaration to the designated competent authorities.

Countries may opt from among the following three types of declaration systems: (i) a written declaration system for all travellers, (ii) a written declaration system for those travellers carrying an amount of currency or BNIs above the threshold and (iii) an oral declaration system. These systems are described below in their pure forms. However, it is not uncommon for countries to opt for a mixed system.[477]

(a) Written declaration system for all travellers: In this system, all travellers are required to complete a written declaration before entering the country. This would include questions on a common or customs declaration form. In practice, travellers

---

477 The Financial Action Task Force (FATF): International Standards on Combating Money Laundering and the financing of terrorism and proliferation, (The FATF Recommendations) 2012, Recommendation 32

must declare whether or not they are carrying currency or BNIs (e.g., by ticking a yes or no box).[478]

(b) Written declaration system for travellers carrying amounts above a threshold: In this system, all travellers carrying an amount of currency or BNIs above a preset designated threshold are required to complete a written declaration form. In practice, travellers who are not carrying currency or BNIs over the designated threshold are not required to fill out any forms.[479]

(c) Oral declaration system for all travellers: In this system, all travellers are required to orally declare if they carry an amount of currency or BNIs above a prescribed threshold. This is usually done at customs entry points where travellers are required to choose between the 'red channel' (goods to declare) and the 'green channel' (nothing to declare). The traveller's choice of channel is considered the oral declaration. In practice, travellers do not declare in writing but are required to actively report to a customs official.[480]

While countries have followed the advice of the FATF, the laws in these countries are not identical. For example, Nigeria and the United Kingdom require all travellers to orally declare if they carry an amount of currency above the prescribed threshold, while the United States requires travellers who carry an amount of currency above a preset designated threshold to complete a written declaration form.

This chapter compares the approach adopted by Nigeria and United Kingdom with that of the United States to determine the best approach. This is likely the one that strikes a fair balance between protecting the financial system against money launderers and upholding equality before the law.

---

478 Ibid.
479 Ibid.
480 Ibid.

9.1 Declaration System

9.1.1 Nigeria

The dual channel system of passenger clearance is operated at Lagos/Abuja International Airports. By choosing a specifically designated exit, the traveller declares either that he is carrying with him an amount less than ten thousand dollars or an amount equivalent to ten thousand dollars or more than ten thousand dollars.

There are two designated exits and a passenger goes through one of the exits with all his baggage loaded on a trolley: -

9.1.1.1 Green Exit

A passenger who is satisfied that he does not have ten thousand dollars or more is to pass through the green exit indicated by a green regular octagon with the words "NOTHING TO DECLARE" in English or "RIEN A DECLARER" in French.

9.1.1.2 Red Exit

A passenger who has ten thousand dollars or more is to pass through the Red channel indicated by a read square with the words "GOODS TO DECLARE" in English or "MERCHANDISES A DECLARER" IN French and to declare such goods to the Customs officer by the Examination bench.

By choosing a channel, a passenger is, by implication, declaring the contents of his baggage.[481]

Any person who falsely declares or fails to make a declaration to the Nigerian Custom Service is guilty of an offence and shall be liable on conviction to forfeit the undeclared funds or negotiable

---

481 Nigeria Customs Service (2017), 'Passenger's Concessions', Available at: https://www.customs.gov.ng/Stakeholders/passengers_concessions.php (accessed 27 December 2017).

instrument or to imprisonment to a term of not less than 2 years or to both.[482]

To effectively enforce this measure, the Nigerian Customs has deployed scanners and X-ray machines at all entry and exit ports to detect cash concealment and other precious metals, in baggage, containerized cargo, vehicles, aircraft and ships. It has also enforced physical examination of cargo to check false bottoms and false declaration.

Customs also screens passengers at check-in counters, follows up intelligence information, acts on suspicion, and makes random checks of travellers at airports and the border station. Other enforcement measures include passenger profiling, using the index list, Interpol, the aircraft's manifest and the passenger advance information system, all of which help a great deal in risk management.

The Nigeria Customs Service has also computerized the AML/CFT Unit in all the designated Area Commands, and enforces the application of relevant software to support the database in generating queries based on passport number, date of birth, destination. Specialized training has also been given to staff who are responsible for enforcing this measure.

The successes so far recorded indicate that the Nigerian cash declaration system is a workable model and this should be encouraged in other Member States in the region. In 2006, when this measure became fully operational in 2006, about 26,487 declarations were recorded; and in 2007 this increased to 33,580. As at October 2007, a total of 60,067 renditions were reported to the Nigerian Financial Intelligence Unit, about 350 of which were suspicious transactions involving amounts above fifty thousand dollars. Cooperation and collaboration between the law enforcement agencies facilitates sharing and exchange of intelligence.[483]

---

482 Money Laundering Prohibition Act 2011 (as amended), s. 2 (5)

483 Inter-Governmental Action Group Against Money Laundering in West Africa (2007), 'TYPOLOGIES REPORT ON CASH TRANSACTIONS AND CASH COURIERS IN WEST AFRICA', Available at: http://www.giaba.org/media/f/107_typologies-report-november-2007.pdf (accessed 13 August 2017).

CASE STUDY: FAILURE TO MAKE A DECLARATION TO THE NIGERIAN CUSTOM SERVICE

Case 9.1: Federal Government of Nigeria v. Rowland Ojukwu and Linus Ngene

A Federal High Court in Lagos had on February 9, 2016 jailed two businessmen, Rowland Ojukwu and Linus Ngene, for two years each for their failure to declare the sums of two million nine hundred thousand dollars and two million five hundred thousand dollars respectively to the Nigerian Customs at the Murtala Muhammed International Airport, Lagos.

The trial judge, Justice Ibrahim Buba, ordered the convicts to forfeit the cash sums to the Federal Government. Ojukwu and Ngene had been separately arraigned on a charge of money laundering by the Economic and Financial Crimes Commission.

The EFCC prosecutor, Vincent Latona, had told the court how Ojukwu, who was on his way to Addis Ababa, Ethiopia on October 8, last year, failed to declare the foreign currency to the Nigerian Customs.

He also told the court during Ngene's trial, that the China-bound convict made partial disclosure to the Customs, claiming that he carried only eleven thousand five hundred dollars while he actually had two million five hundred thousand dollars on him.

According to Latona, Ojukwu and Ngene acted contrary to sections 2, 2 (5) and 3 of the Money Laundering (prohibition) Act 2011 as amended by Act 1 of 2012.

But during their separate arraignment, Ojukwu and Ngene pleaded not guilty.

In a bid to prove his case, Latona called eight witnesses and tendered eight exhibits.

In his judgment on Tuesday, Justice Buba said he was satisfied that the prosecution proved its case against the convicts beyond reasonable doubts.

The judge said it was obvious that the convicts knew what they were doing, stressing that they needed to be punished to send a signal to others who might want to toe their path.

In the case of Ojukwu, the judge held, "There is no doubt that the accused passed the gate without declaring the sum; that evidence stands as tall as the rock of Gibraltar; at all times the accused knew what he was doing.

"Facts are certain, they do not lie. Lies are like bats, once in the dark, they elude everyone but once exposed to the rays of light, they hang stupidly as one of the ugliest creatures.

"This court has no doubt in holding that the prosecution proved its case beyond reasonable doubts; accordingly, the accused is convicted as charged.

"The accused is hereby sentenced to a term of two years imprisonment beginning from February 9, 2016.

"The undeclared sum is ordered to be forfeited to the federal government."[484]

On appeal, the Lagos Division of the Court of Appeal on July 14, 2017 upheld the February 9, 2016 judgment of Justice I.N Buba of the Federal High Court Lagos, which convicted and sentenced Mr. Ngene Linus Chibuike to two years imprisonment and ordered the forfeiture of the undeclared sum of Two Million, Five Hundred and Six Thousand, Nine hundred and Ninety-Eight United States Dollars to the Federal Government of Nigeria.[485]

9.1.2 United States

When entering the United States in-transit to a foreign destination, you will be required to clear U.S. Customs Border Protection (CBP) and Immigration and Customs Enforcement. If you have "negotiable monetary instruments" (i.e. currency, personal checks (endorsed), travellers checks, gold coins, securities or stocks in bearer

---

484 The Punch (2016), 'Money laundering: Two bag four years, forfeits $5.4m', Available at: http://punchng.com/money-laundering-two-bag-four-years-forfeits-5-4m/ (accessed 13 August 2017).

485 Economic and Financial Crimes Commission (2017), 'Appeal Court Affirms Two Years Jail Term, Forfeiture of $ 2,506,988 Against Money Laundering Convict', Available at: https://efccnigeria.org/efcc/news/2669-appeal-court-affirms-two-years-jail-term-forfeiture-of-2-506-988-against-money-laundering-convict (accessed 30 August 2017).

form) valued at ten thousand dollars or more in your possession a "Report of International Transportation of Currency or Monetary Instruments" form FinCEN 105 must be submitted to a CBP Officer upon your entry into the United States.

Monetary instruments that are made payable to a named person but are not endorsed or which bear restrictive endorsements are not subject to reporting requirements, nor are credit cards with credit lines of over ten thousand dollars. Gold bullion is not a monetary instrument for purposes of this requirement. The requirement to report monetary instruments on a FinCEN 105 does not apply to imports of gold bullion.

Failure to declare monetary instruments in amounts of or over ten thousand dollars can result in its seizure.[486]

9.1.3 United Kingdom

When you arrive in the United Kingdom, you'll have to go through customs. Most UK ports and airports have three customs exits or 'channels', while some have only one exit, with a red-point phone for declaring goods.

9.1.3.1 When to Use the Blue Channel

You should use the blue channel if you are travelling from a country within the European Union (EU) and you have no banned or restricted goods.

This exit is not seen present in the Nigerian airports. The reason could be that Nigeria does not differentiate between European citizens and other citizens.

---

486 U.S Department of Homeland Security (2017), 'Declaring currency when entering the U.S in-transit to a foreign destination', Available at: https://help.cbp. gov/app/answers/detail/a_id/778/~/declaring-currency-when-entering-the-u.s.- in-transit-to-a-foreign-destination (accessed 28 December 2017).

9.1.3.2 When to Use the Green Channel

You should use the green channel if you are travelling from outside the EU and have with you less than ten thousand euros (or equivalent) in cash

Customs officials from the UK Border Agency (UKBA) carry out checks on travellers in the green channel and **there are penalties for failing to declare goods. This can include seizure of: duty free allowance goods, any goods in excess of your duty free allowance, any vehicle used to transport the goods**

9.1.3.3 When to Use the Red Channel or Red-Point Phone

You should use the red channel or the red-point phone if you have ten thousand euros or more (or equivalent) in cash.

You'll be able to speak to a UKBA officer either in person or by using the red-point phone. You should tell them everything that you are bringing into the country. The UKBA officer may ask to look inside your luggage.[487]

9.2 Discussion

As stated earlier, Nigeria and the United Kingdom require travellers to orally declare whether they carry an amount of currency above the prescribed threshold, while the United States requires all travellers who carry an amount above a preset designated threshold to complete a written declaration form.

This section determines what the best approach is. The best approach is likely the one that strikes a fair balance between protecting

---

487 HM Revenue and Customs (2017), 'Entering the UK', Available at: http://www.hmrc.gov.uk/customs/arriving/customs-channels.htm (accessed 26 December 2017).

the financial system against money launderers[488] and upholding
equality before the law.[489]

9.2.1 Protecting the Financial System Against Money Launderers and Terrorists

The oral declaration system adopted in Nigeria does not appear to
be working as effectively as it is in the United Kingdom. This could
be because the so-called system has not curtailed the movement of
criminal property by the deadly terrorist group Boko Haram.

Boko Haram primarily uses a system of couriers to move cash
around Nigeria and across the porous borders from neighbouring
African states. This cash is said to be derived from lucrative criminal
activities that involve kidnappings.[490]

Nigeria's use of higher denomination bank notes than those of
the United Kingdom could be one of the reasons why the oral declaration system does not work as effectively. People are able to move
large sums of money around without being detected.

The problem could be solved if the federal government directed
the Central Bank of Nigeria (CBN) to stop the production of higher denomination bank notes. This would enable law enforcement
agents to identify persons carrying large sums of money.

The written declaration system appears to be working effectively
in the United States. So far, there has been little or no record of any
terrorist threat from within the United States, apart from the Boston
bombings.

---

488 The Financial Action Task Force (FATF): International Standards On Combating Money Laundering and the financing of terrorism and proliferation,(The
FATF Recommendations) 2012, Page 9.

489 African Charter on Human and Peoples Rights (1981), Article 2; American
Convention on Human Rights (1969), Article 1, 24; European Convention on
Human Rights (1950) as amended, Article 14; Rehman, J. (2010), *International Hu-
man Rights Law*, 2nd edition (Pearson Education Limited), 214.

490 Stewart, P. and Wroughton, L. (2014), 'How Boko Haram Is Beating
US Efforts to Choke Its Financing', Available at: http://www.reuters.com/ar-
ticle/2014/07/01/us-usa-nigeria-bokoharam-insight-idUSKBN0F636920140701
(accessed August 5, 2014).

9.2.2 Upholding Equality Before the Law

This section will determine if the approaches adopted in Nigeria, the United States and the United Kingdom directly violate the human rights of foreign individuals.

It will determine this by looking into the conditions that must be cumulatively met in order for direct discrimination to be considered to have occurred. These conditions include differential treatment, prohibited grounds, lack of objective and reasonable justification and no reasonable relationship of proportionality.[491]

9.2.2.1 Differential Treatment

One of the conditions that must exist before a situation is considered direct discrimination is that there must be a given difference in treatment that may concern the exercise of any right set forth by law.[492]

The Nigerian approach does create a difference in treatment, as it operates the dual-channel system of passenger clearance. This requires travellers who are carrying amounts of less than ten thousand dollars to go through the green channel exit, while passengers with amounts equivalent to ten thousand dollars or more must go through the red channel exit.

The United Kingdom's approach does create a difference in treatment concerning the exercise of certain rights set forth by law. This is because European Union passengers are required to go through the blue channel, while other passengers choose either the green or red channel, depending on the amount of cash they are carrying.

---

491 Belgian Linguistic Case (1979–80) 1 EHRR 252, Para 10; Swedish Engine Driver's Union v. Sweden (1979–80) 1 EHRR, 617, Para 45, 47, 48; National Union of Belgian Police v. Belgium (1979–80) 1 EHRR 578, Para 44, 46; Engel and Others v. The Netherlands (No.1) (1979–80) 1 EHRR 647, Para 72; The Republic of Ireland v. The United Kingdom (1979–80) 2 EHRR 25, Para 226.

492 Belgian Linguistic Case (1979–80) 1 EHRR 252, Para 10; National Union of Belgian Police v. Belgium (1979–80) 1 EHRR 578 Para 44, 46.

Both Nigeria and the United Kingdom's approaches could interfere with a person's right to privacy, such as when a passenger going through the red channel is forced to reveal confidential information to airport staff. This information can include source of income and source of wealth.

The US approach does create a difference in treatment, as it requires passengers who are carrying amounts over ten thousand dollars to submit a Form FinCEN 105, Report of International Transportation of Currency or Monetary Instruments, to a customs and border patrol officer, while travellers carrying less than ten thousand dollars are not required to submit any such form.

Just like the UK and Nigerian approaches, the US approach could interfere with a person's right to privacy. This can occur when a person filling out Form FinCEN 105 is forced to reveal confidential information to the officer in charge. This information includes source of wealth and source of income.

9.2.2.2 Prohibited Grounds

The respective human rights conventions provide that discrimination could be on the grounds of sex, race, colour, national or social origin, property, birth or other status.[493]

The Nigerian, US and UK approaches do discriminate on the grounds of currency.

9.2.2.3 Without Objective and Reasonable Justification

The third condition for direct discrimination is that the distinction or difference in treatment would have no objective and reasonable justification. The existence of such a justification must be assessed in relation to the aim and effects of the measure under consideration.[494] This means that the aims and objectives of the Nigerian, UK

---

493 African Charter on Human and Peoples Rights (1981) Article 2; American Convention on Human Rights, Article 1; European Convention on Human Rights (1950) as amended, Article 14.

494 Belgian Linguistic Case (1979–80) 1 EHRR 252, Para 10; National Union of

and US approaches must be looked at to determine if they have no reasonable justification.

The aim and objective of the measure in all three countries is to prevent physical cross-border transportation of illegal money.

Persons carrying criminal property into Nigeria and the United Kingdom would be detected at the red channel, while persons carrying criminal property into the United States would be detected once the information provided in Form FinCEN 105 was verified. This justifies the Nigerian and US human rights interference.

The United Kingdom is justified to the extent of its utilization of the green and red channels. The blue channel, however, directly discriminates against citizens who are not Europeans, since the channel is not designed to prevent physical cross-border transportation of illegal money.

There is no need to further determine whether or not the Nigerian, US and UK approaches meet the other direct discrimination requirements.

9.3 Conclusion

In view of these arguments, the following are recommended:

I.   The United Kingdom should adopt the Nigerian approach by operating only the green and red channels.
II. The Nigerian National Assembly should pass a law prohibiting every person from physically carrying more than fifty thousand Nigerian naira. This measure would force people, including cash couriers, to use their debit and credit cards more often, making it easier for banks to monitor financial transactions and report suspicious activities.

Belgian Police v. Belgium (1979–80) 1 EHRR 578, Para 46.

CHAPTER 10

COMPLIANCE OFFICERS

T he Financial Action Task Force (FATF) has advised countries to enact laws that require financial institutions to implement programmes against money laundering and terrorist financing. These programmes should include the appointment of a compliance officer at the management level.[495]

A compliance officer is responsible for the oversight of the firm's anti–money laundering (AML) systems and controls, which include appropriate training for the firm's employees in relation to money laundering and considering each report received from staff to determine whether it gives rise to knowledge, suspicion or reasonable grounds for knowledge or suspicion that another person is engaged in money laundering.[496]

Although countries have followed the advice of the FATF, the enacted laws are not identical. For example, Nigeria and the United States require financial institutions to appoint compliance officers

---

495 The Financial Action Task Force (FATF): International Standards on Combating Money Laundering and the financing of terrorism and proliferation, (The FATF Recommendations) 2012, Recommendation 18

496 Money Laundering Prohibition Act 2011 (as amended), s. 9 (1); Federal Financial Institutions Examination Council (2014), 'Bank Secrecy Act/Anti-Money Laundering Examination Manual', Available at: https://www.occ.treas.gov/publications/publications-by-type/other-publications-reports/ffiec-bsa-aml-examination-manual.pdf (accessed 10 January 2017); Senior Management Arrangements, Systems and Controls (SYSC), 6.3.9 (1) R, see also SYSC, 6.3.7 G.

who receive disclosures from staff and who train staff.[497] The United Kingdom requires financial institutions to appoint compliance officers with the responsibility of training staff,[498] but the duty of receiving disclosures from staff rests on the nominated officer.[499]

This chapter compares the approach adopted in Nigeria and the United States with that of the United Kingdom, with the aim of determining if Nigeria and the United States should adopt the approach of the United Kingdom or if there is no need for reform.

The comparison will be made under two subheadings: 'The Title of the Individual Responsible for Anti–Money Laundering Compliance' and 'Duties and Responsibilities'.

The chapter will later analyse issues that arise from the comparison to determine if there is need for reform.

CASE STUDY: NEED FOR BANKS TO PROVIDE COMPLIANCE OFFICERS WITH SUFFICIENT RESOURCES AND TIME TO OVERSEE ANTI-MONEY LAUNDERING COMPLIANCE

Case 10.1: Financial Crimes Enforcement Network v. Bank of Mingo. Number 2015-08

The Financial Crimes Enforcement Network ("FinCEN") determined that grounds exist to assess a civil money penalty against Bank of Mingo ("Mingo"), pursuant to the Bank Secrecy Act ("BSA") and regulations issued pursuant to that Act.

---

497   Money Laundering Prohibition Act 2011 (as amended), s. 9 (1); Federal Financial Institutions Examination Council (2014), 'Bank Secrecy Act/Anti-Money Laundering Examination Manual', Available at: https://www.occ.treas.gov/publications/publications-by-type/other-publications-reports/ffiec-bsa-aml-examination-manual.pdf (accessed 10 January 2017).

498   Senior Management Arrangements, Systems and Controls (SYSC) 2017, 6.3.9 (1) R, see also SYSC, 6.3.7 G.

499   Proceeds of Crime Act 2002 (as amended), ss. 337, 338; The Money Laundering, Terrorist Financing and Transfer of Funds (Information on the Payer) Regulations 2017, Regulation 21 (3)

A bank is required to designate a person responsible for ensuring day-to-day compliance with BSA requirements. **31 U.S.C. § 5318(h)(1) (B); 31 C.F.R. § 1020.210**. Although Mingo designated a BSA Officer, it did not provide the BSA Officer with sufficient resources and time to adequately oversee Mingo's BSA compliance program. Specifically, Mingo assigned the BSA Officer multiple non-BSA responsibilities that left him unable to adequately fulfill his BSA obligations. Mingo was aware of this situation but failed to designate an additional person to support the BSA Officer or otherwise remedy the situation.

FinCEN determined that the penalty in this matter will be four million five hundred thousand dollars. The penalty will run concurrent with the FDIC three million five hundred thousand dollars penalty, of which two million two hundred thousand dollars is concurrent with the amount forfeited pursuant to the deferred prosecution agreement with the U.S. Attorney's Office for the Southern District of West Virginia.[500]

CASE STUDY: NEED TO PROVIDE ADEQUATE STAFFING TO MITIGATE MONEY LAUNDERING RISKS

Case 10.2: Financial Crimes Enforcement Network v. Ocean Bank. Number 2011-7

Ocean failed to adequately staff the BSA compliance function at the Bank with personnel to ensure day-to-day compliance with the BSA. The unit responsible for monitoring the Bank's domestic and foreign retail customer accounts was understaffed, and personnel lacked the requisite knowledge and expertise to adequately perform their duties. The Bank failed to recognize the risks inherent within its retail business lines and failed to provide adequate staffing to mitigate such risks. The Bank's failure to provide adequate numbers of appropriately trained personnel limited its ability to initiate and complete reviews and file complete, accurate, and timely suspicious activity reports.

---

500 United States of America Department of the Treasury Financial Crimes Enforcement Network (2015), 'IN THE MATTER OF: Bank of Mingo Williamson, West Virginia', Available at: https://www.fincen.gov/sites/default/files/enforcement_action/Mingo_Assessment.pdf (accessed 5 March 2017).

Based on the seriousness of the violations at issue in this matter, and the financial resources available to Ocean, FinCEN determined that the appropriate penalty in this matter is ten million nine hundred thousand dollars.[501]

CASE STUDY: NEED FOR A COMPLIANCE OFFICER TO POSSESS THE NECESSARY SKILLS AND EXPERTISE IN ANTI-MONEY LAUNDERING COMPLIANCE

Case 10.3: Financial Crimes Enforcement Network v. Pamrapo Savings Bank, S.L.A. Number 2010-3

Under the authority of the **Bank Secrecy Act ("BSA")** and regulations issued pursuant to that Act, the Financial Crimes Enforcement Network determined that grounds exist to assess a civil money penalty against Pamrapo Savings Bank, S.L.A. ("Pamrapo" or the "Bank").

The Bank's BSA officer and Compliance officer were unqualified for their positions. The BSA and Compliance officers held other full-time positions within the Bank, did not have experience with or training in BSA requirements, and spent minimal time dealing with BSA matters. The BSA officer did not attend meetings with regulators to discuss examination findings, nor was the BSA officer provided copies of examination reports detailing BSA deficiencies.

Both the BSA officer and Compliance officer were aware for years that certain cash transactions were not appearing on the Large Currency Transaction Report (LCTR), the sole report used for identifying transactions for accurate and complete currency transaction reporting, yet did not take steps to rectify this failure. In fact, the BSA officer, who was also a full-time branch manager, was aware that tellers processed transactions utilizing the code that would negate the transactions from appearing on the LCTR. This resulted in the Bank's failure to file numerous currency transaction reports and

---

501   United States of America Department of the Treasury Financial Crimes Enforcement Network (2011), 'IN THE MATTER OF: OCEAN BANK, MAIMI, FLORIDA)', Available at: https://www.fincen.gov/sites/default/files/enforcement_action/08222011_OceanBank_ASSESSMENT.pdf (accessed 5 May 2017).

failure to file accurate and complete currency transaction reports. Further exacerbating this situation, the LCTR was used by the BSA officer to manually monitor for structuring activity by customers. However, in addition to not capturing numerous transactions due to the coding deficiencies, the LCTR did not capture any cash transactions below ten thousand dollars until 2006, rendering it useless for monitoring for structuring patterns.

Another example of the BSA officer's lack of qualification was reflected in the incorrect classification of over three dozen accounts which were determined by regulators to be MSBs. These accounts were not assessed for risk or appropriately monitored for an extended period of time.

Despite knowing that these individuals were unqualified and that the Bank had systemic BSA problems, Bank management and the Board of Directors did not begin to take corrective action in this area until late 2008.

After considering the seriousness of the violations and the financial resources available to Pamrapo, the Financial Crimes Enforcement Network has determined that the appropriate penalty in this matter is one million dollars.[502]

CASE STUDY: NEED FOR BANKS TO PROVIDE THE NECESSARY LEVEL OF AUTHORITY TO ITS COMPLIANCE OFFICERS

Case 10.4: Financial Crimes Enforcement Network v. Merchants Bank of California. Number 2017-02

Merchants Bank of California failed to provide the necessary level of authority, independence and responsibility to its BSA Officer to ensure day-to-day compliance with the BSA as required.

---

502 United States of America Department of the Treasury Financial Crimes Enforcement Network (2010), 'IN THE MATTER OF: PAMRAPO SAVINGS BANK, S.L.A. BAYONNE, NEW JERSEY', Available at: https://www.fincen.gov/sites/default/files/enforcement_action/PamrapoAssessment.pdf (accessed 27 April 2017).

Merchants's BSA Officer and the compliance staff were not empowered with sufficient authority and autonomy to implement the Bank's AML program. Merchants's interest in revenue compromised efforts to effectively manage and mitigate its deficiencies and risks.

Prior to September 2016, Merchants's leadership had not ensured that the BSA Officer had sufficient authority and resources to administer an effective BSA compliance program by failing to define a permanent BSA department structure and to establish criteria regarding how the BSA Officer roles and responsibilities would successfully be performed. Specifically, the BSA department had relied on other departments within the Bank to make determinations on acceptable risks often without clear guidance from the BSA department. For those BSA responsibilities for which other departments did have specific guidelines, including the collection of customer information, there was no accountability when those departments failed to abide by the AML program. At Merchants, BSA duties were shared among other departments at the Bank, including those associated with specific business lines, where its staff lacked BSA knowledge and experience.

From August 2014 to April 2015, Merchants failed to designate a BSA Officer and had three people sharing the BSA Officer duties without clearly defining each individual's responsibility. The staff assigned these responsibilities were neither BSA knowledgeable nor adequately trained in their BSA duties. Most concerning was the fact that two out of these three individuals were Merchants's executives in charge of bringing businesses to the Bank, particularly MSBs, creating a conflict of interest that impeded them from performing compliance duties on their own customers.

Merchants's leadership did not provide the BSA department with the appropriate level of authority, autonomy, or independence in which to properly and effectively execute its responsibilities to ensure the Bank's compliance with the BSA. For example, despite repeated recommendations to improve its AML program, Merchants continuously failed to establish clear policies for correcting key BSA/AML deficiencies.

From 2009 to September 2016, Merchants did not establish an effective process to ensure management could effectively address adverse findings in compliance reviews. Specifically, the Bank had inadequate policies and procedures to implement corrective actions for its BSA/AML program deficiencies. Because of these failures, Merchants maintained an AML program with repeated, material deficiencies in its risk identification and assessment, controls to mitigate risk, monitoring for suspicious transactions, and collecting sufficient account documentation.

FinCEN had determined that Merchants willfully violated the AML program, reporting, and recordkeeping requirements of the BSA and its implementing regulations as described in the CONSENT, and that grounds exist to assess a civil money penalty for these violations.

FinCEN had determined that the penalty in this matter will be seven million dollars. The penalty will run concurrent with the OCC's one million dollars penalty.[503]

10.1 The Title of the Individual Responsible for Anti Money Laundering Compliance

10.1.1 Nigeria

The individual responsible for coordinating and monitoring day-to-day Anti Money Laundering compliance is known as the compliance officer.[504]

---

503 United States of America Department of the Treasury Financial Crimes Enforcement Network (2017), 'IN THE MATTER OF: MERCHANTS BANK OF CALIFORNIA, N.A. CARSON, CALIFORNIA', Available at: https://www.fincen. gov/sites/default/files/enforcement_action/2017-02-27/Merchants%20Bank%20 of%20California%20Assessment%20of%20CMP%2002.24.2017.v2.pdf (accessed 29 April 2017).

504 Money Laundering Prohibition Act 2011 (as amended), s. 9 (1) (a)

10.1.2 United States

The individual responsible for coordinating and monitoring day-to-day Anti Money Laundering compliance is known as the compliance officer.[505]

10.1.3 United Kingdom

The individual responsible for coordinating and monitoring day-to-day Anti Money Laundering compliance is known as the money laundering reporting officer.[506]

The title given to such individual appears to be different from that of the FATF.

10.2 Duties and Responsiblities

10.2.1 Nigeria

Compliance officers are under a duty: to receive disclosures from staffs in the firm and to train staffs in the firm.[507]

10.2.2 United States

Compliance officers are under a duty: to receive disclosures from staffs in the firm and to train staffs in the firm.[508]

---

505 Federal Financial Institutions Examination Council (2014), 'Bank Secrecy Act/Anti-Money Laundering Examination Manual', Available at: https://www.occ.treas.gov/publications/publications-by-type/other-publications-reports/ffiec-bsa-aml-examination-manual.pdf (accessed 10 January 2017).

506 Senior Management Arrangements, Systems and Controls (SYSC), 6.3.9 (1) R, see also SYSC, 6.3.7 G

507 Money Laundering Prohibition Act 2011 (as amended), s. 9 (1)

508 Federal Financial Institutions Examination Council (2014), 'Bank Secrecy Act/Anti-Money Laundering Examination Manual', Available at: https://www.occ.treas.gov/publications/publications-by-type/other-publications-reports/ffiec-bsa-aml-examination-manual.pdf (accessed 10 January 2017).

10.2.3 United Kingdom

Compliance officers are under a duty to train staffs in the firm.[509] The duty to receive disclosures from staffs in the firm rests on the Nominated Officer.[510]

In practice, the compliance officer and nominated officer will be one and the same person.[511]

10.3 Discussion

The previous section compared the approach in Nigeria with that in the United States and the United Kingdom as it relates to compliance officers. This section will analyse issues that arose to determine if there is a need for reform.

10.3.1 Duties and Responsibilities

As stated earlier, the duties of compliance officers in Nigeria and the United States include receiving disclosures from staff and training staff, while compliance officers in the United Kingdom train staff, but receiving disclosures from staff is the responsibility of the nominated officer.

This section will determine if Nigeria and the United States need to adopt the approach used in the United Kingdom, or if there is no need for reform.

The United Kingdom's approach allows for the responsibilities conferred on compliance officers by the FATF to be shared between two people, thereby reducing the burden of work on the compliance officers. This is not the approach adopted by Nigeria and the United States.

---

509 Senior Management Arrangements, Systems and Controls (SYSC), 6.3.9 (1) R, see also SYSC, 6.3.7 G

510 See the Money Laundering, Terrorist Financing and Transfer of Funds (Information on the Payer) Regulations 2017, Regulation 21 (3), (5)

511 The Joint Money Laundering Steering Group JMLSG, *Prevention of money laundering/combating terrorist financing 2017 Revised Version*, Guidance for the UK financial sector Part I, June 2017 (Amended December 2017), Paragraph 3.4

However, compliance officers in Nigeria and the United States could delegate some of their duties to other competent individuals.[512]

10.4 Conclusion

This chapter compared the approach in Nigeria with that of the United States and the United Kingdom as it relates to compliance officers. It also analysed issues that arose from the comparison to determine that the Nigerian and US money laundering laws do not need to adopt the approach of the United Kingdom.

---

512 Federal Financial Institutions Examination Council (2014), 'Bank Secrecy Act/Anti-Money Laundering Examination Manual', Available at: https://www.occ. treas.gov/publications/publications-by-type/other-publications-reports/ffiec-bsa-aml-examination-manual.pdf (accessed 10 January 2017).

CHAPTER 11

MODERN SLAVERY

Trafficking in persons is a modern form of slavery, and it is the largest manifestation of slavery today. At least 700,000 persons annually, primarily women and children, are trafficked within or across international borders. Approximately 50,000 women and children are trafficked into the United States each year.[513] Many of these persons are trafficked into the international sex trade, often by force, fraud, or coercion.[514] The Home Office UK estimates that there were 10,000 – 13,000 potential victims in the United Kingdom in 2013. The National Crime Agency (NCA) estimates that one third of victims are from UK. The number of referrals of potential victims of trafficking has grown year-on-year for the past 3 years, and the NCA assesses that this trend is likely to continue. There is an intelligence gap on the scale of proceeds of this crime in the UK, but the International Labour Organisation estimates that profits from forced labour worldwide come to one hundred and fifty billion US dollars per year.[515]

---

513 United States Victims of Trafficking and Violence Protection Act of 2000, s. 102 (b) (1)

514 United States Victims of Trafficking and Violence Protection Act of 2000, s. 102 (b) (2)

515 HM Treasury and Home Office (2015), 'UK national risk assessment of money laundering and terrorist financing', Available at: https://www.gov.uk/government/publications/uk-national-risk-assessment-of-money-laundering-and-terrorist-financing (accessed 5 August 2017).

The sex industry has rapidly expanded over the past several decades. It involves sexual exploitation of persons, predominantly women and girls, involving activities related to prostitution, pornography, sex tourism, and other commercial sexual services. The low status of women in many parts of the world has contributed to a burgeoning of the trafficking industry.[516] Trafficking in persons is not limited to the sex industry. This growing transnational crime also includes forced labor and involves significant violations of labor, public health, and human rights standards worldwide.[517] Traffickers primarily target women and girls, who are disproportionately affected by poverty, the lack of access to education, chronic unemployment, discrimination, and the lack of economic opportunities in countries of origin. Traffickers lure women and girls into their networks through false promises of decent working conditions at relatively good pay as nannies, maids, dancers, factory workers, restaurant workers, sales clerks, or models. Traffickers also buy children from poor families and sell them into prostitution or into various types of forced or bonded labor.[518]

Trafficking in persons is increasingly perpetrated by organized, sophisticated criminal enterprises. Such trafficking is the fastest growing source of profits for organized criminal enterprises worldwide. Profits from the trafficking industry contribute to the expansion of organized crime in the United States and worldwide. Trafficking in persons is often aided by official corruption in countries of origin, transit, and destination, thereby threatening the rule of law.[519] Trafficking includes all the elements of the crime of forcible rape when it involves the involuntary participation of another person in sex acts by means of fraud, force, or coercion.[520] Trafficking also

---

516 United States Victims of Trafficking and Violence Protection Act of 2000, s. 102 (b) (2)

517 United States Victims of Trafficking and Violence Protection Act of 2000, s. 102 (b) (3)

518 United States Victims of Trafficking and Violence Protection Act of 2000, s. 102 (b) (4)

519 United States Victims of Trafficking and Violence Protection Act of 2000, s. 102 (b) (8)

520 United States Victims of Trafficking and Violence Protection Act of 2000, s. 102 (b) (9)

involves violations of other laws, including labor and immigration codes and laws against kidnapping, slavery, false imprisonment, assault, battery, pandering, fraud, and extortion.[521]

Trafficking in persons is a transnational crime with national implications. To deter international trafficking and bring its perpetrators to justice, nations including the United States, the United Kingdom and Nigeria have recognized that trafficking is a serious offence. This they have done by prescribing appropriate punishment, giving priority to the prosecution of trafficking offences, and protecting rather than punishing the victims of such offences. This chapter compares the laws of these countries to determine whether they meet the minimum standards for the elimination of trafficking applicable to the government of a country of origin.

The minimum standards for the elimination of trafficking applicable to the government of a country of origin, transit, or destination for a significant number of victims of severe forms of trafficking are:

(1) The government of the country should prohibit severe forms of trafficking in persons and punish acts of such trafficking.

(2) For the knowing commission of any act of sex trafficking involving force, fraud, coercion, or in which the victim of sex trafficking is a child incapable of giving meaningful consent, or of trafficking which includes rape or kidnapping or which causes a death, the government of the country should prescribe punishment commensurate with that for grave crimes, such as forcible sexual assault.

(3) For the knowing commission of any act of a severe form of trafficking in persons, the government of the country should prescribe punishment that is sufficiently stringent to deter and that adequately reflects the heinous nature of the offence.

---

521 United States Victims of Trafficking and Violence Protection Act of 2000, s. 102 (b) (10)

(4) The government of the country should make serious and sustained efforts to eliminate severe forms of trafficking in persons.[522]

11.1 Laws on Trafficking in Persons/Modern Slavery

11.1.1 Nigeria
The laws enacted to combat Modern Slavery in Nigeria include the **Constitution of the Federal Republic of Nigeria 1999 (as amended)** and the **Trafficking in Persons (Prohibition), (Enforcement and Administration) Act, 2015.**

11.1.2 United States
The U.S. Laws on Trafficking in Persons are:

Survivors of Human Trafficking Empowerment Act (Section 115 of the Justice for Victims of Trafficking Act of 2015)

Trafficking Victims Protection Reauthorization Act of 2013 (Title XII of the Violence Against Women Reauthorization Act of 2013)

William Wilberforce Trafficking Victims Protection Reauthorization Act of 2008

Trafficking Victims Protection Reauthorization Act of 2005

Prosecutorial Remedies and Other Tools to End the Exploitation of Children Today Act of 2003 (PROTECT Act)

---

522 United States Victims of Trafficking and Violence Protection Act of 2000, s. 108

Trafficking Victims Protection Reauthorization Act of 2003

U.S. Leadership on HIV/AIDS, Tuberculosis, and Malaria Act of 2003

Victims of Trafficking and Violence Protection Act of 2000

11.1.3 United Kingdom
The law enacted to combat Modern Slavery in the United Kingdom is the **Modern Slavery Act 2015.**

11.2 Interagency Task Force to Monitor and Combat Trafficking/Modern Slavery

11.2.1 Nigeria
The **Trafficking in Persons (Prohibition), (Enforcement and Administration) Act, 2015** establishes the National Agency for the Prohibition of Trafficking in Persons (hereinafter referred to as 'the Agency').[523]

The functions of the Agency shall be to —

(a) enforce and administer the provisions of the **Trafficking in Persons (Prohibition), (Enforcement and Administration) Act, 2015;**

(b) co-ordinate and enforce all other laws on trafficking in persons and related offences;

(c) adopt effective measures for the prevention and eradication of trafficking in persons and related offences;

---

523 Nigeria Trafficking in Persons (Prohibition), (Enforcement and Administration) Act, 2015, s. 2 (1)

(d)   establish co-ordinated preventive, regulatory and investigatory machinery geared towards the eradication of trafficking in persons;

(e)   investigate all cases of trafficking in persons including forced labour, child labour, forced prostitution, exploitative labour and other forms of exploitation, slavery and slavery-like activities, bonded labour, removal of organs, illegal smuggling of migrants, sale and purchase of persons;

(f)   encourage and facilitate the availability and participation of persons who voluntarily, consent to assist in investigations or proceedings relating to trafficking in persons and related offences;

(g)   enhance the effectiveness of law enforcement agents and other partners in the suppression of trafficking in persons;

(h)   create public enlightenment and awareness through seminars, workshops, publications, radio and television programmes and other means aimed at educating the public on the dangers of trafficking in persons;

(i)   establish and maintain communications to facilitate rapid exchange of information concerning offences under the **Trafficking in Persons (Prohibition), (Enforcement and Administration) Act, 2015;**

(j)   conduct research and strengthen effective legal means of international co-operation in suppressing trafficking in persons;

(k)   implement all bilateral and multilateral treaties and conventions on trafficking in persons adopted by Nigeria;

(l)   strengthen co-operation and conduct joint operations with relevant law enforcement and security agencies, international authorities and other relevant partners in the eradication of trafficking in persons;

(m)   co-ordinate, supervise and control—

    (i) the protection, assistance and rehabilitation of trafficked persons; and

    (ii) all functions and activities relating to investigation and prosecution of all offences connected with or relating to trafficking in persons;

(n) adopt measures to identify, trace, freeze, confiscate or seize proceeds, property, funds or other assets derived from trafficking in persons or related offences;

(o) conduct research on factors responsible for internal and external trafficking in persons and initiate programmes and strategies aimed at the prevention and elimination of the problem;

(p) facilitate rapid exchange of scientific and technical information concerning or relating to trafficking in persons;

(q) collaborate with government bodies both within and outside Nigeria whose functions are similar to those of the Agency in the area of the—

    (i) movement of proceeds or properties derived from trafficking in persons and other related offences,

    (ii) identities, location and activities of persons suspected of being involved in trafficking in persons and other related offences, and

    (iii) exchange of personnel and other experts;

(r) establish and maintain a system for monitoring trans-border activities relating to trafficking in persons in order to identify suspicious movements and persons involved;

(s) deal with matters connected with the extradition and deportation of persons involved in trafficking in persons and other mutual legal assistance between Nigeria and any other country in trafficking in persons, subject to the supervision of the Attorney-General of the Federation and Minister of Justice;

(t) initiate, develop and improve special training programmes for personnel of the Agency and relevant law enforcement agents charged with the responsibility of detecting offences created under the **Trafficking in Persons (Prohibition), (Enforcement and Administration) Act, 2015** Act; and

(u) carry out such other activities as are necessary for the efficient discharge of the functions conferred on it under the **Trafficking in Persons (Prohibition), (Enforcement and Administration) Act, 2015**.[524]

---

524 Nigeria Trafficking in Persons (Prohibition), (Enforcement and Administration) Act, 2015, s. 5

11.2.2 United States

Section 105 (a) of the Victims of Trafficking and Violence Protection Act of 2000 requires the President of the United States of America to establish an Interagency Task Force to Monitor and Combat Trafficking. The Task Force shall carry out the following activities:

(1) Coordinate the implementation of this division.

(2) Measure and evaluate progress of the United States and other countries in the areas of trafficking prevention, protection, and assistance to victims of trafficking, and prosecution and enforcement against traffickers, including the role of public corruption in facilitating trafficking. The Task Force shall have primary responsibility for assisting the Secretary of State in the preparation of the reports described in **section 110 of the Victims of Trafficking and Violence Protection Act of 2000**.

(3) Expand interagency procedures to collect and organize data, including significant research and resource information on domestic and international trafficking. Any data collection procedures established under this subsection shall respect the confidentiality of victims of trafficking.

(4) Engage in efforts to facilitate cooperation among countries of origin, transit, and destination. Such efforts shall aim to strengthen local and regional capacities to prevent trafficking, prosecute traffickers and assist trafficking victims, and shall include initiatives to enhance cooperative efforts between destination countries and countries of origin and assist in the appropriate reintegration of stateless victims of trafficking.

(5) Examine the role of the international "sex tourism" industry in the trafficking of persons and in the sexual exploitation of women and children around the world.

(6) Engage in consultation and advocacy with governmental and nongovernmental organizations, among other entities, to advance the purposes of this division.[525]

---

525   United States Victims of Trafficking and Violence Protection Act of 2000, s. 105

11.2.3 United Kingdom

The United Kingdom's Modern Slavery Act 2015 establishes the UK's first ever Independent Anti-Slavery Commissioner to drive forward the law enforcement response and hold them to account at all levels, ensuring that the perpetrators are caught and prosecuted and that the victims of Modern Slavery are swiftly identified so they can get help.[526]

11.3 Prevention of Trafficking/Modern Slavery

11.3.1 Nigeria

Section 11 of the Trafficking in Persons (Prohibition), (Enforcement and Administration) Act, 2015 establishes for the National Agency for the Prohibition of Trafficking in Persons (in this chapter referred to as 'the Agency'), the following Special Departments—

(a) Investigation and Monitoring Department;
(b) Public Enlightenment Department;
(c) Research and Programme Development Department; and
(d) Training and Manpower Development Department.

The Investigation and Monitoring Department shall—

(a) be responsible for the prevention and detection of offences under the **Trafficking in Persons (Prohibition), (Enforcement and Administration) Act, 2015**;
(b) collaborate with the Nigeria Immigration Service and other relevant law enforcement agencies in charge of entry and exit for the purpose of detecting offences under the **Trafficking in Persons (Prohibition), (Enforcement and Administration) Act, 2015**;

---

526   United Kingdom Modern Slavery Act 2015, s. 40, s. 41

(c) investigate, trace and identify the proceeds, assets and properties of persons derived from acts which constitute an offence under the **Trafficking in Persons (Prohibition), (Enforcement and Administration) Act, 2015**; and

(d) effect the confiscation or forfeiture of such proceeds, assets and properties in collaboration with the Legal and Prosecution Department.[527]

The Public Enlightenment Department shall be responsible for—

(a) carrying out information and awareness-raising campaigns, seminars and workshops, radio and television programmes aimed at educating the public on the dangers of trafficking in persons, especially to sectors and groups that are vulnerable to trafficking in persons, in cooperation with the media, non-governmental organizations, labour, market organizations, migrants' organizations and other segments of civil society;

(b) developing educational programmes, in particular for young people, to—

    (i)   address gender discrimination and promote gender equality and respect for the dignity and integrity of every human being,

    (ii)   include trafficking in persons in human rights curricula in schools and universities, and

    (iii)   address the underlying causes of trafficking, such as poverty, under-development, unemployment, lack of equal opportunities and discrimination in all its forms, and improve the social and economic conditions of groups at risk.[528]

---

527 Nigeria Trafficking in Persons (Prohibition), (Enforcement and Administration) Act, 2015, s. 12 (1)

528 Nigeria Trafficking in Persons (Prohibition), (Enforcement and Administration) Act, 2015, s. 12 (3)

The Research and Programme Development Department shall be responsible for—

(i)   researching into factors causing and promoting internal and external trafficking in persons,

(ii)   initiating programmes and developing strategies for addressing the problems of trafficking in persons,

(iii) supporting the Agency in areas of statistics, records, planning, and

(iv) performing such other duties as the Agency may refer to it from time to time.[529]

The Training and Manpower Development Department shall—

(a) initiate, develop or improve specific training programmes for officers of the Agency and relevant law enforcement officers charged with the responsibility for the prevention, detection, investigation, elimination, prosecution, rehabilitation of victims of trafficking and related activities;

(b) collaborate with relevant law enforcement and security agencies and institutions for the purpose of providing training for law enforcement and security officers responsible for the investigation, detection, prevention, elimination of human trafficking and related offences and the rehabilitation of victims of trafficking in persons and related unlawful activities; and

(c) collaborate with, support and keep a register of Non-Governmental Organizations involved in anti-human trafficking activities especially in the area of training, workshop and seminars.[530]

---

529 Nigeria Trafficking in Persons (Prohibition), (Enforcement and Administration) Act, 2015, s. 12 (5)

530 Nigeria Trafficking in Persons (Prohibition), (Enforcement and Administration) Act, 2015, s. 12 (6)

11.3.2 United States
Section 106 of the Trafficking and Violence Protection Act of 2000 requires the President to establish and carry out international initiatives to enhance economic opportunity for potential victims of trafficking as a method to deter trafficking. Such initiatives may include—

(1) microcredit lending programs, training in business development, skills training, and job counseling;
(2) programs to promote women's participation in economic decision making;
(3) programs to keep children, especially girls, in elementary and secondary schools, and to educate persons who have been victims of trafficking;
(4) development of educational curricula regarding the dangers of trafficking; and
(5) grants to nongovernmental organizations to accelerate and advance the political, economic, social, and educational roles and capacities of women in their countries.

11.3.3 United Kingdom
The United Kingdom's Modern Slavery Act 2015 enhances the Court's ability to put restrictions on individuals where it is necessary to protect people from the harm caused by modern slavery offences.

Section 14 of the UK's Modern Slavery Act, 2015 empowers a Court to make a slavery and trafficking prevention order against a person ("the Defendant") where it deals with the Defendant in respect of—

(a) a conviction for a slavery or human trafficking offence,
(b) a finding that the defendant is not guilty of a slavery or human trafficking offence by reason of insanity, or
(c) a finding that the defendant is under a disability and has done the act charged against the defendant in respect of a slavery or human trafficking offence.

The Court may make the order only if it is satisfied that—

(a) there is a risk that the defendant may commit a slavery or human trafficking offence, and
(b) it is necessary to make the order for the purpose of protecting persons generally, or particular persons, from the physical or psychological harm which would be likely to occur if the defendant committed such an offence.

Section 54 requires businesses over a certain size to disclose each year what action they have taken to ensure there is no modern slavery in their business or supply chains.

11.4 Protection and Assistance for Victims of Trafficking/ Modern Slavery

11.4.1 Nigeria

A number of provisions in the **Trafficking in Persons (Prohibition), (Enforcement and Administration) Act, 2015** give protection and assistance to victims of modern slavery. These provisions are contained in Part IX and X of the Act. Key statutory provisions are excerpted below.

Treatment of trafficked persons – Section 61 Trafficking in Persons (Prohibition), (Enforcement and Administration) Act, 2015
Section 61 of the Trafficking in Persons (Prohibition), (Enforcement and Administration) Act, 2015 places a duty on the National Agency for the Prohibition of Trafficking in Persons (in this chapter referred to as 'the Agency') to ensure that—

(a) a trafficked person is not subjected to discriminatory treatment on account of race, colour, gender, sex, age, language, religion, political or other opinion, cultural beliefs or practices, national, ethnic or social origin, property, birth or other status, including his status as a victim of trafficking or having worked in the sex industry;

(b) a trafficked person has access to adequate health and other social services during the period of temporary residence;

(c) a trafficked person has access to the embassy or, consulate of the country of which he is a citizen or, where there is no embassy or consulate, has access to the diplomatic representative of the State that takes charge of the country's interest or any national to protect him;

(d) a trafficked person is able to return home safely, if he wishes and when he is able to do so;

(e) a trafficked person is not denied temporary residence visas during the pendency of any criminal, civil or other legal action;

(f) investigation, detection, gathering and interpretation of evidence are conducted in such a manner as to minimize intrusion into the personal history of a trafficked person;

(g) the identity of a person trafficked is protected;

(h) the use of any person's history of being trafficked to discriminate or cause harm to such person, his family or his friends in any way whatsoever, particularly with regards to freedom of movement, marriage or search for gainful employment is prohibited;

(i) it takes steps to maintain and rehabilitate facilities provided for trafficked persons; and

(j) a trafficked person and his family are protected from intimidation, threats, and reprisals from traffickers and their associates including reprisals from persons in position of authority.

Non-detention or prosecution of a trafficked person in certain circumstances – Section 62 Trafficking in Persons (Prohibition), (Enforcement and Administration) Act, 2015

Where the circumstances so justify, trafficked persons shall not be detained or prosecuted for offences relating to being a victim of trafficking, including non-possession of valid travel documents, use of a false travel or other document.

Rights of a victim to information – Section 63 Trafficking in Persons (Prohibition), (Enforcement and Administration) Act, 2015
A victim of trafficking in person shall be provided with—

(a) information on relevant Court and administrative proceedings;

(b) assistance to enable the victim's views and concerns to be presented and considered at appropriate stages of criminal proceedings against the traffickers; and

(c) counseling and information as regards the victim's legal rights in a language that the victim can understand.

Establishment of Transit Shelter – Section 64 Trafficking in Persons (Prohibition), (Enforcement and Administration) Act, 2015

(1) There shall be established for the Agency Transit Shelters which shall be managed and supervised as homes to cater for rescued trafficked persons particularly women and children.

(2) The Transit Shelters shall be run by staff of the Agency with the aim of providing protection, assistance, counseling, rehabilitation and training for the rescued victims to facilitate their reintegration into the society.

Right to Compensation or Restitution – Section 65 Trafficking in Persons (Prohibition), (Enforcement and Administration) Act, 2015

(1) A trafficked person, irrespective of his immigration status is entitled to compensation, restitution and recovery for economic, physical and psychological compensation or damages which shall be assessed and paid out of forfeited assets of the convicted trafficker.

(2) Where an offender is convicted of an offence under this Act, the Court may order the offender to pay compensation to the victim, in addition to any other punishment ordered by the Court.

(3) Notwithstanding any other provision of this Act, a trafficked person has the right to institute civil action against

a trafficker and any other person including a public officer who may have exploited or abused his person provided that the amount awarded by the Criminal Court shall be taken into consideration in the determination of the amount of compensation to be awarded in the civil suit.

(4)

Establishment of Victims of Trafficking Trust Fund – Section 67 Trafficking in Persons (Prohibition), (Enforcement and Administration) Act, 2015

(1) There is established for the Agency a Victims of Trafficking Trust Fund (in this chapter referred to as 'the Trust Fund'), into which shall be paid:

(a) any take-off grant and special intervention funds as may be provided by the Federal Government;

(b) such moneys as may be appropriated to meet the objectives of the Trust Fund by the National Assembly;

(c) proceeds of the sale of assets and properties derived from acts which constitute an offence under this Act;

(d) aids, grants, gifts, bequests, endowments, donations or assistance from bilateral and multi-lateral international agencies, Non- Governmental Organizations, other donor agencies, partners and the private sector;

(e) any other money which may accrue to the Trust Fund from time to time.

(2) The sources of monies referred to in paragraph (d) of subsection (1) of this section shall be acceptable to the Trust Fund by the Agency except where the terms and conditions attached to the aid, grant, gift, bequest, endowment, donation or assistance are inconsistent with the objective of the Trust Fund or the provisions of this Act.

(3) The Minister shall make regulations and issue guidelines for the management of the Fund established under subsection (1) of this section and related matters.

(4) The Trust Fund shall be utilized—

(a) to pay compensation, restitution and damages to trafficked persons; and

(b) to fund victim support services for trafficked persons.

11.4.2 United States

Section 107 (a) (1) of the Trafficking and Violence Protection Act of 2000 requires the Secretary of State and the Administrator of the United States Agency for International Development, in consultation with appropriate nongovernmental organizations, to establish and carry out programs and initiatives in foreign countries to assist in the safe integration, reintegration, or resettlement, as appropriate, of victims of trafficking. Such programs and initiatives shall be designed to meet the appropriate assistance needs of such persons and their children, as identified by the Task Force.

Section 107 (C) (1) states that Victims of severe forms of trafficking, while in the custody of the Federal Government and to the extent practicable, shall—

(A) not be detained in facilities inappropriate to their status as crime victims;

(B) receive necessary medical care and other assistance; and

(C) be provided protection if a victim's safety is at risk or if there is danger of additional harm by recapture of the victim by a trafficker, including—

    (i) taking measures to protect trafficked persons and their family members from intimidation and threats of reprisals and reprisals from traffickers and their associates; and

    (ii) ensuring that the names and identifying information of trafficked persons and their family members are not disclosed to the public.

Section 107 (C) (3) authorizes Federal law enforcement officials to permit an alien individual's continued presence in the United States, if after an assessment, it is determined that such individual is a victim of a severe form of trafficking and a potential witness to such trafficking, in order to effectuate prosecution of those responsible, and such officials in investigating and prosecuting traffickers shall protect the safety of trafficking victims, including taking measures to protect trafficked persons and their family members from intimidation, threats of reprisals, and reprisals from traffickers and their associates.

11.4.3 United Kingdom

The **United Kingdom's Modern Slavery Act 2015** creates a statutory defence for victims of modern slavery so that they are not inappropriately criminalized.

Section 45 of the Modern Slavery Act 2015 states as follows:

(1) A person is not guilty of an offence under the Modern Slavery Act 2015 if—
   (a) the person is aged 18 or over when the person does the act which constitutes the offence,
   (b) the person does that act because the person is compelled to do it,
   (c) the compulsion is attributable to slavery or to relevant exploitation, and
   (d) a reasonable person in the same situation as the person and having the person's relevant characteristics would have no realistic alternative to doing that act.
(2) A person may be compelled to do something by another person or by the person's circumstances.
(3) Compulsion is attributable to slavery or to relevant exploitation only if—
   (a) it is, or is part of, conduct which constitutes an offence under section 1 or conduct which constitutes relevant exploitation, or
   (b) it is a direct consequence of a person being, or having been, a victim of slavery or a victim of relevant exploitation.

(4) A person is not guilty of an offence if—

    (a) the person is under the age of 18 when the person does the act which constitutes the offence,

    (b) the person does that act as a direct consequence of the person being, or having been, a victim of slavery or a victim of relevant exploitation, and

    (c) a reasonable person in the same situation as the person and having the person's relevant characteristics would do that act.

In addition to the above, the Modern Slavery Act 2015 gives the Courts new powers to order perpetrators of slavery and trafficking to pay Reparation Orders to their victims[531] and;

- Provides for child advocates to support child victims of trafficking;[532]
- Extends special measures so that all victims of modern slavery can be supported through the criminal justice process;[533]
- Provides statutory guidance on victim identification and victim services, including an enabling power to put the relevant processes on a statutory basis;[534] and
- Introduces protections for victims of abuse on an overseas domestic workers visa.[535]

11.5 Prosecution and Punishment of Traffickers/Modern Slavery

---

531 United Kingdom Modern Slavery Act 2015, s. 10
532 United Kingdom Modern Slavery Act 2015, s. 48
533 United Kingdom Modern Slavery Act 2015, s. 46
534 United Kingdom Modern Slavery Act 2015, s. 49, s. 50
535 United Kingdom Modern Slavery Act 2015, s. 53

11.5.1 Nigeria

A number of provisions in the **Trafficking in Persons (Prohibition), (Enforcement and Administration) Act, 2015** target modern slavery, also known as involuntary servitude/slavery or forced labor. These provisions are contained in Part III and IV of the Act. Key statutory provisions are excerpted below.

Prohibition of acts of trafficking in persons – Section 13 Trafficking in Persons (Prohibition), (Enforcement and Administration) Act, 2015

(1) All acts of human trafficking are prohibited in Nigeria.

(2) Any person who recruits, transports, transfers, harbours or receives another person by means of—

    (a) threat or use of force or other forms of coercion,

    (b) abduction, fraud, deception, abuse of power or position of vulnerability, or

    (c) giving or receiving of payments or benefits to achieve the consent of a person having control over another person, for the purpose of exploitation of that person, commits an offence and is liable on conviction to imprisonment for a term of not less than 2 years and a fine of not less than two hundred and fifty thousand naira.

(3) For the purpose of sub-section (2) (c), abuse of a position of vulnerability includes intentionally using or otherwise taking advantage of an individual's personal, situational or circumstantial vulnerability to recruit, transport, transfer, habour or receive that person for the purpose of exploiting him or her, such that the person believes that submitting to the will of the abuser is the only real or acceptable option available to him or her and that this belief is reasonable in the light of the victims situation.

(4) A person who in or outside Nigeria directly or indirectly—

    (a) does or threatens any act preparatory to or in furtherance of an act of trafficking in persons,

    (b) omits to do anything that is reasonably necessary to prevent an act of trafficking in persons,

(c) assists or facilitates the activities of persons engaged in acts of trafficking in persons or is an accessory to any offence under this Act

(d) procures any other person by any means to commit an offence under this Act.

(e) participates as an accomplice in the commission of an offence under this Act, or

(f) promises or induces any other person by any means to commit any of the offences referred to in this Act, **commits an offence under this Act and is liable on conviction to imprisonment for a term of not less than 5 Years and a fine of not less than one million naira.**

(5) The consent of a victim of trafficking in persons to the intended exploitation set forth in the definition of trafficking in persons in this Act shall be irrelevant where any of the means set forth in the definition has been used.

(6) The recruitment, transportation, transfer, harboring or receipt of a child for the purpose of exploitation shall be considered trafficking in persons even if this does not involve any of the means set forth in the definition of trafficking in persons in this Act.

Importation and exportation of person - Section 14 Trafficking in Persons (Prohibition), (Enforcement and Administration) Act, 2015

Any person who—

(a) imports another person into Nigeria, knowing or having reason to know that the person will be forced or induced into prostitution or other forms of sexual exploitation in Nigeria or while in transit or

(b) exports another person from Nigeria, knowing or having reason to know. that the person will be forced or induced into prostitution or other forms of sexual exploitation in the country to which the person is exported or while in transit, commits an offence and is liable on conviction to imprisonment for a term of not less than 5 years and a fine of not less than one million naira.

Procurement of Person for Sexual Exploitation – Section 15 Trafficking in Persons (Prohibition), (Enforcement and Administration) Act, 2015
Any person who—

(a) by the use of deception, coercion, debt bondage or any means, induces any person under the age of 18 years to go from one place to another to do any act with intent that such person may be, or knowing that it is likely that the person will be forced or seduced into illicit intercourse with another person, or

(b) keeps, detains or harbours any other person with intent, knowing or having reason to know that such a person is likely to be forced or induced into prostitution or other forms of sexual exploitation with or by any person or an animal, commits an offence and is liable on conviction to imprisonment for 5 years and a fine of five hundred thousand naira.

Abuse, procurement or recruitment of person under 18 years for prostitution or other forms of Sexual exploitation – Section 16 Trafficking in Persons (Prohibition), (Enforcement and Administration) Act, 2015

(1) Any person who procures or recruits any person under the age of 18 years to be subjected to prostitution or other forms of sexual exploitation with himself, any person or persons, either in Nigeria or anywhere else, commits an offence and is liable on conviction to imprisonment for a term of not less than 7 years and a fine of not less than one million naira.

(2) Any person who procures or recruits any person under the age of 18 years to be conveyed from his usual place of abode,

knowing or having reasons to know that such a person may be subjected or induced into prostitution or other forms of sexual exploitation in any place outside Nigeria, commits an offence and is liable on conviction to imprisonment for a term of not less than 7 years and a fine of not less than one million naira.

Procurement or recruitment of person under the age of 18 years for pornography or brothel – Section 17 Trafficking in Persons (Prohibition), (Enforcement and Administration) Act, 2015

(1) Any person who—
    (a) procures, recruits, uses or offers any person under the age of 18 years for the production of pornography or for pornographic performances,
    (b) allows a person under the age of 18 years to be harboured in a brothel, commits an offence and is liable on conviction to imprisonment for a term of not less than 7 years and a fine of not less than one million naira.

(2) Notwithstanding the punishment prescribed in subsection (1) of this section, a convicted person under this section shall, in addition to the prescribed punishment be liable to a term of not less than 1-year imprisonment where he administered or stupefied the victim with any drug substance.

Foreign travel which promotes prostitution or sexual exploitation – Section 18 Trafficking in Persons (Prohibition), (Enforcement and Administration) Act, 2015

Any person, who organizes, facilitates or promotes foreign travels which promote prostitution or other forms of exploitation of any person or encourages such activity, commits an offence and is liable on conviction to Imprisonment for a term of not less than 7 years and a fine of not less than one million naira.

Procurement or recruitment of person for use in armed conflicts – Section 19 Trafficking in Persons (Prohibition), (Enforcement and Administration) Act, 2015

Any person who trafficks any person for the purpose of forced or compulsory recruitment for use in armed conflict, commits an offence and is liable on conviction to imprisonment for a term of not less than 7 years and a fine of not less than one million naira.

Procurement or recruitment of person for organ harvesting – Section 20 Trafficking in Persons (Prohibition), (Enforcement and Administration) Act, 2015

(1) Any person who—

   (a) through force, deception, threat, debt bondage or any form of coercion -

      (i) abuses a position of power or situation of dominance or authority arising from a given circumstance, or

      (ii) abuses a vulnerable situation, or

   (b) through the giving or receiving of payments or benefits in order to induce or obtain the consent of a person directly or through another person who has control over him; enlists, transports, delivers, accommodates or takes in another person for the purpose of removing the person's organs, commits an offence and is liable on conviction to imprisonment for a term of not less than 7 years and a fine of not less than five million naira.

(2) Without prejudice to the provisions of subsection (1) of this section, a person who procures or offers any person, assists or is involved in anyway-

   (a) in the removal of human organs, or

   (b) buying and selling of human organs, commits an offence and is liable on conviction to imprisonment for a term of not less than 7 years and to a fine of not less than five million naira.

(3) Any person who enlists, transports, delivers, accommodates or takes in another person under the age of 18 years
for the purpose of removing the person's organs, commits
an offence and is liable on conviction to imprisonment for
a term of not less than 7 years and a fine of not less than
five million naira.

**Prohibition of buying or selling of human beings for any purpose –
Section 21 Trafficking in Persons (Prohibition), (Enforcement and
Administration Act), 2015**
Any person who buys, sells, hires, lets or otherwise obtains the possession or disposal of any person with intent, knowing it to be likely
or having reasons to know that such a person will be subjected to
exploitation, commits an offence and is liable on conviction to imprisonment for a term of not less than 5 years and a fine of not less
than two million naira.

**Forced Labour – Section 22 Trafficking in Persons (Prohibition),
(Enforcement and Administration) Act, 2015**
Any person who—

(a) requires, recruits, transports, harbours, receives or hires
out a person to be used for forced labour within or outside
Nigeria, or
(b) permits any place or premises to be used for the purpose of
forced labour, commits an offence and is liable on conviction
to imprisonment for a term of not less than 5 years and a fine
of not less than one million naira.

**Employment of child as domestic worker and inflicting griev-
ous harm – Section 23 Trafficking in Persons (Prohibition),
(Enforcement and Administration) Act, 2015**

(1) Any person who—
(a) employs, requires, recruits, transports, harbours, receives
or hires out a child under the age of 12 years as a domestic

worker, commits an offence and is liable on conviction to imprisonment for a minimum term of 6 months and not exceeding 7 years.

(b) employs, requires, recruits, transports, harbours, receives or hires out a child to do any work that is exploitative, injurious or hazardous to the physical, social and psychological development of the child, commits an offence and is liable on conviction to imprisonment for a minimum term of 2 years but not exceeding 7 years without an option of fine.

(2) Notwithstanding the punishment prescribed in subsection (1) of this section, a convicted person under this section shall, in addition to the prescribed punishment, be liable to—

(a) a term of not less than 2 years imprisonment where the child is denied payment or reasonable compensation for services rendered; or

(b) a term of not less than 3 years where the child is defiled or inflicted with bodily harm.

Trafficking in Slaves – Section 24 Trafficking in Persons (Prohibition), (Enforcement and Administration) Act, 2015

Any person who recruits, imports, exports, transfers, transports, buys, sells, disposes or in any way traffics in any person as a slave or accepts, receives, detains or harbours a person as a slave, commits an offence and is liable on conviction to imprisonment for a term of not less than 7 years and a fine of not less than two million naira.

Slave dealing – Section 25 Trafficking in Persons (Prohibition), (Enforcement and Administration) Act, 2015

Any person who—

(a) deals, keeps, receives or harbours any person for the purpose of holding or treating that person as a slave,

(b) places, receives, harbours or holds any person as a pledge, pawn, in servitude or security for debt or benefits; whether due or to be incurred,

(c) transports, transfers or in any way induces any person to come into Nigeria in order to hold, possess, deal or treat such person as a slave or to be used as a pledge or security for debt, or

(d) enters into any contract or agreement with or without consideration for the purpose of doing or accomplishing any of the purposes enumerated in this section, commits an offence and is liable on conviction to imprisonment for a term of not less than 7 years and to a fine of not less than two million naira.

Offences relating to fraudulent entry of persons – Section 26 Trafficking in Persons (Prohibition), (Enforcement and Administration) Act, 2015

(1) Any person who knowingly, in order to obtain, directly or indirectly, a financial or material benefit, procures the illegal entry of a person into a country of which the person is not a citizen or a permanent resident, commits an offence, and is liable on conviction to imprisonment for a term of not less than 5 years without an option of fine.

(2) Any person who, intentionally in order to obtain a financial or material benefit from another person, engages in fraudulent acts or conducts purportedly for the purpose of procuring, facilitating or promoting the actual or intended entry into, transit across or stay in a country in which that other person is not a national or a permanent resident, commits an offence and is liable on conviction to imprisonment for a term of not less than 5 years without an option of fine and shall refund all monies fraudulently obtained from the victims.

(3) For the purpose of subsection (1) of this section "illegal entry' means crossing borders without complying with the necessary requirements for legal entry into the receiving state.

Conspiracy – Section 27 Trafficking in Persons (Prohibition), (Enforcement and Administration) Act, 2015

Any person who conspires with another to commit all offence under this Act is liable—

    (a) where the offence is committed, to the punishment provided for the commission of the offence; and

    (b) where the offence is not committed, to a punishment which is half the punishment for the offence.

Escape or aiding and abetting escape – Section 28 Trafficking in Persons (Prohibition), (Enforcement and Administration) Act, 2015

Any person who—

    (a) being in lawful custody of the Agency, escapes, or

    (b) aids, facilitates or abets the escape of a person in lawful custody of the Agency, or suspected to have committed an offence under any of the provisions of this Act, commits an offence and is liable on conviction to imprisonment for a term of 5 years.

Attempt to commit an offence under this Act – Section 29 Trafficking in Persons (Prohibition), (Enforcement and Administration) Act, 2015

Any person who attempts to commit any offence under this Act is liable on conviction to half the punishment for the offence.

Offences by a body corporate – Section 31 Trafficking in Persons (Prohibition), (Enforcement and Administration) Act, 2015

    (1) Where an offence under this Act committed by a body corporate is proved to have been committed on the instigation or with the connivance of, or is attributable to any neglect on the part of, a director, manager, secretary of the body corporate or any person purported to act in any such capacity, the officer shall be liable on conviction to the same punishment provided under this Act for individuals committing the offence,

(2) Where a body corporate is convicted of an offence under this Act, it shall be liable to a fine of ten million naira and the Court may issue an order to wind-up the body corporate and its assets and properties transferred to the Victims of Trafficking Trust Fund,

(3) Nothing contained in subsections (1) and (2) of this section shall render any person liable to any punishment if he proves that the offence was committed without his knowledge or that he exercised all due diligence to prevent the commission of such offence.

Responsibility of airlines, commercial carriers, tour operators and travel agents – Section 35 Trafficking in Persons (Prohibition), (Enforcement and Administration) Act, 2015

(1) Every airline operator, sea vessel operator, commercial carrier, tour operator and travel agent are under obligation not to aid and abet facilitate and promote -

(a) trafficking in persons: or

(b) pornography and exploitation in tourism;

(2) Every airline operator. sea vessel operator. commercial carrier, tour operator and travel agent shall notify its clients of its obligation under subsection (1) of this section.

(3) Every airline operator, sea vessel operator, commercial carrier, tour operator and travel agent are required to—

(a) provide a clause in contracts with corresponding suppliers in destination countries, requiring the suppliers to comply with the obligations stated in subsections (1) and (2) of this section;

(b) refrain from utilizing messages on printed materials, video or the internet that could suggest or allude to behaviour incompatible with the objectives of this Act

(c) inform their staff of their obligations under this Act, and

(d) include clauses regarding their obligations under this Act in their conditions of service.

(4) Every airline operator, sea vessel operator, commercial carrier, tour operator and travel agent who violates the provisions of subsections (1) and (2) of this section commits an offence and, in addition to any other penalty provided in any other law or enactment, is liable on conviction to a fine not exceeding ten million naira.

11.5.2 United States

A number of provisions in the U.S. Code target trafficking in persons, also known as involuntary servitude/slavery or forced labor. These provisions are contained in Chapter 77 of Title 18 and are sometimes referred to generally as Chapter 77 offences. The Trafficking Victims Protection Act (TVPA) of 2000 supplemented existing laws, primarily 18 U.S.C. § 1584 (Involuntary Servitude), and also provided new tools to combat trafficking. Key statutes are excerpted below.[536]

Peonage; obstructing enforcement

Summary: Section 1581 of Title 18 makes it unlawful to hold a person in "debt servitude," or peonage, which is closely related to involuntary servitude. Section 1581 prohibits using force, the threat of force, or the threat of legal coercion to compel a person to work against his/her will. In addition, the victim's involuntary servitude must be tied to the payment of a debt.[537]

---

536 The United States Department of Justice (2015), 'Involuntary Servitude, Forced Labor, And Sex Trafficking Statutes Enforced', Available at: https://www.justice.gov/crt/involuntary-servitude-forced-labor-and-sex-trafficking-statutes-enforced (accessed 6 August 2017).

537 The United States Department of Justice (2015), 'Involuntary Servitude, Forced Labor, And Sex Trafficking Statutes Enforced', Available at: https://www.justice.gov/crt/involuntary-servitude-forced-labor-and-sex-trafficking-statutes-enforced (accessed 6 August 2017).

18 U.S.C. § 1581

(a) Whoever holds or returns any person to a condition of peonage, or arrests any person with the intent of placing him in or returning him to a condition of peonage, shall be fined under this title or imprisoned not more than 20 years, or both. If death results from the violation of this section, or if the violation includes kidnapping or an attempt to kidnap, aggravated sexual abuse or the attempt to commit aggravated sexual abuse, or an attempt to kill, the defendant shall be fined under this title or imprisoned for any term of years or life, or both.

(b) Whoever obstructs, or attempts to obstruct, or in any way interferes with or prevents the enforcement of this section, shall be liable to the penalties prescribed in subsection (a).

Involuntary Servitude

Summary: Section 1584 of Title 18 makes it unlawful to hold a person in a condition of slavery, that is, a condition of compulsory service or labor against his/her will. A Section 1584 conviction requires that the victim be held against his/her will by actual force, threats of force, or threats of legal coercion. Section 1584 also prohibits compelling a person to work against his/her will by creating a "climate of fear" through the use of force, the threat of force, or the threat of legal coercion [i.e., If you don't work, I'll call the immigration officials.] which is sufficient to compel service against a person's will.

18 U.S.C. § 1584

Whoever knowingly and willfully holds to involuntary servitude or sells into any condition of involuntary servitude, any other person for any term, or brings within the United States any person so held, shall be fined under this title or imprisoned not more than 20 years, or both. If death results from the violation of this section, or if the violation includes kidnapping or an attempt to kidnap, aggravated sexual abuse or the attempt to commit aggravated sexual abuse, or an attempt to kill, the defendant shall be fined under this title or imprisoned for any term of years or life, or both.

Forced labor

Summary: Section 1589 of Title 18, which was passed as part of the TVPA, makes it unlawful to provide or obtain the labor or services of a person through one of three prohibited means. Congress enacted § 1589 in response to the Supreme Court's decision in United States v. Kozminski, 487 U.S. 931 (1988), which interpreted § 1584 to require the use or threatened use of physical or legal coercion. Section 1589 broadens the definition of the kinds of coercion that might result in forced labor.

18 U.S.C. § 1589

Whoever knowingly provides or obtains the labor or services of a person–

(1) by threats of serious harm to, or physical restraint against, that person or another person;
(2) by means of any scheme, plan, or pattern intended to cause the person to believe that, if the person did not perform such labor or services, that person or another person would suffer serious harm or physical restraint; or
(3) by means of the abuse or threatened abuse of law or the legal process,

shall be fined under this title or imprisoned not more than 20 years, or both. If death results from the violation of this section, or if the violation includes kidnapping or an attempt to kidnap, aggravated sexual abuse or the attempt to commit aggravated sexual abuse, or an attempt to kill, the defendant shall be fined under this title or imprisoned for any term of years or life, or both.

Trafficking with Respect to Peonage, Slavery, Involuntary Servitude, or Forced Labor

Summary: Section 1590 makes it unlawful to recruit, harbor, transport, or broker persons for labor or services under conditions which violate any of the offences contained in Chapter 77 of Title 18.

18 U.S.C. § 1590

Whoever knowingly recruits, harbors, transports, provides, or obtains by any means, any person for labor or services in violation of this chapter shall be fined under this title or imprisoned not more than 20 years, or both. If death results from the violation of this section, or if the violation includes kidnapping or an attempt to kidnap, aggravated sexual abuse, or the attempt to commit aggravated sexual abuse, or an attempt to kill, the defendant shall be fined under this title or imprisoned for any term of years or life, or both.

Sex Trafficking of Children or by Force, Fraud, or Coercion

Summary: Section 1591 criminalizes sex trafficking, which is defined as causing a person to engage in a commercial sex act under certain statutorily enumerated conditions. A commercial sex act means any sex act, on account of which anything of value is given to or received by any person. The specific conditions are the use of force, fraud, or coercion, or conduct involving persons under the age of 18. The punishment for conduct that either involves a victim who is under the age of 14 or involves force, fraud, or coercion is any term of years or life. The punishment for conduct that involves a victim between the ages of 14 and 18 is 40 years.

18 U.S.C. § 1591

Whoever knowingly–

(1) in or affecting interstate or foreign commerce, or within the special maritime and territorial jurisdiction of the United

States, recruits, entices, harbors, transports, provides, or obtains by any means a person; or

(2) benefits, financially or by receiving anything of value, from participation in a venture which has engaged in an act described in violation of paragraph (1), knowing that force, fraud, or coercion described in subsection (c)(2) will be used to cause the person to engage in a commercial sex act, or that the person has not attained the age of 18 years and will be caused to engage in a commercial sex act, shall be punished as provided in subsection (b).

Unlawful Conduct with Respect to Documents in Furtherance of Trafficking, Peonage, Slavery, Involuntary Servitude, or Forced Labor

Summary: **Section 1592 makes it illegal to seize documents in order to force others to work. By expanding its coverage to false documents as well as official documents, § 1592 recognizes that victims are often immobilized by the withholding of whatever documents they possess, even if the documents are forged or fraudulent. Section 1592 expands the scope of federal trafficking statutes to reach those who prey on the vulnerabilities of immigrant victims by controlling their papers.**

18 U.S.C. § 1592

(a) Whoever knowingly destroys, conceals, removes, confiscates, or possesses any actual or purported passport or other immigration document, or any other actual or purported government identification document, of another person–
  (1) in the course of a violation of section 1581, 1583, 1584, 1589, 1590, 1591, or 1594(a);
  (2) with intent to violate section 1581, 1583, 1584, 1589, 1590, or 1591; or
  (3) to prevent or restrict or to attempt to prevent or restrict, without lawful authority, the person's liberty to move or

travel, in order to maintain the labor or services of that person, when the person is or has been a victim of a severe form of trafficking in persons, as defined in section 103 of the Trafficking Victims Protection Act of 2000, *shall be fined under this title or imprisoned for not more than 5 years, or both.*

(b) Subsection (a) does not apply to the conduct of a person who is or has been a victim of a severe form of trafficking in persons, as defined in section 103 of the Trafficking Victims Protection Act of 2000, if that conduct is caused by, or incident to, that trafficking.

Additional provisions of the Trafficking Victims Protection Act (TVPA) of 2000 provide for mandatory restitution (18 U.S.C. § 1593) and forfeiture (18 U.S.C. § 1594(b)), criminalize attempt (18 U.S.C. § 1594(a)), and give victims an avenue for civil lawsuits (18 U.S.C. § 1595).

11.5.3 United Kingdom
Slavery, Servitude, Forced and Compulsory Labour

Section 1 Modern Slavery Act 2015

1. A person commits an offence if:
   1. the person holds another person in slavery or servitude and the circumstances are such that the person knows or ought to know that the other person is held in slavery or servitude, or
   2. the person requires another person to perform forced or compulsory labour and the circumstances are such that the person knows or ought to know that the other person is being required to perform forced or compulsory labour.

2. In subsection (1) the references to holding a person in slavery or servitude or requiring a person to perform forced or compulsory labour are to be construed in accordance with Article 4 of the Human Rights Convention (which prohibits a person from being held in slavery or servitude or being required to perform forced or compulsory labour).

3. In determining whether a person is being held in slavery or servitude or required to perform forced or compulsory labour, regard may be had to all the circumstances.

4. For example, regards may be had -
   1. to any of the person's personal circumstances (such as the person being a child, the person's family relationships, and any mental or physical illness) which may make the person more vulnerable than other persons;
   2. to any work or services provided by the person, including work or services provided in circumstances which constitute exploitation within s. 3(3) to (6) of the Act (for human trafficking for exploitation)

5. The consent of a person (whether adult or child) to any of the acts alleged to constitute holding the person in slavery or servitude, or requiring the person to perform forced or compulsory labour, does not preclude a determination that the person is being held in slavery or servitude or required to perform forced or compulsory labour.

A person guilty of an offence under this section is liable: on summary conviction, to imprisonment for term not exceeding 12 months or a fine or both; and on conviction on indictment, to imprisonment for life.

In this section, "Human Rights Convention" means the Convention for the Protection of Human Rights and Fundamental Freedoms agreed by the Council of Europe at Rome on 4 November 1950. Article 4 states that no one shall be held in slavery or servitude and no one shall be required to perform forced or compulsory labour. The definition of each element of the offence is described below.

This offence can be used in cases where the victim has been exploited in accordance with the **European Convention on Human Rights (ECHR)** definition but was not trafficked, or the trafficking element cannot be proved to the criminal standard. The offence under **s. 1 Modern Slavery Act 2015** has been extended to cover all forms of exploitation relevant to human trafficking. This means that prosecutors should consider any work or services provided in circumstances amounting to exploitation within the meaning of **s.3 of the Act.** This may include, for example, children involved in pickpocketing or begging. However, the circumstances must still be interpreted in accordance with **Article 4 ECHR.**

For offences of Slavery, Servitude, Forced and Compulsory Labour which occurred before 31 July 2015, the following legislation should be used: **Section 71 of the Coroners and Justice Act 2009.**

Exceptions to the offence

Article 4(3) of the ECHR sets out exceptions (below) which are applicable to this offence. For the purpose of this offence the term "forced or compulsory labour" shall not include the following exceptions:

- any work required to be done in the ordinary course of detention imposed according to the provisions of **Article 5 of this Convention** or during conditional release from such detention;
- any service of a military character or, in case of conscientious objectors in countries where they are recognised, service exacted instead of compulsory military service;
- any service exacted in case of an emergency or calamity threatening the life or well-being of the community;
- any work or service which forms part of normal civic obligations. This might include obligations to conduct free medical examinations or participate in medical emergency service.

Whilst there is a range of pre-existing legislation which could cover behaviour relating to servitude and forced or compulsory labour, such as offences of false imprisonment, fraud, blackmail and assault, this offence allows prosecutors to present the full extent of the behaviour, rather than relying on these offences which may not fully reflect the nature of the offending.

Notwithstanding this, prosecutors should also consider charging specific offences in addition to the offence where appropriate (for example where the person has been physically assaulted while subjected to forced labour).

Elements of the offence

Slavery, servitude and forced or compulsory labour are not specifically defined in the Act. In interpreting the offence therefore, police, prosecutors and the courts will need to have regard to existing case-law on **Article 4 ECHR** and international conventions to find guidance defining the parameters of each of the terms. A brief synopsis of the terms follows.

Slavery or Servitude

Slavery is described as the status or condition of a person over whom any or all of the powers attaching the right of ownership are exercised. In essence, characteristics of ownership need to be present for a state of slavery to exist.

Servitude is a linked but much broader term than slavery. In *Siliadin v France* [2005] EHRLR 660 (paragraph 123), the ECHR reaffirmed that servitude "prohibits a particularly serious form of denial of freedom. It includes, in addition to the obligation to provide certain services to another, the obligation on the "serf" to live on the other's property and the impossibility of changing his status". The evidence showed the applicant, an alien who arrived in France at the age of sixteen, had worked for several years for the respondents carrying out household tasks and looking after their three, and subsequently four, children for seven days a week, from 7 am to 10 pm, without receiving any remuneration. She was obliged to follow instructions regarding her working hours and the work to be done, and was not free to come and go as she pleased, though she was allowed out on her own with permission of her employers. The Court unanimously held that there has been a violation of Article 4 of the Convention.

Forced or compulsory labour

The ECHR, in the case of Van der Mussele 8919/80, affirmed that the International Labour Organisation (ILO) conventions were the starting point for interpreting Article 4. The conventions defined forced or compulsory labour as being "all work or service which is exacted from any person under the menace of any penalty and for which the said person has not offered himself voluntarily".

Domestic case law

The case of *William Connors and others* [2013] EWCA Crim 324 offers some further guidance on the distinction between these 3 elements. This case involved a family who, cajoled, bullied and through deception, recruited vulnerable men to work for them. The men worked long hours in very poor conditions 7 days a week, whilst being subjected to violence, threats and abuse. A manifestation of this control was that many of the victims were deprived of the will to leave; others were too demoralised to do so. All five defendants were convicted of a single count of conspiracy to require a person to perform forced or compulsory labour. During the course of the trial, the judge directed the jury to acquit the defendants of conspiracy to hold a person in slavery or servitude. The trial judge had commented that in order for servitude to be established, a court must find that it was impossible for the workers to change their status.[538]

---

538 The Crown Prosecution Service (2017), 'Human Trafficking, Smuggling and Slavery', Available at: http://www.cps.gov.uk/legal/h_to_k/human_trafficking_and_smuggling/ (accessed 8 August 2017).

CASE STUDY ON FORCED OR COMPULSORY LABOUR

Case 11.1: R v. Ayodeji Adewakun and Abimbola Adewakun

Ayodeji Adewakun, 44, (16.6.72) a doctor and her husband Abimbola Adewakun, 48, (13.6.68) a nurse, both from St Katherine's Road in Erith appeared for trial at Southwark Crown Court. They were found guilty on Thursday, 18 May, of one count of trafficking a woman to the United Kingdom for the purposes of exploitation.

The 29-year-old victim was brought by the couple to the UK from Nigeria.

She worked as a domestic worker for the Adewakuns between February 2007 and June 2009.

She was also brought to the UK from Nigeria and was contracted to work from 0700hrs to 1700hrs, Monday to Saturday, looking after the Adewakuns' children for five hundred pounds per month. They didn't pay her anything at all until May 2009, when she confronted Dr Adewakun about her lack of wages. A bank account was subsequently set up for her but even then, only four payments totalling three hundred and fifty pounds were deposited into this account for over two years' worth of work.

She was never given a day off, she worked night and day and eventually her health began to suffer. When she eventually confronted Dr Adewakun about the way she was being treated, her situation worsened. She was no longer permitted to use the family bathroom and was made to wash her clothes by hand. She eventually escaped in June 2009 with the help of a family friend.

The case was referred to the Met's Modern Slavery and Kidnap Unit by Migrant Legal Action (formerly Afro-Asian Advisory Service). On 13 January 2015 Abimbola Adewakun was arrested and interviewed and later released on bail.

On 19 January 2015 Ayodeji Adewakun attended a police station by appointment and was interviewed under caution. She was not arrested.

Both defendants were charged on 10 November 2015 with trafficking for the purpose of exploitation.

Investigating Officer Detective Sergeant Nick Goldwater said: "This couple deceived the victim by promising her a regular wage, which was far higher than her earnings in Nigeria. She hoped that she would be able to send money home and improve her family's standard of living.

"In reality, she was made to work day and night and barely paid anything. She was subject to intimidating behaviour by Dr Adewakun, who exerted control over her by keeping her socially isolated and withholding her passport.

"I hope that these convictions serve as a warning to anyone else committing this crime and encourages anyone being exploited to come forward. I also hope it brings a measure of comfort to the brave victim in this case."

Sentencing has been provisionally set for 16 June.

- Adimbola Adewakun was found not guilty in relation to trafficking charges against a second victim
- The jury did not reach a verdict in the case of Ayodeji Adewakun in relation to trafficking charges against a second victim.[539]

Case 11.2: R v. Emmanuel Edet and Antan Edet

A couple who kept a man in servitude for almost a quarter of a century after illegally bringing him to Britain have been jailed for six years each.

Emmanuel Edet, 61, a former NHS obstetrician, and Antan Edet, 58, a midwife, kept Ofonime Sunday Inuk as a "houseboy" after telling immigration officials he was their teenage son when they arrived from Nigeria in 1989.

Over the next 24 years Inuk worked unpaid up to 17 hours a day looking after the couple's two sons, cooking, cleaning and gardening. For long periods of time he had to sleep on a hall floor.

539 Metropolitan Police (2017), 'Couple convicted of trafficking woman', Available at: http://news.met.police.uk/news/couple-convicted-of-trafficking-woman-242948 (accessed 15 August 2017).

He eventually managed to alert a charity to his plight after the couple went to Nigeria for Christmas in 2013, and they were arrested the following March.

Sentencing them at Harrow crown court on Monday, the judge Graham Arran said their treatment of Inuk, now 40, had left him "conditioned" to his plight.

The judge said: "He was conditioned to the extent that he did not ask for what he wanted because he expected his request to be refused. He was paid the occasional pocket money of perhaps ten pounds. He claims that that was only at Easter and Christmas, and occasionally visitors would give him larger sums. He most certainly was not paid for the work that he was performing for you.

"The most serious aspect of your behaviour towards him was that it went on for an exceptionally long period of time, robbing him of the opportunity of leading a normal life. He suffered as a result of that treatment and has found it difficult to adjust [to] a normal life."

The court heard that the sum he was in theory owed for his years of work ran into hundreds of thousands of pounds.

The couple, of Perivale, north-west London, were found guilty by a jury last month of cruelty to a child under 16, servitude and assisting unlawful immigration. They remained impassive as they were sentenced on Monday.

Caroline Carberry, prosecuting, said Inuk felt that his life had been ruined by his years in the family home. Analysing his victim impact statement, she said: "He has suffered very low self-esteem in regards to interaction with others. He spoke of feeling sad, alone and depressed. He can see no future and thought his life had been wasted and, as such, considered suicide."

The couple were each jailed for three years for child cruelty, six for servitude and one for the immigration offence, all to run concurrently.

Although their mistreatment of Inuk spanned 24 years, servitude only became an offence under the **Coroners and Justice Act 2009,** so they were convicted and sentenced for their actions only between 2010 and 2013. However, the judge said he considered the total length of time Inuk suffered as an aggravating feature.

Inuk told the trial that his passport was confiscated and he was told that if he left the house he would be deported as an illegal immigrant.

The gently spoken victim, who gave his evidence from behind a screen so he could not see his tormentors, said the Edets changed his name and added him to their family passport as their son when they brought him, aged about 13 or 14, to the UK in 1989 via Israel.

He had agreed to go with them because he believed he would be paid and educated. He lived with the couple at several locations including London and Walsall, and kept a diary in which he catalogued his treatment at the hands of people he called "Sir" and "Ma".

He made several attempts to flee. He told the jury that he spoke to a family friend, an MP, and was left feeling "a bit dejected" when he tried to report the Edets to the police in around 2005 only to be told they could not help as it was a "family matter".[540]

Arranging or facilitating the travel of another person with a view to exploitation - Section 2 Modern Slavery Act 2015

1. A person commits an offence if the person arranges or facilitates the travel of another person (V) with a view to V being exploited.
2. It is irrelevant whether the victim consents to the travel (whether V is an adult or child).
3. A person may in particular arrange or facilitate V's travel by recruiting V, transporting or transferring V, harbouring or receiving V, or transferring or exchanging control over V.
4. A person arranges or a person arranges or facilitates V's travel with a view to V being exploited only if
   (a) the person intends to exploit V in any part of the world during or after travel; or
   (b) the person knows or ought to know that another person is likely to exploit V in any part of the world during or after travel.
5. Travel is defined as:
   (a) Arriving in, or entering, any country

---

540 The Guardian (2015), 'Couple jailed after keeping man as slave for 24 years', Available at: https://www.theguardian.com/uk-news/2015/dec/07/doctor-wife-edet-jailed-keeping-man-slave-24-years (accessed 15 August 2017).

(b) Departing from any country, or

(c) Travelling within any country.

6. A person who is a United Kingdom (UK) national commits an offence regardless of where the arranging or facilitating takes place, or where the travel takes place.

7. A person who is not a UK national commits an offence if any part of the arranging or facilitating takes place in the UK, or the travel consists of arrival or entry into, departure from, or travel within the UK.

Section 3 defines the meaning of exploitation for the purposes of section 2. A person is exploited only if one or more of the following apply:

2. Slavery servitude and forced or compulsory labour, where a person is the victim of an offence under section 1 Modern Slavery Act 2015 (see Slavery, Servitude, Forced and Compulsory Labour below).

3. Sexual exploitation, which involves the commission of an offence under
   - Section 1(1)(a) of the Protection of Children's Act 1978 (indecent photographs of children), or
   - Part 1 Sexual Offences Act 2003

which would involve the commission of such an offence if it were done in England and Wales.

4. Removal of organs in circumstances where a person is encouraged required or expected to do anything which involves the commission of an offence under section 32 or 33 of the Human Tissue Act 2004 (prohibition of commercial dealings in organs and restrictions on use of live donors).

5. Securing services etc. by force, threats or deception, where the person is subjected to force, threats or deception designed to induce him or her -
   (a) to provide services of any kind,
   (b) to provide another person with benefits of any kind, or
   (c) to enable another person to acquire benefits of any kind.

6. Securing services etc. from children and vulnerable persons in circumstances where another person uses or attempts to use the person for a purpose within section (5) (a), (b) or (c), having chosen him or her for that purpose on the grounds that -
   (a) he or she is a child, is mentally or physically ill or disabled, or has a family relationship with a particular person, and
   (b) an adult, or a person without the illness, disability, or family relationship, would be likely to refuse to be used for that purpose.

Under sections 3(5) and 3(6) "benefits" is defined as any advantage derived by the trafficker, which could include financial gain, profit, personal benefit or privilege as well as state financial assistance.

This is an either-way offence and on summary conviction is subject to twelve months' imprisonment and/or unlimited fine. On conviction on indictment, it is life imprisonment. The offence is also a "lifestyle offence" for the purposes of the Proceeds of Crime Act 2002. As the offence is likely to lead to a significant sentence on conviction all cases should be tried in the Crown Court.

Section 4 Modern Slavery Act 2015 - Committing an offence with intent to commit an offence under section 2 of the Act

Section 4 creates an offence of committing any offence with the intention to commit an offence of human trafficking under section 2. This includes an offence committed by aiding, abetting, counselling or procuring an offence under section 2. The offence will also capture activity such as supplying false documents to be used to facilitate trafficking. The offence is drawn widely enough to encompass any offence committed by aiding, abetting, counselling or procuring an offence of trafficking.

This is an either-way offence and on summary conviction is subject to twelve months' imprisonment and/or unlimited fine. On conviction on indictment, the maximum sentence is ten years' imprisonment. However, where the offence involves false imprisonment or kidnapping, it is life imprisonment.

For offences of trafficking for sexual exploitation which occurred before 31 July 2015, but after 13 April 2013, the following legislation should be used: Trafficking people for sexual exploitation - section 59A Sexual Offences Act 2003.

For offences of trafficking for sexual exploitation which occurred before 13 April 2013, the following legislation should be used: Trafficking into the UK for sexual exploitation - section 57, 58 and 59 Sexual Offences Act 2003.

For offences of trafficking for all other forms of exploitation (non-sexual exploitation) which occurred before 31 July 2015, the following legislation should be used: Trafficking people for labour and other exploitation - section 4 of the Asylum and Immigration (Treatment of Claimants etc.) Act 2004 (AI (ToC) Act) as amended.

In circumstances where the victim was not trafficked, or the trafficking element cannot be proved to the criminal standard, prosecutors should consider the offence of "holding another person in slavery or servitude" or "requiring them to perform forced or compulsory labour" under section 1 Modern Slavery Act 2015 or, if before 31 July 2015, section 71 of the Coroners and Justice Act 2009.

11.6 Discussion

In the United Kingdom, crimes are classified as summary, indictable and either way offences.[541] Summary offences are the least serious offences, typically what one might view as 'technical monitoring' offences, though also including minor assaults and low value criminal damage. They are tried in the Magistrates' Court. These offences are usually punishable by imprisonment for a maximum term of 6 months and sometimes 12 months.[542]

---

541 Ormerod, D. (2011), Smith and Hogan's Criminal Law (13th Edition Oxford University Press) 32, see also Allen, M. (2011), Criminal Law (11th Edition Oxford University Press) 14.

542 See Reed, A. and Fitzpatrick, B. (2009), Criminal Law (4th Edition Sweet and Maxwell Limited) 5; For Examples of summary offences see Licensing Act 2003, s. 146; Animal Welfare Act 2006, s. 8, Communications Act 2003, s. 127; Criminal Justice and Public Order Act 1994, s. 166; Criminal Justice and Public Order Act 1994, s. 167; Communications Act 2003, s. 363.

Indictable offences are the most serious offences. These offences include murder and rape. These offences are tried in the Crown Court by a judge and jury and are usually punishable with a maximum term in excess of 12 months[543] and as such the double criminality defence would not be applicable in such cases.

Either way offences mean an offence triable either way.[544] It is for the Magistrates' Court to decide whether the offence appears to it more suitable for summary trial or for trial on indictment.[545] The Offence of Forced Labour is an either way offence in the United Kingdom. If the Magistrates' Court decides that it should be tried summarily, and the Defendant is later convicted; he or she would be liable to imprisonment for a term not exceeding 12 months or a fine or both. But if the Magistrates' Court decides that it would tried on indictment, and the Defendant is later convicted; he or she would be liable to imprisonment for life.

The above punishment is in line with Section 108 of the Victims of Trafficking and Violence Protection Act of 2000 (as amended) which requires the government of any country to prescribe punishment that is sufficiently stringent to deter modern slavery and that adequately reflects the heinous nature of the offence.

The **United States** also prescribes punishment that is sufficiently stringent to deter modern slavery. Under the United States Human Trafficking Law, a person guilty of the offence of 'Forced Labour' shall be fined or imprisoned not more than 20 years, or both. If death results from the violation of the section criminalizing 'Forced Labour' or if the violation includes kidnapping or an attempt to kidnap, aggravated sexual abuse or the attempt to commit aggravated

---

543 Reed, A. and Fitzpatrick, B. (2009), Criminal Law (4th Edition Sweet and Maxwell Limited) 5, See also Monaghan, N. (2012), Criminal Law Directions (2nd Edition Oxford University Press) 6. For examples of Indictable offences see Theft Act 1968, s. 7, s. 8, s. 9 and s. 10.

544 Crime and Disorder Act 1998, s. 51

545 Reed, A. and Fitzpatrick, B. (2009), Criminal Law (4th Edition Sweet and Maxwell Limited) 5; For examples of Either way offences see Bribery Act 2010, s. 11 (1); Copyright, Designs and Patents Act 1988, s. 107 (4); Trade Marks Act 1994, s. 92 (6).

sexual abuse, or an attempt to kill, the Defendant shall be fined or imprisoned for any term of years or life, or both.

Both the United Kingdom and the United States cater for situations where the offence of 'Forced Labour' may be less serious or very serious. Nigeria, on the other hand, does not cater for situations where the offence of 'Forced Labour' is very serious. A person guilty of Forced Labour in Nigeria is liable on conviction for a term of not less than 5 years and a fine of not less than one million naira. This punishment is ineffective for very serious offences like Kidnapping and Rape.

11.7 Conclusion

Based on the arguments canvassed in this chapter, the following reforms to the **Nigerian Modern Slavery Law/Approach** are recommended:

I.   The Nigerian Modern Slavery Law does not prescribe punishment commensurate with that for grave crimes, such as forcible sexual assault. Although the Prosecution could fix this problem by drawing up a charge that accommodates grave crimes like Rape, it is advisable that the National Assembly should amend the **Trafficking in Persons (Prohibition), (Enforcement and Administration) Act, 2015** to provide effective, proportionate and dissuasive criminal sanctions for very serious offences of Modern Slavery.

II. There is need for the National Agency for the Prohibition of Trafficking in Persons (NAPTIP) to create more awareness through publications and television programmes and other means aimed at educating the public on the dangers of trafficking in persons. This measure may go a long way in preventing and eradicating human trafficking and slave trade of Nigerians in Libya. The Vanguard Newspapers recently reported that NAPTIP is making arrangements to introduce "Traffic in Persons (TIP)" subject into the curriculum of primary and secondary schools in Nigeria. Mrs Ebele Ulasi,

Assistant Director, Public Enlightenment, NAPTIP, told the Vanguard on January 15, 2018 in Abuja, that NAPTIP was collaborating with the Nigerian Educational Research and Development Council (NERDC) on the proposal. The aim of this proposal is to create awareness and sensitise the masses on the prevalence and dangers associated with human trafficking.[546] This is indeed a good development.

---

546 The Vanguard (2018), 'NAPTIP takes `Traffic in Person' subject to schools', Available at: https://www.vanguardngr.com/2018/01/naptip-takes-traffic-person-subject-schools/ (accessed 17 January 2018).

CHAPTER 12

THE OFFENCE OF BRIBERY

The Financial Action Task Force (FATF) has advised countries to apply the crime of money laundering to all serious offences, with a view of including the widest range of predicate offences.[547]

A predicate offence is any offence that generates proceeds that may become the subject of an offence of money laundering.[548] They include the offences of bribery and corruption.[549]

Bribery can be defined as the promising, offering or giving to a public official, directly or indirectly, an undue advantage for the official, or another person or entity, in order to cause that official to act or refrain from acting in the exercise of official duties.[550]

This chapter starts by briefly highlighting the relevant bribery laws and regulations in Nigeria, the United States and the United Kingdom. Then it will compare the bribery laws in the United Kingdom with those of the United States and Nigeria.

---

547 The Financial Action Task Force (FATF): International Standards on Combating Money Laundering and the Financing of Terrorism and Proliferation, (The FATF Recommendations) 2012, Interpretive Note to Recommendation 3

548 United Nations Convention against Transnational Organized Crime and the Protocol Thereto (2004), Article 2 (h).

549 United Nations Convention against Transnational Organized Crime and the Protocol Thereto (2004), Article 8.

550 United Nations Convention against Transnational Organized Crime and the Protocol Thereto (2004), Article 8 (1) (a).

The comparison will be done under three subheadings: 'Strict Liability', 'Extraterritorial Jurisdiction' and 'Penalties'.

12.1 Relevant Bribery Laws and Regulations

12.1.1 United Kingdom
The law enacted to combat bribery and corruption in the United Kingdom is the Bribery Act 2010.

12.1.2 United States
The law enacted to combat bribery and corruption in the Unites States is the **Foreign Corrupt Practices Act 1977 (as amended)**.

12.1.3 Nigeria
The laws enacted to combat bribery and corruption in Nigeria includes the **Criminal Code Act** and the **Corrupt Practices and Other Related Offences Act 2000**.

12.2 Strict Liability
The United Kingdom Bribery Act makes it a strict liability offence for a company to fail to prevent bribery. This proviso is not present in the Nigerian and US bribery laws.[551]

The strict liability offence of failing to prevent bribery does not require knowledge, intention or recklessness. All it requires is that a person associated with the commercial organization acted on behalf of that organization with the intention of retaining a business or an advantage for the organization.[552]

---

551 Corrupt Practices and Other Related Offences Act (2000), s 8, 9; Foreign Corrupt Practices Act (1977), 15 USC, s. 78 dd-1 (a).
552 Bribery Act 2010, s. 7 (1).

What this means is that if someone were instructed by a company to negotiate business on its behalf, and that person paid a bribe to the individual or company being negotiated with without being told to do so and the company did not have adequate procedures in place, the company would be liable for failing to prevent bribery—even if the person who paid the bribe failed to reveal the deed to the company. This would definitely offend the principle governing the agency and principal relationship, which requires that an agent must act on the instructions of the principal and if he does not do so he is acting on his own behalf.[553] It could also offend the principle of vicarious liability if such a person were not an employee.[554]

This will likely have a serious impact on commercial insurance broker firms that are regulated by the Financial Conduct Authority (FCA), which was formally the Financial Services Authority (FSA).[555] The FCA released a report with regard to its visits to seventeen broker firms, which confirmed that commercial insurance broker firms could not demonstrate that adequate procedures were in place to prevent bribery.[556] This means that if a bribe were committed by a third party in a commercial insurance broker firm, three parties would likely be affected: the broker firm, the parent company (if it's a subsidiary to one) and the firm it acts for. Let's take, for example, the case between the FSA and Aon Limited (an insurance broker/intermediary). In January 2009, Aon Limited was fined five million, two hundred and fifty thousand pounds by the FSA for failures in its antibribery systems and controls. The firm was said to have made suspicious payments

553 See Elliott, C. and Quinn, F. (2009), *Contract Law*, 7th edition (Pearson Education Limited), 279 for the principles governing Agency/Principal Relationship.

554 Horsey, K. and Rackley, E. (2011), *Tort Law*, 2nd edition (Oxford University Press), 328 states that an employer can only be liable for acts of employees and the Bribery Act extends this to anyone acting on its behalf. See also Kidner, R. (2012), *Casebook on Torts*, 12th edition (Oxford University Press), 217–218.

555 See Yeoh, P. (2012), *Bribery Act 2010: Implications for Regulated Firms* (Legislative Comment) 20 (3), JFR and C, 264–277 for details on the new status of the Financial Services Authority (FSA).

556 Financial Crime: A Guide for Firms, Part 2: A Firm's Guide to Preventing Financial Crime by the Financial Conduct Authority April 2013.

totalling seven million pounds to overseas firms and individuals who helped generate business in higher-risk jurisdictions. No due diligence was carried out, the company did not have a risk-based system and the company failed to train its staff on bribery.[557]

Based on the new offence of 'failure to prevent' in the UK Bribery Act, in addition to the fine imposed by the FCA, the company would also be fined under the Bribery Act. The fine could be justified, since the company deliberately did not do any due diligence on the third parties and this has given other firms the opportunity to compete in the market. What may not be justified is that the parent company of Aon Limited, Aon Corporation,[558] could also be fined under the Bribery Act for failing to prevent Aon Limited from committing bribery if the prosecutors were able to establish that Aon Limited was acting on behalf of Aon Corporation. This could be even worse if Aon Limited told the authorities that they were acting on behalf of the parent company when, in actual fact, they were not.

Another party that could be affected is the principal Aon Limited actually worked for, since Aon Limited is an insurance broker. If the principal is a firm, then it could face the same challenges as Aon Corporation.

This law could be regarded as good in a situation where Aon Corporation had knowledge that Aon Limited was acting on its behalf, or it could be good if the principal Aon Limited acted for knew that Aon was acting on its behalf. What may not be good is if neither party had any knowledge whatsoever of the bribery. This is even the case when neither party had control over the other. This, on its own, not only offends the agency and principal relationship, but the principle of vicarious liability.

Another case was between the FSA and Willis Limited. Willis was also an insurance broker and was fined for not having antibribery systems and controls in place to prevent bribery.[559] Willis's parent

557 Ibid.

558 Aon Plc (2017), 'About Aon', Available at: http://www.aon.com/about-aon/about-aon.jsp, (accessed 20 December 2017).

559 Financial Crime: a guide for firms Part 1: A firm's guide to preventing financial crime by the Financial Conduct Authority, April 2013.

company (Willis Group Holdings)[560] could share the same fate as Aon Corporation. An interesting discovery was that Willis Limited is a Lloyds broker.[561] If action was brought under the Bribery Act, Lloyds could be indicted for failing to prevent bribery. This would be unjustified if Lloyds did not know anything.

In the unregulated sector, the impact will likely be higher, based on the fact that the majority of people working for the company could be trying to win contracts for the company, as seen in SEC v. Lucent Technologies Inc., Case No 07-cv-2301 (DDC 21 Dec 2007) ECF no 1 and other similar cases, and the company may not be able to prevent it.[562] If a third party were to bribe someone on the company's behalf, two parties will likely be affected: the subsidiary and the parent companies.

Take, for example, the KBR/Halliburton scandal.[563] Stanley, then the CEO of KBR, paid bribes on the company's behalf to secure contracts from Nigeria. KBR was charged under the anti-bribery provisions of the Foreign Corrupt Practices Act (FCPA), and Halliburton was only charged under the accounting provisions. Although the SEC did not give its reasons for withholding this charge, some writers have argued that Halliburton was not charged under the antibribery provisions because it had no knowledge of what went down, and the FCPA requires that such

---

560 Willis Limited (2017), 'Willis Limited', Available at: http://www.willis.com/ Regulation/ (accessed 15 May 2017).

561 Ibid.

562 See SEC v. Alcatel-Lucent, SA Case No 10–cv–24620 (SD Fla Dec 27 2010) ECF No. 1, see SEC v. ABB LTD, Case No 10, 10-cv-1648, (DDC Sep 29 2009) ECF No 1; SEC v. RAE Sys Inc Case No 10-Cv-2093 (DDC Dec 10 2010) ECF No 1; SEC v. ABB Ltd, Case No 4-cv-1141 (DDC July 6 2004) ECF No.1; SEC v. UTS Starcom Inc No 09-cv-6094 (ND Cal Dec 31 2009) ECF No 1; SEC v. Schering–Plough Corp No 4-cv-945 (DDC June 9 2004) ECF No 1; SEC v. Innospec Inc, No 10-cv-448 (DDC March 18 2010) ECF No 1; SEC v. Technip No 10-cv-2289. (SD Tex June 28 2010) ECF No 1; United States v. JGC Corp No 11-cv-260 (SD Tex Apr 6 2011) ECF No 1. See also Growing Beyond: A Place for Integrity 12th Global Survey by Ernst and Young whose survey revealed that 15 percent versus 9 percent employees would like to commit bribery to win business.

563 SEC v. Halliburton Company and KBR INC Civil Action, 4:09–399.

knowledge be established.[564] This can be supported by the fact that Stanley was asked by senior officials in Halliburton about the money, and Stanley failed to disclose that it was paying bribes on its behalf.

If such a situation were to happen under the Bribery Act, Halliburton would definitely be charged under the antibribery provisions. The question is: Would it be right for the Serious Fraud Office (SFO)[565] to charge Halliburton? One could argue, based on the fact that Halliburton did take efforts to mitigate the risk by conducting due diligence on the UK agent, that it wouldn't be legitimate for the SFO to fine them. But a now-retired senior Halliburton legal officer said that Halliburton approved the use of the agent, despite the fact that the investigation had failed to learn significant information about it. Because Halliburton also did not do due diligence on the Japanese agent, one can confidently say that the United Kingdom would be right to charge Halliburton.

A similar situation happened in SEC v. Magyar Telekom Plc and Deutsche Telekom AG.[566] In that case, Deutsche Telekom, the parent company to Magyar, was in charge of the due-diligence procedure but failed to prevent bribery. In such a case, it would be right for the SFO to charge them.

It would have been a different case if KBR was an indirect subsidiary to Halliburton and Halliburton knew nothing about the use of the UK and Japanese agents, even though its policy governed the use of its agents. This can be seen in the case of SEC v. ENI, SPA and Snamprogetti Netherlands,[567] where Snamprogetti was an indirect subsidiary to ENI. Although ENI's policy governed Snamprogetti's

---

564 Cassin, R.L. (2009), *'Understanding the KBR Halliburton Charges'* (The FCPA Blog), Available at: http://fcpablog.squarespace.com/blog/2009/2/24/understanding-the-kbr-halliburton-charges.html (accessed 16 May 2013).

565 The Joint Prosecution Guidance of the Director of the Serious Fraud Office(SFO) and the Director of Public Prosecutions states that the SFO is the lead agency for the prosecution of overseas corruption (this includes bribery), which is a part of it.

566 SEC v. Magyar Telekom Plc and Deutsche Telekom AG Case No 11-cv-9646 (S.D.N.Y Dec 29 2011) ECF No 1.

567 SEC v. ENI S.P.A and Snamprogetti Netherlands BV Case No 10-cv-2414.

use of agents, it had no idea that Snamprogetti was using those particular agents for the transaction, and it was not the one in charge of doing due diligence. In such a situation, it wouldn't be right for the SFO to charge Halliburton. But in a situation where the parent company had active control over its subsidiary, knew that the subsidiary used a particular agent for a particular transaction, and was in charge of doing due diligence for those agents, then it would be right for the SFO to charge that company.

12.3 Extraterritorial Jurisdiction

As stated earlier, it is an offence under **Section 7 (1) of the UK Bribery Act** for a relevant commercial organization to fail to prevent bribery.[568] However, **Section 7 (5) (b) and (d)** defines a commercial organization as a body corporate that carries on business or part of its business in the United Kingdom.[569] This means that, provided the organization is incorporated or formed in the United Kingdom or the organization carries on a business or part of a business in the United Kingdom—wherever in the world it may be incorporated or formed—then UK courts will have jurisdiction to prosecute that company whether an offence is committed in the United Kingdom or elsewhere.

This would mean that if a company that carries on business in the United Kingdom operates in another country, and the law of that country allows for the bribery of an official in accordance with business practices or customs, the foreign company would not be subject to such domestic law based on the fact that it carries on business in the United Kingdom. For example, Korean law permits the bribery of an official where such a bribe is done in accordance with accepted business practices.[570] This means that a Korean company doing business in Cambodia that carried on business two years ago in the United Kingdom and that plans to return to the United

568 Bribery Act 2010, s. 7 (1).

569 Bribery Act 2010. s. 7 (5) b and d.

570 Republic of Korea Criminal Act, No. 293, Sep 18 1953 as last amended by Act No 10259 April 15 2010, Article 20, Article 133.

Kingdom when there are favourable conditions might be liable for the offence of bribery where an agent of the Korean company bribes an agent of the Cambodian company. This is because Section 7 of the UK Bribery Act extends to bribery of officials and not just foreign officials.[571]

Another example could be where a Cambodian company gave an expensive gift to a company situated in Korea in accordance with a particular custom and tradition. Under the new Cambodian anti-corruption law, gifts are allowed to be given to officials in accordance with custom and tradition.[572] While the Cambodian company would not have been liable if it never carried on business in the United Kingdom, it would be liable if it did carry on business there. This provision could infringe on principles of comity.[573]

The same could be said when the law of another country allows an extent of bribery when certain payments are made to foreign officials. The most common is facilitation payments.[574] While the United Kingdom does not allow for facilitation payments, the United States, Australia and Korea do to some extent.[575] The antibribery law of the United States contains a narrow exception for 'facilitation payments' made in furtherance of routine governmental actions. The exception only applies when a payment is made to further 'routine governmental action' that involves

---

571 Bribery Act 2010, s. 7 (3).

572 ADB/OECD (2010), '*The Criminalisation of Bribery in Asia and the Pacific*', *Available at:* http://www.oecd.org/site/adboecdanti-corruptioninitiative/46587127.pdf *(accessed 26 December 2017).*

573 Marshall, P. (2003), *Part 7 of the Proceeds of Crime Act 2002: Double Criminality, Legal Certainty, Proportionality and Trouble Ahead*, 11 (2) JFC 111–126.

574 See Bribery Act 2010: Joint Prosecution Guidance of the Director of the Serious Fraud Office and the Director of Public Prosecutions, which defines facilitation payments as unofficial payments made to public officials to secure or expedite the performance of a routine governmental action.

575 Foreign Corrupt Practices Act of 1977 (FCPA) 15 USC, s. 78dd-2(b); Australia's Criminal Code Act 1995, s. 70 (4); The Act on Preventing Bribery of Foreign Public Officials in International Business Transactions (FBPA) 1998, Article 3 (2) (b).

nondiscretionary acts.[576] Examples include processing visas.[577] This means that if a US company that carries on business in the United Kingdom were to do business in places such as South Africa, Malawi, Congo, Mozambique, Zambia and Zimbabwe where surveys show that facilitation payments are paid at a high level because foreign officials are highly corrupt,[578] then the US company could not make such payment even to process a visa. If the company did make such a payment, it would be prosecuted by the SFO. The same can be said for companies that are incorporated in Australia or Korea where the bribery laws allow for small facilitation payments to an extent.[579] It means that companies operating there cannot make such facilitation payments.

The same could be said of laws that allow for bribery of a foreign official where it is in accordance with business practices. This can be seen in Korean law.[580] If someone in a company that is organized under the laws of Korea pays a foreign official money in China to improve the personal relationship for business purposes, this act could lead to an offence under the UK law. This is wrong because, in China, the value of personal relationships and the concept of *guanxi* are the focal points of business culture. *Guanxi* is best described as a personal connection between two people and is typically established by providing personal favours such as gifts, entertainment and other benefits.[581] There is no way

576 Foreign Corrupt Practices Act of 1977 (FCPA) 15 USC, s. 78dd-2 (b).

577 *FCPA: A Resource Guide to the US Foreign Corrupt Practices Act* by the Criminal Division of the US Department of Justice and the Enforcement Division of the US Securities and Exchange Commission, November 14, 2012.

578 *Daily Lives and Corruption: Public Opinion in Southern Africa* by Transparency International 2011.

579 Australia's Criminal Code Act 1995, s 70 (4); FBPA: The Act on Preventing Bribery of Foreign Public Officials in International Business Transactions (1998), Article 3 (2) (b).

580 FBPA: The Act on Preventing Bribery of Foreign Public Officials in International Business Transactions (1998), Article 3 (1) makes it an offence to bribe a foreign officer, while the Republic of Korea Criminal Act, No 293, Sep 18 1953 as last amended by Act No 10259 April 15, 2010, Article 20, allows for an exception where business practices accept such bribes.

581 Hebert Smith Asia's anticorruption report, issue 1, Summer 2012

that the agent of the Korean company would have known that the United Kingdom would see such a payment as a bribe.

This provision seems to go beyond the scope of the Organization for Economic Co-operation and Development (OECD) convention, which requires its parties to cover foreign bribery committed partly in their own territories.[582] Not only does the United Kingdom extend its jurisdiction of foreign bribery over acts that are not committed in the United Kingdom, it even exercises jurisdiction over commercial bribery.[583] This goes further than the United States. The FCPA applies to SEC issuers (US and foreign companies),[584] domestic concerns[585] and certain foreign nationals or entities that act within the United States.[586]

Such broad provisions made Jessica A. Lordi ask the question: Is this extraterritorial provision even legal under international law? Lordi argues that if the United Kingdom uses this provision as a means of prosecuting bribery anywhere in the world against companies with any level of connection to the United Kingdom, the law could reach permissible extraterritorial jurisdiction and effectively establish universal jurisdiction for bribery offences. According to Lordi, the United Kingdom should not use such jurisdiction as it is often used for egregious acts, piracy, war crimes, genocide and terrorism. Bribery is not as serious as these offences. She also argues that various countries have amended and updated their antibribery laws, but none reach the level of prosecutorial discretion or extraterritorial reach that the Bribery Act

---

582   OECD Convention on Combating Bribery of Foreign Officials in International Business Transactions (1997), Article 4 (1). See also United Nations Convention against Corruption 2004, Article 42 (1), which does not cover the type of jurisdiction the United Kingdom is using. See also the Nigerian Criminal Code Act 2004, s 12, which implements Article 4 (1) of the OECD Convention. Nwadialo S.A.N, F. (1987), The *Criminal Procedure of the Southern States of Nigeria*, 2nd edition (MIJ Professional Publishers Limited) 14–15.

583   Bribery Act 2010, s. 1.

584   Foreign Corrupt Practices Act (1977), 15 USC, s. 78 dd-1; Securities Exchange Act (1934) 1, Section 30 A.

585   Foreign Corrupt Practices Act (1977), 15 USC, s. 78 dd-2.

586   Ibid.

employs. Lastly, she argues that since bribery is widely defined, it would be wrong to apply universal jurisdiction to it. Universal jurisdiction applies when the crime is universally identified, and there is no need for the United Kingdom to operate on behalf of the international community to prosecute bribery.[587]

While the definition of bribery may be too wide to fit into the universal jurisdiction principle, bribery is arguably as serious as war crimes and piracy, and universal jurisdiction could be used. Bribery, which is a part of corruption, is an insidious plague that has a wide range of corrosive effects on societies. It undermines democracy and the rule of law and leads to violations of human rights.[588] If this were the only criteria, the SFO would be justified in using universal jurisdiction. However, since it does offend the customs of others, leads to confusion and has a negative impact on business, universal jurisdiction should not be used.

12.4 Penalties

The UK bribery law is such that if a company is convicted of failing to prevent bribery, it will be liable, upon indictment, to an unlimited fine.[589]

Nigeria and the United States, on the other hand, impose a limit on the penalty.[590]

It is unclear what method the courts in the United Kingdom intend to use to calculate the penalty. This definitely leads to a lot of uncertainty in that regard. The reason the exact amount is not

---

587 Lordi, J. A. (2012), '*The United Kingdom Bribery Act: Endless Jurisdictional Liability on Corporate Violators*', Vol. 44 Case W Res J Int LL, 955; Evans, M. D. (2010), *International Law*, 3rd edition (Oxford University Press, 2010), 326–327. This also emphasises the fact that universal jurisdiction is applied to serious crimes like war crimes and piracy. Gardiner, R. K. (2003), *International Law*, first published (Pearson Education Ltd), 312, describes the *universal principle* as determining jurisdiction by reference to the place where the offence was committed.

588 United Nations Convention against Corruption 2004 (Foreword).

589 Bribery Act 2010, s. 11(3).

590 Corrupt Practices and Other Related Offences Act 2000, s 17; Foreign Corrupt Practices Act of 1977 (FCPA) 15 USC, s. 78dd-2 (g).

specified may be that the scope of the Bribery Act is much wider than the FCPA, and it wouldn't be fair to impose the same penalty on a company where the agent bribed an official as on a company where the agent bribed a foreign official. While this may be a creative approach, the courts may still end up doing what they sought to avoid. The courts are likely to interpret cases differently and, therefore, could impose a serious penalty on one company, and then impose a lesser penalty on another, even when the facts of the cases are similar. This could even conflict with **Article 3 (1) of the OECD Convention**, which requires that such sanctions should be proportionate.[591] If the court is able to treat everyone fairly, then there may be no issue.

12.5 Conclusion

We have seen that **Section 7 of the UK Bribery Act** can cause many issues for firms, both in the regulated and unregulated sectors. Firms with no knowledge of an act can pay unwarranted fines. Also, the extraterritorial reach of the act conflicts with other countries' domestic and foreign laws, making it illegal to an extent. One can confidently say that there is need for reform.

Cecilia Wells has suggested that Section 7 be amended to allow for vicarious liability with a due-diligence defence,[592] while the Law Commission suggested that the act allow for negligence in failing to prevent bribery, subject to adequate procedures.[593] Wells's suggestion is recommended, along with an amendment to the definition of associated persons to restrict it to companies incorporated under UK law.

With regard to whether facilitation payments should remain prohibited, some have argued against distinguishing between a facilitation payment and a bribe, while others have argued that

---

591 OECD Convention Article 3 (1).

592 Wells, C. (2009), *'Bribery: corporate liability under the draft bill 2009'*, 7, Criminal Law Review, 479–487.

593 The Law Commission (2008), (LAW Com No. 313): Reforming Bribery, Paragraph 6.1.

facilitation payments should be allowed on the basis that they may be solicited under threat, making refusal difficult.[594] Facilitation payments should not be prohibited due to uncertainty, and should be made a defence, as long as it is not wide enough to create uncertainty. The United Kingdom could adopt the approach of the United States by limiting facilitation payments to routine governmental actions.

---

594 Drinnan, R. (2012), 'Australia: proposed reform to Australian foreign bribery legislation', 2, IELR, 40–42.

CHAPTER 13

FRAUD

F raud can be broadly defined as a false representation of a matter of fact – whether by words or by conduct, by false or misleading allegations, or by concealment of what should have been disclosed – that deceives and is intended to deceive another so that the individual will act upon it to her or his legal injury.[595]

The criminal activities that most commonly generate significant sums for laundering are large-scale financial frauds (for example, the Enron, Parmalat, and Madoff scandals), corruption (such as the regimes of the Philippines' President Marcos and Zaire's President Mobutu), tax evasion, and narcotics production and trafficking.[596] Unlike drug trafficking, fraud proceeds rarely start off as a cash purchase. The transactions typically occur through normal, regulated financial channels and are intended to appear as legitimate. Criminals will, however, use check cashers, money transmitters, automated teller machines (ATMs), and normal withdrawals or transfers from bank or brokerage accounts to cash out fraud proceeds.[597]

---

595 Ross, I. (2015), 'Exposing Fraud: Skills, Process and Practicalities', Wiley Corporate F&A. 35

596 Hagan, S. and Myers, J. (2009), 'Stepping Up the Fight Against Money Laundering and Terrorist Financing', Available at: https://blogs.imf.org/2009/12/17/money-laundering-and-terrorist-financing/ (accessed 23 August 2017).

597 U.S. Department of the Treasury (2015), 'National Money Laundering Risk Assessment', Available at: https://www.treasury.gov/resource-center/terrorist-illicit-finance/Documents/National%20Money%20Laundering%20Risk%20Assessment%20%E2%80%93%2006-12-2015.pdf (accessed 11 August 2017).

Fraud is increasingly conducted online. Non- and under-reporting by individuals and some business sectors makes the true scale difficult to estimate. The number of reported frauds is rising, although this may be a consequence of improved reporting through Action Fraud rather than an actual increase in crime. Her Majesty's Revenue and Customs (HMRC) estimate that four billion four hundred million pounds was lost to criminal attacks against the tax system in 2012/13, with a further four billion one hundred million pounds lost to tax evasion. Excise duty fraud (particularly targeting tobacco, alcohol and fuel) and Value Added Tax (VAT) fraud are the principal threats.[598]

13.1 Criminal Fraud
This section compares the anti-fraud laws in Nigeria with those of the United States and the United Kingdom, and provides a number of case studies that illustrate various ways that people can be exploited for fraudulent purposes.
Fraud is a predicate offence leading to money laundering.

13.1.1 Nigeria
In Nigeria, criminal fraud is mainly dealt with in the Advance Fee Fraud and other Fraud Related Offences Act 2006. Key statutory provisions are excerpted below.

Section 1 – Obtaining property by false pretence, etc

(1) Notwithstanding anything contained in any other enactment or law, any person who by any false pretence, and with intent to defraud

598 HM Treasury and Home Office (2015), 'UK national risk assessment of money laundering and terrorist financing', Available at: https://www.gov.uk/government/uploads/system/uploads/attachment_data/file/468210/UK_NRA_October_2015_final_web.pdf (accessed 13 August 2017).

(a) obtains, from any other person, in Nigeria or in any other country for himself or any other person;

(b) induces any other person, in Nigeria or in any other country, to deliver to any person; or

(c) obtains any property, whether or not the property is obtained or its delivery is induced through the medium of a contract induced by the false pretence,

commits an offence under this Act.

(2) A person who by false pretence, and with the intent to defraud, induces any other person, in Nigeria or in any other country, to confer a benefit on him or on any other person by doing or permitting a thing to be done on the understanding that the benefit has been or will be paid for commits an offence under this Act.

(3) A person who commits an offence under subsection (1) or (2) of this section is liable on conviction to imprisonment for a term of not more than 20 years and not less than seven years without the option of a fine.

CASE STUDY ON OBTAINING PROPERTY BY FALSE PRETENCE

Case 13.1: Federal Government of Nigeria v. Mallam Umaru Kankani (Unreported)

The Economic and Financial Crimes Commission, EFCC, arraigned one Mallam Umaru Kankani before Justice Sa'ad Muhammad of the Gombe State High Court on a two-count charge bordering on forgery and obtaining by false pretence.

Kankani's journey to the dock followed a petition by one Dr. Salisu Ahmed of Federal Teaching Hospital, Gombe alleging that sometimes in June, 2016, he was defrauded by the accused to the tune two million three hundred thousand naira over a parcel of land situated at Federal Low-cost, Gombe, which ownership the accused claimed was his, but was later discovered to be a scam.

Investigation by operatives of the EFCC revealed that the documents used in the transaction were forged by the accused person.

Count two of the charge reads:

"That you, Mallam Umaru Kankani sometimes between June to September 2016 or thereabout, at Gombe, Gombe State within the jurisdiction of this Honourable Court, did obtain the sum of Two Million, Three Hundred Thousand Naira only (N2,300,000.00), from one Dr Salisu Ahmed under the false Pretence that the said sum was for the purchase of a landed property situate at Federal Low-cost Gombe, Gombe State knowing fully well that the said landed property does not belong to you and thereby committed an offence contrary to Section 1 (1) (b) and Punishable under Section 1 (3) of the Advance Fee Fraud and other Fraud Related Offences Act 2006."

The accused person pleaded guilty to the charge.

Upon his plea, counsel to the EFCC, Zarami Muhammad, urged the court "to convict the accused person in accordance with the law under which he was charged since the High Court has to conduct summary trial".

In response, Kankani's counsel, M. A. Ghalaya, however, opposed Muhammad's submission on the grounds that "the High Court has no jurisdiction to conduct summary trial under Criminal Procedure Code (CPC)".

At this point, Justice Muhammad adjourned to July 18, 2017 to enable the prosecution to respond and ordered the accused person to be remanded in prison custody.[599]

599 Economic and Financial Crimes Commission (2017), 'Man Pleads Guilty to N2.3m Land Scam', Available at: https://efccnigeria.org/efcc/news/2672-man-pleads-guilty-to-n2-3m-land-scam (accessed 30 August 2017).

Section 2 – Other related offences.
A person who—

(a) with intent to defraud, represents himself as capable of producing, from a piece of paper or from any other material,
any currency note by washing, dipping or otherwise treating
the paper or material with or in a chemical substance or any
other substance; or

(b) with intent to defraud, represents himself as possessing the power or as capable of doubling or otherwise increasing any sum of
money through scientific or any other medium of invocation of
any juju or other invisible entity or of anything whatsoever; or

(c) not being the Central Bank of Nigeria, prints, makes or issues, or represents himself as capable of printing, making or
issuing any currency note, commits an offence and is liable
on conviction to imprisonment for a term not more than 15
years and not less than five years without the option of a fine.

Section 3 – Use of premises
A person who, being the occupier or is concerned in the management of any premises, causes or knowingly permits the premises to
be used for any purpose which constitutes an offence under this Act
commits an offence and is liable on conviction to imprisonment for
a term of not less more than 15 years and not less than five years
without the option of a fine.

Section 4 – Fraudulent invitation.
A person who by false pretence, and with the intent to defraud any
other person, invites or otherwise induces that person or any other
person to visit Nigeria for any purpose connected with the commission of an offence under this Act commits an offence and is liable on
conviction to imprisonment for a term not more than 20 years and
not less than seven years without the option of a fine.

Section 5 – Receipt of fraudulent document by victim to constitute attempt.

(1) Where a false pretence which constitutes an offence under this Act is contained in a document, it shall be sufficient in a charge of an attempt to commit an offence under this Act to prove that the document was received by the person to whom the false pretence was directed.

(2) Notwithstanding anything to the contrary in any other law, every act or thing done or omitted to be done by a person to facilitate the commission by him of an offence under this Act shall constitute an attempt to commit the offence.

Section 6 – Possession of fraudulent document to constitute attempt.

A person who is in possession of a document containing a false pretence which constitutes an offence under this Act commits an offence of an attempt to commit an offence under this Act if he knows or ought to know, having regard to the circumstances of the case, the document contains the false pretence.

Section 7 – Laundering of fund obtained through unlawful activity, etc.

(1) A person who conducts or attempts to conduct a financial transaction which in fact involves the proceeds of a specified unlawful activity -

    (a) with the intent to promote the carrying on of a specified unlawful activity; or

    (b) where the transaction is designed in whole or in part -

        (i) to conceal or disguise the nature, the location, the source, the ownership or the control of the proceeds of a specified unlawful activity; or

(ii) to avoid a lawful transaction under Nigerian law, commits an offence under this Act if he knows or ought to know, having regard to the circumstances of the case, that the property involved in the financial transaction represents the proceeds of some form of unlawful activity.

(2) A person who commits an offence under subsection (1) of this section, is liable on conviction -

(a) in the case of a financial institution or corporate body, to a fine of N 1 million and where the financial institution or corporate body is unable to pay the fine, its assets to the value of the fine shall be confiscated and forfeited to the Federal Government; or

(b) in the case of a director, secretary or other officer of the financial institution or corporate body or any other person, to imprisonment for a term, not more than 10 years and not less than five years.

(3) When as a result of negligence, or regulation in the internal control procedures, a financial institution fails to exercise due diligence as specified in the Banks and Other Financial Institutions Act, 1991 as amended or the Money Laundering (Prohibition) Act, 2004 in relation to the conduct of financial transactions which in fact involve the proceeds of unlawful activity-

(a) the financial institution commits an offence and is liable on conviction to refund the total amount involved in the financial transaction and not less than N100.000 sanction by the appropriate financial regulatory authority;

(b) a director, secretary, employee or other staff of the financial institution who facilitates, contributes or otherwise is involved in the failure to exercise due diligence as stipulated under this section, commits an offence and is liable on conviction to imprisonment for a term not less than three years and may also be liable to be banned indefinitely for a period of three years from exercising the profession which provided the opportunity for the offence to be committed.

(4) A person who transports or attempts to transport a monetary instrument or funds from a place in Nigeria to or through a place outside Nigeria or to a place in Nigeria from or through a place outside Nigeria -

(a) with the intent to promote the carrying on of specified unlawful activity; or

(b) where the monetary instrument or funds involved in the transportation represent the proceeds of some form of unlawful activity and the transportation is designed in whole or in part -

  (i) to conceal or disguise the nature, the location, the source, the ownership, or the control of the proceeds of a specified unlawful activity; or

  (ii) to avoid a lawful transaction under Nigerian law, commits an offence under this Act, if he knows or ought to know, having regard to the circumstances of the case, that the monetary instrument or funds involved in the transportation are the proceeds of some form of unlawful activity and the intent of the transaction

(5) A person who commits an offence under subsection (3) of this section is liable on conviction to a fine of ₦500.000 or twice the value of the monetary instrument or funds involved in the transportation, whichever is higher, or imprisonment for a term of not less than 10 years or to both such fine and imprisonment.

(6) In this section -

(a) "conducts" includes initiating, being involved, connected with, concluding, or participating in initiating or concluding a transaction;

(b) "financial institution" means banks, body association or group of persons, whether corporate or incorporate which carries on the business of investment and securities, a discount house, insurance institutions, debt factorization and conversion firms, bureau de change, finance company, money brokerage firm whose principal business includes factoring, project financing, equipment leasing, debt administration, fund management, private ledger services, investment management, local purchase order financing, export finance, project consultancy, financial consultancy, pension funds management and such other businesses as the Central Bank of Nigeria or other appropriate regulatory authorities may from time to time designate.

(c) "financial transaction" means -

(i) a transaction involving the movement of funds by wire or other means or involving one or more monetary instruments, which in any way or degree affects foreign monetary instruments; or

(ii) a transaction involving the use of a financial institution which is engaged in, or the activities of which affect, foreign commerce in any way or degree;

(d) "knows or ought to know that the property involved in a financial transaction represents the proceeds of some form of unlawful activity" means that the person knew or ought to have known that the property involved in the transaction represented proceeds from some form, though not necessarily which form, of activity that constitutes an offence under this Act;

(e) "monetary instrument" means coin or currency of Nigeria or of any other country, traveller's cheque, personal cheque, bank cheque, money order, investment security in bearer form or otherwise in such form that title thereto passes upon delivery;

(f) "proceeds" means any property derived or obtained, directly or indirectly through the commission of an offence under this Act;

(g) "property" includes assets, monetary instruments and instrumentalities used in the commission of an offence under this Act;

(h) "specified unlawful activity" means -

(i) any act or activity constituting an offence under this Act;

(ii) with respect to a financial transaction occurring in whole or in part in Nigeria, an offence against the laws of a foreign nation involving obtaining property by fraud by whatever name called;

(i) "transaction" includes a purchase, sale, loan, pledge, gift, transfer, delivery, or other disposition, and with respect to a financial institution, includes a deposit, withdrawal, transfer between accounts, exchange of currency, loan, extension of credit, purchase or sale of any stock, bond, certificate of deposit or other monetary instrument, or any other payment, transfer, or delivery by, through, or to a financial institution, by whatever means effected.

Section 8 – Conspiracy, aiding, etc.
A person who -

(a) conspires with, aids, abets, or counsels any other person to commit an offence; or

(b) attempts to commit or is an accessory to an act or offence; or

(c) incites, procures or induces any other person by any means whatsoever to commit an offence, under this Act, commits the offence and is liable on conviction to the same punishment as is prescribed for that offence under this Act.

Section 9 – Conviction for alternative offences.

(1) Where a person is charged with an offence under this Act and the evidence establishes an attempt to commit that offence, he may be convicted of having attempted to commit that offence although the attempt is not separately charged and such a person shall be punished as is prescribed for that offence under this Act

(2) Where a person is charged with an attempt to commit an offence under this Act, but the evidence establishes the commission of the full offence, the offender shall not be entitled to acquittal but shall be convicted of the offence and punished as provided under this Act.

Section 10 – Offences by bodies cooperate.

(1) Where an offence under this Act which has been committed by a body corporate is proved to have been committed on the instigation or with the connivance of or attributable to any neglect on the part of a director, manager, secretary or other similar officer of the body corporate, or any person purporting to act in any such capacity, he, as well as the body corporate, where practicable, shall be deemed to have committed that offence and shall be liable to be proceeded against and punished accordingly.

(2) Where a body corporate is convicted of an offence under this Act, the High Court may order that the body corporate shall thereupon and without any further assurance, but for such order, be wound up and all its assets and properties forfeited to the Federal Government.

Section 11 – Restitution.

(1) In addition to any other penalty prescribed under this Act, the High Court shall order a person convicted of an offence under this Act to make restitution to the victim of the false pretence or fraud by directing that person-

(a) where the property involved is money, to pay to the victim an amount equivalent to the loss sustained by the victim;

in any other case -

> > (i) to return the property to the victim or to a person designated by him; or
> >
> > (ii) to pay an amount equal to the value of the property, where the return of the property is impossible or impracticable.
>
> (2) An order of restitution may be enforced by the victim or by the prosecutor on behalf of the victim in the same manner as a judgment in a civil action.

CASE STUDY ON RESTITUTION ORDERS

Case 13.2: Federal Government of Nigeria v. Bike John Niye (Unreported)

A 22 years old internet fraudster, Bike John Niye was sentenced to one and half years imprisonment by a Lagos State High Court sitting in Ikeja, for defrauding one Laura Wallmam of Indiana, United States of America the sum of fifty-three thousand five hundred dollars. Justice A Akinlade slammed the prison term on Niye having found him guilty of the four-count charge bordering on obtaining money by false pretense and attempt to obtain money by false pretense, preferred against him by the Economic and Financial Crimes Commission, EFCC.

Reports showed that Niye presented himself to Wallmam as businessman who operates a 'moving' company and needed money to get some of his goods out of storage. He met Wallmam in a dating site and has been in a relationship with her using a fictitious name, Toby Encore.

His journey to prison began on May 27th, 2010 when officials of the National Drug Law Enforcement Agency, NDLEA and DHL Courier Services intercepted a suspicious parcel containing a Teddy Bear and a Blackberry handset sent from the USA to the convict by Wallmam. The parcel was examined and it was discovered that it contained the sum of forty thousand dollars, a Blackberry handset, and a white lady's photograph concealed in the Teddy Bear. The parcel was to be delivered to an address in Alapere, a suburb of Lagos with the name Tobi Encore and a Nigerian phone number also belonging to the same recipient. With the phone number, the convicted fraudster was traced and upon finding him, he was handed over to the EFCC for further investigations.

Upon investigation, Operatives of the Commission discovered that the name Tony Encore was used by the fraudster to deceive the American in order to defraud her. It was found out that his real name is Bike John Niye. The operatives also discovered that it was Niye who instructed the victim to conceal all the items in a Teddy Bear.

Investigations also revealed that Niye has been receiving various sums of money from the victim via Western Union totaling about twenty-five thousand dollars before the parcel which finally landed him in jail. To enable him collect the sent funds via Western Union, findings revealed that Niye obtained a Driver's license with a forged identity bearing the name Nathan Omarkeh. He usually destroys the identity card after collecting money sent to him.

In addition to the one and half year jail term, Niye is to refund the sum of forty-eight thousand five hundred dollars as restitution to the victim.[600]

Section 14 – Jurisdiction to try offences, etc.
The Federal High Court or the High Court of the Federal Capital Territory and the High Court of the State shall have jurisdiction to try offences and impose penalties under this Act

---

600 Uwujaren, W. (2012), 'Court Jails Fraudster Over $53,500 Romance Scam', Available at: https://efccnigeria.org/efcc/news/84-court-jails-fraudster-over-53-500-romance-scam (accessed 30 August 2017).

Section 15 – Possession of pecuniary resources not accounted for.
In a trial for an offence under this Act, the fact that a person

    (a) is in possession of pecuniary resources or property for which he cannot satisfactorily account and which is disproportionate to his known sources of income; or

    (b) that he had at or about the time of the alleged offence obtained an accretion to his pecuniary resources or property for which he cannot satisfactorily account,

        may be proved and may be taken into consideration by the High Court as corroborating the testimony of a witness in the trial.

Section 16 – Power to control property of an accused person.

    (1) Where at any stage of a trial, the High Court is satisfied that a prima facie case has been made out against a person, the High Court may by an order and for such time as it may direct or require -

    (a) prohibit any disposition of property, movable or immovable, by or on behalf of that person, whether or not the property is owned or held by that person or by any other person on his behalf, except to such extent and in such manner as may be specified in the order; addressed to the manager of the bank or to the head office of the bank where the person has an account or is believed to have account, direct the manager or the bank

        (i) to stop all outward payments, operations or transactions *(including any bill of exchange)* for the time being specified in the order;

        (ii) to supply any information and produce books and documents, in respect of the account of that person; and

    (b) where necessary or expedient, vest in the High Court or otherwise acquire the custody of, any property, movable or immovable, of the person, for the preservation of the property, pending the determination of the proceedings.

(2) An order under subsection (1) of this section shall have effect as specified therein, but the order may at any time thereafter be varied or annulled by the High Court.

(3) Failure to comply with the requirement of an order under this section shall be an offence punishable on conviction

(a) in the case of an individual, by imprisonment for a term of not less than two years or more than five years without the option of a fine;

(b) in the case of any group of persons not being a body corporate, by the like punishment of each of such persons as is prescribed in paragraph (a) of this subsection;

(c) in the case of a body corporate, by a fine of an amount equal to two times the estimated value of the property affected by the non-compliance or ₦500,000, whichever is higher.

Section 17 – Power to make order of forfeiture without conviction for an offence.

(1) Where any property has come into the possession of any officer of the Commission as unclaimed property or any unclaimed property is found by any officer of the Commission to be in the possession of any other person, body corporate or financial institution or any property in the possession of any person, body corporate or financial institution is reasonably suspected to be proceeds of some unlawful activity under this Act, the Money Laundering Act of 2004, the Economic and Financial Crimes Commission Act of 2004 or any other law enforceable under the Economic and Financial Crime Commission Act of 2004, the High Court shall upon application made by the Commission, its officers, or any other person authorized by it and upon being reasonably satisfied that such property is an unclaimed property or proceeds of unlawful activity under the

Acts stated in this subsection make an order that the property or the proceeds from the sale of such property be forfeited to the Federal Government of Nigeria.

(2) Notwithstanding the provision of subsection (1) of this section the High Court shall not make an order of forfeiture of the property or the proceeds from the sale of such property to the Federal Government of Nigeria until such notice or publication as the High Court may direct has been given or made for any person, corporate or financial institution in whose possession the property is found or who may have interest in the property or claim ownership of the property to show cause why the property should not be forfeited to the Federal Government of Nigeria.

(3) Application under subsection (1) above shall first be made by a motion ex parte for interim forfeiture order of the property concerned and the giving of the requisite notice or publication as required in subsection (2) of this section.

(4) At the expiration of 14 days or such other period as the High Court may reasonably stipulate from the date of the giving of the notice or making of the publication stated in subsection (2) and (3) of this section, an application shall be made by a motion on notice for the final forfeiture of the property concerned to the Federal Government of Nigeria.

(5) In this section:

"financial institution" shall have the same meaning as in section 7 of this Act.

"property" includes assets whether moveable or immovable, money, monetary instruments, negotiable instruments, securities, shares, insurance policies, and any investments.

(6) An order of forfeiture under this section shall not be based on a conviction for an offence under this Act or any other law.

Section 18 – Power to arrest.

The power of arrest in respect of an offence under this Act shall be in accordance with the provisions of the Criminal Procedure Act or the Criminal Procedure Code, the case may be.

Section 19 – Power to grant bail.

The courts shall have power to grant bail to an accused person charged with an offence under this Bill or any other law triable by the Courts upon such terms and conditions as the Courts may deem fit.

Fraud is also criminalized under the Dishonored Cheques (Offences) Act, Cap D11, Laws of the Federation, 2004. Key statutory provisions are excerpted below.

1. Offences in relation to dishonoured cheques, etc.

(1) Any person who-
- (a) obtains or induces the delivery of anything capable of being stolen either to himself or to any other person; or
- (b) obtains credit for himself or any other person, by means of a cheque that, when presented for payment not later than three months after the date of the cheque, is dishonoured on the ground that no funds or insufficient funds were standing to the credit of the drawer of the cheque in the bank on which the cheque was drawn, shall be guilty of an offence and on conviction shall-
    - (i) in the case of an individual be sentenced to imprisonment for two years, without the option of a fine; and
    - (ii) in the case of a body corporate, be sentenced to a fine of not less than ₦5,000.

(2) For the purposes of subsection (1) of this section-
- (a) the reference to anything capable of being stolen shall be deemed to include a reference to money and every

other description of property, things in action and other intangible property;

(b) a person who draws a cheque which is dishonoured on the ground stated in the subsection and which was issued in settlement or purported settlement of any obligation under an enforceable contract entered into between the drawer of the cheque and the person to whom the cheque was issued, shall be deemed to have obtained credit for himself by means of the cheque, notwithstanding that at the time when the contract was entered into, the manner in which the obligation would be settled was not specified.

(3) A person shall not be guilty of an offence under this section if he proves to the satisfaction of the court that when he issued that cheque he had reasonable grounds for believing, and did believe in fact, that it would be honoured if presented for payment within the period specified in subsection (1) of this section.

CASE STUDY: DUD CHEQUE

Case 13.3: Federal Government of Nigeria v. Aliyu Zakari (Unreported)

Justice Yusuf Ubale of the Kano State High Court on April 7, 2015 sentenced one Aliyu Zakari to two years imprisonment on a 2-count charges bordering on Issuance of dud cheque brought against him by the Economic and Financial Crimes Commission, EFCC.

The convict who is chief executive of AZH Enterprises Limited, was arrested by the Commission following a petition alleging that he refused to pay part of the value of premium motor spirit and automotive gas oil sold to him by the petitioner, and that the cheques he issued to settle the debt were returned unpaid owing to insufficient funds in his account.

Count one reads, "That you AZH Enterprises Limited and Aliyu Zakari being the Chairman, CEO of AZH Enterprises Limited and the sole signatory to the Company's First Bank account on or about 30th June, 2010 in kano within the judicial division of the High Court of Justice of kano State did issue a First Bank Plc cheque No: 42199661 in the sum of N9,000,000.00 (Nine Million Naira only) to one Alhaji Magaji Ubale which when presented sometimes in July, 2010 was dishonoured on the ground that no sufficient funds were standing to the credit of the account upon which the cheque was drawn and you thereby committed an offence contrary to section 1(1) (a) and punishable under Section 1 (1) (b) (i)(ii) of the Dishonoured Cheques (Offences) Act, Cap. D11 Laws of the Federation, 2004".

When the charge was read to the accused person, he pleaded guilty. Consequently, the prosecution counsel A.T. Habib urged the court to convict him.

In view of his plea, Justice Ubale convicted and sentenced him to two years imprisonment without an option of fine. The Judge however imposed a fine of ten thousand naira only against the company.[601]

Case 13.4: Federal Government of Nigeria v. Hussien Tahir (Unreported)

Justice Lawan Faruk of Kano State High Court, Kano convicted and sentenced one Hussien Tahir to twenty-four months imprisonment for Issuance of dud cheque.

The convict, who was arraigned on October 15, 2014, had in 2009 approached the complainant with a proposal to jointly fund the execution of a capital project which he claimed was awarded to him by the Nigeria Customs Service. The complainant decided to take part in the project and invested twenty-two million Naira, with the expectation of a return of ten million naira on his investment.

But upon successful completion of the project, the complainant said he neither received the agreed profit nor get a refund of his investment. He further stated that upon insistence on getting a

---

601 Economic and Financial Crimes Commission (2015), 'Man Bags Two Years Imprisonment for Dud Cheque', Available at: https://efccnigeria.org/efcc/news/1280-man-bags-two-years-imprisonment-for-dud-cheque (accessed 1 September 2017).

refund, the convict gave him five different cheques totalling twenty-two million Naira, which were returned unpaid.

In his ruling, Justice Faruk sentenced the accused to 24 months imprisonment with the option of two million Naira fine. He was also ordered him to pay a sum of Thirty-Two Million Six Hundred and Fifty Thousand Naira only as restitution to the victim, or risk five years in prison.[602]

Case 13.5: Federal Government of Nigeria v. Dora Gilmaska (Unreported)

Justice Abubakar Umar of the Federal Capital Territory (FCT) High Court sitting in Maitama, Abuja on Thursday, September 29, 2016, convicted one Dora Gilmaska, a pole, alongside her company, Icon Media and Marketing Agency Limited, on one-count charge of fraud brought against her by the Economic and Financial Crimes Commission, EFCC.

Gilmaska was found guilty of forging and issuing a dud cheque of nine million naira to one Tayo Olugbemi sometime in 2012.

She was arraigned on November 7, 2012, and upon arraignment pleaded not guilty to the charge.

After diligent prosecution, Justice Umar found Gilmaska guilty and she was consequently convicted.[603]

2. Offences by body corporate

Where any offence under this Act by a body corporate is proved to have been committed with the consent of or connivance of, or to be attributable to any neglect on the part of any director, manager,

---

602 Economic and Financial Crimes Commission (2014), 'Lebanese Bags 2 Years for Issuance of N22m Dud Cheque', Available at: https://efccnigeria.org/efcc/news/1664-lebanese-bags-2-years-for-issuance-of-n22m-dud-cheque (accessed 1 September 2017).

603 Economic and Financial Crimes Commission (2016), 'Court Convicts Polish Woman for N9m Fraud', Available at: https://efccnigeria.org/efcc/news/2085-court-convicts-polish-woman-for-n9m-fraud (accessed 1 September 2017).

secretary or other similar officer, servant or agent of the body corporate (or any person purporting to act in any such capacity), he, as well as the body corporate, shall be deemed to be guilty of the offence and may be proceeded against and punished in the same manner as an individual.

3. Procedure for trial of offences

(1) Offences under this Act shall be triable summarily by the High Court of the State where the offence was committed and the procedure applicable in the case of summary trial of offences before such court shall apply to the same extent for the purposes of trials for offences under this Act.

(2) Authority to exercise the powers of the Attorney-General of the Federation under section 160 of the Constitution of the Federal Republic of Nigeria, 1999 (which relates to the initiation and conduct of criminal proceedings for offences under an enactment) is hereby, in respect of any offence under this Act committed in a State, conferred on the Attorney-General of that State, but nothing in this subsection shall be construed as precluding the Attorney-General of the Federation from exercising any of the powers to which this subsection relates.

CASE LAW

In *Onwudiwe v. F.R.N* (2006) 10 N.W.L.R. (Pt. 988) 382 S.C at 429 - 430. Per Niki Tobi, J.S.C. held:

"A fraudulent action or conduct conveys an element of deceit to obtain some advantage for the owner of the fraudulent action or conduct or another person or to cause loss to any other person. In fraud, there must be a deceit or an action or an intention to deceive flowing from the fraudulent action or conduct to the victim of that action or conduct."

See generally *Kettlewell v. Watson* (1882) 21 Ch.D 685 at 685; *R v. Reigels* (1932) 11 NLR 33; *Welham v. DPP* (1960) 44 Cr. App. R. 124; *R v. Odiakosa* (1944) 10 WACA 247; *R v. Bassey* (1931) 22 Cr. App. R. 160. An offence is said to be committed fraudulently, in the context of the appeal before us, if the action or conduct is a deceit to make, obtain or procure money illegally. By the fraudulent action or conduct, the accused deceives his victim by pretending to have abilities or skills that he does not really have. In one word, he is an imposter."

In *Adamu v. State* (2014) 10 N.W.L.R. (Pt. 1416) 441 at 465, Per Ariwoola, J.S.C held that:

"It is a fundamental principle of our criminal law that in all cases, the burden of proving that any person has been guilty of crime or wrongful act, subject to certain exceptions, is on the prosecution. And if the commission of a crime is directly in issue in any civil or criminal proceeding, it must be proved beyond reasonable doubt. See; *R v. Basil Ranger Lawrence* (1932) U.N.L.R. 6, *per* Lord Atkin: *Abeke Onafowokan v. The State* (1987) 3 N.W.L.R. (Pt.61) 538; (1987) L.P.E.L.R. 266 (S.C.)."

In *Ugheneyovwe v. State* (2004) 12 N.W.L.R. (Pt. 888) 626 at 652 – 653, Per Augie, J.C.A held:

"It is an elementary principle of law that any allegation of commission of crime in a proceeding, whether civil or criminal must be proved beyond reasonable doubt and the burden of so proving that any person committed the crime is on the person who asserts it. If the prosecution proves such commission beyond reasonable doubt, the burden of proof then shifts to the accused. Upon the whole evidence however, if the Court were left in a state of doubt, the prosecution would have failed to discharge the onus of proof, which the law lays upon it and the accused is entitled to an acquittal."

In *Shuaibu v. Muazu* (2014) 8 N.W.L.R. (Pt. 1409) 207 at 317, Per Oredola, J.C.A., held:

> "It has long been settled that the burden of proof in an allegation of fraud lies on the person who asserts the same. Also, that the standard just as in all criminal cases, is beyond reasonable doubt. Thus, all elements of the offence of fraud or deceit must be proved beyond reasonable doubt in order to substantiate/sustain the allegation. See: *Terab v. Lawan* (1992) 3 N.W.L.R. (Pt. 231) 569."

In *Bassey v. State (2012) 12 N.W.L.R.* (Pt. 1314) 209 at 228, Rhodes-Vivour, J.S.C. held:

> "Proof beyond reasonable doubt does not mean proof beyond all doubt, or all shadow of doubt. It means the prosecution establishing the guilt of the accused person with compelling evidence which is conclusive. It means a degree of compulsion which is consistent with a high degree of probability. Proof beyond reasonable doubt is not achieved by the prosecution calling several witnesses to testify, rather the Court is only interested in the testimony of a quality witness. If the Court convicts on the extra judicial confessional statement of an accused person, proof beyond reasonable doubt would be achieved if and only if the statement was made voluntary and the accused person did not retract from his confessional statement when he gave evidence in Court on oath."

13.1.2 United States

In the United States of America, criminal fraud is mainly dealt with in Title 18 of the United States Code. Key statutory provisions are excerpted below.

18 U.S. Code § 1001 – Statements or entries generally

(a) Except as otherwise provided in this section, whoever, in any matter within the jurisdiction of the executive, legislative, or judicial branch of the Government of the United States, knowingly and willfully—

    (1) falsifies, conceals, or covers up by any trick, scheme, or device a material fact;

    (2) makes any materially false, fictitious, or fraudulent statement or representation; or

    (3) makes or uses any false writing or document knowing the same to contain any materially false, fictitious, or fraudulent statement or entry;

        shall be fined under this title, imprisoned not more than 5 years or, if the offence involves international or domestic terrorism (as defined in section 2331), imprisoned not more than 8 years, or both. If the matter relates to an offence under chapter 109A, 109B, 110, or 117, or section 1591, then the term of imprisonment imposed under this section shall be not more than 8 years.

(b) Subsection (a) does not apply to a party to a judicial proceeding, or that party's counsel, for statements, representations, writings or documents submitted by such party or counsel to a judge or magistrate in that proceeding.

(c) With respect to any matter within the jurisdiction of the legislative branch, subsection (a) shall apply only to—

    (1) administrative matters, including a claim for payment, a matter related to the procurement of property or services, personnel or employment practices, or support services, or a document required by law, rule, or regulation to be submitted to the Congress or any office or officer within the legislative branch; or

(2) any investigation or review, conducted pursuant to the authority of any committee, subcommittee, commission or office of the Congress, consistent with applicable rules of the House or Senate.

18 U.S. Code § 1030 – Fraud and related activity in connection with computers

(a) Whoever—

(1) having knowingly accessed a computer without authorization or exceeding authorized access, and by means of such conduct having obtained information that has been determined by the United States Government pursuant to an Executive order or statute to require protection against unauthorized disclosure for reasons of national defense or foreign relations, or any restricted data, as defined in paragraph y. of **section 11 of the Atomic Energy Act of 1954**, with reason to believe that such information so obtained could be used to the injury of the United States, or to the advantage of any foreign nation willfully communicates, delivers, transmits, or causes to be communicated, delivered, or transmitted, or attempts to communicate, deliver, transmit or cause to be communicated, delivered, or transmitted the same to any person not entitled to receive it, or willfully retains the same and fails to deliver it to the officer or employee of the United States entitled to receive it;

(2) intentionally accesses a computer without authorization or exceeds authorized access, and thereby obtains—

(A) information contained in a financial record of a financial institution, or of a card issuer as defined in section 1602(n) of title 15, or contained in a file of a consumer reporting agency on a consumer, as such terms are defined in the Fair Credit Reporting Act (15 U.S.C. 1681 et seq.);

(B) information from any department or agency of the United States; or

(C) information from any protected computer;

(3) intentionally, without authorization to access any nonpublic computer of a department or agency of the United States, accesses such a computer of that department or agency that is exclusively for the use of the Government of the United States or, in the case of a computer not exclusively for such use, is used by or for the Government of the United States and such conduct affects that use by or for the Government of the United States;

(4) knowingly and with intent to defraud, accesses a protected computer without authorization, or exceeds authorized access, and by means of such conduct furthers the intended fraud and obtains anything of value, unless the object of the fraud and the thing obtained consists only of the use of the computer and the value of such use is not more than $5,000 in any 1-year period;

(5)

(A) knowingly causes the transmission of a program, information, code, or command, and as a result of such conduct, intentionally causes damage without authorization, to a protected computer;

(B) intentionally accesses a protected computer without authorization, and as a result of such conduct, recklessly causes damage; or

(C) intentionally accesses a protected computer without authorization, and as a result of such conduct, causes damage and loss.

(6) knowingly and with intent to defraud traffics (as defined in section 1029) in any password or similar information through which a computer may be accessed without authorization, if—

(A) such trafficking affects interstate or foreign commerce; or

(B) such computer is used by or for the Government of the United States;

(7) with intent to extort from any person any money or other thing of value, transmits in interstate or foreign commerce any communication containing any—

(A) threat to cause damage to a protected computer;

(B) threat to obtain information from a protected computer without authorization or in excess of authorization or to impair the confidentiality of information obtained from a protected computer without authorization or by exceeding authorized access; or

(C) demand or request for money or other thing of value in relation to damage to a protected computer, where such damage was caused to facilitate the extortion;

      shall be punished as provided in subsection (c) of this section.

(b) Whoever conspires to commit or attempts to commit an offence under subsection (a) of this section shall be punished as provided in subsection (c) of this section.

(c) The punishment for an offence under subsection (a) or (b) of this section is—

(1) (A) a fine under this title or imprisonment for not more than ten years, or both, in the case of an offence under subsection (a)(1) of this section which does not occur after a conviction for another offence under this section, or an attempt to commit an offence punishable under this subparagraph; and

(B) a fine under this title or imprisonment for not more than twenty years, or both, in the case of an offence under subsection (a)(1) of this section which occurs after a conviction for another offence under this section, or an attempt to commit an offence punishable under this subparagraph;

(2) (A) except as provided in subparagraph (B), a fine under this title or imprisonment for not more than one year, or both, in the case of an offence under subsection (a)(2), (a)(3), or (a)(6) of this section which does not occur

after a conviction for another offence under this section, or an attempt to commit an offence punishable under this subparagraph;

(B) a fine under this title or imprisonment for not more than 5 years, or both, in the case of an offence under subsection (a)(2), or an attempt to commit an offence punishable under this subparagraph, if—

    (i) the offence was committed for purposes of commercial advantage or private financial gain;

    (ii) the offence was committed in furtherance of any criminal or tortious act in violation of the Constitution or laws of the United States or of any State; or

    (iii) the value of the information obtained exceeds $5,000; and

(C) a fine under this title or imprisonment for not more than ten years, or both, in the case of an offence under subsection (a)(2), (a)(3) or (a)(6) of this section which occurs after a conviction for another offence under this section, or an attempt to commit an offence punishable under this subparagraph;

(3) (A) a fine under this title or imprisonment for not more than five years, or both, in the case of an offence under subsection (a)(4) or (a)(7) of this section which does not occur after a conviction for another offence under this section, or an attempt to commit an offence punishable under this subparagraph; and

(B) a fine under this title or imprisonment for not more than ten years, or both, in the case of an offence under subsection (a)(4), or (a)(7) of this section which occurs after a conviction for another offence under this section, or an attempt to commit an offence punishable under this subparagraph;

(4) (A) except as provided in subparagraphs (E) and (F), a fine under this title, imprisonment for not more than 5 years, or both, in the case of—

(i) an offence under subsection (a)(5)(B), which does not occur after a conviction for another offence under this section, if the offence caused (or, in the case of an attempted offence, would, if completed, have caused)—

    (I)   loss to 1 or more persons during any 1-year period (and, for purposes of an investigation, prosecution, or other proceeding brought by the United States only, loss resulting from a related course of conduct affecting 1 or more other protected computers) aggregating at least $5,000 in value;

    (II) the modification or impairment, or potential modification or impairment, of the medical examination, diagnosis, treatment, or care of 1 or more individuals;

    (III) physical injury to any person;

    (IV) a threat to public health or safety;

    (V)   damage affecting a computer used by or for an entity of the United States Government in furtherance of the administration of justice, national defense, or national security; or

    (VI) damage affecting 10 or more protected computers during any 1-year period; or

(ii) an attempt to commit an offence punishable under this subparagraph;

(B) except as provided in subparagraphs (E) and (F), a fine under this title, imprisonment for not more than 10 years, or both, in the case of—

(i) an offence under subsection (a)(5)(A), which does not occur after a conviction for another offence under this section, if the offence caused (or, in the case of an attempted offence, would, if completed, have caused) a harm provided in subclauses (I) through (VI) of subparagraph (A)(i); or

(ii) an attempt to commit an offence punishable under this subparagraph;

(C) except as provided in subparagraphs (E) and (F), a fine under this title, imprisonment for not more than 20 years, or both, in the case of—

    (i) an offence or an attempt to commit an offence under subparagraphs (A) or (B) of subsection (a)(5) that occurs after a conviction for another offence under this section; or

    (ii) an attempt to commit an offence punishable under this subparagraph;

(D) a fine under this title, imprisonment for not more than 10 years, or both, in the case of—

    (i) an offence or an attempt to commit an offence under subsection (a)(5)(C) that occurs after a conviction for another offence under this section; or

    (ii) an attempt to commit an offence punishable under this subparagraph;

(E) if the offender attempts to cause or knowingly or recklessly causes serious bodily injury from conduct in violation of subsection (a)(5)(A), a fine under this title, imprisonment for not more than 20 years, or both;

(F) if the offender attempts to cause or knowingly or recklessly causes death from conduct in violation of subsection (a)(5)(A), a fine under this title, imprisonment for any term of years or for life, or both; or

(G) a fine under this title, imprisonment for not more than 1 year, or both, for—

    (i) any other offence under subsection (a)(5); or

    (ii) an attempt to commit an offence punishable under this subparagraph.

(d) (1) The United States Secret Service shall, in addition to any other agency having such authority, have the authority to investigate offences under this section.

(2) The Federal Bureau of Investigation shall have primary authority to investigate offences under subsection (a)(1) for any cases involving espionage, foreign counterintelligence,

information protected against unauthorized disclosure for reasons of national defense or foreign relations, or Restricted Data (as that term is defined in section 11y of the Atomic Energy Act of 1954 (42 U.S.C. 2014(y)), except for offences affecting the duties of the United States Secret Service pursuant to section 3056(a) of this title.

(3) Such authority shall be exercised in accordance with an agreement which shall be entered into by the Secretary of the Treasury and the Attorney General.

(e) As used in this section—

(1) the term "computer" means an electronic, magnetic, optical, electrochemical, or other high-speed data processing device performing logical, arithmetic, or storage functions, and includes any data storage facility or communications facility directly related to or operating in conjunction with such device, but such term does not include an automated typewriter or typesetter, a portable hand-held calculator, or other similar device;

(2) the term "protected computer" means a computer—

(A) exclusively for the use of a financial institution or the United States Government, or, in the case of a computer not exclusively for such use, used by or for a financial institution or the United States Government and the conduct constituting the offence affects that use by or for the financial institution or the Government; or

(B) which is used in or affecting interstate or foreign commerce or communication, including a computer located outside the United States that is used in a manner that affects interstate or foreign commerce or communication of the United States;

(3) the term "State" includes the District of Columbia, the Commonwealth of Puerto Rico, and any other commonwealth, possession or territory of the United States;

(4) the term "financial institution" means—

(A) an institution, with deposits insured by the Federal Deposit Insurance Corporation;

(B)   the Federal Reserve or a member of the Federal Reserve including any Federal Reserve Bank;

(C)   a credit union with accounts insured by the National Credit Union Administration;

(D)   a member of the Federal home loan bank system and any home loan bank;

(E)   any institution of the Farm Credit System under the **Farm Credit Act of 1971**;

(F)   a broker-dealer registered with the Securities and Exchange Commission pursuant to **section 15 of the Securities Exchange Act of 1934**;

(G)   the Securities Investor Protection Corporation;

(H)   a branch or agency of a foreign bank (as such terms are defined in paragraphs (1) and (3) of **section 1(b) of the International Banking Act of 1978**); and

(I)   an organization operating under section 25 or section 25(a) [1] of the Federal Reserve Act;

(5)   the term "financial record" means information derived from any record held by a financial institution pertaining to a customer's relationship with the financial institution;

(6)   the term "exceeds authorized access" means to access a computer with authorization and to use such access to obtain or alter information in the computer that the accesser is not entitled so to obtain or alter;

(7)   the term "department of the United States" means the legislative or judicial branch of the Government or one of the executive departments enumerated in section 101 of title 5;

(8)   the term "damage" means any impairment to the integrity or availability of data, a program, a system, or information;

(9)   the term "government entity" includes the Government of the United States, any State or political subdivision of the United States, any foreign country, and any state, province, municipality, or other political subdivision of a foreign country;

(10) the term "conviction" shall include a conviction under the law of any State for a crime punishable by imprisonment for more than 1 year, an element of which is unauthorized access, or exceeding authorized access, to a computer;

(11) the term "loss" means any reasonable cost to any victim, including the cost of responding to an offence, conducting a damage assessment, and restoring the data, program, system, or information to its condition prior to the offence, and any revenue lost, cost incurred, or other consequential damages incurred because of interruption of service; and

(12) the term "person" means any individual, firm, corporation, educational institution, financial institution, governmental entity, or legal or other entity.

(f) This section does not prohibit any lawfully authorized investigative, protective, or intelligence activity of a law enforcement agency of the United States, a State, or a political subdivision of a State, or of an intelligence agency of the United States.

(g) Any person who suffers damage or loss by reason of a violation of this section may maintain a civil action against the violator to obtain compensatory damages and injunctive relief or other equitable relief. A civil action for a violation of this section may be brought only if the conduct involves 1 of the factors set forth in subclauses (I), (II), (III), (IV), or (V) of subsection (c)(4)(A)(i). Damages for a violation involving only conduct described in subsection (c)(4)(A)(i)(I) are limited to economic damages. No action may be brought under this subsection unless such action is begun within 2 years of the date of the act complained of or the date of the discovery of the damage. No action may be brought under this subsection for the negligent design or manufacture of computer hardware, computer software, or firmware.

(h) The Attorney General and the Secretary of the Treasury shall report to the Congress annually, during the first 3 years following the date of the enactment of this subsection, concerning investigations and prosecutions under subsection (a)(5).

(i) (1) The court, in imposing sentence on any person convicted of a violation of this section, or convicted of conspiracy to violate this section, shall order, in addition to any other sentence imposed and irrespective of any provision of State law, that such person forfeit to the United States—

    (A) such person's interest in any personal property that was used or intended to be used to commit or to facilitate the commission of such violation; and

    (B) any property, real or personal, constituting or derived from, any proceeds that such person obtained, directly or indirectly, as a result of such violation.

(2) The criminal forfeiture of property under this subsection, any seizure and disposition thereof, and any judicial proceeding in relation thereto, shall be governed by the provisions of section 413 of the Comprehensive Drug Abuse Prevention and Control Act of 1970 (21 U.S.C. 853), except subsection (d) of that section.

(j) For purposes of subsection (i), the following shall be subject to forfeiture to the United States and no property right shall exist in them:

(1) Any personal property used or intended to be used to commit or to facilitate the commission of any violation of this section, or a conspiracy to violate this section.

(2) Any property, real or personal, which constitutes or is derived from proceeds traceable to any violation of this section, or a conspiracy to violate this section.

CASE STUDY: MAIL FRAUD

Allen Weintraub, 48, of Boynton Beach, was sentenced on April 24, 2014 by U.S. District Judge Donald Graham to 111 months in prison, three years of supervised release, and was ordered to forfeit one hundred forty thousand two hundred eighty dollars and forty-seven cents and to pay the same amount in restitution to two victims of a scheme to sell Facebook shares.

In February 2014, Weintraub pled guilty to two counts of mail fraud. According to an agreed factual proffer, in February 2012, Weintraub, using an alias, steered potential investors seeking to purchase pre-IPO stock of Facebook to the website of Private Stock Transfer Inc. by posting a response on www.quora.com. In that post, Weintraub claimed that he had purchased Facebook stock from Private Stock Transfer Inc. When victims went to the website and sought information on purchasing Facebook stock, Weintraub responded representing that Private Stock Transfer Inc. had thousands of Facebook shares available for purchase. He directed that various forms be completed which represented that victims were purchasing shares described as "Facebook Inc. by and through PST Investment III, Inc. Class A shares on a one for one conversion basis." PST Investment III Inc. was another company associated with Weintraub. After the victims sent payment to Weintraub's bank accounts, Weintraub issued and mailed stock certificates for PST Investment III shares that would convert to Facebook shares on a one-for-one basis once Facebook went public. In reality, neither Weintraub nor Private Stock Transfer Inc. had any Facebook shares. The two victims were defrauded a total of four hundred and fourteen thousand dollars.

This case was prosecuted by Assistant U.S. Attorney Lois Foster-Steers.[604]

CASE STUDY: MEDICARE FRAUD

A Houston woman and a California man were ordered to federal prison for conspiring to defraud Medicare through so-called diagnostic testing labs in the Houston area. Zaven "George" Sarkisian,

---

604 Federal Bureau of Investigation (2014), 'Facebook Fraudster Sentenced', Available at: https://www.fbi.gov/contact-us/field-offices/miami/news/press-releases/facebook-fraudster-sentenced (accessed 6 September 2017).

55, of Fresno, California, and Konna Hanks, 48, of Houston, pleaded guilty Dec. 9 and 2, 2015, respectively.

On June 1, 2017, U.S. District Judge Keith P. Ellison ordered Sarkisian to serve the statutory maximum of 10 years in prison. In handing down the sentence, Judge Ellison imposed enhancements for obstruction of Medicare's administrative investigation, leadership role, abuse of Medicare's trust, sophisticated means and loss to a federal health care program of more than one million dollars. The court noted Sarkisian's conspiracy was plotted over a long period of time and was "extremely serious." For her role, Hanks will serve a total of 37 months in prison. As part of their pleas, Sarkisian and Hanks acknowledged they caused actual losses in the amounts of four million four hundred twelve thousand nine hundred forty-four dollars and two million five hundred sixty-nine thousand five hundred thirty dollars, respectively. Both defendants were also ordered to pay full restitution to Medicare.

"The sentence imposed today demonstrates the gravity of Sarkisian's actions," said Martinez. "He created an elaborate scheme and used others to bilk millions out of Medicare even after they attempted to cut his federal funding."

From 2012 to August 2014, Sarkisian formed 11 diagnostic testing "clinics" that the conspirators used to fraudulently bill Medicare for services and diagnostic tests that were not actually performed or were medically unnecessary. Hanks worked with Sarkisian at seven of the clinics and recruited and paid Medicare beneficiaries to attend his clinics.

Marketers such as Hanks paid Medicare beneficiaries to attend the clinics so they could use their Medicare numbers to fraudulently bill Medicare. Sarkisian paid these marketers eighty dollars to a hundred dollars cash, knowing they would keep part of this fee and pay the rest to the beneficiary.

Sarkisian told co-conspirators to order ultrasounds, allergy tests and pulmonary function tests for each beneficiary, regardless of circumstances. He also instructed others to ensure every beneficiary had poor circulation, shortness of breath, heart problems and allergies written in their chart.

Medicare eventually put Sarkisian's first clinic on pre-payment review, thus drastically slowing down the flow of Medicare payments. He then recruited others to form new clinics and to open bank accounts in their names even though Sarkisian would actually be the owner of the clinics and who received proceeds.

Sarkisian was taken into custody following the sentencing today where he will remain pending transfer to a U.S. Bureau of Prisons facility to be determined in the near future. Hanks had been previously on bond but was later ordered into custody for violating her conditions of release.

Two others - Darryl Johnson, 33, of Richmond, and Hmyak "Hamlet" Samsonyan, 47, of Katy, also pleaded guilty and are awaiting sentencing.

The FBI Health Care Fraud Task Force, Texas Attorney General's Medicaid Fraud Control Unit and the Department of Health and Human Services - Office of Inspector General, Office of Investigations conducted the investigation. Assistant U.S. Attorneys Michael Chu and Jason Smith are prosecuting the case.[605]

CASE STUDY: CONSPIRACY TO COMMIT WIRE AND SECURITIES FRAUD

Like many successful con men, William C. Lange made people believe that he really cared about them—even as he looked them in the eye and took their money.

The 67-year-old Washington state businessman was sentenced in March, 2015 to 22 years in federal prison for swindling more than 300 investors in the U.S. and overseas out of ten million dollars. He had befriended some of his victims at Rotary Club functions. Many thought they would be getting loans to rebuild after the devastation of Hurricane Katrina in 2005.

"Unfortunately, this type of white-collar crime is all too common," said Special Agent Ben Williamson, who investigated the case

---

605   United States Department of Justice (2017), 'Medicare Fraudster Given Maximum Prison Sentence', Available at: https://www.justice.gov/usao-sdtx/pr/medicare-fraudster-given-maximum-prison-sentence (accessed 5 September 2017).

with Special Agent Mike Brown from the FBI's Seattle Field Office. "Some investors lost their life savings."

Lange and his co-conspirators, including his son, operated two companies that were "based entirely on lies," Brown said. Lange founded the Harbor Funding Group, Inc. (HFGI) in 2006, and not long after began to target real estate developers and their clients seeking to rebuild after Hurricane Katrina. The pitch was that HFGI had access to lenders and millions of dollars in funds to finance real estate projects. To get that money, however, HFGI required investors to place 10 percent of the loan amount in an escrow account.

In reality, HFGI had neither lenders nor funds. And as soon as the money was placed in escrow, Lange took it to finance his own lavish lifestyle.

That advance fee scheme netted more than nine million dollars, which Lange spent on salaries, fishing and hunting trips, landscaping for his new house, Harley-Davidson motorcycles, and other business ventures. After the money was gone, Lange set up another sham business—Black Sand Mine, Inc. (BSMI)—with the supposed intention of mining gold and other precious metals on an Alaskan island.

Beginning in 2009, Lange convinced investors—through lies and misrepresentations—to purchase BSMI stock. Almost one million dollars was collected, but instead of using it to mine for gold, the money was spent on salaries and other personal expenses for Lange and his crew.

The FBI began to receive complaints about Lange's business dealings, and in 2009 partnered with the U.S. Postal Inspection Service, which had also begun looking into his activities. During the investigation, countless financial documents were reviewed, victims were interviewed, and cooperating witnesses were engaged to help unravel the frauds. Lange was arrested in 2011.

In September 2014, Lange pled guilty to conspiracy to commit wire and securities fraud and admitted his leadership role in both the advance fee fraud and the gold mine investment schemes. Other co-conspirators have already been convicted or pled guilty in related cases, Williamson said, "but clearly Lange was the mastermind behind these crimes."

Both Williamson and Brown are pleased that Lange received a lengthy jail term, but they also remember the hundreds of victims in the case.

One individual who lost nearly one hundred thousand dollars in the HFGI scheme wrote in a victim impact statement for the court, "Our life savings have gone—we have nothing. Life financially has been horrific for us." Another HFGI victim wrote, "We live in England, and this property investment opportunity was widely publicized here as a way to make a positive contribution to rebuilding the Katrina affected area as well as making a financial return."

"We are glad that Lange is off the streets," Brown said, "and unable to victimize anyone else."[606]

How to Avoid Becoming a Victim of financial fraud

FBI agents who specialize in financial fraud stress that investors need to exercise common sense before giving someone their money. "There are no quick ways to get rich," said Special Agent Ben Williamson. "If an investment opportunity seems too good to be true, it probably is."

Before investing your money, it's always a good idea to:

- Do your research. Who are you dealing with? Check for complaints with the Better Business Bureau and elsewhere online.
- Talk to as many people as you can about the investment. Get second opinions.
- Don't rush into any decisions.
- If you are engaging in risky investments, be willing to lose what you put in.[607]

---

606 Federal Bureau of Investigation (2015), 'Lengthy Prison Term for Advance Fee Fraudster', Available at: https://www.fbi.gov/news/stories/advance-fee-fraudster (accessed 5 September 2017).

607 Federal Bureau of Investigation (2015), 'Lengthy Prison Term for Advance Fee Fraudster', Available at: https://www.fbi.gov/news/stories/advance-fee-fraudster (accessed 5 September 2017).

13.1.3 United Kingdom

In England and Wales, criminal fraud is mainly dealt with in the **Fraud Act 2006 (FA 2006)**.

Section 1 of the Act establishes a new general offence of fraud, which can be committed in three ways: fraud by false representation; fraud by failing to disclose information; and fraud by abuse of position. These are set out in sections 2, 3 and 4 respectively.

There are two basic requirements which must be met before any of the three limbs of the new offence can be charged. First, the behaviour of the defendant must be dishonest. Second it must also be his intention to make a gain, or cause a loss to another. However, there will no longer be any need to prove that a gain or loss has been made, or that any victim was deceived by the defendant's behaviour. Each of the three limbs of the offence carries a maximum sentence of 10 years.

Section 2 makes it an offence to commit fraud by false representation in any form. For a representation to be false, the representation being made must be wrong or misleading, and the person making it must know that it is, or might be, wrong or misleading. For example, a section 2 offence would be committed by a "phisher", i.e. a person who sends emails to large groups of people falsely representing that the email has been sent by a legitimate financial institution. The email prompts the reader to provide information such as credit card and bank account numbers so that the "phisher" can gain access to their assets. It makes no difference if the representation is made to a machine or to a person. For example, a false representation involving the inputting of a number into a CHIP and PIN machine would also be covered by the offence.

*Section 3_* makes it an offence for a person to fail to disclose information to another person where there is a legal duty to disclose the information. It would be a section 3 offence for example if a doctor failed to disclose to a hospital that certain patients referred by him for treatment are private patients, thereby avoiding a charge for the services provided.

*Section 4_* makes it an offence to commit fraud by abuse of one's position; meaning taking advantage of a position where one is expected to safeguard another's financial interests. The offence can be committed by omission or by a positive action, so that a failure to act in the interests of another could be caught by section 4, (provided, as in each of the sections 2-4, that the behaviour was dishonest and aimed at making a gain or causing a loss). Section 4 would cover, for example, a case where an employee of a software company uses his position to clone software products with the intention of selling the products to make a profit for himself, or a case where an employee copies his employer's client database for the purpose for setting up a rival company. It would also cover a case where a person is employed to care for an elderly or disabled person has access to that person's bank account and abuses his position by transferring funds to invest in a high-risk business venture of his own.

Section 6 makes it an offence to possess articles for use in frauds. So far as fraud is concerned, it replaces section 25 of the Theft Act 1968, which makes it an offence for a person to have with him, when not at his place of abode, any article for use in the course of any burglary, theft or cheat. The types of articles that could be caught by the offence include lists of other peoples' credit card details, or software used for producing blank utility bills. "For use" is a key phrase in both provisions and it requires a general, not a specific, intent to commit fraud to be proved. The crucial difference between the offences is that section 6 also applies to articles found in the offender's home. The offence carries a maximum sentence of 5 years.

Section 7 makes it an offence to make or supply articles for use in frauds, and carries a sentence of 10 years. It is designed to catch, for example, those who supply personal financial details for use in frauds to be carried out by other people. It is also designed to catch those who manufacture devices, such as software programmes for generating credit card numbers, which are to be used in frauds by other people.

Section 9 mirrors the fraudulent trading offence in section 458 of the Companies Act 1985 which covers UK companies. Section 9 is a new offence which applies to businesses not caught by the Companies Act offence - meaning sole traders, partnerships, trusts, companies registered overseas, etc. Section 9 is an "activity" offence, meaning that it captures a course of conduct, and is not limited to specific transactions. The offence (and section 458) will carry a maximum sentence of 10 years. An example of fraudulent trading would be a pattern of behaviour by a dishonest roof repairer who consistently inflated bills and charged for work he had not done.

Section 11 makes it an offence to obtain services dishonestly, thus creating a new "theft-like" offence to cover services, which addresses the current loophole which exists because services cannot be stolen under the Theft Acts and because the current offence of obtaining of services 'by deception' cannot be charged when services are obtained from machines. The offence covers, for example, the situation where a person attaches a decoder to a television to enable viewing access to cable / satellite television channels for which a charge is made but which he has no intention of paying.[608]

CASE STUDY: IMPERSONATION FRAUD

A group of fraudsters who spent four years taking driving tests for other people were sentenced to three years in prison.

The group, headed by Dzemail Trstena, aged 45, from Belgium, charged provisional licence holders up to two thousand five hundred pounds to sit theory or practical driving tests for them at centres all around the Home Counties and West Midlands.

A joint investigation between the National Crime Agency (NCA) and Met Police's Organised Crime Partnership (OCP) and the Driving Vehicle Standards Agency (DVSA) identified that the same person, Emil Petkov, aged 30, from Bulgaria, was the subject of a large number of impersonation reports being filed by test centres. Closed-circuit television (CCTV) footage confirmed Petkov being turned away from over 30 theory tests between 2010 and 2014 when the photographic identity document (ID) he presented was not his.

---

608 Home Office (2006), 'The Fraud Act 2006: repeal of the deception offences in the Theft Acts 1968 – 1996', Available at: https://www.gov.uk/government/publications/the-fraud-act-2006-repeal-of-the-deception-offences-in-the-theft-acts-1968-1996 (accessed 23 August 2017).

Investigators identified two further impersonators, Musa Matluma, aged 34, from Macedonia, who was arrested on 30 June 2014 whilst fraudulently sitting a theory test, and Colin Julian, aged 42, a bus driver from the UK.

Trstena and Julian were arrested at their homes on 1 July 2014, while Petkov handed himself in to Leytonstone Police Station later that day. Searches found them to be in possession of a large number of provisional licences and theory test booking documents.

Julian and Trstena are known to have been responsible for a successful practical driving test impersonation at Kettering in June 2014, however the total number of successful tests cannot be quantified.

Seven provisional licence holders, whose documents were found in the group's possession, have also been prosecuted. Investigators believe their main motivation in using impersonators was to bypass the language restriction of taking the test in English or Welsh.

Trstena, Petkov and Julian were sentenced on 12 August at Blackfriars Crown Court to 15, 12 and 9 months respectively. Matluma was sentenced along with the seven provisional licence holders in March 2016 at the same court. Full details below.

Spencer Barnett from the Organised Crime Partnership said:

"These men conspired to make a criminal profit with no regard for the risk that they were helping potentially dangerous and unskilled drivers onto Britain's roads.

"Trstena was the coordinator, ferrying his fake candidates to test centres around the country and adopting the role of 'instructor' as part of the fraud.

"We will never know how many tests they successfully cheated, but they were brazen and persistent in their repeated attempts. I have no doubt that they would have kept going had we not stopped them when we did."

Andy Rice, Head of Counter-Fraud & Investigations at DVSA said:

"Although instances of impersonation fraud are rare in relation to over 3m theory and practical driving tests which are taken each year, DVSA continues to take them seriously, and work closely with the police and NCA to bring offenders to justice."

"Impersonators taking tests on behalf of others allow untested and unqualified drivers onto our roads. These unqualified individuals pose a real risk to other road users and pedestrians as they have never been tested to ensure that they meet the minimum standards for driving and are unsafe."[609]

CASE STUDY: WINE AND MORTGAGE FRAUD

The National Crime Agency had seized assets worth six hundred thousand pounds from an organised crime group linked to wine and mortgage fraud.

NCA officers seized two flats and the freehold title for the flats' building after making a civil recovery order under the Proceeds of Crime Act 2002.

The properties were believed to be bought with the proceeds of crime by the defendants John George Evans, 34, his wife Josephine Evans, 34, his brother Richard Lee Evans, 29, and their mother Joan Ann Evans, 58.

Officers also seized two hundred eighty-eight thousand three hundred forty-one pounds from bank accounts belonging to John Evans, his wife and mother.

The money was what remained from the sale of a property in Bromley bought through mortgage fraud.

It is the NCA's belief that the properties were funded by fraudulent trading, money laundering, tax evasion and mortgage fraud.

One fraud involved two apparent wine investment companies, Fine Wine Vintners Limited and Beaumont Vintners Limited, which took customers' money but rarely provided their wine.

John Evans ran Fine Wine Vintners but was disqualified in 2013 from being a director for 12 years.

---

609 National Crime Agency (2016), 'Fraudsters took driving tests for £2,500', Available at: http://www.nationalcrimeagency.gov.uk/news/901-fraudsters-took-driving-tests-for-2-500 (accessed 4 September 2017).

He and his brother Richard received money from both wine companies.

In response to the NCA's investigation, the family agreed to settle by handing over the money and two properties in Sidcup Hill, Sidcup, Kent.[610]

13.2 Discussion

This section discusses some current fraud trends and risks, and provides tips on how to guard against them.

13.2.1 Protecting Your Mobile Device Against "Sim Swap Fraud"

There is a new and little-reported scam which overrides the additional security introduced by banks to protect customer transactions. It is called "sim swap fraud". Fraudsters can complete cash transfers from a stranger's account by accessing one-time Personal Identification Number (PIN) codes and Short Message Service (SMS) notifications.

Criminal gangs obtain an individual's bank details by bamboozling them with a phishing email, or by purchasing them from organised crime networks.

They then open a parallel business account with the same bank, in the customer's name, since this involves fewer security checks if the account holder is already a customer.

Having worked out possible answers to security questions from the victim's social media accounts, they call the victim's mobile phone provider, posing as the customer, to report that their phone is lost or damaged.

Provided they can answer basic security questions, the old sim is cancelled and a new one activated. From then on they can commandeer their victim's mobile account, intercepting or initiating calls,

---

610 National Crime Agency (2017), 'NCA seizes properties from fine wine and mortgage fraudsters', Available at: http://www.nationalcrimeagency.gov.uk/news/1107-nca-seizes-properties-from-fine-wine-and-mortgage-fraudsters (accessed 5 September 2017).

texts and authorisations such as those used for cash transfers. They can also request that security settings are changed to stop the victim gaining access to their account.

The first the victim will know of a problem is when their mobile stops working and they report it to their provider. In the meantime, their bank account may have been emptied.[611]

The American Bankers Association recommends following these tips to keep your information – and your money – safe, and to guard against 'sim swap fraud.'

- **Keep personal information personal.** Hackers can use social media profiles to figure out your passwords and answer those security questions in the password reset tools. Lock down your privacy settings and avoid posting things like birthdays, addresses, mother's maiden name, etc. Be wary of requests to connect from people you do not know.

- **Use the passcode lock on your smartphone and other devices.** This will make it more difficult for thieves to access your information if your device is lost or stolen.

- **Log out completely when you finish a mobile banking session.**

- **Protect your phone from viruses** and malicious software, or malware, just like you do for your computer by installing mobile security software.

- **Use caution when downloading apps.** Apps can contain malicious software, worms, and viruses. Beware of apps that ask for unnecessary "permissions."

- **Download the updates for your phone and mobile apps.**

- **Avoid storing sensitive information** like passwords or a social security number on your mobile device.

- **Tell your financial institution immediately if you change your phone number or lose your mobile device.**

---

611 The Guardian (2015), 'Sim swap' gives fraudsters access-all-areas via your mobile phone', Available at: https://www.theguardian.com/money/2015/sep/26/sim-swap-fraud-mobile-phone-vodafone-customer (accessed 23 August 2017).

- **Be aware of shoulder surfers.** The most basic form of information theft is observation. Be aware of your surroundings especially when you're punching in sensitive information.
- **Wipe your mobile device before you donate, sell or trade it** using specialized software or using the manufacturer's recommended technique. Some software allows you to wipe your device remotely if it is lost or stolen.
- **Beware of mobile phishing.** Avoid opening links and attachments in emails and texts, especially from senders you don't know. And be wary of ads (not from your security provider) claiming that your device is infected.
- **Watch out for public Wi-Fi.** Public connections aren't very secure, so don't perform banking transactions on a public network. If you need to access your account, try disabling the Wi-Fi and switching to your mobile network.
- **Report any suspected fraud to your bank immediately.**[612]

13.2.2 Protecting Yourself Against Vanity Fraud

Academicians must be wary of vanity fraud. It involves a non-peer review journal impersonating itself as a peer review journal and sending you an email inviting you to submit your article for peer review and then asking you to pay a processing fee of about two hundred dollars. It happens a lot nowadays and most banks unwillingly allow the transaction to go through because it looks very real. The peer review journals have legit websites with legit emails but fake names. Most put Pakistan as the place of business of the Editor-in-Chief so that he or she cannot be traced. Research has shown millions being laundered in the process. Banks won't term it high risk since little cash is involved in the process.

There are many ways to detect vanity fraud.

- A peer review journal would not normally review an article in two weeks. It takes months for that to happen. The fake

---

612 American Bankers Association (2017), 'Protecting Your Mobile Device', Available at: http://www.aba.com/Consumers/Pages/Protect-Mobile.aspx (accessed 23 August 2017).

online journal is likely to tell you that it can reveal your article in a week or two.

- The fake online journal may provide names not known to the public eye. You may see strange names listed on the editorial board of the online journal. Try and do some research using google to find out if that professor really belongs to the University that the website claims he belongs to. You can also find out if it is reputable University and if it is, you should try and contact the individual to ask him whether or not he is aware that his name is on the editorial board of the journal.

- You can check with Thomas Reuters on the impact factor of the journal. You can also send a mail to a reputable University asking it to confirm if the journal is among those recognized by that University.

13.2.3 ATM Safety Tips

Criminals are now using sophisticated methods to uncover card information.

The following case concerns a technique used by computer experts to uncover the PIN CODE of Automated Teller Machine (ATM) cards. Proceeds generated from these crimes are used to purchase iPhones, laptops, wristwatches, a Blackberry phone and a ring.

CASE STUDY: USING SOFTWARE TO UNCOVER AN ATM'S CARD PIN CODE

A driver, Mayowa Adenuga, was arrested on September 9, 2016 by operatives of the Lagos State Police Command for allegedly stealing his boss' Automated Teller Machine (ATM) card and withdrawing over two million seven hundred thousand naira.

Also arrested were suspected accomplices in the crime – Adewale Opeyemi, 18, and Jeremiah Iyitoye, 29.

PUNCH Metro gathered that 25-year-old Adenuga, who is also a computer expert, was employed as a driver by a lecturer at the University of Lagos (UNILAG), Prof. Simbo Banjoko.

It was learnt that the suspect had driven Banjoko to the Bells University on the day of the incident.

While waiting for his boss on the university premises, the driver found Banjoko's Zenith Bank ATM card in the car and hid it.

PUNCH Metro gathered that when the victim did not notice that his ATM card was missing, Adenuga used software to uncover the card's Personal Identification Number (PIN) code.

After withdrawing two hundred thousand naira from the bank account through the ATM, he allegedly bought four iPhones, valued at four hundred and ninety-five thousand naira; one Macbook laptop, valued at four hundred and fifteen thousand naira; 10 wristwatches, a Blackberry and a ring.

It was learnt that a total of two million seven hundred twenty-eight thousand two hundred fifty-five naira was withdrawn from the victim's bank account.

The theft of the ATM card was said to have been referred to the Rapid Response Squad (RRS), which later transferred the case to the Anti-Vice Section of the State Criminal Investigation and Intelligence Department (SCIID), Yaba.

A source said the prime suspect, Adenuga, perfected the crime by blocking his boss' telephone line so that he would not see the alert of transactions conducted on his account.

He said, "The suspect is the lecturer's driver. He is also a computer expert. He hid the ATM card for three days and when he saw that the man did not look for it, he used software to get the PIN. He called Adewale (Opeyemi) and handed over the card to him for safekeeping, saying it belonged to his sister.

"When he drove his boss out again at another time, he had access to the man's phone and deliberately entered the wrong Personal Unblocking Key (PUK) number three times which led to the blockage of the line."

PUNCH Metro was told that having succeeded in blocking the line, the suspect contacted Opeyemi and linked him up with another friend, Iyitoye.

He allegedly asked the duo to make transactions with the card on his behalf.

The two men were said to have gone to Shoprite, Ikeja, and Mega Plaza, Victoria Island, where they withdrew two hundred thousand naira and purchased the iPhones, Macbook laptop, wristwatches and other items through Point of Sale (POS) transactions.

It was gathered that the loot was shared among the three men.

A police source explained that Banjoko, who noticed that his telephone line had been blocked, took it to a telecoms centre, where it was reactivated.

"At that point, he received 30 alerts that a total of two million seven hundred twenty-eight thousand two hundred fifty-five naira had been withdrawn from his account. He reported the matter to the police, and the case was transferred to the RRS.

"When the matter got to the Anti-Vice Section of the SCIID, the police arrested the driver and after interrogation, he confessed to the crime and named his accomplices.

"The police recovered two iPhones 6S Plus, two iPhones SSE, one Macbook laptop, seven GT Shock wristwatches, one Blackberry Z10, one ring and two bags," the source added.

The suspects were arraigned at the Yaba Magistrate's Court on two counts of stealing.

The charge read in part, "That you, Mayowa Adenuga, Adewale Opeyemi and Jeremiah Iyitoye, on July 2, 2016, on Olanireti Fesan Street, Magodo, Isheri, Lagos, in the Lagos Magisterial District, did steal the sum of two million seven hundred twenty-eight thousand two hundred fifty-five naira only, property of one Professor Simbo Banjoko."

The police said the offence was punishable under sections 409 and 285 of the Criminal Law of Lagos State, Nigeria, 2011.

The defendants pleaded not guilty to the charge.

The magistrate, Mrs. O.A. Erinle, admitted them to bail in the sum of eight hundred thousand naira with two sureties in like sum.

She added that one of the sureties must be a blood relation of the defendants, who must be a landlord within the jurisdiction of the court.[613]

---

613 The Punch (2016), 'Driver steals UNILAG lecturer's ATM card, withdraws N2.7m', Available at: http://punchng.com/driver-steals-unilag-lecturers-atm-card-withdraws-n2-7m/ (accessed 30 August 2017).

Protecting Your ATM Card

Always protect your ATM card and keep it in a safe place, just like you would cash, credit cards or checks.

- Do not leave your ATM card lying around the house or on your desk at work. No one should have access to the card but you. Immediately notify your bank if it is lost or stolen.
- Keep your Personal Identification Number (PIN) a secret. Never write it down anywhere, especially on your ATM card.
- Never give any information about your ATM card or PIN over the telephone. For example, if you receive a call, supposedly from your bank or possibly the police, wanting to verify your PIN, do not give that information. Notify the police immediately.

Using an ATM

- Be aware of your surroundings, particularly at night. If you observe or sense suspicious persons or circumstances, do not use the machine at that time.
- Have your ATM card ready and in your hand as you approach the ATM. Don't wait to get to the ATM and then take your card out of your wallet or purse.
- Visually inspect the ATM for possible skimming devices. Potential indicators can include sticky residue or evidence of an adhesive used by criminals to affix the device, scratches, damaged or crooked pieces, loose or extra attachments on the card slot, or noticeable resistance when pressing the keypad.
- Be careful that no one can see you enter your PIN at the ATM. Use your other hand or body to shield the ATM keyboard as you enter your PIN into the ATM.
- To keep your account information confidential, always take your receipts or transaction records with you.

- Do not count or visually display any money you received from the ATM. Immediately put your money into your pocket or purse and count it later.
- If you are using a drive-up ATM, be sure passenger windows are rolled up and all doors are locked. If you leave your car and walk to the ATM, lock your car.

Special Precautions for Using an ATM at Night

- Park close to the ATM in a well-lighted area.
- Take another person with you, if at all possible.
- If the lights at the ATM are not working, don't use it.
- If shrubbery has overgrown or a tree blocks the view, select another ATM and notify your bank.[614]

13.2.4 Protecting Yourself Online

Though the internet has many advantages, it can also make users vulnerable to fraud, identity theft and other scams. According to a Norton Cybercrime Report, 378 million adults worldwide were victims of cybercrime in 2013.

This section uses the "Ighofose Oyoma case study" to illustrate the vulnerability of the internet to online scams.

Case 13.6: Federal Government of Nigeria v. Ighofose Oyoma (Unreported)

A Federal High Court sitting in Warri, Delta State has convicted and sentenced to two years imprisonment one Ighofose Oyoma. Ighofose was first arraigned by the Economic and Financial Crimes Commission, EFCC, on 3rd May, 2016 on a seven-count

614 American Bankers Association (2017), 'ATM Safety Tips', Available at: http://www.aba.com/Consumers/Pages/CNC_contips_atm.aspx (accessed 23 August 2017).

charge bordering on Conspiracy, Forgery and Obtaining Money by False Pretence to the tune of Nine Thousand Two Hundred United States Dollars.

Upon his arraignment, the convict pleaded not guilty to the charge, but later changed his plea to "guilty".

Justice E. A. Obile consequently convicted Ighofose and sentenced him to two years imprisonment with an option of three hundred thousand naira fine to be forfeited to Federal Government. He also ordered that the payment receipt be deposited to the court registry.

Ighofose was arrested sometime in May, 2015 in Calabar, Cross River State following intelligence report on his involvement in internet scams.

During investigation different scam mails which he used in defrauding his victims, mostly foreign women by presenting himself as Mike Anderson, an American businessman, were recovered.

Count one of the charge reads: "that you Ighofose Oyoma (a k a) Mike Anderson on or about the month of May, 2014, at Warri, Delta State within the jurisdiction of this Honorable court did possess documents containing false representation as Mike Anderson, which said representation you made to Sandra 'M' and obtained the sum of one thousand two hundred dollars under false pretence, a pretext you knew to be false and thereby committed an offence contrary to section 1 (1) (a) of the Advance Fee Fraud and Other Related Offences Act, 2006 and punishable under section 1 (3) of the said Act".[615]

Tips to keep you safe online
Having the latest security software, web browser, and operating system are the best defenses against viruses, malware, and other online

---

615 Economic and Financial Crimes Commission (2016), 'Internet Fraudster Bags Two Years Jail Term In Delta State', Available at: https://efccnigeria.org/efcc/news/2082-internet-fraudster-bags-two-years-jail-term-in-delta-state (accessed 1 September 2017).

threats. Turn on automatic updates so you receive the newest fixes as they become available and

- **Set strong passwords**. A strong password is at least eight characters in length and includes a mix of upper and lowercase letters, numbers, and special characters.
- **Watch out for phishing scams.** Phishing scams use fraudulent emails and websites to trick users into disclosing private account or login information. Do not click on links or open any attachments or pop-up screens from sources you are not familiar with.
- **Keep personal information personal**. Hackers can use social media profiles to figure out your passwords and answer those security questions in the password reset tools. Lock down your privacy settings and avoid posting things like birthdays, addresses, mother's maiden name, etc. Be wary of requests to connect from people you do not know.
- **Secure your internet connection**. Always protect your home wireless network with a password. When connecting to public Wi-Fi networks, be cautious about what information you are sending over it.
- **Shop safely.** Before shopping online, make sure the website uses secure technology. When you are at the checkout screen, verify that the web address begins with https. Also, check to see if a tiny locked padlock symbol appears on the page.
- **Read the site's privacy policies.** Though long and complex, privacy policies tell you how the site protects the personal information it collects. If you don't see or understand a site's privacy policy, consider doing business elsewhere.[616]

13.2.5 Protecting Your Identity

Identity theft continues to be one of the fastest growing crimes in Nigeria and the United States. In 2013, an American fell victim to identity fraud every two seconds.

The following case concerns a technique used by fraudsters to obtain peoples' data.

This case study aims to help build awareness with the regulatory, enforcement and customs authorities as well as reporting entities about risks and vulnerabilities of disclosing your Personal Identification Number (PIN) to others, and how to mitigate them.

Case 13.7: Federal Government of Nigeria v. Akinade Tofunmi (UNREPORTED)

Akinade Tofunmi who operates with the identity of her victims raked in about three million naira within 24 hours in her last operation. Her target is usually possible victims in ATM Points and Point of Sales (POS) machines across the country.

One of the methods employed by the suspected fraudster is to politely approach people having difficulty using the ATM and offering to help, only to dupe them after obtaining their personal identification numbers.

This was the scenario that played out on Friday, June 3, 2016, when a woman identified simply as Alhaja attempted to use the ATM in Ibadan, Oyo state while her husband waited for her in the car. Tofunmi observing that the elderly lady had some difficulty, offered to help. In the process, she obtained her PIN number, and after the transaction, swapped her card with another in her possession.

Armed with the card and the PIN as well as the knowledge that the account had a credit balance of three million naira, she made several ATM withdrawals and carried out PoS transactions.

Having exceeded the daily withdrawing limit, Tofunmi waited for a few minutes into the following day which was a Saturday.

Shortly after midnight, she made another round of withdrawals to the tune of one hundred and fifty thousand naira which was also the withdrawal limit for that day.

Since it was a weekend when most are banks officially closed for business, Alhaja and her husband were helpless as debit alerts start coming in torrent.

Not satisfied with what she had stolen, the fraudster started transferring funds out of the account.

In desperate need of where and how to empty the balance in the account, Tofunmi went to a night club where she met a motorcycle transporter, popularly known as Okada rider whom she approached for help.

Her decoy was that she had enough money in her account, but could not access it having exceeded her daily withdrawal limit.

She showed the bike man her balance and pleaded with him to give her his ATM card, account details and PIN for a quick teller transfer from her (Alhaja's) account. With that, she was able to transfer some of Alhaja's money to the bike man's account thereby stealing the identity of the unsuspecting bike man.

To further cover her tracks and ensure a total clear out of the victim's account, she got the motorcyclist to take her to a hotel.

At the hotel reception while paying for her accommodation which was ten thousand naira for a night, she deliberately credited the hotel's account with one hundred and one thousand naira feigning a mistake and demanded a refund of ninety-one thousand naira as overpayment. This was also done with Alhaja's ATM card through the PoS machine at the Hotel.

To further conceal her identity, Tofunmi provided fake personal details in the hotel and gave the hotel the bike man's account detail when the hotel management requested for an account to deposit the refund.

All these happened on a Saturday.

By Sunday, Alhaja's funds had been moved to the fraudster (through both cash withdrawals and transfers to the bike man's account domiciled in the same bank). All the while, the fraudster was in possession of ATM cards of both Alhaja (the first victim) and the bike man (the second victim).

The bike man was arrested on Monday June 5, when he could no longer reach the fraudster on phone and went to the bank to request for another ATM card.

The suspect has allegedly defrauded others and has been spotted in other parts of the country.[617]

Keeping your information Safe

Don't provide your Social Security number or account information to anyone who contacts you online or over the phone. Protect your PINs and passwords and do not share them with anyone. Use a combination of letters and numbers for your passwords and change them periodically. Do not reveal sensitive or personal information on social networking sites and

- **Shred sensitive papers.**

Shred receipts, banks statements and unused credit card offers before throwing them away.

- **Keep an eye out for missing mail.**

Fraudsters look for monthly bank or credit card statements or other mail containing your financial information. Consider enrolling in online banking to reduce the likelihood of paper statements being stolen. Also, don't mail bills from your own mailbox with the flag up.

- **Use online banking to protect yourself.**

Monitor your financial accounts regularly for fraudulent transactions. Sign up for text or email alerts from your bank for certain types of transactions, such as online purchases or transactions of more than $500.

- **Monitor your credit report.**

---

617 Economic and Financial Crimes Commission (2016), 'EFCC Raises the Alarm on Identity Theft', Available at: https://efccnigeria.org/efcc/news/2028-efcc-raises-the-alarm-on-identity-theft (accessed 1 September 2017).

Order a free copy of your credit report every four months from one of the three credit reporting agencies at annualcreditreport.com.

- **Protect your computer.**

Make sure the virus protection software on your computer is active and up to date. When conducting business online, make sure your browser's padlock or key icon is active. Also look for an "s" after the "http" to be sure the website is secure.

- **Protect your mobile device.**

Use the passcode lock on your smartphone and other devices. This will make it more difficult for thieves to access your information if your device is lost or stolen. Before you donate, sell or trade your mobile device, be sure to wipe it using specialized software or using the manufacturer's recommended technique. Some software allows you to wipe your device remotely if it is lost or stolen. Use caution when downloading apps, as they may contain malware and avoid opening links and attachments – especially for senders you don't know.

- **Report any suspected fraud to your bank immediately.**

What to do if you are a victim

- Call your bank and credit card issuers immediately so they can close your accounts.[618]

Further Reading
Refer to Exposing Fraud: Skills, Process and Practicalities (Wiley Corporate F&A) by Ian Ross for guidance on applying sound

618 American Bankers Association (2017), 'Protecting Your Identity', Available at: http://www.aba.com/Consumers/Pages/Protect-ID.aspx (accessed 23 August 2017).

techniques for fraud investigation and detection and related project management. The book is available for sale on Amazon.

In this book, Author Ian Ross (a noted expert in financial fraud and corporate corruption) goes beyond a basic review of investigative approaches and shows how to apply the techniques in real–life situations. Designed to be practical, the book approaches fraud investigation from a project management perspective. I am proud to be a part of such an outstanding project.

Ian Ross gained his initial experience in fraud investigation in the UK police before extending his skills and competencies into the financial and insurance industries, Now with over 20 years' experience, Ian is an established prominent fraud risk specialist and investigator of financial crime, with added supporting skills of asset tracing and intelligence handling to meet modern challenges in countering fraud trends and threats.

Holding a Masters Degree in Fraud and Corruption Studies, supported by professional accreditation, Ian's main focus is on situational corporate fraud, financial fraud, money laundering and cyber-fraud risk.

CHAPTER 14

Tax Evasion: The New Corporate Offence of Failure to Prevent Facilitation of Tax Evasion

Our banking system's vulnerability to money laundering is once again a focal point of debate in the wake of recent disclosures that billions of dollars were siphoned out of Nigeria, the United States and the United Kingdom into accounts at off shore tax havens. Internal data leaked from Panama-based law firm Mossack Fonseca showed that more than five hundred banks, their subsidiaries and branches, including HSBC, Credit Suisse, UBS, Société Générale and RBS-owned Coutts, registered nearly fifteen thousand six hundred shell companies for their customers through the Panama-based law firm Mossack Fonseca.[619]

The United Kingdom has responded viciously to this new revelation by introducing two new criminal offences to tackle corporate facilitation of tax evasion. They are:

1. **The domestic fraud offence** – which criminalises corporations, based anywhere in the world, who fail to put in place

---

619 Moore, S. (2016), 'Panama papers: Banks including HSBC and Credit Suisse deny helping clients avoid tax using offshore companies', Available at: http://economia.icaew.com/news/april-2016/panama-papers-banks-deny-helping-clients-avoid-tax-using-offshore-companies (accessed 23 April 2016), see also Franklin, J and Nebehay, S. (2016), 'Europe's banks under scrutiny as regulators look into Panama Papers', Available at: http://www.reuters.com/article/us-panama-tax-swiss-idUSKCN0X40QG (accessed 23 April 2016).

reasonable procedures to prevent their representatives from criminally facilitating tax evasion.[620]

2. **The overseas fraud offence** – which criminalises corporations carrying out a business in the UK, who fail to put in place reasonable procedures to prevent their representatives facilitating tax evasion in another jurisdiction.[621]

These offences address gaps in the existing law which can act as a disincentive for large multinational businesses to exercise due diligence over their representatives.

At present those deliberately helping others to commit tax evasion take advantage of gaps between domestic criminal justice systems to avoid prosecution, for example by operating out of jurisdictions that do not recognise tax evasion as a criminal offence. Applying the new corporate offences beyond the borders of the UK helps to address this. The Government is aiming for the new offence to act as a deterrent to corporations from providing services for this purpose, and incentivising them to ensure their agents aren't complicit in illegal activity.

For the corporation to be liable under the new offence, there must have been:

i. **Stage one**: criminal tax evasion by a taxpayer (either an individual or an entity) under the existing law.

ii. **Stage two**: criminal facilitation of this offence by a representative of the corporation, as defined by the **Accessories and Abettors Act 1861**.

iii. **Stage three**: the corporation failed to prevent its representative from committing the criminal act outlined at stage two.

The corporation may choose to put forward a defence (on the balance of probabilities) of having put in place "reasonable procedures" to prevent the action at stage two.[622]

---

620 Criminal Finances Act 2017, s. 45
621 Criminal Finances Act 2017, s. 46
622 Criminal Finances Act 2017, s. 45 (2), s. 46 (3)

The United States and Nigeria do not make facilitation of tax evasion illegal. It is necessary that they make it a crime if companies fail to put in place measures to stop economic crime, such as tax evasion. The measure would help to tackle those professionals and corporations who facilitate tax evasion across borders.

Tax evasion is a predicate offence leading to money laundering. Failing to report knowledge or suspicions relating to such an activity is an offence under the UK Criminal Finances Act.[623]

14.1 How Does This New Measure Apply to Nigeria and the United States?

If a corporation is operating in Nigeria and the United States and a person providing services for that corporation is deliberately and dishonestly facilitating the evasion of taxes in the UK, then that corporation would be liable under the new offence, regardless of the fact that the corporation is operating in Nigeria or the United States.

If that corporation is based in Nigeria and the United States but is carrying out part of a business in the UK, and a person providing services for that corporation is deliberately and dishonestly facilitating the evasion of taxes in Kenya, then that corporation will be liable in the UK by virtue of carrying out a business activity in the UK.

Similarly, if an individual is providing services for a corporation based in Nigeria deliberately and dishonestly facilitates a tax evasion whilst physically present in the UK, then that corporation is liable.

---

623 The Joint Money Laundering Steering Group JMLSG, Prevention of money laundering/combating terrorist financing 2017 Revised Version, Guidance for the UK financial sector Part I, June 2017 (Amended December 2017), Paragraph 5.1.12

CHAPTER 15

CONFISCATION AND PROVISIONAL MEASURES

The Financial Action Task Force has advised countries to adopt measures similar to those set forth in the Vienna Convention and the Palermo Convention, including legislative measures, to enable their competent authorities to freeze or seize and confiscate the following, without prejudicing the rights of *bona fide* third parties: (a) property laundered, (b) proceeds from, or instrumentalities used in or intended for use in money laundering or predicate offences, (c) property that is the proceeds of, or used in, or intended or allocated for use in, the financing of terrorism, terrorist acts or terrorist organisations, or (d) property of corresponding value.[624]

Such measures should include the authority to: (a) identify, trace and evaluate property that is subject to confiscation; (b) carry out provisional measures, such as freezing and seizing, to prevent any dealing, transfer or disposal of such property; (c) take steps that will prevent or void actions that prejudice the country's ability to freeze or seize or recover property that is subject to confiscation; and (d) take any appropriate investigative measures.[625]

According to the FATF, Countries should consider adopting measures that allow such proceeds or instrumentalities to be confiscated without requiring a criminal conviction (non-conviction based confiscation), or which require an offender to demonstrate the

---

624   The FATF Recommendations 2012, Recommendation 4
625   Ibid.

lawful origin of the property alleged to be liable to confiscation, to the extent that such a requirement is consistent with the principles of their domestic law.[626]

Chapter 5 of this book analysed the policies and procedures involved in the seizure/forfeiture of terrorist property as it relates to Nigeria, the United States and the United Kingdom. This chapter examines the policies and procedures involved in the seizure/forfeiture and confiscation of property laundered or proceeds from, or instrumentalities used in or intended for use in money laundering or predicate offences as it relates to Nigeria, the United States and the United Kingdom.

15.1 Nigeria

Nigeria law provides for the confiscation of laundered properties which represent proceeds from, instrumentalities used in and instrumentalities intended to be used for the commission of money laundering, and other illegal acts and property of corresponding value. At the moment, the types of measures for recovery of proceeds of crime in Nigeria are Criminal Judicial Forfeiture and non-conviction based asset forfeiture.

15.1.1 Criminal Judicial Forfeiture

Confiscation, freezing and seizure measures are provided for in **sections 20 to 26 of the Economic and Financial Crimes Commission (Establishment) Act, 2004 (EFCC Act, 2004)**. While Section 34 with its schedule B specifies the procedure for freezing suspects' accounts in a bank or other financial institution, Section 26 deals with seizure of property pursuant to arrest, search or confiscation. The specific provisions on confiscation are found in Sections 20 – 25 of the same EFCC Act.

In addition to this general statutory framework, other legislation has provisions that empower the authorities to freeze, seize

---

626 The FATF Recommendations 2012, Recommendation 4

and confiscate laundered assets through a court order. For example, **sections 27 to 33 of the National Drug Law Enforcement Agency Act 1989 as amended (NDLEA Act)** cover situations where the source of the proceeds is from trafficking in narcotics, and **sections 37 and 38 of the Corrupt Practices and other Related Offences Act, 2000 (ICPC Act, 2000)**, where the source is from corruption. The legal frameworks do not only deal with proceeds of the laundered assets and properties but also the instrumentalities used for the commission of money laundering offences. From the statutory provisions, the following authorities are involved in taking specific provisional actions at various levels – the Economic and Financial Crimes Commission (EFCC), National Drug Law Enforcement Agency (NDLEA), Customs, Police, the Attorney General, Independent Corrupt Practices and Other Related Offences Commission (ICPC), and the financial supervisory authorities such as the Central Bank of Nigeria (CBN) and the Nigerian Financial Intelligence Unit (NFIU).

Each institution can apply for an interim order. The court may, under **section 29 (b) of the EFCC Act** make an interim order of forfeiture where there is prima facie evidence that the property is liable to forfeiture. Under **section 30 of the EFCC Act**, once a conviction is secured, the EFCC can apply to the court for the order of confiscation.[627] The Commission then sells the property and pays the proceeds to the Consolidated Fund of the Federation.

The Attorney-General under **S. 31 (4) of the EFCC Act** is empowered to make rules or regulations for the sale of confiscated properties. Apart from the **NDLEA Act**, neither the **EFCC Act** nor the **Money Laundering Prohibition Act 2011 (as amended)** defines the terms: "freezing', "seizure' and "confiscation". These concepts constitute critical enforcement stages in any Anti-Money Laundering/ Countering the Financing of Terrorism (AML/CFT) regime.

---

627 Also note that where the accused is discharged and acquitted by a Court of the offences charged, the Court is empowered under section 33 of the EFCC Act to revoke the interim order of attachment." See Dangabar v. F.R.N. (2014) 12 N.W.L.R. (Pt. 1422) 575 at 603 for more on this issue.

Other types of measures for recovery of proceeds of crime include seizure and forfeiture of cash and assets either through plea bargaining or through a court order.[628]

BOX 15.1.1: POWER OF EFCC TO SEIZE AND ATTACH ASSETS AND PROPERTIES AND CONDITION PRECEDENT TO MAKING INTERIM ORDER OF FORFEITURE OF SUCH ASSETS

Under section 28 of the EFCC Act, the Economic and Financial Crimes Commission is empowered not only to arrest any person suspected to have committed an offence under the EFCC Act but also to trace and attach all the assets and properties of the accused person or persons suspected to have been acquired as a result of such economic or financial crime and subsequently cause to be obtained an interim attachment order from Court. Section 28 therefore confers a ready-made license to the EFCC to attach or seize any property suspected by it to have been acquired by committing any offence under EFCC Act. This is the one single method provided for in the EFCC Act for immediate attachment or seizure of any property suspected to have been acquired through any means constituting an offence under the EFCC Act. The provision of section 28 could, therefore, hardly be divorced from the next immediate provision of section 29 of the same law. Particularly, paragraph (a) thereof makes a clear link between the two provisions by making reference to seizure of assets or properties of any person arrested for an offence under the EFCC Act. While paragraph (b) refers to assets or properties otherwise seized by the EFCC that is with or without arresting the suspects, the EFCC is required after

628 The Inter-Governmental Action Group against Money Laundering in West Africa (**GIABA**) (2008), 'Mutual Evaluation Report: Anti-Money Laundering and Combating the Financing of Terrorism', Available at: http://www.giaba.org/media/f/299_Mutual%20Evaluation%20Report%20of%20Nigeria.pdf (accessed 2 January 2016).

the attachment or seizure of property under paragraph (a) or (b) of section 29 to apply ex-parte for an interim order of attachment forfeiting the property concerned to the Federal Government. It is only upon such an ex-parte application that the Court is empowered by the said section 29 to make an interim order for forfeiture of the already seized property to the Federal Government, if it is satisfied that there is prima facie evidence that the property concerned is liable to forfeiture.[629]

BOX 15.1.2: PROCEDURE FOR FORFEITURE OF PROPERTIES UNDER THE EFCC ACT

The first step as provided by section 28 of the EFCC Act is for the EFCC to attach any property or asset suspected to have been acquired by way of committing an offence under the Act, and later apply to Court for an interim attachment order. It is however not open for the EFCC to jump this simple and friendly procedure to simply apply for interim forfeiture of the various properties of the accused persons to the Federal Government thereby putting the cart before the horse. The power of the EFCC to make an application for forfeiture only matures upon lawful seizure of the property as provided by section 28 of the EFCC Act.[630]

The seizure of property by the EFCC is therefore a necessary precondition to a competent *ex-parte* motion for an interim order of forfeiture of property to the Federal Government. It further follows that the application by which the interim order for forfeiture was granted by the Court below was incompetent since it was made without valid seizure of the property and assets in question.[631]

629 Dangabar v. F.R.N. (2014) 12 N.W.L.R. (Pt. 1422) 575 at 599 – 600; Nwaigwe v. F.R.N. (2009) 16 N.W.L.R. (Pt. 1166) 169 at 190; Nwude v. Chairman, EFCC (2005) All F.W.L.R. (Pt. 276) page 740.
630 Nwaigwe v. F.R.N. (2009) 16 N.W.L.R. (Pt. 1166) 169 at 191 - 192.
631 Nwaigwe v. F.R.N. (2009) 16 N.W.L.R. (Pt. 1166) 169 at 191

15.1.2. Non-Conviction Based Asset Forfeiture

A "non-conviction based asset forfeiture" usually begins when the Economic and Financial Crimes Commission (EFCC) or the Independent Corrupt Practices and Other Related Offences Commission (ICPC) seizes an asset identified during the course of a criminal investigation. Once the asset is seized, the EFCC/ICPC will get an interim forfeiture order from the Court via a motion ex parte[632] and invite anyone who owns such properties to come and establish proof of ownership. The Court would normally give a directive to the attorneys for the EFCC/ICPC that the interim order should be published in a national newspaper.[633] The Court will then adjourn the case for any interested party to appear before the Judge and show cause why the orders should not be made absolute. If no one files a claim after the expiration of 14 days or such other period as the High Court may reasonably stipulate from the date of the giving of the notice or making of the publication provided in the notice, an application shall be made by a motion on notice for the final forfeiture of the property concerned to the Federal Government of Nigeria.[634] The "non-conviction based asset forfeiture" concept is very similar to the 'administrative forfeiture' concept being adopted in the United States of America. This concept will be explained in more detail in paragraph 15.2.

The real-life case studies below show how the "non-conviction based asset forfeiture" concept works.

CASE STUDY: TEMPORARY FORFEITURE

Justice Chuka Obiozor of the Federal High Court in Ikoyi, Lagos, on July 19, 2017 ordered the temporary forfeiture of a thirty-seven million five hundred thousand dollars property at Banana Island bought by a former Minister of Petroleum Resources, Diezani Alison-Madueke, in 2013.

---

632   Advance Fee Fraud and other Fraud Related Offences Act 2006, s. 17 (3)

633   Advance Fee Fraud and other Fraud Related Offences Act 2006, s. 17 (2)

634   Advance Fee Fraud and other Fraud Related Offences Act 2006, s. 17 (4), s. 17 (1)

According to the court papers argued by the Economic and Financial Crimes Commission (EFCC), the property, which has 24 apartments, 18 flats and six penthouses, is located at Building 3, Block B, Bella Vista Plot 1, Zone N, Federal Government Layout, Banana Island Foreshore Estate.

Apart from the property, the court also ordered the temporary forfeiture of the sums of two million seven hundred forty thousand one hundred ninety-seven dollars and ninety-six cents and eighty-four million five hundred thirty-seven thousand eight hundred forty naira and seventy kobo, said to be part of the rent collected on the property.

The funds were said to have been found in a Zenith Bank account number 1013612486.

Anselem Ozioko, counsel for the EFCC, had told the judge that the EFCC reasonably suspected that the property was acquired with proceeds of alleged unlawful activities of the Minister.

He said an investigation by the EFCC revealed that Mrs. Alison-Madueke made the thirty-seven million five hundred thousand dollars payment for the purchase of the property in cash, adding that the money was moved straight from her house in Abuja and paid into the seller's First Bank account in Abuja.

"Nothing could be more suspicious than someone keeping such huge amounts in her apartment," he said. "Why was she doing that, to avoid attention?"

He continued: "We are convinced beyond reasonable doubt because as of the time this happened, Mrs. Diezani Alison-Madueke was still in public service as the Minister of Petroleum Resources."

The ex-parte application taken before the judge was filed pursuant to **Section 17 of the Advance Fee Fraud and Other Related Offences Act, No. 14, 2006** and **Section 44(2) (k) of the Constitution.**

Listed as respondents in the application are Mrs. Alison-Madueke, a legal practitioner, Afamefuna Nwokedi, and a company, Rusimpex Limited.

In a 41-paragraph affidavit attached to the application, an investigative officer with the EFCC, Abdulrasheed Bawa, explained that

Nwokedi, in connivance with Mrs. Alison-Madueke, purposely incorporated the company, Rusimpex Limited, on September 11, 2013 to facilitate the alleged fraud scheme.

According to Bawa, when Nwokedi was questioned by the EFCC, the lawyer explained that he had approached Mrs. Alison-Madueke for opportunities in the Oil and Gas industry but the ex-minister told him that being a lawyer, she did not have any such opportunity for him and asked him whether he could in the alternative manage landed properties, an offer which Nwokedi accepted.

Bawa said Nwokedi later registered Rusimpex Limited at the Corporate Affairs Commission (CAC), wherein a lawyer in his law firm, Adetula Ayokunle, and a Russian, Vladmir Jourauleu, were listed as the directors of the company, while the address of Nwokedi's law firm in Ikoyi, Lagos was registered as the business address of Rusimpex Limited.

The investigator added that when Ayokunle was questioned by the EFCC, he explained that he only appended his signature on the CAC documents at his boss' instruction, while Jourauleu denied knowledge of the company.

The investigator explained: "Sometime in 2013, the former Minister of Petroleum Resources, Mrs. Diezani Alison-Madueke, invited Barrister Afamefuna Nwokedi, the Principal Counsel of Stillwaters Law Firm, to her house in Abuja for a meeting where she informed the said Barrister Afamefuna Nwokedi to incorporate a company and use same as a front to manage landed properties on her behalf without using her name in any of the incorporation documents."

He further explained that Mrs. Alison-Madueke further directed Mr. Afamefuna Nwokedi to meet with Mr. Bisi Onasanya, the Group Managing Director of First Bank of Nigeria Plc for that purpose.

"Mr. Stephen Onasanya was invited by the commission and he came and volunteered an extrajudicial statement wherein he stated that he marketed a property at Bella Vista, Banana Island, Ikoyi, Lagos, belonging to Mr. Youseff Fattau of Ibatex Nigeria Limited to Mrs. Diezani Alison-Madueke and Mrs. Diezani Alison-Madueke later bought the property from Mr. Youseff Fattau, through her lawyer,

Mr. Afamefuna Nwokedi (who she introduced to him) and that payment for the said property was made through the Abuja office of First Bank of Nigeria Plc.

"First Bank of Nigeria Plc, through Mr. Barau Muazu, wrote to the commission and also volunteered an extra-judicial statement in writing that they made the payments totaling thirty-seven million five hundred thousand dollars to Ibatex Nigeria Limited & YF Construction Development and Real Estate Limited on behalf of Mrs. Diezani Alison-Madueke and that they collected the entire cash from Mrs. Diezani Alison-Madueke at her residence of No. 10, Fredrick Chiluba Close of Jose Marti Street, Asokor, Abuja and paid into the First Bank of Nigeria Plc accounts of Ibatex and YF Construction Development and Real Estate Limited on her instruction."

After listening to the EFCC lawyer, Ozioko on Tuesday, Justice Obiozor made an order temporarily seizing the property and the funds.

He then directed that the order should be published in a national newspaper. He adjourned till August 7, 2017 for anyone interested in the property and funds to appear before him.[635]

CASE STUDY: PERMANENT FORFEITURE

Justice Muslim Hassan of the Federal High Court, Lagos, on June 6, 2017, ordered the permanent forfeiture to the Federal Government the sums of forty-three million four hundred forty-nine thousand nine hundred forty-seven dollars, twenty-seven thousand eight hundred pounds and twenty-three million two hundred eighteen thousand naira recovered from No. 16, Osborne Road, Flat 7B Osborne Towers, Ikoyi, Lagos.

The funds had been stashed in iron cabinets and "Ghana-must-go" bags in the apartment before they were recovered on April 11, 2017 by the Economic and Financial Crimes Commission.

---

635 Sahara Reporters (2017), 'Court Orders Forfeiture Of Diezani Alison-Madueke's $37.5m Banana Island Property', Available at: http://saharareporters.com/2017/07/19/court-orders-forfeiture-diezani-alison-maduekes-375m-banana-island-property (accessed 20 August 2017).

The anti-graft agency had earlier on April 13, 2017 obtained an interim court order temporarily forfeiting the funds to the Federal Government.

Mr. Hassan, who granted the interim order, had given 14 days for anyone interested in the funds to appear before him to show cause why the money should not be permanently forfeited to the Federal Government.

However, no one came before the judge to claim the money on May 5, 2017, when the matter came up.

A private legal practitioner, Olukoya Ogungbeje, appeared before the judge, with an application, urging the judge to suspend the final forfeiture proceedings pending when a three-man panel constituted by President Muhammadu Buhari in relation to the funds would submit its report.

The panel, headed by the Vice-President, Yemi Osinbajo, was to probe the claim and counter-claim of the Nigeria Intelligence Agency and Rivers State Government to the funds.

But the EFCC had opposed Mr. Ogungbeje's application and urged Mr. Hassan to dismiss it and go ahead with the forfeiture proceedings.

Ruling on Tuesday, Justice Hassan upheld the EFCC's submission and dismissed Mr. Ogungbeje's application for lacking in merit.

The judge described the application as "totally strange", noting that "having not appealed against the interim forfeiture order, Mr. Ogungbeje had no right to seek a stay of proceedings in the case."

The judge, who noted that Mr. Ogungbeje was not a party in the suit filed by the EFCC, described the lawyer as a "meddlesome interloper" and a "busybody", adding that "his application was strange to law."

He advised the lawyer to explore the Freedom of Information Act if he wanted information from the Federal Government on the findings of the Osinbajo's panel.

Having dismissed Mr. Ogungbeje's application, the judge subsequently made an order permanently forfeiting the funds to the Federal Government, noting that no one had appeared to show cause why the permanent forfeiture order should not be made.

In his ruling, the judge held, "I am in complete agreement with the submission of the learned counsel for the applicant (EFCC) that the property sought to be attached are reasonably suspected to be proceeds of unlawful activities and that by every standard this huge sum of money is not expected to be kept without going through a designated financial institution; more so, nobody has shown cause why the said sum should not be forfeited to the Federal Government of Nigeria. Having regard to the foregoing, I have no other option but to grant this application as prayed," Mr. Hassan said.

"For the avoidance of any doubt, I hereby make the following orders: 1. A final order is made forfeiting the sums of forty-three million four hundred forty-nine thousand nine hundred forty-seven dollars found by the Economic and Financial Crimes Commission at Flat 7B of No. 16 Osborne Road, Osborne Towers, Ikoyi, Lagos, which sum is reasonably suspected to be proceeds of unlawful activities to the Federal Government of Nigeria," the judge held.

The judge made the same order in respect of the twenty-seven thousand eight hundred pounds and twenty-three million two hundred and eighteen thousand naira.

The EFCC had, while arguing the application for final forfeiture order on May 5, named the wife of the National Intelligence Agency (NIA) Director General, Folashade Oke as the owner of Flat 7B, No. 13, Osborne Road, Osborne Towers, Ikoyi, Lagos, where the funds were recovered.

The EFCC said it found out that Mrs. Oke made a cash payment of $1.658m for the purchase of the flat between August 25 and September 3, 2015.

She was said to have purchased the property in the name of a company, Chobe Ventures Limited, to which she and her son, Master Ayodele Oke Junior, were directors. Payment for the purchase of the flat was said to have been made to one Fine and Country Limited.

The EFCC stated that Mrs. Oke made the cash payment in tranches of seven hundred thousand dollars, six hundred and fifty thousand dollars and three hundred and fifty-three thousand seven hundred dollars to a Bureau de Change company, Sulah Petroleum and Gas Limited, which later converted the sums into three hundred and sixty million naira and subsequently paid it to Fine and Country Limited for the purchase of the property.

The anti-graft agency had tendered the receipt issued by Fine and Country Limited to Chobe Ventures Limited as an exhibit before the Federal High Court in Lagos, where it is seeking an order of final forfeiture of the recovered money to the Federal Government.

"The circumstances leading to the discovery of the huge sums stockpiled in Flat 7B, Osborne Towers, leaves no one in doubt that the act was pursuant to an unlawful activity.

"The very act of making cash payment of one million six hundred thousand dollars without going through any financial institution by Mrs. Folashade Oke for the acquisition of Flat 7B, Osborne Towers, is a criminal act punishable by the Money Laundering (Prohibition) Amendment Act. I refer My Lord to **sections 1(a), 16(d) and 16(2)(b) of the Money Laundering (Prohibition) Amendment Act**," a counsel for the EFCC, Rotimi Oyedepo, told the court on Friday.

In an affidavit filed before the court, a Detective Inspector with the EFCC, Mohammed Chiroma, stated that "Chobe Ventures Limited is not into any business but was merely incorporated to retain proceeds of suspected unlawful activities of Mrs. Folashade Oke."

While urging Justice Hassan to order the permanent forfeiture of the funds to the Federal Government, the EFCC lawyer, Mr. Oyedepo, had argued that the fact that Flat 7B, Osborne Towers was purchased in a criminal manner, made the thirteen billion naira recovered therein "extremely suspicious to be proceeds of unlawful acts."

The lawyer noted that despite the newspaper advertisement of the initial order of April 13, 2017 temporarily forfeiting the money to the Federal Government, no one showed up in court to show cause why the money should not be permanently forfeited to the Federal Government.

Mr. Oyedepo also observed that Chobe Ventures Limited, in whose apartment the huge sums were recovered, did not come to court to challenge the forfeiture order, despite being served with the motion on notice at its registered address of No. 18, Ogunmodede Street, off Allen Avenue, Ikeja, Lagos.

Mr. Oyedepo said the court papers were received at the stated address, which is also the house of the Okes, by one Bola, who signed for them on May 3, 2017.

"The failure of Chobe Ventures Limited, in whose custody these properties we are seeking to forfeit were found, to show cause before My Lord today why the property (money) should not be forfeited to the Federal Government of Nigeria, Your Lordship should hold that Chobe Ventures Limited has admitted all the facts deposed to in our affidavit and order the final forfeiture of the property to the Federal Government," Mr. Oyedepo said.[636]

15.2 United States

U.S. law provides for the confiscation of laundered properties which represent proceeds of crime. At the moment, the types of measures for recovery of proceeds of crime in the U.S. is Administrative Forfeiture, Civil (Non-Conviction Based) Judicial Forfeiture and Criminal Judicial Forfeiture.

15.2.1 Administrative Forfeiture

Each year, the majority, generally over 60 percent, of federal forfeitures in the U.S. are obtained through administrative forfeiture. The reason is that most seizures are not contested. This may seem strange at first, but when one considers that most of the property seized for forfeiture in the U.S. constitutes large bundles of cash, it is readily apparent why many seizures are not challenged, particularly if the person from whom the cash was seized is not arrested or later indicted. No one really wants to come forward to swear that he or she has an interest in such large amounts of generally quite unexplained U.S. currency. Administrative forfeiture is not used for real property or businesses. Since 1990, the Customs laws (19 U.S.C. § 1607, et

---

636 Premium Times (2017), 'Court orders permanent forfeiture of N13 billion recovered from Ikoyi property', Available at: http://www.premiumtimesng.com/news/top-news/233203-court-orders-permanent-forfeiture-of-n13-billion-recovered-from-ikoyi-property.html (accessed 20 August 2017).

seq.) have permitted administrative forfeiture of currency and monetary instruments without limit, and of other personal property up to a value of $500,000.

An administrative forfeiture usually begins when a federal law enforcement agency seizes an asset identified during the course of a criminal investigation. The investigation may be a purely federal one, or may be a task force which also involves state and/or local law enforcement agencies. The asset seizure must be based upon "probable cause" to believe that the property is subject to forfeiture. Once the asset is seized, attorneys for the seizing agency are required by the **Civil Asset Forfeiture Reform Act (CAFRA) of 2000** to send notice to any persons whom the government has reason to believe may have an interest in the property. Such notice must be sent within 60 days of the seizure if a federal agent seized the property. An administrative forfeiture can also be based upon an "adoptive seizure," where a state or local officer has seized the property under the authority of state or local law, but then transfers it to federal custody for forfeiture. In that case, the federal adopting agency has 90 days after the seizure within which to send notice. Notice is usually sent by Certified Mail or Federal Express, so that the agency has proof of delivery. The agency must also publish its intent to forfeit for three successive weeks in a newspaper of general circulation in the area where the property was seized, or via a government internet publication website. A person receiving notice has 30 days within which to file a sworn claim with the seizing agency, asking for one of two types of relief: (1) the opportunity to challenge the forfeiture in court; or (2) remission or mitigation from the forfeiture. In the second option, the property owner is basically acknowledging the forfeiture, but claiming some mitigating circumstance. If a timely claim is filed under the first option, the seizing agency refers the matter to the appropriate U.S. Attorney's Office to file a judicial forfeiture action in the case. If no one files a claim after the deadlines provided in the notice and publication expire, the property is summarily forfeited to the United States. Remission or mitigation may be provided if certain guidelines are met.[637]

---

637 Weld, J.B. (2009), 'Forfeiture Laws and Procedures in the United States of America', RESOURCE MATERIAL SERIES No.83, p. 20

15.2.2 Civil (Non-Conviction Based) Judicial Forfeiture in the U.S.

In the United States, non-conviction based ("NCB") forfeiture is known as "civil forfeiture." This judicial process may be brought at any time prior to or after criminal charges are filed, or even if criminal charges are never filed.[638]

In a civil judicial case, the Government may take possession of personal property with an arrest warrant in rem. The procedure for issuing an arrest warrant in rem is set forth in the **Federal Rules of Civil Procedure Supplemental Rules for Admiralty or Maritime Claims and Asset Forfeiture Actions (Rule G(3))**.

Under the Supplemental Rules, no arrest warrant is needed if the property is already subject to a pre-trial restraining order. In all other cases, however, the Government must obtain an arrest warrant in rem and serve it on the property, generally by actual or constructive seizure of the property, to ensure that the court obtains in rem jurisdiction.

The procedure for issuing the warrant differs depending on whether the property is already in the Government's custody at the time the complaint is filed. If the property is already in the Government's custody, the warrant may be issued by the clerk of the court without any finding of probable cause by a judge or magistrate judge, but if the effect of the warrant will be to take the property out of the hands of a non-Government entity, the warrant must be issued by a court upon a finding of probable cause. *See* Rule G(3)(b). Once the warrant is issued, it must be delivered "to a person or organization authorized to execute it." Rule G(3)(C).

A second form of process for seizing forfeitable property is the warrant of seizure authorized by **21 U.S.C. § 881(b) and 18 U.S.C. § 981(b)(2)**. This form of process requires a judicial determination of probable cause.

The seizure of property pursuant to a civil seizure warrant issued under **section 981(b)** or warrant of arrest in rem under **Supplemental Rule G(3)(b)(ii)** provides a valid basis for the Government's physical

---

638 Weld, J.B. (2009), 'Forfeiture Laws and Procedures in the United States of America', RESOURCE MATERIAL SERIES No.83, p. 20 -21

possession of property pending the outcome of a criminal forfeiture proceeding. But this is so only as long as the civil forfeiture matter is pending, including if the civil proceeding is stayed during the pendency of the case. If someone files a claim in an administrative forfeiture proceeding, the Government has 90 days in which to (1) commence a civil forfeiture action; (2) commence a criminal forfeiture action; or (3) return the property. *See* **18 U.S.C. § 983(a) (3)(B)**. It is perfectly appropriate for the Government to file both a civil action and a criminal action within the 90-day period, or to file a civil action within such period and file a criminal action later. In such cases, the civil seizure warrant provides a valid basis for the Government's continued possession of the property.

But **section 983(a)(3)(C)** provides that if "criminal forfeiture is the only forfeiture proceeding commenced by the Government, the Government's right to continued possession of the property shall be governed by the applicable criminal forfeiture statute." In other words, if there are parallel civil and criminal proceedings, the civil seizure warrant will provide a sufficient basis for holding the property either with a criminal seizure warrant issued pursuant to **21 U.S.C. § 853(f)**, or with an order issued pursuant to **21 U.S.C. § 853(e)**.

The 90-day deadline provision in the **Civil Asset Forfeiture Reform Act (CAFRA) of 2000**, of course, only applies to cases where the property was initially seized for the purpose of "non-judicial" (i.e., administrative) forfeiture. *See* **section 981(a) (1) (A)**. If the property was seized pursuant to a civil forfeiture seizure warrant under section 981(b) or a warrant of arrest in rem under **Supplemental Rule G(3)(b)(ii)**, but it was not seized for the purpose of administrative forfeiture, the prescriptions found in **section 983(a)(3)** regarding the 90-day deadline and the need to re-seize property already in Government possession do not apply. Nevertheless, even in such cases, if the Government proceeds only with a criminal forfeiture action, it may not lawfully maintain possession of the property pursuant to a civil seizure warrant alone, but must obtain either a criminal seizure warrant or a pre-trial restraining order.[639]

639 Asset Forfeiture and Money Laundering Section (AFMLS) (2016), 'Asset Forfeiture Policy Manual', Available at: https://www.justice.gov/criminal-afmls/file/839521/download (accessed 15 October 2017).

15.2.3 Criminal Judicial Forfeiture in the U.S.

Criminal forfeiture in the United States is dependent upon a conviction of a defendant for a crime which provides a basis for the forfeiture. For example, if a defendant is charged with securities fraud and income tax evasion, and is convicted of the tax evasion charges, but not the fraud offences, there can be no forfeiture because U.S. law does not provide for forfeiture based upon tax evasion. Over the years, United States criminal forfeiture laws have gradually expanded, and in 2000, CAFRA added **28 U.S.C. § 2461(c)** which provides that if any law provides for civil forfeiture, then the prosecutor may also include a criminal forfeiture for the property in a criminal indictment. Now prosecutors often seek parallel civil and criminal proceedings against the same property.

Criminal forfeiture is in personam, against the defendant. One drawback to this type of forfeiture under U.S. law is that only property in which the defendant has a true interest may be forfeited criminally. Property which is held by "nominees" or straw owners on behalf of the defendant may be forfeited criminally, but the government must prove that the defendant is the true owner. Any property which is truly owned by other parties who are not convicted as part of the criminal case, such as a spouse or other family member or business partners, may not be forfeited criminally. Such property may be forfeited only in an in rem civil action.[640]

Property subject to criminal forfeiture is occasionally seized pursuant to a criminal seizure warrant issued under **21 U.S.C. § 853(f).** More often, property named in a criminal indictment or information is in the custody of the Government because it was seized pursuant to a civil seizure warrant issued under section 981(b), a warrant of arrest in rem under Supplemental Rule G(3)(b)(ii), or because it was seized as evidence in the underlying criminal investigation.

It is not necessary for the Government to have the property subject to criminal forfeiture in its possession during the pendency of a criminal forfeiture proceeding. To the contrary, the criminal

---

640 Weld, J.B. (2009), 'Forfeiture Laws and Procedures in the United States of America', RESOURCE MATERIAL SERIES No.83, p. 21-22

forfeiture statutes contemplate that the property will, in most cases, remain in the possession of the defendant—albeit pursuant to a pre-trial restraining order—until the court enters a preliminary order of forfeiture. *See* **21 U.S.C. § 853(g)** ("Upon entry of an order of forfeiture under this section, the court shall authorize the Attorney General to seize all property ordered forfeited...."). Cases where the Government takes physical possession of property subject to criminal forfeiture with a criminal seizure warrant prior to the entry of a preliminary order of forfeiture are relatively rare.

But the Government could have physical possession of the property subject to criminal forfeiture before any preliminary order of forfeiture is entered in the criminal case. Such possession may be the result of a seizure pursuant to a civil seizure warrant issued pursuant to section 981(b), a warrant of arrest in rem issued pursuant to Supplemental Rule G(3)(b)(ii), or a seizure for the purpose of civil forfeiture that was based on probable cause. It also could be the consequence of the seizure of the property for evidence, with or without a warrant.[641]

15.3 United Kingdom

The **Proceeds of Crime Act 2002 (POCA)** set out the powers under which the Government could seize the proceeds of a criminal's activities. It represented the rationalisation of various pieces of legislation which enabled law-enforcement bodies to pursue proceeds of crime. The Home Office stated that "the aim of the asset recovery scheme in POCA is to deny criminals the use of their assets, recover the proceeds of crime, and deter and disrupt criminality".

In its recent report analysing the confiscation elements of POCA, the Royal United Services Institute (RUSI) summarised the four key elements of recovery:

---

641 Asset Forfeiture and Money Laundering Section (AFMLS) (2016), 'Asset Forfeiture Policy Manual', Available at: https://www.justice.gov/criminal-afmls/file/839521/download (accessed 15 October 2017).

(1) **Criminal confiscation**: Part 2 of the POCA sets out powers to confiscate the proceeds of crime following a criminal conviction as part of the sentencing process.[642]

(2) **Civil recovery**: Part 5 (Chapter 2) of the POCA sets out a system for confiscating the proceeds of crime in the absence of a criminal conviction through the civil courts.[643]

(3) **Cash forfeiture**: Part 5 (Chapter 3) of the POCA sets out powers to seize and forfeit cash, through a civil process, where there are reasonable grounds to suspect that it is the proceeds of crime.[644]

(4) **Criminal taxation**: Part 6 of the POCA allows the National Crime Agency to access revenue powers to tax income which it has reasonable grounds to suspect are the proceeds of crime.[645]

On 27 April 2017 the UK parliament passed an important provision of the Criminal Finance Bill that introduces a powerful new weapon into the anti-corruption arsenal: Unexplained Wealth Orders.[646] This follows action already taken in Australia and Ireland. This provision is not seen present in the Nigerian and the United States laws on civil recovery.

The provision specifically targets red flag situations where a person buying expensive items, like property or jewels, doesn't appear to be wealthy enough to make the purchase. It could be a politician in Russia or a small business owner in Brussels who buys a multi-million-pound property in central London. If the person has links to serious crime or access to public money, then the authorities can act.

The UK law enforcement agencies can now use an Unexplained Wealth Order to investigate the source of that money, and, if it is

---

642 Proceeds of Crime Act 2002 (as amended), s. 6, s. 7, s. 8, s. 9, s. 10, s. 11, s. 12, s. 13

643 Proceeds of Crime Act 2002 (as amended), sections 243 to 280

644 Proceeds of Crime Act 2002 (as amended), sections 289 to 303

645 Proceeds of Crime Act 2002 (as amended), sections 317 to 326

646 Criminal Finances Act 2017, s. 1, s. 2, s. 3, s. 4, s. 5, s. 6

found to be corrupt money, more easily return it to those from whom it has been stolen.

This is something that Transparency International UK and other anti-corruption groups in the UK have been working hard to bring about since the UK has been identified as one of the key destinations for corrupt money.[647]

15.4 Discussion

The Nigeria asset recovery scheme is likely to be more effective when the **Proceeds of Crime Bill, 2017** becomes law.

The Bill passed second reading in the Senate on May 17, 2017. The Bill has been referred to the Committee on Judiciary, Human Rights and Legal Matters for further legislative input and is expected to report back within four weeks.

The Nigerian Proceeds of Crime Bill seeks to provide the legal and institutional framework for the recovery and management of proceeds of crime in such a manner that is more organised, coordinated and allows the country to benefit from rather than lose the value of the property obtained from these illegal activities.

What we have now creates a very consuming system that have left both the victim, the state as losers as the values recovered by agencies of government end up decrepit and decaying with little or no accountability or ultimate responsibility.

This Bill is aimed at providing the necessary consolidation of the existing provisions on the recovery of proceeds of assets across our law enforcement agencies and creates the institutional structures that will eliminate corruption in the handling of proceeds of crime while allowing law enforcement to focus on their key role of arrest, investigation and prosecution of cases.

---

647 Transparency International (2017), 'Unexplained Wealth Orders: How to catch the corrupt and corrupt money in the UK', Available at: https://www.transparency.org/news/feature/unexplained_wealth_orders_how_to_catch_the_corrupt_and_corrupt_money_in_the (accessed 18 August 2017).

The objectives of the bill therefore are to:

I. Provide for an effective legal and institutional framework for the recovery and management of proceeds of crime or benefits derived from unlawful activities;

II. Deprive a person of the proceeds of an unlawful activity and other benefits derived from an offence committed within or outside Nigeria;

III. Prevent the reinvestment of proceeds of unlawful activities in the furtherance of criminal enterprise;

IV. Harmonize and consolidate existing legislative provisions on the recovery of proceeds of crime and related matters in Nigeria; and

V. Make comprehensive provisions for the restraint, seizure, confiscation and forfeiture of property derived from unlawful activities and any instrumentalities used or intended to be used in the commission of such unlawful activities.

The bill has 164 clauses into 12 parts namely;

Part 1- This part sets out the objectives and application of the law

Part 2- Civil Forfeiture

Part 3- Additional Investigation Powers in Civil Recovery

Part 4- Recovery of Cash Being Imported or Exported

Part 5- Criminal Forfeiture and Confiscation

Part 6- Proceeds of Crime Recovery and Management Agency

Part 7- Investigation, Search and Seizure

Part 8- Administration

Part 9- Confiscated and Forfeiture Properties Account

Part 10- Jurisdiction

Part 11- General Provisions Relating to Legal Proceedings Miscellaneous

Part 12- The benefits of the Bill are enormous:

The bill will enable a prosecuting agency to identify properties which are proceeds of crime and commence forfeiture proceedings against the properties in situations where the defendant cannot be prosecuted either because he is dead or out of jurisdiction.

The Assets forfeiture law is today one of the key missing links to our fight against corruption. Therefore, the proceeds of crime Bill we have here today has the potential to radically swing the pendulum of the anti-corruption war firmly in the favour of the country. We are today struggling to recover or confiscate the proceeds of corruption that we have identified and even moved against both home and abroad. With this law we will be better equipped to deal with the proceeds of this kind of activities and make it easier for our anti-graft agencies to not only prosecute and jail economic criminals but also to effectively recover for the country the value that may have been taken and more.

The assets recovery and forfeiture agency set up under this law will be empowered to administer the proceeds of crime and as well as establish special account for the recovery and safe keeping of monies recovered from as proceeds of crime.

This bill is part of the action plan of the government to prosecute criminal activities within and outside the nation's border as well as fulfil its commitment to the international community especially the Financial Action Task Force and the International Government Action Group against Money Laundering in West Africa (GIABA) to enact some identified critical laws to tackle criminal activities globally. Countries like India, USA, UK, Australia, Trinidad and Tobago, Jamaica and Kenya have all enacted this legislation in compliance with the FATF requirement.

15.5 Conclusion

This chapter compared the asset recovery measures in Nigeria with those of the United States and the United Kingdom. It has also analysed issues that arose from the comparison to determine the need for reform. This section focuses on those areas that need reform.

Based on the arguments canvassed in section 15.1 to section 15.3 of this chapter, the following reforms are recommended:

i. Nigeria should adopt the UK's approach by revising the **Proceeds of Crime Bill, 2017** to include Unexplained Wealth Orders, where individuals whose assets are disproportionate to their known income will need to explain the origin of their wealth. The United States should also amend its existing laws to include Unexplained Wealth Orders.

ii. The **Proceeds of Crime Bill, 2017** should be given accelerated consideration in the Nigerian National Assembly based on its urgency and significance for the anti-corruption war. Civil (Non-Conviction Based) Judicial Forfeiture is an essential tool in the fight against corruption to deprive offenders of the proceeds of their criminal conduct; to deter the commission of further offences; and to reduce the profits available to fund further corrupt or criminal enterprises.

CHAPTER 16

PLEA BARGAINING

The Financial Action Task Force (FATF) has advised countries to adopt measures that enable their competent authorities to freeze or seize and confiscate laundered property.[648] These measures include the introduction of the concept of plea bargaining into a country's criminal justice system. This measure ensures that all criminal proceeds are confiscated.

In a plea bargain deal, both sides gain something from the arrangement. The prosecution gains a conviction without the time and expense of a trial, while the defendant might get a reduced sentence or have some of the charges dropped. In some cases, for example, the prosecution will offer a plea deal so that the victim does not have to go through the drama and stress of testifying at a trial.[649]

While countries have adopted the concept of plea bargaining into their criminal justice system, the application of the concept in these countries is not identical.

This chapter seeks to compare the approach in Nigeria with those of the United States and the United Kingdom to determine the best approach. This is likely the one that achieves the highest

---

648 The Financial Action Task Force (FATF): International Standards on Combating Money Laundering and the Financing of Terrorism and Proliferation, (The FATF Recommendations) 2012, Interpretive Note to Recommendation 4

649 Montaldo, C. (2017), 'The plea bargain stage of a criminal case, stages of the criminal justice system', Available at: http://crime.about.com/od/Crime_101/a/The-Plea-Bargain-Stage-Of-A-Criminal-Case.htm (accessed 26 December 2017).

number of convictions without necessarily interfering with a person's right to a jury trial.[650]

This chapter will start by defining what plea bargaining is and giving a brief introduction of the history and nature of plea bargaining. Then it will compare the approach adopted in Nigeria with those of the United States and the United Kingdom.

16.1 Definition of Plea Bargaining

To a layman on the street, plea bargaining in the Nigerian context is a system in which room is provided for unfettered looting of public treasury at all levels of governance in our country. This is done in such a way that billions of naira is stolen, and some paltry millions are returned to the coffers of the government, while a large chunk of the looted public funds at the end of the day is left for the looter and his/her unborn generations.[651]

But to an Advocate of Legal Practice, plea bargaining consists of the exchange of official concessions for a defendant's act of self-conviction. These concessions may relate to the sentence imposed by the Court or recommended by the prosecution, the offence charged, or a variety of other circumstances; they may be explicit or implicit; and they may proceed from any of a number of officials.[652] The benefit offered by the defendant, however is always the same: entry of[653] a plea of guilty. This definition excludes unilateral exercises of prosecutorial or judicial discretion, such as an unqualified dismissal or reduction of charges. It also excludes the exchange of official concessions for actions other than entry of a guilty plea, such as offering restitution to the victim of a

---

650 Note that a judge can only make a confiscation order after a conviction has been secured.

651 Joseph, O. (2012), 'Why encourage plea bargaining?', Available at: http://www.punchng.com/opinion/letters/why-encourage-plea-bargaining/ (accessed 3rd July 2014).

652 Alschuler, A. (1979), 'Plea Bargaining and its History', 79 Columbia Law Review 1, 3

653 Ibid

crime, giving information or testimony concerning other alleged offenders, or resigning from public office following allegations of misconduct.[654]

Black's Law Dictionary defines plea bargain as follows:

A negotiated agreement between a prosecutor and a criminal defendant whereby the defendant pleads guilty to a lesser offence or to one of multiple charges in exchange for some concession by the prosecutor[655]

16.2 History of Plea Bargaining

The plea bargain was a prosecutorial tool used only episodically before the 19th century. ''In America,'' Fisher says, ''it can be traced almost to the very emergence of public prosecution – and public prosecution, although not exclusive to the United States., developed earlier and more broadly in the United States than in most places.''

Below is a summary of the history of plea bargaining from the 16th century to the 19th century:

1633: Galileo gets house arrest from the Inquisition in exchange for his reciting penitential psalms weekly and recanting Copernican heresies.

1931: Al Capone brags about his light sentence for pleading guilty to tax evasion and Prohibition violations. The judge then declares that he isn't bound by the bargain, and Capone does seven and a half years in Alcatraz.

1969: To avoid execution, James Earl Ray pleads guilty to assassinating Martin Luther King Jr. and gets 99 years.

---

654 Alschuler, A. (1979), '*Plea Bargaining and its History*', 79 Columbia Law Review 1, 4

655 Garner, B.A. (2004): *Black's Law Dictionary* (8th Edition West, a Thomson business) 1190

1973: Spiro Agnew resigns the vice presidency and pleads no contest to the charge of failing to report income; he gets three years' probation and ten thousand dollars fine (roughly one-third of the amount at issue).

1990: Facing serious federal charges of insider trading, Michael Milken pleads to lesser charges of securities fraud; soon after, his 10-year sentence is reduced to 2 years.[656]

16.3 The Nature of Plea Bargaining

There are two basic types of plea bargaining: charge bargain and sentence bargain. In the case of charge bargain, it is arranged in a way that the prosecutor agrees to drop some of the counts or reduce the charge to a less serious offence in exchange for a plea of either guilty or no contest from the defendant.

In the case of sentence bargain, the prosecutor agrees to recommend a lighter sentence in exchange for a plea of either guilty or no contest from the defendant.[657]

16.4 Discussion

The previous sections defined plea bargaining and discussed the history and nature of plea bargaining.

This section compares the approach to plea bargaining in Nigeria with those of the United States and the United Kingdom. The aim of this comparison is to determine what the best approach is, which is the one that achieves the highest number of convictions without necessarily interfering with a person's right to a jury trial.

---

656 Olin, D. (2002), '*The Way We Live Now: 9-29-02: Crash Course; Plea Bargain*', *Available at:* http://www.nytimes.com/2002/09/29/magazine/the-way-we-live-now-9-29-02-crash-course-plea-bargain.html (accessed 3rd July 2014).

657 Garner, B.A. (2004): Black's Law Dictionary (8th Edition West, a Thomson business) 1190.

16.4.1 Nigeria

The practice of plea bargain is obviously very embryonic in Nigeria. It was never part of any Nigerian law until 2004 when the Economic and Financial Crimes Commission was established.

The provision of **Section 14 (2) of the Economic and Financial Crimes Commission (Establishment) Act, 2004** indicates that when a defendant agrees to give up money stolen by him, the Commission may compound any offence for which such a person is charged under the Act.

The Administration of Criminal Justice Act 2015 lays down guidelines that the prosecution must follow when entering into a plea agreement with the defendant.

Section 270 of the Administration of Criminal Justice Act 2015 is to the effect that:

(1) Notwithstanding anything in this Act or in any other law, the Prosecutor may:

(a) receive and consider a plea bargain from a defendant **charged with an offence** either directly from that defendant or on his behalf; or

(b) offer a plea bargain to a defendant **charged with an offence**

(2) The prosecution may enter into plea bargaining with the defendant, with the consent of the victim or his representative during or after the presentation of the evidence of the prosecution, but before the presentation of the evidence of the defence, provided that all of the following conditions are present:

(a) the evidence of the prosecution is insufficient, to prove the offence charged beyond reasonable doubt;

(b) where the defendant has agreed to return the proceeds of the crime or make restitution to the victim or his representative; or

(c) where the defendant, in a case of conspiracy, has fully cooperated with the investigation and prosecution of the crime by providing relevant information for the successful prosecution of other offenders.

(3) Where the prosecutor is of the view that the offer or accep-tance of a plea bargain is in the interest of justice, the public interest, public policy and the need to prevent abuse of legal process, he may offer or accept the plea bargain.

(4) The prosecutor and the defendant or his legal practitioner may, before the plea to the charge, enter into an agreement in respect of:

(a) the term of the plea bargain which may include the sentence recommended within the appropriate range of punishment stipulated for the offence or a plea of guilty by the defendant to the offence charged or a lesser offence of which he may be convicted on the charge: and

(b) an appropriate sentence to be imposed by the court where the defendant is convicted of the offence to which he intends to plead guilty.

(5) The prosecutor may only enter into an agreement contem-plated in subsection (3) of this section:

(a) after consultation with the police responsible for the in-vestigation of the case and the victim or his representa-tive; and

(b) with due regard to the nature of and circumstances relat-ing to the offence, the defendant and public interest;

Provided that in determining whether it is in the pub-lic interest to enter into a plea bargain, the prosecution shall weigh all relevant factors, including:

(i)   the defendant's willingness to cooperate in the in-vestigation or prosecution of others,

(ii)   the defendant's history with respect to criminal activity,

(iii)   the defendant's remorse or contrition and his will-ingness to assume responsibility for his conduct,

(iv)   the desirability of prompt and certain disposition of the case,

(v)   the likelihood of obtaining a conviction at trial and the probable effect on witnesses,

      (vi)   the probable sentence or other consequences if the defendant is convicted,

      (vii)   the need to avoid delay in the disposition of other pending cases,

      (viii)   the expense of trial and appeal, and

      (ix)   the defendant's willingness to make restitution or pay compensation to the victim where appropriate.

(6) The prosecution shall afford the victim or his representative the opportunity' to make representations to the prosecutor regarding:

(a) the content of the agreement; and

(b) the inclusion in the agreement of a compensation or restitution order.

(7) An agreement between the parties contemplated in subsection (3) of this section shall be reduced to writing and shall:

(a) state that, before conclusion of the agreement, the defendant has been informed:

      (i)   that he has a right to remain silent,

      (ii)   of the consequences of not remaining silent, and

      (iii)   that he is not obliged to make any confession or admission that could be used in evidence against him;

(b) state fully, the terms of the agreement and any admission made;

(c) be signed by the prosecutor, the defendant, the legal practitioner and the inteipreter, as the case may be; and

(d) a copy of the agreement forwarded to the Attorney-General of the Federation.

(8) The presiding judge or magistrate before whom the criminal proceedings are pending shall not participate in the discussion contemplated in subsection (3) of this section.

(9) Where a plea agreement is reached by the prosecution and tire defence, the prosecutor shall inform the court that the parties have reached an agreement and the presiding judge or magistrate shall then inquire from the defendant to confirm the terms of the agreement.

(10) The presiding judge or magistrate shall ascertain whether the defendant admits the allegation in the charge to which he has pleaded guilty' and whether he entered into the agreement voluntarily and without undue influence and may where:

(a) he is satisfied that the defendant is guilty' of the offence to which he has pleaded guilty, convict the defendant on his plea of guilty to that offence, and shall award the compensation to the victim in accordance with the term of the agreement which shall be delivered by the Court in accordance with section 308 of this Act; or

(b) he is for any reason of the opinion that the defendant cannot be convicted of the offence in respect of which the agreement was reached and to which the defendant has pleaded guilty or that the agreement is in conflict with the defendant's right referred to in subsection (6) of this section, he shall record a plea of not guilty in respect of such charge and order that the trial proceed.

(11) Where a defendant has been convicted under subsection (9) (a), the presiding judge or magistrate shall consider tire sentence as agreed upon and where he is:

(a) satisfied that such sentence is an appropriate sentence, impose the sentence;

(b) of the view that he would have imposed a lesser sentence than the sentence agreed, impose the lesser sentence; or

(c) of the view that the offence requires a heavier sentence than the sentence agreed upon, he shall inform the defendant of such heavier sentence he considers to be appropriate.

(12) The presiding Judge or Magistrate shall make an order that any money, asset or property agreed to be forfeited under the plea bargain shall be transferred to and vest in the victim or his representative or any other person as may be appropriate or reasonably feasible.

(13) Notwithstanding the provisions of the Sheriffs and Civil Process Act, the prosecutor shall take reasonable steps to ensure that any money, asset or property agreed to be forfeited or returned by the offender under a plea bargain are transferred to or vested in the victim,-Iris representative or other person lawfully entitled to it.

(14) Any person who, willfully and without just cause, obstructs or impedes the vesting or transfer of any money, asset or property under this Act, commits an offence and is liable on conviction to imprisonment for 7 years without an option of fine.

(15) "Where the defendant has been informed of the heavier sentence as contemplated in subsection (11) (c) of this section, the defendant may:

(a) abide by his plea of guilty as agreed upon and agree that, subject to the defendant's right to lead evidence and to present argument relevant to sentencing, the presiding judge or magistrate proceed with the sentencing; or

(b) withdraw from his plea agreement, in which event the trial shall proceed de novo before another presiding judge or magistrate, as the case may be.

Plea bargaining has secured convictions in high-profile cases, including *Federal Republic of Nigeria v. Cecilia Ibru, Federal Republic of Nigeria v. Alamieyeseigha, Federal Republic of Nigeria v. Tafa Balogun and Federal Republic of Nigeria v. Lucky Igbinedion.*

In the case of *Federal Republic of Nigeria v. Cecilia Ibru*, the commission had charged Mrs Cecilia Ibru with a twenty-five-count criminal information offence bordering on financial crimes before the court. However, she entered into a plea bargain with the prosecution and pleaded guilty to a lesser three-count charge. The court thereafter convicted Ibru on the three-count charge and ordered the forfeiture of her assets, which amounted to about one hundred and ninety-one billion naira. She was sentenced to six months in prison for each of the three counts, to be served concurrently. In effect, Ibru was expected to spend only six months in jail.[658]

Another plea bargain under the EFCC Act was the former governor of Bayelsa State, Alamieyeseigha, who stood trial on a thirty-three-count charge of corruption, money laundering, illegal acquisition of property and false declaration of assets. He pleaded guilty to a six-count charge of money laundering brought by the commission and forfeited properties worth billions of naira in exchange for the lesser sentence. The former governor entered into a plea bargain with the commission, gave up his right to a trial and pleaded guilty to the charges. Rather than serving a prolonged prison term if convicted, he accepted the commission's offer for a guilty plea. However, because he had completed almost two years in jail before accepting the bargain, he was released a few days after his conviction.[659]

Other beneficiaries of plea bargains in Nigeria include Tafa Balogun, the former inspector general of police and Mr Lucky Igbinedion, the former governor of Edo State.[660]

As shown in the cases cited, plea bargaining has proven useful in Nigeria's criminal justice system by saving time and avoiding the necessity of public trials, thereby protecting innocent victims of crime from the ordeal of giving evidence during trials. The use of plea bargaining in these cases has yielded fruits, one of which was the reduction of public expenditure that would have been incurred during prolonged trials.

If the cases had gone to full trial, there would have been an unacceptable waste of state resources as trials are so costly. Lawyers are paid appearance fees each time they appear in court for a case. The commission usually hires the services of senior advocates of Nigeria, so one can imagine how much money would have been spent if these cases had gone to full trial. So we can appreciate Tafa Balogun and the rest who chose to accept the plea bargains.

---

658 Oladele, K. (2010), *'Plea bargaining and the criminal justice system in Nigeria'*, *Available at:* http://www.vanguardngr.com/2010/10/plea-bargaining-and-the-criminal-justice-system-in-nigeria/ (accessed July 4, 2014).
659 Ibid.
660 Ibid.

This has also helped decongest prisons. Overcrowding in Nigeria's prisons is no longer news. The prisons have poor sanitary systems, and they rarely have facilities; where facilities do exist, they are dilapidated and unhygienic.

Despite the advantages noted above, the concept of plea bargaining has been criticized by a number of people. The most notable among them is the former chief justice of Nigeria (CJN), Justice Dahiru Musdapher, who was reported to have criticized the commission for smuggling the plea bargain concept into Nigerian criminal jurisprudence and also said that the concept had 'dubious' origins. The former CJN explained that he meant that the concept had a dubious origin in Nigeria.

When I described the concept of 'dubious origin', I was not referring to the original raison d'être or the juridical motive behind its conception way back, either in the United States or in England in the early nineteenth century; I was referring to the sneaky motive behind its introduction into our legal system, or its evident fraudulent application. You will learn that plea bargain is not only 'condemnation without adjudication', as John Langbien decried it; it is, as some other critics say, 'a triumph of administrative and organizational interests over justice'. At its very best, it penalizes the innocent who may be tempted to plead guilty to avoid being actuated by judicial default, and, at its most obnoxious extent, it grants 'undue leniency' as reward to criminals simply for pleading their guilt. You will see also that plea bargain is not only a flagrant subordination of the public's interest to the interest of 'criminal justice administration', but, worst of all, the concept generally promotes a cynical view of the entire legal system. I have said that our wavering disposition on the ethical standards set by your noble profession guarantees or jeopardizes our peace, security and progress. And it is the reason that I have chosen this occasion to speak—with all sense of solemnity—on a matter that has continued to eat away at even the modest gains that we seem to be making in reforming both the infrastructure and the overall judicial template of the Nigerian Judiciary.[661]

---

661 Akintimoye, D.A. (2012), *'Should plea bargaining be abolished or encouraged in Nigeria?', Available at:* http://community.vanguardngr.com/profiles/blogs/should-plea-bargaining-be-abolished-or-encouraged-in-nigeria (accessed January 2, 2014).

The commission did not smuggle the concept into Nigeria. The law-makers carved laws around the concept of plea bargaining, and the commission capitalized on those provisions to the country's advantage by applying them to the cases they were dealing with for the benefit of Nigeria and Nigerians.

The concept of plea bargaining did not have a 'dubious' origin in the sense that there was not a sneaky motive behind its introduction into Nigeria's legal system, nor was its application fraudulent. This is a new age in which alternative dispute resolutions are taking the place of litigation. Plea bargaining is like the alternative dispute resolution that is used in a civil trial. It saves the court time and money.

Plea bargaining does, however, penalize the innocent who may be tempted to plead guilty. Prosecutors could try to intimidate defendants by drawing up countless numbers of charges, thus forcing innocent defendants to submit to the plea bargain offers, which is complete injustice. This can be avoided if the defendants become more enlightened about the bag of tricks the prosecutors could attempt to play on them.

16.4.2 United States

The **Federal Rules of Criminal Procedure 2010,** and in specific, **Rule 11 (c),** recognizes and codifies the concept of plea agreements in the United States.

One recent estimate indicated that guilty pleas account for the disposition of as many as 95% of all criminal cases in United States. A substantial number of these are the result of plea discussions.[662]

While some scholars have interpreted the above statistics to mean that the process of plea bargaining is been abused in the American Criminal Justice System.[663] The statistics could be interpreted to mean that the concept of plea bargaining has been properly administered in the United States.

---

662 Fields, G. and Emshwiller, J.R. (2012), *'Federal Guilty Pleas, Soar As Bargains Trump Trials', Available at:* http://online.wsj.com/news/articles/SB10000872396390 4435893045776376100097206808 (accessed 7th October 2014).

663 Lynch, T. (2003),*'The Case against Plea Bargaining'* (Regulation Fall) 24

The basis for such interpretation lies in **subdivision (c) Rule 11** of the **U.S. Federal Rules of Criminal Procedure 2010.**

The procedure described in subdivision (c) is designed to prevent abuse of plea discussions and agreements by providing appropriate and adequate safeguards.

Subdivision (c) (1) specifies that the "attorney for the government and the attorney for the defendant or the defendant when acting pro se may" participate in plea discussions. The inclusion of "the defendant when acting pro se" is intended to reflect the fact that there are situations in which a defendant insists upon representing himself. It may be desirable that an attorney for the government not enter plea discussions with a defendant personally. If necessary, counsel can be appointed for purposes of plea discussions.

Subdivision (b) (2) makes it mandatory that the court inquire of the defendant whether his plea is the result of plea discussions between him and the attorney for the government. This is intended to enable the court to reject an agreement reached by an unrepresented defendant unless the court is satisfied that acceptance of the agreement adequately protects the rights of the defendant and the interests of justice.

Apparently, it is the practice of most prosecuting attorneys to enter plea discussions only with defendant's counsel. Discussions without benefit of counsel increase the likelihood that such discussions may be unfair. Some courts have indicated that plea discussions in the absence of defendant's attorney may be constitutionally prohibited.[664]

Subdivision (c) (2) provides that the judge shall require the disclosure of any plea agreement in open court.

Upon notice of the plea agreement, the court is given the option to accept or reject the agreement or defer its decision until receipt of the presentence report.

The judge may, and often should, defer his decision until he examines the presentence report. This is made possible by rule

---

664 See Anderson v. North Carolina, 221 F.Supp. 930, 935 (W.D.N.C.1963); Shape v. Sigler, 230 F.Supp. 601, 606 (D.Neb. 1964)

32 which allows a judge, with the defendant's consent, to inspect a presentence report to determine whether a plea agreement should be accepted.

The plea agreement procedure does not attempt to define the criteria for the acceptance or rejection of a plea agreement. Such a decision is left to the discretion of the individual trial judge.

Subdivision (c) (4) makes is mandatory, if the court decides to accept the plea agreement, that it inform the defendant that it will embody in the judgment and sentence the disposition provided in the plea agreement, or one more favourable to the defendant. This serves the purpose of informing the defendant immediately that the agreement will be implemented.

Subdivision (c) (5) requires the court, if it rejects the plea agreement, to inform the defendant of this fact and to advise the defendant personally, in open court, that the court is not bound by the plea agreement. The defendant must be afforded an opportunity to withdraw his plea and must be advised that if he persists in his guilty plea or plea of nolo contendere, the disposition of the case may be less favourable to him than that contemplated by the plea agreement.

If the court rejects the plea agreement and affords the defendant the opportunity to withdraw the plea, the court is not precluded from accepting a guilty plea from the same defendant at a later time, when such plea conforms to the requirements of rule 11.

In addition to Rule 11 (c) of the Federal Rules of Criminal Procedure, there are a number of cases decided by the U.S. Supreme Court on 21ˢᵗ March 2012, which support the above interpretation.

In the first case, *Missouri v. Frye,* defendant Galin Frye was charged with felony driving without a licence after several repeated offences. The State offered to reduce the charge to a misdemeanour with maximum jail time of one year in exchange for a guilty plea. Although prosecutors communicated this offer to Mr. Frye's attorney, the attorney made no effort to relay the offer to his client. As a result, the offer expired without Mr. Frye ever knowing of its existence. Mr. Frye later pled guilty without any agreement with the State, and he was sentenced to three years in prison.

The Supreme Court held that Mr. Frye was entitled to the effective assistance of counsel during plea negotiations and that **Strickland v. Washington** provides the appropriate standard for evaluating such a claim. Consequently, a prisoner pursuing such a claim must prove both deficient performance and prejudice. Citing to a number of sources, including the **ABA Criminal Justice Standards,** the Court found that an attorney's failure to communicate a plea offer to his client may constitute deficient performance. While evaluating deficient performance in Mr. Frye's case, the Court noted that there was no evidence that any effort was made to communicate the offer or that Mr. Frye interfered in any way with the communication of the offer.

Having found deficient performance, the Court then analysed whether Mr. Frye was prejudiced by his attorney's actions. In order to prove prejudice, the Court held that Mr. Frye must show a "reasonable probability" that 1) he would have accepted the offer had it been made known to him; 2) acceptance of the offer would have resulted in a less severe sentence; 3) the state would not have withdrawn or changed the offer; and 4) the trial court would have sentenced him according to the agreement. Although the Court found that Mr. Frye had likely satisfied the first two requirements, it expressed serious doubts that the State would not have withdrawn the offer or that the trial court would not have rejected it. Writing for the majority, Justice Kennedy pointed out a number of considerations, such as the fact that Mr. Frye was charged with another instance of the same offence while the case was pending and that Missouri law allows a trial judge to disregard a plea agreement during sentencing. Ultimately the Court found that the issue of prejudice in Mr. Frye's case turned on questions of state law and remanded the case for further proceedings.

A companion case, **Lafler v. Cooper,** was decided the same day as **Frye.** Anthony Cooper was charged by the state of Michigan with attempted murder for shooting a woman in her buttocks and leg. The prosecution offered a reduced sentence in exchange for a guilty plea, but Mr. Cooper's attorney advised him not to take it, erroneously instructing him that he could not be convicted of attempted murder because the victim was shot below the waist. Consequently, Mr. Cooper's case went to trial, where he was convicted and sentenced to a term 3.5 times longer than the sentence offered in the plea bargain. During state post-conviction proceedings, the court rejected the claim of ineffective assistance of counsel, its analysis turning on whether Mr. Cooper's rejection of the offer was voluntary. Mr. Cooper then filed a habeas petition with the federal district court, which applied the **Strickland** standard and found that he had been denied his Sixth Amendment right to counsel. The Sixth Circuit affirmed the district court's decision and ordered that Mr. Cooper be sentenced to the terms of the original plea offer.

The Supreme Court affirmed the Sixth Circuit's decision in part, holding that if a plea bargain is offered, a criminal defendant has a constitutional right to effective assistance of counsel in considering whether to accept that offer. It rejected the State's argument that a fair trial and sentencing by jury could correct the earlier constitutional error, noting that "the constitutional rights of criminal defendants . . . are granted to the innocent and the guilty alike." Again, writing for the majority, Justice Kennedy limited his analysis to the question of prejudice and the appropriate remedy, because both parties conceded deficient performance.

Examining the same factors discussed in **Frye,** the Court agreed with the Sixth Circuit, finding Mr. Cooper had satisfied the prejudice prong of **Strickland**. The Court found that the Sixth Circuit erred, however, in determining the appropriate remedy. It held that, in this instance, the State should re-offer the plea bargain, and if accepted by the defendant, the trial court could then exercise its discretion in issuing a sentence. Justice Kennedy suggested that this discretion is very broad, indicating that the court may issue a sentence ranging anywhere from the terms of the plea agreement to the original sentence being challenged by the defendant. He declined to discuss the "boundaries of proper discretion," finding that this would be best informed by state law. The Court vacated the Sixth Circuit's judgment and remanded for further proceedings.

Both cases were decided by a 5-4 majority of the court, with Justice Scalia writing dissents in each case joined by Justices Thomas and Roberts, and Justice Alito dissenting separately in **Lafler.**[665]

16.4.3 United Kingdom

The concept of 'plea bargaining' traditionally has no legal standing in the law of England and Wales. However, informal 'discussions' between Counsel on both sides will often lead to an 'offer' by the defence to enter a plea of guilty to either a lesser count or to an agreed basis of plea.

Normally, the first occasion at which a defendant is required to enter a plea is at the Plea and Case Management Hearing in the Crown Court. The defendant may enter a guilty plea at the hearing, and may subsequently change his plea to guilty at any time before a trial commences or even during the trial process.

A plea of guilty must be entered voluntarily. If the accused is deprived of a genuine choice as to plea and in consequence purports to plead guilty, the plea is a nullity and the conviction can be quashed on appeal.[666]

The above procedure ensures that plea discussions are not being abused in the United Kingdom's Criminal Justice System.

Some recent developments have sought to formalise the process of plea bargaining in the United Kingdom. A 'Goodyear application' enables the accused to seek, and the Judge, if he feels it appropriate, to provide an indication of sentence. The following guidelines are given in *R v. Goodyear* **[2005] 1 WLR 2532:**

   i.   A Court should not give an indication of sentence unless one has been sought by the accused

   ii. The Court remains entitled to exercise the power to indicate that the sentence, or type of sentence, on the accused would

---

665 Williams, E.M. (2012), *'U.S. Supreme Court Recognizes Right to Effective Counsel in Plea Bargains', Available at:* http://www.americanbar.org/publications/project_press/2012/spring/plea_bargains.html (accessed 1st October 2014).
666 The SFO Operational Handbook 2012.

be the same whether the case proceeds as a plea of guilty or goes to trial with a resulting conviction. The Court is also entitled to remind the defence advocate that the accused is entitled to seek an advance indication of sentence.

iii. Where an indication is sought, the Court may refuse altogether to give an indication, or may postpone doing so, with or without giving reasons.

iv. Where the Court has it in mind to defer an indication, the probability is that the Judge would explain his reasons, and further indicate the circumstances in which, and when he would be prepared to respond to a request for a sentence indication.

v. If the Court refuses to give an indication it remains open to the defence to make a further request for an indication at a later stage. The Court should not normally initiate the process, except where appropriate to indicate that the circumstances have changed sufficiently to permit a renewed application for an indication.

vi. Once an indication has been given, it is binding.

vii. If the accused does not plead guilty, the indication will cease to have effect.

viii. Where appropriate, there must be an agreed, written basis of plea, otherwise the Judge should refuse to give an indication.[667]

The process laid down in *R v. Goodyear* [2005] 1 WLR 2532 is somewhat similar to plea bargaining, but it is not plea bargaining.

There is no actual agreement between the judge and the defendants to reduce the sentence if the defendants plead guilty. Also, there is no actual agreement between the prosecutors and the defendants to reduce the number of charges if the defendants plead guilty.

The only agreement is for the judge to reveal the details of judgment before the prescribed time.

---

667 The SFO Operational Handbook 2012

16.5 Conclusion

The concept of plea bargaining has not been abused in Nigeria, the United States or the United Kingdom. Rather, it has been utilized in a coordinated way and, in the process, has made a positive impact on the criminal justice system of these countries. Plea bargaining has saved time and state resources, and although it has its disadvantages, the advantages completely outweigh them.

The United States has secured the highest number of convictions compared to Nigeria and the United Kingdom.

Therefore, Nigeria and the United Kingdom are recommended to adopt the US approach.

CHAPTER 17

CUSTOMER DUE DILIGENCE

'Customer due diligence/know your customer' is intended to enable a financial institution to form a reasonable belief that it knows the true identity of each of its customers and, with an appropriate degree of confidence, knows the types of business and transactions the customer is likely to undertake.

The financial institution should have procedures in place to: (i) identify and verify the identity of each customer on a timely basis, (ii) take reasonable risk-based measures to identify and verify the identity of any beneficial owner and (iii) obtain appropriate additional information to understand the customer's circumstances and business, including the expected nature and level of transactions.[668]

Financial institutions are required to undertake customer due-diligence (CDD) measures when: (i) establishing business relations, (ii) carrying out occasional transactions above the applicable designated threshold (fifteen thousand US dollars or Euros) or that are wire transfers, (iii) there is a suspicion of money laundering or terrorist financing or (iv) the financial institution has doubts about the veracity of adequacy of previously obtained customer identification data.

---

668 FATF Guidance on the Risk Based Approach to Combating Money Laundering and Terrorist Financing, (High Level Principles and Procedures) (2007), Paragraph 3.10.

The principle that financial institutions should conduct CDD should be set out in law. Each country may determine how it imposes specific CDD obligations, either through law or enforceable means.[669]

This chapter compares the approaches adopted in Nigeria, the United Kingdom and the United States as they relate to the application of CDD measures to determine what the best approach is.

The comparison falls under the following subheadings: 'Customer Information Required', 'Verification through Documents' and 'Verification through Non-Documentary Methods'.

17.1 Customer Information Required

17.1.1 Nigeria

Financial institutions are required to obtain the following information in relation to natural persons:

i. Legal name and any other names used (such as maiden name);
ii. Permanent address (full address shall be obtained and the use of a post office box number only, is not sufficient);
iii. Telephone number, fax number and email address;
iv. Date and place of birth;
v. Nationality
vi. Occupation, public position held and name of employer;
vii. An official personal identification number or other unique identifier contained in an unexpired official document such as passport, identification card, residence permit, social security records or drivers licence that bears a photograph of the customer;

---

669 The Financial Action Task Force (FATF): International Standards on Combating Money Laundering and the Financing of Terrorism and Proliferation, (The FATF Recommendations) 2012, Interpretive Note to Recommendation 10

viii. Type of account and nature of the banking relationship; and
ix. Signature.[670]

A financial institution shall make an initial assessment of a customer's risk profile from the information provided and particular attention shall be focused on those customers identified as having a higher risk profile and any additional inquiries made or information obtained in respect of those customers shall include:

i.   Evidence of an individual's permanent address sought through a credit reference agency search, or through independent verification by home visits;
ii. Personal reference by an existing customer of the same institution;
iii. Prior bank reference and contact with the bank regarding the customer;
iv. Source of wealth; and
v.   Verification of employment and public position held where appropriate.[671]

17.1.2 United States

Financial institutions are required to obtain the following information in relation to natural persons:

i.   Name;
ii. Date of birth;

---

670 CBN (Anti-Money Laundering and Combating the Financing of Terrorism in Banks and Other Financial Institutions in Nigeria) Regulations, 2013, Schedule II Paragraph 1 (1)

671 CBN (Anti-Money Laundering and Combating the Financing of Terrorism in Banks and Other Financial Institutions in Nigeria) Regulations, 2013, Schedule II Paragraph 1 (5)

iii. Address;

iv. Identification number.[672]

Customers that pose higher money laundering or terrorist financing risks present increased exposure to banks; due diligence policies, procedures, and processes should be enhanced as a result. Enhanced due diligence (EDD) for higher-risk customers is especially critical in understanding their anticipated transactions and implementing a suspicious activity monitoring system that reduces the bank's reputation, compliance, and transaction risks. Higher-risk customers and their transactions should be reviewed more closely at account opening and more frequently throughout the term of their relationship with the bank.

The bank may determine that a customer poses a higher risk because of the customer's business activity, ownership structure, anticipated or actual volume and types of transactions, including those transactions involving higher-risk jurisdictions. If so, the bank should consider obtaining, both at account opening and throughout the relationship, the following information on the customer:

i. Purpose of the account;

ii. Source of funds and wealth;

iii. Individuals with ownership or control over the account, such as beneficial owners, signatories or guarantors;

iv. Occupation or type of business (of customer or other individuals with ownership or control over the account);

v. Financial statements;

vi. Banking references;

vii. Domicile (where the business is organized);

viii. Proximity of the customer's residence, place of employment, or place of business to the bank;

---

672 Federal Financial Institutions Examination Council (2014), 'Bank Secrecy Act/Anti-Money Laundering Examination Manual', Available at: https://www.occ. treas.gov/publications/publications-by-type/other-publications-reports/ffiec-bsa-aml-examination-manual.pdf (accessed 10 January 2017).

ix. Description of the customer's primary trade area and whether international transactions are expected to be routine;

x. Description of the business operations, the anticipated volume of currency and total sales, and a list of major customers and suppliers;

xi. Explanations for changes in account activity.[673]

17.1.3 United Kingdom

Firms are required to obtain the following information in relation to natural persons:

i. Full name;
ii. Residential address;
iii. Date of birth.[674]

When someone becomes a new customer, or applies for a new product or service, or where there are indications that the risk associated with an existing business relationship might have increased, the firm should, depending on the nature of the product or service for which they are applying, request information as to:

i. The customers residential status;
ii. Employment and salary details;
iii. Other sources of income or wealth (e.g., inheritance, divorce settlement, property sale).[675]

---

673 Federal Financial Institutions Examination Council (2014), 'Bank Secrecy Act/Anti-Money Laundering Examination Manual', Available at: https://www.occ.treas.gov/publications/publications-by-type/other-publications-reports/ffiec-bsa-aml-examination-manual.pdf (accessed 10 January 2017).

674 The Joint Money Laundering Steering Group JMLSG, *Prevention of money laundering/combating terrorist financing 2017* Revised Version, Guidance for the UK financial sector Part I, June 2017 (Amended December 2017), Paragraph 5.3.71

675 The Joint Money Laundering Steering Group JMLSG, *Prevention of money laundering/combating terrorist financing 2017* Revised Version, Guidance for the UK financial sector Part I, June 2017 (Amended December 2017), Paragraph 5.5.6

17.2 Verification Through Documents

17.2.1 Nigeria

Financial institutions shall verify the information referred to in subsection 9.1.1 by at least one of the following methods:

i.   Confirming the date of birth from an official document (such as birth certificate, passport, identity card, social security records);

ii. Confirming the permanent address (such as utility bill, tax assessment, bank statement, a letter from a public authority).[676]

17.2.2 United States

A bank using documentary methods to verify a customer's identity must have procedures that set forth the minimum acceptable documentation.

Banks shall verify the information referred to in subsection 9.1.2 by at least one of the following methods:

i.   A Driver's licence;

ii. Passport.[677]

17.2.3 United Kingdom

If identity is to be verified from documents, this should be based on: Either a government-issued document which incorporates:

---

676   CBN (Anti-Money Laundering and Combating the Financing of Terrorism in Banks and Other Financial Institutions in Nigeria) Regulations, 2013, Schedule II Paragraph 1 (2) (a) (b)

677   Federal Financial Institutions Examination Council (2014), 'Bank Secrecy Act/Anti-Money Laundering Examination Manual', Available at: https://www.occ. treas.gov/publications/publications-by-type/other-publications-reports/ffiec-bsa-aml-examination-manual.pdf (accessed 10 January 2017).

    i.   The customer's full name and photograph, and;

   ii. Either his residential address;

  iii. Or his date of birth.

Or a government-issued document (without a photograph) which incorporates the customer's full name, supported by a second document, either government-issued, or issued by a judicial authority, a public-sector body or authority, a regulated utility company, or another FCA-regulated firm in the UK financial services sector, or in an equivalent jurisdiction, which incorporates:

    i.   The customer's full name and;

   ii. Either his residential address;

  iii. Or his date of birth.

Government-issued documents with a photograph include:

    i.   Valid passport;

   ii. Valid photo card driving licence (full or provisional);

  iii. National identity card;

  iv. Firearms certificate or shotgun licence;

   v. Identity card issued by the Electoral Office for Northern Ireland.

Government-issued documents without a photograph include:

    i.   Valid (old style) full UK driving licence;

   ii. Recent evidence of entitlement to a state or local authority-funded benefit (including housing benefit and council tax benefit), tax credit, pension, educational or other grant.

Other documents include

    i.   Instrument of a Court appointment (such as liquidator, or grant of probate);

ii. Current council tax demand letter, or statement;[678]

iii. Current bank statements, or credit/debit card statements, issued by a regulated financial sector firm in the United Kingdom, EU or an equivalent jurisdiction (but not ones printed off the internet);

iv. Utility bills (but not ones printed off the internet).[679]

17.3 Verification Through Non-Documentary Methods

17.3.1 Nigeria
Financial institutions may verify the information referred to in sub-section 9.1.1 by at least one of the following methods:

i. Contacting the customer by telephone, by letter or by email to confirm the information supplied after an account has been opened (such as a disconnected phone, returned mail, or incorrect e-mail address shall warrant further investigation);

ii. Confirming the validity of the official documentation provided through certification by an authorized person such as embassy official, notary public.[680]

17.3.2 United States
Banks are not required to use non-documentary methods to verify a customer's identity. However, a bank using non-documentary

---

678 The Joint Money Laundering Steering Group JMLSG, *Prevention of money laundering/combating terrorist financing 2017* Revised Version, Guidance for the UK financial sector Part I, June 2017 (Amended December 2017), Paragraph 5.3.75

679 The Joint Money Laundering Steering Group JMLSG, *Prevention of money laundering/combating terrorist financing 2017* Revised Version, Guidance for the UK financial sector Part I, June 2017 (Amended December 2017), Paragraph 5.3.76

680 CBN (Anti-Money Laundering and Combating the Financing of Terrorism in Banks and Other Financial Institutions in Nigeria) Regulations, 2013, Schedule II Paragraph 1 (2) (c) (d)

methods to verify a customer's identity must have procedures that set forth the methods the bank will use.

Non-documentary methods may include:

i.   Contacting a customer;
ii. Independently verifying the customer's identity through the comparison of information provided by the customer with information obtained from a customer reporting agency, public data base, or other source;
iii. Checking references with other financial institutions; and
iv. Obtaining a financial statement.[681]

17.3.3 United Kingdom

When using an electronic/digital source to verify a customer's identity, firms should ensure that they are able to demonstrate that they have both verified that the customer exists, and satisfied themselves that the individual seeking the business relationship is, in fact, that customer (or beneficial owner).[682]

Electronic verification may be carried out by the firm either direct, using as its basis the customer's full name, address and date of birth, or through an organisation which meets the criteria in **paragraphs 5.3.51 and 5.3.52 of the JMLSG Guidance for the UK financial sector Part I, June 2017 (Amended December 2017)**.[683]

A number of commercial agencies which access many data sources are accessible online by firms, and may provide firms with a composite and comprehensive level of electronic verification through a

---

681 Federal Financial Institutions Examination Council (2014), 'Bank Secrecy Act/Anti-Money Laundering Examination Manual', Available at: https://www.occ. treas.gov/publications/publications-by-type/other-publications-reports/ffiec-bsa-aml-examination-manual.pdf (accessed 10 January 2017).

682 The Joint Money Laundering Steering Group JMLSG, *Prevention of money laundering/combating terrorist financing* 2017 Revised Version, Guidance for the UK financial sector Part I, June 2017 (Amended December 2017), Paragraph 5.3.79

683 The Joint Money Laundering Steering Group JMLSG, *Prevention of money laundering/combating terrorist financing* 2017 Revised Version, Guidance for the UK financial sector Part I, June 2017 (Amended December 2017), Paragraph 5.3.80

single interface. Such agencies use databases of both positive and negative information, and many also access high-risk alerts that utilise specific data sources to identify high-risk conditions, for example, known identity frauds or inclusion on a sanctions list. Some of these sources are, however, only available to closed user groups.[684]

Positive information (relating to full name, current address, date of birth) can prove that an individual exists, but some can offer a higher degree of confidence than others. Such information should include data from more robust sources - where an individual has to prove their identity, or address, in some way in order to be included, as opposed to others, where no such proof is required.[685]

Negative information includes lists of individuals known to have committed fraud, including identity fraud, and registers of deceased persons. Checking against such information may be necessary to mitigate against impersonation fraud.[686]

For an electronic check to provide satisfactory evidence of identity on its own, it must use data from multiple sources, and across time, or incorporate qualitative checks that assess the strength of the information supplied. An electronic check that accesses data from a single source (e.g., a single check against the Electoral Roll) is not normally enough on its own to verify identity.[687]

Before using a commercial agency for electronic verification, firms should be satisfied that information supplied by the data provider is considered to be sufficiently extensive, reliable and accurate.

---

684 The Joint Money Laundering Steering Group JMLSG, *Prevention of money laundering/combating terrorist financing* 2017 Revised Version, Guidance for the UK financial sector Part I, June 2017 (Amended December 2017), Paragraph 5.3.46

685 The Joint Money Laundering Steering Group JMLSG, *Prevention of money laundering/combating terrorist financing* 2017 Revised Version, Guidance for the UK financial sector Part I, June 2017 (Amended December 2017), Paragraph 5.3.47

686 The Joint Money Laundering Steering Group JMLSG, *Prevention of money laundering/combating terrorist financing* 2017 Revised Version, Guidance for the UK financial sector Part I, June 2017 (Amended December 2017), Paragraph 5.3.49

687 The Joint Money Laundering Steering Group JMLSG, *Prevention of money laundering/combating terrorist financing* 2017 Revised Version, Guidance for the UK financial sector Part I, June 2017 (Amended December 2017), Paragraph 5.3.50

This judgement may be assisted by considering whether the provider meets all the following criteria:

i.   it is recognised, through registration with the Information Commissioner's Office, to store personal data;
ii. it uses a range of positive information sources that can be called upon to link an applicant to both current and previous circumstances;
iii. it accesses negative information sources, such as databases relating to identity fraud and deceased persons;
iv. it accesses a wide range of alert data sources; and
v.   it has transparent processes that enable the firm to know what checks were carried out, what the results of these checks were, and what they mean in terms of how much certainty they give as to the identity of the subject.[688]

In addition, a commercial agency should have processes that allow the enquirer to capture and store the information they used to verify an identity.[689]

CASE STUDY ON THE ADVANTAGES OF A CUSTOMER IDENTIFICATION PROGRAM

Case 17.1: Financial Crimes Enforcement Network v. North Dade Community Development Federal Credit Union Number 2014-07

As part of its anti-money laundering compliance program, a credit union must implement a written Customer Identification Program ("CIP") appropriate for its size and type of business. The program must include

---

688 The Joint Money Laundering Steering Group JMLSG, *Prevention of money laundering/combating terrorist financing* 2017 Revised Version, Guidance for the UK financial sector Part I, June 2017 (Amended December 2017), Paragraph 5.3.52

689 The Joint Money Laundering Steering Group JMLSG, *Prevention of money laundering/combating terrorist financing* 2017 Revised Version, Guidance for the UK financial sector Part I, June 2017 (Amended December 2017), Paragraph 5.3.53

risk-based identity verification, recordkeeping, and retention procedures, as well as procedures to determine whether an account is being opened for a government-designated terrorist or terrorist organization and to take appropriate follow-up action if a customer is designated. **31 U.S.C. § 5318(l); 31 C.F.R §§ 1020.210, 1020.220; 12 C.F.R. § 748.2(b)(2).** CIP helps a financial institution determine the risks posed by a particular customer, allowing the institution to ensure that it has the proper controls in place, including suspicious activity monitoring procedures, and to monitor and report on the risks of a particular client.

In relation to the Vendor's MSB clients, North Dade had no procedures in place to address CIP requirements. While North Dade management discussed the high risk posed by this business line as early as March 2010, North Dade's staff and management never reviewed, researched, or verified the identities of the holders of any of the MSB accounts. Instead, North Dade relied exclusively on the Vendor to perform CIP functions. A credit union may rely on another financial institution only in instances where the credit union and the financial institution share customers, and the financial institution is regulated by a federal functional regulator. **31 C.F.R. § 1020.220(a)(6).** In this case, North Dade should not have relied on the Vendor for CIP compliance because, as an MSB, the Vendor was not regulated by a federal functional regulator. By not knowing its members, North Dade was not capable of understanding their expected transactional behavior and thus was unable to appropriately monitor for suspicious activities.

FinCEN determined that North Dade willfully violated the program, reporting, and recordkeeping requirements of the Bank Secrecy Act and its implementing regulations, as described in this ASSESSMENT, and that grounds exist to assess a civil money penalty for these violations. **31 U.S.C. § 5321 and 31 C.F.R. § 1010.820.** FinCEN has determined that the penalty in this matter will be three hundred thousand dollars.[690]

---

690   United States of America Department of the Treasury Financial Crimes Enforcement Network (2014), 'IN THE MATTER OF: North Dade Community Development Federal Credit Union Miami Gardens, Florida', Available at: https://www.fincen.gov/sites/default/files/enforcement_action/NorthDade_Assessment.pdf (accessed 3 January 2017).

17.4 Discussion

The previous sections compared the approaches adopted in Nigeria, the United Kingdom and the United States as they relate to the application of CDD measures.

This section will determine issues that arise from such a comparison.

17.4.1 Bank Verification Number

Nigeria has a centralized biometric identification system for the banking industry tagged Bank Verification Number (BVN), while the UK and US do not have this kind of system in place.

This system was launched by the Central Bank of Nigeria (the apex financial regulator in Nigeria) through the Bankers' Committee and in collaboration with all banks in Nigeria on February 14, 2014. The BVN project, which involved capturing biometrics of customers, was intended to protect bank customers and further strengthen the Nigerian banking system. It was also expected to minimise the incidences of fraud and money laundering in the banking industry. Every account holder is expected to do the BVN biometrics registration because it gives each bank depositor a unique identity, which can be verified at any bank where the customer has accounts.

The biometric identification system has helped curb payroll fraud in the Nigerian civil service. A 2016 Punch Report revealed that 43,000 ghost workers were discovered through the use of the Bank Verification Number. According to the Honourable Minister of Finance, Mrs. Kemi Adeosun, the use of BVN exposed the links of some individuals in the civil service to multiple accounts, while, in other instances, the name on the BVN was inconsistent with that on the payroll.

The Bank Verification Number also helped to expose how a former Chief of Defence Staff, Air Chief Marshal Alex Badeh (retd.), was linked to two hundred and forty-million-naira worth of property in Abuja.

The biometric identification system has also helped to curb money laundering. On October 17, 2017, a Federal High Court in Abuja ordered the forfeiture of all monies in bank accounts owned by corporate organisations, government agencies and individuals without the BVN. It is believed that most of these accounts are owned by corrupt public officials who used fictitious names to open accounts for the purpose of laundering their ill-gotten wealth.

The forfeiture order, which was issued by Justice Dimgba Igwe, while ruling on an ex parte application filed by the Federal Government through the Office of the Attorney General of the Federation, is not final yet.

Despite the successes being recorded by the Bank Verification Number project as noted above, a recent report by the Economic and Financial Crimes Commission (the designated Financial Intelligence Unit in Nigeria) revealed that some banks are helping corrupt government officials to operate secret accounts without Bank Verification Numbers. The report accused banks of not reporting suspicious transactions in line with statutory regulations. This revelation epitomises systemic failure aggravated by the Central Bank of Nigeria's weak regulation.

This year alone, the Financial Crimes Enforcement Network (the delegated administrator of the **United States Bank Secrecy Act**) and the Financial Conduct Authority (the conduct regulator for 56,000 financial services firms and financial markets in the UK and the prudential regulator for over 18,000 of those firms) have all brought enforcement actions against a number of financial institutions for violations of the reporting, recordkeeping, or other requirements of the Financial Action Task Force Recommendations 2012.

For example, the Financial Conduct Authority (FCA) had on the 31st of January, 2017, fined Deutsche Bank AG (Deutsche Bank) £163,076,224 for failing to maintain an adequate anti-money laundering (AML) control framework during the period between 1 January 2012 and 31 December 2015. This is the largest financial penalty for AML controls failings ever imposed by the FCA, or its predecessor, the Financial Services Authority (FSA).

According to the FCA, "Deutsche Bank exposed the UK financial system to the risks of financial crime by failing to properly oversee the formation of new customer relationships and the booking of global business in the UK. As a consequence of its inadequate AML control framework, Deutsche Bank was used by unidentified customers to transfer approximately $10 billion, of unknown origin, from Russia to offshore bank accounts in a manner that is highly suggestive of financial crime."

On or about February 2017, the Financial Crimes Enforcement Network (FinCEN) had determined that grounds exist to assess a civil money penalty against Merchants Bank of California, N.A. (Merchants or the Bank), pursuant to the **Bank Secrecy Act (BSA) and regulations** issued pursuant to that Act.

According to FinCEN, "Merchants willfully violated the BSA's program and reporting requirements from March 2012 to September 2016. As described below, Merchants failed to (a) establish and implement an adequate AML program; (b) conduct required due diligence on its foreign correspondent accounts; and (c) detect and report suspicious activity. Merchants's failures allowed billions of dollars in transactions to flow through the U.S. financial system without effective monitoring to adequately detect and report suspicious activity. Many of these transactions were conducted on behalf of money services businesses (MSBs) that were owned or managed by Bank insiders who encouraged staff to process these transactions without question or face potential dismissal or retaliation."

In view of the above stated facts, FinCEN determined that the penalty in this matter would be $7 million. The penalty will run concurrent with the Office of the Comptroller of the Currency, OCC's $1 million penalty.

The Central Bank of Nigeria, on the other hand, has brought no enforcement action against any financial institution in Nigeria despite disturbing revelations from the EFCC and the media.

17.4.2 Meaning of 'Customer'

As stated above, financial institutions are required to apply the necessary CDD measures to their customers.

The term 'customer' is not expressly defined in the Nigerian or UK Money Laundering Regulations as it is defined in the **US Bank**

Secrecy Act/Anti–Money Laundering Examination Manual 2014. Its meaning must be inferred from the definitions of 'business relationship' and 'occasional transaction', the context in which it is used in the United Kingdom and Nigerian Money Laundering Regulations and its everyday dictionary meaning.[691]

In general, the customer is the party, or parties, with whom the business relationship is established, or for whom the transaction is carried out. Where, however, there are several parties to a transaction, not all will necessarily be customers.[692]

A "business relationship" is defined under in the ML Regulations as a business, professional or commercial relationship between a financial institution/credit institution and a customer, which arises out of the business of the financial institution/credit institution, and is expected by the financial institution/credit institution, at the time when contact is established, to have an element of duration.[693]

A relationship where the financial institution/credit institution is asked to form a company for its customer is to be treated as a business relationship for the purpose of the UK's Money Laundering Regulations, whether or not the formation of the company is the only transaction carried out for that customer.[694] An estate agent is to

---

691 The Joint Money Laundering Steering Group JMLSG, *Prevention of money laundering/combating terrorist financing* 2017 Revised Version, Guidance for the UK financial sector Part I, June 2017 (Amended December 2017), Paragraph 5.3.3

692 The Joint Money Laundering Steering Group JMLSG, *Prevention of money laundering/combating terrorist financing* 2017 Revised Version, Guidance for the UK financial sector Part I, June 2017 (Amended December 2017), Paragraph 5.3.4

693 For United Kingdom laws, see the Money Laundering, Terrorist Financing and Transfer of Funds (Information on the Payer) Regulations 2017, Regulation 4 (1). See also the Joint Money Laundering Steering Group JMLSG, *Prevention of money laundering/combating terrorist financing* 2017 Revised Version, Guidance for the UK financial sector Part I, June 2017 (Amended December 2017), Paragraph 5.3.5. For Nigerian laws, see Money Laundering Prohibition Act 2011 (as amended), s. 25. See also CBN (Anti–Money Laundering and Combating the Financing of Terrorism in Banks and Other Financial Institutions in Nigeria) Regulations, 2013, Regulation 132.

694 The United Kingdom Money Laundering, Terrorist Financing and Transfer of Funds (Information on the Payer) Regulations 2017, Regulation 4 (2)

be treated as entering into a business relationship with a purchaser (as well as with a seller), at the point when the purchaser's offer is accepted by the seller.[695]

An 'occasional transaction' means a transaction which is not carried out as part of a business relationship.[696]

The United States, on the other hand, defines a customer as a person (an individual, a corporation, partnership, a trust, an estate or any other entity recognized as a legal person) who opens a new account; an individual who opens a new account for another individual who lacks legal capacity; or an individual who opens a new account for an entity that is not a legal person (e.g., a civic club). A customer does not include a person who does not receive banking services, such as a person whose loan application is denied. The definition of customer also does not include an existing customer as long as the bank has a reasonable belief that it knows the customer's true identity. Excluded from the definition of customer are federally regulated banks, banks regulated by a state bank regulator, governmental entities and publicly traded companies (as described in 31 CFR 103.22 (d) (2) (ii) through (iv).[697]

In view of the above facts, the US approach is far better than the United Kingdom and the Nigerian approach, because it leaves no room for ambiguity.

---

695   The United Kingdom Money Laundering, Terrorist Financing and Transfer of Funds (Information on the Payer) Regulations 2017, Regulation 4 (3)

696   For United Kingdom laws, see the Money Laundering, Terrorist Financing and Transfer of Funds (Information on the Payer) Regulations 2017, Regulation 3 (1); See also the Joint Money Laundering Steering Group JMLSG, *Prevention of money laundering/combating terrorist financing* 2017 Revised Version, Guidance for the UK financial sector Part I, June 2017 (Amended December 2017), Paragraph 5.3.6. For Nigerian laws, see Money Laundering Prohibition Act 2011 (as amended), s. 25.

697   Federal Financial Institutions Examination Council (2014), 'Bank Secrecy Act/Anti-Money Laundering Examination Manual', Available at: https://www.occ. treas.gov/publications/publications-by-type/other-publications-reports/ffiec-bsa-aml-examination-manual.pdf (accessed 10 January 2017).

17.4.3 Direct Discrimination

This section aims to determine if the approaches adopted in Nigeria, the United States and the United Kingdom in relation to the application of CDD measures directly violate the human rights of customers.

We will look into the conditions that must be cumulatively met in order to be considered direct discrimination. These conditions include differential treatment, prohibited grounds, without objective and reasonable justification and no reasonable relationship of proportionality.[698]

17.4.3.1 Differential Treatment

One of the conditions that must exist in direct discrimination is that there must be a given difference in treatment, which may concern the exercise of any right set forth by law.[699]

It could be argued that the UK law does create a difference in treatment by using the word *his* in paragraph 5.3.100 of its money laundering guidelines. That could imply that the CDD measures apply only to men, and not women.

However, since the law implements the FATF's Money Laundering Recommendations, which apply all anti–money laundering measures to both men and women, it does not discriminate.

The UK approach does not directly discriminate against customers, and, on that note, there is no need to further determine whether or not it meets the other direct discrimination requirements.

The US and Nigerian money laundering laws also do not directly discriminate against customers since both laws, unlike the UK law, never use the word *he.*

---

698 Belgian Linguistic Case, (1979–80) 1 EHRR 252, Para 10; Swedish Engine Driver's Union v. Sweden (1979–80) 1 EHRR, 617, Para 45, 47, 48; National Union of Belgian Police v. Belgium (1979–80) 1 EHRR 578, Para 44, 46; Engel and Others v. The Netherlands (No.1) (1979–80) 1 EHRR 647, Para 72; The Republic of Ireland v. The United Kingdom (1979–80) 2 EHRR 25, Para 226.

699 Belgian Linguistic Case (1979–80) 1 EHRR 252, Para 10; National Union of Belgian Police v. Belgium (1979–80) 1 EHRR 578 Para 44, 46.

17.4 Conclusion

In view of the arguments in the previous section, the following are recommended:

I. Nigeria and the United Kingdom should amend their money laundering laws by defining who a customer is.

II. The United Kingdom should amend its money laundering laws by removing the word *his*.

CHAPTER 18

RECORD KEEPING

The Financial Action Task Force (FATF) has advised countries to enact laws that mandate financial institutions to keep all records obtained through CDD measures (e.g., copies or records of official identification documents like passports, identity cards, driving licences or similar documents); account files and business correspondence, including the results of any analysis undertaken (e.g., inquiries to establish the background and purpose of complex, unusual large transactions) for at least five years after the business relationship ends or after the date of the occasional transaction.

Financial institutions should be required by law to maintain records on transactions and information obtained through the CDD measures. The CDD information and the transaction records should be available to domestic competent authorities upon appropriate authority.[700]

Although there is no material difference in the approaches adopted by Nigeria, the United States and the United Kingdom in relation to record-keeping requirements, it is still necessary to discuss this topic.

This chapter critically analyses the rule-based approach that is applied to record-keeping requirements under the subheading 'The Risk-Based Approach to Record-Keeping Requirements'.

---

700 The Financial Action Task Force (FATF): International Standards on Combating Money Laundering and the Financing of Terrorism and Proliferation, (The FATF Recommendations) 2012, Interpretive Note to Recommendation 11

18.1 The Risk-Based Approach to Record-Keeping Requirements

The FATF requires financial institutions to apply a rule-based approach to record-keeping requirements. In other words, financial institutions are required by law to maintain records on transactions and information obtained through the CDD measures for a minimum period of five years.

A risk-based approach may be a preferable option to a rule-based approach.

A risk-based approach is designed to make it more difficult for money launderers and terrorist organizations to make use of financial institutions due to the increased focus on the identified higher-risk activities that are undertaken by these criminal elements.[701]

Countries should not be allowed to stipulate a minimum time frame for financial institutions to maintain records. Rather, the period should depend on whether or not the customer is high risk.

For customers who have been designated as higher risk by a firm, financial institutions should be allowed to keep records of information obtained through CDD measures for ten years or more. For customers designated as lower risk, financial institutions should be allowed to keep records of information obtained through CDD measures for as little as two years.

Keeping information for five years may lead to an unnecessary interference with a person's right to a private life, and such interference cannot be justified.

18.2 Conclusion

In view of the arguments canvassed in section 18.1 of this chapter, a risk-based approach to record-keeping requirements is the preferable approach.

---

701 FATF Guidance on the Risk Based Approach to Combating Money Laundering and Terrorist Financing, (High Level Principles and Procedures) (2007), paragraph 1.17.

CHAPTER 19

LEVEL OF COMPLIANCE

The previous chapters focused on the anti–money laundering measures implemented by Nigeria, the United States and the United Kingdom for the purpose of combating money laundering and terrorist financing.

This chapter will determine the level of compliance with anti–money laundering measures in those countries.

19.1 Nigeria

In a letter to banks and discount houses titled 'Status and Reporting Line of Chief Compliance Officers of Banks', with reference number: BSD/DIR/GEN/LAB/07/013, the Central Bank of Nigeria (CBN) stated that information available to it revealed that the qualifications of chief compliance officers of some banks and discount houses were below the grade of general manager that was required by the CBN.

Equally worrisome, the apex bank wrote, is that most of the compliance officers do not report directly to the board of directors, which is 'a flagrant disregard to the extant laws and regulations on the subject'.[702]

---

702 Nweze, C. (2014), *'CBN laments skills gap of Compliance Officers', Available at:* http://thenationonlineng.net/new/cbn-laments-skills-gap-compliance-officers/ (accessed October 1, 2014).

19.2 United States

Examination authority over banks and other depository institutions for **Bank Secrecy Act** compliance has been delegated by FinCEN to the industry's five functional regulators.

These regulators include the Board of Governors of the Federal Reserve System (Federal Reserve), the Federal Deposit Insurance Corporation, the National Credit Union Association, the Office of the Comptroller of the Currency and the Office of Thrift Supervision. State-chartered private banks, trust companies and credit unions without federal insurance have no federal functional regulators and come under the purview of the IRS SB/SE Division for purposes of BSA examination.

In the second half of 2004, US federal banking regulators completed forty-four public enforcement actions involving **Bank Secrecy Act (BSA)** violations.

Among the problems most often cited was the lack of independent testing to validate BSA compliance. In about 60 percent of the BSA cases that were closed in the second half, a bank was ordered to arrange for testing or was cited for failure to do so. In recent years, several banks have faced severe criminal and civil penalties as a consequence of BSA lapses.[703]

19.3 United Kingdom

The Financial Conduct Authority's 2011 thematic review of the management of high money laundering risk situations found that three quarters of the banks reviewed, including a number of major banks, were not managing this risk effectively. Around a third of banks, including the private banking arms of some major banking groups,

---

703 Department of the Treasury (2005), 'US Money Laundering Threat Assessment', Available at: https://www.treasury.gov/resource-center/terrorist-illicit-finance/Documents/mlta.pdf (accessed 26 December 2017). See also Department of the Treasury (2015), 'National Money Laundering Risk Assessment', Available at: https://www.treasury.gov/resource-center/terrorist-illicit-finance/Documents/National%20Money%20Laundering%20Risk%20Assessment%20%E2%80%93%202006-12-2015.pdf (accessed 26 December 2017).

appeared willing to accept high levels of money laundering risk if the immediate reputational and regulatory risk was acceptable.[704]

Over half the banks the Financial Conduct Authority (FCA) visited failed to apply meaningful enhanced due-diligence (EDD) measures in higher-risk situations and so failed to identify or record adverse information about the customer or the customer's beneficial owner. Around a third of them dismissed serious allegations about their customers without adequate review. More than a third of the banks visited failed to put effective measures in place to identify customers as PEPs.[705]

Three quarters of the banks in the FCA's sample failed to take adequate measures to establish the legitimacy of the source of wealth and source of funds to be used in the business relationship. This was of particular concern where the bank was aware of significant adverse information about the customer's or beneficial owner's integrity.[706]

More recently, the FCA's thematic review of the control of financial crime risks in trade finance found that most banks, including a number of major UK banks, were not giving adequate attention to money laundering red flags in trade finance transactions. There was an inconsistent approach to risk assessment and only a few banks had conducted a specific trade finance money laundering risk assessment.[707]

About half of the banks had no clear policies or procedures document for dealing with trade-based money laundering risks. As a result, some banks failed to implement adequate controls to identify potentially suspicious transactions. Many banks were unable to demonstrate that money laundering risk had been taken into account when processing particular transactions. In particular, trade

---

704 Financial Conduct Authority: Anti–Money Laundering annual report (2013), Paragraph 6.2.

705 Financial Conduct Authority: Anti–Money Laundering annual report (2013), Paragraph 6.3.

706 Financial Conduct Authority: Anti–Money Laundering annual report (2013), Paragraph 6.4.

707 Financial Conduct Authority: Anti–Money Laundering annual report (2013), Paragraph 6.6.

processing staff in most banks made inadequate use of customer due-diligence information that the relationship managers or trade sales teams gathered. In addition, systems and controls over dual-use goods were inadequate at most banks. However, a minority of banks used some innovative and effective techniques to assess money laundering risk in trade finance transactions, which other banks could usefully follow.[708]

The root cause of these problems is often a failure in governance of money laundering risk, which leads, among other things, to inadequate anti–money laundering resources and a lack of (or poor quality) assurance work across the firm. This often focuses on whether processes have been followed rather than on the substance of whether good AML judgments are being made.[709]

The weakness the FCA sees in dealings with high-risk customers and PEPs is a serious and persistent problem in firms of all sizes. However, this issue manifests itself in different ways in different types of firms. Small firms often fail to collect enhanced due-diligence information, as required under the MLR 2007. Large firms, including those that have been subject to Systematic Anti–Money Laundering Programme (SAMLP) examinations, often collect adequate information but fail to assess it properly and/or make poor judgments about the money laundering risk this information exposes, particularly where potential profits are high.[710]

The FCA also found weaknesses in firms of all sizes in establishing and corroborating the source of wealth or funds for high-risk customers. Too much reliance is often placed on the customers' explanations, even when they are subject to serious and credible allegations of criminal activity.[711]

---

708 Financial Conduct Authority: Anti–Money Laundering annual report (2013), Paragraph 6.7.

709 Financial Conduct Authority: Anti–Money Laundering annual report (2013), Paragraph 6.8.

710 Financial Conduct Authority: Anti–Money Laundering annual report (2013), Paragraph 6.9.

711 Financial Conduct Authority: Anti–Money Laundering annual report (2013), Paragraph 6.10.

19.4 Discussion

The previous section summarized the findings from regulated authorities on the degree of anti–money laundering compliance in Nigeria, the United States and the United Kingdom.

This section analyses the issues that arose from such findings, with the aim of determining if there is need for reform.

19.4.1 Qualification of Compliance Officers

The problem the United Kingdom seems to be facing with regard to compliance is that many banks refuse to apply meaningful enhanced due-diligence measures in higher-risk situations.

In the United States, the problem most often cited is the lack of independent testing to validate BSA compliance.

In Nigeria, the problem appears to be much bigger. The people who ought to be responsible for coordinating and monitoring day-to-day anti–money laundering compliance in financial institutions lack the required expertise to undertake the job.

The CBN has attempted to fix the problem by issuing a circular requiring all deposit money banks and discount houses to ensure:

I.   That no chief compliance officer in the institution is below the grade of general manager without prior CBN approval.
II. That the chief compliance officer reports to the board of directors with dotted lines to the MD/CEO and without interlocking roles.

Accordingly, the particulars of all current chief compliance officers along with evidence of the CBN's approval and the reporting lines should be forwarded to the director of banking supervision within one week from the date of the circular, which was 23 May 2014.[712]

The CBN approach appears to be similar to that of the FCA's approach. In the United Kingdom, the role of a compliance officer

---

712 CBN: *Circular on Status and Reporting Line of Chief Compliance Officers of Banks* (2014).

has been designated by the FCA as a controlled function under section 59 of the Financial Services and Markets Act 2000 (FSMA). As a result, any person invited to perform that function must be individually approved by the FCA, on the application of the firm, before performing the function.[713]

19.5 Conclusion

In view of the arguments canvassed in section 19.4 of this chapter, the CBN should adopt the approach of the FCA by conducting annual thematic reviews of banking operations. This would keep them updated on the performance level of these institutions.

---

713 Financial Conduct Authority Handbook, SYSC 6.3.10 G. See also The Joint Money Laundering Steering Group JMLSG, *Prevention of money laundering/combating terrorist financing* 2017 Revised Version, Guidance for the UK financial sector Part I, June 2017, Paragraph 3.10

APPENDIX 1

THE NIGERIAN MONEY LAUNDERING (PROHIBITION) ACT, 2011 (AS AMENDED)

ARRANGEMENT OF SECTIONS

MONEY LAUNDERING (PROHIBITION) ACT, 2011 (AS AMENDED)
(Act No. 11, 2011 and Act No. 1, 2012)
SECTION:

PART 1—PROHIBITION OF MONEY LAUNDERING

1. Limitation to make or accept cash payment.
2. Duty to report international transfer of funds and securities.
3. Identification of customers.
4. Duties incumbent upon casinos.
5. Occasional cash transaction by designated non-Financial Institutions.
6. Suspicious transaction reporting.
7. Preservation of records.
8. Communication of information.
9. Internal procedures, policies and controls.
10. Mandatory disclosure by financial institutions.
11. Prohibition of numbered or anonymous accounts, accounts in fictitious names and shell banks.

MONEY LAUNDERING (PROHIBITION) ACT, 2011 (AS AMENDED)

AN ACT TO REPEAL THE MONEY LAUNDERING (PROHIBI-TION) ACT 2004 AND ENACT THE MONEY LAUNDERING (PRO-HIBITION ACT, 2011 TO ENHANCE THE SCOPE OF MONEY LAUNDERING OFFENCES AND CUSTOMER DUE DILIGENCE MEASURES, AND FOR RELATED MATTERS

[3rd Day of June, 2011]

Enacted by the National Assembly of the Federal Republic of Nigeria as follows—

PART 1—PROHIBITION OF MONEY LAUNDERING

1. Limitation to Make or Accept Cash Payment

No person or body corporate shall, except in a transaction through a Financial Institution, make or accept cash payment of a sum exceeding-

  (a) ₦5,000,000.00 or its equivalent, in the case of an individual; or
  (b) ₦10,000,000.00 or its equivalent, in the case of a body corporate.

2. Duty to Report International Transfer of Funds and Securities

  (1) A transfer to or from a foreign country of funds or securities by a person or body corporate including a Money Service Business of a sum exceeding US$10,000 or its equivalent shall be reported to the Central Bank of Nigeria, Securities and Exchange Commission or the Commission in writing within 7 days from the date of the transaction.

  (2) A report made under subsection (1) of this section shall indicate the nature and amount of the transfer, the names and addresses of the sender and the receiver of the funds or securities.

  (3) Transportation of cash or negotiable instruments in excess of US$10,000 or its equivalent by individuals in or out of the country shall be declared to the Nigerian Customs Service.

  (4) The Nigeria Customs Service shall report any declaration made pursuant to subsection (3) of this section to the Central Bank and the Commission.

  (5) Any person who falsely declares or fails to make a declaration to the Nigerian Customs Service pursuant to section 12 of the Foreign Exchange (Monitoring and Miscellaneous Provisions) Act, Cap. F34, LFN, 2004 is guilty of an offence and shall be liable on conviction to forfeit the undeclared funds or negotiable instrument or to imprisonment to a term of not less than 2 years or to both.

3. Identification of Customers

(1) A Financial Institution and a Designated Non-Financial Institution shall—

    (a) identify a customer, whether permanent or occasional, natural or legal person or any other form of legal arrangements, using identification documents as may be prescribed in any relevant regulation;

    (b) verify the identity of that customer using reliable, independent source documents, data or information; and

    (c) identify the beneficial owner and take reasonable measures to verify the identity of the beneficial owner using relevant information or data obtained from a reliable source such that the Financial Institution or the Designated Non- Financial Institution is satisfied that it knows who the beneficial owner is.

(2) Financial Institutions and Designated Non-Financial Institutions shall undertake customer due diligence measures when—

    (a) establishing business relationships;

    (b) carrying out occasional transactions above the applicable designated threshold prescribed by relevant regulations, including transactions carried out in a single operation or in several operations that appear to be linked;

    (c) carrying out occasional transactions that are wire transfers;

    (d) there is a suspicion of money laundering or terrorist financing, regardless of any exemptions or thresholds; or

    (e) the Financial Institution or Designated Non-Financial Institution has doubts about the veracity or adequacy of previously obtained customer identification data.

(3) Financial Institutions or Designated Non-Financial Institutions shall—

    (a) conduct ongoing due diligence on a business relationship;

    (b) scrutinise transactions undertaken during the course of the relationship to ensure that the transactions are consistent with the institution's knowledge of the customer, their business and risk profile and where necessary, the source of funds; and

(c) ensure that documents, data or information collected under the customer due diligence process is kept up-to-date and relevant by undertaking reviews of existing records, particularly for higher risk categories of customers or business relationships.

(4) Financial Institutions and Designated Non-Financial Institutions shall take enhanced measures to manage and mitigate the risks and—

(a) where higher risks are identified, take enhanced measures to manage and mitigate the risks;

(b) where lower risks are identified, take simplified measures to manage and mitigate the risks, provided that simplified customer due diligent measures are not permitted whenever there is suspicion of money laundering or terrorist financing;

(c) in the case of cross-border correspondent banking and other similar relationships and in addition to carrying out customer due diligence measures—

(i) gather sufficient information about a respondent institution;

(ii) assess the respondent institution's anti-money laundering and combating the financing of terrorism controls;

(iii) document respective responsibilities of each institution in this regard; and

(iv) obtain management approval before establishing new correspondent relationships.

(5) A casual customer shall comply with the provisions of subsection (2) of this section for any number or manner of transactions including wire transfer involving a sum exceeding US$ 1,000 or its equivalent if the total amount is known at the commencement of the transaction or as soon as it is known to exceed the sum of US$1,000 or its equivalent.

(6) Where a Financial Institution or Designated Non-Financial Institution suspects or has reasonable grounds to suspect that the amount involved in a transaction is the proceeds of a crime or an illegal act, it shall require identification of the customer notwithstanding that the amount involved in the transaction is less than US$1,000 or its equivalent.

(7) Where the customer is a politically exposed person, the Financial Institution or Designated Non-Financial Institution shall in addition to the requirements of subsection (1) and (2) of this section—

(a) put in place appropriate risk management systems; and

(b) obtain senior management approval before establishing and during any business relationship with the politically exposed person.

4. Duties Incumbent upon Casinos

(1) A Casino shall—

(a) verify the identity of any of its customers carrying out financial transactions by requiring its customer to present a valid original document bearing his name and address;

(b) record all transactions under this section in chronological order including—

(i) the nature and amount involved in each transaction; and

(ii) each customer's surname, forenames and address, in a register forwarded to the Ministry for that purpose.

(2) A register kept under subsection (1) (b) of this section shall be preserved for at least 5 years after the last transaction recorded in the register.

5. Occasional Cash Transaction by Designated Non-Financial Institutions

(1) A Designated Non-Financial Institution whose business involves cash transaction shall—

(a) in the case of—

   (i) a new business, before commencement of the business;

   (ii) an existing business, within 3 months from the commencement of this Act, submit to the Ministry a declaration of its activities;

(a) prior to any transaction involving a sum exceeding US$1,000 or its equivalent, identify the customer by requiring him to fill a standard data form and present his international passport, driving license, national identity card or such other document bearing his photograph as may be prescribed by the Ministry;

(b) record all transactions under this section in chronological order, indicating each customer's surname, forenames and address in a register numbered and forwarded to the Ministry.

(2) The Ministry shall forward the information received pursuant to subsection (1) of this section to the Commission within 7 days of its receipt.

(3) A register kept under subsection (1) of this section shall be preserved for at least 5 years after the last transaction recorded in the register.

(4) The Minister may make regulations for guiding the operations of Designated Non-Financial Institutions under this section.

(5) Notwithstanding the provisions of subsection (2) of this section, the Commission shall have powers to demand and receive reports directly from Designated Non-Financial Institutions.

(6) A Designated Non-Financial Institution that fails to comply with the requirements of customer identification and the submission of returns on such transaction as specified in this Act within 7 days from the date of the transaction commits an offence and is liable to—

(a) a fine of ₦250,000 for each day during which the offence continues; and

(b) suspension, revocation or withdrawal of license by the appropriate licensing authority as the circumstances may demand.

6. Suspicious Transaction Reporting —

(1) Where a transaction—
   (a) involves a frequency which is unjustifiable or unreasonable;
   (b) is surrounded by conditions of unusual or unjustified complexity;
   (c) appears to have no economic justification or lawful objective; or
   (d) in the opinion of the Financial Institution or Designated Non-Financial Institution involves terrorist financing or is inconsistent with the known transaction pattern of the account or business relationship;

   that transaction shall be deemed to be suspicious and the Financial Institution involved in such transaction shall seek information from the customer as to the origin and destination of the fund, the aim of the transaction and the identity of the beneficiary.

(2) A Financial Institution or Designated Non-Financial Institution shall immediately after the transaction referred to in sub-section (1) of this section—
   (a) draw up a written report containing all relevant information on the matters mentioned in subsection (1) of this section together with the identity of the principal and where applicable, of the beneficiary or beneficiaries;
   (b) take appropriate action to prevent the laundering of the proceeds of a crime or an illegal act; and
   (c) report any suspicious transaction and actions taken to the Economic and Financial Crimes Commission.

(3) The provisions of subsections (1) and (2) of this section shall apply whether the transaction is completed or not.

(4) The Economic and Financial Crimes Commission shall acknowledge receipt of any disclosure, report or information received under this section and may demand such additional information as it may deem necessary.

(5) (a) The acknowledgement of receipt shall be sent to the Financial Institution or Designated Non-Financial Institution within the time allowed for the transaction to be undertaken and it may be accompanied by a notice deferring the transaction for a period not exceeding 72 hours.

(b) Notwithstanding the provisions of paragraph (a) of this subsection, the Chairman of the Economic and Financial Crimes Commission or his authorised representative shall place a Stop Order not exceeding 72 hours, on any account or transaction if it is discovered in the course of their duties that such account or transaction is suspected to be involved in any crime.

(6) If the acknowledgment of receipt is not accompanied by a stop notice, or where the stop notice has expired and the order specified in subsection (7) of this section to block the transaction has not reached the Financial Institution or Designated Non-Financial Institution, it may carry out the transaction.

(7) Where it is not possible to ascertain the origin of the funds within the period of stoppage of the transaction, the Federal High Court may, at the request of the Commission or other persons or authority duly authorized in that behalf, order that the funds, accounts or securities referred to in the report be blocked.

(8) An order made by the Federal High Court under this subsection (7) of this section shall be enforced forthwith.

(9) A Financial Institution or Designated Non-Financial Institution which fails to comply with the provisions of subsections (1) and (2) of this section commits an offence and is liable on conviction to a fine of ₦1,000,000 for each day during which the offence continues.

(10) The Directors, Officers and Employees of Financial Institutions and Designated Non-Financial Institutions who carry out their duties under this Act in good faith shall not be liable to any civil or criminal liability or have any criminal or civil proceedings brought against them by their customers.

7. Preservation of Records

A Financial Institution and Designated Non-Financial Institution shall preserve and keep at the disposal of the authorities specified in section 8 of this Act—

(a) the record of a customer's identification for a period of at least 5 years after the closure of the account or the severance of relations with the customer; and

(b) the record and other related information of a transaction carried out by a customer and the report provided for in section 6 of this Act shall be preserved, for a period of at least 5 years after carrying out the transaction or making of the report as the case may be.

8. Communication of Information

The records referred to in section 7 of this Act shall be communicated on demand to the Central Bank of Nigeria or the National Drug Law Enforcement Agency (in this Act referred to as the "Agency") and such other regulatory authorities or judicial persons as the Commission may specify from time to time, by order published in the Gazette.

9. Internal Procedures, Policies and Controls

(1) Every Financial Institution and Designated Non-Financial Institution shall develop programmes to combat the laundering of the proceeds of a crime or other illegal acts, and these shall include—

(a) the designation of compliance officers at management level at its headquarters and at every branch and local office;

(b) regular training programmes for its employees;

(c) the centralization of the information collected; and

(d) the establishment of an internal audit unit to ensure compliance with and effectiveness of the measures taken to enforce the provisions of this Act.

(2) Notwithstanding the provision of this Act or any other Law, the Central Bank of Nigeria, Securities and Exchange Commission, National Insurance Commission or any other relevant regulatory authority may—

(a) impose a penalty of not less than ₦1,000,000 for capital brokerage and other financial institutions and ₦5,000,000 in the case of a Bank; and

(b) in addition, suspend any licence issued to the Financial Institution or Designated Non-Financial Institution, for failure to comply with the provisions of subsection (1) of this section.

10. Mandatory Disclosure by Financial Institutions

(1) Notwithstanding anything to the contrary in any other law or regulation, a Financial Institution or Designated Non-Financial Institution shall report to the Economic and Financial Crimes Commission in writing within 7 days, any single transaction, lodgement or transfer of funds in excess of—

(a) ₦5,000,000 or its equivalent, in the case of an individual; or

(b) ₦10,000,000 or its equivalent, in the case of a body corporate.

(2) A person other than a Financial Institution may voluntarily give information on any transaction, lodgement or transfer of funds in excess of—

(a) ₦1,000,000 or its equivalent, in the case of an individual; or

(b) ₦5,000,000 or its equivalent, in the case of a body corporate.

(3) Any Financial Institution or Designated Non-Financial Institution that contravenes the provisions of this section is guilty of an offence and is on conviction liable to a fine of not less ₦250,000 and not more than ₦1 million for each day the contravention continues.

11. Prohibition of numbered or anonymous accounts, accounts in fictitious names and shell banks

(1) The opening or maintaining of numbered or anonymous accounts by any person, Financial Institution or body corporate is prohibited.

(2) A person shall not establish or operate a shell bank in Nigeria.

(3) A financial institution shall—

(a) not enter into or continue correspondent banking relationships with shell banks; and

(b) satisfy itself that a respondent financial institution in a foreign country does not permit its accounts to be used by shell banks.

(4) Any person, Financial Institution or body corporate that contravenes the provisions of subsections (1), (2) and (3) of this section, commits an offence and is liable on conviction to—

(a) in the case of an individual, a term of imprisonment of not less than 2 years but not more than 5 years; or

(b) in the case of a financial institution or body corporate, a fine of not less than ₦10,000,000 but not more than ₦50,000,000, in addition to:

(i) the prosecution of the principal officers of the body corporate, and

(ii) the winding up and prohibition of its constitution or incorporation under any form or guise.

12. Liability of directors, employees of Financial Institutions, Designated Non-Financial Institutions, Financial Intelligence Unit, Regulators, the Commission and the Agency.
Where funds are blocked under subsection (7) of section 6 of this Act and there is evidence of conspiracy with the owner of the funds, the Financial Institution or the Designated Non-Financial Institution involved shall not be relieved of liability under this Act and criminal proceedings for all offences arising there from, may be brought against its director and employees involved in the conspiracy.

13 Surveillance of Bank Accounts

(1) The Commission, Agency, Central Bank of Nigeria or other regulatory authorities pursuant to an order of the Federal High Court obtained upon an ex-parte application supported by a sworn declaration made by the Chairman of the Commission or an authorized officer of the Central Bank of Nigeria or other regulatory authorities justifying the request, may in order to identify and locate proceeds, properties, objects or other things related to the commission of an offence under this Act, the Economic and Financial Crimes Commission (Establishment) Act or any other law—

    (a) place any bank account or any other account comparable to a bank account under surveillance;

    (b) obtain access to any suspected computer system;

    (c) obtain communication of any authentic instrument or private contract, together with all bank, financial and commercial records, when the account, the telephone line or computer system is used by any person suspected of taking part in a transaction involving the proceeds of a financial or other crime.

(2) The Agency may exercise the powers conferred under subsection (1) of this section where it relates to identifying or locating properties, objects or proceeds of narcotic drugs or psychotropic substances.

(3) In exercising the power conferred under subsection (2) of this section, the Agency shall promptly make a report to the Commission.

(4) Banking secrecy or preservation of customer confidentiality shall not be invoked as a ground for objecting to the measures set out in subsection (1) and (2) of this section or for refusing to be a witness to facts likely to constitute an offence under this Act, the Economic and Financial Crimes Commission (Establishment), etc.) Act or any other law.

14. Determination of flow of transactions

The Commission shall in consultation with the Central Bank and the Corporate Affairs Commission determine the flow of transaction and the identities of beneficiaries under this Act including the beneficiaries of individual accounts and of corporate accounts.

Part II—OFFENCES

15. Money Laundering Offences

(1) Money laundering is prohibited in Nigeria.

(2) Any person or body corporate, in or outside Nigeria, who directly or indirectly—
  (a) conceals or disguises the origin of;
  (b) converts or transfers;
  (c) removes from the jurisdiction; or
  (d) acquires, uses, retains or takes possession or control of; any fund or property, knowingly or reasonably ought to have known that such fund or property is, or forms part of the proceeds of an unlawful act; commits an offence of money laundering under this Act.

(3) A person who contravenes the provisions of subsection (2) of this section is liable on conviction to a term of not less than 7 years but not more than 14 years imprisonment.

(4) A body corporate who contravenes the provisions of subsection (2) of this section is liable on conviction to—

(a) a fine of not less than 100% of the funds and properties acquired as a result of the offence committed; and

(b) withdrawal of licence.

(5) Where the body corporate persists in the commission of the offence for which it was convicted in the first instance, the Regulators may withdraw or revoke the certificate or licence of the body corporate.

(6) The unlawful act referred to in subsection (2) of this section includes participation in an organized criminal group, racketeering, terrorism, terrorist financing, trafficking in persons, smuggling of migrants, sexual exploitation, sexual exploitation of children, illicit trafficking in narcotic drugs and psychotropic substances, illicit arms trafficking, illicit trafficking in stolen goods, corruption, bribery, fraud, currency counterfeiting, counterfeiting and piracy of products, environmental crimes, murder, grievous bodily injury, kidnapping, hostage taking, robbery or theft, smuggling (including in relation to customs and excise duties and taxes), tax crimes (related to direct taxes and indirect taxes), extortion, forgery, piracy, insider trading and market manipulation or any other criminal act specified in this Act or any other law in Nigeria.

(7) A person who commits an offence under subsection (2) of this section shall be subject to the penalties specified in this section notwithstanding that the various acts constituting the offence were committed in different countries or places.

16. Other Offences

(1) Without prejudice to the penalties provided under section 15 of this Act, any person who—

(a) being a director or employee of a Financial Institution warns or in any other way intimates the owner of the funds involved in the transaction referred to in section 6 of this Act about the report he is required to make or the action taken on it or who refrains from making the report as required;

(b) destroys or removes a register or record required to be kept under this Act;

(c) carries out or attempts under a false identity to carry out any of the transactions specified in sections 1 to 5 of this Act;

(d) makes or accepts cash payments exceeding the amount authorized under this Act;

(e) fails to report an international transfer of funds or securities required to be reported under this Act; or

(f) being a director or an employee of a Financial Institution or Designated Non-Financial Institution contravenes the provisions of sections 2, 3, 4, 5, 6, 7, 9, 10, 12, 13 or 14 of this Act, commits an offence under this Act.

(2) A person who commits an offence under subsection (1) of this section—

(a) paragraph (a), is liable on conviction to imprisonment for a term of not less than 2 years or a fine of not less than ₦10,000,000; and

(b) paragraphs (b) — (f), is liable to imprisonment for a term of not less than 3 years or a fine of ₦10,000,000 or to both, in the case of individual and ₦25,000,000, in the case of a body corporate.

(3) A person found guilty of an offence under this section may also be banned indefinitely or for a period of 5 years from practicing the profession, which provided the opportunity for the offence to be committed.

(4) Where as a result of a serious oversight or a flaw in its internal control procedures, a Financial Institution or person designated under subsection (1) (a) of section 9 of this Act, fails to meet any of the obligations imposed by this Act, the disciplinary authority responsible for the Financial Institution or the person's professional body may, in addition to any penalty in this Act take such disciplinary action against the Financial Institution or persons as is in conformity with its professional and administrative regulations.

17. Retention of Proceeds of a Criminal Conduct

Any person who—

(a) conceals, removes from jurisdiction, transfers to nominees or otherwise retains the proceeds of a crime or an illegal act on behalf of another person knowing or suspecting that other person to be engaged in a criminal conduct or has benefited from a criminal conduct or conspiracy, aiding, etc.; or

(b) knowing that any property either in whole or in part directly or indirectly represents another person's proceeds of a criminal conduct, acquires or uses that property or possession of it, commits an offence under this Act and is liable on conviction to imprisonment for a term not less than 5 years or to a fine equivalent to 5 times the value of the proceeds of the criminal conduct or both such imprisonment and fine.

18. Conspiracy, aiding and abetting

A person who—

(a) conspires with, aids, abets or counsels any other person to commit an offence;

(b) attempts to commit or is an accessory to an act or offence; or

(c) incites, procures or induces any other person by any means whatsoever to commit an offence under this Act, commits an offence and is liable on conviction to the same punishment as is prescribed for that offence under this Act.

19. Offences by a body corporate

(1) Where an offence under this Act which has been committed by a body corporate is proved to have been committed on the instigation or with the connivance of or attributable to any neglect on the part of a director, manager, secretary or other similar officer of the body corporate, or any person purporting to act in any such capacity, he, as well as the body corporate where

applicable, shall be guilty of that offence and shall be liable to be proceeded against and punished accordingly.

(2) Where a body corporate is convicted of an offence under this Act, the court may order that the body corporate shall thereupon and without any further assurances, but for such order, be wound up and all its assets and properties forfeited to the Federal Government.

PART III—MISCELLANEOUS

20. Jurisdiction to try offences under this Act

(1) The Federal High Court shall have jurisdiction to—
(a) try offences under this Act or any other related enactment; and
(b) hear and determine proceedings arising under this Act whether or not the offence was commenced in Nigeria and completed outside Nigeria and the victim is—
  (i) a citizen or resident of Nigeria;
  (ii) not a citizen of any country but ordinarily resident in Nigeria;
  (iii) in transit or has a link with Nigeria; and
  (iv) dealing with or on behalf of the Government of Nigeria, or a citizen of Nigeria or an entity registered in Nigeria; or
  (v) the alleged offender is in Nigeria and not extradited to any other country for prosecution.

(2) The Federal High Court shall have jurisdiction to impose any penalty provided for an offence under this Act or any other related enactment.

(3) In any trial for an offence under this Act, the Court shall have power, notwithstanding anything to the contrary in any other enactment, to adopt all legal measures necessary to avoid unnecessary delays and abuse in the conduct of matters.

(4) Subject to the provisions of the Constitution of the Federal Republic of Nigeria, an application for stay of proceedings in

respect of any criminal matter brought under this Act shall not be entertained until judgment is delivered.

21. Power to demand and obtain records

For the purpose of this Act, the Director of Investigation or an officer of the Ministry, Commission, or Agency duly authorized in that behalf may demand, obtain and inspect the books and records of the Financial Institution or Designated Non-Financial Institution to confirm compliance with the provisions of this Act.

22. Obstruction of the Commission or authorized officers

A person who wilfully obstructs officers of the Ministry, the Commission, the Agency or any authorized officer in the exercise of the powers conferred on the Ministry, the Commission or the Agency by this Act commits an offence and is liable on conviction—

(a) in the case of an individual, to imprisonment for a term of not less than 2 years and not exceeding 3 years; and

(b) in the case of a financial institution or other body corporate, to a fine of ₦1,000,000.

23. Regulations

(1) The Attorney-General may make orders, rules, guidelines or regulations as are necessary for the efficient implementation of the provisions of this Act.

(2) Orders, rules, guidelines or regulations made under subsection (1) of this section may provide for the—

(a) method of custody of video and other electronic recordings of suspects apprehended under this Act;

(b) method of compliance with directives issued by relevant international institutions on money laundering and terrorism financing counter measures;

(c) procedure for freezing, unfreezing and providing access to frozen funds or other assets;

(d) procedure for the prosecution of all money laundering cases in line with international human rights standards; and

(e) any other matter the Attorney-General may consider necessary or expedient for the purpose of the implementation of this Act.

24. Repeal of the Money Laundering (Prohibition) Act 2004

(1) The Money Laundering (Prohibition) Act 2004 is repealed.

(2) The repeal of the enactment specified in subsection (1) of this section shall not affect anything done or purported to be done under or pursuant to that enactment.

25. Interpretation

1.   In this Act—
     "Account" means a facility or arrangement by which a Financial Institution—
     (a) accepts deposits of currency;
     (b) allows withdrawals of currency or transfers into or out of the account;
     (c) pays cheques or payment orders drawn on a Financial Institution or cash dealer by a person or collect cheques or payment orders on behalf of a person; or
     (d) supplies a facility or an arrangement for a safe deposit box;

"Agency" means National Drug Law Enforcement Agency;

"Beneficiary" includes a natural or legal person or any other form of legal arrangement identified by the originator as the receiver of the requested wire transfer;

"Beneficial owner" refers to—

(a) the natural person who ultimately owns or controls a customer;

(b) the natural person on whose behalf a transaction is being conducted; and

(c) a person who exercises ultimate effective control over a legal person or arrangement;

"Business relationship" means an arrangement between a person and a Financial Institution or Designated Non-Financial Institution for the purpose of concluding a transaction;

"Central Bank" means the Central Bank of Nigeria;

"Commission" means the Economic and Financial Crimes Commission;

"Competent authority" means any agency or institution concerned with combating money laundering and terrorist financing under this Act or under any other law or regulation;

"Correspondent banking" means the provision of banking services by one bank (the correspondent bank) to another bank (the respondent bank);

"Designated Non-Financial Institution" include dealers in jewellery, cars and luxury goods, chartered accountants, audit firms, tax consultants, clearing and settlement companies, legal practitioners, hotels, casinos, supermarkets, and such other businesses as the Federal Ministry of Industry, Trade and Investment or appropriate regulatory authorities may from time to time designate;

"False Declaration" refers to a misrepresentation of—

(a) the value of the currency or bearer negotiable instrument being transported ; and

(b) other relevant data required for submission in the declaration or otherwise requested by the authorities;

"Financial Institution" include banks, body corporates, associations or group of persons, whether corporate or incorporate which carries on the business of investment and securities, a discount house, insurance institution, debt factorization and conversion firm, bureau de change, finance company, money brokerage firm whose principal business includes factoring, project financing, equipment leasing, debt administration, fund management, private ledger service, investment management, local purchase order financing, export finance, project consultancy, financial consultancy, pension funds management and such other business as the Central Bank or other appropriate regulatory authorities may from time to time designate;

"Funds" refers to assets of every kind whether tangible or intangible, movable or immovable, howsoever acquired and legal documents or instruments in any form, including electronic or digital, evidencing title to or interest in such assets, including bank credits, travellers cheques, bank cheques, money orders, shares, securities, bonds, drafts or letters of credit;

"Minister" means the Minister charged with responsibility for matters pertaining to Trade and Investment;

"Ministry" means the Federal Ministry of Industry, Trade and Investment;

"Money Service Business" includes currency dealers, money transmitters, cheque cashers, and issuers of travellers' cheques, money orders or stored value;

"Nigerian Financial Intelligence Unit (NFIU)" refers to the central unit responsible for the receiving, requesting, analyzing and disseminating to the competent authorities disclosures of financial information concerning the suspected proceeds of crime and potential financing of terrorism;

"Other Regulatory Authorities" means the Securities and Exchange Commission, and the National Insurance Commission;

"Physical Presence" in relation to shell banks, means having structure and management located within a country and not merely the existence of a local agent or low level staff;

"Politically exposed persons ('PEPs')" includes—

(a) individuals who are or have been entrusted with prominent public functions by a foreign country, for example Heads of State or Government, senior politicians, senior government, judicial or military officials, senior executives of State owned corporations and important political party officials;

(b) individuals who are or have been entrusted domestically with prominent public functions, for example Heads of State or of Government, senior politicians, senior government, judicial or military officials, senior executives of State owned corporations and important political party officials; and

(c) persons who are or have been entrusted with a prominent function by an international organization and includes members of senior management such as directors, deputy directors and members of the board or equivalent functions other than middle ranking or more junior individuals;

"Proceeds" means property derived from or obtained, directly or indirectly through the commission of an offence;

"Property" means assets of every kind, whether corporeal or incorporeal, moveable or immoveable, tangible or intangible and legal documents or instruments evidencing title to or interest in such assets;

"Public Officers" means individuals who are or have been entrusted with prominent public function, both within and outside Nigeria and those associated with them;

"Regulators" means competent regulatory authorities responsible for ensuring compliance of Financial Institutions and Designated Non-Financial Institutions with requirements to combat money laundering and terrorist financing;

"Shell bank" means a bank that is not physically located in the country in which it is incorporated and licensed and which is unaffiliated with a regulated financial group that is subject to effective consolidated supervision;

"Suspicious" means a matter which is beyond mere speculations and is based on some foundation;

"Terrorism Financing means financial support, in any form, of terrorism or of those who encourage, plan or engage in terrorism;

"Transaction" means—

(a) acceptance of deposit and other repayable funds from the public;
(b) lending;
(c) financial leasing;
(d) money transmission service;
(e) issuing and managing means of payment (for example, credit and debit cards, cheques, travellers' cheque and bankers' drafts etc.);
(f) financial guarantees and commitment;
(g) trading for account of costumer (spot-forward, swaps, future options, etc.) in—
    (i)   money market instruments (cheques, bills of exchange, etc.);
    (ii) foreign exchange;
    (iii) exchange interest rate and index instruments;
    (iv) transferable securities; and (v) commodity futures trading;

(h) participation in capital markets activities and the provision of financial services related to such issues;

(i) individual and collective portfolio management;

(j) safekeeping and administration of cash or liquid securities on behalf of clients;

(k) life insurance and all other insurance related matters; and

(l) (l) money changing.

"Wire transfer" means any transaction carried out on behalf of a natural person or legal originator through a Financial Institution by electronic means with a view to making an amount of money available to a beneficiary person at another financial institution, irrespective of whether the originator and the beneficiary are the same person.

26. Citation

This Act may be cited as the Money Laundering (Prohibition) Act, 2011 (as Amended).

Explanatory Memorandum

(This Memorandum does not form part of the above Act but is intended to explain its purport)

This Act provides for the repeal of the Money Laundering Act, 2004 and enacts the Money Laundering (Prohibition) Act, 2011 to make comprehensive provisions to prohibit the financing of terrorism, the laundering of the proceeds of crime or illegal acts, expand the scope of money laundering offences, enhance customer due diligence measures, provide appropriate penalties and expand the scope of supervisory and regulatory authorities to address the challenges faced in the implementation of the anti-money laundering regime in Nigeria.

Printed and Published by The Federal Government Printer, Lagos, Nigeria.

FGP 93/92013/650 (OL 119)

APPENDIX 2

Central Bank of Nigeria (Anti-Money Laundering and Combating the Financing of Terrorism in Banks and Other Financial Institutions in Nigeria) Regulations, 2013

ARRANGEMENT OF REGULATIONS
Regulation:

PART III—OFFENCES, MEASURES AND SANCTIONS

PART IV—CUSTOMER DUE DILIGENCE, HIGHER RISK CUSTOMERS AND ACTIVITIES OF POLITICALLY EXPOSED PERSONS

PART V—MAINTENANCE OF RECORDS

PART VIII—GENERAL INFORMATION

PART IX—FINANCIAL EXCLUSION FOR THE SOCIALLY OR FINANCIALLY DISADVANTAGED APPLICANTS

CENTRAL BANK OF NIGERIA (ANTI-MONEY LAUNDERING AND COMBATING THE FINANCING OF TERRORISM IN BANKS AND OTHER FINANCIAL INSTITUTIONS IN NIGERIA) REGULATIONS, 2013

In exercise of the powers conferred upon me by the provisions of section 51(1) of the Banks and Other Financial Institutions Act, 2004 and all other powers enabling me in that behalf, I, SANUSI LAMIDO SANUSI, Governor of the Central Bank of Nigeria, make the following Regulations—

Commencement. [29th August. 2013]

PART I—OBJECTIVES, SCOPE AND APPLICATIONS

1. Objective

The objectives of these Regulations are to—

(a) provide Anti-Money Laundering and Combating the Financing of Terrorism ("AML/CFT") compliance guidelines for financial institutions under the regulatory purview of the Central Bank of Nigeria ("CBN") as required by relevant provisions of the Money Laundering (Prohibition) Act. 2011 (as amended), the Terrorism Prevention Act, 2011 (as amended) and other relevant laws and Regulations;

(b) enable the CBN to diligently enforce AML/CFT measures and ensure effective compliance by financial institutions; and

(c) provide guidance on Know Your Customer ("KYC") measures to assist financial institutions in the implementation of these Regulations.

2. Scope

(1) These Regulations cover the relevant provisions of the Money Laundering (Prohibition) Act, 2011 (as amended), the Terrorism Prevention Act, 2011 (as amended) and any other relevant laws or Regulations.

(2) These Regulations cover—

     (a) the key areas of Anti-Money Laundering and Combating the Financing of Terrorism (AML/CFT) Policy:

     (b) development of Compliance Unit and function;

     (c) Compliance Officer designation and duties;

     (d) the requirement to co-operate with the competent or supervisory authorities;

     (e) conduct of Customer Due Diligence;

     (f) monitoring and filing of suspicious transactions to the Nigerian Financial Intelligence Unit ("NFIU") and other reporting requirements;

     (g) reporting requirements;

     (h) record keeping; and

     (i) AML/CFT employee training.

3. Application

These Regulations shall apply to banks and other financial institutions in Nigeria within the regulatory purview of the Central Bank of Nigeria.

Part II—Anti-Money Laundering and Combating the Financing of Terrorism Directives

4. AML/CFT Institutional Policy Framework

     (1) A financial institution shall adopt policies stating its commitment to comply with Anti-Money Laundering ('AML') and Combating Financing of Terrorism ('CFT') obligations under subsisting laws, regulations and regulatory directives and to actively prevent any transaction that otherwise facilitates criminal activities, money laundering or terrorism.

     (2) A financial institution shall formulate and implement internal controls and other procedures to deter criminals from using its facilities for money laundering and terrorist financing.

     (3) Financial Institutions shall adopt a risk-based approach in the identification and management of their AML/CFT risks in line with the requirements of these Regulations.

(4)   Financial Institutions shall comply promptly with requests made pursuant to current AML/CFT legislations and provide information to the Central Bank of Nigeria ("CBN"), Nigeria Financial Intelligence Unit ("NFIU") and other competent authorities.

(5)   Financial Institutions shall not in any way inhibit the implementation of the provisions of these Regulations and shall co-operate with the regulators and law enforcement agencies in the implementation of a robust AML/CFT regime in Nigeria.

(6)   Financial institutions shall render statutory reports to appropriate authorities as required by law and shall guard against any act that will cause a customer or client to avoid compliance with AML/CFT Legislations.

(7)   Financial institutions shall identify, review and record other areas of potential money laundering and terrorist financing risks not covered by these Regulations and report same to the appropriate authorities.

(8)   Financial institutions shall reflect AML/CFT policies and procedures in their strategic policies.

(9)   Financial institutions shall conduct on-going Due Diligence and where appropriate, enhanced Due Diligence on all business relationships and shall obtain information on the purpose and intended nature of the business relationship of their potential customers.

(10)   Financial institutions shall ensure that their employees, agents and others doing business with them, clearly understand the AML/CFT programme.

5. Risk Assessment

A financial institution shall—

(a) take appropriate steps to identify, assess and understand its Money Laundering ('ML') and the Financing of Terrorism ('FT') risks for customers, countries or geographic areas of its operations, products, services and delivery channels;

(b) document its risk assessments profile;

(c) consider all relevant risk factors before determining the overall level of risk and the appropriate level and type of mitigation to be applied;

(d) keep the assessments in this regulation up to date; and

(e) have, the appropriate mechanisms to provide risk assessments reports to regulatory, supervisory and competent authorities, and Self-Regulatory Organizations ('SROs').

6. Risk Mitigation

A financial institution shall—

(a) have policies, controls and procedures which are approved by its board of directors to enable it manage and mitigate the risks that have been identified (either by the country or by the financial institution);

(b) monitor the implementation of the controls in this regulation and enhance them, where necessary; and

(c) take enhanced measures to manage and mitigate the risks where higher risks are identified.

7. Designation and Duties of AML/CFT Compliance Officer

(1) A Financial institution shall designate its AML/CFT Chief Compliance Officer with the relevant competence, authority and independence to implement the institution's AML/CFT compliance programme.

(2) The AML/CFT Compliance Officer shall be appointed at management level and shall report directly to the Board on all matters under these Regulations.

(3) The duties of the AML/CFT Compliance Officer referred to in sub-regulation (1) of this regulation shall include—

(a) developing an AML/CFT Compliance Programme;

(b) receiving and vetting suspicious transaction reports from staff;

(c) filing Suspicious Transaction Reports ("STRs") with the NFIU;

(d) filing other regulatory returns with the CBN and other relevant regulatory and supervisory authorities;

(e) rendering "nil" reports to the CBN and NFIU, where necessary to ensure compliance;

(f) ensuring that the financial institution's compliance programme is implemented;

(g) co-ordinating the training of staff in AML/CFT awareness, detection methods and reporting requirements; and

(h) serving both as a liaison officer between his institution, the CBN and NFIU and a point-of-contact for all employees on issues relating to money laundering and terrorist financing.

8. Co-operation with Competent Authorities

(1) A financial institution shall give an undertaking that it shall comply promptly with all the requests made pursuant to the provisions of relevant AML/CFT laws and Regulations and provide all requested information to the CBN, NFIU and other competent authorities.

(2) A financial institution's procedures for responding to authorized requests for information on ML and FT shall meet the following—

(a) searching immediately the financial institution's records to determine whether it maintains or has maintained any account for, or has engaged in any transaction with any individual, entity or organization named in the request;

(b) reporting promptly to the requesting authority the outcome of the search; and

(c) protecting the security and confidentiality of such requests.

PART III—OFFENCES, MEASURES AND SANCTIONS

9. Scope of Offences

(1) A financial institution shall identify and file suspicious transaction reports to the NFIU, where funds, assets or property are suspected to have been derived from any of the following criminal activities—

   (a)   participation in an organized criminal group and racketeering;

   (b)   terrorism, including terrorist financing;

   (c)   trafficking in persons and migrant smugglings;

   (d)   sexual exploitation, including sexual exploitation of children;

   (e)   illicit trafficking in narcotic drugs and psychotropic substances;

   (f)   illicit arms trafficking;

   (g)   illicit trafficking in stolen and other goods;

   (h)   corruption;

   (i)   bribery;

   (j)   fraud;

   (k)   currency counterfeiting;

   (l)   counterfeiting and piracy of products;

   (m) environmental crime;

   (n)   murder;

   (o)   grievous bodily injury;

   (p)   kidnapping, illegal restraint and hostage-taking;

   (q)   robbery or theft;

   (r)   smuggling, including smuggling done in relation to customs and excise duties and taxes);

   (s)   tax crimes, related to direct taxes and indirect taxes;

   (t)   extortion;

   (u)   forgery:

   (v)   piracy;

   (w) insider trading and market manipulation, or

(x) any other predicate offence under the Money Laundering (Prohibition) Act, 2011 (as amended) and the Terrorism Prevention Act 2011 (as amended).

10. Terrorism Financing Offences

(1) Terrorism financing offences extend to any person or entity who solicits, acquires, provides, collects, receives, possesses or makes available funds, property or other services by any means to terrorists or terrorist organizations, directly or indirectly with the intention or knowledge or having reasonable grounds to believe that such funds or property shall be used in full or in part to carry out a terrorist act by a terrorist or terrorist organization in line with section 1 of the Terrorism (Prevention) Act 2011 (as amended).

(2) Under these Regulations, terrorism financing offences are predicate offences for money laundering and shall apply regardless of whether the person or entity alleged to have committed the offence is in the same country or a different country from the one in which the terrorist or terrorist organization is located or the terrorist act occurred or will occur.

11. Targeted Financial Sanctions related to Terrorism Financing and Proliferation

(1) A financial institution shall report to the NFIU any assets frozen or actions taken in compliance with the prohibition requirements of the relevant United Nations Security Council Resolutions ('UNSCRs') on terrorism, financing of proliferation of weapons of mass destruction, any future successor resolutions and the Terrorism Prevention (Freezing of International Terrorist Funds and Other Related Issues) Regulation, 2013, and any amendments that may be reflected by the competent authorities.

(2) The reports in sub-regulation (1) of this regulation shall include all transactions involving attempted and concluded transactions in compliance with the Money Laundering (Prohibition) Act 2011 (as amended), Terrorism (Prohibition) Act, 2011 (as amended) and the Terrorism Prevention (Freezing of International Terrorist Funds and Other Related Issues) Regulation, 2013, and any amendments that may be reflected by the competent authorities.

(3) The administrative sanctions contained in Schedule 1 to these Regulations or in the Terrorism Prevention (Freezing of International Terrorist Funds and Other Related Measures) Regulations. 2013 shall be imposed by the CBN on institutions under its regulatory purview.

12. I.imitation of Secrecy and Confidentiality Laws

(1) Financial institutions' secrecy and confidentiality laws shall not in any way, be used to inhibit the implementation of the requirements of these Regulations having regard to the provisions of section 38 of Economic and Financial Crimes Commission Act. 2004; section 13 of Money laundering (Prohibition) Act, 2011 (as Amended) and section 33 of the CBN Act, 2007.

(2) The relevant laws cited in sub-regulation (1) of this regulation have given the relevant authorities the powers required to access information to properly perform their functions in combating money laundering and financing of terrorism, the sharing of information between competent authorities, either domestically or internationally, and the sharing of information between financial institutions necessary or as may be required.

(3) Banking secrecy or preservation of customer confidentiality shall not be invoked as a ground for objecting to the measures set out in these Regulations or for refusing to be a witness to facts likely to constitute an offence under these Regulations, the relevant provisions of the Money Laundering (Prohibition) Act, 2011 (as amended), the

Terrorism Prevention Act, 2011 (as amended) and any other relevant subsisting laws or Regulations.

PART IV—CUSTOMER DUE DILIGENCE, HIGHER RISK CUSTOMERS AND ACTIVITIES OF POLITICALLY EXPOSED PERSONS

13. Customer Due Diligence ("CDD") measures

(1) A financial institution shall undertake Customer Due Diligence ('CDD') measures when—

(a) business relationships are established;

(b) carrying out occasional transactions above the applicable and designated threshold of US$1,000 or its equivalent in other currencies or as may be determined by the CBN from time to time, including where the transaction is carried out in a single operation or several operations that appear to be linked;

(c) carrying out occasional transactions that are wire transfers, including those applicable to cross-border and domestic transfers between financial institutions and when credit or debit cards are used as a payment system to effect money transfer;

(d) there is a suspicion of money laundering or terrorist financing, regardless of any exemptions or any other thresholds referred to in these Regulations; or

(e) there are doubts on the veracity or adequacy of previously obtained customer identification data.

(2) The measures in paragraphs (a), (b) and (c) of sub-regulation (1) of this regulation, shall not apply to payments in respect of—

(i) any transfer flowing from a transaction carried out using a credit or debit card so long as the credit or debit card number accompanying such transfers flow from the transactions such as withdrawals from a bank account through an ATM machine, cash advances from a credit card or payment for goods.

(ii) Inter-financial institution transfers and settlements where both the originator-person and the beneficial-person are financial institutions acting on their own behalf.

(3) Financial institutions, must not after obtaining all the necessary documents and being so satisfied, repeatedly perform identification and verification exercise every' time a customer conducts a transaction except there is a suspicion that the previously obtained information is not complete or has changed.

14. Identification and verification of identity of Customers

(1) A financial institution shall identify their customers, whether permanent or occasional, natural or legal persons, or legal arrangements, and verify the customers' identities using reliable, independently sourced documents, data or information

(2) A financial institution shall carry out the full range of the CDD measures contained in these Regulations, the relevant provisions of the Money Laundering (Prohibition) Act, 2011 (as amended), and any other relevant laws or Regulations.

(3) Financial institutions shall apply the CDD measures on a risk-sensitive basis.

(4) Types of customer information to be obtained and identification data to be used to verify the information are contained in Schedule 11 to these Regulations.

(5) Where the customer is a legal person or a legal arrangement, the financial institution shall—

(a) identify any person purporting to have been authorized to act on behalf of that customer by obtaining evidence of the customer's identity and verifying the identity of the authorized person; and

(b) identify and verify the legal status of the legal person or legal arrangement by obtaining proof of incorporation from the Corporate Affairs Commission ('CAC') or similar evidence of establishment or existence and any other relevant information.

15. Verification of Beneficial Ownership

(1) A financial institution shall identify' and take reasonable steps to verify the identity of a beneficial-owner, using relevant information or data obtained from a reliable source to satisfy itself that it knows who the beneficial-owner is through methods including—

(a) for legal persons:

    (i) identifying and verifying the natural persons, where they exist, that have ultimate controlling ownership interest in a legal person, taking into cognizance the fact that ownership interests can be so diversified that there may be no natural persons (whether acting alone or with others) exercising control of the legal person or arrangement through ownership;

    (ii) to the extent that it is manifestly clear under sub-paragraph (i) of this paragraph that the persons with the controlling ownership interest are the beneficial owners or where no natural person exerts control through ownership interests, identify and verify the natural persons, where they exist, exercising control of the legal person or arrangement through other means; and

    (iii) where a natural person is not identified under sub-paragraph (i) or (ii) of this paragraph, financial institutions shall identify and take reasonable measures to verify the identity of the relevant natural person who holds senior management position in the legal person.

(b) for legal arrangements - such as trust arrangement, financial institutions shall identify and verify the identity of the settlor, the trustee, the protector where they exist, the beneficiaries or class of beneficiaries, and any other natural person exercising ultimate or effective control over the trust including through a chain of control or ownership; and

(c) for other types of legal arrangements, the financial institutions shall identify and verify persons in equivalent or similar positions.

(2) Financial institutions shall in respect of all customers, determine whether a customer is acting on behalf of another person or not and where the customer is acting on behalf of another person, take reasonable steps to obtain sufficient identification data and verify the identity of the other person.

(3) A financial institution shall take reasonable measures in respect of customers that are legal persons or legal arrangements to—

(a) understand the ownership and control structure of such a customer; and

(b) determine the natural persons that ultimately own or control the customer.

(4) In the exercise of its responsibility under this regulation, a financial institution shall take into account that natural persons include those persons who exercise ultimate or effective control over the legal person or arrangement and factors to be taken into consideration to satisfactorily perform this function include—

(a) for companies - the natural persons shall own the controlling interests and comprise the mind and management of the company; and

(b) for trusts - the natural persons shall be the settlor, the trustee or person exercising effective control over the trust and the beneficiaries.

(5) Where a customer or an owner of the controlling interest is a company listed on a stock exchange and subject to disclosure requirements (either by stock exchange rules or by law or other enforceable means) which impose requirements to ensure adequate transparency of beneficial ownership, or is a majority-owned subsidiary of such a company, it is not

necessary to identify and verify the identity of any shareholder or beneficial owner of the company.

(6)   The relevant identification data referred to in the foregoing regulation may be obtained from a public register, the customer and other reliable sources, and for this purpose, ownership of 5% interest or more in a company is applicable.

(7)   A financial institution shall obtain information on the purpose anti intended nature of the business relationship of its potential customers.

(8)   A financial institution shall conduct on-going Due Diligence on a business relationship.

(9)   The conduct of on-going Due Diligence includes scrutinizing the transactions undertaken by the customer throughout the course of the financial institution and customer relationship to ensure that the transactions being conducted are consistent with the financial institution's knowledge of the customer, his business, risk profiles and the source of funds.

(10)   A financial institution shall ensure that documents, data or information collated under the CDD process are kept up-to-date and relevant by undertaking regular periodic reviews of existing records, particularly the records in respect of higher-risk business-relationships or customer categories.

16. Application of Enhanced Due Diligence to Higher Risk Customers and Activities

A financial institution shall perform Enhanced Due Diligence for higher-risk customers, business relationship or transactions including—

(a) non-resident customers;

(b) private banking customers;

(c) legal persons or legal arrangements such as trusts that are personal assets-holding vehicles;

(d) companies that have nominee-shareholders or shares in bearer form;

(e) Politically Exposed Persons ('PEPs'), cross-border banking and business relationships, amongst others;

(f) cross-border banking and business relationships, and

(g) any other businesses, activities or professionals as may be prescribed by regulatory, supervisory or competent authorities.

17. Attention to High Risk Countries

(1) A financial institution shall give special attention to business relationships and transactions with persons, including legal persons and other financial institutions; from countries which do not or insufficiently apply the FATF recommendations.

(2) A financial institution shall report transactions that have no apparent economic or visible lawful purpose to competent authorities with the background and purpose of such transactions as far as possible, examined and written findings made available to assist competent authorities.

(3) A financial institution that does a business with foreign institutions which do not apply the provisions of FATF recommendations shall take measures, including the following—

(a) stringent requirements for identifying clients and enhancement of advisories, including jurisdiction-specific financial advisories to financial institutions for identification of the beneficial owners before business relationships are established with individuals or companies from that jurisdiction;

(b) enhance relevant reporting mechanisms or systematic reporting of financial transactions on the basis that financial transactions with such countries are more likely to be suspicious;

(c) in considering requests for approving the establishment of subsidiaries or branches or representative offices of financial institutions, in countries applying the counter measure shall take into account the fact that the relevant financial institution is from a country that, does not have adequate AML/CFT systems; and

(d) warn that non-financial sector businesses that transact with natural or legal persons within that country might run the risk of money laundering; limiting business relationships or financial transactions with the identified country or persons in that country.

18. Politically Exposed Poisons (PEP)

(1) Politically Exposed Persons ('PEPs') are individuals who are or have been entrusted with prominent public functions in Nigeria or in foreign countries, and people or entities associated with them and include—

(a) Heads of State or Government;

(b) State Governors;

(c) Local Government Chairmen;

(d) senior politicians;

(e) senior government officials;

(f) judicial or military officials;

(g) senior executives of slate owned corporations;

(h) important political party officials;

(i) family members or dose associates of PEPs; and

(j) members of royal families.

(2) PEPs also include persons who are or have been entrusted with a prominent function by an international organization, including members of senior management including directors, deputy directors and members of the hoard or equivalent functions other than middle ranking or more junior individuals.

(3) Financial institutions shall in addition to performing CDD measures, to put in place appropriate risk management systems to determine whether a potential customer or existing customer or the beneficial-owner is a PEP.

(4) Financial institutions shall obtain senior management approval before they establish business relationships with a PEP

and shall render monthly returns on all transactions with PEPs to the CBN and NFIU.

(5) Where a customer has been accepted or has an ongoing relationship with a financial institution and the customer or beneficial-owner is subsequently found to be or becomes a PEP, the financial institution shall obtain senior management approval to continue the business relationship.

(6) A financial institution shall take reasonable measures to establish the source of wealth and the source of funds of customers and beneficial-owners identified as PEPs.

(7) A financial institution that is in a business relationship with a PEP shall conduct enhanced and on-going monitoring of that relationship and in the event of any transaction that is abnormal, a financial institution shall flag the account and report the transaction immediately to the NFIU as a suspicious transaction.

19. Cross-Border and Correspondent Banking

(1) For cross-border and correspondent banking and other similar relationships, a financial institution shall, in addition to performing the normal CDD measures, take the following measures

(a) gather sufficient information about a respondent institution to understand fully the nature of its business and determine from publicly available information, the reputation of the institution and the quality of supervision, including whether or not it has been subject to a money laundering or terrorist financing investigation or regulatory action;

(b) assess the respondent institution's AML/CFT controls and ascertain that they are in compliance with FATF standards;

(c) obtain approval from senior management before establishing correspondent relationships; and

(d) document the respective AML/CFT responsibilities of the respondent institution.

(2) Where a correspondent relationship involves the maintenance of payable through-account, the financial institution shall be satisfied that—

(a) its customer (the respondent bank or financial institution) has performed the normal CDD obligations on its customers that have direct access to the accounts of the correspondent financial institution; and

(b) the respondent financial institution is able to provide relevant customer identification data upon request to the correspondent financial institution.

20. New Technologies and Non-Face-to-face Transactions

(1) A financial institution shall identify and assess the money laundering or terrorist financing risks that may arise in relation to the development of new products and new business practices (including new delivery mechanisms) and the use of new or developing technologies for both new and pre-existing products.

(2) Financial institutions are to ensure that any risk assessment to be undertaken is carried out prior to the launch of the new products, business practices or the use of new' or developing technologies are to be documented and appropriate measures taken to manage and mitigate such risks.

(3) A financial institution shall have policies and procedures in place to address any specific risk associated with non-face-to-face business relationships or transactions.

(4) The policies and procedures required to be taken shall be applied automatically when establishing customer relationships and conducting on-going Due Diligence and measures for managing the risks are to include specific and effective CDD procedures that apply to non-face-to-face customers.

21. Money or Value Transfer (MVT) Services

(1) All natural and legal persons performing Money or Value Transfer Service ('MVTS operators') shall be licensed by the Banking and Payment Systems Department of the CBN and shall be subject to the provisions of these Regulations, the relevant provisions of the Money Laundering (Prohibition) Act, 2011 (as amended), the Terrorism Prevention Act 2011 (as amended) and any other relevant laws or Regulations.

(2) MVTS Operators shall maintain a current list of their agents and render quarterly returns to the CBN and the NF1U.

(3) In addition to the requirement specified in this regulation, MVTS Operators shall gather and maintain sufficient information about their agents and correspondent operators or any other operators or institutions they are or likely to do business with.

(4) MVTS Operators shall
  (a) assess their agents' and correspondent operators' AML/CFT controls and ascertain that such controls arc adequate and effective;
  (b) obtain approval from the CBN before establishing new correspondent relationships; and
  (c) document and maintain a checklist of the respective AML/CFT responsibilities of each of their agents and correspondent operators.

22. Foreign Branches and Subsidiaries

(1) A financial institution shall ensure that its foreign branches and subsidiaries observe AML/CFT measures consistent with the provisions of these Regulations and apply the measures to the extent that the local or host country's laws and Regulations permit.

(2) Financial institutions shall ensure that the principle referred to in sub-regulation (1) of this regulation is observed by their

branches and subsidiaries in countries which do not or insufficiently apply the requirements of these Regulations.

(3) Where the minimum AML/CFT requirements contained in these Regulations and those of the host country differ, branches' and subsidiaries of Nigerian financial institutions in the host country shall apply the higher standard provided in these Regulations and such standards shall be applied to the extent that the host country's laws, regulations or other measures permit.

(4) A financial institution shall inform the CBN in writing when their foreign branches or subsidiaries are unable to observe the appropriate AML/CFT measures where they are prohibited to observe such measures by the host country's laws, regulations or other measures.

(5) Financial institutions shall subject to the AML/CFT principles contained in these Regulations, apply consistently the CDD measures at their group levels, taking into consideration the activity of the customer with the various branches and subsidiaries.

23. Wire Transfers

(1) For every wire transfer of US$1,000 or more, the ordering financial institution shall obtain and maintain the following information relating to the originator of live wire transfer—
   (a) the name of the originator;
   (b) the originator's account number (or a unique reference number where no account number exists); and
   (c) the originator's address (which address may be substituted with a national identity number).

(2) For every wire transfer of' US$1,000 or more, the ordering financial institution shall obtain and verify the identity of the originator in accordance with the CDD requirements contained in these Regulations.

(3) For cross-border wire transfers of US$1,000 or more, the ordering financial institution shall include the full originator

information in sub-regulation (1) of this regulation in the message or the payment form accompanying the wire transfer.

(4) Where however, several individual cross-border wire transfers of US$1,000 or more from a single originator are bundled in a batch-life for transmission to beneficiaries in another country, the ordering financial institution should only include the originator's account number or unique identifier on each individual cross-border wire transfer, provided that the batch-file (in which the individual transfers are batched) contains full originator information that is fully traceable within the recipient country.

(5) For every domestic wire transfer, the ordering financial institution shall—

(a) include the full originator information in the message or the payment form accompanying the wire transfer; or

(b) include only the originator's account number or a unique identifier, within the message or payment form.

(6) The inclusion of the originator's account number or the originator's unique identifier alone should be permitted by a financial institution only where the originator's full information can be made available to the beneficiary financial institution and to the appropriate authorities within three business days of receiving the request.

(7) Each intermediary and beneficiary financial institution in the payment chain shall ensure that all the originator's information that accompanies a wire transfer is transmitted with the transfer.

(8) Where technical limitations prevent the full originator information accompanying a cross-border wire transfer from being transmitted with a related domestic wire transfer (during the necessary time to adapt payment systems), a record shall be kept for five years by the receiving intermediary financial institution of all the information received from the ordering financial institution.

(9) Beneficiary's financial institution shall adopt effective risk-based procedures for identifying and handling wire transfers that arc not accompanied by complete originator's information.

(10) The lack of complete originator's information is considered as a factor in assessing whether a wire transfer or related transactions are suspicious.

(11) Financial institutions shall file a Suspicious Transaction Report on wire transfers with incomplete originator's information to the NFIU.

(12) The beneficiary's financial institution shall restrict or even terminate its business relationship with the financial institutions that fail to meet the standards specified in this regulation.

(13) Cross-border and domestic transfers between financial institutions are not applicable to the following types of payments

(a) any transfer that flows from u transaction carried out using a credit or debit card so long as the credit or debit card number accompanies all transfers flowing from the transaction, such as withdrawals from a bank account through an ATM machine, cash advances from a credit card or payments for goods and services, provided that where credit or debit cards are used as a payment system to effect a money transfer the necessary information should be included in the message; and

(b) transfers and settlements between financial institution where both the originator person and the beneficiary person are financial institutions acting on their own behalf.

24. Simplified Due Diligence Applicable to Lower Risk Customers Transactions or Products

(1) Where there are low risks, financial institution shall apply reduced or simplified measures.

(2) There are low risks in circumstances where—

(a) the risk of money laundering or terrorist financing is lower;

(b) information on the identity of the customer and the beneficial owner of a customer is publicly available; or

    (c) adequate checks and controls exist elsewhere in the national systems.

(3) In circumstances of low-risk, financial institution shall apply the simplified or reduced CDD measures when identifying and verifying the identity of their customers and the beneficial-owners.

(4) The circumstances which the simplified or reduced CDD measures refer to in sub-regulation (3) of this regulation are applicable include cases of—

    (a) Financial institutions—provided they are subject to the requirements for the combat of money laundering and terrorist financing which are consistent with the provisions of those Regulations and are supervised for compliance with them;

    (b) Public companies (listed on a stock exchange or similar situations) that are subject to regulatory disclosure requirements;

    (c) Insurance policies for pension schemes where there is no surrender-value clause and the policy cannot he used as collateral; and

    (d) a pension, superannuation or similar scheme that provides retirement benefits to employees, where contributions arc made by way of deduction from wages and the scheme rules do not permit the assignment of a member's interest under the scheme.

(5) Financial institution shall not apply the simplified CDD measures to a customer where there is suspicion of money laundering or terrorist financing or specific higher risk scenarios and in such a circumstance, enhanced Due Diligence is mandatory.

(6) Financial institutions shall adopt CDD measures on a risk sensitive-basis and have regard to risk involved in the type of customer, product, transaction or the location of the customer and where there is doubt; they are directed to clarity with the CBN.

25. Timing of Verification

(1) A financial institution shall obtain and verify the identity of the customer, beneficial-owner and occasional customers before or during the course of establishing a business relationship or conducting transactions for them.

(2) Financial institutions are permitted to complete the verification of the identity of the customer and beneficial owner following the establishment of the business relationship, only where—

(a) this can take place as soon as reasonably practicable;

(b) it is essential not to interrupt the normal business conduct of the customer in cases of non-face-to-face business, securities transactions and others; or

(c) the money laundering risks can be effectively managed.

(3) Where a customer is permitted to utilize the business relationship prior to verification, financial institutions shall adopt risk management procedures relevant to the conditions under which this may occur.

(4) The procedures contemplated under sub-regulation (3) of this regulation shall include a set of measures such as—

(a) limitation of the number, types or amount of transactions that may be performed; and

(b) the monitoring of large or complex transactions being carried out outside the expected norms for that type of relationship.

26. Existing Customers

(1) A financial institution shall apply CDD requirements to existing customers on the basis of materiality and risk, and continue to conduct Due Diligence on such existing relationships at appropriate times.

(2) The appropriate time to conduct CDD by financial institutions is where –

(a) a transaction of significant value takes place;

(b) a customer documentation standards change substantially;

(c) there is a material change in the way that the account is operated; or

(d) the institution becomes aware that it lacks sufficient information about an existing customer.

(3) A financial institution shall properly identify the customer in accordance with the criteria contained in these Regulations and the customer identification records shall be made available to the AML/CFT compliance officer, other appropriate staff and competent authorities.

27. Failure to complete CDD

(1) A financial institution that fails to comply with the CDD measures pursuant to these Regulations shall

(a) not be permitted to open the account, commence business relations or perform the transaction; and

(b) be required to render a Suspicious Transaction Report to the NF1U.

(2) The financial institution that has commenced the business relationship shall terminate the business relationship and render Suspicious Transaction Reports to the NFIU.

(3) Where, a financial institution suspects that transactions relate to money laundering or terrorist financing, during the establishment or course of the customer relationship, or when conducting occasional transactions, it shall immediately—

(a) obtain and verify the identity of the customer and the beneficial owner, whether permanent or occasional, irrespective of any exemption or any designated threshold that might otherwise apply; and

(b) render a Suspicious Transaction Report ("STR") to the NFIU without delay.

(4) Where a financial institution suspects that a transaction relates to money laundering or terrorist financing and it believes that performing the CDD process shall tip-off the customer, it shall

(a) not pursue the CDD process, and

(b) file an STR to the NFIU without delay.

(5) A financial institution shall ensure that its employees are aware of, and sensitive to the issues mentioned under this regulation.

(6) When assessing risk, financial institution shall consider all the relevant risk factors before determining the level of overall risk and the appropriate level of mitigation to be applied.

(7) Financial institutions are allowed to differentiate the extent of measures, depending on the type and level of risk for the various risk factors and in a particular situation they may—

(a) apply the normal CDD for customer acceptance measures;

(b) enhanced CDD for on-going monitoring; or

(c) apply any of the procedures as may be considered appropriate in the circumstance.

28. Reliance on Intermediaries and Third Parties on CDD Function

(1) A financial institution that relies upon a third party to conduct its CDD shall—

(a) immediately obtain the necessary information concerning the property which has been laundered or which constitutes proceeds from instrumentalities used in or intended for use in the commission of money laundering and financing of terrorism or other relevant offences; and

(b) satisfy itself that copies of identification data and other relevant documentation relating to the CDD requirements shall be made available from the third party upon request without delay.

(2) The financial institution shall satisfy itself that a third party- is a regulated and supervised institution and that it has

measures in place to comply with requirements of CDD reliance on intermediaries and other third parties on CDD as contained in these Regulations.

(3) Financial institutions relying on intermediaries or other third parties who have no outsourcing, agency, business relationships, accounts or transactions with it or their clients shall perform some of the elements of the CDD process on the introduced business.

(4) The criteria to be met in carrying the elements of the CDD process by the financial institution referred to in sub-regulation (3) of this regulation are to—

   (a) immediately obtain from the third party the necessary information concerning certain elements of the CDD process;

   (b) take adequate steps to satisfy itself that copies of identification data and other relevant documentation relating to CDD requirements shall be made available from the third party upon request without delay;

   (c) satisfy themselves that the third party is regulated and supervised in accordance with Core Principles of AML/CFT and has measures in place to comply with the CDD requirements set out in these Regulations; and

   (d) ensure that adequate Know Your Customer ("KYC") provisions are applied to the third party in order to obtain account information for competent authorities.

(5) Notwithstanding the conditions specified in this regulation, the ultimate responsibility for customer identification and verification shall be with the financial institution relying on the third party.

PART V—MAINTENANCE OF RECORDS

29. Maintenance of Records on Transactions

(1) A financial institution shall maintain all necessary records of transactions, both domestic and international for at least five years after completion of the transaction or such longer

period as may be required by the CBN and NFIU, provided that this requirement shall apply regardless of whether the account or business relationship is on-going or has been terminated.

(2) The components of records of transaction to be maintained by financial institutions include the—

    (a) records of customer's and beneficiary's names, addresses or other identifying information normally recorded by the intermediary;

    (b) nature and date of the transaction;

    (c) type and amount of currency involved; and

    (d) type and identifying number of any account involved in the transaction.

(3) Financial institutions shall maintain records of the identification data, account files and business correspondence for at least five years after the termination of an account or business relationship or such longer period as may be required by the CBN and NFIU.

(4) A financial institution shall ensure that all customer-transaction records and information art- available on a timely basis to the CBN and NFIU.

30. Attention on Complex and unusual large Transactions

(1) A financial institution shall pay special attention to all complex, unusually large transactions or unusual patterns of transactions that have no visible economic or lawful purpose.

(2) A financial institution shall Investigate suspicious transactions and report its findings to the NFIU immediately, in compliance with the provision of section 6(2)(c) of Money Laundering (Prohibition) Act, 2011 (as amended).

(3) For the purpose of sub-regulation (1) of this regulation, complex or unusually large transaction' or 'unusual pattern of transactions' include significant transactions relating to a relationship, transactions that exceed certain limits, very high account turnover inconsistent with the size of the balance or

transactions which fall outside the regular pattern of the account's activity.

31. Suspicious Transaction Monitoring

(1) Where a transaction—
  (a) involves a frequency which is unjustifiable or unreasonable;
  (b) is surrounded by conditions of unusual or unjustified complexity;
  (c) appears to have no economic justification or lawful objective; or
  (d) in the opinion of the financial institution involves terrorist financing or is inconsistent with the known transaction pattern of the account or business relationship, the transaction shall be deemed to be suspicious and the financial institution shall seek information from the customer as to the origin and destination of the fund, the aim of the transaction and the identity of the beneficiary.

(2) Where a financial institution suspects that the funds mentioned under sub-regulation (1) of this regulation—
  (a) are derived from legal or illegal sources but are intended to be used for an act of terrorism;
  (b) are proceeds of a crime related to terrorist financing; or
  (c) belong to a person, entity or organization considered as terrorists, it shall immediately and without delay report the matter to the NFIU and shall not be liable for violation of the confidentiality rules and banking secrecy obligations for any lawful action taken in furtherance of this obligation.

(3) A financial institution shall immediately and without delay; but not later than within 24 hours—
  (a) draw up a written report containing all relevant information on the transaction, together with the identity of the principal and where applicable, of the beneficiary or beneficiaries;

(b) take appropriate action to prevent the laundering of the proceeds of a crime, an illegal act or financing of terrorism; and

(c) report to the NFIU any suspicious transaction stating clearly the reasons for the suspicion and actions taken.

(4) The obligation on financial institutions provided for in this regulation shall apply whether the transaction is completed or not.

(5) A financial institution that fails to comply within the stipulated timeframe with the provisions of—

(a) sub-regulation (1) of this regulation is liable to a fine of '₦1,000,000 for each day the offence subsists; or

(b) sub-regulation (2) of this regulation is liable to sanction as stipulated under the Terrorism (Prevention) Act, 2011 (as amended).

(6) Any person who being a director or employee of a financial institution warns or in any other way intimates the owner of the funds involved in a suspicious transaction report, or who refrains from making the report as required, is liable to a fine of not less than ₦10,000,000 or banned indefinitely or for a period of not less than 5 years from practicing his profession.

(7) The directors, officers and employees of financial institutions who carry out their duties in good faith shall not be liable to any civil or criminal liability, or have any criminal or civil proceedings brought against them by their customers.

32. Procedure for the Monitoring and Reporting or Suspicious Transactions

(1) A financial institution shall have a written Policy Framework that guides and enables its staff to monitor, recognize and respond appropriately to suspicious transactions in addition to the list of Money Laundering "Red Flags" provided for in the Third Schedule to these Regulations.

(2) Every financial institution shall appropriately designate an officer as the AML/CFT Compliance Officer to supervise

the monitoring and reporting of terrorist financing and suspicious transactions, among other duties.

(3)   Financial institutions shall be alert to the various patterns of conduct that are known to be suggestive of money laundering, and shall maintain and disseminate a checklist of such transactions to the relevant staff.

(4)   When any staff of a financial institution detects any "red flag" or suspicious money laundering or terrorist financing activity, the institution shall promptly institute a "Review Panel" under the supervision of the AML/CFT Compliance Officer and every action taken shall be recorded.

(5)   A financial institution and its staff shall maintain confidentiality in respect of any investigation conducted in pursuance of these Regulations and any suspicious transaction report that may be filed with the NFIU consistent with the provision of the Money Laundering (Prohibition) Act, 2011 (as amended) and the Terrorism (Prevention) Act, 2011 (as amended), and shall not say anything that might "tip off any person or entity that is under suspicion of money laundering.

(6)   A financial institution that suspects or has reason to suspect that funds are the proceeds of a criminal activity or are related to terrorist financing shall promptly report its suspicions to the NFIU.

(7)   All suspicious transactions, including attempted transactions are to be reported regardless of the amount involved.

(8)   The requirement to report suspicious transactions applies regardless of whether they are considered to involve tax matters or other matters.

(9)   Financial institutions, their directors, officers and employees whether permanent or temporary, are prohibited from disclosing the fact that a report of a transaction shall be filed with the competent authorities.

(10) In compliance with the Terrorism (Prevention) Act, 2011 (as amended), financial institutions are also required to, forward to the NFIU without delay but not later than within 24 hours, reports of suspicious transactions relating to—

(a) funds derived from illegal or legal sources are intended to be used for any act of terrorism;

(b) proceeds of a crime related to terrorism financing; or

(c) proceeds belonging to a terrorist, terrorist entity or organization.

PART VI—MONITORING, INTERNAL CONTROLS, PROHIBI-TIONS AND SANCTIONS

33. Internal Controls, Compliance and Audit

(1) A financial institution shall establish and maintain internal procedures, policies and controls to prevent money laundering and financing of 'terrorism and to communicate these to their employees.

(2) The procedures, policies and controls established by financial institution shall cover operational matters including the CDD, record retention, the detection of unusual and suspicious transactions and the reporting obligation.

(3) The AML/CFT Compliance Officer and appropriate staff are to have timely access to customer identification data, CDD information, transaction records and other relevant information.

(4) Financial institutions are accordingly required to develop programs against money laundering and terrorist financing, such as—

(a) the development of internal policies, procedures and controls, including appropriate compliance management arrangement and adequate screening procedures to ensure high standards when hiring employees;

(b) on-going employee training programs to ensure that employees are kept informed of new developments, including information on current ML and FT techniques, methods and trends;

(c) providing clear explanation of all aspects of AML/CFT laws and obligations, and in particular, requirements concerning CDD and suspicious transaction reporting; and

(d) adequately resourced and independent audit function to test compliance with the procedures, policies and controls.

(5) A financial institution shall put in place a structure that ensures the operational independence of the Chief Compliance Officer ('CCO') and Branch Compliance Officers.

34. Sanctions and Penalties for Non-Compliance

(1) Failure to comply with the provisions contained in these Regulations shall attract appropriate sanction in accordance with the provisions of the MLPA. 2011 (as amended), existing laws on AML/CFT and as provided for under the provisions of the Second Schedule to these Regulations.

(2) A financial institution, its officers or employees shall not benefit from any violation of extant AML/CFT laws and Regulations.

(3) A financial institution that fails to comply with, or contravenes the provisions in these Regulations, shall be subject to sanctions by the CBN (including the suspension or withdrawal of its operating licence).

(4) Any individual, being an official of a financial institution, who fails to take reasonable steps to ensure compliance with the provisions of these Regulations shall be sanctioned accordingly based on relevant provisions of the Money Laundering (Prohibition) Act 2011 (as amended), the Terrorism (Prevention) Act, 2011 (as amended) and any other relevant law or Regulations, the extant administrative sanction regime issued by the Central Bank of Nigeria or direction by the Attorney-General of the Federation; including revocation, suspension or withdrawal of professional licences by appropriate self- regulatory organizations.

(5) Criminal cases involving officers and the financial institutions shall be referred to the relevant law enforcement agencies for prosecution and the offender shall be liable to forfeit any pecuniary benefit obtained as a result of the violation or breach.

(6) Incidence of false declaration, false disclosure, non-declaration or non-disclosure of returns to be rendered under these Regulations by a financial institution or its officers shall be subject to administrative review and sanctions as stipulated in these or other Regulations and the appropriate administrative or civil penalties applied.

35. Prohibition of Numbered or Anonymous Accounts, Accounts in Fictitious names and Shell banks

(1) A financial institution shall not keep anonymous accounts or accounts in fictitious names.

(2) A financial institution shall not establish correspondent relationships with high risk foreign banks, including shell banks with no physical presence in any country or with correspondent banks that permit their accounts to be used by such banks.

(3) Shell banks are prohibited from operating in Nigeria as provided in Money Laundering (Prohibition) Act, 2011 (as amended).

(4) A financial institution shall—

    (a) not enter into or continue respondent or correspondent banking relationships with shell banks; and

    (b) satisfy itself that a respondent financial institution in a foreign country does not permit its accounts to be used by shell banks.

(5) A financial institution, corporate body or any individual that contravenes the provisions of this regulation shall on conviction be liable to a fine of not less than ₦10,000,000 and in addition to the—

    (a) prosecution of the principal officers of the corporate body; and

(b) winding up and prohibition of its re-constitution or in-corporation under any form or guise.

(6) A financial institution shall take all necessary measures to satisfy itself that respondent financial institutions in a foreign country do not permit their accounts to be used by shell banks.

36. Other forms of Reporting

(1) A financial institution shall report in writing any single transaction, lodgment or transfer of funds in excess of ₦5,000,000 and ₦10,000,000 or their equivalent made by an individual and corporate body respectively to the NFIU in accordance with section 10 (1) of the Money Laundering (Prohibition) Act, 2011 (as amended).

(2) In compliance with section 2(1) of the Money Laundering (Prohibition) Act, 2011 (as amended) financial institutions shall render reports in writing on transfers to or from a foreign country of funds or securities by a person or body corporate including a Money Service Business of a sum exceeding US$10,000 or its equivalent to CBN, Securities and Exchange Commission ('SEC') and the NFIU within 7 days from the date of the transaction.

(3) Details of a report sent by a financial institution to the NFIU shall not be disclosed by the institution or any of its officers to any other person.

37. AML/CFT Employee-education and Training Programme

(1) A financial institution shall design comprehensive employee education and training programmes, to make employees fully aware of their obligations and also to equip them with relevant skills required for the effective discharge of their AML/CFT tasks.

(2) The timing, coverage and content of the employee training programme shall be tailored to meet the needs of the

financial institution to ensure compliance with the requirements and provisions of these Regulations.

(3) A financial institution shall provide comprehensive training programmes for staff covering compliance officers and as part of the orientation programmes for new staff and those posted to the front office, banking operations and branch office staff, particularly cashiers, account opening, mandate, and marketing staff, internal control and audit staff and managers.

(4) A financial institution shall render quarterly returns on their level of compliance on their education and training programmes to the CBN and NFIU

(5) An employee training programme shall be developed under the guidance of the AML/CFT Compliance Officer in collaboration with the top Management.

(6) The basic elements of the employee training programme of financial institutions shall include—

(a) AML Regulations and offences;

(b) the nature of money laundering;

(c) money laundering 'red flags' and suspicious transactions, including trade-based money laundering typologies;

(d) reporting requirements;

(e) Customer Due Diligence;

(f) risk-based approach to AML and CFT; and

(g) record keeping and retention policy.

(7) A financial institution shall submit its annual AML/CFT employee training programme for the following year to the CBN and NFIU at the end of June and December every financial year.

38. Monitoring of employee conduct

(1) A financial institution shall monitor their employees' accounts for potential signs of money laundering.

(2) A financial institution shall subject employees' accounts to the same AML/CFT procedures as applicable to other customers' accounts.

(3) The requirement specified in sub-regulation (2) of this regulation shall be performed under the supervision of the AML/CFT Chief Compliance Officer and the account of this officer is in turn to be reviewed by the Chief Internal Auditor or a person of adequate and similar seniority.

(4) Compliance reports including findings shall be rendered to the CBN and NFIU at the end of June and December of every year.

(5) The AML/CFT performance review of staff shall be part of employees' annual performance appraisals.

39. Protection of Staff Who Report Violations

(1) A Financial institution shall make it possible for employees to report any violations of the institution's AML/CFT compliance programme to the AML/CFT Compliance Officer.

(2) A financial institution shall direct its employees in writing to always co-operate fully with the Regulators and law enforcement agents and to promptly report suspicious transactions to the NFIU.

(3) Where the violations involve the Chief Compliance Officer, employees shall report the violations to a designated higher authority such as the Chief Internal Auditor, the Managing Director or in confidence to the CBN or to the NFIU.

(4) A financial institution shall inform its employees in writing to make their reports confidential and to assure employees of protection from victimization as a result of making any report.

40. Additional areas of AML/CFT Risks

(1) A financial institution shall review, identify and record other areas of potential money laundering risks not covered by these Regulations and report the risk quarterly to the CBN and NFIU.

(2) A financial institution shall review its AML/CFT frameworks from time to time with a view to determining their adequacy and identifying other areas of potential risks not covered by the AML/CFT Regulations.

41. Additional Procedures and Mitigants

After carrying out the review of the AML/CFT framework and identified new areas of potential money laundering vulnerabilities arid risks, financial institution shall design additional procedures and mitigants as contingency plan in their AML/CFT Operational Manuals with indication on how such potential risks shall be appropriately managed where they crystallize and details of the contingency plan rendered to the CBN and NFIU on the 31st December of every financial year.

42. Testing for the adequacy of the AML/CTF Compliance

(1) A financial institution shall make a policy commitment and subject its AML/CFT Compliance Programme to independent-testing or require its internal audit function to determine the adequacy, completeness and effectiveness of the programme.

(2) Report of compliance by a financial institution shall be rendered to the CBN and NFIU by 31st December of every financial year and any identified weaknesses or inadequacies promptly addressed by a financial institution.

43. Formal Board approval of the AML/CFT Compliance

(1) The ultimate responsibility for AML/CFT compliance is placed on the Board and top Management of every financial institution in Nigeria.

(2) The Board of a financial institution shall ensure that a comprehensive operational AML/CFT Policy and Procedure is formulated annually by Management and presented to the Board for consideration and Formal approval.

(3) Copies of the approved AML/CFT Policy and Procedure referred to in sub-regulation (2) of this regulation shall be forwarded to the CBN and NFIU within six months of the release of these Regulations.

(4) Monthly reports on the AML/CFT compliance status of a financial institution shall be presented to the board by the Chief Compliance Officer for its information and necessary action.

44. Culture of compliance

Every financial institution shall have a comprehensive AML/CFT—compliance programme to guide its efforts and to ensure the diligent implementation of its programme, to entrench in the institution a culture of compliance, to minimize the risks of being used to launder the proceeds of crime and also to provide protection against fraud, reputation and financial risks.

Part VII—Guidance on Know Your Customer ("KYC")

45. Three Tiered KYC Requirements

(1) To further deepen financial inclusion, a three-tiered KYC standard shall be utilized to ensure application of flexible account opening requirements for low-value and medium value accounts which shall be subject to caps and restrictions as the amounts of transactions increase where the account opening requirements shall increase progressively with less restrictions on operations stated in this regulation.

(2) Tier one for which—
    (a)   basic customer information required to be provided are:
        (i)   passport photograph;
        (ii)   name, place and date of birth;
        (iii) gender, address, telephone number, etc;
    (b)   information in paragraph (a) of this sub-regulation may be sent electronically or submitted onsite in bank's branches or agent's office;

(c)   evidence of information provided by a customer or verification of same is not required;

(d)   the accounts shall be closely monitored by the financial institution;

(e)   the accounts may be opened at branches of the financial institutions by the prospective customer or through banking agents;

(f)   no amount is required for opening of accounts;

(g)   such accounts may cover Mobile Banking products, issued in accordance with the CBN Regulatory Framework for Mobile Payments Services in Nigeria;

(h)   deposits may be made by account holder and 3rd parties while withdrawal is restricted to account holder only;

(i)   may be linked to mobile phone accounts;

(j)   operation is valid only in Nigeria;

(k)   limited ATM transactions are allowed;

(l)   a maximum single deposit amount is limited to ₦20,000 and maximum cumulative balance of ₦200,000 at any point in time;

(m)   International funds transfer is prohibited; and

(n)   accounts are strictly savings;

(3) Tier two for which—

(a)   evidence of basic customer information such as passport photograph, name, place and date of birth, gender and address is required;

(b)   items in paragraph (a) of this regulation may be forwarded electronically or submitted on-site in banks' branches or agents' offices;

(c)   customer information obtained shall be against similar information contained in the official data-bases such as National Identity Management Commission (NIMC). Independent National Electoral Commission (INEC) Voters Register, Federal Road Safety Commission (FSRC) among others;

(d) accounts may be opened face to face at any branch of a bank by agents for enterprises used for mass payroll or by the account holder;

(e) evidence of basic customer information is required at this level and identification, verification and monitoring by financial institutions are also required;

(f) accounts may be contracted by phone or at the institution's website;

(g) accounts may be linked to a mobile phone;

(h) may be used for funds transfers within Nigeria only;

(i) the accounts are strictly savings;

(j) no amount is required for opening of the accounts;

(k) such accounts cover Mobile Banking products (issued in accordance with the CBN Regulatory Framework for Mobile Payments Services in Nigeria);

(l) maximum single deposit of ₦50,000 and a maximum cumulative balance of ₦400,000 are allowed at any time; and

(m) withdrawal shall be denied where cross-checking of client's identification information is not completed at the point of account opening.

(4) Tier three for which—

(a) a financial institution shall obtain, verify and maintain copies of all the required documents for opening of accounts in compliance with the KYC requirements contained in these Regulations;

(b) no amount is required for opening of the accounts;

(c) there is no limit on cumulative balance, deposit and transactions, and

(d) KYC requirements shall apply.

46. Duty to Obtain Identification Evidence

(1) A Financial institution shall not establish a business relationship until the relevant parties to the relationship have been identified, verified, and the nature of the business they intend to conduct ascertained.

(2) Where an on-going business relationship is established, any activity that is not consistent to the business relationship shall be examined to determine whether or not there are elements of money laundering, terrorist financing or any suspicion activity.

(3) The first requirement of knowing your customer for money laundering and terrorist financing purposes, is for the financial institution to be satisfied that a prospective customer is who he claims to be.

(4) A Financial institution shall not engage in any financial business or provide advice to a customer or potential customer except where the financial institution is sure or certain as to who that person actually is.

(5) Where a customer is acting on behalf of another in a situation where funds are supplied by someone else or the investment is to be held in the name of someone else, a financial institution shall verify the identity of the customer, the agent or trustee except where the customer is itself a Nigerian regulated financial institution.

(6) A Financial institution shall obtain evidence of identification of its customers.

(7) A financial institution shall identify all relevant parties to a business relationship from the beginning in accordance with the general principles of obtaining satisfactory identification evidence set out in these Regulations.

47. Nature and Level of the Business

(1) A financial institution shall obtain sufficient information on the nature of the business that its customer intends to undertake, including expected or predictable pattern of transactions.

(2) The information obtained before the commencement of the business shall include—

    (a) purpose for opening the account or establishing the relationship;

(b) nature of the activity that is to be undertaken;

(c) expected origin of the funds to be used during the relationship; and

(d) details of occupation, employment or business activities and sources of wealth or income.

(3) A financial institution shall take reasonable steps to keep the information up-to-date as the opportunities arise, include where an existing customer opens a new account.

(4) Any information obtained during any meeting, discussion or other communication with a customer shall be recorded and kept in a customer's file to ensure, as far as practicable, that current customer information is readily accessible by the Anti-Money Laundering Compliance Officers ('AMLCOs') or relevant regulatory bodies.

48. Application of Commercial Judgment

(1) A financial institution shall take a risk-based approach of KYC requirements.

(2) A financial institution shall decide on the number of times to verify the customers' records during the relationship, the identification evidence required and when additional checks arc necessary and its decisions shall be recorded.

(3) A financial institution shall for personal account relationships, identify and verify all joint-account holders.

(4) A financial institution shall for private company or partnership, identify and verify the principal owners or controllers.

(5) The identification evidence obtained from the beginning of a business relationship shall be reviewed against the inherent risks in the business or service.

49. Identification

(1) The customer identification process shall continue to exist throughout the duration of the business relationship.

(2) The process of confirming and updating identity and address, and the extent of obtaining additional KYC information collected may differ from one type of financial institution to another.

(3) The general principles for establishing the identity of legal and natural persons and the guidance on obtaining satisfactory identification evidence set out in these Regulations are not exhaustive.

50. Factors to consider in identification

In determining a customer's identity under these Regulations, the following shall be considered—

(a) the name used;

(b) date of birth;

(c) the residential address at which the customer can be located;

(d) in the case of a natural person, the date of birth shall be obtained as an important identifier in support of the name and there shall be no obligation to verify the date of birth provided by the customer; and

(e) where an international passport, driver's licence, INEC voter's card or national identity card is taken as evidence of identity, the number, date and place or country of issue (as well as expiry date in the case of international passport and driver's licence) shall be recorded.

51. Time for Verification of Identity

(1) The identity of a customer shall be verified whenever a business relationship is to be established, on account opening, during one-off transaction or where a series of linked transactions takes place.

(2) In these Regulations, "transaction" include the giving of advice and "advice" under this regulation shall not apply where information is provided on the availability of products or services and when a first interview or discussion prior to establishing a relationship takes place.

(3) Where the identification procedures have been completed and business relationship established, as long as contact or activity is maintained and records concerning that are complete and kept, no further evidence of identity shall be undertaking when another transaction or activity is subsequently undertaken.

(4) Where an investor finally realizes the investment made (wholly or partially), where the amount payable is US$1,000 or its equivalent or above or such other monetary amounts as may, from time to time be stipulated by any applicable money laundering legislation or Regulations, the identity of the investor shall be verified and recorded where this had not been done previously.

(5) Where there is a redemption or surrender of an investment (wholly or partially), a financial institution shall take reasonable measures to establish the identity of the investor where payment is made to—

   (a) the legal owner of the investment by means of a cheque crossed "account payee"; or

   (b) a bank account held (solely or jointly), in the name of the legal owner of the investment by any electronic means.

52. Verification of Identity

(1) Financial institutions shall obtain sufficient evidence of the client's identity to ascertain that the client is the person he claims to be.

(2) Where a person is acting on behalf of another, the obligation is to obtain sufficient evidence of identities of the two persons involved.

53. Exceptions

(1) Notwithstanding the provisions of regulation 52 of these Regulations, in situation of consortium lending, the lead-manager or agent shall supply a confirmation letter as evidence that he has obtained the required identity.

(2) There is no obligation to look beyond the client where—

(a) the client is acting on its own account (rather than for a specific client or group of clients);

(b) the client is a bank, broker, fund manager or other regulated financial institutions; or

(c) all the businesses are to be undertaken in the name of a regulated financial institution.

54. Additional Verification Requirements

In other circumstances, except where the client is a regulated financial institution acting as agent on behalf of one or more underlying clients within Nigeria, and has given written assurance that it has obtained the recorded evidence of identity to the required standards, identification evidence shall be verified for —

(a) the named account holder or person in whose name an investment is registered;

(b) any principal beneficial owner of funds being invested who is not the account holder or named investor;

(c) the principal controller of an account or business relationship including those who regularly provide instructions; and

(d) any intermediate parties including cases where an account is managed or owned by an intermediary.

55. Identification of Directors and other Signatories

A financial institution shall identify directors and all the signatories to an account.

56. Joint Account Holders

Identification evidence shall be obtained for all joint applicants or account holders.

57. Verification of Identity for High Risk Business

For higher risk business undertaken for private companies including those not listed on the stock exchange sufficient evidence of identity and address shall be verified in respect of—

(a) the principal underlying beneficial owner(s) of the company with 5% interest and above; and

(b) those with principal control over the company's assets (e.g. principal controllers or directors).

58. Duty to keep watch of significant changes in nature of business
A financial institution shall—

(a) be at alert in circumstances that may indicate any significant changes in the nature of a business or its ownership and shall make enquiries accordingly; and

(b) observe the additional provisions for High Risk Categories of Customers under AML/CFT directive in these Regulations.

59. Verification of identity of Person providing Funds for Trust

(1) A financial institution shall obtain and verify the identity of those providing funds for Trusts.

(2) The identity of those providing funds for Trust envisaged under these regulations include the settlor and those who are authorized to invest, transfer funds or make decisions on behalf of the Trust such as the principal trustees and controllers who have power to remove the Trustees.

60. Savings schemes and investments in third parties' names
Where an investor sets up a savings account or a regular savings scheme whereby, the funds are supplied by one person for investment in the name of another (such as in the case of a spouse or a child), the person who funds the subscription or makes deposits into the savings scheme is for all intent and purposes, the applicant for the business in question and for such person, identification evidence shall be obtained in addition to that of the legal owner.

61. Personal Pension Schemes

(1) Identification evidence shall be obtained at the outset for all investors, except personal pensions connected to a policy of insurance taken out by virtue of a contract of employment or pension scheme.

(2) Personal pension advisers are charged with the responsibility of obtaining the identification evidence on behalf of the pension fund provider and confirmation that identification evidence has been taken shall be provided on the transfer of a pension to another pension fund provider.

62. Timing of Identification Requirements

(1) An acceptable time-span for obtaining satisfactory evidence of identity is determined by the nature of the business, the geographical location of the parties and the possibility of obtaining the evidence before commitments are entered into or actual monies given or received.

(2) Any business conducted before satisfactory evidence of identity has been obtained shall only be in exceptional cases and under circumstances that can be justified with regard to the risk and in such a case, financial institution shall—

    (a) obtain identification evidence as soon as reasonably practicable after it has contact with a client with a view to agreeing with the client to carry out an initial transaction or reaching an understanding, whether binding or not, with the client that it may carry out future transactions; and

    (b) where the client does not supply the required information as stipulated in paragraph (a) of this regulation, the financial institution shall discontinue any activity it is conducting for the client and bring to an end any understanding reached with the client.

(3) A financial institution shall also observe the provision in the timing of verification under the AML/CFT directive contained in these Regulations.

(4) A financial institution may however start processing the business or application immediately, provided that it—

   (a) promptly takes appropriate steps to obtain identification evidence; and

   (b) does not transfer or pay any money out to a third party until the identification requirements are carried out.

63. Consequence of failure to provide satisfactory Identification Evidence

(1) The failure or refusal of an applicant to provide satisfactory identification evidence within a reasonable time and without adequate explanation may lead to a suspicion that the depositor or investor is engaged in money laundering.

(2) A financial institution under the situation stipulated in sub-regulation (1) of this regulation shall immediately make an STR to the NFIU based on the information in its possession before the funds involved are returned to the potential client or original source of the funds.

(3) A financial institution shall have in place written and consistent policies of closing an account or unwinding a transaction where satisfactory evidence of identity cannot be obtained.

(4) A financial institution is also required to respond promptly to inquiries made by competent authorities and financial institutions on the identity of their customers.

64. Identification Procedures

(1) A financial institution shall ensure that it is dealing with a real person or organization whether natural, corporate or legal, by obtaining sufficient identification evidence.

(2) Where reliance is placed on a third party to identify or verify the identity of an applicant, the overall responsibility for

obtaining satisfactory identification evidence rests with the account holding Financial institution.

(3) In all cases, it is mandatory to obtain satisfactory evidence that a person lives at the address he provided and that the applicant is that person or that the company has identifiable owners and that its representatives can be located at the address provided.

(4) The identification process should be cumulative, as no single form of identification can be fully guaranteed as genuine or representing correct identity.

(5) The procedures adopted to verify the identity of private individuals, whether or not identification was done face-to-face or remotely, shall be stated in the customer's file and the reasonable steps taken to avoid single, multiple fictitious applications, substitution (impersonation) or fraud shall be stated also by the financial institution in the client's file.

(6) An introduction from a respected customer, a person personally known to a Director or Manager or a member of staff often provides comfort but shall not replace the need for identification evidence requirements to be complied with as set out in this Regulation.

(7) Details of the person who initiated and authorized the introduction should be kept in the customer's mandate file along with other records and the Directors or Senior Managers shall insist on the prescribed identification procedures for every applicant.

65. New Business for Existing Customers

(1) Where an existing customer closes one account and opens another or enters into a new agreement to purchase products or services, it shall not be necessary to verify the identity or address for such a customer unless the name or the address provided does not tally with the information in the financial institution's records, provided that procedures are put in place to guard against impersonation or fraud.

(2) The opportunity of opening the new account referred to in sub-regulation (1) of this regulation shall be utilized to ask the customer to confirm the relevant details and to provide any missing KYC information and where—

(a) there was an existing business relationship with the customer and identification evidence had not previously been obtained;

(b) there had been no recent contact or correspondence with the customer within the past three months; or

(c) a previously dormant account is re-activated.

(3) In the circumstances in sub-regulation (2) of this regulation, details of the previous account and any identification evidence previously obtained or any introduction records shall be linked to the new account-records and retained for the prescribed period in accordance with the provisions of these Regulations.

66. Certification of Identification Documents

(1) In order to guard against the dangers of postal-interception and fraud, prospective customers shall not be asked to send originals of their valuable personal identity documents including international passport, identity card, driver's licence, by post.

(2) Where there is no face-to-face contact with a customer and documentary' evidence is required, certified true copies by a lawyer, notary public or court of competent jurisdiction, banker, accountant, senior public servant or their equivalent in the private sector shall be obtained provided that the person undertaking the certification is known and capable of being contacted. In the case of a foreign national, a copy of international passport, national identity card or documentary evidence of his address shall be certified by—

(a) the-embassy, consulate or high commission of the country of issue;

(b) a senior official within the account opening institution; or

(c) a lawyer or notary public.

(3) Certified True Copies of identification evidence are to be stamped, dated and signed "original sighted by me" by a senior officer of the financial institution.

(4) A financial institution shall always ensure that a good production of the photographic evidence of identity is obtained provided that where this is not possible, a copy of evidence certified as providing a good likeness of the applicant is acceptable in the interim.

67. Recording Identification Evidence

(1) Records of the supporting evidence and methods used to verify identity shall be retained for a minimum period of five years after the account is closed or the business relationship ended.

(2) Where the supporting evidence cannot be copied at the time it was presented, the reference numbers and other relevant details of the identification evidence shall be recorded to enable the documents to be obtained later.

(3) Confirmation of evidence in sub-regulation (2) of this regulation shall be provided that the original documents were seen by certifying either on the photocopies or on the record that the details were taken down as evidence.

(4) Where checks are made electronically, a record of the actual information obtained or where it can be re-obtained shall be retained as part of the identification evidence.

(5) The record in sub-regulation (4) of this regulation shall make the reproduction of the actual information that would have been obtained before, less cumbersome.

68. Concession in respect of Payment made by Post

(1) Where the money laundering risk is assessed to be low, concession may be granted for product or services in respect of long-term life insurance business or purchase of personal investment products.

(2) Where payment is to be made from an account held in a customer's name or jointly with one or more other persons, at a regulated financial institution, no further evidence of identity shall be necessary.

(3) Additional verification requirements for postal or electronic transactions shall apply to the following—

    (a) products or accounts where funds may be transferred to other types of products or accounts which provide cheque or money transfer facilities;

    (b) situations where funds may be repaid or transferred to a person other than the original customer; and

    (c) investments where the characteristics of the product or account may change subsequently to enable payment to be made to third parties.

(4) Postal concession shall not be an exemption from the requirement to obtain satisfactory evidence of a customer's identity and payment debited from an account in the customer's name shall be capable of constituting the required identification evidence in its own right.

(5) To avoid proceeds of crime from being laundered by a customer who uses a third-party cheque, draft or electronic payment drawn on a bank, payment from joint accounts shall be considered acceptable for this purpose where the name of the account-holder from where the funds have been provided shall be clearly indicated on the record reflecting the payment or receipt, provided that a financial institution may rely upon the required documentary evidence of a third party, without further verification of the identity, where there is no apparent inconsistency between the name in which an application is made and the name on the payment instrument.

(6) In the case of a mortgage institution's cheque or banker's draft, it shall only be possible to rely on the concession in sub-regulation (5) of this regulation where the holder of the account from which the money is drawn is confirmed to have met the KYC requirements by the

mortgage institution or bank, and payment by direct debit or debit card shall be relied upon except the authentication procedure identifies the name of the account holder from which the payment is drawn and confirms the customer's address.

(7)   In respect of direct debits, it shall not be assumed that the account-holding bank or institution may carry out any form of validation of the account name and number or that the mandate shall be rejected where they do not match.

(8)   Where payment for the product is to be made by direct debit or debit card or notes, and the applicant's account details have not previously been verified through sighting of a bank statement or cheque drawn on the account, repayment proceeds shall only be returned to the account from which the debits were drawn.

(9)   Records shall be maintained indicating how a transaction arose, including details of the financial institution's branch and account number from which the cheque or payment is drawn.

(10)   The concession in this regulation may apply both where an application is made directly to the financial institution and where a payment is passed through a regulated intermediary.

(11)   A financial institution that has relied on the postal concession to avoid additional verification requirements, which shall be so indicated on the customer's file, cannot introduce that customer to another financial institution for the purpose of offering bank accounts or other products that provide cheque or money transmission facilities.

(12)   Where the customer in sub-regulation (11) of this regulation wishes to migrate to an account that provides cheque or third-party transfer facilities, additional identification checks shall be undertaken at that time, and where these circumstances occur on a regular basis a financial institution shall identify all the parties to the relationship at the outset.

69. Term Deposit Account ('TDA')

Term Deposit Accounts ('TDA') can be broadly classified as a one-off transaction provided that a financial institution shall note that concession is not available for TDAs opened with cash where there is no audit trail of the source of funds or where payments to or from third parties are allowed into the account.

70. Investment Funds

Where the balance in an investment fund account is transferred from one funds manager to another and the value at that time is above $1,000 or its equivalent and identification evidence has not been taken or confirmation obtained from the original fund manager, such evidence shall be obtained at the time of the transfer.

PARI VIII GENERAL INFORMATION

71. Establishing Identity

Establishing identity under these Regulations is divided into three broad categories, namely—

(a) private individual customers;
(b) quasi corporate customers; and
(c) pure corporate customers.

72. Private Individuals— General Information

(1) The following information shall be established and independently validated for all private individuals whose identities need to be verified—
(a) Lite full name used; and
(b) the permanent home address, including landmarks and postcode, where available.
(2) The information obtained shall provide satisfaction that a person of that name exists at the address given and that the applicant is that same person so indicated, and where an

applicant has recently moved from his residence, the previous address shall be validated.

(3) The date of birth shall be obtained as required by the law enforcement agencies, provided that the information need not be verified and the residence or nationality of a customer is ascertained to assist risk assessment procedures.

(4) A risk-based approach shall be adopted when obtaining satisfactory evidence of identity.

(5) The extent and number of checks may vary depending on the perceived risk of the service or business sought and whether the application is made in person or through a remote medium such as telephone, post or the internet.

(6) The source of funds of how the payment was made, from where and by whom shall always be recorded to provide an audit trail, provided that for high risk products, accounts or customers, additional steps shall be taken to ascertain the source of wealth or funds.

(7) For low-risk accounts or simple investment products such as deposit or savings accounts without cheque-books or automated money transmission facilities, the financial institution shall satisfy itself as to the identity and address of the customer.

73. Private Individuals Resident in Nigeria

(1) The confirmation of name and address shall be established by reference to a number of sources.

(2) The checks shall be undertaken by cross-validation that the applicant exists at the stated address either through the sighting of actual documentary evidence or by undertaking electronic checks of suitable databases or by a combination of the two.

(3) The overriding requirement to ensure that the identification evidence is satisfactory shall rest with the financial institution opening the account or providing the product or service.

74. Documenting Evidence of Identity

(1) To guard against forged or counterfeit documents, care shall be taken to ensure that documents offered are originals.

(2) Copies that are dated and signed 'original seen' by a senior public servant or equivalent in a reputable private organization may be accepted in the interim, pending presentation of the original documents.

(3) Suitable documentary evidence for private individuals resident in Nigerian as contained in the Second Schedule to these Regulations.

(4) Checking of a local or national telephone directory may be used as additional corroborative evidence but shall not be used as a primary check.

75. Physical Checks on Private Individuals Resident in Nigeria

(1) A financial institution shall establish the true identity and address of its customer and carryout effective checks to protect the institution against substitution of identities by applicants.

(2) Additional verification of a customer's identity and the fact that the application was made by the person identified shall be obtained through one or more of the following procedures—

(a) direct mailing of account opening documentation to a named individual at an independently verified address;

(b) an initial deposit cheque drawn on a personal account in the applicant's name in another financial institution in Nigeria;

(c) telephone contact with the applicant prior to opening of the account on an independently verified home or business number or a "welcome call" to the customer before transactions are permitted, utilizing a minimum of two pieces of personal identity information that had previously been provided during the setting up of the account;

(d) internet sign-on following verification procedures where the customer uses security codes, tokens, or other

passwords which had been set up during account opening and provided by mail or secure delivery, to the named
individual at an independently verified address; or

(e) card or account activation procedures.

(3) A financial institution shall ensure that additional information on the nature and level of the business to be conducted
and the origin of the funds to be used within the relationship
are obtained from the customer.

76. Electronic Checks

(1) An applicant's identity, address and other available information may be checked electronically by accessing other
data-bases or sources, as an alternative or supplementary to
documentary evidence of identity or address.

(2) A financial institution shall use a combination of electronic,
documentary and physical checks to confirm different sources of the same information provided by a customer.

(3) In respect of electronic checks, confidence as to the reliabil-
ity of information supplied shall be established by the cumulative nature of checking across a range of sources, preferably
covering a period of time or through qualitative checks that
assess the validity of the information supplied.

(4) The number or quality of checks to be undertaken shall vary
depending on the diversity as well as the breadth and depth
of information available from each source.

(5) Verification that the applicant is the data-subject shall be
conducted within the checking process.

(6) Suitable electronic sources of information include—
   (a) an electronic search of the electoral register not be used
       as a sole identity and address check;
   (b) access to internal or external account database; and
   (c) an electronic search of public records where available.

(7) Application of the process and procedures in this regulation shall assist financial institutions to guard against impersonation, invented-identities and the use of false addresses

provided that where an applicant is a non face-to-face person, one or more additional measures shall be undertaken for re-assurance.

PART IX—FINANCIAL EXCLUSION FOR THE SOCIALLY OR FINANCIALLY DISADVANTAGED APPLICANTS

77. "Financial Exclusion" for the socially or financially disadvantaged Applicants Resident in Nigeria

(1) Notwithstanding that access to basic banking facilities and other financial services is a necessary requirement for most adults, the socially or financially disadvantaged shall not be precluded from opening accounts or obtaining other financial services merely because they do not possess evidence to identify themselves.

(2) The socially or financially disadvantaged shall not be precluded from opening accounts or obtaining other financial services merely because they do not possess evidence to identify themselves since access to basic banking facilities and other financial services is a necessary requirement for most adults.

(3) Where the socially or financially disadvantaged cannot reasonably comply with sub-regulation (1) of this regulation, the internal procedures of the financial institution shall make allowance for such persons by way of providing appropriate advice to staff on how the identities of such group of persons may be confirmed and what checks shall be made under these exceptional circumstances.

(4) Where a financial institution has reasonable grounds to conclude that an individual client is not able to produce the detailed evidence of his identity and cannot reasonably be expected to do so; the institution may accept as identification evidence, a letter or statement from a person in a position of responsibility such as solicitors, doctors, ministers of religion and teachers who know the client, confirming that the client is who he says he is and his permanent address.

(5) When a financial institution has decided to treat a client as "financially excluded", it shall record the reasons for doing so along with the account opening documents, and returns of same shall be rendered to the CBN and NFIU quarterly.

(6) Where a letter or statement is accepted from a person in position of responsibility, it shall include a telephone number where the person can be contacted for verification and the financial institution shall verify from an independent source the information provided by that person so as to satisfy itself that such customer is the person he claims to be.

(7) A financial institution shall include in its internal procedures the "alternative documentary evidence of personal identity and address" that may he accepted to guard against "financial exclusion" and to minimize the use of the exception procedure.

78. Private Individuals not resident in Nigeria

(1) International passports or national identity cards shall generally be available as evidence of the name of a customer and reference numbers, date and country of issue shall be obtained and recorded in the customer's file as part of the identification evidence in respect of prospective customers who are not resident in Nigeria but who make face-to-face contact.

(2) A Financial institution shall obtain separate evidence of an applicant's permanent residential address from the best available evidence, preferably from an official source.

(3) A Post Office Box number ("P.O.Box Number") alone shall not be accepted as evidence of address and the applicant's residential address shall be such that it may be physically located by way of a recorded description or other means.

(4) Relevant evidence shall be obtained by the financial institution directly from the customer or through a reputable

credit or financial institution in the applicant's home
country or country of residence, provided that particular care shall be taken when relying on identification evidence obtained from other countries.

(5)   A financial institution shall ensure that a customer's true
identity and current permanent address are actually confirmed. In such cases, copies of relevant identity documents shall be sought and retained.

(6)   Where a foreign national has recently arrived in Nigeria,
reference may be made to his employer, university, evidence of traveling documents, etc. to verify the applicant's identity and residential address.

(7)   For a private individual not resident in Nigeria, who wishes to supply documentary information by post, telephone
or electronic means, a risk-based approach shall be taken
where the financial institution shall obtain one separate
item of evidence of identity in respect of the name of the
customer and one separate item for the address.

(8)   Documentary evidence of name and address may be obtained from—

(a) an original documentary evidence supplied by the
customer;

(b) a certified copy of the customer's passport or national identity card and a separate certified document including utility bill and driving licence, verifying the
customer's address; or

(c) a branch, subsidiary', head office of a correspondent
bank.

(9)   Where an applicant does not already have a business relationship with the financial institution that is supplying
the information or the financial institution is outside
Nigeria, certified copies of relevant underlying documentary evidence shall be sought, obtained and retained
by the institution.

(10)   An additional comfort shall be obtained by confirming
the customer's true name, address and date of birth from

a reputable credit institution in the customer's home country, where necessary.

(11) A financial institution shall use requirements in this regulation in conjunction with the First Schedule to these Regulations.

79. Non-face- to-face Identification

(1) In respect of a non-face-to-face customer, an additional measure or check shall be undertaken to supplement the documentary or electronic evidence to ensure that an applicant is who he claims to be and these additional measures shall apply whether the applicant is resident in Nigeria or elsewhere and shall be particularly robust where the applicant is requesting a bank account or other product or service that offers money transmission or third party payments.

(2) Procedures to identify and authenticate a customer shall ensure that there is sufficient evidence either documentary or electronic, to confirm his address and personal identity and to undertake at least one additional check to guard against impersonation or fraud.

(3) The extent of the identification evidence required in this regulation shall depend on the nature and characteristics of the product or service and the assessed risk, provided that care shall be taken to ensure that the same level of information is obtained for internet customers and other postal or telephone customers.

(4) Where reliance is placed on intermediaries to undertake the processing of applications on the customer's behalf, checks shall be undertaken to ensure that the intermediaries are regulated for money laundering prevention and that the relevant identification procedures are applied.

(5) A financial institution shall conduct regular monitoring of internet-based business or clients and where a significant proportion of the business is operated electronically, computerized monitoring systems or solutions that are designed

to recognize unusual transactions and related patterns of transactions shall be put in place to recognize suspicious transactions.

(6) In all cases, evidence as to how identity has been verified shall be obtained and retained with the account opening records.

(7) AML/CFT compliance officers shall review these systems or solutions, record exemptions and report same quarterly to the NFIU.

80. Refugees or Asylum Seekers

(1) Where a refugee or asylum seeker requires a basic bank account without being able to provide evidence of identity, authentic references from the Nigerian Immigration Services endorsed by the State Security Services shall be used in conjunction with other readily available evidence.

(2) Additional monitoring procedures shall be undertaken in respect of sub- regulation (1) of this regulation to ensure that the use of the account is consistent with the customer's circumstances.

81. Students and Minors

(1) When opening accounts for students or other young people, the normal identification procedures set out in these Regulations shall be followed and where such procedures may not be relevant or do not provide satisfactory Identification evidence, verification may be obtained through -

(a) the home address of the parent;

(b) confirming the applicant's address from his institution of learning; or

(c) seeking evidence of a tenancy agreement or student accommodation contract.

(2) An account for a minor may be opened by a family member or guardian and where the adult opening the account does not already have an account with the financial institution,

the identification evidence for that adult or of any other person who will operate the account shall be obtained in addition to obtaining the birth certificate and passport of the child, provided that strict monitoring shall be undertaken.

(3) For accounts opened through a school-related scheme, the school shall provide the date of birth and permanent address of the pupil and complete the standard account opening documentation on behalf of the pupil.

(4) Account of a minor shall be constantly monitored to ensure that it is not used for the purposes of money laundering or terrorist financing and that the transaction does not exceed an amount that should be determined by the financial institution.

82. Quasi Corporate Customers

Trusts, nominee companies and fiduciaries are popular vehicles for criminals wishing to avoid the identification procedures and mask the origin of the dirty money they wish to launder. The particular characteristics of Trust that attract the genuine customer, the anonymity and complexity of structures that they can provide are also highly attractive to money launderers.

PART X—TRUST, POLICY, RECEIPT AND PAYMENT OF FUNDS

83. Trust, Nominees and Fiduciaries

(1) Trusts, nominees and fiduciary accounts present a higher money laundering risk than others.

(2) Identification and "Know Your Customer's Business" procedures shall be set and managed in accordance with the perceived risk.

(3) The principal objective of money laundering prevention trusts, nominees and fiduciaries shall be to verify the identity of the provider of funds such as the settlor, and those who have control over funds like the trustees and any controllers who have the power to remove the trustees.

(4) For discretionary or offshore trust, the nature and purpose of the trust and the original source of funding shall be ascertained.

(5) Whilst reliance may be placed on other financial institutions that are regulated for money laundering prevention to undertake the checks or confirm identity, the responsibility to ensure that this is undertaken shall vest with the financial institution and the underlying evidence of identity shall be made available to law enforcement agencies in the event of an investigation.

(6) Identification shall be obtained and not waived for any trustee who does not have authority to operate an account and cannot give relevant instructions concerning the use or transfer of funds.

84. Offshore Trusts

(1) Since offshore trusts present a higher money laundering risk, additional measures shall be needed for Special Purpose Vehicles (SPVs) or International Business Companies connected to trusts.

(2) Where trusts are set up in offshore locations with strict bank, secrecy or confidentiality rule, those created in jurisdictions without equivalent money laundering procedures in place shall warrant additional enquiries.

(3) Except an applicant for business is a regulated financial institution, measures shall be taken to identify the trust company or the corporate service provider in line with the requirements for professional intermediaries or companies generally.

(4) Certified copies of the documentary evidence of identity for the principals including settlors and controllers on whose behalf the applicant for business is acting shall be obtained.

(5) For overseas trusts, nominee and fiduciary accounts, where the applicant is a financial institution that is regulated for money laundering purposes—

(a) reliance may be placed on an introduction or intermediary certificate letter stating that evidence of identity exists for all underlying principals and confirming that there are no anonymous principals;

(b) the trustees or nominees shall be asked to state from the outset the capacity' in which they are operating or making the application; and

(c) documentary evidence of the appointment of the current trustees shall be obtained.

(6) Where the evidence is not retained in Nigeria, enquiries shall be made to determine, that there is no overriding bank secrecy or confidentiality constraint that shall restrict access to the documentary evidence of identity, shall it be needed in Nigeria.

(7) An application to open an account or undertake a transaction on behalf of another without the applicant identifying his trust or nominee capacity shall be regarded as suspicious and shall lead to further enquiries and rendition of reports to the NFIU.

(8) Where a bank in Nigeria is the applicant for an offshore trust on behalf of a customer, where the corporate trustees are not regulated, the Nigerian bank shall undertake due diligence on the trust itself.

(9) Where funds have been drawn upon an account that is not under the control of the trustees, the identity of two of the authorized signatories and their authority to operate the account shall be verified except where the identity of beneficiaries have not previously been verified and verification shall be carried out where payments are made to them.

85. Conventional Family and Absolute Nigerian Trusts

(1) For Conventional Nigerian Trusts, identification evidence shall be obtained for—

(a) those who have control over the funds, the principal trustees, who can include the settlor;

(b) the providers of the funds, the settlors, except where they are deceased; and

(c) where the settlor is deceased, written confirmation shall be obtained for the source of funds, grant of probate or copy of the Will or other document creating the Trust.

(2) Where a corporate trustee such as a bank acts jointly with a co-trustee, any non-regulated co-trustee shall be verified even where the corporate trustee is covered by an exemption and the relevant guidance contained in these Regulations for verifying the identity of persons, institutions or companies shall be followed.

(3) A financial institution may not review an existing trust but the bank confirmation of the settlor and the appointment of any additional trustees shall be obtained.

(4) Copies of any underlying documentary evidence shall be certified as true copies and a check shall be carried out to ensure that any bank account on which the trustees have drawn funds is in their names.

(5) Where a risk-based approach is adopted, consideration shall be given as to whether the identity of any additional authorized signatories to the bank account may be verified.

(6) A payment for any trust property shall be made to a trustee and as a matter of practice, some life assurance companies make payments directly to beneficiaries on receiving a request from the trustees, payment shall be made to the named beneficiary by way of a crossed cheque marked "account payee only" or a bank transfer direct to an account in the name of the beneficiary in such circumstances.

86. Receipt and payment of Funds

(1) Where money is received on behalf of a trust, reasonable steps shall be taken to ensure that the source of funds is properly identified and the nature of the transaction or instruction is understood.

(2) A Payment shall be properly authorized in writing by the trustees.

87. Identification of new Trustees

Where a trustee who has been verified is replaced, the identity of the new trustee shall be verified before he is allowed to exercise control over funds of the Trust.

88. Life policies placed in Trust

Where a life policy is placed in trust, an applicant for the policy is also a trustee and where the trustees have no beneficial interest in the funds, it shall verify the identity of the person applying for the policy except that the remainder of the trustees shall be identified in a situation where policy proceeds were being paid to a third party not identified in the trust deed.

89. Powers of Attorney and Third-Party Mandates

(1) The authority to deal with assets under a Power of Attorney and Third-Party Mandates constitute a business relationship.

(2) At the start of a relationship, identification evidence shall be obtained from a holder of Power of Attorney and third-party mandates in addition to the customer or subsequently on a later appointment of a new attorney, where advised, within one year of the start of the business relationship.

(3) An attorney for corporate or trust business shall be verified and a financial institution shall always ascertain the reason for the granting of a power of attorney.

(4) A record of a transaction undertaken in accordance with a Power of Attorney shall be maintained as part of the client's record.

PARI XI—EXECUTORSHIP, CLIENT ACCOUNTS, UNINCORPO-RATED AND CORPORATED ORGANIZATIONS

90. Executorship Accounts

(1) Where a bank account is opened for the purpose of winding up the estate of a deceased person, the identity of the executor or administrator of the estate shall be verified.

(2) Identification evidence shall not be required for the executors or administrators where payment is made from an established bank or mortgage institution's account in a deceased's name, solely for the purpose of winding up the estate in accordance with the grant of probate or letter of administration.

(3) Where a life policy pays out on death, identification evidence shall not be obtained for the legal representatives.

(4) A Payment to beneficiaries in sub-regulations (1) (2) and (3) of this regulation on the instructions of the executor or administrator may be made without additional verification requirements, except that where a beneficiary wishes to transact business in his own name, then identification evidence shall be required.

(5) Where suspicion is aroused in respect of the nature or origin of assets comprising an estate that is being wound up, such suspicion shall be reported to the NFIU.

91. "Client Accounts" Opened by Professional Intermediaries

(1) Stockbrokers, fund managers, solicitors, accountants, estate agents and other intermediaries frequently hold Funds on behalf of their clients in "client accounts" opened with a financial institution.

(2) Accounts in sub-regulation (1) of this regulation may be general omnibus accounts holding the funds of many clients or they may be opened specifically for a single client.

(3) In each case, it is the professional intermediary who is the financial institution's customer. These situations shall be distinguished from those where an intermediary introduces a client who himself becomes a customer of the financial institution.

(4) Where a professional intermediary is covered and is indeed monitored under the money laundering Regulations or AML/CFT supervisors or their equivalent, identification may be waived on production of evidence.

(5) Notwithstanding sub-regulation (4) of this regulation, where the professional intermediary' is not regulated by money laundering Regulations or their equivalent, the financial institution shall verify the identity of the professional inter-mediary and also verify the identity of the person on whose behalf the professional intermediary is acting.

(6) Where it is impossible for a financial institution to establish the identity of the person for whom a solicitor or accoun-tant is acting, it shall take a commercial decision based on its knowledge of the intermediary, as to the nature and extent of business that they are prepared to conduct, where the pro-fessional firm is not itself covered by these Regulations.

(7) Financial institutions shall make reasonable enquiries about transactions passing through client-accounts that give cause for concern and shall report any suspicion to the NFIU.

92. Un-incorporated Business or Partnership

(1) Where an applicant is an un-incorporated business or a partnership whose principal partners or controllers do not already have a business relationship with the financial institu-tion, identification evidence shall be obtained in respect of the principal beneficial owners or controllers and any signa-tory in whom significant control has been vested by the prin-cipal beneficial owners or controllers.

(2) Evidence of the address of a business or partnership shall be obtained and where a current account is being opened, a visit to the place of business may be made to confirm the true nature of the business activities and a copy of the latest report and audited accounts shall be obtained.

(3) The nature of the business or partnership shall be verified to ensure that it has a legitimate purpose.

(4) Where a formal partnership arrangement exists, a mandate from the partnership authorizing the opening of an account or undertaking of the transaction shall be obtained.

93. Limited Liability Partnership

A limited liability partnership shall be treated as a corporate customer for verification of identity and know your customer purposes.

94. Pure Corporate Customers

(1) The legal existence of an applicant-company shall be verified from official documents or sources to ensure that persons purporting to act on its behalf are fully authorized.

(2) Where the controlling principals cannot be identified, enquiries shall be made to confirm that the legal person is not merely a "brass-plate company".

95. The identity of a corporate company

(1) (1) The identity of a corporate company shall comprise of—
(a) registration number;
(b) registered corporate name and any trading names used;
(c) registered address and any separate principal trading addresses;
(d) directors;
(e) owners and shareholders; and
(f) the nature of the company's business.

(2) The extent of identification measures required to validate the information or the documentary evidence to be obtained in this regulation depends on the nature of the business or service that the company requires from the financial institution and a risk-based approach shall be taken.

(3) Information as to the nature of the normal business activities that the company expects to undertake with the financial institution shall be obtained.

(4) Before a business relationship is established, measures shall be taken by way of company search at the Corporate Affairs

Commission (CAC) and other commercial enquiries undertaken to check that the applicant-company's legal existence has not been or is not-in the process of being dissolved, struck off, wound up or terminated.

96. Non-face-to-Face Business

(1) Additional procedures shall be undertaken to ensure that the applicant's business, company or society exists at the address provided and it is for a legitimate purpose because of the risks with non-face-to-face business, as with the requirements for private individuals.

(2) Where the characteristics of the product or service permit, steps shall be taken to ensure that relevant evidence is obtained to confirm that any individual representing the company has the necessary authority to do so.

(3) Where the principal owners, controllers or signatories need to be identified within the relationship, the relevant requirements for the identification of personal customers shall be followed.

97. Public Registered Companies

(1) Corporate customers that are listed on the stock exchange are considered to be publicly-owned and generally accountable and there is no need to verify the identity of the individual shareholders.

(2) The Identity of the directors of a quoted company may not be verified.

(3) A financial institution shall make appropriate arrangements to ensure that an officer or employee, past or present, is not using the name of the company or its relationship with the financial institution for a criminal purpose.

(4) The Board resolution or other authority for a representative to act on behalf of the company in its dealings with the financial institution shall be obtained.

(5) Phone calls may be made to the Chief Executive Officer of a company in sub-regulation (4) of this regulation to intimate him of the application to open the account in the financial institution.

(6) Further steps shall not be taken to verify identity more than the usual commercial checks where the applicant company is listed on the stock exchange or there is independent evidence to show that it is a wholly owned subsidiary or a subsidiary under the control of such a company.

(7) Due Diligence shall be conducted where the account or service required falls within the category of higher risk business.

98. Private Companies

Where the applicant is an unquoted company and none of the principal directors or shareholders already have an account with the financial institution, to verify the business, the following documents shall be obtained from an official or a recognized independent source—

(a) a copy of the certificate of incorporation or registration, evidence of the company's registered address and the list of shareholders and directors;

(b) a search at the CAC or an enquiry through a business information service to obtain the information on the company;

(c) an undertaking from a firm of lawyers or accountants confirming the documents submitted to the CAC;

(d) a financial institution shall pay attention to the place or origin of the documents and background against which they were produced; and

(e) where comparable documents cannot be obtained, verification of principal beneficial owners or controllers shall he undertaken.

99. Higher Risk Business Applicant

Where a higher-risk business applicant is seeking to enter into a full banking relationship or any other business relationship where third party funding and transactions are permitted, the following evidence shall be obtained either in documentary or electronic form—

(a) for established companies that are incorporated for 18 months or more, a set of the latest report and audited accounts shall be produced;

(b) a search report at the CAC or an enquiry through a business information service or an undertaking from a firm of lawyers or accountants confirming the documents submitted to the CAC;

(c) a certified copy of the resolution of the Board of Directors to open an account and confer authority on those who will operate it; and

(d) the Memorandum and Articles of Association of the company.

100. Higher Risk Business Relating to Private Companies

(1) Where a private company is undertaking a higher risk business, in addition to verifying the legal existence of the business, the principal requirement is to look behind the corporate entity to identify those who have ultimate control over the business and the company's assets.

(2) What constitutes significant shareholding or control for the purpose of this regulation depends on the nature of the company and identification evidence shall be obtained for shareholders with interests of 5% or more.

(3) Identification evidence shall be obtained for the principal-beneficial owner of the company and any other person with principal control over the company's assets.

(4) Where the principal owner is another corporate entity or trust, it shall take measures that look behind that company or vehicle and verify the identity of the beneficial-owner or settlers and where a financial institution is aware that the principal-beneficial owners or controllers have changed, they are required to verify the identities of the new owners.

(5) Financial institutions shall identify directors who are not principal controllers and signatories to an account for risk-based approach purpose.

(6) Financial institutions shall visit the place of business to confirm the existence of such business premises and the nature of the business conducted.

(7) Where suspicions are aroused by a change in the nature of the business transacted or the profile of payments through a bank or investment account, further checks shall be made to ascertain the reason for the changes.

(8) In full banking relationships, periodic enquiries shall be made to establish changes to controllers, shareholders or the original nature of the business or activity.

(9) Particular care shall be taken to ensure that full identification and KYC requirements are met if the company is an International Business Company (IBC) registered in an offshore jurisdiction and operating out of a different jurisdiction.

101. Foreign Financial Institutions

(1) For a foreign financial institution, the confirmation of existence and regulated status shall be checked by—

  (a) checking with the home country's Central Bank or relevant supervisory body;

  (b) checking with another office, subsidiary, branch, or correspondent bank in the same country;

  (c) checking with Nigerian regulated correspondent bank of the overseas institution; or

  (d) obtaining evidence of its license or authorization to conduct financial and banking business from the institution itself.

(2) Additional information on banks all over the world may be obtained from various international publications and directories or any of the international business information services.

(3) The publications referred to in sub-regulation (2) of this regulation shall not replace the confirmation evidence requirements under these Regulations.

102. Bureau De Change

(1) A Bureau De Change ("BDC") is subject to the provisions of these Regulations and shall be verified in accordance with the procedures for other financial institutions, and satisfactory evidence of identity, ownership structure, source of funds and a certified copy of the applicant's operating license shall be obtained.

(2) A financial institution shall consider the risks associated with doing business with BDCs before entering into a business relationship with them.

103. Designated Non-Financial Businesses and Professions (DNFBPs)

(1) As part of KYC documentation for designated non-financial businesses and professions, the certificate of registration with Special Control Unit against Money Laundering in the Federal Ministry of Trade and Investment or a certificate from a self-regulatory organization as defined under the relevant Designated Non-Financial Business and Professions ("DNFBP") Regulations shall be obtained including identities of at least two of the directors.

(2) Where an application is made on behalf of a club or society, a financial institution shall take reasonable steps to satisfy itself as to the legitimate purpose of the organization by sighting its constitution and the identity of at least two of the principal contact persons or signatories shall be verified in line with the requirements for private individuals and where signatories are changed, a financial institution shall verify the identity of at least two of the new signatories.

(3) Where the purpose of a club or a society is to purchase the shares of a regulated investment company or where all the

members are regarded as individual clients, all the members in such cases shall be identified in line with the requirements for personal customers on a case-by-case basis.

104. Occupational Pension Schemes

(1) Where transactions carried out on behalf of an Occupational Pension Scheme, where the transaction is not in relation to a long-term policy of insurance, the identities of both the principal employer and the Trust shall be verified.

(2) In addition to the identity of the principal employer, the source of funding shall be verified and recorded to ensure that a complete audit trail exists if the employer is dissolved or wound up.

(3) For the Trustees of Occupational Pension Schemes, satisfactory identification evidence shall be based on the inspection of formal documents concerning the Trust which confirm the names of the current Trustees and their addresses for correspondence and in addition to the documents, confirming the Trust identification shall be based on extracts from Public Registers or references from Professional Advisers or Investment Managers.

(4) Any payment of benefits by or on behalf of the Trustees of an Occupational Pension Scheme will not require verification of identity of the recipient.

(5) Where individual members of an Occupation Pension Scheme are to be given personal investment advice, their identities shall be verified but where the Trustees and principal employer have been satisfactorily identified (and the information is still current) it can be appropriate for the employer to provide confirmation of the identity of individual employees.

105. Registered Charity Organizations

(1) A financial institution shall adhere to the identification procedures requirements for opening of accounts on behalf of charity organizations; and the confirmation of the authority to act in the name of the organization.

(2) The opening of accounts on behalf of charity organizations in Nigeria shall be carried out by a minimum of two signatories, duly verified and documentation evidence shall be obtained.

(3) When dealing with an application from a registered charity organization, a financial institution shall obtain and confirm the name and address of the organization concerned.

(4) Where a person making an application, or undertaking a transaction is not the official correspondent or the recorded alternate, a financial institution shall send a letter to the official correspondent, informing him of the charity organizations' application before it and the official correspondent shall respond as a matter of urgency where there is any reason to suggest that the application has been made without authority.

(5) An application on behalf of un-registered charity organization shall be made in accordance with the procedures for clubs and societies as set out in these Regulations.

(6) Where a charity organization is opening a current account, the identity of all signatories shall be verified and where the signatories change, identities of the new signatories shall be verified.

106. Religious Organizations (ROs)

A Religious Organization ("RO") shall have a CAC, and SCUML registered numbers and its identity may be verified by reference to the CAC. appropriate headquarters or regional area of the denomination, and the identity of at least two signatories to its account shall be verified.

107. Three-Tiers of Government and Parastatals

(1) Where the applicant for business is a legal person, a financial institution shall verify the legal standing of the applicant, including its principal ownership and address.

(2) A certified copy of the resolution or other documents which authorise an official representing the body to open an account or undertake any transaction shall be obtained.

(3) A financial institution shall telephone the Chief Executive Officer of the organization or parastatal concerned, to verify and confirm the application to open an account with the financial institution.

(4) An authorization from the Federal or State Accountant-General shall be obtained before any of the three tiers of government or parastatals can open accounts with a financial institution in Nigeria.

108. Foreign Consulates

The authenticity of an applicant who requested to open accounts or undertake transactions in the name of Nigerian-resident foreign consulates and any documents of authorization presented in support of the application shall be checked with the Ministry of Foreign Affairs and the relevant authorities in the Consulate's home country or as confirmed by the Head of the High Commission of that country in Nigeria.

109. Intermediaries or other third parties to verify identity or to introduce business

Whilst the responsibility to obtain satisfactory identification evidence rests with the financial institution that is entering into a relationship with a client, it is reasonable, in a number of circumstances, for reliance to be placed on another financial institution to—

(a) undertake the identification procedure when introducing a customer and to obtain any additional KYC information from the client;

(b) confirm the identification details where the customer is not resident in Nigeria; or

(c) confirm that the verification of identity has been carried out where an agent is acting for a principal.

PART XII — INTRODUCTIONS, APPLICATIONS AND FOREIGN INTERMEDIARIES

110. Introductions from Authorized Financial Intermediaries

(1) Where an intermediary introduces a customer and then withdraws from the ensuing relationship altogether, then the underlying customer has become the applicant for the business and shall be identified in line with the requirements for personal, corporate or business customers as appropriate.

(2) An introductory' letter shall be issued by the introducing financial institution or person in respect of each applicant for business.

(3) To ensure that product-providers meet their obligations, satisfactory identification evidence shall be obtained and retained for the necessary statutory period.

(4) Each introductory letter shall either be accompanied by certified copies of the identification evidence obtained in line with the usual practice of certification of identification documents or by sufficient details and reference numbers that will permit the actual evidence obtained to be re-obtained at a later stage.

111. Written Applications

(1) Where other arrangements have been made, the service provider shall verify the identity itself and financial intermediary shall provide along with each application, the customer's introductory letter together with certified copies of the evidence of identity which shall be placed in the customer's file.

(2) Where these procedures are followed, a product provider, stockbroker or investment banker shall be considered to have fulfilled its own identification obligations.

(3) Where the letter is not forthcoming from the intermediary, or the letter indicates that the intermediary has not verified

the identity of the applicant, the service provider shall satisfy its obligation by applying its own direct identification procedures.

112. Non-Written Application

(1) A Unit Trust Manager and other product providers receiving non-written applications from a financial intermediary, where a deal is made over a telephone or by other electronic means, shall verify the identity of such a customer and ensure that the intermediary provides specific confirmation that identity has been verified.

(2) The answers given by the intermediary shall be recorded and retained for a minimum period of 5 years.

(3) The answers constitute sufficient evidence of identity in the hands of the service provider.

113. Foreign Intermediaries

Where business is introduced or received from a regulated financial intermediary who is outside Nigeria, the reliance that shall be placed on that intermediary to undertake the verification of identity-check shall be assessed by the AMLCO or some other competent persons within the financial institution, on a case-by-case basis based on the knowledge of the intermediary.

114. Corporate Group Introductions

(1) Where a customer is introduced by one part of a financial sector group to another, identity shall not be re-verified and neither shall the records be duplicated except—

(a) the identity of the customer has been verified by the introducing parent company, branch, subsidiary or associate in line with the money laundering requirements of equivalent standards and taking account of any specific requirements such as separate address verification;

(b) no exemptions or concessions have been applied in the original verification procedures that would not be available to the new relationship;

(c) a group introduction letter is obtained and placed with the customer's account opening records; and

(d) in respect of group introducers from outside Nigeria, in which case arrangements shall be put in place to ensure that identity is verified in accordance with requirements and that the underlying records of identity in respect of introduced customers are retained for the necessary' period.

(2) Where a financial institution has day-to-day access to all the group's KYC information and records, there is no need to identify an introduced customer or obtain a group introduction letter where the identity of that customer has been verified previously.

(3) Where an identity of a customer has not previously been verified, then any missing identification evidence will need to be obtained and a risk-based approach taken on the extent of KYC information that is available on whether or not additional information shall be obtained.

(4) A financial institution shall ensure that there is no secrecy or data protection legislation that would restrict free access to the records on request or by law enforcement agencies under court order or relevant mutual assistance procedures.

(5) Where such restrictions apply, copies of the underlying records of identity shall, wherever possible, be sought and retained.

(6) Where identification records are held outside Nigeria, it shall be the responsibility of the financial institution to ensure that the records available meet the requirements in these Regulations.

115. Business Conducted by Agents

(1) Where an applicant is dealing in its own name as agent for its own client, a financial institution shall, in addition to verifying the agent, establish the identity of such a client.

(2) A financial institution shall accept or admit evidence as sufficient where it has established that the client is—

    (a) bound by and has observed these Regulations or the provisions of the Money Laundering (Prohibition) Act, 2011 (as amended); and

    (b) acting on behalf of another person and has given a written assurance that he has obtained and recorded evidence of the identity of the person on whose behalf he is acting.

(3) Where another financial institution deals with its own client regardless of whether or not such a client has disclosed to the financial Institution, then where—

    (a) the agent is a financial institution, there is no requirement to establish the identity of such a client or to obtain any form of written confirmation from the agent concerning the due diligence undertaken on its underlying clients;

    (b) a regulated agent from outside Nigeria deals through a customer omnibus account or for a named customer through a designated account, the agent shall provide a written assurance that the identity of all the underlying clients has been verified in accordance with their local requirements; and

    (c) such an assurance cannot be obtained, then the business shall not be undertaken.

(4) Where an agent is either unregulated or is not covered by the money laundering legislation, then each case shall be treated on its own merits.

(5) The knowledge of the agent shall determine the type of the Due Diligence standards to apply and risk-based approach shall be observed by a financial institution.

116. Syndicated Lending

Where there is a syndicated lending arrangement, the verification of identity and any additional KYC requirements rest with the lead-manager or agent to supply the normal confirmation letters.

117. Correspondent Relationship

(1) Transactions conducted through correspondent relationships shall be managed, in accordance with a risk-based approach; and "Know Your Correspondent" procedures shall be established to ascertain whether or not the correspondent bank or the counter-party is itself regulated for money laundering prevention; and where regulated, the correspondent shall verify the identity of its customers in accordance with FATF standards; and where this is not the case, additional due diligence shall be required to ascertain and assess the correspondent's internal policy on money laundering prevention and KYC procedures.

(2) The volume and nature of transactions flowing through correspondent accounts with a financial institution, from high risk jurisdictions or those with inadequacies or material deficiencies shall be monitored against expected levels and destinations and any material variances shall be checked.

(3) A financial institution shall maintain records and ensure that sufficient due diligence has been undertaken by the remitting bank on the underlying client and the origin of the funds in respect of the funds passed through their accounts.

(4) A financial institution shall guard against establishing correspondent relationships with high risk foreign banks such as shell banks or with correspondent banks that permit their accounts to be used by such banks.

(5) Staff dealing with correspondent banking accounts shall be trained to recognize higher risk circumstances and be prepared to challenge the correspondents over irregular activity whether isolated transactions or trend and to submit a suspicious activity report to the NFIU.

(6) A financial institution shall terminate an account with a correspondent bank that fails to provide satisfactory answers to questions including confirming the identity of customers involved in unusual or suspicious circumstances.

118. Acquisition of one financial institution and business by another

(1) Where a financial institution acquires a business and accounts of another financial institution, it will not be necessary for the identity of all the existing customers to be re-identified, provided that all the underlying customers' records are acquired with the business, but it shall carry out due diligence enquiries to confirm that the acquired institution had conformed with the requirements of the provisions of these Regulations.

(2) Verification of identity shall be undertaken for all the transferred customers who were not verified by the transferor, in line with the requirements for existing customers that open new accounts, where the—

   (a) money laundering procedures previously undertaken have not been in accordance with the requirements of these Regulations;

   (b) procedures shall be checked; or

   (c) customer-records are not available to the acquiring financial institution.

119. Vulnerability of Receiving Bankers and Agents

(1) A receiving financial institution can be used by money launderers in respect of offers for sale where new issues are oversubscribed and their allotment is scaled down; the money launderer is not concerned if there is a cost involved in laundering dirty money.

(2) New issues that trade at a discount will, therefore, still prove acceptable to the money launderer.

(3) Criminal funds can be laundered by way of the true beneficial-owner of the funds providing the payment for an application in another person's name, specifically to avoid the verification process and to break the audit trail with the underlying crime from which the funds are derived.

120. Categories of persons to be Identified

(1) A receiving financial institution shall obtain satisfactory identification evidence of a new applicant, including such applicants in a rights issue, where the value of a single transaction
or a series of linked transactions is $1,000 or its equivalent or
as per the tiered KYC directive issued by the CBN.

(2) Where funds to be invested are being supplied by or on behalf of a third party, the identification evidence for both the
applicant and the provider of the funds shall be obtained to
ensure that, the audit trail for the funds is preserved.

121. Applications Received through Brokers

(1) Where an application is submitted, payment made by a broker or an intermediary acting as agent, no steps shall be
taken to verify the identity of the underlying applicants, the
following standard procedures shall apply—
   (a) the lodging agent's stamp shall be affixed on the application form or allotment letter; and
   (b) application and acceptance forms and cover letters submitted by lodging agents shall be identified and recorded in the bank's records.

(2) The terms and conditions of the issue shall state that any
requirements to obtain identification evidence are the responsibility of the broker lodging the application and not
the receiving financial institution.

(3) Where the original application has been submitted by a regulated broker, no additional identification evidence shall be
conducted for subsequent calls in respect of shares issued
and partly paid.

122. Applications Received from Foreign Brokers

Where a broker or other introducer is a regulated person or institution (including an overseas branch or a subsidiary) from a country

with equivalent legislation and financial sector procedures, and the broker or introducer is subject to anti-money laundering laws or regulations, then a written assurance shall be taken from the broker that he has obtained and recorded evidence of identity of any principal and underlying beneficial owner that is introduced.

123. Multiple Family Applications

(1) Where multiple family applications are received supported by one cheque and the aggregate subscription price is US$1,000 or more: and $1,000 or more for an individual person, then identification evidence will not be required for—

    (a) a spouse or any other person whose surname and address are the same as those of the applicant who has signed the cheque;

    (b) a joint account holder; or

    (c) an application in the name of a child where the relevant company's Articles of Association prohibit the registration in the names of minors and the shares are to be registered with the name of the family member of full age on whose account the cheque is drawn and who has signed the application form.

(2) Identification evidence of the signatory of the financial instrument shall be required for any multiple family applications for more than $1,000 or its equivalent; or as per the tiered KYC directive issued by the CBN, where such application is supported by a cheque signed by someone whose name differs from that of the applicant.

(3) Other monetary amounts or more shall, from time to time, be stipulated by any applicable money laundering legislation and guidelines.

(4) Where an application is supported by a financial institution's branch cheque or brokers' draft, the applicant shall state the name and account number from which the funds were drawn -

(a) on the front of the cheque;

(b) on the back of the cheque together with a branch stamp; or

(c) attaching other supporting documents.

PART XIII—LINKED TRANSACTIONS, FOREIGN ACCOUNTS AND INVESTMENT

124. Linked Transactions

(1) Where a person handling applications that a number of single applications under $1,000 or its equivalent in different names are linked, such as payments from the same financial institution account apart from the multiple family applications above, identification evidence shall be obtained in respect of parties involved in each single transaction.

(2) Installment payment issues shall be treated as linked transactions where it is known that total payments will amount to $1,000 or its equivalent or such other monetary amounts as may, from time to time, be stipulated by any applicable money laundering legislation or guidelines; and either from the beginning or when a particular point has been reached, identification evidence shall be obtained.

(3) An application that is believed to be linked with money laundering shall be processed on a separate batch for investigation after allotment and registration have been completed.

(4) The returns with the documentary evidence shall be rendered to the NFIU accordingly.

(5) Copies of the supporting cheques, application forms and any repayment-cheques shall be retained to provide an audit trail until the receiving financial institution is informed by CBN, NFIU or the investigating officer that the records are of no further interest.

125. Foreign Domiciliary Account (FDA)

(1) Where a customer wishes to open a Domiciliary Account (DA) or make a wholesale deposit by means of cash or inter-bank transfer, a financial institution shall obtain identification evidence in accordance with the requirements for private individuals, companies or professional intermediaries operating on behalf of third parties as appropriate.

(2) A financial institution shall satisfy itself that the transferring institution is regulated for money laundering prevention in its country of origin.

126. Safe Custody and Safety Deposit Boxes

(1) Precautions shall be taken in relation to requests to hold boxes, parcels and sealed envelopes in a safe custody.

(2) Where such facilities are made available, the identification procedures set out in these Regulations shall be followed, depending on the type of individual involved or risks associated with the business relationship.

127. Customer's Identity Not Properly Obtained

Where a customer's identity was not properly obtained as contained in these Regulations and the requirements for Account Opening Procedure, a financial institution shall re-establish the customer's identity in line with the provisions of these Regulations.

128. Exemption from Identification Procedures

Identification evidence shall not be required where the applicant for business is a Nigerian financial institution or person covered and persons regulated by the requirements of these regulations.

129. One-off Cash Transaction, Remittances and Wire Transfers

(1) Cash remittances and wire transfers either inward or outward or other monetary instruments that are undertaken against

payment in cash for customers who do not have an account or other established relationship with the financial institution such as walk in customers, present a high risk for money laundering purposes.

(2) Adequate procedures shall be established to record the transaction and relevant identification evidence taken; and where such transactions form a regular part of the financial institution's business, the limits for requiring identification evidence of US$1,000 or its equivalent for foreign transfers shall be observed.

130. Re-investment of Income

The proceeds of a one-off transaction due can be paid to a customer or be further re-invested where records of his identification requirements were obtained and kept. In the absence of this, his identification requirements shall be obtained before the proceeds are paid to him or be re-invested on his behalf in accordance with the relevant provision of these Regulations.

131. Amendment or revocation of these Regulations

(1) The Central Bank of Nigeria may, as it considers appropriate, amend or revoke the provisions of these Regulations which amendment or revocation shall be published in the Gazette.

(2) The Central Bank of Nigeria (Anti-Money Laundering/ Combating the Financing of Terrorism (AML/CFT) Regulations, 2009 (as amended) is hereby revoked.

(3) The revocation of the Regulations specified in sub-regulation (2) of this regulation shall not affect anything done or purported to be done under or pursuant to these Regulations.

132. Interpretation

In these Regulations-

'*AMCLO*' means Anti-Money Laundering Complaince Officer;

Applicant for Business means a person or company seeking to establish a 'business relationship' or an occasional customer undertaking a 'one-off' transaction whose identity must be verified;

'Batch transfer' means a transfer comprising a number of individual wire transfers that are being sent to the same financial institution, but may or may not be ultimately intended for different persons;

'BDC' means Bureau De Change;

'Beneficial owner' includes a natural person who ultimately owns or controls a customer or a person on whose behalf a transaction is being conducted and the persons who exercise ultimate control over a legal person or arrangement;

'Beneficiary' includes a natural person who receives charitable, humanitarian or other types of assistance through the services of a Non-Profit Organization (NPO), all trusts other than charitable or statutory permitted non-charitable trusts which may include the settlor, and a maximum time, known as the perpetuity period, normally of 100 years;

'Business Relationship' means any arrangement between the financial institution and the applicant for business the purpose of which is to facilitate the carrying out of transactions between the parties on a 'frequent, habitual or regular' basis and where the monetary value of dealings in the course of the arrangement is not known or capable of being ascertained at the outset;

'Cross-border transfer' means any wire transfer where the originator and beneficiary institutions are located in different jurisdictions. This term also refers to any chain of wire transfers that has at least one cross-border element:

'Designated categories of offences' includes—

(a) participation in an organized criminal group and racketeering;

(b) terrorism, including terrorist financing;

(c) trafficking in human beings and migrant smuggling;

(d) sexual exploitation, including sexual exploitation of children;

(e) illicit trafficking in narcotic drugs and psychotropic substances;

(f) illicit arms trafficking;

(g) illicit trafficking in stolen and other goods;

(h) corruption and bribery;

(i) fraud;

(j) counterfeiting currency;

(k) counterfeiting and piracy of products;

(l) environmental crime;

(m) murder, grievous bodily injury;

(n) kidnapping, illegal restraint and hostage-taking;

(o) robbery or theft;

(p) smuggling (including in relation to customs and excise duties and taxes);

(q) tax crimes (related to direct taxes and indirect taxes);

(r) extortion;

(s) forgery;

(t) piracy;

(u) insider trading and market manipulation; and

(v) all other predicate offences as contained in section 15 of Money Laundering (Prohibition) Act, 2011 (as amended).

"Designated non-financial businesses and professions" includes any institution as designated by the Minister of Trade and Investment, MLPA, 2011 (as amended) and CBN AML/CFT Regulations, 2013;

'Domestic transfer' means any wire transfer where the originator and beneficiary institutions are both located in Nigeria. This term therefore, refers to any chain of wire transfers that takes place entirely within Nigeria's borders, even though the system used to effect the wire transfer may be located in another jurisdiction;

'False declaration or disclosure' means failing to declare or, *to* misrepresent the value of currency or bearer negotiable instruments being transported, or a misrepresentation of other relevant data requested for by the authorities;

'FATF' means Financial Action Task Force;

'FATF Recommendations' means the revised FATF Recommendations issued by the Financial Action Task Force;

'Financial institutions' include any person or entity who conducts as a business one or more of the following activities on behalf of a customer—

(a) acceptance of deposits and other repayable funds from the public;

(b) lending;

(c) financial leasing;

(d) the transfer of money or value;

(e) issuing and managing means of payment such as credit and debit cards, cheques, travelers' cheques, money orders and bankers' drafts, electronic money;

(f) financial guarantees and commitments;

(g) trading in—

    (i) money market instruments (cheques, bills, CDs, derivatives etc.);

    (ii) foreign exchange;

    (iii) exchange, interest rate and index instalments;

    (iv) transferable securities; and

    (v) commodity futures trading;

(h)   participation in securities issues and the provision of finan-
      cial services related to such issues;

(i)   individual and collective portfolio management;

(j)   safekeeping and administration of cash or liquid securities
      on behalf of other persons;

(k)   otherwise investing, administering or managing funds or
      money on behalf of other persons;

(l)   underwriting and placement of life insurance and other in-
      vestment related insurance; and

(m)   money and currency changing.

The list is not exhaustive but subject to the definition contained in
BOFIA 2004;

'Financing of terrorism' extends to all acts so defined under the
Terrorism (Prevention) Act, 2011 (as amended) and the Terrorism
Prevention ((Freezing of International Terrorists Funds and other
Related Measures) Regulations, 2013;

'Funds' include assets of every kind, tangible or intangible, movable
or immovable however acquired, legal documents or Instruments
in any form, electronic or digital evidencing title or interest in such
assets, bank credits, travelers cheques, bank cheques, money orders,
shares, securities, bonds, drafts and letters of credit;

'Funds transfer' means any transaction carried out on behalf of an
originator person, both natural and legal through a financial institution by electronic means with a view to making an amount of money
available to a beneficiary person at another financial institution and
the originator and the beneficiary may be the same person;

'Legal arrangement' means express trusts or other similar legal
arrangements;

'Legal persons' mean bodies corporate, foundations, partnerships, or
associations, or any similar bodies that can establish a permanent

customer relationship with a financial institution or otherwise own property;

'*Money or value transfer services (MVTS)*' include financial services that involve the acceptance of cash, cheques, other monetary instruments or other stores of value and the payment of a corresponding sum in cash or other form to a beneficiary by means of a communication, message, transfer or through a clearing network to which the MVTS provider belongs and transactions performed by such services can involve one or more intermediaries and a final payment to a third party, and may include any new payment methods. Sometimes these services have ties to particular geographic regions and are described using a variety of specific terms, including *hawala, hundi, and feichen;*

'*Non-profit/non-governmental Organization*' means a legal entity or organization that primarily engages in raising or disbursing funds for purposes such as charitable, religious, cultural, educational, social or fraternal purposes, or for the carrying out of other types of good works;

'*Originator*' means an account holder or where there is no account, the person natural or legal that places the order with the financial institution to perform the wire transfer;

'*one-off transaction*' means any transaction carried out other than in the course of an established business relationship. It is important to determine whether an applicant for business is undertaking a one-off transaction or whether the transaction is or will be a part of a business relationship as this can affect the identification requirements;

'*Payable through account*' means correspondent accounts that are used directly by third parties to transact business on their own behalf;

'*Proceeds*' mean any property or value derived from or obtained, directly or indirectly, through the commission of an offence;

'Property' means assets of every kind, whether corporeal or incorporeal, moveable or immoveable, tangible or intangible, and legal documents or instruments evidencing title to or interest in such assets;

'Risk' means the risk of money laundering and/or terrorist financing;

'SCUML' means Special Control Unit against Money Laundering in the Federal Ministry of Trade and Investment;

'Settlors' Settlors include persons or companies who transfer ownership of their assets to trustees by means of a trust deed and where the trustees have some discretion as to the investment and distribution of the trust's assets, the deed may be accompanied by a non-legally binding letter setting out what the settlor wishes to be done with the assets;

'Shell bank' means a bank that has no physical presence in the country in which it is incorporated and licensed, and which is unaffiliated with a regulated financial service group that is subject to effective consolidated supervision;

'Physical presence' means meaningful mind and management located within a country and the existence simply of a local agent or low-level staff does not constitute physical presence;

'Terrorist" has the same meaning as in Terrorism (Prevention) Act, 2011 (as amended);

'Terrorist act' has the same meaning as in Terrorism (Prevention) Act, 2011 (as amended);

'Terrorist organization' 'has the same meaning as in Terrorism (Prevention) Act, 2011 (as amended);

'Terrorist property' includes a property which—

(a) has been, is being or is likely to be used for any act of terrorism;
(b) has been, is being or is likely to be used by a proscribed organization;
(c) is the proceeds of an act of terrorism; and
(d) is provided or collected for the pursuit of or in connection with an act of terrorism;

'Those who finance terrorism' include any person, group, undertaking or other entity that provides or collects, by any means, directly or indirectly, funds or other assets that may be used, in full or in part, to facilitate the commission of terrorist acts, or to any persons or entities acting on behalf of, or at the direction of such persons, groups, undertakings or other entities and those who provide or collect funds or other assets with the intention that they should be used or in the knowledge that they are to be used, in full or in part, in order to carry out terrorist acts;

'Trustees' include paid professionals or companies or unpaid persons who hold the assets in a trust fund separate from their own assets. They invest and dispose of them in accordance with the settlor's trust deed, taking account of any letter of wishes. There may also be a protector who may have power to veto the trustees' proposals or remove them, or a custodian trustee, who holds the assets to the order of the managing trustees;

'Unique identifier' means any unique combination of letters, numbers or symbols that refers to a specific originator; and

'Wire transfer' means any transaction carried out on behalf of an originator both natural and legal person, through a financial institution by electronic means, with a view to making an amount of money available to a beneficiary person at another financial institution; where the originator and the beneficiary may be the same person.

133. Citation
These Regulations may be cited as Central Bank of Nigeria (Anti-Money Laundering and Combating Financing of Terrorism for Banks and Other Financial Institutions in Nigeria), Regulations. 2013.

SCHEDULES
Schedule 1—Sanctions and Penalties

Sanctions
Sections 15 and 16 of the Money Laundering (Prohibition) Act, 2011 (as amended) provide for lines or term of imprisonment or both upon committing money laundering or aiding and abetting money laundering activities. The administrative sanctions outlined in this document will be imposed consequent upon the examination of a financial institution and observance of contraventions by CBN Examiners and other agencies.

In determining the sanctions to apply, all the circumstances of the case will be taken into account, including -

1. Nature and seriousness of contravention/exception(s) observed

(a) Whether the contravention was deliberate, dishonest or reckless;

(b) The duration and frequency of the contravention;

(c) The amount of any benefit gained or loss avoided due to the contravention;

(d) Whether the contravention reveals serious or systemic weaknesses of the management systems or internal rules relating to all or part of the business; and

(e) The nature and extent of any AML/CFT crime facilitated, occasioned or otherwise attributable to the contravention—

    (i) whether there are a number of smaller issues, which individually may not justify administrative sanction, but which do so when taken collectively; and

(ii) Any potential or pending criminal proceedings in respect of the contravention which will be prejudiced or
barred if a monetary penalty is imposed pursuant to the
Administrative Sanctions Procedure.

2. The conduct of the regulated financial institution or person concerned in its management after the contravention

(a) How quickly, effectively and completely the financial institution or person concerned in its management brought the
contravention to the attention of the CBN or any other relevant regulatory authority;

(b) The degree of co-operation with CBN Examiners or other
agency provided during the examination;

(c) Any remedial steps taken since the contravention was identified, including: taking disciplinary action against staff involved (where appropriate); addressing any systemic failures;
and taking action designed to ensure that similar problems
do not arise in the future;

(d) The likelihood that the same type of contravention will reoc-
cur if no administrative sanction is imposed; and

(e) Whether the contravention was admitted or denied.

3. The previous record of the financial institution or person concerned in its management

(a) Whether CBN has taken any previous action resulting in a
settlement, sanctions or whether there are relevant previous
criminal convictions;

(b) Whether the financial institution or person concerned in its
management has previously been requested to take remedial
action; and

(c) General compliance history.

4. General considerations

(a) Prevalence of the contravention;

(b) Action taken by CBN in previous similar cases; and

(c) Any other relevant consideration.

PENALTIES

The penalties that the CBN shall apply for contraventions of the MLPA 2011 (as amended), Terrorism Prevention Act (TPA), 2011 (as amended), Terrorism Prevention (Freezing of International Terrorists Funds and Other Related Measures) Regulations, 2013 and CBN AML/CFT Regulation 2013 (comprise revocation or suspension of the operating license, non-monetary and financial penalties) shall be as permitted by BOFIA or any other relevant laws or any regulations issued by the Attorney General of the Federation.

SCHEDULE II
INFORMATION TO ESTABLISH IDENTITY

1. Natural Persons

(1) For natural persons, the following information shall be obtained, where applicable

(a) legal name and any other names used (such as maiden name);

(b) permanent address (full address shall be obtained and the use of a post office box number only, is not sufficient);

(c) telephone number, fax number, and e-mail address;

(d) date and place of birth;

(e) nationality;

(f) occupation, public position held and name of employer;

(g) an official personal identification number or other unique identifier contained in an unexpired official document such as passport, identification card, residence permit, social security records or drivers' licence that bears a photograph of the customer;

(h) type of account and nature of the banking relationship; and

(i) signature.

(2) The Financial Institution shall verify the information referred to in paragraph 1 of this Appendix, by at least one of the following methods—

(a) confirming the date of birth from an official document (such as birth certificate, passport, identity card, social security records);

(b) confirming the permanent address (such as utility bill, tax assessment, bank statement, a letter from a public authority);

(c) contacting the customer by telephone, by letter or by e-mail to confirm the information supplied after an account has been opened (such as a disconnected phone, returned mail, or incorrect e-mail address shall warrant further investigation):

(d) confirming the validity of the official documentation provided through certification by an authorized person such as embassy official, notary public.

(3) The examples quoted above are not the only possibilities. There may be other documents of an equivalent nature which may be produced as satisfactory evidence of customers' identity.

(4) A Financial Institution shall apply equally, effective customer identification procedures for non-face-to-face customers as for those available for interview.

(5) A Financial Institution shall make an initial assessment of a customer's risk profile from the information provided and particular attention shall be focused on those customers identified as having a higher risk profile and any additional

inquiries made or information obtained in respect of those customers shall include—

(a) evidence of an individual's permanent address sought through a credit reference agency search, or through independent verification by home visits;

(b) personal reference by an existing customer of the same institution;

(c) prior bank reference and contact with the bank regarding the customer;

(d) source of wealth; and

(e) verification of employment and public position held where appropriate.

(6) The customer acceptance policy shall not be so restrictive to amount to a denial of access by the general public to banking services, especially for people who are financially or socially disadvantaged.

2. Institutions

The term "Institution" includes any entity that is not a natural person and in considering the customer identification guidance for the different types of institutions, particular attention shall be given to the different levels of risk involved.

3. Corporate Entities

(1) For corporate entities such as corporations and partnerships, the following information shall be obtained—

(a) name of the institution;

(b) principal place of the institution's business operations;

(c) mailing address of the institution;

(d) contact telephone and fax numbers;

(e) some form of official identification number, if available such as tax identification number;

(f) the original or certified copy of the certificate of incorporation and memorandum and articles of association;

(g) the resolution of the board of directors to open an account and identification of those who have authority to operate the account; and

(h) nature and purpose of business and its legitimacy.

(2) The Financial Institution shall verify the information referred to in paragraph 7(1) of this Schedule by at least one of the following methods—

(a) for established corporate entities, reviewing a copy of the latest report and audited accounts, if available;

(b) conducting an enquiry by a business information service or an undertaking from a reputable and known firm of lawyers or accountants confirming the documents submitted;

(c) undertaking a company search and/or other commercial enquiries to see that the institution has not been, or is not in the process of being dissolved, struck off, wound up or terminated;

(d) utilising an independent information verification process, such as accessing public and private databases;

(e) obtaining prior bank references;

(f) visiting the corporate entity; and

(g) contacting the corporate entity by telephone, mail or e-mail.

(3) The Financial Institution shall also take reasonable steps to verify the identity and reputation of any agent that opens an account on behalf of a corporate customer, if that agent is not an officer of the corporate customer.

4. Corporation or Partnership

(1) For Corporations or Partnerships, the principal guidance is to look behind the institution to identify those who have control over the business and the company's or partnership's assets, including those who have ultimate control.

(2) For corporations, particular attention shall be paid to shareholders, signatories or others who inject a significant

proportion of the capital or financial support or exercise control and where the owner is another corporate entity or trust, the objective is to undertake reasonable measures to look behind that company to verify the identity of the principals.

(3) What constitutes control for this purpose shall depend on the nature of a company and may rest in those who are mandated to manage the funds, accounts or investments without requiring further authorization, and who would be in a position to override internal procedures and control mechanisms.

(4) For partnerships, each partner shall be identified and it shall identify immediate family members that have ownership control.

(5) Where a company is listed on a recognized stock exchange or is a subsidiary of a listed company, the company itself may be considered to be the principal to be identified and where a listed company is effectively controlled by an individual, group of individuals, another corporate entity or trust, those in control of the company are considered to be principals and shall be identified accordingly.

5. Other types of Institution

(1) The following information shall be obtained in addition to that required to verify the identity of the principals in respect of Retirement Benefit Programmes, Mutual or Friendly Societies, Cooperatives and Provident Societies, Charities, Clubs and Associations, Trusts and Foundations and Professional Intermediaries:

(a) name of account;

(b) mailing address;

(c) contact telephone and fax numbers;

(d) some form of official identification number, such as tax identification number;

(e) description of the purpose or activities of the account holder as stated in a formal constitution; and

(f) copy of documentation confirming the legal existence of the account holder such as register of charities.

(2) The Financial Institution shall verify the information referred to in paragraph 6(1) of this Schedule by at least one of the following -

(a) obtaining an independent undertaking from a reputable and known firm of lawyers or accountants confirming the documents submitted;

(b) obtaining prior bank references; and

(c) accessing public and private databases or official sources.

6. Retirement Benefit Programme

Where an occupational pension programme, employee benefit trust or share option plan is an applicant for an account, the trustee and any other person who has control over the relationship such as the administrator, programme manager, and account signatories shall be considered as principals and the financial institution shall take steps to verify their identities.

7. Mutual or Friendly, Cooperative and Provident Societies

Where Mutual or Friendly, Cooperative and Provident Societies is an applicant for an account, the principals to be identified shall be considered to be those persons exercising control or significant influence over the organisation's assets. This often includes board members, executives and account signatories.

8. Charities, Clubs and Associations

(1) In the case of accounts to be opened for charities, clubs, and societies, the financial institution shall take reasonable steps to identify and verify at least two signatories along with the institution itself. The principals who shall be identified shall be considered to be those persons exercising control or significant influence over the organization's assets. These include members of the governing body or committee, the President, board members, the treasurer, and all signatories.

(2) In all cases, independent verification shall be obtained that the persons involved are true representatives of the institution and independent confirmation shall also be obtained of the purpose of the institution.

9. Trusts and Foundations

(1) When opening an account for a Trust, the financial institution shall take reasonable steps to verify the trustee, the settlor of the trust (including any persons settling assets into the trust) any protector, beneficiary and signatories.

(2) Beneficiaries shall be identified when they are defined. In the case of a foundation, steps shall be taken to verify the founder, the managers or directors and the beneficiaries.

10. Professional Intermediaries

(1) Where a professional intermediary opens a client account on behalf of a single client, that client shall be identified and Professional intermediaries shall open "pooled" accounts on behalf of a number of entities; and where funds held by the intermediary are not co-mingled but there are "sub-accounts" which shall be attributable to each beneficial owner, all beneficial owners of the account held by the intermediary shall be identified.

(2) Where the funds are commingled, the financial institution shall look through to the beneficial-owners but there may be circumstances that the Financial Institution may not look beyond the intermediary such as when the intermediary is subject to the same due diligence standards in respect of its client base as the financial institution.

(3) Where such circumstances apply and an account is opened for an open or closed ended investment company (unit trust or limited partnership) also subject to the same due diligence standards in respect of its client base as the financial institution, the following shall be considered as

principals and the Financial Institution shall take steps to identity:

(a) the fund itself;

(b) its directors or any controlling board, where it is a company;

(c) its trustee, where it is a unit trust;

(d) its managing (general) partner, where it is a limited partnership;

(e) account signatories; and

(f) any other person who has control over the relationship such as fund administrator or manager.

(4) Where other investment vehicles are involved, the same steps shall be taken as in above where it is appropriate to do so and in addition, all reasonable steps shall be taken to verify the identity of the beneficial owners of the funds and of those who have control over the funds.

(5) Intermediaries shall be treated as individual customers of the financial institution and the standing of the intermediary shall be separately verified by obtaining the appropriate information itemized above.

SCHEDULE III
MONEY LAUNDERING AND TERRORIST FINANCING "RED FLAGS"

1. Suspicious Transactions "Red Flags"

Potential Transactions which may be referred to as 'Red Flags' shall be categorized as follows—

(a) potential transactions perceived or identified as being suspicions which among others shall include:

(i) transactions involving high-risk countries vulnerable to money laundering, subject to this being confirmed;

(ii) transactions involving shell companies;

(iii) transactions with correspondents that have been identified as higher risk;

     (iv)   large transaction activities involving monetary instruments such as traveler's cheques, bank drafts, money order, particularly those that are serially numbered; and

     (v)   transaction activities involving amounts that are just below the stipulated reporting threshold or enquiries that appear to test an institution's own internal monitoring threshold or controls.

(b) money laundering using cash transactions which among others shall include:

     (i)   significant increases in cash deposits of an individual or corporate entity without apparent cause, particularly where such deposits are subsequently transferred within a short period out of the account to a destination not normally associated with the customer;

     (ii)   unusually large cash deposits made by an individual or a corporate entity whose-normal business is transacted by cheques and other non-cash instruments;

     (iii)   frequent exchange of cash into other currencies;

     (iv)   customers who deposit cash through many deposit slips such that the amount of each deposit is relatively small but the overall total is quite significant;

     (v)   customers whose deposits contain forged currency notes or instruments;

     (vi)   customers who regularly deposit cash to cover applications for bank drafts;

     (vii)   customers making large and frequent cash deposits with cheques always drawn in favour of persons not usually associated with their type of business;

     (viii)   customers who request to exchange, large quantities of low denomination banknotes for those of higher denominations;

     (ix)   branches of banks that tend to have far more cash transactions than usual, even after allowing for seasonal factors; and

(x)   customers transferring large sums of money to or from overseas locations with instructions for payment in cash.

(c) money laundering using deposit accounts, especially where they are inconsistent with a customer's legitimate business, which among others shall include:

    (i)   minimal, vague or fictitious information provided by a customer that the money deposited in the bank is not in a position to be verified;

    (ii)   lack of reference or identification in support of an account opening application by a person who is unable or unwilling to provide the required documentation;

    (iii)   a prospective customer who does not have a local residential or business address and there is no apparent legitimate reason for opening a bank account;

    (iv)   customers maintaining multiple accounts in a bank or in different banks for no apparent legitimate reason or business rationale whether the accounts are in the same names or have different signatories;

    (v)   customers depositing or withdrawing large amounts of cash with no apparent business source or in a manner inconsistent with the nature and volume of the business;

    (vi)   accounts with large volumes of activity but low balances or frequently overdrawn positions;

    (vii)   customers making large deposits and maintaining large balances with no apparent rationale;

    (viii)   customers who make numerous deposits into accounts and soon thereafter request for electronic transfers or cash transactions from those accounts to other accounts, locally or internationally, leaving only small balances which typically are transactions that are not consistent with the customers' legitimate business needs;

    (ix)   Sudden and unexpected increase in account activity or balance arising from deposit of cash and non-cash items which typically are accounts opened with small amounts but subsequently increase rapidly and significantly;

(x)   accounts used as temporary repositories for funds that are subsequently transferred outside the bank to foreign accounts which accounts often have low activity;

(xi)   customer requests for early redemption of certificates of deposit or other investment soon after the purchase, with the customer being willing to suffer loss of interest or incur penalties for premature realization of investment;

(xii)   customer requests for disbursement of the proceeds of certificates of deposit or other investments by multiple cheques, each below the stipulated reporting threshold;

(xiii) retail businesses which deposit many cheques into their accounts but with little or no withdrawals to meet daily business needs;

(xiv)   frequent deposits of large amounts of currency, wrapped in currency straps that have been stamped by other banks;

(xv)   substantial cash deposits by professional customers into client, trust or escrow accounts;

(xvi)   customers who appear to have accounts with several institutions within the same locality, especially when the institution is aware of a regular consolidation process from such accounts prior to a request for onward transmission of the funds;

(xvii) large cash withdrawals from a previously dormant or inactive account, or from an account which has just received an unexpected large credit from abroad;

(xviii) greater use of safe deposit facilities by individuals, particularly the use of sealed packets which are deposited and soon withdrawn;

(xix)   substantial increase in deposits of cash or negotiable instruments by a professional firm or company, using client accounts or in-house company or trust accounts, especially where the deposits are promptly transferred between other client company and trust accounts;

(xx)   large numbers of individuals making payments into the same account without adequate explanation;

(xxi)   high velocity of funds that reflects the large volume of money flowing through an account;

(xxii)   an account opened in the name of a money changer that receives deposits; and

(xxiii) an account operated in the name of an off-shore company with structured movement of funds.

(d) trade-based money laundering which among others shall include—

    (i)   over and under-invoicing of goods;

    (ii)   multiple invoicing of goods and services;

    (iii)   over and under-invoicing of goods and services;

    (iv)   falsely described goods and services and "phantom" shipments whereby the exporter does not ship any goods at all after payments had been made, particularly under confirmed letters of credit;

    (v)   transfer pricing;

    (vi)   transaction structure which appear unnecessarily complex and designed to obscure the true nature of the transaction;

    (vii)   items shipped which are inconsistent with the nature of the customer's normal business and transaction which lack an obvious economic rationale;

    (viii)   customer requests payment of proceeds to an unrelated third party; and

    (ix)   significantly amended letters of credit without reasonable justification or changes to the beneficiary or location of payment.

(e) lending activities which among others include:

    (i)   customers who repay problem loans unexpectedly;

    (ii)   a customer who is reluctant or refuses to state the purpose of a loan or the source of repayment or provides a questionable purpose or source of repayment;

   (iii) loans secured by pledged assets held by third parties unrelated to the borrower;

   (iv) loans secured by deposits or other readily marketable assets, such as securities particularly when owned by apparently unrelated third parties;

   (v) loans made for or paid on behalf of a third party with no reasonable explanation; and

   (vi) loans lacking a legitimate business purpose, provide the bank with significant fees for assuming minimal risk, or tend to obscure the movement of funds (e.g. loans made to a borrower and immediately sold to an entity related to the borrower);

(f) terrorist financing "red flags" which among others include:

   (i) persons involved in currency transactions who share an address or phone number, particularly when the address is also a business location or does not seem to correspond to the stated occupation such as student, unemployed, or self-employed;

   (ii) financial transaction by a nonprofit or charitable organisation, for which there appears to be no logical economic purpose or for which there appears to be no link between the stated activity of the organisation and other parties in the transaction;

   (iii) a safe deposit box opened on behalf of a commercial entity when the business activity of the customer is unknown or such activity does not appear to justify the use of a safe deposit box;

   (iv) where large numbers of incoming or outgoing funds transfers take place through a business account, and there appears to be no logical business or other economic purpose for the transfers, particularly when this activity involves designated high-risk locations;

   (v) where the stated occupation of the customer is inconsistent with the type and level of account activity;

(vi)   where funds transfer does not include information on the originator, or the person on whose behalf the transaction is conducted, the inclusion of which should ordinarily be expected;

(vii)   multiple personal and business accounts or the accounts of nonprofit organisations or charities are used to collect and funnel funds to a small number of foreign beneficiaries;

(viii)   foreign exchange transactions which are performed on behalf of a customer by a third party, followed by funds transfers to locations having no apparent business connection with the customer or to high-risk countries; and

(ix)   funds generated by a business owned by persons of the same origin or by a business that involves persons of the same origin from designated high-risk countries.

(g) other unusual or suspicious activities which among others include:

(i)   where employee exhibits a lavish lifestyle that cannot be justified by his/her salary;

(ii)   where employee fails to comply with approved operating guidelines, particularly in private banking;

(iii)   where employee is reluctant to take a vacation;

(iv)   safe deposit boxes or safe custody accounts opened by individuals who do not reside or work in the institution's service area despite the availability of such services at an institution closer to them;

(v)   customer rents multiple safe deposit boxes to store large amounts of currency, monetary instruments, or high value assets awaiting conversion to currency, for placement in the banking system;

(vi)   customer uses a personal account for business purposes;

(vii)   where official embassy business is conducted through personal accounts;

(viii)   where embassy accounts are funded through substan-
         tial currency transactions; and
(ix)   where embassy accounts directly fund personal ex-
         penses of foreign nationals.

MADE at Abuja this 29th Day of August, 2013.

Sanusi Lamido Sanusi

Governor of the Central Bank of Nigeria

EXPLANATORY NOTE

(This note does not form part of these Regulations but is intended
to explain its purports)

These Regulations seek to ensure that the Banking Industry and
other financial institutions comply with subsisting Anti-Money
Laundering and Combating the Financing of Terrorism Legislation.

APPENDIX 3

ECONOMIC AND FINANCIAL CRIMES COMMISSION (ESTABLISHMENT) ACT, 2004

ARRANGEMENT OF SECTIONS
SECTION:

ENACTED by the National Assembly of the Federal Republic of Nigeria –

PART I - ESTABLISHMENT OF THE ECONOMIC AND FINANCIAL CRIMES COMMISSION, ETC

1. Establishment of the Economic and Financial Crimes Commission

(1) There is established a body to be known as the Economic and Financial Crimes Commission (in this Act referred to as "the Commission") which shall be constituted in accordance with and shall have such functions as are conferred on it by this Act.

(2) The Commission -

    a. shall be a body with perpetual succession and a common seal

    b. may sue or be sued in its corporate name and may, for the purpose of its function Commission acquire, hold or dispose of property (whether movable or immovable);

    c. is the designated Financial Intelligence Unit (FIU) in Nigeria, which is charged with the responsibility of co-ordinating the various institutions involved in the fight against money laundering and enforcement of all laws dealing with economic and financial crimes in Nigeria.

2. Composition of the Commission

(1) The Commission shall consist of the following members –

    (a) a chairman, who shall -

        (i)   be the Chief Executive and Accounting Officer of the Commission.

        (ii)   be a serving or retired member of any government security or law enforcement agency not below the rank of Assistant Commissioner of Police or equivalent; and

(iii)   Possess not less than 15 years cognate experience

(b) the Governor of the Central Bank or his representative; and

(c) a representative each of the following Federal Ministries—
(i)   Foreign Affairs,
(ii) Finance,
(iii) Justice,

(d) the Chairman National Drug Law Enforcement Agency or his representative;

(e) the Director General of –
(i)   the National Intelligence Agency,
(ii) the Department of State Security Services or his representative;

(f) the Registrar-General of the Corporate Affairs Commission or his Representative;

(g) the Director-General, Securities and Exchange Commission or his representative;

(h) the Managing- Director, Nigeria- Deposit Insurance Corporation or his representative

(i) the Commissioner for Insurance or his representative;

(j) the Postmaster-General of the Nigerian Postal Services or his representative;

(k) the Chairman, Nigerian Communications Commission or his representative;

(l) the Comptroller-General, Nigeria Customs Services or his representative;

(m) the Comptroller-General Nigeria Immigration Services or his representative;

(n) an Inspector General of Police or his representative;

(o) four eminent Nigerians with cognate experience in any of the following, that is finance, banking or accounting; and

(p) the Secretary to the commission who shall be the head of administration

(2) The members of the Commission, other than the Chairman and the Secretary shall be part time members

(3) The Chairman and members of the Commission other than ex-officio members shall be appointed by the President and appointment shall be subject to the confirmation of the Senate.

3. Tenure of Office

(1) The Chairman and members of the Commission other than ex-officio members shall hold office for a period of four years and may be re-appointed for a further term of four years and no more

(2) A member of the Commission may at any time be removed by the President for inability to discharge the functions of his office (whether arising from infirmity of mind or body or any other cause) or for misconduct or if the President is satisfied that it is not in the interest of the Commission or the interest of the public that the member should continue in office.

(3) A member of the Commission may resign his membership by notice in writing addressed to the President and that member shall, on the date of the receipt of the notice by the President, cease to be member.

4. Vacancy in membership

Where a vacancy occurs in the membership of the Commission, it shall be filled by the appointment of a successor to hold office for the remainder of the term of office of his predecessor, so however that the successor shall represent the same interest as his predecessor.

5. Standing Orders

The Commission may take standing orders from regulating its proceedings or those of any of its committees

PART II – FUNCTIONS OF THE COMMISSION

6. Functions of the Commission

The Commission shall be responsible for -

(a)   the enforcement and the due administration of the provisions of this Act;

(b)   the investigation of all financial crimes including advance fee fraud, money laundering, counterfeiting, illegal charge transfers, futures market fraud, fraudulent encashment of negotiable instruments, computer credit card fraud, contract scam, etc.;

(c)   the co-ordination and enforcement of all economic and financial crimes laws and enforcement functions conferred on any other person or authority;

(d)   the adoption of measures to identify, trace, freeze, confiscate or seize proceeds derived from terrorist activities, economic and financial crimes related offences or the properties the value of which corresponds to such proceeds;

(e)   the adoption of measures to eradicate the commission of economic and financial crimes;

(f)   the adoption of measures which includes coordinated preventive and regulatory actions, introduction and maintenance of investigative and control techniques on the prevention of economic and financial related crimes;

(g)   the facilitation of rapid exchange of scientific and technical information and the conduct of joint operations geared towards the eradication of economic and financial crimes;

(h)   the examination and investigation of all reported cases of economic and financial crimes with a view to identifying individuals, corporate bodies or groups involved;

(i)   the determination of the extent of financial loss and such other losses by government, private individuals or organizations;

(j)   collaborating with government bodies both within and outside Nigeria carrying on functions wholly or in part analogous with those of the Commission concerning -

    (i)   the identification, determination, of the where-abouts and activities of persons suspected of being involved in economic and financial crimes,

    (ii)   the movement of proceeds or properties derived from the commission of economic and financial and other related crimes;

    (iii)   the exchange of personnel or other experts,

    (iv)   the establishment and maintenance of a system for monitoring international economic and financial crimes in order to identify suspicious transactions and persons involved,

    (v)   maintaining data, statistics, records and reports on person, organizations, proceeds, properties, documents or other items or assets involved in economic and financial crimes;

    (vi)   undertaking research and similar works with a view to determining the manifestation, extent, magnitude, and effects of economic and financial crimes and advising government on appropriate intervention measures for combating same

(k)   dealing with matters connected with the extradition, deportation and mutual legal or other assistance between Nigeria and any other country involving Economic and Financial Crimes;

(l)   The collection of all reports relating suspicious financial transactions, analyse and disseminate to all relevant Government agencies;

(m)   taking charge of, supervising, controlling, coordinating all the responsibilities, functions and activities relating to the current investigation and prosecution of all offences connected with or relating to economic and financial crimes;

(n) the coordination of all existing economic and financial crimes, investigating units in Nigeria;

(o) maintaining a liaison with office of the Attorney-General of the Federation, the Nigerian Customs Service, the Immigration and Prison Service Board, the Central Bank of Nigeria, the Nigeria Deposit Insurance Corporation, the National Drug Law Enforcement Agency, all government security and law enforcement agencies and such other financial supervisory institutions in the eradication of economic and financial crimes;

(p) carrying out and sustaining rigorous public and enlightenment campaign against economic and financial crimes within and outside Nigeria and;

(q) carrying out such other activities as are necessary or expedient for the full discharge of all or any of the functions conferred on it under this Act.

7. Special powers of the Commission

(1) The Commission has power to –

    (a) cause investigations to be conducted as to whether any person, corporate body or organization has committed any offence under this Act or other law relating to economic and financial crimes

    (b) cause investigations to be conducted into the properties of any person if it appears to the commission that the person's lifestyle and extent of the properties are not justified by his source of income;

(2) The Commission is charged with the responsibility of enforcing the provisions of –

    (a) the Money Laundering Act 2003; 2003 No.7 1995 N0. 13

    (b) the Advance Fee Fraud and Other Fraud Related Offences Act 1995;

    (c) the Failed Banks (Recovery of Debts) and Financial Malpractices in Banks Act 1994, as amended;

(d) The Banks and other Financial Institutions Act 1991, as amended; and

(e) Miscellaneous Offences Act

(f) Any other law or regulations relating to economic and financial crimes, including the Criminal code of penal code

PART III – STAFF OF THE COMMISSION

8. Appointment of the Secretary and other staff of the Commission

(1) There shall be established for the Commission a Secretariat that shall be headed by secretary who shall be appointed by the President.

(2) The secretary shall be–

(a) the head of the Secretariat of the Commission;

(b) responsible for the administration of the Secretariat and the keeping of the books and records of the Commission;

(c) appointed for a term of five years in the first instance and may be reappointed for a further term of five years subject to satisfactory performance; and

(d) subject to the supervision and control of the Chairman and the Commission

(3) The Commission may, from time to time, appoint such other staff or second officers from government security or law enforcement agencies or such other private or public services as it may deem necessary, to assist the Commission in the performance of its functions under this Act.

(4) The staff of the Commission appointed under subsection (3) of this section, shall be appointed upon such terms and conditions as the Commission may, after consultation with the Federal Civil Commission, determine.

(5) For the purpose of carrying out or enforcing the provisions of this act, all officers of the Commission involved in the enforcement of the provisions of this act shall have the same powers, authorities, privileges (including power to bear arms) as are given by law to members of the Nigerian Police.

9. Staff regulations

(1) The Commission may, subject to the provision of this Act, make staff regulations relating generally to the conditions of service of the employees of the Commission and without prejudice to the generality of the foregoing, the regulations may provide for –

(a) the appointment, promotion and disciplinary control (including dismissal) of employees of the Commission; and

(b) appeals by such employees against dismissal or other disciplinary measures, and until the regulations are made, any instrument relating to the conditions of services of officers in the Civil Service of the Federation shall be applicable, with such modifications as may be necessary, to the employees of the Commission.

(2) Staff regulations made under subsection (1) of this section shall not have effect until approved by the Commission, and when so approved the regulations may not be published in the Gazette but the Commission shall cause them to be brought to the notice of all affected persons in such manner as it may, from time to time, determine.

10. Pensions, Cap 346 LFN 1990

(1) Service in the commission shall be public service for the purpose of the Pensions Act and, accordingly, officers and other persons employed in the commission, shall in respect of their service in the Commission, be entitled to pension, gratuities and other retirement benefits as are prescribed thereunder, so however that nothing in this act shall prevent the appointment of a person to any office on terms which preclude the grant of pension or gratuity in respect of that office.

(2) For the purpose of the application of the provisions of the Pensions Act, any power exercisable under the Act by a Minister or other authority of the Government of the

Federation (not being the power to make regulations under Section 23 thereof) is hereby vested in and shall be exercisable by the Commission and not by any other person or authority.

11. Training Programme

The Commission shall initiate, develop or improve specific training programmes for its law enforcement and other personnel charged with responsibility for the eradication of offences created by this Act and such programmes shall include –

(a) methods used in the detection of offences created under this Act;

(b) techniques used by persons involved in offences created under this Act and appropriate counter-measures;

(c) detection and monitoring of the movement of proceeds and property derived from economic and financial malpractices intended to be used in the commission of offences under this Act;

(d) methods used for the transfer, concealment or disguise of such proceeds, property and instrumentalities;

(e) collection of evidence;

(f) law enforcement techniques;

(g) Legal prosecution and defence;

(h) dissemination of information on economic and financial crimes and related offences.

12. Establishment of Special units etc

(1) For the effective conduct of the functions of the Commission, there shall be established the following units–

    (a) the General and Assets Investigation Unit;

    (b) the Legal and Prosecution Unit;

    (c) the Research Unit;

    (d) the Administration Unit; and

    (e) the Training Unit.

(2) Notwithstanding the provisions of subsection (1) of this section, the Commission has power to set up any committee as may be necessary to assist the Commission in the performance of its duties and functions under this Act.

13. Special duties of the units

(1) The General and Assets Investigation Units shall be charged with responsibilities for–

(a) The prevention and detection of offences in violation of the provisions of this Act;

(b) The arrest and apprehension of economic and financial crime perpetrators;

(c) The investigation of assets and properties of persons arrested for committing any offence under this Act;

(d) The identification and tracing of proceeds and properties involved in any offence under this Act and the forfeiture of such proceeds and properties to the Federal Government; and

(e) Dealing with matters connected with extradition and mutual assistance in criminal matters involving economic and financial offences.

(2) The Legal and Prosecution Unit shall be charged with responsibility for -

(a) Prosecuting offenders under this Act;

(b) Supporting the general and assets investigation unit by providing the unit with legal advice and assistance whenever it is required;

(c) Conducting such proceedings as may be necessary towards the recovery of any assets or property forfeited under this Act;

(d) Performing such other legal duties as the Commission may refer to it from time to time.

(3) There shall be appointed for each of the Units a principal officer who shall be known by such designation as the Commission may determine.

PART IV – OFFENCES

14. Offences relating to financial malpractices

(1) A person who, being an officer of a bank or other financial institution or designated non-financial institution -

   (a) fails or neglects to secure compliance with the provisions of this Act; or

   (b) fails or neglects to secure the authenticity of any statement submitted pursuant to the provisions of this act, commits an offence and is liable on conviction to imprisonment for a term not exceeding 5 years or to a fine of Five Hundred Thousand Naira (N500,000) or to both such imprisonment and fine.

(2) Subject to the provision of Section 174 of the Constitution of the Federal Republic of Nigeria 1999 (which relates to the power of the Attorney-General of the Federation to institute, continue or discontinue criminal proceedings against any persons in any court of law), the Commission may compound any offence punishable under this Act by accepting such sums of money as it thinks fit, not exceeding the amount of the maximum fine to which that person would have been liable if he had been convicted of that offence.

(3) All moneys received by the Commission under the provisions of subsection (2) of this section shall be paid into the Consolidated Revenue Fund of the Federation.

15. Offences relating to terrorism

(1) A person who willfully provides or collects by any means, directly or indirectly, any money by any other person with intent that the money shall be used for any act of terrorism commits an offence under this Act and is liable on conviction to imprisonment for life.

(2) Any person who commits or attempts to commit a terrorist act or participates in or facilitates the commission of a

terrorist act, commits an offence under this Act and is liable
on conviction to imprisonment for life.

(3) Any person who makes funds, financial assets or economic
resources or financial or other related services available for
use of any other person to commit or attempt to commit,
facilitate or participate in the commission of a terrorist act is
liable on conviction to imprisonment for life.

16. Offences relating to false information

(1) Any person who, in the discharge of his duty under this Act,
gives information which is false in any material particular,
commits an offence under this Act and the onus shall lie on
him to prove that such information was supplied to him by
another person and that he exercised all diligence to prevent
the commission of the offence having regard to the nature
of his functions in that capacity and in all the circumstances.

(2) The penalty for offences under subsection (1) of this section
shall be imprisonment for a term not less than 2years and
not exceeding 3years provided that where the offender is a
public officer the penalty shall be imprisonment for a term
not less than 3 years and not more than 5 years

(3) Without prejudice to the provisions of any other enactment,
any regulatory agency or body in the financial sector shall
in the exercise of its functions, liaise with the Commission
to investigate and monitor the commission of economic and
financial crimes.

17. Retention of Proceeds of a criminal conduct

A person who –

(a) whether by concealment, removal from jurisdiction, transfer
to nominees or otherwise or otherwise retains the control of
the proceeds of a criminal conduct or an illegal act on behalf
of another person knowing that the proceeds is as a result of
criminal conduct by the principal; or

(b) knowing that any property is in whole or in part directly or indirectly represents another person' s proceeds of a criminal conduct, acquires or uses that property or has possession of it, commits an offence and is liable on conviction to imprisonment for a term not less than 5 years or to a fine equivalent to 5 times the value of the proceeds of the criminal conduct or to both such imprisonment and fine.

18. Offences in relation to economic and financial crimes and petitions

(1) A person who, without lawful authority –
   (a) engages in the acquisition, possession or use of property knowing at the time of its acquisition, possession or use that such property was derived from any offence under this Act; or
   (b) engages in the management, organisation or financing of any of the offences under this Act; or
   (c) engages in the conversion or transfer of property knowing that such property is derived from any offence under this Act; or
   (d) engages in the concealment or disguise of the true nature, source, location, disposition, movement, rights, with respect to or ownership of property knowing such property is derived from any offence referred under this Act commits an offence under this Act and is liable on conviction to the penalties provided in Subsection (2) of this section.
(2) The penalties provided for offences under subsection (1) of this section shall be imprisonment for a term not less than two years and not exceeding three years.

19. Jurisdiction and special powers of the court

(1) The Federal High Court or High Court of a state of the Federal Capital Territory has jurisdiction to try offenders under this Act.

(2) The Court shall have power, notwithstanding anything to the contrary in any other enactment,

    (a) to impose the penalties provided for in this Act.

    (b) To ensure that all matters brought before the court by the Commission against any person, body or authority shall be conducted with dispatch and given accelerated hearing

    (c) To adopt all legal measures necessary to avoid unnecessary delays and abuse in the conduct of matters brought by the Commission before it or against any person, body or authority.

(3) The Chief Judge of the Federal High Court or a High Court of a State of the High Court of The Federal Capital Territory Abuja, as the case may be shall order under his hand, designate a court or judge he shall deem appropriate to hear and determine all cases under this act or other related offences under this Act.

(4) A court or judge so designated shall give such matters priority over other matter pending before it.

(5) In any trial for an offence under this act, the fact that an accused person is in possession of pecuniary resources or property for which he cannot satisfactorily account and which is disproportionate to his known sources of income, of that he had at or about the time of the alleged offence obtained an accreditation to his pecuniary resources or property for which he cannot satisfactorily account, may be proved and taken into consideration by the Court as corroborating the testimony of any witness in the trial.

20. Forfeiture after conviction in certain cases

(1) A person convicted of an offence under this Act shall forfeit to the Federal Government -

    (a) all the assets and properties which may or are the subject of an interim order of the Court after an attachment by the Commission as specified in section 26 of this Act;

(b) any asset or property confiscated, or derived from any proceeds, the person obtained directly or indirectly, as a result of such offences not already disclosed in the Assets Declaration Form specified in Form A of the Schedule to this Act or not falling under paragraph (a) of this subsection;

(c) any of the person's property or instrumentalities used in any manner to commit or to facilitate the commission of such offence not already disclosed in the Declaration of Assets Form or not falling under paragraph (a) of this subsection.

(2) The Court in imposing a sentence on any person under this section, shall order, in addition to any other sentence imposed pursuant to Section 11 of this Act, that the person forfeit to the Federal Government all properties described in subsection (1) of this section.

(3) In this section, "proceeds" means any property derived or obtained, directly, through the commission of an offence under this Act.

21. Forfeiture in property

For the avoidance of doubt and without any further assurance than this Act; all the properties of a person of a person convicted of an offence under this Act and shown to be derived or acquired from such illegal act and already the subject of an interim order shall be forfeited to the Federal Government.

22. Foreign Assets

(1) Where it is established that any convicted person has assets or properties in a foreign country, acquired as a result of such criminal activity, such assets or properties, subject to any treaty or arrangement with such foreign country, shall be forfeited to the Federal Government.

(2) The Commission shall, through the office of the Attorney-General of the Federation, ensure that the forfeited assets

or properties are efficiently transferred and vested in the Federal Government.

23. Forfeiture of Passports

The passport of any person convicted of an offence under this Act shall be forfeited to the Federal Government and shall not be returned to that person till he has served any sentence imposed or unless or until the President directs otherwise after the grant of pardon or on the exercise of the prerogative of mercy under the constitution of the Federal Republic of Nigeria1999

24. Property subject to forfeiture

Any property

(a) Whether real or personal, which represents the gross receipts a person obtains directly as a result of the violation of this Act or which is traceable to such gross receipts;

(b) Within Nigeria which represents the proceeds of an offence under the laws of a foreign country within whose jurisdiction such offence of activity would be punishable by imprisonment for a term exceeding one year and which would be punishable by imprisonment under this Act if such act or activity had occurred within Nigeria, is subject to forfeiture to the Federal Government and no other property rights shall exist on it.

25. Further Provisions as to the forfeiture of Property

Without prejudice to the provision of any other law permitting the forfeiture of property, the following shall also be subject to forfeiture under this Act and no proprietary right shall exist in them -

(a) all means of conveyance, including aircraft, vehicles, or vessels which are used or are intended for use to transport or in any manner, to facilitate the transportation, sale, receipt, possession or concealment of economic or financial crime except that-

(i) No means of conveyance used by any person as a common carrier in the transaction of business as a common carrier shall be forfeited under this section unless it shall appear that the owner or other person in the charge of such means of conveyance was a consenting party or privy to a violation of this Act;

(ii) No means of conveyance shall be forfeited under this section by reason of any act established by the owner thereof to have been committed by any person other than such owner while such means of conveyance was unlawfully in the possession of a person other than the owner in violation of the criminal laws of Nigeria or any part thereof, and

(iii) No means of conveyance shall be forfeited under this section to the extent of an interest of an owner, by reason of any act established by that owner to have been committed without the knowledge, consent or willful connivance of that owner;

(b) all books, records, research and data used or intended to be used in violation of any provision of this Act;

(c) all monies, negotiable instruments, securities or other things of value furnished or intended to be furnished by any person in exchange for any illegal act or in violation of this Act or all proceeds traceable to such an exchange, and all monies, negotiable instruments and securities used or intended to be used to facilitate any violation of this Act;

(d) all real property, including any right, title and interest (including any leasehold interest) in the whole or any piece or parcel of land and any improvements or appurtenances which is used or intended to be used, in any manner or part to commit, or facilitate the commission of an offence under this Act.

26. Seizure of Property

(1) Any property subject to forfeiture under this Act may be seized by the Commission in the following circumstances –

(a) the seizure incidental to an arrest or search; or

(b) in the case of property liable to forfeiture upon process issued by the Court following an application made by the Commission in accordance with the prescribed rules.

(2) Whenever property is seized under any of the provisions of this Act, the Commission may –

(a) place the property under seal; or

(b) remove the property to a place designed by the Commission.

(3) Properties taken or detained under this section shall be deemed to be in the custody of the Commission, subject only to an order of a Court.

PART V – FORFEITURE OF ASSETS OF PERSONS ARRESTED FOR OFFENCES UNDER THIS ACT

27. Disclosure of Assets and Properties by an arrested person etc

(1) Where a person is arrested for committing an offence under this Act, such a person shall make full disclosure of all his assets and properties by completing the declaration of Assets Form as specified in form A of the Schedule to this Act.

(2) The completed Declaration of Assets Form shall be investigated by the Commission

(3) Any Person who –

(a) knowingly fails to make full disclosure of his assets and liabilities; or

(b) knowingly makes a declaration that is false; or

(c) fails, neglects or refuses to make a declaration or furnishes any information required, in the Declaration of Assets Form; commits an offence under this Act and is liable on conviction to imprisonment for a term of five years.

(4) Subject to the provisions of section 24 of this Act, whenever the assets and properties of any person arrested under this Act are attached, the General and Assets Investigation Unit

shall apply to the Court for an interim forfeiture order under the provision of this Act.

(5) The Chairman of the Commission shall have powers to make changes or modifications to the Declaration of Assets Form specified in Form A of the Schedule to this Act as may become necessary in order to give effect to the provisions of this Act

28. Investigation of assets and properties of a person arrested of an offence under this Act etc

Where a person is arrested for an offence under this Act, the Commission shall immediately trace and attach all the assets and properties of the person acquired as a result of such economic and financial crime and shall thereafter cause to be obtained an interim attachment order from the Court.

29. Interim forfeiture order

Where:

(a) the assets or properties of any person arrested for an offence under this Act has been seized; or

(b) any assets or property has been seized by the Commission under this Act, the Commission shall cause an application to be made to the Court for an interim order forfeiting the property concerned to the Federal Government and the Court shall, if satisfied that there is Prima Facie evidence that the property concerned is liable to forfeiture, make an interim order forfeiting the property to the Federal Government.

30. Final Order

Where a person is convicted of an offence under this Act, the Commission or any authorized officer shall apply to the Court for the order of confiscation and forfeiture of the convicted person's assets and properties acquired or obtained as a result of the crime already subject to an interim under this Act.

31. Final Disposal of forfeited property

(1) A copy of every final order forfeiting the asset and property of a person convicted under this Act shall be forwarded to the Commission.

(2) Upon receipt of a final order pursuant to this section, the Secretary to the Commission shall take steps to dispose of the property concerned by sale or otherwise and where the property is sold, the proceeds thereof shall be paid into the Consolidated Revenue Fund of the Federation.

(3) Where any part of the property included in a final order is money in a bank account or in the possession of any person, the Commission shall cause a copy of the order to be produced and served on the manager or any person in control of the head office or branch of the bank concerned and that manager or person shall forthwith pay over the money to the Commission without any further assurance than this Act and the Commission shall pay the money received into the Consolidated Fund of the Federation.

(4) The Attorney General of the Federation may make rules or regulations for the disposal or sale of any property or assets forfeited pursuant to this Act.

32. Offences in relation to forfeiture orders

(1) Any person who, without due authorization by the Commission, deals with, sells or otherwise disposes of any property or assets which is the subject of an attachment, interim order or final order commits an offence and is liable on conviction to imprisonment for a term of five years without the option of a fine.

(2) Any manager or person in control of the head office or branch of a bank or other financial institution who fails to pay over to the Commission upon the production to him of a final order commits an offence under this Act and is liable on conviction to imprisonment for a term of not less

than one year and not more than three years, without the option of a fine.

33. Consequences of an acquittal in respect of assets and properties

(1) Where a person is discharged or acquitted by a Court of an offence under this Act, the Court may make an order of revocation or confirmation as the case may be, of an interim order made pursuant to this Act whichever order is considered just, appropriate or reasonable within the circumstances.

(2) The property may be attached where a discharge is merely given on technical grounds.

(3) Where an interim order is revoked by a Court under subsection (1) of this section, all assets and properties of the person concerned shall be released to him by the Commission.

34. Freezing order on banks or other financial institutions

(1) Notwithstanding anything contained in any other enactment or law, the Chairman of the Commission or any officer authorized by him may, if satisfied that the money in the account of a person is made through the commission of an offence under this Act or any enactments specified under section 6 (2) (a)-(f) of this Act, apply to the Court exparte for power to issue or instruct a bank examiner or such other appropriate regulatory authority to issue an order as specified in Form B of the Schedule to this Act, addressed to the manager of the bank or any person in control of the financial institution where the account is or believed by him to be or the head office of the bank or other financial institution to freeze the account.

(2) The Chairman of the Commission, or any officer authorized by him may by an order issued under subsection (1) of this section, or by any subsequent order, direct the bank or other financial institution to supply any information and produce books and documents relating to the account and to stop all outward

payments, operations or transactions (including any bill of exchange) in respect of the account of the arrested person.

(3) The manager or any other person in control of the financial institution shall take necessary steps to comply with the requirements of the order made pursuant to subsection (2) of this section.

(4) In this section –

    a. "bank" has the meaning given to it in the Banks and other Financial Institutions Act 1999 as amended; 1991 No. 25

    b. the reference to an order issued includes a reference to any order, direction or requirement addressed to the manager of a bank or any other officer of a bank which directs the manager or such officer to stop all outward payments, operations or transactions in respect of any account with that bank.

PART VI – FINANCIAL PROVISIONS

35. Funds of the Commission

(1) The Commission shall establish and maintain a fund from which shall be defrayed all expenditure reasonably incurred by the Commission for the execution of its functions under this Act.

(2) There shall be paid and credited to the fund established pursuant to subsection (1) of this section, such monies as may in each year be approved by the Federal Government for the purpose of the Commission.

(3) The Commission may accept gifts of land, money or other property (whether within or outside Nigeria) upon such terms and conditions, if any, as may be specified by the person or organization making the gift provided that the terms and conditions are not contrary to the objectives and functions of the Commission under this Act.

36. Accounts and Audit

(1) The Commission shall keep proper accounts, in a form, which conforms to accepted commercial standards of its receipts, payments, assets and liabilities and shall submit the accounts annually, for auditing by a qualified auditor appointed from the list of auditors and in accordance with the guidelines supplied by the Auditor-General of the Federation.

37. Annual Report

The Commission shall, not later than 30th September in each year, submit to the National Assembly, a report of its activities during the immediately preceding year and shall include in such report the audited accounts of the Commission.

PART VII – MISCALLENOUS PROVISIONS

38. Power to receive information without hindrance

(1) The Commission shall seek and receive information from any person, authority, corporation or company without let or hindrance in respect of offences it is empowered to enforce under this Act.

(2) A person who –

(a) willfully obstructs the Commission or any authorized officer of the Commission in exercise of any of the powers conferred on the Commission by this Act; or

(b) fails to comply with any lawful enquiry or requirements made by any authorized officer in accordance with the provision of this Act, commits an offence under this Act and is liable on conviction to imprisonment for a term not exceeding five years or to a fine of twenty thousand naira or to both such imprisonment and fine.

39. Protecting informants and information, etc and Penalty for false information

(1) Officers of the Commission cannot be compelled to disclose the source of information or identity of their informants except by the order of the court

(2) Any person who makes or causes any other person to make to an officer of the Commission or to any other Public Officer, in the course of the exercise by such Public officer of the duties of his office, any statement which to the knowledge of the person making the statement, or causing the statement to be made—

(a) is false, or intended to mislead or is untrue in any material particular; or

(b) is not consistent with any other statement previously made by such person to any other person having authority or power under any law to receive, or require to be made such other statement notwithstanding that the person making the statement is not under any legal or other obligation to tell the truth, shall be guilty of an offence and shall on conviction be liable to a fine not exceeding one hundred thousand naira or to imprisonment for a term not exceeding two (2) years or to both such fine and imprisonment.

(c) Where any person who has made a statement to an officer of the Commission or to the Attorney-General, in the course of such officer or Attorney-General exercising any power conferred by this Act, subsequently thereto makes any other statement to any person having authority or power under any law to receive or require to be made such other statement regardless of whether or not the person making the statement is under a legal or other obligation to tell the truth, he shall, if such other statement is inconsistent with any statement previously made to an officer of the Commission or such other Public Officer, be guilty of an offence and shall on conviction be liable to a fine not exceeding ten thousand Naira or to an imprisonment for a term not exceeding two years or both.

(d) For the purpose of sub-section (1) and (2), any statement made in the course of any legal proceedings before any court, whether civil or criminal, or any statement made by any person in the course of any disciplinary proceedings, whether such legal proceedings or disciplinary proceedings are against the person making the statement or against any other person, shall be deemed to be a statement made to a person having authority or power under the law to receive the statement so made.

40. Appeals against interlocutory ruling, etc.

Subject to the provisions of the constitution of the Federal Republic of Nigeria 1999, an application for stay of proceedings, in respect of any criminal matter brought by the commission before the High Court shall not be entertained until judgment is delivered by the High Court.

41. Immunities

Subject to the provisions of this Act, an officer of the Commission when investigating or prosecuting a case under this Act, shall have all the powers and immunities of a Police Officer under the Police Act and any other law conferring power on the police or empowering and protecting law enforcement agencies.

42. General Savings

Any offence committed or proceedings instituted before the commencement of this Act under the provisions of the –

(a) Miscellaneous Offences Act;
(b) the Banks and Other Financial Institutions Act 1991 as amended;
(c) Failed Banks (Recovery of Debt and Financial Malpractices in Banks) Act; as amended;

(d) the Advance Fee Fraud and Other Related Offences Act

(e) the Money Laundering Act; and

(f) any other law or regulation relating to Economic and Financial Crimes shall as the case may require be enforced or continue to be enforced by the Economic and Financial Crimes Commission Established under this Act

43. Regulations

The Attorney General of the Federation may make rules or regulations with respect to the exercise of any of the duties, functions or powers of the Commission under this Act

44. Repeal of No.5, 2002

The Economic and Financial Crimes Commission (Establishment Act) No 5 2002 is repealed.

45. Savings

The repeal of the Act specified in section 43 of this Act shall not affect anything done or purported to be done under or pursuant to the Act.

46. Interpretation

In this Act -

"Commission" means the Economic and Financial Crimes Commission established by Section 1 of this Act;

"Court" means the Federal High Court or the High court of the Federal Capital Territory or the High Court of a State;

"Designated non-financial institutions means dealers in "jewellery, cars and luxury goods, chartered accountants, audit firms, tax consultants, clearing and settlement companies, legal practitioners, hotels, casinos, supermarkets or such other business as the Federal Ministry of Commerce or appropriate regulatory authorities may from time to time designate"

"Economic and Financial Crimes" means the non-violent criminal and illicit activity committed with the objectives of earning wealth illegally either individually or in a group or organized manner thereby violating existing legislation governing the economic activities of government and its administration and includes any form of fraud, narcotic drug trafficking, money laundering, embezzlement, bribery, looting and any form of corrupt malpractices, illegal arms deal, smuggling, human trafficking and child labour, illegal oil bunkering and illegal mining, tax evasion, foreign exchange malpractices including counterfeiting of currency, theft of intellectual property and piracy, open market abuse, dumping of toxic wastes and prohibited goods, etc.;

"Financial Institution" means banks, body, association or group of persons whether corporate or incorporate which carries the business of investments and securities, a discount house, insurance institutions, debt factorization and conversion firms, bureau de Change, finance Company, Money brokerage firms whose principal business includes factoring, project financing equipment leasing, debt administration, fund management, private ledger services, investment services, local purchase order financing, export finance, project consultancy, pension funds management and other business as the Central Bank or other appropriate regulatory authorities may from time to time designate.

"other appropriate regulatory authorities" includes the Securities and Exchange Commission, National Insurance Commission and the Federal ministry of Commerce;

"Terrorism" means

(a) any act which is a violation of the Criminal Code or the Penal Code and which may endanger the life, physical integrity or freedom of, or cause serious injury or death to, any person, any number or group of persons or causes or may cause damage to public property, natural resources, environmental or cultural heritage and is calculated or intended to

     (i)   intimidate, put in fear, force, coerce, or induce any government, body, institution, the general public or any segment thereof, to do or abstain from doing any act or to adopt or abandon a particular standpoint, or to act according to certain principles, or

    (ii) disrupt any public service, the delivery of any essential service to the public or to create a public emergency, or

    (iii) create general insurrection in a state;

(b) any promotion, sponsorship of, contribution to, command, aid incitement, encouragement, attempt threat, conspiracy, organization or procurement of any person, with the intent to commit any act referred to in paragraph (a) (i), (ii) and (iii).

47. Short Title

This Act may be cited as the Economic and Financial Crimes Commission (Establishment, Etc) Act, 2004.

APPENDIX 4

UNITED STATES BANK SECRECY ACT LAWS AND REGULATIONS: AN OVERVIEW

Statutes

<u>12 USC 1829b</u>, <u>12 USC 1951–1959</u>, and <u>31 USC 5311</u>, *et seq.* — "The Bank Secrecy Act"

<u>12 USC 1818(s)</u> — "Compliance with Monetary Recordkeeping and Report Requirements"

Requires that the appropriate federal banking agencies shall prescribe regulations requiring insured depository institutions to establish and maintain procedures reasonably designed to assure and monitor the compliance of such depository institutions with the requirements of the BSA. In addition, this section requires that each examination of an insured depository institution by the appropriate federal banking agency shall include a review of the procedures, and that the report of examination shall describe any problem with the procedures maintained by the insured depository institution. Finally, if the appropriate federal banking agency determines that an insured depository institution has either 1) failed to establish and maintain procedures that are reasonably designed to assure and monitor the institution's compliance with the BSA; or 2) failed to correct any problem with the procedures that a report of examination or other written supervisory communication identifies as requiring communication to the institution's board of directors or senior management as a matter that must be corrected, the agency shall issue an order requiring such depository institution to cease and desist from the violation of the statute and the regulations prescribed thereunder. Sections 1818(b)(3) and (b)(4) of Title 12 of the USC extend section 1818(s) beyond insured depository institutions.

12 USC 1786(q) — "Compliance with Monetary Recordkeeping and Report Requirements"

Requires that the NCUA Board prescribe regulations requiring insured credit unions to establish and maintain procedures reasonably designed to assure and monitor the compliance of such credit unions with the requirements of the BSA. In addition, this section requires the NCUA Board to examine and enforce BSA requirements.

Regulations

U.S. Treasury/FinCEN

31 CFR Parts 1000-1099 — "Financial Recordkeeping and Reporting of Currency and Foreign Transactions"

Sets forth FinCEN regulations that promulgate the BSA. Select provisions are described below.

31 CFR 1010.100 — "Meaning of Terms"

Sets forth the definitions used throughout 31 CFR Chapter X.

31 CFR 1025.320 — "Reports by Insurance Companies of Suspicious Transactions"

Sets forth the requirements for insurance companies to report suspicious transactions of $5,000 or more.

31 CFR 1020.320 — "Reports by Banks of Suspicious Transactions"

Sets forth the requirements for banks to report suspicious transactions involving or aggregating $5,000 or more.

31 CFR 1010.311 — "Reports of Transactions in Currency"
Sets forth the requirements for financial institutions to report currency transactions in excess of $10,000. Includes 31 CFR 103.22(d) — "Transactions of Exempt Persons," which sets forth the requirements for financial institutions to exempt transactions of certain persons from currency transaction reporting requirements.

31 CFR 1010.340 — "Reports of Transportation of Currency or Monetary Instruments"
Sets forth the requirements for filing a Report of International Transportation of Currency or Monetary Instruments (CMIR).

31 CFR 1010.350 — "Reports of Foreign Financial Accounts"
Sets forth the requirement that each person having a financial interest in, or signature or other authority over, a financial account in a foreign country must file a report with the IRS annually.

31 CFR 1010.306 — "Filing of Reports"
Sets forth the filing and recordkeeping requirements for CTRs, CMIRs, and Report of Foreign Bank and Financial Accounts (FBAR).

31 CFR 1010.312 — "Identification Required"
Sets forth the requirement that financial institutions verify the identity of persons conducting currency transactions in excess of $10,000.

31 CFR 1010.415 — "Purchases of Bank Checks and Drafts, Cashier's Checks, Money Orders, and Traveler's Checks"
Sets forth the requirements that financial institutions maintain records relating to purchases of monetary instruments with currency in amounts between $3,000 and $10,000, inclusive.

31 CFR 1010.420 — "Records to Be Made and Retained by Persons Having Financial Interests in Foreign Financial Accounts"
Sets forth the requirement that persons having a financial interest in, or signature or other authority over, financial account in a

foreign country maintain records relating to foreign financial bank accounts reported on an FBAR.

31 CFR 1020.410 — "Records to Be Made and Retained by Financial Institutions"

Sets forth recordkeeping and retrieval requirements for financial institutions, including funds transfer recordkeeping and transmittal requirements.

31 CFR 1020.410 — "Additional Records to Be Made and Retained by Banks"

Sets forth additional recordkeeping requirements for banks.

31 CFR 1010.430 — "Nature of Records and Retention Period"

Sets forth acceptable forms of records required to be kept and establishes a five-year record-retention requirement.

31 CFR 1022.380 — "Registration of Money Services Businesses"

Sets forth the requirements for money services businesses to register with the U.S. Treasury/FinCEN.

31 CFR 1010.820 — "Civil Penalty"

Sets forth potential civil penalties for willful or negligent violations of 31 CFR Chapter X.

31 CFR 1010.840 — "Criminal Penalty"

Sets forth potential criminal penalties for willful violations of 31 CFR Chapter X.

31 CFR 1010.314 — "Structured Transactions"

Prohibits the structuring of transactions to avoid currency transaction reporting requirement.

31 CFR 1010.520 — **"Information Sharing Between Federal Law Enforcement Agencies and Financial Institutions"**
Establishes procedures for information sharing between federal law enforcement authorities and financial institutions to deter terrorist activity and money laundering.

31 CFR 1010.540 — **"Voluntary Information Sharing Among Financial Institutions"**
Establishes procedures for voluntary information sharing among financial institutions to deter terrorist activity and money laundering.

31 CFR 1021.100 — **"Anti-Money Laundering Program Requirements for Financial Institutions Regulated by a Federal Functional Regulator or a Self-Regulatory Organization, and Casinos"**
Establishes, in part, the standard that a financial institution regulated only by a federal functional regulator satisfies statutory requirements to establish an AML program if the financial institution complies with the regulations of its federal functional regulator governing such programs.

31 CFR 1020.220 — **"Customer Identification Programs for Banks, Savings Associations, Credit Unions, and Certain Non-Federally Regulated Banks"**
Sets forth the requirement for banks, savings associations, credit unions, and certain non-federally regulated banks to implement a written Customer Identification Program.

31 CFR 1025.210 — **"Anti-Money Laundering Programs for Insurance Companies"**
Sets forth the requirement for insurance companies that issue or underwrite "covered products" to develop and implement a written AML program that is reasonably designed to prevent the insurance company from being used to facilitate money laundering or financing of terrorist activity.

31 CFR 1010.610 — "Due Diligence Programs for Correspondent Accounts for Foreign Financial Institutions"
Sets forth the requirement for certain financial institutions to establish and apply a due diligence program that includes appropriate, specific, risk-based, and, where necessary, enhanced policies, procedures, and controls that are reasonably designed to enable the financial institution to detect and report known or suspected money laundering activity conducted through or involving any correspondent account established, maintained, administered, or managed by the financial institution in the United States for a foreign financial institution.

31 CFR 1010.630 — "Prohibition on Correspondent Accounts for Foreign Shell Banks; Records Concerning Owners of Foreign Banks and Agents for Service of Legal Process"
Prohibits a covered financial institution from establishing, maintaining, administering, or managing a correspondent account in the United States for or on behalf of a foreign shell bank, and requires the financial institution to maintain records identifying the owners of foreign financial institutions and regarding a person resident in the United States who is authorized to and has agreed to be an agent to receive service of legal process.

31 CFR 1010.620 — "Due Diligence Programs for Private Banking Accounts"
Sets forth the requirement for certain financial institutions to establish and maintain a due diligence program that includes policies, procedures, and controls that are reasonably designed to detect and report any known or suspected money laundering or suspicious activity conducted through or involving any private banking account that is established, maintained, administered, or managed in the United States for a non-U.S. person.

31 CFR 1010.670 — "Summons or Subpoena of Foreign Bank Records; Termination of Correspondent Relationship"
Requires a financial institution to provide foreign financial institution records upon the request of an appropriate law enforcement

official and to terminate a correspondent relationship with a foreign financial institution upon receipt of written notice from the U.S. Secretary of the Treasury or the U.S. Attorney General.

"Certification Regarding Correspondent Accounts for Foreign Banks".
Voluntary certification form to be obtained by a bank that establishes, maintains, administers, or manages a correspondent account in the United States for or on behalf of a foreign bank. Form is available on FinCEN's website (www.fincen.gov).

"Recertification Regarding Correspondent Accounts for Foreign Banks"
Voluntary re-certification form to be obtained by a bank that establishes, maintains, administers, or manages a correspondent account in the United States for or on behalf of a foreign bank. Form is available on FinCEN's website (www.fincen.gov).

Board of Governors of the Federal Reserve System

Regulation H — 12 CFR 208.62 — "Suspicious Activity Reports"
Sets forth the requirements for state member banks for filing a SAR with the appropriate federal law enforcement agencies and the U.S. Treasury.

Regulation H — 12 CFR 208.63 — "Procedures for Monitoring Bank Secrecy Act Compliance"
Sets forth the requirements for state member banks to establish and maintain procedures to ensure and monitor their compliance with the BSA.

Regulation K — 12 CFR 211.5(k) — "Reports by Edge and Agreement Corporations of Crimes and Suspected Crimes"
Sets forth the requirements for an Edge and agreement corporation, or any branch or subsidiary thereof, to file a SAR with the appropriate federal law enforcement agencies and the U.S. Treasury.

Regulation K — 12 CFR 211.5(m) — "Procedures for Monitoring Bank Secrecy Act Compliance"

Sets forth the requirements for an Edge and agreement corporation to establish and maintain procedures reasonably designed to ensure and monitor compliance with the BSA and related regulations.

Regulation K — 12 CFR 211.24(f) — "Reports of Crimes and Suspected Crimes"

Sets forth the requirements for an uninsured branch, an agency, or a representative office of a foreign financial institution operating in the United States to file a SAR with the appropriate federal law enforcement agencies and the U.S. Treasury.

Regulation K — 12 CFR 211.24(j) — "Procedures for Monitoring Bank Secrecy Act Compliance"

Sets forth the requirements for an uninsured branch, an agency, or a representative office of a foreign financial institution operating in the United States to establish and maintain procedures reasonably designed to ensure and monitor compliance with the BSA and related regulations.

Regulation Y — 12 CFR 225.4(f) — "Suspicious Activity Report"

Sets forth the requirements for a bank holding company or any nonbank subsidiary thereof, or a foreign bank that is subject to the Bank Holding Company Act or any nonbank subsidiary of such a foreign bank operating in the United States to file a SAR with the appropriate federal law enforcement agencies and the U.S. Treasury.

Federal Deposit Insurance Corporation

12 CFR 326 Subpart B — "Procedures for Monitoring Bank Secrecy Act Compliance"

Sets forth requirements for state nonmember banks to establish and maintain procedures to ensure and monitor their compliance with the BSA.

12 CFR 353 — "Suspicious Activity Reports"

Establishes requirements for state nonmember banks to file a SAR when they detect a known or suspected violation of federal law, a suspicious transaction relating to a money laundering activity, or a violation of the BSA.

National Credit Union Administration

12 CFR 748 — "Security Program, Report of Crime and Catastrophic Act and Bank Secrecy Act Compliance"

Requires federally insured credit unions to maintain security programs and comply with the BSA.

12 CFR 748.1 — "Filing of Reports"

Requires federally insured credit unions to file compliance and Suspicious Activity Reports.

12 CFR 748.2 — "Procedures for Monitoring Bank Secrecy Act (BSA) Compliance"

Ensures that all federally insured credit unions establish and maintain procedures reasonably designed to assure and monitor compliance with the recordkeeping and reporting requirements in the BSA.

Office of the Comptroller of the Currency

Effective July 21, 2011, the Office of Thrift Supervision was integrated into the Office of the Comptroller of the Currency.

12 CFR 21.11 — "Suspicious Activity Report"

Ensures that national banks file a Suspicious Activity Report when they detect a known or suspected violation of federal law or a suspicious transaction related to a money laundering activity or a violation of the BSA. This section applies to all national banks as well as any federal branches and agencies of foreign financial banks licensed or chartered by the OCC.

12 CFR 163.180 — "Suspicious Activity Reports and Other Reports and Statements"
Sets forth the rules for savings associations or service corporations for filing a SAR with the appropriate federal law enforcement agencies and the U.S. Treasury.

12 CFR 21.21 — "Procedures for Monitoring Bank Secrecy Act (BSA) Compliance"
Requires all national banks and savings associations to establish and maintain procedures reasonably designed to assure and monitor their compliance with the requirements of subchapter II of chapter 53 of title 31, United States Code, and the implementing regulations promulgated thereunder by the Department of the Treasury at 31 CFR Chapter X (formerly 31 CFR part 103). Effective June 16, 2014, the OCC amended 12 CFR 21.21 to make it applicable to both national banks and savings associations and rescinded 12 CFR 163.177 (refer to 79 Fed. Reg. 95, May 16, 2014).

Source: Federal Financial Institutions Examination Council (2017), 'Bank Secrecy Act Anti-Money Laundering Examination Manual', Available at: https://www.ffiec.gov/bsa_aml_infobase/pages_manual/OLM_101.htm **(accessed 6 January 2017).**

APPENDIX 5

THE UNITED KINGDOM'S CRIMINAL FINANCES ACT 2017: AN OVERVIEW

What is in the Act?

Measures to enhance the UK's ability to investigate the proceeds of crime (Part 1 Chapter 1)

- The Act introduces Unexplained Wealth Orders, where individuals whose assets are disproportionate to their known income will need to explain the origin of their wealth.
- The Act extends Disclosure Orders to money laundering investigations and provides an effective, efficient and flexible means of obtaining information.

Measures to strengthen the Suspicious Activity Report regime (Part 1 Chapter 2)

- The Act enables extensions of the moratorium period, in situations where the National Crime Agency (NCA) has refused consent for a transaction to proceed. The current 31-day period is sometimes not enough, particularly when the law enforcement agency needs to obtain evidence, or to secure formal letters of request from overseas authorities.
- It permits firms in the regulated sector to share information between themselves, to allow them to work together to build

a clearer picture of how money launderers operate, and use
that to inform the NCA and to protect themselves.

- It allows the NCA to follow up on a suspicious activity report,
where further information is needed to allow the NCA to
conduct effective and informed analysis.

**Measures to improve the UK's capability to recover the proceeds of
crime (Part 1 Chapter 3)**

- Current legislation allows law enforcement agencies to take
swift and effective action against criminal cash, but a gap in
the law prevents them from being able to do so if criminals
store the proceeds of crime in bank accounts or other means,
such as precious metals and jewels. The Act creates new civil
powers to close this gap.

Measures to combat the financing of terrorism (Part 2)

- The Act makes complementary changes to the legislation
governing the law enforcement response to the threats from
terrorist financing.
- The Government is committed to ensuring that the law enforcement capabilities in respect of terrorist finance are as
strong as those for countering money laundering.

Measures to prevent the facilitation of tax evasion (Part 3)

- Whilst individual employees may face criminal charges for
facilitating tax evasion, their employer often sits beyond the
easy reach of the criminal law.
- These new offences of corporate failure to prevent the facilitation of tax evasion address this difficulty.

APPENDIX 6

GLOSSARY OF TERMINOLOGY

Accountable institutions

'Accountable institutions' include:

1. A legal practitioner
2. A board of executors or a trust company or any other person that invests, keeps in safe custody, controls or administers trust property
3. An estate agent
4. An authorised user of an exchange
5. A person who carries on the 'business of a bank'
6. A mutual bank
7. A person who carries on a 'long-term insurance business'
8. A person who carries on the business of making available a gambling activity
9. A person who carries on the business of dealing in foreign exchange.
10. A person who carries on the business of lending money against the security of securities
11. A person who carries on the business of a financial services provider, to provide advice and intermediary services in respect of the investment of any financial product and a health service benefit provided by a medical scheme
12. A person who issues, sells or redeems travellers' cheques, money orders or similar instruments.
13. A person who carries on the business of a money remitter.

Confiscation

The term *confiscation,* which includes forfeiture where applicable, means the permanent deprivation of funds or other assets by order of a competent authority or a court. Confiscation or forfeiture takes place through a judicial or administrative procedure that transfers the ownership of specified funds or other assets to be transferred to the State. In this case, the person(s) or entity(ies) that held an interest in the specified funds or other assets at the time of the confiscation or forfeiture loses all rights, in principle, to the confiscated or forfeited funds or other assets. Confiscation or forfeiture orders are usually linked to a criminal conviction or a court decision whereby the confiscated or forfeited property is determined to have been derived from or intended for use in a violation of the law.

Currency

Currency refers to banknotes and coins that are in circulation as a medium of exchange.

Designated nonfinancial businesses and professions

Designated non-financial businesses and professions means:

a) Casinos
b) Real estate agents.
c) Dealers in precious metals.
d) Dealers in precious stones.
e) Lawyers, notaries, other independent legal professionals and accountants – this refers to sole practitioners, partners or employed professionals within professional firms. It is not meant to refer to 'internal' professionals that are employees of other types of businesses, nor to professionals working for government agencies, who may already be subject to AML/ CFT measures.
f) Trust and Company Service Providers refers to all persons or businesses that are not covered elsewhere under these Recommendations, and which as a business, provide any of the following services to third parties:

- acting as a formation agent of legal persons;
- acting as (or arranging for another person to act as) a director or secretary of a company, a partner of a partnership, or a similar position in relation to other legal persons;
- providing a registered office; business address or accommodation, correspondence or administrative address for a company, a partnership or any other legal person or arrangement;
- acting as (or arranging for another person to act as) a trustee of an express trust or performing the equivalent function for another form of legal arrangement;
- acting as (or arranging for another person to act as) a nominee shareholder for another person.

Economic and Financial Crimes

Economic and Financial Crimes means the non-violent criminal and illicit activity committed with the objectives of earning wealth illegally either individually or in a group or organized manner thereby violating existing legislation governing the economic activities of government and its administration and includes any form of fraud, narcotic drug trafficking, money laundering, embezzlement, bribery, looting and any form of corrupt malpractices, illegal arms deal, smuggling, human trafficking and child labour, illegal oil bunkering and illegal mining, tax evasion, foreign exchange malpractices including counterfeiting of currency, theft of intellectual property and piracy, open market abuse, dumping of toxic wastes and prohibited goods, etc.

Established customer

An *established customer* is a person with an account with the financial institution, including a loan account or deposit or other asset account, or a person with respect to which the financial institution has obtained and maintains on file the person's name and address, as well as taxpayer identification number(e.g., social security or employer identification number) or, if none, alien identification number or passport number and country of issuance, and to which the financial institution provides financial services relying on that information.

Financial institutions

Financial institutions mean any natural or legal person who conducts as a business one or more of the following activities or operations for or on behalf of a customer:

1. Acceptance of deposits and other repayable funds from the public.
2. Lending.
3. Financial leasing.
4. Money or value transfer services.
5. Issuing and managing means of payment (e.g. credit and debit cards, cheques, traveller's cheques, money orders and bankers' drafts, electronic money).
6. Financial guarantees and commitments.
7. Trading in:
   (a) money market instruments (cheques, bills, certificates of deposit, derivatives etc.);
   (b) foreign exchange;
   (c) exchange, interest rate and index instruments;
   (d) transferable securities;
   (e) commodity futures trading.
8. Participation in securities issues and the provision of financial services related to such issues.
9. Individual and collective portfolio management.
10. Safekeeping and administration of cash or liquid securities on behalf of other persons.
11. Otherwise investing, administering or managing funds or money on behalf of other persons.
12. Underwriting and placement of life insurance and other investment related insurance.
13. Money and currency changing.

Money Service Business
Money Service Business includes currency dealers, money transmitters, cheque cashers, and issuers of travellers' cheques, money orders or stored value.

Shell Company
The term shell company generally refers to an entity without a physical presence in any country.

Smurfing
Smurfing is the act of breaking down a transaction into smaller transactions to avoid regulatory requirements or an investigation by the authorities.

Structure (structuring)
A person structures a transaction if that person, acting alone, or in conjunction with, or on behalf of, other persons, conducts or attempts to conduct one or more transactions in currency, in any amount, at one or more financial institutions, on one or more days, in any manner, for the purpose of evading the reporting requirements. "In any manner" includes, but is not limited to, the breaking down of a single sum of currency exceeding $10,000 into smaller sums, including sums at or below $10,000, or the conduct of a transaction, or series of currency transactions at or below $10,000. The transaction or transactions need not exceed the $10,000 reporting threshold at any single financial institution on any single day in order to constitute structuring within the meaning of this definition.

Terrorist
The term *terrorist* refers to any natural person who: (i) commits, or attempts to commit, terrorist acts by any means, directly or indirectly, unlawfully and wilfully; (ii) participates as an accomplice in terrorist acts; (iii) organises or directs others to commit terrorist acts; or (iv) contributes to the commission of terrorist acts by a group of

persons acting with a common purpose where the contribution is made intentionally and with the aim of furthering the terrorist act or with the knowledge of the intention of the group to commit a terrorist act.

Terrorist act

A *terrorist act* includes:

i.   an act which constitutes an offence within the scope of, and as defined in one of the following treaties: (i) Convention for the Suppression of Unlawful Seizure of Aircraft (1970); (ii) Convention for the Suppression of Unlawful Acts against the Safety of Civil Aviation (1971); (iii) Convention on the Prevention and Punishment of Crimes against Internationally Protected Persons, including Diplomatic Agents (1973); (iv) International Convention against the Taking of Hostages (1979); (v) Convention on the Physical Protection of Nuclear Material (1980); (vi) Protocol for the Suppression of Unlawful Acts of Violence at Airports Serving International Civil Aviation, supplementary to the Convention for the Suppression of Unlawful Acts against the Safety of Civil Aviation (1988); (vii) Convention for the Suppression of Unlawful Acts against the Safety of Maritime Navigation (2005); (viii) Protocol for the Suppression of Unlawful Acts against the Safety of Fixed Platforms located on the Continental Shelf (2005); (ix) International Convention for the Suppression of Terrorist Bombings (1997); and (x) International Convention for the Suppression of the Financing of Terrorism (1999).

ii. any other act intended to cause death or serious bodily injury to a civilian, or to any other person not taking an active part in the hostilities in a situation of armed conflict, when the purpose of such act, by its nature or context, is to intimidate a population, or to compel a Government or an international organisation to do or to abstain from doing any act.

APPENDIX 7

Ehi's Publications

BOOKS

- Esoimeme, E.E. (2015), 'The Risk-Based Approach to Combating Money Laundering and Terrorist Financing', Eric Press; Available on Amazon: https://www.amazon.co.uk/Risk-Based-Combating-Laundering-Terrorist-Financing/dp/9789486030/ref=sr_1_2?ie=UTF8&qid=1437508453&sr=8-2&keywords=ehi+eric+esoimeme
- Esoimeme, E.E. (2014), 'A Comparative Study of the Money Laundering Laws/Regulations in Nigeria, the United States and the United Kingdom', Eric Press; Available on Amazon: https://www.amazon.co.uk/Comparative-Laundering-Regulations-Nigeria-Kingdom-ebook/dp/B00OC2X7HK/ref=sr_1_8?s=digital-text&ie=UTF8&qid=1413235091&sr=1-8&keywords=money+laundering
- Onwudiwe, C.C. and Esoimeme, E.E. (2016), 'Banker-Customer Relationship: A Practical Legal Guide', Bank Customers Association of Nigeria.

ARTICLES

- Esoimeme, E.E. (2018), 'The money laundering risks and vulnerabilities associated with MMM Nigeria', Journal of Money Laundering Control, Vol. 21 Issue: 1, pp.112-119, http://www.emeraldinsight.com/doi/full/10.1108/JMLC-01-2017-0002

- Esoimeme, E.E. (2017), 'A critical analysis of the effects of the Central Bank of Nigeria foreign exchange policy on financial inclusion, anti-money laundering measures and fundamental rights', Journal of Money Laundering Control, Vol. 20 Issue: 4, pp.417-427, https://doi.org/10.1108/JMLC-05-2016-0020
- Esoimeme, E.E. (2017), "The Nigerian Money Laundering (Prevention and Prohibition) Bill, 2016: a critical appraisal", Journal of Money Laundering Control, Vol. 20 Issue: 1, pp.79-88, https://doi.org/10.1108/JMLC-07-2016-0025
- Esoimeme, E.E. (2017), 'A Critical Analysis of the Anti-Corruption Policy of the Federal Executive Council of Nigeria', Journal of Money Laundering Control – Emerald.
- Esoimeme, E.E. (2017), 'A Comparative Analysis of the Prepaid Card Laws/Regulations in Nigeria, the United Kingdom, the United States and India', Journal of Money Laundering Control – Emerald.
- Esoimeme, E.E. (2017), 'A Critical Analysis of the Anti-Corruption Policy of the National Judicial Council of Nigeria', Journal of Money Laundering Control – Emerald.
- Esoimeme, E.E. (2016), 'Wealth Management, Tax Evasion and Money Laundering: The Panama Papers Case Study', Law Digest Issue 11 Autumn 2016. Available at Law Digest: https://issuu.com/nglawdigest/docs/law_digest_issue_11_autumn_2016
- Esoimeme, E.E. (2016), 'Balancing Anti-Money Laundering/Counter-Terrorist Financing Requirements and Financial Inclusion for Migrants: A Case Study of Germany', Available at SSRN: https://ssrn.com/abstract=2710097
- Esoimeme, E.E. (2015), 'The Death Penalty: An Effective Anti-Corruption Mechanism?', Available at SSRN: https://ssrn.com/abstract=2621268
- Esoimeme, E.E. (2015), 'A Critical Analysis of the Anti-Money Laundering Measures Adopted by BitGold Inc', Available at SSRN: https://ssrn.com/abstract=2604721 or http://dx.doi.org/10.2139/ssrn.2604721

- Esoimeme, E.E. (2015), 'A Critical Analysis of the Bank Verification Number Project Introduced by the Central Bank of Nigeria', Available at SSRN: https://ssrn.com/abstract=2544934 or http://dx.doi.org/10.2139/ssrn.2544934
- Esoimeme, E.E. (2013), 'A Critical Analysis of the Effect of the Double Criminality Test on the Investigation Team and the Prosecution's Case', Available at SSRN: https://ssrn.com/abstract=2514719
- Esoimeme, E.E. (2014), 'A Comparative Study of the Money Laundering Laws/Regulations in Nigeria, the United States and the United Kingdom: Cash Couriers', The PUNCH, VOL 38 NO. 20,733, 20,739 PAGE 25, 29. Available at SSRN: https://ssrn.com/abstract=2476587
- Esoimeme, E.E. (2013), 'A Critical Analysis of the Effect of the Double Criminality Test on Nominated Officers and Money Laundering Reporting Officers (MLRO) in the Regulated Sector', Available at SSRN: https://ssrn.com/abstract=2462952
- Esoimeme, E.E. (2014), 'Has the Concept of Plea Bargaining Been Abused in Nigeria's Criminal Justice System?', The Legal Aid Journal Volume 1. Available at SSRN: https://ssrn.com/abstract=2462307
- Esoimeme, E.E. (2015), 'A Comparative Study of the Money Laundering Laws/Regulations in Nigeria, the United States and the United Kingdom: Reporting Requirements', Professionals Center for Business Research Volume 2 – June 2015 (06). Available at SSRN: https://ssrn.com/abstract=2441086
- Esoimeme, E.E. (2013), 'The Importance of Why Firms Dealing with PEPs Must Adopt a Risk-Based Approach to Their Compliance Programmes', Available at SSRN: https://ssrn.com/abstract=2430972

Ehi Esoimeme has also peer reviewed the following publications:

- Ross, I. (2015), 'Exposing Fraud: Skills, Process and Practicalities', Wiley Corporate F&A. Available on Amazon: https://www.amazon.co.uk/Exposing-Fraud-Process-Practicalities-Corpo-

rate-ebook/dp/B01CJK4Z8Q/ref=sr_1_fkmr0_2?ie=UTF8&qi
d=1493990138&sr=8-2-fkmr0&keywords=ian+ross+on+fraud

- Nwachukwu, E. (2015), 'Academic Excellence in 21 Days',
  Partridge Africa. Available on Amazon: https://www.ama-
  zon.co.uk/Academic-Excellence-Days-Eric-Nwachukwu/
  dp/1482826224/ref=sr_1_1?ie=UTF8&qid=1493990393&
  sr=8-1&keywords=eric+nwachukwu

INDEX

REFERENCES ARE TO PARAGRAPH NUMBERS

C

CONDITIONS FOR VOLUNTARY DISCLOSURES WITHIN THE UK REGULATED SECTOR

MONEY LAUNDERING, 3.3.6.1.1

TERRORIST FINANCING, 3.3.6.1.2

CASH COURIERS

DECLARATION SYSTEM, 9.1

DIFFERENTIAL TREATMENT, 9.2.2.1

PROTECTING THE FINANCIAL SYSTEM AGAINST MONEY LAUNDERERS AND TERRORISTS, 9.2.1

PROHIBITED GROUNDS, 9.2.2.2

UPHOLDING EQUALITY BEFORE THE LAW, 9.2.2

WITHOUT OBJECTIVE AND REASONABLE JUSTIFICATION, 9.2.2.3

COMPLIANCE OFFICERS

DUTIES AND RESPONSIBLITIES, 10.2, 10.3.1

THE TITLE OF THE INDIVIDUAL RESPONSIBLE FOR ANTI MONEY LAUNDERING COMPLIANCE, 10.1

REPORTING REQUIREMENTS FOR UNITED STATES
CONFIDENTIALITY OF SARS/TIPPING OFF (GENERAL RULE), 3.2.2.4
CONFIDENTIALITY OF SARS/TIPPING OFF (EXCEPTIONS), 3.2.2.5
PENALTIES, 3.2.2.6
WHAT TO FILE, 3.2.2.1
WHERE TO FILE, 3.2.2.2
WHEN TO FILE, 3.2.2.3

REPORTING REQUIREMENTS FOR UNITED KINGDOM
CONFIDENTIALITY OF SARS/TIPPING OFF (GENERAL RULE), 3.2.3.4
CONFIDENTIALITY OF SARS/TIPPING OFF (EXCEPTION), 3.2.3.5
PENALTIES, 3.2.3.6
WHAT TO FILE, 3.2.3.1
WHERE TO FILE, 3.2.3.2
WHEN TO FILE, 3.2.3.3

RISK ASSESSMENT FOR FINANCIAL INSTITUTIONS
CLIENT RISK, 2.2.1
BUSINESS RELATIONSHIP RISK, 2.2.2
DELIVERY CHANNEL RISK, 2.2.4
EMPLOYEE RISK, 2.2.6
GEOGRAPHIC LOCATION RISK, 2.2.5
INTERNAL CONTROLS, 2.2.7
PRODUCT/SERVICE RISK, 2.2.3

ROLE OF GOVERNMENT AGENCIES IN NIGERIA IN IMPLEMENTING AML/CFT REGULATIONS
CENTRAL BANK OF NIGERIA, 1.5.1.1
FEDERAL MINISTRY OF TRADE AND INVESTMENT, 1.5.1.3
NIGERIAN FINANCIAL INTELLIGENCE UNIT, 1.5.1.2
SPECIAL CONTROL UNIT AGAINST MONEY LAUNDERING (SCUML), 1.5.1.4

About the Author

"Ehi Eric Esoimeme has a clear ability to interpret and explain complex or substantive anti–money laundering and related legislation into clear and understandable language, but not oversimplifying the topics (as many texts do). Full learning value emits from Ehi's works and is of immense support to both law and industry practitioners. Ehi Eric Esoimeme's academic record and suitability is, beyond doubt, of a very high standard. When measured in academic terms, Ehi demonstrates subject-matter expertise with a balance of strong legal knowledge and practical commentary and handling of the topics. He references his work appropriately (using the Harvard system), and his publications and works are fully indexed. Acknowledgements and quotations are correctly attributed. Given also that Ehi's works are published before the legal and financial industry professions, the formal academic requirements standards in this regard are well met.

Ehi and I have peer-reviewed each other's work, which includes our books and articles. We have also exchanged information and dialogue on related publications on risk and money laundering. Moreover, my regard for Ehi's high caliber approach is demonstrated by him featuring in my own book, and reciprocally I have read and reviewed his excellent book on risk and money laundering, along with all of his other publications. Reviews on Ehi's work in that regard are highly positive and comment about how valuable his work is for learning, even helping to inform some best practices in anti–money laundering risk issues and tasks for organizations.

Ehi has keen analytical skills and has an ability when reviewing the law and the stated cases to fill in the learning gaps left by the parties and provide thorough and discursive commentary on the cases, thereby making a rare contribution by expanding the knowledge and understanding of vital precedent cases in English law (which are merely listed and accounted in case or legal textbooks), and he most confidently commits to structuring and explaining his rationale to go to open publication, whereby most legal authors and commentators prefer to "stay on the fence" to quote a phrase. Ehi shows a confidence to balance his knowledge with practical and cogent argument and reasoning. His review of jurisdictional legislation and related judicial powers shows a flexible approach and makes key connections with local/national provisions and affecting issues.

Another key competence of Ehi's skill set is his originality. The title of his book, *The Risk-Based Approach to Combating Money Laundering and Terrorist Financing*, is one such example. Among the many books on money laundering and risk, Ehi's work stands out and demonstrates input and conceptual thinking around core themes and the legal framework. There is a mark of individuality on all his publications.

Ehi's impressive record of publications demonstrates perseverance in achieving objectives. Combined with his professionalism and project management competence, Ehi remains focused on his objectives and produces quality outcomes. Equally, his professional role in his publishing company demonstrates his professional competences of standards, relationship building, and his commitment to keeping up with modern challenges in combating money laundering, corruption, et al.

Regarding weaknesses, in my view, Ehi has no weaknesses which would have bearing on him delivering in the second edition of this book.

Ehi has a complete professional approach and undoubted subject matter expertise. Combined, these qualities make Ehi Esoimeme

more than ably equipped to be able to write this excellent book. Refer to Appendix 7 of this book for the full list of Ehi's publications."
—Ian Ross, compliance, financial-crime specialist and trainer, Intersol Global (UK)
Accredited counter fraud specialist (ACFS)
Certified internal controls auditor (CICA)
International Academy of Investigative Psychology

"Ehi is a good writer and researcher on anti–money laundering discourse. I have worked closely with him in one of his recent publications as a peer reviewer. This book has received many commendations from both academic researchers and AML professionals."
—Emmanuel Oluwasina Sotande (PhD, Leeds), senior special assistant to executive chairman at the Economic and Financial Crimes Commission (EFCC)